THE BEARDS'
NEW BASIC HISTORY OF
THE UNITED STATES

THE BEARDS'

New Basic History
of the United States

— ☆ —

CHARLES A. BEARD
and
MARY R. BEARD

Revised and brought up to date
by their son
WILLIAM BEARD

DOUBLEDAY & COMPANY, INC.
Garden City, N.Y.

PREFATORY NOTE TO THE
BEARDS' BASIC HISTORY
OF THE UNITED STATES
(published in 1944)

With this book we bring to a close our many years of co-operative efforts in seeking to interpret the long course of American history. As its title indicates, the volume deals with fundamental activities, ideas, and interests which have entered into the development of American society from the colonial period to the contemporary age. Whatever may be added to the record here presented, a consideration of these activities, ideas, and interests is basic, we believe, to any understanding of American history.

Although compact in form and directed to the general public, the book is no mere summary or digest of our previous works. Nor is it a collection of excerpts from any or all of them. On the contrary it is newly designed and newly written to express the historical judgment which we have reached after more than forty years devoted to the study of documents and the observation of life at first hand in all parts of the United States, rural and urban, and in parts of the Old World and the Orient.

CHARLES A. BEARD
MARY R. BEARD

New Milford,
Connecticut.

PREFACE TO THE
BEARDS' NEW BASIC HISTORY
OF THE UNITED STATES

THE last volume completed by Charles A. and Mary R. Beard which undertook to describe and interpret America's past was their *Basic History of the United States.*

Since the volume's appearance in 1944, the flow of events has been swift and powerful. For example, the technology of warfare has been profoundly altered by the appearance of nuclear explosives and long-range missiles to carry them. The smashing of the Axis has destroyed the old "balance of power" and contributed toward an unstable new alignment, in which the United States and other nations have drawn together for protection against Communist aggression, leaving America deeply enmeshed in global politics. Within the United States, the Republicans fought their way into the presidency after twenty years of uninterrupted defeat, hot contests developed over civil rights, and technological advances, such as in automation, were affecting the lives and fortunes of millions of Americans.

Until shortly before his death in 1948, my father, Charles A. Beard, remained a close observer and analyzer of such developments and discussed them with me at considerable length. Several years after his passing, my mother, Mary R. Beard, undertook to link the 1944 edition of the *Basic History* with our own times through a formal revision of the volume, with my close co-operation. After death cut short her labors, in 1958, I did my best to weave into the fabric of the present revision my father's thinking, my mother's contributions, and my own work, to produce the co-operative account bound within these covers.

Practically all of the material on activities, ideas, and interests my parents deemed fundamental for the period up to 1944 has been left unchanged in the 1960 edition. However, advantage has been taken of a complete resetting of the type for the volume to correct several small errors, to supply a new start for the chapter on exploration, and to make a few other minor adjustments.

To cover the years since 1944, the chapter dealing with World War II, in the previous edition, has been carried through the surrender of the Axis powers. It has been followed by a new chapter bearing Mary R. Beard's suggested title, "The Atomic Age Unfolds," to extend the record into the year 1960. Lastly, the Appendix has been updated.

WILLIAM BEARD, PH.D.
*Formerly Assistant Professor
of Political Science
University of Wisconsin*

Scottsdale, Ariz.
Feb. 1, 1960

CONTENTS

MAPS AND DIAGRAMS

ILLUSTRATIONS

THE BEARDS'
NEW BASIC HISTORY OF
THE UNITED STATES

SOME FAMOUS VOYAGES OF EXPLORATION

Chapter 1

EXPLORATION, TERRITORIAL CLAIMS, AND COLONIZING AGENCIES

IMPELLING CURIOSITY was one of the prime forces that drove adventuresome Europeans to sail westward across the uncharted Atlantic, centuries ago, to come by surprise upon the great wilderness later called America. Impelling curiosity, too, induced European settlers in America and their descendants to investigate with growing success the complex laws of the physical world about them. Finally, impelling curiosity led Americans, enriched with the new accumulation of knowledge, to undertake the ultimate in exploration—the probing of the vastnesses of the mighty universe itself. In 1959 a device built and launched in the United States shot past the moon into permanent orbit around the Sun, millions of miles from the Earth. It was followed by an American electronic complex that observed the planet Venus, and by a later probe that flashed photographs of Mars back to Earth by radio. Work has begun on vehicles to carry men to the moon, perhaps to be followed by human visits to Mars. Once the solar system has been conquered, what will stand in the way of going even deeper into the dim immensities of space?

Plunging into this great stream of exploration near its source, where the details of our story may properly begin, we find Europeans of the late fifteenth century contemplating a daring project. It was that of sailing westward across the Atlantic, defying unknown hazards, in quest of new routes to old lands, and perhaps finding hitherto unsuspected regions along the way. Then as now, major exploratory projects were expensive. Like the space probes of our own times, they were government-financed, and considered by many as important to the maintenance of national prestige.

While it has been claimed that Leif Ericson might have reached North America around the year 1000, the first major exploratory expedition westward across the Atlantic to produce lasting results was that of Christopher Columbus, financed largely by the Spanish royal treasury and actively backed by Queen Isabella, who saw the possibilities of the enterprise. With her good wishes and a small fleet Columbus and a motley crew left Spain and came upon islands well off the southeastern coast of what is now the United States. The year was 1492.

Within a short time, other European nations entered the exploratory race, in quest of fame and fortune. Of particular interest to Americans was the project of King Henry VII of England, which assigned to John Cabot, an Italian navigator, and his three sons, the task of seeking hitherto unknown heathen lands to the west, on the way to Cipango (Japan) and China via the Atlantic.

In carrying out his orders, Cabot reached the shores of what is now Canada, in the region where the mighty St. Lawrence River pours forth into the sea. There, in 1497, he landed and planted the banner of the English king, claiming for his sponsor what he supposed was the east coast of Asia. With news of his labors, he went back to England. The next year Cabot was sent out again. This time he sighted the east coast of Greenland but his sailors mutinied against pushing north into the strange, icy seas that interested him. To satisfy the crew, he headed southward, coming to the continent of North America and following its shores to a point in the neighborhood of what is now called Chesapeake Bay. Unable to find a rich people with goods for profitable trade, he returned to England deeply disappointed.

On the basis of Cabot's discoveries, the King laid claim to a domain of unknown size and character in North America on which the history of the United States was to unfold. By this simple act, he opened for the English the greatest real estate and investment opportunity in the history of Western civilization.

But nearly a century passed before the English began to take full advantage of that opportunity. In the interval numerous and wide voyages by Portuguese, Italian, Spanish, French, and English explorers led to mapping, if roughly, the contours of a large part of the two Americas. And as an outcome Spanish, Portuguese, and French rulers also laid claims to large shares of land in the Western Hemisphere.

Intrepid explorers under the flag of Spain, by innumerable journeys, were the first to penetrate the mainlands. Spanish conquerors led by Hernando Cortes and Francisco Pizarro invaded Mexico and Peru, robbed them of gold, silver, and precious stones, and excited all Europe by reports of wealth in the New World. Between 1539 and 1542 Hernando de Soto traveled overland from the coast of Florida, with his mounted companions, to the Mississippi River and some distance beyond. During those years Francisco Vásquez de Coronado, with an armed band of horsemen, toiled his way northward from Mexico into the heart of the region lying west of the Mississippi, looking for more treasure in the rumored Indian cities of Cibola. In 1565 the Spanish planted the settlement of St. Augustine in Florida.

By the middle of the sixteenth century the Spaniards seemed about to take possession of the newly discovered world. Though they had not found more gold and silver in regions above Mexico or the elixir of youth sought in Florida by Ponce de Leon, by 1550 the ruler of Spain, Charles V, could claim as his property many islands in the Caribbean; Mexico by right of conquest; all of South America except Brazil, which the Portuguese had seized; and an immense area, if indefinite as to boundaries, north of the Gulf of Mexico and the Rio Grande. To back up his claim he had at his command a big navy, a large merchant marine, and many hardy soldiers. With his conquering hosts were associated dauntless Catholic priests to aid in establishing a New Spain in the New World—a state, church, and feudal aristocracy all resting on the labor of subject peoples.

Before the English government began to develop its territorial rights by occupation the monarchs of France had also become interested in the New World. Francis I laughed at Spain and Portugal for pretending to own so much of it, and declared that he wanted to see the will of Father Adam, the first proprietor, bequeathing to them the inheritance they claimed. In 1524, while Henry VIII, who had succeeded his father in 1509, was neglecting the patrimony won by Cabot's voyages, Francis sent an Italian seaman, John Verrazano, across the Atlantic to hunt for a northwest passage to the Orient. Verrazano did not find the passage, but he did sail along the coast of North America and gave Francis good grounds for asserting that he too owned a big share of the new continent. Several years later Francis sent Jacques Cartier forth on two successive voyages. They resulted in explorations of the St. Lawrence River region, the bestowal of the name Montreal on an Indian village, and a more definite claim to a huge area in that neighborhood.

Such were the rights asserted by England, Spain, and France to enormous masses of land in the New World when Queen Elizabeth came to the throne of England in 1558. Her father, Henry VIII, had done nothing to develop the real estate nominally acquired through the voyages of Cabot. Busy with intrigues on the continent of Europe, his marital troubles, and his quarrels with the Pope, he had continued to neglect his opportunities in the New World. During the reigns of his son Edward VI and his daughter Mary, England had been torn by religious disputes, and the exploitation of land over the sea had been slighted by English statesmen.

With the accession of Queen Elizabeth, however, many things incited English enterprisers to develop the real estate and investment opportunity opened to them by the voyages of Cabot under Henry VII. Elizabeth was high-spirited, well educated in the secular learning of the Renaissance, and greatly interested in adding to the riches and power of her realm. She was determined that her people should be kept Protestant in religion under the Church of England, firmly united, and strong enough to break the dominion of her Catholic rival, the King of Spain, in the Atlantic Ocean. Elizabeth gathered around her Protestant statesmen of the same mind, fostered the growth of the English navy, and encouraged her sea captains to plunder Spanish ships and colonies wherever they could.

The new temper of the Elizabethan age was imperiously displayed in 1577–80 when the English "sea dog," Francis Drake, sailed around the world plundering cities and Spanish ships laden with treasure as he went —down along the east coast of South America, up along the west coast, to the shores of California, and all the way home.

From this exploit English capitalists got an inkling of the investment opportunity before them, on and across the seas. Money for Drake's expedition had been supplied by a corporation in which Elizabeth held shares. The company's original investment was £5000. In return for the stockholders' risk, Drake's treasure ships brought them £600,000 in profits—enough to satisfy the most expectant investor. As a prudent ruler Elizabeth used her portion of the proceeds to pay off the debts owed by the Crown. According to careful estimates, the numerous raids on Spanish ships and colonies during Elizabeth's reign netted the handsome sum of £12,000,000.

With news of splendid returns on investment undertakings at sea ringing in their ears, English merchant capitalists, including investors among fair ladies, began to take a serious interest in the real estate of the English Crown in the New World. Since it was undeveloped real estate—not land occupied by peoples abounding in wealth—its exploitation demanded colonization by the English people themselves and the founding of a "New England" under the Crown of the old England. Having this project in view, Queen Elizabeth gave Sir Walter Raleigh, one of the favorites at her court, a patent to all the territory he might colonize, on condition that he pay to the Crown one fifth of the returns from the mining of precious metals.

Under this patent Raleigh sent out in 1584 an expedition which visited the island of Roanoke off the coast of North Carolina and brought back reports of a favorable climate and country—"the most plentiful, sweet, fruitful, and wholesome of all the world." The next year Raleigh dispatched seven ships and 108 colonists to Roanoke, but the colonial experiment was a failure. Raleigh made another attempt in 1587, only to fail again. The colonists who shared in that venture utterly disappeared from the scene, leaving behind them not even a clue to their fate. The sixteenth century came to a close without the creation of a single permanent English settlement in America.

But the century did not close until the English navy, aided by a terrible storm at sea, had destroyed in 1588 the Spanish Armada, a mighty fleet sent by the King of Spain to crush the rising power of England. Though this victory, by eliminating powerful enemy forces, would have facilitated the settlement of America, the English did not immediately follow up their advantage with a wave of colonization.

While the English rested, three rival powers made the most of the lull to strengthen their positions in America. Following Hudson's trip in 1609, up the river now bearing his name, his Dutch employers laid claim to the surrounding territory. As "New Netherland" this holding became an important farming and trading community with what is now New York City as its chief port. Farther to the North, in Canada, French fur traders set up temporary quarters which were followed, in 1608, by the establishment of Canada's oldest permanent community—Quebec. From this base, French missionaries journeyed westward, creating missions all the way to the Great Lakes by 1616. Meanwhile Spain expanded from her Florida base to build posts and missions along the Atlantic Coast as far north as what is now the State of South Carolina. On the other side of the Mississippi River, Spaniards went from Mexico northward into what is now the State of New Mexico, in 1598. By 1610 their settlements were being governed from a capital at Santa Fe, a community that has come down to our own times to serve as the capital of a modern State.

By the time the English finally got around to exploiting in earnest the territory nominally under the English Crown, the French, Spanish and Dutch already had good footholds in the New World. To cope with these established rivals, England now most urgently needed large, permanent, and prosperous colonies, something new to British experience. Beside this complicated undertaking the spectacular dispatch of Drake on a voyage of exploration and the sensational robbery of Spanish vessels were mere theatrical displays of power and daring. To arm a few ships, shoot up Spanish galleons, loot them, and send them to the bottom of the ocean was an operation that required little money—mainly skill in navigation and the fighting spirit.

LAND GRANTS BY JAMES I IN 1606

Great pieces of real estate were granted to the London Company and the Plymouth Company. In the shaded portion of the map both Companies could make settlements provided their plantations were at least 100 miles apart.

Qualities and courage of a different sort were necessary to create large and orderly societies in a wilderness. This business demanded huge capital. It was more than men's work: women in great numbers had to be associated with it. All the ideals, arts, and sciences of civilization were involved in it.

Not fully aware of all that colonization implied but eager to exploit the real estate in America, English merchant capitalists sought that privilege from the Crown at the beginning of the seventeenth century. They had already formed trading companies to engage in commerce with Russia, the Levant, and the East Indies. In corporate enterprises of that type they had demonstrated their ingenuity. Besides they had accumulated much capital for investment. This capital they now proposed to use in colonial enterprise, about which they knew so little. Only one aspect of it was clear to them: individual farmers, merchants, artisans, and their families, with small savings or none at all, could not embark unaided on any such undertaking as large-scale colonization.

Under English law all the territory claimed in America belonged to the

Crown. The monarch could withhold it from use, keep any part of it as a royal domain, or grant it, by charter or patent, in large or small blocks, to privileged companies or private persons. It was to the Crown, therefore, that English enterprisers bent on colonizing America turned for grants of land and powers of government. And in making such grants by charter or patent, the Crown created two types of legal agencies for colonization: the corporation and the proprietary.

The corporate type of colonizing agency was the company, or group of individuals merged into a single "person" at law by a royal charter. The charter named the original members of the company and gave them the right to elect officers, frame bylaws, raise money, and act as a body. It granted to the company an area of territory and conferred upon it certain powers: to transport emigrants, govern its settlements, dispose of its land and other resources, and carry on commerce, subject to the laws of England. Such a corporation was akin to the modern joint-stock company organized for profit-making purposes.

The proprietary agency for colonizing consisted of one or more persons to whom were given a grant of territory and various powers of government by the Crown. The proprietor or proprietors thus endowed with special privileges had authority to found a particular colony and enjoy property, commercial, governing, and other rights similar in character to those vested in a company by royal charter.

Companies and proprietors did not, however, have a completely free hand in managing their colonial affairs. They were limited by the terms of their charters or patents and were compelled to confer upon free settlers certain liberties and immunities enjoyed by English people at home, including a share in the making of local laws.

Various motives inspired English leaders to form companies or embark on careers as proprietors in America. Among the motives was the desire to extend English power, to make money out of trading privileges and land sales, and to convert the Indians to Christianity. For some companies and proprietors the idea of establishing religious liberty in America for members of persecuted sects was also among the primary considerations in their colonizing activities. Still another purpose entering into the plans of companies or proprietors was that of giving poor and otherwise unfortunate persons in England a chance to work and live better in a new country so open to opportunity. In other words, political, economic, religious, and charitable motives induced English leaders to devote their energies to the business of colonization.

The systematic beginnings of all the American colonies were made by companies or proprietors or under their jurisdiction. By 1733, the year in which the last colony, Georgia, was started at Savannah, there were thirteen colonies under the Crown at London, legally known as the British Crown after the Union of England and Scotland in 1707. These colonies, taken arbitrarily in geographical order, with references to origins, were:

New Hampshire—partly an offshoot of Massachusetts, given a separate status in 1679.

Massachusetts—founded in 1630 by Puritans under the Massachusetts Bay Company; with it became associated in 1691 the colony of Plymouth, established by the Pilgrims in 1620 on land belonging to the Plymouth Company chartered by James I in 1606.

Rhode Island—incorporating two offshoots from Massachusetts, Rhode Island and Providence Plantations, to which, as a single colony, a royal charter was given in 1663.

Connecticut—originating partly in offshoots from Massachusetts planted in the Connecticut River valley in 1635 and partly in settlements on the shore, united under a royal charter in 1662.

New York—founded as New Netherland under the Dutch West India Company in 1624; seized by the English in 1664 and given the name of New York.

New Jersey—founded under Dutch auspices, seized by the English in 1664, and afterward named New Jersey.

Delaware—first settled by the Dutch under the Dutch West India Company and by Swedes under the Swedish South Company; taken by the English in 1664 and placed under the proprietorship of William Penn in 1682.

Pennsylvania—granted to William Penn as proprietary by Charles II in 1681; first settlement at Philadelphia in 1682.

Maryland—granted to Lord Baltimore as proprietary in 1632 and started by settlements on Chesapeake Bay in 1634.

Virginia—founded by settlement at Jamestown in 1607, made under the London Company chartered by James I in 1606.

North Carolina—early settlements made by pioneers from other colonies; passed under an association of proprietors in 1665 by a royal grant covering all the Carolina region, formerly within the jurisdiction of the Virginia Company; given a separate status as the royal province of North Carolina in 1729.

South Carolina—granted to proprietors in 1665; settlements made at Albemarle Point in 1670 and near Charleston in 1672; an independent royal province after 1729.

Georgia—granted to a board of trustees, or company, by George II in 1732; Savannah founded in 1733.

This listing of some of the corporate and proprietary agencies under which English colonization took place, does not give an adequate impression of the amount of free movement by individuals and groups in America, especially after the first settlements had been planted. Nothing less than an encyclopedia could do that.

Take for example North Carolina. Virginians had made a permanent settlement in that region at least five years before it was granted to proprietors in 1665, and other pioneers, mainly Scotch, Scotch-Irish, and Germans from Pennsylvania, went down into North Carolina on their own motion.

Again, take New Hampshire in the far north. An independent settlement was established there as early as 1623 under a royal grant. Other beginnings in New Hampshire had been made before the Puritans came to Massachusetts Bay in 1630. When Puritans pushed over into the New Hampshire region and claimed it as a part of their grant, they encountered stout opposition from the forerunners. Only after many disputes was a final separation from Massachusetts effected by New Hampshire in 1679.

But independent undertakings and individual or group migrations from colony to colony, significant as they were in colonial beginnings, had relatively little influence on the rise of self-governing colonies. It was under companies and proprietors holding grants of land subject to the English Crown that systematic colonization on a large scale was made possible. It was under companies and proprietors that the foundations of all the colonies were securely laid. Crown, companies, and proprietors—their work in colonization was to have from the outset a profound influence on the course of affairs which eventuated in the formation of the continental United States.

Chapter 2

IMMIGRATION TO THE COLONIES

THE VARIOUS English corporations and proprietors possessing royal grants of land along the eastern seaboard of what is now the United States ultimately went to work on a grand scale to put their properties to some kind of productive use. They raised funds. They had to purchase quantities of livestock, food, seed, tools, and other items of freight. They acquired ships and hired crews. They drew up many plans. They did their best to find the thousands upon thousands of men, women, and children who might turn these things to good account in the New World. Then they moved articles, animals, and people across the Atlantic in what were, by modern standards, very small craft, in one of the most amazing and important migrations of all times.

Basic to the success of this vast enterprise, of course, was the selection of desirable settlers. Only able-bodied men and women possessing many skills, familiar with numerous arts and sciences, could be expected to produce the food, clothing, shelter, and other prime ingredients for a relatively self-sufficient society in a distant wilderness.

But trading corporations and proprietors, even aided by the English government, could not simply commandeer farmers, mechanics, artisans, and managers for colonial adventures. In the nature of things, most of the men and women for the undertaking had to be persons who were willing, even eager, to cross the sea. They had to be volunteers moved by one reason or many reasons to tear up their roots in the Old World and brave the perils and toil of transplanting themselves across the wide ocean into the lonely territory claimed by the English Crown.

The bulk of the white men and women who came to North America between the founding of Jamestown in Virginia in 1607 and the eve of the American revolt against Great Britain came voluntarily. Even those who indentured, or bound, themselves by contract to labor for a term of years as servants, in order to pay their passage, were in the main volunteers.

It is true that many white laborers were kidnaped in England for shipment to the American colonies and that Negroes were dragged out of Africa for that purpose by slave traders. Forced migration of laborers was undoubtedly extensive. Yet the overwhelming majority of immigrants came to America of their own choice.

What lay behind this choice? The whole history of Europe. The long struggle between barbarism and civilization since the beginning of human societies in the Old World. Immediately influential were the convulsions of the age in which the emigrants lived. From the opening of the seventeenth century to the close of the colonial period the Old World was in turmoil—physical, intellectual, moral, religious, military, economic, and political. The feudal order of the Middle Ages was breaking up amid fierce resistance to change.

The years of the great migration from the Old World to the English colonies in the New World were marked by international wars, civil wars, religious controversies and persecutions, political disputes, displays of royal despotism, and social dislocation, accompanied by growing poverty and the enactment of barbaric criminal laws against the poor.

None of these events was sharply separated from others. All were interrelated. For example, wars were connected with national jealousies, ambitions of monarchs, religious hatreds, and rivalries over trade and territory. Religious clashes were associated with the political interests of kings and queens, Catholic and Protestant, with the conflicts of nations over commerce and empire in the Old World and beyond the seas, and with the struggles of classes.

An impression of the almost endless wars waged in Europe between 1618 and 1776 may be derived from the following list of the major conflicts:

1618–48—The Thirty Years' War, involving Bohemia, Denmark, Sweden, France, German princes, Spain, and other Powers; large parts of Germany were devastated by battles, burnings, and lootings; Protestants and Catholics both engaged in it.

1648–59—France and Spain, two Catholic monarchies, continued the Thirty Years' War, between themselves.

1667–68—The War of Devolution; the King of France, Louis XIV, waged war to wrest neighboring territories from Spain.

1672–78—France waged war on Holland.

1689–97—War of the Palatinate; French, Dutch, and English struggled for power on the Continent; called in America King William's War.

1702–14—War of the Spanish Succession; France, England, Spain, Holland, and other Powers fought over territory on the Continent and over colonial possessions; known in American colonies as Queen Anne's War.

1739–48—War of Jenkins' Ear, between England and France; widened out into the War of the Austrian Succession, involving England, France, Spain, Austria, Prussia, and other Powers; known in the American colonies as King George's War.

1756–63—The Seven Years' War, involving England, France, Spain, Prussia, and other countries; contest between England and France over dominion in Canada, India, and other places; known in America as the French and Indian War.

These major wars, covering in all more than eighty years between 1618 and 1776, to say nothing of many local wars such as short fights between the English and the Dutch, spread ruin in several parts of western Europe. And one reason for the extent of this ruin was a revolution in the "art of war."

In the Middle Ages almost endless wars had been fought largely by a relatively few feudal lords and their retainers—by dukes, earls, barons, knights, and esquires. Into feudal armies workers on the land and merchants in the towns had not been drafted wholesale. With the discovery of gunpowder and the invention of cannon, muskets, and other powerful implements of destruction, however, a new kind of army—the standing army—was organized in Europe.

The standing army could be extended by summoning tens of thousands of men to its ranks, thus far exceeding in size any feudal army. To fill the ranks of the new and bigger armies sturdy young men were caught and dragged to the barracks for training if they could not be got otherwise. Princes drafted their subjects en masse for their own wars and sometimes sold them in large blocks, as mercenaries, to other princes in need of soldiers.

With this transformation in the character of armies, the actual snatching of men for wars and the fear of being snatched made life a genuine terror for innumerable men of military age, their families, and young marriageable women. Moreover the death and destruction spread by wars on a large scale made the "art of war" so practiced more terrible to noncombatants. For all such reasons British and European workers in town and country, as well as yeomen and merchants, could regard the perils and hardships of resettlement in America, in a strange land, as offering trials slight in comparison.

To wars between nations were added conflicts within nations arising from religious and political sources. In the Middle Ages the people of all countries in western Europe were members of one church—the Catholic

Church, and belonged to one faith—the Catholic faith. Dissent from that faith, heresy, was forbidden and if it appeared was put down by Church and State.

But during the opening years of the sixteenth century a revolt, known as the Protestant Reformation, broke out against the Pope and the Catholic Church of which he was the head. In southern Germany, Italy, and Spain, the Church and the princes managed to suppress religious uprisings and keep most of the people loyal to the Catholic religion. France, long torn by religious wars, found peace for a time when the King was able to make a truce in 1598—by granting a limited toleration to the Huguenots, Protestant followers of John Calvin. In Holland, Scandinavia, and the countries of northern Germany, the revolt against the Pope ended in the establishment of independent Protestant churches under the various rulers.

The religious quarrels in England took a peculiar turn. After the power of the Pope was finally cast off under Queen Elizabeth, a state church—the Church of England—was established by act of Parliament and everybody in the realm was ordered to become a member of it under pain of fine or physical punishment. But this official church had scarcely been set up, and Catholics had barely been suppressed, when more religious protests arose among the people.

Some of the new objectors merely wanted to reform, or "purify," the English Church; they were known as Puritans. Others, generally called Dissenters, spurned the English Church entirely and asserted the right of individuals and groups of individuals to form churches of their own and worship God according to their consciences. This was the view taken by Presbyterians, Baptists, and Quakers, for example.

Nowhere in the Old World at the beginning of American colonization was there anything like religious toleration in the modern sense of the term: that is, the right of every person to join any church he or she pleases, or none at all, and to express his or her opinions freely on matters of religion. In the Catholic countries, except France, Protestantism was forbidden and Protestants were persecuted. Even in France the limited toleration of Huguenots was abolished by the King in 1685, and they were subjected to persecution. On the other hand, in Protestant countries Catholicism was forbidden and Catholics were persecuted. In England persecution cut two ways. The government of that country meted out stern punishment to Catholics who clung to their faith and also to Protestants who wanted to "purify" the English Church or to found independent churches. As far as the strict letter of English law was concerned there could be no Catholics at all in England or any Protestants outside the Church of England. Although many religious objectors defied or winked at the law, they were liable at any time to be arrested and fined, imprisoned, mutilated, or put to death.

Religious disputes in England were embittered by a political struggle which broke out between the Parliament and James I, shortly after his accession in 1603. High-tempered and arrogant, James tried to make laws and lay taxes without the consent of Parliament, and Parliament resisted his encroachments on its rights.

Under his successor, Charles I, the quarrel developed into a civil war and a revolution, led by Oliver Cromwell with the general support of the Puritans. The struggle ended temporarily in the execution of Charles, the exile of his son, the flight of many members of the aristocracy, and the establishment of a dictatorship by Cromwell.

In the course of the civil conflict a flood of radical, or "leveling," ideas was let loose in England. It was boldly said that no King or House of Lords was needed at all; that every man should have the right to vote for members of the House of Commons; that all the people had "natural rights" which no government could take away from them.

Shortly after the death of Cromwell the monarchy was restored by the coronation of Charles II, in 1660. But this brought only a few years of internal peace to England. Even then religious and political unrest continued beneath the surface of social peace. It emerged in a revolt soon after Charles II died and his brother, James II, an avowed Catholic, came to the throne. James tried to rule England as autocratically as his grandfather had done, and in 1688 he was driven out in a popular uprising.

Late in that year, William, the Prince of Orange, and his wife, Mary, the elder daughter of James II, were called to England. Under an act of Parliament they were crowned king and queen of the realm. In the general settlement which went with the revolution of 1688 the supremacy of Parliament as the lawmaking body of England was acknowledged, a bill of rights for English subjects was proclaimed, and a limited tolerance was granted to Protestant Dissenters—though not to Catholics.

During the many years of this strife in England migration to America was stimulated; and the colonies that had already been founded were deeply affected by rapid changes in the mother country. Resenting the autocratic rule of James I and Charles I, thousands of Puritans and Dissenters fled from the kingdom in search of more political and religious freedom for themselves. While the Puritans under Cromwell's leadership were in power in England, hundreds of their opponents, loosely called "Cavaliers," took refuge in America, especially in Virginia. And all the while news of the disputes in England over the political rights of the people and over religious toleration circulated from one end of the colonial settlements to the other, affecting judgments respecting politics and religion on this side of the Atlantic.

Amid the wars, religious revolts, persecutions, and political upheavals which kept the Old World in convulsions, the feudal order inherited from the Middle Ages was disintegrating. In that order government had been in the hands of kings and princes, supported by the clergy and nobility, as a rule. The land of the various kingdoms and principalities had been held by great landlords, lay and clerical; and most of the earth had been tilled by serfs bound to the soil on which they labored, so that they were unable to leave it even if they desired to do so. The number of merchants was relatively small and they counted for little in the class valuations of early feudal times. Stated in another way, feudal society was a class society in which each class, from serfs at the bottom to princes at the top, had a fixed and permanent place. The mass of the people were not free to move around as they pleased, even in the region in which they lived, or to emigrate to any other country.

But wars, religious upheavals, and the growth of commerce finally shook this rigid class order apart. In England the process of dissolution began early and went forward rapidly, particularly after the Protestant revolt opened in the sixteenth century. Under Henry VIII great landed estates held by the Catholic Church were seized by the Crown and many of them were parceled out among the King's favorites, thus increasing the number of English landlords. About the same time landlords discovered that they could make more money by raising sheep and exporting wool to the continent of Europe than they could by having the soil tilled for the production of crops. So they turned a vast acreage into sheep pastures and evicted serfs and laborers from the land, forcing them, homeless and forlorn, to search for other work in the towns.

By the beginning of Elizabeth's reign England was swarming with "free" men and women, hunting in the streets and highways for employment or begging for charity. Cruel laws were enacted against them. They were harshly punished for begging, driven into poorhouses, or forced to labor at anything they could find to do at wages fixed by government officials.

In some of the English towns at the opening of the seventeenth century as high as one third of all the inhabitants were paupers dependent for a living on the charity of their neighbors. Although paupers were unequally distributed over England, the number was enormous and their plight was nothing short of horrible.

Everywhere even those fathers and mothers who earned a fair livelihood could see that their children had slight chances of getting along at all or of bettering their condition and that their families might easily fall into the great mass of pauperism. Since most of the English land was monopolized by great landlords it was difficult for anyone to buy a farm; and the oversupply of labor in the cities made competition for jobs an agonizing struggle.

When the cry that cheap land, even free land, was offered to immigrants in America rang through the streets of English towns and cities and through the byways of the English countryside, it awakened in the imagination of multitudes of nameless men and women a dream of liberty, security, and advancement such as had never before come to toiling masses in the Old World. Even the homeless and propertyless were stirred by news from some of the colonies that, if they would bind themselves to service for a term of five years, they would receive at the end of their indenture at least fifty acres of land for their own.

Such were the Old World backgrounds for migration to America. It was in these circumstances, according to estimates from fragmentary records, that about 750,000 people, for one reason or another or for many reasons, journeyed over the ocean between 1600 and 1770 to seek a way of life on this continent. Relatively few of them were from the permanent class of helpless English paupers created by the heartless eviction of peasants from the lands their ancestors had tilled; for paupers did not always have the energy or skills required for successful farming that made them desirable indentured servants. Approximately two thirds of the immigrants belonged to families able to meet the cost of the journey and make a start of some kind in the new country. The other third, composed of indentured servants, although lacking in money or property, had skills and talents which they could apply in making their way in a land of opportunity.

The motives provoking men and women to brave the perils of the sea voyage in slow sailing vessels overcrowded with passengers and to risk their lives and fortunes in a strange continent, far from their native habitats, were no doubt various. But historical records justify such a summary as the following:

A desire to get away from the devastations of the endless wars and conflicts in Europe.

A resolve to flee from the snatching and selling of men for service in the armies of kings and princes constantly engaged in wars.

A longing for an opportunity to find honest and honorable work and create better homes for themselves and their children.

An eagerness to escape religious persecutions and to found communities in which they could worship God in their own ways, free from the domination of church and government officials trying to enforce conformity to other faiths.

In addition to one or more of these motives, immigrants had a quality for which no name can be found. Countless men and women who lived amid the wars, persecutions, and poverty of the Old World and suffered from them as did the emigrants, stayed at home and continued to endure them. If the Old World backgrounds in themselves had supplied the sole motives for migration, then more millions would also have broken away and joined the voyagers bound for the New World. It follows, therefore, that there was something in the spirit of the men and women who voluntarily made the break and migrated, a force of character not simply determined by economic, political, or religious conditions —a force that made them different from their neighbors who remained in the turmoil and poverty of the Old World. That something was a quality of energy, enterprise, daring, or aspiration that was to be a power in the course of American history, immediately and by transmission through coming generations.

The strength of the several motives for migration doubtless varied from immigrant to immigrant, from group to group. The assignment of specific weights to the motives is impossible. But among them a desire to win a larger religious freedom was widely acknowledged as significant and impelling by many immigrants and their descendants. Practically all the immigrants were members of some church or adherents to some religious faith. The overwhelming majority were Protestants—but Protestants who objected, as much as Catholics did, to the faith and government of the Church of England. On this point of objection Quakers, Baptists, Presbyterians, and Lutherans agreed in spite of their differences on other matters. In any event, religious considerations entered into the founding and development of every colony from New Hampshire to Georgia.

The early settlers of Virginia were members of the Church of England and it was the practices of their church which were to be observed in the colony. This church soon became and long remained the Established Church of Virginia, supported by taxation. Nevertheless, in the course of time Protestants of other denominations went into Virginia though, theoretically, they had no legal right to be there. A few Catholics also found their way quietly into the Old Dominion and officers of the law merely winked at their presence. Thus a kind of toleration grew up in practice. But it was far from universal religious liberty and was often marred by persecutions fostered by the Virginia government and Established Church.

The neighboring colony of Maryland, often spoken of as a free refuge for Catholics persecuted in England, was in fact at the outset nothing of the sort. It is true that the first Lord Baltimore, who received the grant of land from King Charles I, was a Catholic in spite of the prohibitory English law, favored and protected by the King. It is true that many Catholics from the British Isles were able to settle in Maryland and enjoy a high degree of religious liberty, although according to English law Catholics were not supposed to exist anywhere under the English Crown. But the second Lord Baltimore, who on the death of his father started the settlements on Chesapeake Bay, was interested in more than a religious refuge. He wanted to develop a prosperous colony by selling his lands to farmers, and he invited Protestants as well as Catholics to migrate to Maryland.

Within a short time the Protestants in Maryland outnumbered the Catholics and prepared to abolish the toleration that had quietly become a custom in the colony. To avoid a disruptive religious conflict, leaders in Maryland arranged for the colonial assembly to pass, in 1649, what is known as the Toleration Act. The term is inexact. It did not establish universal religious liberty in Maryland. It granted freedom of religious worship only to those who professed faith in Jesus Christ, thereby excluding Jews, unbelievers, Deists, and Unitarians from the benefit of this freedom.

In the case of the Massachusetts Bay Colony, religious affairs took a course unlike that in Virginia or Maryland. Although, like Virginians, the Puritans who settled on the bay were members of the Church of England when they arrived, they had wanted to alter some of its practices and soon they separated from it entirely in their new home. After the separation each town set up a church of its own, called Congregational, and taxpayers were required by law to support it. For a long time every voter in Massachusetts had to be a member of a Congregational church.

Strenuous efforts were made to bar immigrants belonging to other religious denominations. Dissenters and critics who appeared among the Puritans were frowned upon and sometimes severely punished, executed, or exiled into the wilderness. In short Puritans came to Massachusetts to develop, among other things, religious liberty for themselves, not to establish an ideal of toleration for all religions—a liberty utterly unknown as practice in the England they had left.

The first English colony in America to grant general religious liberty as a matter of law and principle was an offshoot from Massachusetts, at first called the Rhode Island and Providence Plantations. It was not founded by settlers coming directly from England but by inhabitants of Massachusetts who rebelled against the teachings and practices of Puritan preachers and magistrates. In 1636 Roger Williams, ordered to conform or get out, fled with a few friends into the wilderness and founded the town of Providence at the head of Narragansett Bay. Two years afterward Anne

Hutchinson, also outlawed by the Puritan clergy of Boston for her religious and general independence, took refuge with her companions for a while at Portsmouth on Rhode Island.

Both Roger Williams and Anne Hutchinson believed that the government should not force any form of religion by law on anybody; that every person should be free to worship God according to his conscience. This rule of broad tolerance, extended to Quakers and Jews, was retained in the Providence and Rhode Island plantations after all the townships were united in an independent colony—by a charter from Charles II granted in 1663. It made Rhode Island unique among the colonies.

No such general religious liberty was permitted in the second offshoot from Massachusetts, the colony of Connecticut, founded about the same time as Providence. The expedition of Puritans who built the towns of Hartford, Windsor, and Wethersfield in the Connecticut River valley was led by a preacher rightly deemed broad-minded for his time, Thomas Hooker. But neither he nor his companions accepted the liberal toleration proclaimed by Roger Williams and Anne Hutchinson. Likewise strict in their views of religious discipline under government control were the Puritans who made settlements at New Haven and other places on Long Island Sound.

Before and after the two groups of towns were united in a single colony as Connecticut, under a charter granted by Charles II in 1662, the Congregational Church was the established church in each town, and it remained so established by law through the Revolution down to 1818. Catholics, Protestant dissenters of various kinds, especially Quakers, and even members of the Church of England encountered hostility in Connecticut. Immigrants who were not Congregationalists in faith filtered into the colony here and there but full toleration and equality were not accorded to them as a matter of principle and law.

A wide, though not complete, religious toleration was adopted in Pennsylvania under the leadership of the Quaker proprietor, William Penn. By his faith Penn was committed to the principle that religion is a matter for the conscience of the individual and is not to be imposed on anybody by law and government officials. But from the beginning of his settlement at Philadelphia in 1682 Penn opened his colony only to immigrants who professed belief in God. As a proprietor Penn, like Lord Baltimore, was eager to have immigrants settling in his colony, buying farms carved out of the land granted to him by the King, and engaging in lucrative commerce. In his quest for settlers he made special efforts to encourage the migration of Scotch-Irish Presbyterians and German Protestants, as hardy folk with skills and crafts.

Religious considerations entered into the rise and growth of settlements in other parts of America. It was in search of freedom for their form of religious worship as well as a livelihood that the Pilgrims, persecuted in England and for a time exiles in Holland, went to Plymouth in 1620. After the English seized the Dutch holdings in 1664 and renamed them New York, the practice of granting toleration to Protestants of all denominations was followed in New York, although the Anglican Church was established in certain counties of the colony as the official church. Quakers and Presbyterians took part in filling up New Jersey and a similar toleration became the general practice there. Under the Penn proprietorship the inhabitants of Delaware shared the almost unlimited religious freedom established by William Penn for Pennsylvania. While the proprietors of North Carolina and South Carolina were favorable to the Anglican Church, settlers of various Protestant faiths, including French Huguenots, were welcomed and allowed to worship God according to their creeds. In Georgia, founded as an experiment in philanthropy, a rule of religious liberty akin to that in South Carolina soon prevailed generally.

As long as shipping was controlled by companies and proprietors, it was relatively easy to keep people of "undesirable" religious sects out of any colony. But after ports and inland towns were well developed, owners of ships were fairly free to make independent voyages to America. Then colonial barriers crumbled and immigrants of all faiths found easier entrance into all colonies. Ship captains in search of emigrants who could pay their passage were prone to disregard laws on religion or colonial restrictions on the ingress of religious refugees.

Indeed, to promote passenger traffic ship captains offered to carry over to America emigrants who had no money to pay their way, and collected the cost, with a profit, by selling the labor and skills of their passengers to employers for a term of years. Colonists who engaged these laborers were inclined to be more interested in strong bodies and stable characters than in the theological opinions of their servants.

Thus it came about that by 1776 there was a great difference between the surface appearance of things, as evidenced by the existence of established churches, and the realities of religious practice in America. By law, the Church of England was the official church in six colonies—Virginia, Maryland, the two Carolinas, Georgia, and New York. In three other colonies—Massachusetts, Connecticut, and New Hampshire—the Congregational Church, supported in each town by taxation, remained established as the official church. Yet generally throughout the colonies there were large numbers of people of English origin who were Christian dissenters from the official churches—Presbyterians, Baptists, Quakers, Catholics, and members of other sects. To these were added many German Lutherans and a small quantity of French Protestants, or Huguenots. Even Jews, severely oppressed nearly everywhere in the Old World, were able to find shelter from persecution in several seaboard towns and to erect synagogues in which to conduct their religious rites.

Colonial Americans, then, by 1776 enjoyed a degree of religious liberty such as had not been witnessed in England and Western Europe for centuries. Yet while Americans had gone far on the road to the kind of universal religious freedom they enjoy today, they had not completed the journey. Still to be overcome, for example, was the colonial practice of excluding followers of certain faiths, notably Catholics, from voting and holding political office.

Chapter 3

AGRICULTURAL BEGINNINGS

THE PRIME TASK confronting the stream of immigrants, of varied national origins, backgrounds, and religious faiths, who poured into the English colonies in America, was that of establishing a substantially self-sufficient agricultural society in the New World. This was to be a laborious enterprise.

A few emigrants at the beginning of the seventeenth century, it is true, were lured by the original dream of the London Company that gold and silver for quick riches would be found in its territory. A year before the tiny settlement had been planted on the James River, an actor in the English metropolis had declared on the stage that the Indians' dripping pans were of "pure golde," that their "chaines with which they chained up their streets were of massive golde," that their prisoners were "fettered in golde," and that they "goe forth on holy days to gather rubies and diamonds by the seashore." But neither in Virginia nor anywhere in the colonies were the English to discover, conquer, and loot Indian societies fabulously rich in rare treasures, such as the Spaniards had found in Mexico and Peru. So all the pioneers had to come down to hard earth and create the real wealth which was alone valuable for life—farms, houses, food, clothing, and all the material commodities necessary for the living of civilized people. They had to cherish the values of a working society, one firmly based on agriculture.

In the new environment the pioneers confronted primitives such as they had never seen before. All along the shores from Maine to Georgia were scattered tribes of native Indians ranging in degrees of social organization from marauding nomads to more or less settled communities engaged in practicing the economic arts of forest, stream, field, and domesticity. With the Indians the pioneers entered into varied relations: from peace and friendship to treachery and massacre on both sides.

In terms of peace the newcomers sometimes bought lands from the Indians, giving them in exchange such English goods as cloth, beads, hoes, knives, axes, and other implements. For example, when Roger Williams founded his first plantation in Rhode Island in 1636, he displayed good will toward the Indians at once and bought from them the land on which he settled with his companions. Sometimes colonial leaders, occasionally in connection with the purchase of land, made treaties of amity with the Indians. William Penn, for instance, besides protecting the Indians of his colony from the rapacity of white traders, made treaties of friendship with them which they faithfully kept. By the marriage of John Rolfe to Pocahontas, daughter of the warlike chief, Powhatan, in 1614, peace was brought to the settlers of Virginia for eight years. More than once an English settlement was saved from starvation by timely supplies of food furnished by neighboring tribes.

From red Indians "the palefaces" recovered some of the primitive arts of survival which had been lost to the English since their own primitive times. Indian women were farmers, cooks, and practitioners of other domestic arts, and from them English women learned how to handle native foodstuffs, especially Indian corn, and provide nutritious meals. Indian men also had their arts of hunting, fishing, and woodworking, and from them English men acquired various new skills which, combined with their own, enabled them to make rapid progress in every form of economic operation. As hunters adept in the ways of wild animals, Indians knew how to procure fish, game, and furs for their own people. By studying the hunting arts of the Indians and by trading with them, white pioneers were able to get meat more quickly and stocks of furs.

Unhappily, relations with the Indians were not all confined to genial exchanges of arts and commodities. Human nature, red and white, also displayed cruelty and stupidity. From time immemorial Indian tribes had fought among themselves, the warlike nomads preying upon the tribes that tilled the soil, the settled tribes trying to defend themselves, tribes battling against other tribes for other reasons or without rationality. Under the thin veneer of their civilization the barbaric greed and brutality of innumerable whites led them to rob, murder, betray, and try to enslave Indians. White traders sold them whisky and firearms and cheated them in transactions over furs and the purchase of lands. Thus the whites incited retaliations even among Indians formerly disposed to be friendly.

So sporadic brawls, local conflicts, and general wars punctuated the relations of whites and Indians all along the line from North to South and all through the years from the early days in Virginia to the close of the colonial period. After the whites had introduced the Indians to "fire water" and guns the fighting became more desperate and bloody as the years passed and as the frontier advanced upon the Indian hunting grounds. Nothing but stockades, militiamen, and eternal vigilance prevented the Indians from exterminating many of the early settlements and keeping the frontier constantly aflame.

Besides encountering the strange aborigines, the first English settlers found themselves in the presence of new and wide variations of climate. In their old home they had been accustomed to a moderate temperature. Now they had before them a great range of climate from the cold coasts of Maine to the hot savannahs of Georgia, with all the gradations from the far North to the deep South. To the exigencies of these variations, all the immigrants, from the British Isles as well as the Continent, had to adapt their economy and ways of living. Wherever the colonists set to work in clearing land for tillage, building houses, sowing and reaping, and producing the commodities required for living, they had to take into account the conditioning element of climate.

The soil at their feet was likewise a conditioning feature of their life in America. It, too, presented variations, from the small fields in narrow valleys, the rocky ground and steep hillsides of New England, through the broad and fertile valleys of the middle colonies, to the pine barrens, swamps, clay, and shallow loam of the deep South. Yet in every colony settlers could find land on which to produce all the grains, vegetables, and fruits for their staple foodstuffs and grasses for the grazing of livestock. Nothing was needed to furnish a generous and diverse food supply from the cultivation of the earth except implements, skills, good management, and hard labor.

While the soil for the most part was favorable to multiform agricultural production, clay beds and quarries yielded bricks, stones, and marble for building purposes. Primeval forests provided additional means of a livelihood more abundant than that of workers on the land in England or Western Europe. In every section the amazing array of trees offered materials for every kind of shelter from quickly constructed cabins to carefully built great manor houses, for barns and workshops, for the making of furniture and other household equipment, and for the output of staves, barrels, and lumber to be shipped to England in payment of debts partly incurred by the purchase of the finer grades of manufactured goods.

In the forests were also wild animals in a great variety, the furs and skins of which were useful for domestic purposes and profitable for export. In the forests was wild game for food—turkeys, deer, rabbits, and squirrels, for instance—and more meat and more kinds of meat could be procured than the plain peoples had ever enjoyed in the Old World, at first without asking the permission of any lord or gamekeeper or poaching secretly on private preserves. In the forests were nuts, berries, grapes, and other wild fruits available to agile climbers and pickers, aids to a balanced diet and free as the air.

Moreover the rivers, brooks, ponds, and lakes teemed with fish easy even for children to catch, while off the long coast were deep-sea fish accessible to professional fishermen.

Most of the immigrants who came to the colonies, rich and poor alike, knew more about agriculture than about any other practical art; and in turning to the creation of real wealth, by inclination and necessity, they found ways and means of applying this knowledge in old and new forms. At home the English had been accustomed to the production of a few standard commodities—a few grains, fruits, vegetables, and meats. In the colonies, owing to the variations in climate and soil, they were able to produce new and special crops. In many respects this very fact had decisive influences on the branches of agriculture which they developed, on types of commodities entering into the trade with the mother country, on the growth of wealth in America, and on the social characteristics of the several regions from Maine to Georgia.

Besides possessing extraordinary resources for the food, clothing, and shelter required in daily living, the South from Maryland to Georgia had climate and soil especially suitable for the raising of certain staples which supplemented the agricultural economy of England, provided cargoes for English vessels, and business for English merchants. First among these staples was tobacco. While Virginia was still an infant settlement the raising of tobacco became almost a mania.

Zeal for tobacco production quickly spread all along the Southern coastal plains as new colonies were founded and as supplies of indentured white laborers and servile laborers—Negro slaves—increased. Planters gathered great fortunes from tobacco and the prospect of larger fortunes led them to push into the interior even up into the foothills. News of the prosperity to be won by tobacco growing stimulated the immigration of capitalistic planters and merchants ever ready to handle cargoes. Tobacco planters became land speculators and engrossers of small freehold plots. Until the eve of the American Revolution, Southern riches rested largely on this crop.

A second Southern staple from which flowed new wealth was rice. The settlement near Charleston, South Carolina, founded in 1672, was little more than ten years old when it was discovered that rice could be grown luxuriantly in the swampy lands of the coast and along the rivers. In favorable years planters could make as high as a forty per cent return on their capital invested in rice fields and slave labor. Here, too, was a staple which England and European countries did not produce and hence it furnished a profitable article of export for which there was a large demand. Between 1713 and 1724 exports of rice through Charleston rose from 3000 barrels a year to 124,000 barrels. As the death rate of slaves in the rice swamps was high, rice production fostered the importation of slaves and furnished business for British and New England shippers, adding to their wealth.

Near the middle of the eighteenth century a third staple was added to Southern economy—indigo. This was a precious dyestuff, one of the most important until the rise of modern chemistry, and indispensable to the English textile industry. The successful production of this staple was due to the perseverance of Eliza Lucas, who in her youth took over the management of three plantations owned by her father, then governor of Antigua.

Securing indigo seeds from her father in the West Indies, Miss Lucas tested them on her own land. Previous attempts by others had been failures, but by persistence she demonstrated that crops could be produced successfully in South Carolina. Indigo grown on one of her plantations served as a wedding dower when she married Charles Pinckney, of Charleston, in 1744. Pinckney encouraged his neighbors to go into the business. Four years later the British Parliament voted a bounty of sixpence per pound to producers. With this aid and a fair price in England, planters could make a profit ranging from thirty to fifty per cent a year. So valuable did indigo become that small cubes of it were used for money during the Revolution when all forms of paper currency became worthless.

Far to the North, in New England, climate and soil confined colonists to the production of agricultural commodities practically identical with those which could be raised in England. Moreover the narrow valleys, rocky hills, and stony yet often fertile land were unfavorable to the establishment of plantations or great landed estates of any type. There were, in truth, many extensive land holdings in parts of New England, especially in early days, but there was available no cheap and adequate supply of labor by which they could be tilled with large profits to owners. Besides, New England was peopled mainly by yeomen used to owning and tilling small farms and by farm laborers eager to get possession of land in their own right.

So in respect of agriculture New England became a region of small holdings on which farming families produced for their own use nearly all the commodities necessary to a comfortable living. Although iron, salt, some tools, and finer cloths, if any were bought, had to come from the towns, practically everything else was grown or made on the farm. Life on such farms was hard—toil from sun to sun. Out of it came no large accumulations of wealth or cargoes of grain, flour, or meat for export. Yet it yielded a high degree of economic well-being and freedom from dependence on the fortunes of British commerce. With it went a spirit

of impatience at most forms of official control from above which interfered with the course of farm and community affairs. If New England
agriculture produced no great riches for English merchants or investors,
it did produce wealth for the support of a large farming population,
sturdy, educated, and owing neither rents nor obeisance to overlords.

In the middle colonies between New England and the South, agriculture took other forms. The soil, more level and fertile than that of New
England, was adapted to the production of similar crops on a larger
scale, but the climate was not favorable to the establishment of plantations for raising tobacco, rice, or indigo in the Southern style. There were
many great estates in New York, tilled by tenants under terms akin to
feudal bondage. Landlords and speculators—Dutch, English, and American—managed, by investment, chicanery, and corruption, to engross from
one half to two thirds of the land in the colony. Enormous holdings,
comparable in size to great plantations in the South, were in the hands
of a relatively few families, for example, the Van Rensselaers, the Van
Cortlandts, the Schuylers, the Phillipses, the Beekmans, the Livingstons,
and the Morrises. The estate of the Beekmans embraced 240,000 acres,
that of the Van Cortlandts 140,000 acres, and the holdings of the Van
Rensselaers about Albany no less then 700,000 acres.

Often the landed families of New York combined agriculture with shipping and merchandising, sometimes by intermarriage. For instance, Frederick Phillipse, a rich Dutch landlord of the Hudson Valley, while traveling at sea on a packet line operated by Margaret Hardenbroeck, a Dutch
landowner and merchant, was captivated by her personality and enterprise. Soon afterward, in 1662, they were married, and united in a single
household landlordism with zeal for commercial undertakings. While
Frederick looked after his estates and later engaged in shipping so irregularly that he was charged with being involved in the piratical activities
of Captain Kidd, Margaret attended principally to regular mercantile undertakings and proved to be "a very desirable business partner."

After New Jersey was taken from the Dutch in 1664 and turned over
to English proprietors, efforts were made to create large estates there. The
proprietors themselves engaged in land speculation, established titles to
huge areas in their own names, and in their eagerness to sell land in
large blocks carved out many holdings of considerable size. But the inhabitants of New Jersey, especially of the western part, almost rose in
arms against this land policy. Even the proprietors came to see, at least
dimly, that to increase the population and wealth of the colony provision
must be made for selling, even giving, land in small plots to actual settlers
prepared to cultivate them.

In Pennsylvania the proprietor had the right, like the proprietor of
Maryland, under his charter, to lay out and sell great estates, manors,

in his colony and he did in fact lend some encouragement to great land-lordism. But most of Pennsylvania was divided into farms that could be tilled by their owners aided only by one or a few extra laborers, if any. Furthermore large numbers of pioneers simply settled on the frontier without asking the permission of Penn or anybody else. Thus farming on a small or moderate scale became the general rule in Pennsylvania agriculture.

With agriculture the population of all the colonies became self-sustaining as regards food products; and by the tens of thousands farmers grew prosperous, as prosperity was rated, in tilling their own soil; not rich in gold coins or paper claims, but secure in real wealth—houses, barns, stock, tools, and all the means of commodious living. The great areas of level land in the middle colonies, free from stones and covered by a fertile top-soil, enabled them to produce a surplus of grains, beef, pork, and bacon for export. Thus they could pay for imported manufactures and enter into competition with British agriculture in respect of its principal staples.

Inasmuch as even the planters of the South usually combined the production of foodstuffs, for their slaves and for their own use, with the raising of special staples for the British market, all the colonies were, therefore, soon independent of the Old World with regard to these primary essentials of living. There were few if any landlords in New England as rich as the largest Southern planters; but from New York to the borders of Virginia there were landlords who could vie in wealth with the greatest Southern planters. Indeed as the soil on the coastal plains of the South was worn down by intensive cultivation and returns from tobacco raising diminished, the relative position of landlords in New York and Pennsylvania improved.

Closely connected with the agricultural pursuits was domestic manufacturing in the strict sense of that phrase—making things by hand at home. This was especially true in the colonies north of Maryland which produced no great staples that were not also produced in Great Britain. Southern planters did raise crops, such as tobacco, rice, and indigo, that did not compete with British agriculture and could therefore be readily exchanged for British manufactured goods, since those crops were desired by British buyers. But from Pennsylvania northward and in all the back-country regions farming families, having no such staples to sell to English merchants, had to make many things themselves or go without them. And countless families refused to be deprived of necessities and comforts of a manufactured kind. Many men and women among them were Jacks-of-all-trades, meaning "artists in living," and they made living an art by their domestic manufacturing. Even great planters in the South established workshops on their estates in which commodities for household use, for supplying slaves, and for other purposes were manufactured out of materials at hand.

The extent to which manufacturing combined with agriculture could go was represented on the estates of Robert Carter, of Virginia, the grandson of a rich planter, colonial officer, land speculator, and businessman in Virginia. Carter's land holding, including his family seat in Westmoreland County, embraced about 70,000 acres (his grandfather had owned some 300,000 acres) and his slaves numbered more than five hundred. Besides raising tobacco and other agricultural produce, he maintained many shops on his properties for making cloth and salt, grinding grain, baking bread, and working iron. Agriculture and manufacturing he supplemented by selling goods as a merchant, lending money at interest like a banker, and sending ships to and fro carrying goods. At his great mansion, so large that it took twenty-eight fireplaces going full blast to warm it in wintertime, Carter whiled away his leisure hours with balls, music, reading, and dinner parties. Yet, with the aid of overseers and superintendents, and his wife's co-operation, he managed to hold all his agricultural, manufacturing, and trading enterprises together and keep them in successful and profitable operation.

On farms and plantations from New Hampshire to Georgia men usually made and repaired farm implements—plows, sleds, wagons, and hoes. Out of furs and skins they made shoes, hats, and caps. Out of wood they fashioned furniture, churns, spinning wheels, and looms. Where wrought iron was available they manufactured nails, shovels, and chains. At the same time women generally turned their skills and wits to making cloth, rugs, soap, candles, bedding, coverlets, tablecloths, and garments. They also operated processing plants, in which bread was baked, meat was packed, fruits and vegetables were dehydrated and preserved, and butter was churned.

As a rule the products of home workshops were used on the farm or plantation but in time women developed an industry which turned out goods for community and colonial markets. With flax for linen at their command and, in the Northern colonies, wool from sheep, they set to work spinning and weaving with such vim that their output soon alarmed British merchants, who wanted the textile markets free for their own manufactures. While most of the cloth produced by women at their homes was coarse in quality and used mainly for "working clothes," the finer linens and woolens compared well with the grades offered by British merchants. As time went on women so improved the textile art that they made it possible for Americans to clothe themselves well, if not in the finest goods, and to achieve a high degree of economic independence in one primary line of manufacturing.

☆

For the development of agriculture and domestic manufacturing, an abundant and increasing supply of labor, skilled and unskilled, was furnished by the migration of free whites and indentured white laborers and the importation of Negro slaves. On the small farm owned and operated by the freehold family, the husband, wife, and children did all the work in fields, forest, workshops, and the house. At harvest time and on other special occasions, the family might have the co-operative help of neighbors in return for similar labor, but it carried the main burden of its own self-support.

After crossroad settlements and villages arose as centers for stores and craftsmen who made things on order, the farm family could be relieved from certain tasks at home by exchanging farm produce with the smith or woodworker for "odd jobs" or manufactured goods. As colonization proceeded, itinerant artisans—tinkers, smiths, weavers, bakers, tailors, and carpenters—wandered from community to community and worked for their board, lodging, and payments in coin. Yet even in the most populous of the rural regions there was little specialization. The farm family supplied most of the labor for agriculture and domestic manufacturing.

On the larger farms of the North the labor of the owner and his family was often supplemented by the labor of one or more indentured servants. Such a servant was a person bound by contract to work for an employer for a term of years, ranging from four to seven as a rule, in return for board, lodging, and clothing, and some gift or gifts on the expiration of the service. Many men, women, and children kidnaped by gangsters in Great Britain or taken from prisons were shipped over against their will for sale into servitude. But nearly all indentured servants were immigrants who had freely chosen their hard lot in the hope of eventual advantages. They preferred this choice to remaining in the Old World where they could either find no work at all or had to toil all their lives with no prospects of more than subsistence wages.

In all the colonies from early days there were indentured servants, mainly farmers but often household workers and craftsmen. Although the number was small in New England, it was large in Virginia and the middle colonies. Eighteen years after the founding of Jamestown in 1607 more than one third of Virginia's inhabitants were indentured servants. During the closing years of the seventeenth century more than one third of all the immigrants in Pennsylvania were of this class and the proportion did not decrease for a long time.

After they had finished their term of service indentured servants were free to make their way as best they could. Those who were skillful, industrious, and fortunate either acquired farms of their own in the neighborhood or went west to the frontier to settle on new land. Or, if they were especially ingenious in the crafts, they went to the towns and set up shops for themselves or found employment with merchants and master craftsmen. At all events no stigma of servitude rested upon them and, as far as the law was concerned, they could and often did rise to good fortune and even honors in their colony. The fact that they had started near the bottom put no bar against their advancement. Although thousands of servants, on the expiration of their indentures, joined the "poor whites," South and North, the great majority of them merged with the population of farmers and artisans and shared their labors and advantages as free citizens.

In an entirely different position were the Negroes imported from Africa and sold into bondage. As early as 1619 Negroes were brought to Virginia and soon slavery became an established institution under the law. Before many years it spread to all the colonies, and by 1770 about one sixth of the entire population were Negro slaves.

In the North, however, climate, soil, and types of agriculture made slavery on a large scale unprofitable; and, comparatively speaking, the proportion of Negro slaves remained small. In the colony of New York, by way of illustration, it amounted to only about one seventh of the population at the end of the colonial period. On the other hand the climate, soil, staple crops, and plantation system of the South favored the use of slave labor. White bond servants were often intractable, their terms of service made them impermanent laborers, and the most enterprising among them valiantly struggled to get land for themselves as soon as they became free. Negro slaves by contrast had to work for their masters as long as they lived and could be bought in great numbers as the slave traffic increased. Only by slavery, planters insisted, was it possible for them to expand rapidly the cultivation of the soil and make profits in large amounts. At all events, two thirds of the inhabitants of South Carolina were slaves at the close of the colonial period, and along the Southern seaboard the labor of Negroes underlay the wealth and power of masters.

By such means in the great rural resettlement the colonists were able to build up a strong agricultural economy that long continued to be the principal basis of American security. At the end of the colonial age at least nine tenths of the people, from New Hampshire to Georgia, lived on the land and produced for themselves the commodities necessary to a good, if often simple, living. A few thousand great landlords, North and South, grew rich on tenant and slave labor and lived luxuriously. But the overwhelming majority of the white people belonged to families that owned, frequently under mortgage it is true, small farms and worked with their own hands in fields, forests, farmhouses, and little shops.

Their life was toilsome, no doubt, but by their mode of living, their self-supporting economy, and their spirit of independence they made a rural order different from the Old World orders of tenantry, feudalism, and serfdom. In self-sustaining industry, character, and love of their freedom, they formed a body of working people such as had never appeared before in the history of Western civilization.

Chapter 4

THE RISE OF COLONIAL COMMERCE AND INDUSTRY

ALTHOUGH THE population in the colonial age continued to be predominantly agricultural, the character of American life, the evolution of American society, and the total power of American economy, as it gathered force, represented a combination of agriculture, commerce, and industry.

From the beginning of colonization, commerce was integrated with agriculture. It carried over the sea certain raw materials of the colonies and brought back from England tools and other finished commodities that increased the productivity of agriculture and raised the standard of rural life. It speeded up the circulation of commodities within and among the colonies, giving outlets to surplus domestic manufactures and acquainting the people of each section with the people, customs, and economic activities of other sections. Besides pouring commodities into commercial channels, industry evoked the energies of local enterprise, enabled Americans to produce many kinds of things hitherto imported, and demonstrated to discerning persons the immense potentialities of American resources. Together, commerce and industry permitted the accumulation of large capitals in American hands, decreasing dependence on British investors.

The promotion of commerce was an essential element of the mercantilist policy under which the English government operated, and was among the purposes of the companies and proprietors that led in colonization. A provision of the Virginia charter issued in 1606 granted to the London Company special privileges in trade, by laying heavy duties on the commerce of outsiders, English and foreign, and turning the revenue into its treasury for a term of years. To meet the cost of the expedition that brought the Pilgrims to Plymouth in 1620, a large sum was borrowed from English capitalists and the debt could only be paid by gathering in articles of commerce, such as fish and furs, which could be sent back to England. The royal patent of 1681 constituting William

Penn proprietor of Pennsylvania also gave him the right to build harbors and docks for commercial purposes and to lay customs duties on goods "to be laded and unladed" at such ports and places. If colonization was to be profitable to English investors, cargoes had to be provided for the return voyages of ships that transported immigrants and their goods to America.

The early newcomers to America were under obligations to look about for objects of commerce almost as soon as they landed. The first ship which deposited settlers in Virginia carried home a cargo of wooden staves prepared for it under the direction of Captain John Smith. Lumber and its by-products became commodities for export from Virginia before settlers in that colony learned to produce, cure, and pack tobacco.

Long before any colonies had been started, English sailors had embarked on large-scale fishing off the coasts of Newfoundland, and the early explorers had excited English interest in this business by glowing reports of haddock, cod, mackerel, and whales in unlimited quantities in the waters of that region. The Pilgrims at Plymouth and the Puritans at Massachusetts Bay, shortly after their arrival, began to build small boats and send out fishing expeditions. In time Boston, Salem, Marblehead, and a few other towns became busy ports for the fishing industry; and all down the coast fishing became a source of lucrative trading.

Besides furnishing supplies to American markets, fishermen cured and packed huge quantities for export. But the English themselves were extensively engaged in this industry, and American fishermen had to seek other than British markets. They found them principally in France, Portugal, Spain, and the West Indies. On the basis of this exchange an immense business was built up. The fish shipped to Spain, for example, were exchanged for citrus fruits and specie, and the specie was used to pay for English manufactures. The fish sent to the West Indies were traded for sugar and specie; a part of the sugar went to the colonies and another part, with the specie, went to England to pay debts and buy manufactures.

With particular doggedness the fishermen of New England turned to whaling. At first they concentrated their efforts largely in the waters off Newfoundland, but in time they pushed their enterprise all over the Atlantic, using the ports of New Bedford and Nantucket as their chief bases of operation.

So extensive were their whaling voyages and so daring were their undertakings that Edmund Burke, when in 1775 he warned the British Parliament against "ill-considered" tampering with the strength and independence of Americans, paused to give a dramatic picture of their whaling industry: "Look at the manner in which the people of New England have of late carried on the whale fishery. Whilst we follow them among the tumbling mountains of ice, and behold them penetrating into the deepest frozen recesses of Hudson's Bay and Davis's Straits, whilst we are looking for them beneath the Arctic circle, we hear that they have pierced into the opposite region of polar cold, that they are at the antipodes, and engaged under the frozen serpent of the South. . . . Nor is the equinoctial heat more discouraging to them, than the accumulated winter of both the poles.

"We know that whilst some of them draw the line and strike the harpoon on the coast of Africa, others run the longitude, and pursue their gigantic game along the coast of Brazil. No sea but what is vexed by their fisheries. No climate that is not witness to their toils. Neither the perseverance of Holland, nor the activity of France, nor the dexterous and firm sagacity of English enterprise, ever carried this most perilous mode of hard industry to the extent to which it has been pushed by this recent people; a people who are still, as it were, but in the gristle, and not yet hardened into the bone of manhood."

Although the British at home caught plenty of fish for themselves and took relatively little from American exporters, they were short of one prime raw material which the colonies had in abundance—timber. They had exhausted many of their forest areas in building houses, shops, and ships, and in supplying charcoal for their iron industries. British shortage of timber was thus an opportunity for the colonists and they made haste to meet it. Almost at the outset of settlement they had to cut down trees in clearing land for cultivation and they saved many choice logs—especially oak, pine, and walnut—for shipment to England.

Within a few years little sawmills were built along the streams and rivers, and enterprising merchants began to produce lumber in various forms for the English market. New England, New York, Pennsylvania, and North Carolina became the main centers of such undertakings.

In time Americans were supplying finished and semifinished timber products for local, intercolonial, and English markets, such as masts and spars for ships, shingles, and staves for barrels and casks. By developing the lumber industry Americans were enabled to discharge debts in England, buy English manufactures, accumulate profits for new investments in colonial lands and business adventures.

Furs and skins furnished another immensely profitable group of articles for commerce. For some time they were readily procured by colonists near their settlements or from Indian hunters who brought them to the very doors of houses, as soon as they learned that they could exchange otter, mink, bear, fox, beaver, and deer furs or skins for beads, metal knives, hoes, hatchets, cloth, and trinkets. Able to buy furs for so little and sell them overseas at enormous prices, white traders reaped golden rewards from this business. Farmers could supplement agriculture by gathering in furs without giving much time to it. Nor did they need capital for the easy traffic. While settlers clung to the shores and forests still stood at the back doors of cabins, dealing in furs was a simpler transaction than the catching and selling of fish or the cutting and shipping of lumber.

But as forests were cleared for farming and settlements pushed inland, the fur business became more restricted for farmers who were not located on the frontier. Now organized enterprise steadily pressed into the collecting and bundling of furs for shipment. Monopolies of the trade in certain regions were sought and sometimes obtained by personal initiative or through government grants. Among the Dutch, who preceded the English as settlers in the Hudson River valley, fur monopolies were rich prizes over which merchants and officials waged many a lusty contest.

Even in favorable circumstances hunters, woodsmen, and trappers who roamed the frontiers freely in search of furs were finally at the mercy of fur merchants who usually fixed the prices at their own pleasure. As the frontier was pushed westward and forests were cleared, the fur business needed ever larger amounts of capital to pay for scouting and the maintenance of trading stations in the far backwoods. So the traffic in furs gradually became highly organized and tended to concentrate in the hands of a few merchants, British and American. By the close of the colonial period competition between them for mastery over this trade often broke out in political quarrels at colonial capitals and in London.

With the expansion of fishing, lumbering, and fur trading, opportunities widened for the sale of ships, iron products, and other commodities that were not supplied by domestic manufacturers. This in turn stimulated the establishment of native manufacturing industries in the neighborhood of farms and plantations, especially in the North. Three industries attained first rank: shipbuilding, ironworking, and flour milling.

So abundant in the colonies were ship timber and naval stores, including tar, that shipbuilding soon became an important business. Being British subjects, Americans enjoyed the benefits of British navigation laws; ships built in the colonies and manned by Americans belonged to the merchant marine of the mother country and had the same rights in the shipping business. And special circumstances favored American shipbuilding. It was cheaper to build vessels in the colonies, where materials were abundant, than in England, for the English had to import a large part of their ship timber and naval stores. The rapid growth of the fishing industry also made a local demand for ships.

In response to these opportunities and needs, shipyards sprang up all along the coast, especially north of Maryland; a lucrative industry gave employment to ship carpenters and yielded profits to investors. Before long Americans were building ships as stout and swift as any that sailed the seas.

In its turn shipbuilding spurred other industries, particularly the production of ship timber, tar, chains, rope, anchors, and nails. Now there was a demand for ironworking on a scope larger than that needed for making the few types of agricultural implements then in use.

Here again the state of things in England had to be considered. The English had iron ore in abundance and their iron industry had reached a high stage of development. But they used charcoal for smelting ore and were exhausting their local wood supply. On the other hand, Americans had iron ore in almost every colony and their charcoal sources were practically unlimited.

In these circumstances English interest called for the importation of pig, or rough, iron to be transformed in English foundries into finished products for English usage and for export to the colonies. The Americans could, of course, supply the pig iron to English merchants. But they also had skill for working iron into products necessary to their own agriculture and industry and could approach self-sufficiency in that line.

Iron ore was discovered by the first settlers in Virginia and they sent a large quantity of it to England in 1608. Within a few years they were smelting ore and working iron in the colony and might have gone far with it if tobacco raising had not proved to be a quicker way of making large profits. Puritans also early unearthed iron ore. By 1644 Massachusetts had an ironworks in operation. In the other New England colonies and in the middle colonies the discovery of iron deposits was quickly followed by the building of furnaces for ore smelting and mills for hammering, rolling, and slitting iron.

At the middle of the eighteenth century American ironmasters were making iron products of nearly every kind—chains, anchors, guns, kettles, axes, knives, nails, iron bars, and pipes. For fine iron products, such as the best cutlery, needles, and carpenters' tools, the colonies depended largely on imports from England. But the arts of iron manufacture were being steadily improved; so steadily, in fact, that British merchants grew worried over American competition in the colonial market.

Flour and lumber milling industries rose and flourished as agriculture and shipbuilding advanced. Right at hand was wood for water wheels and mills, and hard stone for millstones. Almost everywhere streams rushing down to the sea could be used for power. With the increase in the production of grain for home consumption, the crude labor of pounding, grinding, and bolting wheat, corn, and rye in domestic shops became so burdensome that farmers welcomed the release from it. As the export of grain from the middle colonies enlarged, merchants saw a chance to add to their profits by substituting flour in barrels for the shipment of grain in the raw state. Very early the demands of shipbuilding outran the supply of lumber which could be sawed slowly by hand, and as prospering colonists prepared to move from log cabins to frame houses local needs for lumber and shingles were multiplied.

So on the streams from New Hampshire to Georgia, mills were built to process grain and saw logs into various types of lumber. Sometimes the two processes were combined at a single mill; often they were separated. In Pennsylvania enterprising flour millers barreled their flour for shipment and even erected shops for baking bread and manufacturing the famous hardtack biscuits served to sailors on naval and merchant vessels.

From the farms and plantations, from the gathering of raw materials, from the ironworks, from mills for grinding grain and sawing timber flowed a swelling stream of various commodities to be marketed in the colonies or abroad and exchanged for colonial or British manufactures. Here were expanding opportunities for specialized merchants and shippers. Often, if not usually, the merchant was a shipowner, and combined the business of buying and selling with the business of transporting. But whatever the form of operation, American commercial enterprise had a spacious theater in which to distribute goods and accumulate gains. At home it could use the coastal waters and navigable streams penetrating interior regions. Before it was the Atlantic Ocean, touching all the ports of Europe and Africa, as well as those of Great Britain.

As the population of America rose—from about 300,000 in 1700 to about 2,500,000 in 1770—trade and shipping were extended. In the beginning most of this business was in the hands of merchants resident in England, who operated personally or through agents in the colonies; but it was not long before Americans entered into a vigorous competition with them. Colonists could build and navigate ships, as well as keep accounts and handle commercial transactions. What was to hinder them from gathering more and more of the business into their own hands? As events proved, nothing could.

Five main avenues of trade were open to American merchants and shippers. One branch of their commerce was with Great Britain. Another was with European ports—French, Spanish, and Portuguese—in certain commodities. A third was with the British West Indies and, often illegally, with the French West Indies. Intercolonial trade also flourished from port to port along the Atlantic coast and from point to point along the navigable rivers reaching into the interior. In prosecuting the slave trade, merchants and shippers, particularly from New England and New York, visited the shores of Africa and carried away cargoes of Negroes for the plantations of the West Indies and the South and to supply the smaller markets of the Northern colonies. When wars were raging—frequently the case in the seventeenth and eighteenth centuries—shipowners could embark on privateering, sometimes akin to piracy, and prey upon French, Dutch, or Spanish commerce.

With the wealth garnered from transporting goods was thus combined the loot of commercial wars. When George III ascended the throne in 1760 American merchants and shippers in the great colonial ports were numerous enough, rich enough, and powerful enough to vie with the stoutest merchants of Bristol and London.

The development of commerce and industry encouraged an increasing immigration of workers who specialized in the several crafts, including shipbuilding; and in the course of time the line between purely domestic artisans and industrial mechanics became sharper in the rural districts and very definite in the towns. At the end of the colonial period the colonies thus had an important, if small, body of industrial workers engaged solely in the manufacture of goods for the markets.

Carpenters, masons, smiths, and woodworkers were among the earliest immigrants in the seventeenth century. Some were freemen. Others were indentured servants. With the rise of shipbuilding, ironworking, flour milling and other industries, the stream of artisans, free and indentured, swelled in size, though it was never large enough in the opinion of business enterprisers in the colonies. Workers from the British Isles, from Germany, Holland, Sweden, Switzerland, and France crowded the incoming ships and played a vital part in the building up of industry, commerce, and the standard of living.

Besides regular workers competent in using wood, stone, and other materials for the construction of simple buildings and the manufacture of articles necessary to a commodious living, there were in all the colonies designers and artisans of special and higher skills. Among them were architects, woodcarvers, silversmiths, wheelwrights, potters, pewterers, and makers of glassware, watches, leatherware, coaches, and cabinets.

After the first years of pioneering were over, architects began to design and erect fine mansions for great landlords and merchants, stately buildings for public purposes, and handsome churches for religious worship. So solid, beautiful, indeed exquisite, was much of their work that it became the pride of discriminating colonists and their descendants. In the designing and making of elegant furniture, objects of glass, panels for walls and doors, mantels, carvings for cornices and porticoes, iron gates and grills, silver ornaments of tableware, masters of such arts could satisfy fastidious taste and at the same time supply markets with goods at prices which enabled even small farmers, storekeepers, and mechanics to incorporate some refinements into their simple ways of living.

Out of the economic activities of numberless men and women, white and black, especially out of the export and import trade in all its branches, developed specialized centers of settlement on the seacoast and at favorable points on inland waters. By 1690 the foundations of flourishing cities had been laid at Boston, Newport, New York, Philadelphia, and Charleston. According to careful estimates, the population of these towns at that time was as follows:

Boston, founded in 1630, 7000.
Newport, founded in 1639, 2600.
New York, founded as New Amsterdam in 1625, 3900.
Philadelphia, founded in 1682, 4000.
Charleston, founded in 1672, 1100.

On the eve of the Revolution in 1774, Philadelphia, serving as a leading port of entry for immigrants and for the shipping of surplus produce from a great hinterland, had forged to the top. With almost 40,000 inhabitants, it stood first in population and was second only to London among the cities of the British Empire. Boston had about 20,000 inhabitants; Newport 12,000; New York between 25,000 and 30,000; and Charleston about 10,000. Except in the case of Boston these were only estimates but, however out of line on one side or the other, they corresponded roughly to the facts.

Among other growing centers of trade on the coast or inland were Salem, Providence, New Haven, Perth Amboy, Baltimore, Richmond, and Savannah. Among the minor towns, as yet little more than overgrown villages but increasing in size, were Albany, Princeton, Trenton, Germantown, Lancaster, Annapolis, Norfolk, and Wilmington in North Carolina. Although the population of all the cities having more than 8000 inhabitants was less than three per cent of the total population of the colonies, their importance in wealth and as centers of economic, social, political, and intellectual activity outweighed the mere number of their inhabitants.

Of the total wealth produced by all the economic activities of men, women, and children in all the colonies from year to year between 1607, the founding of Virginia, and 1774, on the eve of the rift with Great Britain, no official census was ever taken. Nor were any figures recorded from which more than the roughest guesses could be made. The first census taken by the United States, in 1790, gave only the population— 3,172,000 whites and 700,000 Negroes. Of this population, according to reckonings by family names, 75.2% were English, Scotch, and Scotch-Irish in origins; 3.7% South Irish; 8.7% Germans, and the rest Dutch, Swedish, French, and miscellaneous.

Although no economic census was taken in colonial times, two well-established facts indicate that the annual output of wealth was immense and on the increase. It was great enough to provide the main support of the rapidly growing population, particularly with regard to the primary staples of living, and a surplus for export. That the output was rising swiftly was disclosed by figures for the trade with Great Britain. In his address to the House of Commons in 1775 *On Conciliation with America*, Edmund Burke presented the following table:

The whole export trade of England, including that to colonies in 1704 . . . . £6,509,000.
Export to the colonies alone [including Canada and the West Indies] in 1772 . . . .£6,024,000

Well could Burke exclaim: "The trade with America alone is now within less than £500,000 of being equal to what this great commercial nation, England, carried on at the beginning of this century with the whole world!"

The exact amount of the English export to the thirteen American colonies was not separated in Burke's figures from the trade with Canada and the British West Indies; but there was no doubt about its magnitude. No longer were the Americans puny colonists almost wholly dependent on Great Britain for capital, primary supplies, and manufactures. They had built up on this continent a great society and provided for it an economic underwriting of unquestionable strength. What was more: they saw extraordinary chances for the expansion of their enterprise and were determined to take advantage of them.

Chapter 5

GROWTH OF SOCIAL AND INTELLECTUAL
AUTONOMY

WHATEVER may have been the visions of English kings who
chartered companies and granted patents to proprietors for the
purpose of founding colonies in America;

Whatever may have been the intentions of the companies and proprietors who planted settlements;

Whatever may have been the dreams of the English leaders who hoped
to see a New England established beyond the sea;

Whatever may have been the hopes of immigrants who acquired great
estates and became mighty landlords or turned to commerce and became
rich merchants able to compete with the most powerful merchants of
London;

Whatever may have been the aspirations of the men and women engaged in tilling the soil and building up domestic manufactures, or of the
artisans devoted to developing industries and creating the refinements of
living;

However much of the Old World heritage the immigrants brought with
them to the New World;

There were from the beginning social and intellectual tendencies which
reinforced the separatist qualities and energies that had led to migration
and worked in the direction of consolidation and autonomy in the
colonies.

Giving form and force to these autonomous tendencies were certain
elemental facts. In America emigrants from England did not reproduce
the whole social order of England—king, lords, established church, and
peasantry with no hope of owning land. Nor did they reproduce the whole
intellectual outlook of England. Neither did they begin anew, from
primitive origins, the history of civilization in the Old World and thus
start repeating that history as it had been from the days of savagery. The
overwhelming majority of the emigrants to America, from the early years
to the close of the colonial period, were dissenters from the Church of

England, whether they were English, Scotch, French, or German. No less opposed to that religious establishment were the English and Irish Catholics who found refuge in the colonies. Despite claims to aristocratic origins made by proud descendants, the overwhelming majority of the emigrants to America were from the "middling orders"—agricultural, mercantile, and artisan. And for their activities in America, whatever the ambitions and hopes of any or all the immigrants, there were two conditioning material realities which helped to shape their fortunes—a virgin continent vast in extent and resources, and three thousand miles of water separating them from the world they had left behind.

Helping to sustain autonomous tendencies and strengthen them as they developed were, first, the qualities of the immigrants as such and, second, the knowledge and ideas acquired from the Old World, out of which they came, and modified for their purposes, in the course of colonial evolution. This truth was firmly grasped by Mercy Otis Warren, herself a colonial, born at Barnstable, Massachusetts, in 1728 and long a resident of Plymouth. "The first emigrations to North America," she wrote, "were not composed of a strolling banditti of rude nations, like the first people of most other colonies in the history of the world." On the contrary, she declared, speaking out of direct knowledge: "The early settlers in the newly discovered continent were as far advanced in civilization, policy, and manners; in their ideas of government, the nature of compacts, and the bands of civil union, as any of their neighbors at that period among the most polished nations of Europe." While recognizing that vices of Europe had also come with virtues, Mrs. Warren maintained that "the progress of everything had there [in America] been remarkably rapid from the first settlement of the country. Learning was cultivated, knowledge disseminated, politeness and morals improved, and valor and patriotism cherished, in proportion to the rapidity of her population."

The qualities of mind and character to which Mrs. Warren referred we abundantly illustrated in the little colony of Plymouth, founded in 1620. Two outstanding leaders among the Pilgrims were Elder William Brewster and William Bradford. Brewster was the son of a local bailiff and postmaster in Yorkshire and had spent some time at Cambridge University in his youth. His library, as a biographer has said, "proves him to have been well read in history, philosophy, and religious poetry and shows that he continued to buy books throughout his life." Bradford, brought up in his youth to follow the plow, was a self-educated man of wide learning who, in his intellectual explorations, read among other books the *Republic* by Jean Bodin, French writer on government and society— a critique of Plato's idealistic and communistic theories. Both Brewster and Bradford displayed qualities of statesmanship, if in a small community, in dealing with lawless and discontented men who made grave troubles for the Pilgrims before and after they landed.

To Massachusetts Bay, during the early years, came more than one hundred graduates of Cambridge and Oxford universities. John Winthrop, the first governor of that colony, was the son of a lawyer and had studied at Cambridge. Roger Williams, who, in rebellion against the government of Massachusetts Bay, founded a freer community at Providence, belonged to a mercantile family of London, had graduated from Cambridge with honors, and was a philosophic thinker of humanist inclinations. Some of the later colonists, notably Charles Carroll, born in Maryland in 1737, were educated at the best Catholic institutions in Europe. Among the leaders in all the colonies were men who had studied law at the Temple in London, or theology, natural philosophy, the classics, medicine, and other branches of learning at the best institutions in Great Britain, on the Continent, or in both places.

From first to last colonial women in large numbers were well educated —though not in universities. Anne Hutchinson, evicted like Roger Williams from Boston for her independence of mind, was the daughter of a Puritan clergyman and wife of a well-to-do merchant, a mother of fourteen children, known for her learning and the vigor of her intellect—the reason for her eviction. Anne Bradstreet—ancestor of Oliver Wendell Holmes and Wendell Phillips—who arrived at Massachusetts Bay in 1630, was the daughter of Thomas Dudley, deputy governor under Winthrop, and the wife of Simon Bradstreet, a graduate of Cambridge. Eight tutors had been employed by her parents in starting her education and the poetry that she composed in America displayed her familiarity with Raleigh's *History of the World*, with Plutarch, Usher, and contemporary French literature. In every colony were numerous women of English, Dutch, Huguenot, and other national origins who had been trained in the classics and modern literature—women of the planting and professional circles, women of the great landed and mercantile families. And a stream of hired tutors in the prosperous families maintained this standard of the proprieties for sons and daughters.

As the sprawling and widely separated settlements grew into populous and orderly colonies, social and intellectual changes of weighty meaning for the future took place. In every colony members of the classes drew together for social and intellectual intercourse and formed permanent ties of customs, manners, and views. In the South the planting and merchant families led in this concentration; generally, in the North, clerical and merchant families took the leadership; in New York and Pennsylvania landlord, merchant, and professional families were preëminent.

In every colony intermarriage strengthened the social ties of the respective communities and intercolonial marriages fortified the enlarging sense of continental solidarity. As generation succeeded generation, memories of family bonds with the Old World grew dimmer and sentiments of attachment to the here and now deepened in their hold upon the minds and hearts of the people. Also, among small farmers and mechanics, increasing density of population was accompanied by multiplying points of contact, and by opportunities for intermarriage and concerted thinking and action relative to common interests. While in many respects these classes were at times in conflict in their communities, in other respects they had common ideas and grew accustomed to think of themselves as Americans.

Among the problems which marked the evolution of the American mind was the question of the permanence of the social system in each colony at each period of its development and the place of that system in the greater British society of which it was a political and economic part. Was this social system impervious to changes under the impacts of changing social facts and ideas? Was it to be defended through thick and thin against encroachments from below and within, and against encroachments from Great Britain—social as well as economic, religious, and political? If its permanence was to be secured, by whom was the feat to be accomplished and under what ideas and declarations?

Arrayed on the side of permanence for the patrician features of the inherited social system was the congenial association between royal governors and proprietors or their agents and the lords of land and trade. At imitation royal courts in the capitals of royal and proprietary colonies social preferment was given to the colonial upper classes and it deepened their affection for "the seasoned culture" of the British social order deemed the best and safest of all social orders. This relationship was dual: it strengthened ties with the mother country and confirmed loyalty to a social hierarchy in America. At such courts were formed centers of resistance to the turbulence of popular demands for a break with the fixations of the class structure in the colonies and the class domination of British rule.

The fine mansions of royal governors and proprietors or their agents were matched or surpassed by the mansions of the wealthy planters and merchants. To dwellers in such mansions mutual hospitality was extended. The menial services required for lavish entertainments were performed, alike for the governors and the governed, by servants, indentured, free, or slave. Similar raiment of fine woolens, silks, and laces gave distinction to the upper circles. The same manners, customs, and pretensions tightened the cords of unity between British and colonial "aristocrats."

If a royal governor or proprietary agent and his retinue of subordinate officials asserted high prerogatives, though flamboyantly, many of the colonial courtiers accepted the assertion as a part of British security and their own security within the aristocratic political and social system. When Governor Thomas Boone, shortly after his arrival in South Carolina in 1761, installed in his mansion at Charleston a woman who was not his wife the gentlemen of Charleston accepted his invitations as a necessary recognition of his privilege and their security, though the ladies boycotted his dinners.

Of the wealthy planting class that sought permanence in the order of special privilege, yet without servility to a royal governor, William Byrd II, of Virginia, was a pungent example. He was the grandson of a London goldsmith and the son of an Englishman who had amassed a great fortune in Virginia as a tobacco planter, merchant, slave trader, and land speculator. Inheriting that fortune, he established his family at Westover, not far from Jamestown. He had spent some time in England, studying law at the Temple and making friends in the ruling circles there. On his large estate at Westover, Byrd lived the life of a leisured country gentleman in a magnificent dwelling famous throughout the colony for its size and elegance, its splendid furnishings, and its exceptionally large and well-selected library, the largest private library in Virginia if not in all the colonies, containing about four thousand volumes.

For the struggling pioneers on the Carolina border Byrd developed a strong contempt, evident in the diary which he kept and in other writings. If his scorn for the small farmers who labored with their own hands in Virginia was less, he was determined that they should submit to government by gentlemen. For his own rights and property he stood up like a landed warrior. When the royal governor, Alexander Spotswood, tried to establish a high judicial court filled with his own appointees, Byrd went to England and protested with success to the Board of Trade. It was tyranny insufferable, in his opinion, for a governor to choose judges with power "to determine concerning not only the lives and liberties, but also concerning the whole estates" of the Virginia gentlemen.

A similar attitude toward an aristocratic order—permanence and conformity—was illustrated in Massachusetts, before and after it became a royal province in 1691, by a contemporary of Byrd, Samuel Sewall, a rich merchant and public official of that Northern colony. Sewall was the grandson of an English merchant. After graduation from Harvard College he entered upon a mercantile career in which he augmented the family patrimony. Like Byrd he was an omnivorous reader and kept a diary, besides writing on various subjects.

When Massachusetts lost its independence and was compelled to bow before a royal governor, Sewall accepted the new system and wrote in defense of it. He once said that it was "intolerable" for "private persons to print reflections and censures on the highest acts of government." Though he objected to gross corruption in politics, he declared: "I was for upholding Government whether in or out of it." As Vernon Parrington has said of Sewall in his volume, *The Colonial Mind*: "He desired no innovation in church or state; established forms answered his needs and filled the measure of his ideal. The existing system was approved by all the respectable people of the community; there was everything to gain in upholding it."

While the conservatism of Byrd was tempered by a will to resist official interference with his personal interests, and the conservatism of Sewall rejected supine acceptance of corruption in government, that of Jonathan Boucher went to the extreme of advocating servile obedience to duly constituted authorities, British and American. Boucher, the son of a poor English schoolteacher, arrived in Virginia in 1759 and soon afterward was ordained a clergyman in the Anglican Church. For a time he preached in Virginia and then moved with some of his slaves to Annapolis, Maryland, where he served as rector of Saint Anne's.

To restive Americans Boucher taught this doctrine: "Obedience to Government is every man's duty, because it is every man's interest, but it is particularly incumbent on Christians, because it is enjoined by the positive commands of God." If government is mild and free, Boucher argued, the people must be grateful; if it be less liberal than it ought to be in reason, "still it is our duty not to disturb the peace of the community, by becoming refractory and rebellious subjects, and *resisting the ordinances of God*." In the sermons and writings of Boucher conservatism reached its pinnacle.

Had the order of things which Byrd, Sewall, Boucher, and men of their type defended been unchanging and unchallenged, the conformity which they taught might have been indefinitely accepted. But that order had been and was changing; it was challenged by hard facts and by bold advocates of change. In England the rapid growth of the mercantile class in numbers and wealth was weakening the hold of the old landed gentry and clergy on English government and policy. In the colonies where land was abundant, no class could monopolize all of it as the landlords of Virginia and the Hudson River valley were inclined to engross the land of their regions. On the frontiers freehold farmers who worked with their own hands were increasing in numbers and evolving ideas of their own.

Nowhere were the class lines absolutely rigid. Many, if not most, of the Southern planters had sprung from mercantile or farming families of England and new merchant immigrants were rising into their class. Farmers and artisans in the North were embarking on careers as merchants, lawyers, or clergymen. Indentured servants, as they worked out their terms of service, were becoming freehold farmers and winning elections to colonial legislatures, even in Virginia.

In other words a leveling of individuals and families proceeded rapidly in the colonies soon after the first settlements were planted. According to Voltaire, "History is full of the sound of wooden shoes going upstairs and the patter of silken slippers coming downstairs." In Great Britain and Europe this process—or its reverse—filled the seventeenth and eighteenth centuries with tumult and revolution. In the colonies wooden shoes seemed to be climbing up the stairs steadily as farms and industries multiplied and as commerce expanded.

In no way was the process better illustrated than in the case of indentured white servants. After their term of service expired some of them were able to climb the social stairs by marrying into already prosperous families. Others were able to get land by outright purchase or on mortgage or merely by going to the frontier and settling down upon it as "squatters." Indentured artisans and merchants' clerks, by the hundreds, went into industry or trade for themselves as soon as they were released from their obligations to those who had bought their labor. In the seventeenth century, it is estimated, at least 100,000 servants rose from bondage to freedom. Many, no doubt, continued to be laborers on farms or in towns, but thousands either acquired land or an established position as craftsmen or merchants; and occasionally they became planters or clergymen.

Generally speaking, this leveling up process, which intruded upon the order cherished by landlords and merchants of patrician temper, South and North, went on quietly, but at times it was accompanied by disturbances bordering on revolution. Mutterings appeared early. In the very cabin of the *Mayflower*, as it rode in the harbor of Plymouth, some of the members of the Pilgrim band made "discontented and mutinous speeches" and threatened that they "would use their own liberty" when they landed. Such mutterings had something to do with the decision to draw up the Mayflower Compact binding the Pilgrims to that plan of government.

Nearly everywhere independent pioneers and indentured workers made trouble by running off to the frontier, building homes of their own in the wilderness fringes of the colonies, and demanding from the older communities protection and equal rights in colonial government. In Virginia in 1676 frontier discontent with the policy and actions of the royal governor broke out in a rebellion led by Nathaniel Bacon; it was only suppressed, after a long struggle, by desperate measures on the part of the governor. During the spring and summer of 1766 farmers and tenants of great landlords in the Hudson River valley raised "the great rebellion" against the exactions of landed monopolists and were not put down until troops had been called out against them.

The leveling up process as facts and ideas controverted the system and ideas of government which Byrd, Sewall, and Boucher supported in their conformity to upper-class law and order of the British type. With the steady increase in the number of small farmers the representation of farmers in colonial legislatures grew in strength and the very basis of government was examined by inquiring minds in the colonies. On what did government rest—the prescriptive rights of king, lords, clergy, and merchants?

No, said John Wise, of Ipswich, Massachusetts, in 1717. Wise was the son of an indentured servant, born in 1652, while many founders of the colony were still living. Educated at Harvard College, he entered the Congregational ministry. As a young man he resisted the attempts of the temporary royal governor, Edmund Andros, to impose taxes on the people of his town, was arrested, tried, convicted, and put under bonds to keep the peace. But after Andros was ousted and until his death in 1725 Wise battled for popular rights.

With reference to government, Wise took the ground that "democracy" is "the form of government which the light of nature does highly value, and often directs to as most agreeable to the just and natural prerogatives of human beings. . . . The natural equality amongst men must be duly favored. . . . government was never established by God or nature, to give one man a prerogative to insult over another. . . . The end of all good government is to cultivate humanity, and promote the happiness of all, and the good of every man in his rights, his life, liberty, estate, honor, etc., without injury or abuse to any." In effect, as early as 1717, John Wise rejected the very basis of government by privileged classes then defended in England and the colonies by conformists in State and Church.

A few years after John Wise died a son was born to Joseph and Mary Baker Allen, at Litchfield, Connecticut, in 1738. They named him Ethan. It is said that he was preparing to enter college when the death of his father threw upon him the burden of fending for himself. After serving in the French and Indian War, he went to the frontier of New Hampshire, to the region soon to be known as Vermont, where he engaged in land speculation and farming.

Somehow, somewhere, Allen learned to read and write and acquired the habit of reading books. Writing autobiographically about his reading, he said: "Ever since I arrived at the state of manhood and acquainted myself with the general history of mankind, I have felt a sincere passion for liberty. The history of nations doomed to perpetual slavery, in consequence of yielding up to tyrants their natural-born liberties, I read with a sort of philosophical horror; so that the first systematical and bloody attempt, at Lexington, to enslave America, thoroughly electrified my mind, and fully determined me to take part with my country."

Whether the leveling process went on silently or amid uproar, it was accompanied by "subversive" ideas no less definite and positive than the conventional ideas expressed by Byrd, Sewall, Boucher, and gentlemen of their school—ideas of a different type, based not on theological mandates or the mere legal rights of Englishmen. While yeomen of New Jersey were waging a ten-year conflict between 1745 and 1754 against the claims of great landlords, they uttered provocative doctrines. "No man," they declared, "is naturally entitled to a greater proportion of the earth than another," and land "was made for the equal use of all." By what right then could any person claim the ownership of land? Their answer to this question rested not on existing "law and order" but on what they called "natural justice." A person may appropriate land, they contended, "by the improvement of any part of it lying vacant"; and after a man has thus bestowed his labor upon such a piece of land, it cannot afterward be taken away from him, "without breaking thro' the rule of natural justice; for thereby he would be actually deprived of the fruits of his industry."

In the young colonial societies where the majority of the people belonged to freehold farming families and where class lines, though marked, were so fluid that former indentured servants could and did rise to membership in legislative assemblies, radical sentiments and ideas respecting life and labor, differing from those in England, gained in force. In the mother country, where land was limited in amount and all privately owned, most workers on the soil were tenants or day laborers on the estates of great landlords; and the social lines between the upper classes and the masses of the people were sharply drawn. Essentially true was an old couplet, even if there was something ironical in it:

> God bless the squire [landlord] and his relations,
> And keep us all in our proper stations.

To the majority of American farmers and artisans, who had no fixed "station," such sentiments were not only unreal but offensive. To American merchants they were equally objectionable. Americans by the hundreds of thousands, amid different circumstances, held tenaciously to other views of themselves, their opportunities, and their duties. And as the colonies grew older—more populous, more self-sustaining in agriculture, commerce, and industry—intellectual leaders formulated American doctrines into a systematic program of thought about American affairs.

In their searching, thinking, speaking, and writing, these intellectual leaders touched upon every major theme that interested reflective colonists and had a bearing on their growth in economic, political, intellectual, and moral power. They raised and answered in their way at least four fundamental questions: What is the origin of human government and by what right does one set of men make laws for, and govern, all the rest of the people? What is the place of the colonists in the British Empire and what rights do they and should they enjoy as British subjects in America and primarily as human beings? What are the sciences, arts, and opportunities of commerce which will promote the economic and social welfare of the American people? What, after all, are the great ends of human life and how may men and women best attain them?

To these questions in one form or another American minds directed their attention and gave answers which in sum made up an American ideology that clashed with the ideology of the British governing class and their allies in the American colonies. The nature of this great American inquiry and the duty of Americans to pursue it were eloquently described by John Adams in 1765:

"Let us dare to read, think, speak and write. Let every order and degree among the people rouse their attention and animate their resolution. Let them all become attentive to the grounds and principles of government, ecclesiastical and civil. Let us study the law of nature; search into the spirit of the British constitution; read the histories of ancient ages; contemplate the great examples of Greece and Rome; set before us the conduct of our own British ancestors, who have defended for us the inherent rights of mankind against foreign and domestic tyrants and usurpers, against arbitrary kings and cruel priests; in short, against the gates of earth and hell.

"Let us read and recollect and impress upon our souls the views and ends of our own more immediate forefathers, in exchanging their native country for a dreary, inhospitable wilderness. Let us examine into the nature of that power, and the cruelty of that oppression, which drove them from their homes. Recollect their amazing fortitude, their bitter sufferings,—the hunger, the nakedness, the cold, which they patiently endured, —the severe labors of clearing their grounds, building their houses, raising their provisions, amidst dangers from wild beasts and savage men, before they had time or money or materials for commerce. Recollect the civil and religious principles and hopes and expectations which constantly supported and carried them through all hardships with patience and resignation. Let us recollect it was liberty, the hope of liberty for themselves and us and ours, which conquered all discouragements, dangers, and trials. . . .

"Let the pulpit resound with the doctrines and sentiments of religious liberty. Let us hear the danger of thralldom to our consciences from ignorance, extreme poverty, and dependence, in short, from civil and political slavery. Let us see delineated before us the true map of man. Let us hear the dignity of his nature, and the noble rank he holds among the works of God,—that consenting to slavery is a sacrilegious breach of trust, as offensive in the sight of God as it is derogatory from our own honor or interest or happiness,—and that God Almighty has promulgated from heaven, liberty, peace, and good will to man!

"Let the bar proclaim, 'the laws, the rights, the generous plan of power' delivered down from remote antiquity—inform the world of the mighty struggles and numberless sacrifices made by our ancestors in defense of freedom. Let it be known that British liberties are not the grants of princes or parliaments but original rights, conditions of original contracts, are coequal with prerogative, and coeval with government; that many of our rights are inherent and essential, agreed on as maxims, and established as preliminaries, even before a parliament existed. Let them search for the foundations of British laws and government in the frame of human nature, in the constitution of the intellectual and moral world. There let us see that truth, liberty, justice, and benevolence, are its everlasting basis; and if these could be removed, the superstructure is overthrown of course.

"Let the colleges join their harmony in the same delightful concert. Let every declamation turn upon the beauty of liberty and virtue, and the deformity, turpitude, and malignity, of slavery and vice. Let the public disputations become researches into the grounds and nature and ends of government, and the means of preserving the good and demolishing the evil. Let the dialogues, and all the exercises, become the instruments of impressing on the tender mind, and of spreading and distributing far and wide, the ideas of right and the sensations of freedom.

"In a word, let every sluice of knowledge be opened and set a-flowing. The encroachments upon liberty in the reigns of the first James and the first Charles, by turning the general attention of learned men to government, are said to have produced the greatest number of consummate statesmen which has ever been seen in any age or nation. The Brookes, Hampdens, Vanes, Seldens, Miltons, Nedhams, Harringtons, Nevilles, Sidneys, Lockes, are all said to have owed their eminence in political knowledge to the tyrannies of those reigns. The prospect now before us in America, ought in the same manner to engage the attention of every man of learning, to matters of power and of right, that we may be neither led nor driven blindfolded to irretrievable destruction."

The business of making these inquiries into fundamentals of intellectual and social life was not monopolized by any small class of persons. It was carried on, as John Adams urged, by "every order and degree among the people"—by multitudes of people in homes, taverns, churchyards, town meetings, and at crossroads stores; by men and women of humble origins and occupations as well as by those who enjoyed the advantages of leisure and higher education. Yet four groups of persons led the great inquest into American rights, duties, and problems: clergymen, lawyers, physicians, and publishers and publicists. And all members of these groups had audiences to hear what they had to say or to read what they wrote in pamphlets, books, and newspaper articles. Furthermore, in homes, in secondary schools, and in colleges, from generation to generation, new leaders were given the rudiments of learning upon which to build in carrying on inquiries and formulating answers.

Primarily charged with the care of souls, clergymen devoted themselves mainly to religious affairs. But then, as ever, no clear line was drawn between the things that belonged to God and the things assigned to Caesar. The Anglican Church, a state church in England and in several colonies, was associated with English policies of state. But the immense majority of the colonists belonged to dissenting and non-conformist denominations. Early in the history of New England, the Puritans became independents in religion and stoutly resisted all encroachments by the English Crown and Church. Presbyterians objected with equal vigor to the doctrines and methods of the Anglican Church and insisted on having liberty for their faith and worship. Besides, many of them had suffered under English legislation directed against their economic interests in their old home in the north of Ireland and had carried to the colonies piercing remembrances of that experience. Baptists and Quakers had undergone persecution in England and strove against any tightening of the English grip on the religious life of the colonies.

Outside the Anglican communion, accordingly, the clergy were concerned with increasing the dissidence of dissent, educating their flocks in dissidence, and fortifying non-conformity. While their sermons and writings were largely theological, many clergymen were interested in all the great questions of human rights, government, and social duty raised in the growth of American economy. They preached on such subjects to congregations from one end of the colonies to the other. They taught their doctrines in the schools over which they presided and wrote pamphlets for general circulation.

The eighteenth century had not advanced far when lawyers began to dispute the intellectual preëminence of the clergy. In the early stages of settlement there was little business for lawyers and dislike for their profession existed in many circles. Throughout the colonial period, in fact, Puritan divines were inclined to look down upon them as a lower order of human beings. When, for instance, the Reverend William Smith learned that his daughter was inclined toward marriage with John Adams, he was distressed; for young Adams was not only the son of a dirt farmer; he was also a lawyer. On principle, the Quakers were opposed to lawyers; they insisted that disputes among members of the meeting should always be settled by private negotiation. It was in Virginia and South Carolina that lawyers were first heartily welcomed and given high standing in the best society.

Yet as the colonies approached maturity, lawyers were prominent everywhere in the cities from Boston to Charleston, and were scattered around in the inland regions. In New England the litigation connected with commerce had become too complicated for field-stump and corner-store justice. In Philadelphia, where Quakers were growing worldly, lawyers flourished and were famous throughout the North for their learning, shrewdness, and boldness. At Williamsburg and Charleston, the Bar was crowded by distinguished attorneys.

Lawyers, if intellectually enterprising, were more than students of law and government. Engaged in litigation for their clients, they were accustomed to preparing briefs—or statements of facts and law—and making oral arguments before judges and juries. They were acquainted with the art of public speaking and many of them studied the art as represented in the speeches of Cicero and the speeches of statesmen in the British Parliament. Wherever there was a controversy, public or private, lawyers were interested and the best of them could "make a powerful case" for the side on which they were enlisted; that is, marshal facts, lay down ruling principles applicable to the facts, and order facts and principles in a logical form, appealing to sentiments of their supporters and commanding the attention, if not always the respect, of their opponents.

For the practice of law in any case, some intellectual preparation was necessary. There was no law school in any of the colonies and there was no professorship of law at any of the colleges. But leading lawyers usually had some preliminary training at a college and often young men of wealthy families, especially in the South, studied at the Inns of Court in London. Whatever their early education, lawyers had to read one or more legal treatises and the statutes of their colony. The ablest and most intellectual among them read widely in the classics, in works on history, jurisprudence, government, and the relation of the law to the people and the economy of the society in which it was made and enforced.

As the colonial period drew toward a close physicians were also outstanding among intellectual leaders, especially at Philadelphia, the great medical center of the colonies. About 1750, it is estimated, at least eighty-two physicians and surgeons were practicing in that city, many of them trained at the medical school of Edinburgh or on the Continent. While some of them adhered strictly to the professional line, many others took a keen interest in civic affairs and allied themselves with the autonomous tendencies. The latter promoted the arts, music, higher education, the establishment of libraries, and the building of social institutions such as hospitals and homes for the impoverished. Thomas Bond, for example, who had completed his medical education abroad and long practiced with success, joined the Revolutionary Committee of Safety in 1776 and rendered service to the Revolutionary army. Benjamin Rush, distinguished in the medical profession, took an interest in most great public questions from education to the abolition of slavery, was elected to the Continental Congress, signed the Declaration of Independence, and for a time was surgeon general of the Middle Department armies.

Important as were clergy, lawyers, and physicians in shaping American opinion and forming the ideology of American autonomy, they had able assistants in independent editors and publicists who wrote articles for newspapers and pamphlets for general circulation. Among all the colonists so engaged, Benjamin Franklin, the publisher and businessman, was especially versatile, active, and influential. For the Pennsylvania *Gazette* and for *Poor Richard's Almanack*, which he published, he wrote articles, short and long, on nearly every subject—scientific, moral, and economic —bearing on the affairs of the colonists. These he supplemented by pamphlets on various topics, such as the vital money question. Although his publishing house was in Philadelphia, his writings circulated widely in the North and the South.

Intellectual leaders in America, from those of local or colony-wide prestige to those of intercolonial or international reputation, had at their command, to inform, inspire, and strengthen their minds, a growing literature on American themes. In this literature, by 1750, there were actually thousands of printed titles, running from large volumes to pamphlets, tracts, and broadsides. When intellectual and social autonomy approached its maturity, there was scarcely a nook or cranny of the seaboard region that had not been explored and described by able writers; scarcely a branch of American economy and social life that had not been written up with more or less fullness; scarcely an American institution or custom on which information was lacking to inquiring minds; scarcely an American idea or aspiration unrecorded in print for the instruction of those who searched for enlightenment on that score.

This immense literature included: histories of individual settlements and colonies—such as Robert Beverly, *History of Virginia* (1705), William Smith, *History of the Province of New York* (1757), and Thomas

Prince, *A Chronological History of New England* in two volumes (1736–55); books of travel and surveys describing various parts of the colonial dominion—for example, John Archdale, *A New Description . . . of Carolina* (1707), and John Bartram, *Observations on the Inhabitants, Climate, Soil, Rivers, Production, Animals and Other Matters Worthy of Notice* from Pennsylvania to Canada (1751); books on natural philosophy and the practical arts—for instance, Samuel Johnson, *An Introduction to the Study of Philosophy, Exhibiting a General View of All the Arts and Sciences* (1743); books on social morality, including John Woolman, *Considerations on Pure Wisdom, and Human Policy; on Labour . . .* (1768); works on phases of economy and government—as illustrations, Benjamin Franklin, *A Modest Enquiry into the Nature and Necessity of a Paper Currency* (1729) and *An Historical Review of the Constitution and Government of Pennsylvania* (1759). If, as had been said in ancient times, "knowledge is power," American colonials were fortunate in having ample stores of it within their reach.

Intellectual leaders intent on exploring theories of society in general and American relations to the government of Great Britain in particular also had at hand works which they had imported from abroad and kept in their libraries, private and public, for ready use. From these they selected germinal ideas, gave to them meaning in the light of their peculiar experiences in a New World, and applied them, so interpreted, to the accomplishment of their purposes.

Among the imported works generally read in the colonies by assiduous students and thinkers, four were of unquestioned influence on American intellectual leadership:

1628—Edward Coke, *Coke upon Littleton.* Treatise on the legal rights of English subjects, defending them against encroachments by Crown and Church. A textbook on common law for colonial students of law.

1690—John Locke, *Treatise of Government.* Philosophic justification of the Revolution of 1688 in England. Traced the origin of government to a compact among the people made for the protection of their lives and property and asserted the right of revolution to assure such protection against tyranny.

1748—Montesquieu, *Esprit des Lois.* Soon in translations. Dealt with the material and social backgrounds of law and government. An early treatise on "sociological jurisprudence."

1757—Adam Ferguson, *An Essay on the History of Civil Society.* A work on the origins and progress of civil societies (civilization), on social relations, and on human beings as active, creative, and progressive creatures.

Americans of searching intellectual curiosity also had at their command, either imported or from their own presses, books reflecting all the main tendencies of thought in the Old World respecting the nature of mankind's universe. They read, discussed, and wrote about these tendencies so widely that the chief ideas which were shaking Great Britain and Europe became common in all the colonies. And what were these chief ideas?

The rationalism in the work of Sir Isaac Newton that eliminated arbitrary interferences of God in the physical universe, the old basis of astrology and other superstitions.

Deism—rejecting the Hebraic and Miltonic interpretation of the cosmos and substituting, for Jehovah, the universal God of all mankind. As Alexander Pope expressed it:

> *Father of all! in every age,*
> *In every clime adored,*
> *By saint, by savage, and by sage . . .*

The idea of progress—now fortified by the new science and by Voltaire's social history, which rejected the theological view that the earth is a temporary place of misery and maintained that advance in arts, sciences, and social improvement is the supreme destiny of mankind.

The doctrine of natural rights—that all people everywhere, whatever their status, are entitled to the rights of life, liberty, property, and the pursuit of happiness.

The idea of the pursuit of happiness on earth as a legitimate and worthy aspiration of the human spirit. "O happiness! our being's end and aim! Good, pleasure, ease, content! whate'er thy name," wrote Pope in his *Essay on Man*.

The doctrine of utility—that usefulness in well-being is the test of things, institutions, and actions.

As these ideas circulating in Europe presented a revolutionary contradiction to the ideology of kings, lords, clergy, peasants, and serfs, so in America they ran counter to the conservative practices of British overlordship. Not only that. They acquired additional force in America on account of the fact that Americans, as contrasted with Europeans, were in possession of the natural resources that made possible the easier realization of these ideas.

So in America, as in the Old World, the Battle of the Books raged. If William Byrd, in Virginia, could read his *Lucian*, the Greek satirist of the second century, A.D., laugh at the follies of mankind, and learn contempt for everything except his own pleasure and interests, Thomas Jefferson in Virginia could draw from the new writers—Locke, Ferguson, and Pope —a faith in mankind and human progress that prepared him in letter and spirit to write and proclaim the declaration of complete autonomy —independence.

☆

It was not merely to a small, exclusive set of upper-class persons that writers on American matters directed their articles, pamphlets, and books. They wrote for a large audience, for a popular audience, for men and women belonging to farming and artisan classes as well as to the ranks of clergymen, lawyers, professors, physicians, schoolmasters, planters, and merchants.

No census of the number of colonists over ten years of age who could read and write was ever taken, but the number was certainly large. The extensive sale of books, pamphlets, almanacs, magazines, and newspapers was one indication that there was a wide reading public in all parts of America. Foreign travelers in the eighteenth century were deeply impressed by the amount of reading that was done in homes and in taverns "on the house," and they contrasted this mental alertness with the stolidity of the ignorant masses in their own countries. So plainly were American writers taking the people at large into account, as readers, that strangers interested in classes and masses seldom failed to make note of it as a sign of distinction in the intellectual development of the colonies.

How had the large public learned to read? To Protestantism must be attributed the main source of this wide literacy. The colonial population was overwhelmingly Protestant and a tenet of dissenting faith was the right of everyone to read the Bible for himself instead of listening merely to its exposition by priests. Hence the Protestant clergy, especially among Puritans, Baptists, and Presbyterians, made it one of their prime duties to see that children of their sects acquired the ability to read and actually carried reading forward, as they grew up, with a sense of religious obligation.

In extending literacy by means of public schools New England stood apart. Homogeneity in population and religious faith characterized that region. There legislation, beginning with the Massachusetts statute of 1642, required the towns to make some provision for giving the rudiments of learning to those children who did not get them at home. In many places this fiat was more honored in the breach than by observance, but in time all the better New England communities had public primary schools of some type. In other parts of colonial America, dissenting sects —Baptist, Quaker, Presbyterian, Lutheran, and Huguenot—also established town and field schools in which children learned elementary reading, writing, and arithmetic. Such schools were supplemented by private enterprise. Schoolmasters and schoolmistresses conducted private elementary schools, usually in their homes; and itinerant teachers journeyed about "holding school" for short periods of the year wherever a few pupils could be collected and fees obtained.

In thickly populated districts, especially in the larger towns, to elementary schools were added grammar schools and academies at which boys and girls were taught more advanced subjects. Secondary schools founded by private interests often catered to sons and daughters of the upper classes, especially boys on their way to college and girls preparing for the life of "polite society"; their curricula included the classics, mathematics, English literature, and frequently French. But secondary schools were not all of that type. Perhaps more generally, particularly in the middle colonies, they adapted their instruction to the needs of boys and girls who had to look forward early to earning a livelihood by their own efforts. At all events secondary schools gave thousands of Americans a more than elementary training for reading newspapers, pamphlets, and books; for taking part in the discussions of public affairs; and for sharing in the growth of social and intellectual autonomy.

It was mainly to religious motives that colleges, like elementary schools, owed their foundations. Massachusetts was only a few years old when, in 1636, Harvard College was established, primarily to train "learned and godly Ministers." A similar purpose led to the creation of a college at Killingworth in Connecticut in 1701—an institution afterward moved to New Haven and in 1718 given the name of Yale College. William and Mary, organized in Virginia in 1693, and King's College, founded in New York City in 1754, were intended as centers for the advanced education of Anglican men. The College of New Jersey, started in 1747 and removed to Princeton in 1756, relied mainly on Presbyterians for support and guidance. Dartmouth College began to function in 1767 as a Puritan mission to the Indians.

Two colonial colleges were less exclusive in sectarian sponsorship: Brown, founded in Rhode Island in 1764, was interdenominational; a majority of its board of trustees were Baptists, but Congregationalists, Anglicans, and Quakers were included in the membership. The Philadelphia Academy, forerunner of the University of Pennsylvania, formally opened in 1751, also admitted to its board of trustees members of various faiths; and Benjamin Franklin, its arch promoter, would have turned it into secular channels if he could have kept its control in his hands. Franklin, however, was outmaneuvered by the provost, William Smith, an invincible Anglican who gradually managed to dominate this institution.

The instruction offered by colleges included secular learning. The presidents and the professors were generally ministers of religion but, whatever their professions of faith, they opened the gateways to the accumulated knowledge of the ages and colonial writings on every theme. Young men admitted to the colleges all had an opportunity to master classical languages and were given access to the learning of antiquity, for example, to the politics and morals of Aristotle and Plato and the ethics of Seneca and Plutarch as well as the historical writings of Tacitus and the constitutional works of Cicero. Thin as they were, modeled on Oxford and Cambridge patterns, the colonial college curricula contained instruction in the elements of moral or natural philosophy, contemporary science, and a drill in logic that sharpened young men's wits for inquiry and argumentation, in the event that they made use of this drill. Within college walls leaders were trained for all the intellectual activities that marked the growth of the colonies into mature and autonomous societies.

Yet in the acquisition of learning, the development of intellectual powers, and the spread of knowledge and conceptual thought, formal education played a minor role in colonial times. Relatively speaking, only a few men had the benefit of college education and those who did gained from it only a limited body of knowledge. On entering business, professional, or political careers, college graduates often found themselves in intellectual competition with men of little formal training who were their peers, if not their superiors, in mental power. Thomas Jefferson was a graduate of William and Mary College; John Marshall was not a graduate of any college. John Adams attended Harvard; Benjamin Franklin was among the founders of a college, never a student in one. All over the country, in communities large and small, on farms and plantations as well as in towns and cities, men and women who had got the rudiments of an education from their fathers and mothers or hired tutors spent laborious days and nights lifting their education by their own efforts, inspired by their intellectual curiosities and other desires.

Self-education on the higher levels was especially the way of women, to whom the doors of colleges were closed. Eliza Pinckney, of South Carolina, which had no college, went on reading and learning, after her youthful studies in England, as the impulse of her own mind and spirit directed. Abigail Adams and Mercy Otis Warren, of Massachusetts, could not go to Harvard; and Abigail lamented the lack of equal education for women, but how well she could think and write is attested by her letters to her husband and family and friends. Mercy Otis had studied the same subjects under the same tutors as her brother, James Otis, previous to his departure for Harvard. She could not follow him there despite their close intellectual companionship, but she did follow where her mind continued to lead her, learning all the time independently. Anna Maulin Zenger, of New York, who took over the publication of John Peter Zenger's New York *Weekly Journal,* after his death in 1746, must have acquired her education and competence for editing largely by her own efforts, like the numerous other women journalists in the colonies. And even in lonely cabins on the frontiers women as well as men frequently educated themselves and opened for their children the paths leading to the knowledge that enabled them to win high places in the public service. From his mother George Wythe, born on a Virginia plantation in 1726, learned the Latin language and he eventually studied jurisprudence by himself. He was of great influence in the intellectual development of Jefferson.

☆

Books, pamphlets, and tracts that passed from reader to reader, formal instruction in schools, the dissemination of learning by fathers and mothers, training at home by private tutors, formed only a part of the process by which Americans were equipped with knowledge and ideas for dealing with affairs private and public. After the opening of the eighteenth century, newspapers added instruction on current issues to the colonial college curriculum dealing mainly with the past. In April 1704 John Campbell at Boston brought out the first number of the first American newspaper, the Boston *News-Letter*, a periodical so hardy that it lasted till independence was declared. In 1719 Andrew Bradford established in Philadelphia the *American Mercury*. In November 1725 the New York *Gazette* came from the press of William Bradford.

From these beginnings, journalism spread to other colonies in the following order of time:

> 1727—Annapolis, Maryland.
> 1732—Charleston, South Carolina.
> 1732—Newport, Rhode Island.
> 1736—Williamsburg, Virginia.
> 1755—New Haven, Connecticut.
> 1755—New Bern, North Carolina.
> 1762—Wilmington, Delaware.
> 1763—Savannah, Georgia.
> 1777—Burlington, New Jersey.

Among the early newspapers the rate of change and mortality was high as competitors appeared in the leading cities; but this signified a growth and persistence in journalism—signs of new thinking and action for those who could see them.

In the columns of newspapers Americans could learn about many things that were going on in the colonies as well as overseas. The small pages of these papers contained brief notes on British and European "occurrences," reports of happenings in the neighborhood and in other colonies, advertisements of commodities in bewildering varieties for sale at merchants' shops, letters from pleased and irate readers on questions of public interest, and essays on events, manners, morals, customs, and politics. Always under the watchful eyes of royal governors, proprietors, or politicians, colonial editors had to be circumspect in discussing disputes among Americans or between Americans and British officials, but as time passed they became more adroit in their retreating and advancing maneuvers. From the journals of other colonies, local editors in each town clipped notices of general interest and made reports to their communities. Ship captains sailing from port to port and postboys traveling from point to point carried news for editors to use. When, for example, the great agrarian rebellion of 1766 occurred in the Hudson Valley, accounts of it appeared in the newspapers of Boston and Philadelphia as well as in the New York press. Provincial journalism was merging into American journalism.

The dissemination of knowledge and ideas, news, information, and misinformation was facilitated by the rise and growth of a colonial postal system. As early as 1639 the legislature of Massachusetts made provision for a local post office and this example was followed by other colonies as they grew in size and population. Under a royal patent of 1692 an intercolonial postal service was established as a private enterprise. Fifteen years later it was taken over by the English government and developed under successive postmasters general, Benjamin Franklin assuming that office in 1753.

In the course of time post roads were extended, new local offices established, the speed of transmission increased, and packet lines to England and to coastal ports were started. Day and night, through the years, post riders, stages, and coastal ships kept communications throughout the colonies open. Correspondence among citizens, once local and restricted, became general. Newspapers issued for local circulation reached out in influence beyond their communities and broadened the scope of their contents accordingly. The circulation of knowledge and ideas was being enlarged. The provincial mind was becoming American in its range of interest and in the subject matter of its concern.

Chapter 6

PRACTICING THE ARTS OF
SELF-GOVERNMENT

ACCOMPANYING the growth of autonomy in agriculture, commerce, industry, social relations, and intellectual pursuits, indeed mingled with every phase of it, was a training in the arts of self-government which prepared colonists for asserting their political and economic rights against British authorities and for managing their own affairs when they had the opportunity.

From the beginning, government played an essential and formative role in the life of the colonies. At the outset, the Crown granted charters and privileges to companies and proprietors, laying down the principles upon which they were to manage the great domains committed to their care. It was also the Crown that made actual grants of real estate to corporations and proprietors, and it was this same Crown which set forth the manner in which land should be divided and sold. The government guided and encouraged commerce between the colonies and European countries as well as with the motherland. Without such commerce the colonies could not have become prosperous and powerful. During the entire colonial period, too, London furnished military and naval assistance in wars with the French and Spanish in America, and at times in coping with the Indians on the frontiers. In civilian and military affairs, government was indispensable at every stage of colonial development.

This was true, of course, of the Spanish and French colonies but there was one fundamental difference between the policy of the French and Spanish governments and the policy of the English government. French and Spanish colonies were ruled absolutely by royal governors who held office at royal pleasure. In those colonies the inhabitants were not allowed to take an active part in making their own laws, laying taxes, choosing officials, and deciding how public affairs were otherwise to be managed. On the other hand, in all the English colonies a considerable portion of the inhabitants enjoyed a large measure of self-government; in some, from the very beginning and in others after they were securely established. To the development of independence and liberty, exercising the rights of self-government in some measure at least was as essential as the activities in agriculture, industry, business enterprise, and every other phase of autonomous unfolding.

To appreciate the importance of political privileges in the making of the American nation, it is only necessary to imagine what would have happened if every colony had been governed solely by a royal agent from London, endowed with dictatorial powers to make and enforce laws of every kind—laws for dividing and selling the lands; for laying out towns and managing farms and industries; for imposing and collecting taxes as heavy or heavier than the people could bear; for controlling speech, press, and religious worship; for regulating the kinds of work to be done and assigning people to their tasks. If wholly autocratic policies had been pursued by the English government in the colonies, the American people would have felt crushed, and liberty might have been stifled. What is more, the colonists would not have learned the arts of self-government so necessary to the establishment and maintenance of independence, the making of popular constitutions, and the management of local, national, and foreign affairs.

Running through the long period from the founding of Jamestown in 1607 to the declaring of independence in 1776 were two opposing tendencies in colonial government. The first was for the government to grow upward from native roots, through the election by qualified colonial voters of members of the lower branches of the colonial legislatures and various other officials including, in two colonies, even the governors. The second tendency was for the Crown to reach downward, extending and strengthening its grip by converting company and proprietary colonies into royal provinces, and appointing their governors.

It was in Virginia that the tendency for government to grow upward from native roots first found a major outlet. The Virginia colony was only a few years old when the London Company decreed that the power of its local governor and council should be limited by a local assembly, called the House of Burgesses, to be elected by the voters. In 1619 members of the House of Burgesses were chosen; and the legislature, duly assembled, began to make laws respecting the management of local affairs.

Before the Pilgrims actually set to work at Plymouth in 1620, the men of that little band met in the cabin of the *Mayflower* and drew up a document celebrated in history as the Mayflower Compact. By solemn written agreement they bound themselves together in a "civil body politic," to make "just and equal laws" for the government of the colony, and promised to obey such laws when enacted. The founders of Massachusetts Bay, who followed the Pilgrims to America ten years later, brought their charter with them. After governing themselves directly for a time by meetings of the members, they established in 1634 an assembly composed of representatives from each town.

Even proprietors could not be complete autocrats in the domains granted them by the King. The charter which gave Lord Baltimore the right to found his colony in Maryland required him in due course to seek the consent of the freemen in making laws. Within a short time after the first settlements were made, in 1635, an assembly representing the freemen was set up in Maryland.

In 1639 the men of the towns founded on the Connecticut River by emigrants from Massachusetts drew up for their colony the "Fundamental Orders of Connecticut"—a document called "the first written constitution known to history which created a government." The Orders provided for a general assembly, or "Court," composed of representatives from each of the towns, and for a governor and magistrates to be elected annually. The people of the colony were thus bound together as "one public State or Commonwealth" and they were "to be guided and governed" in their civil affairs by the laws, orders, and decrees properly made by the government so organized.

In contemplation of growth, the Orders provided that new towns were to be given representation in the assembly, reasonably proportioned to the number of their freemen. Four years later, in 1643, the settlements on Long Island Sound united with New Haven in creating a representative legislature. Finally, the royal charter of 1662, which joined the two groups of settlements in Connecticut, made provision for popular government consisting of a governor, assistants, and representatives, all elected by the qualified voters. A similar system was established in Rhode Island.

As popular assemblies came into existence in the other colonies, one after another, they were formed on a common model. Representatives were assigned to each town, city, borough or county, and they were all to be elected by the voters who had the qualifications fixed by law.

The qualifications for the suffrage varied from place to place and from time to time. But on the eve of the Revolution the right to vote was generally restricted to men who owned property of specified amounts. In New York, for instance, voters for members of the assembly had to be freeholders of land or tenements to the value of £40 free from all encumbrances, except in New York City and Albany where all men formally admitted to civic rights as "freemen" could vote. In Pennsylvania the suffrage was restricted to the owners of fifty acres of land "well seated" with twelve acres "cleared," or other property worth at least £50 in lawful money. According to Virginia law the voter had to own at least fifty acres of land if there was no house on it or twenty-five acres with a house at least twelve feet square; or if a dweller in a town, he had to own a plot of ground with a house at least twelve feet square.

As a result of the various limitations on the suffrage a large proportion of the people in each colony were deprived of the vote; and many who were entitled to that privilege failed to exercise it in elections. In the rural districts of Pennsylvania about one person in ten had the right to vote and in Philadelphia only about one in fifty owned enough property to qualify for the exercise of the suffrage. At times in Massachusetts and Connecticut, where approximately sixteen per cent of the population were enfranchised, only two per cent took the trouble to vote. Similar conditions prevailed elsewhere. It was therefore only a small proportion, even of the freemen, who actually participated in the government of their respective colonies.

Nevertheless, there were in America, at the end of the colonial period, thousands of men who were acquainted practically with voting, managing local campaigns, and taking part in elections; and there were hundreds of men who were serving, or had served, as members of legislatures, in the making of laws and the supervision of law enforcement. When important issues were up for action, campaigns were often exciting. Even men and women who could not vote formed opinions about questions under popular consideration and shared in the discussions that went on in country and town.

But as a rule, by the end of the colonial period, the popular assembly was checked by an upper house or council. In seven of the eight royal provinces, members of the council were appointed by the royal governor; in Massachusetts they were elected by the lower house. In Connecticut all high authorities—governor, assistants, and representatives in the legislature—were elected by the voters. Of the proprietary colonies, Maryland alone had a legislative council, a kind of upper chamber, composed of councilors selected by the proprietor or his deputy; the legislature in Pennsylvania and Delaware consisted of a single house based on popular election.

Generally speaking, councilors or assistants were selected from prominent and wealthy families in the colony and exercised large powers in respect of lawmaking and the conduct of executive business. In the royal provinces they were, with some exceptions, warmly attached to the royal governor and the Crown and acted as a conservative force in blocking the desires and demands of the elected representatives in the lower house.

The powers possessed by the colonial legislature in the beginning, or acquired by practice, were extensive. It could make laws respecting the general and local affairs of the colony. It could lay various kinds of taxes for the support of the colonial government. It could appropriate money for public purposes, including the salaries of the governor and other officers. Speaking broadly, it was limited only by the provision that its acts must not be contrary to the laws of England or the terms of the colony's charter. Otherwise the assembly was fairly free to legislate on all matters pertaining to life, liberty, and property, subject to the veto of the governor in the royal and proprietary colonies and ultimately of the Crown in England.

The second important tendency in the history of colonial government was for the Crown to reach downward, extending and strengthening its grip by converting company and proprietary colonies into royal provinces with governors chosen by the King, and hence subject to stronger royal control. The progress of this development is traced in the following table giving the dates when certain areas became royal provinces:

    1624—Virginia
    1679—New Hampshire
    1685—New York
    1691—Massachusetts
    1702—New Jersey, with a separate governor in 1728
    1729—South Carolina
    1729—North Carolina
    1752—Georgia

ROYAL, PROPRIETARY, AND CHARTER COLONIES ON THE EVE OF THE REVOLUTION

Yet the trend was never carried all the way to completion. By 1752, eight of the thirteen colonies, it is true, were royal provinces, but Connecticut and Rhode Island had governors elected by assemblies of voters, and three were still under the management of proprietors.

The Penns were able to hold fast to Pennsylvania and Delaware until the Revolution broke their proprietorship. Although they and their deputy governors had troubles enough, by twisting and turning and making concessions to the legislature the Penns kept their property until the rupture with Great Britain.

The career of the Baltimores in Maryland was more stormy. Between 1660 and 1689 they encountered four or five open revolts among their subjects. As a result Maryland was made a royal province. Not until a Protestant heir appeared in the Baltimore family was the colony restored to it, in 1715, and then Catholics in Maryland were disfranchised.

The influence of the Crown, whether exerted directly through governors in the royal provinces, or indirectly through proprietors, played an important role in colonial affairs.

The powers enjoyed and exercised by the King's governor in the royal province were both extensive and highly effective. He was really the viceroy of the King and exercised in the colony all the civil and military authority vested in him by the Crown. As chief executive he enforced the laws of England applicable to the colony and all the laws passed by the colonial legislature. He appointed, usually with the consent of the council, the important civil officers and directed them in the discharge of their duties. He acted as the head of the highest court in the colony, which tried important cases at first hand and heard appeals from the lower courts. The power of granting pardons and issuing reprieves was entrusted to him. In military affairs he was commander in chief of the colonial forces and appointed officers of high rank.

In relation to the legislature the royal governor also had many prerogatives. Not only did he choose in all the royal provinces, except Massachusetts, the members of the council which served as the upper house of the legislature. He could summon, adjourn, and dissolve the assembly, lay before it projects of law which the Crown or he himself deemed desirable, and veto bills. He could hear and approve or reject petitions from the assembly, send messages to it, and try to influence its members by methods both public and secret.

Governors in the proprietary colonies had controls and wielded powers resembling those possessed by royal governors. When the proprietor was a resident of his colony he was in fact "a petty king" and could exercise executive authority in person. But most proprietors remained in England and acted through deputies whom they chose to direct their colonial affairs. Naturally the proprietary agent in a colony had less of pomp and circumstance than a royal governor. Yet he had similar legal powers: to appoint members of the council, if there was one; to choose military and civil officers; to grant lands; to veto acts of the legislature; and to supervise the enforcement of the laws. Like the royal governor, he might be on good terms or bad terms with the colonial legislature. Usually, in the best of conditions, he was more or less in open conflict with it.

In all save two colonies, Connecticut and Rhode Island, where the governors were popularly elected, the colonial executive, royal or proprietary, was, formally at least, above responsibility to the people. If he wished or dared, he could defy public opinion.

Many of the governors at the head of royal and proprietary provinces were men of wisdom and moderation who tried to deal amicably with the colonists. Yet they were all periodically in sharp conflict with the colonial assembly. Whatever their personal merits and views, they were expected to promote, if they could, the interests of the British government or of the proprietors, and to enforce, if they could, British law applicable to the colonies. Placed as they were between two fires—British masters and local assemblies—they were fortunate if a year passed without a quarrel of some kind. If a governor was stiff-necked, the colony over which he presided was likely to be in more or less of an uproar during his entire administration. Examples of such disturbances will illustrate the nature of the difficulties that arose between British governors and the colonists bent on having the substance as well as the form of self-government.

In 1642 Charles I sent over Sir William Berkeley to serve as royal governor of Virginia and for about thirty-five years Berkeley held that post. Along many lines he labored zealously for the welfare of the colony but in other respects he was a martinet. He was almost savage in persecuting Quakers and Puritans who ventured to settle in Virginia. He was opposed to newspapers and free schools and thanked God that Virginia had neither. With an iron hand he tried to keep all branches of the government under his own control. He insulted and cursed Virginians who were brash enough to resist his actions and object to his policies.

As the years passed, things went from bad to worse. When in 1676 he failed to take effective measures against marauding Indians, Berkeley found himself in the midst of an armed rebellion led by Nathaniel Bacon and was driven out of Jamestown. Recovering power for a short time, he put to death so many leaders in the rebellion that even the King of England was disgusted with him and appointed another governor to supersede him. "The old fool," Charles II was quoted as saying, "has killed more people in that naked country than I have done for the murder of my father."

A second illustration of the kind of serious troubles that could arise between a royal governor and colonial leaders occurred in New York under Governor William Cosby, who arrived to take office in 1732. In his dealings with the colonial assembly, Cosby managed to avoid bringing on a revolution, though he was brusque in manner and profane in language. But he quarreled fiercely with some members of his council and with leaders in local politics over jobs and money. He ousted from power the chief justice of New York. The displaced man, aided by rich friends, helped John Peter Zenger, a local printer, to establish a newspaper in New York City and attack the governor's policies in print.

Angered by attacks in Zenger's paper, Cosby took steps to have Zenger arrested and brought to trial for criminal libel. To the defense of Zenger came Andrew Hamilton, of Philadelphia, a lawyer from that more liberal center. Appealing eloquently to the jury in the name of a free press and the right to publish the truth, Hamilton won a verdict of "not guilty" amid cheers from the people who had crowded into the courtroom. Thus by an effort to curb a printer, Cosby helped to make freedom of the press a cherished privilege in the American colonies, whether he was right or wrong on his points of law.

Another type of royal governor and dispute appeared in Massachusetts in 1771 when Thomas Hutchinson was placed at the head of that province. Hutchinson was born in Boston in 1711, educated at Harvard, and, as a member of a rich and powerful family of merchants, quickly rose to an influential position in colonial politics. Though conservative in temper and loyal to the King, he opposed many acts of Parliament, such as the Stamp Act, as bad policy, and sought to pursue a moderate course. Yet he did not deny the right of Parliament to tax and govern the colonies according to its own desires; as governor he secretly encouraged British authorities to adopt strong measures in dealing with colonial agitators. He quarreled with the Massachusetts assembly and with Samuel Adams, leader in local resistance to British actions. In an address to the legislature he declared that the supremacy of Parliament must be admitted and that "the mere exercise of its authority can be no grievance." Though a man of personal honor and courage, eager to exert a moderating influence, Hutchinson added fuel to the fires of discontent in Massachusetts. In 1774, after the Boston Tea Party, he left for England and was never able to return to America.

In contests with royal and proprietary governors and in the ordinary management of legislative business, Americans by the hundreds learned to practice and think about the arts of government. They acquired training in drawing up bills and resolutions expressing their grievances, ideals, or demands. They could stand upon the floors of assemblies, defend the projects they favored, argue with their opponents, and carry on business in accordance with the rules of parliamentary law. They could draft petitions to the governor and appear before him to support their demands upon the executive. They could investigate the measures and deeds of officials in charge of law enforcement, and often compel the governor to remove them, by threats of withholding the money for the payment of their salaries.

No form or function of government in fact escaped their thought or experience. With the theory, practice, and arts of lawmaking and administration they became familiar. There was no work of that type in which they were wholly untrained; there were no mysteries veiled to their understanding. Thus through the years, if not wholly aware of it, Americans were equipping themselves to take over all branches of government, and to direct, as persons adept in the business, the public affairs of America.

As members of legislatures gained in political dexterity and wisdom, they insisted on having, holding, and exercising certain fundamental powers of government. Sometimes, in this respect, they gained ground; at other times they lost it. The lines of the battle with royal and proprietary governors swayed to and fro. But to many rights legislatures clung so stoutly that only a hardheaded and stubborn governor could override them for any long period. Among the claims asserted by the legislatures, nine were regarded by colonists as basic to liberty and self-government:

To introduce and enact bills on all matters of local and general interest in the colony, subject to the terms of the charter and English laws.

To fix the kinds and amounts of taxation to be laid on the people.

To pass upon the governor's actions in the nature of legislation.

To control the voting of money to pay salaries, including the governor's, and audit the disbursement of funds.

To create courts of law and regulate the salaries of judges.

To choose and pay agents charged with lobbying for or against measures pending in the Parliament or before royal officers in London.

To elect the speaker of the lower house.

To decide disputes over contested seats and check any resort to corruption on the part of the governor in elections.

To have elections of members held at intervals fixed by law at from two to five years.

Although members of the colonial legislature generally agreed on their rights as against the government of Great Britain, its agents, and the deputies of proprietors, they often differed violently respecting the way in which their colonial affairs were to be conducted. Representatives from districts occupied by owners of small farms were frequently at loggerheads with representatives from districts in which great landlords and merchants were numerous and powerful.

In part the roots of this conflict were sectional. From New York to Georgia, along the coastal plain and up to the headwaters of rivers emptying into the Atlantic, big landlords and merchants were usually in the ascendancy, clever enough to keep an upper hand in politics. In the frontier regions back of this coastal strip, small farmers were dominant.

Many and various were the grounds of strife between representatives of the seaboard and representatives of the frontier. As a rule the people of the seaboard had more representatives in the legislature than their numbers warranted and they wanted to run the colony to suit their ideas and interests. On the other hand, farmers from the back regions demanded more representatives in the assembly and more consideration of their ideas and interests. So within each colony, despite agreement on rights as against Great Britain, there were endless controversies over the concrete issues of representation, taxation, the disposition of Western lands, defense against the Indians, and matters of local government. In such controversies also, Americans gained experience in debating, lawmaking, and law enforcement.

In local or community affairs, Americans in each colony were steadily educated and trained in the arts of self-government if on a small scale. Most of the people were engaged in agriculture and duly qualified men in large numbers shared in the local government of rural districts—towns or counties as the case might be.

Throughout New England and parts of the middle colonies the unit of government was the town—a small rural region, usually with a village or crossroads group of houses as a center. Such a town or township was governed by a meeting of the voters who chose its officers, levied taxes, appropriated money, and passed laws pertaining to roads, schools, bridges, and other local matters. There were counties in New England but they were mainly for judicial purposes. At the county seat a court held sessions for trying important civil and criminal cases and hearing appeals from town justices of the peace.

In Pennsylvania and the colonies to the south, the county was the chief unit of local administration. There local business was carried on by sheriffs, justices of the peace, coroners, and other officials, usually chosen by the governor of the colony.

So well entrenched was the system of local government that it was generally retained during and after the Revolution; indeed, it still exists, with some modifications here and there. Thus town and county "schools of government" furnished abundant opportunities for Americans to practice the arts of lawmaking and law enforcement. In the local schools of politics, leaders acquired training for action in the larger realm, colonial or intercolonial.

At many places cities and boroughs grew up in the course of colonial development. In New England they were governed by town meetings modeled on those existing in rural districts. In the middle and southern colonies, it became a custom to incorporate populous centers, such as New York, Albany, Trenton, Philadelphia, and Norfolk; that is, to give them charters and provide a kind of independent municipal government. As a rule the city charter was granted by the colonial governor. By charters qualified voters in a majority of the cities were given the right to elect members of the council and board of aldermen, who in turn chose the mayor and other city officials. In a few places, for example Philadelphia, Annapolis, and Norfolk, members of the city council were named in the original charter and empowered to choose their own successors as vacancies occurred.

Although the suffrage in cities was limited as a rule to the well-to-do classes and in some places there were no popular elections at all, many inhabitants had some share in conducting municipal affairs. Besides, urban residents, if they owned enough property to qualify for the suffrage, took part in electing members to the colonial assembly. So, for one reason or another, townspeople became "politically minded." Nowhere were they just an inert mass ruled by agents of royal governors.

Active as thousands of Americans were in the local and central governments of their respective colonies, they had little to do with the relations of the colonies to one another. Laws regulating intercolonial commerce were made by the British government. Although a large amount of freedom to engage in such commerce was given to all colonists, dominion over it remained in the hands of superior British authorities. In addition, control over the relations of the colonies to foreign countries was a complete monopoly of the British government. As to the management of intercolonial and foreign affairs, therefore, Americans enjoyed little or no power and were relatively inexperienced during the colonial age.

Yet in regard to intercolonial relations, Americans were not wholly ignorant or indifferent. Nor were they totally without experience, or devoid of the desire to foster closer connections. Indeed many things conspired to draw the colonies closer together: the need for defense against Indians; participation in the numerous wars waged by Great Britain against France and Spain, partly on colonial frontiers; the necessity of co-operating in raising troops and supplies for such wars; and the growth of travel, trade, and intercourse along the seaboard.

As early as 1643, Massachusetts Bay, Plymouth, Connecticut, and New Haven formed the New England Confederation. They united in a "firm and perpetual league of friendship and amity for offense and defense, mutual advice and succor, upon all just occasions, both for preserving and propagating the truth and liberties of the Gospel and for their own mutual safety and welfare." For about twenty years the Confederation was active in carrying out the purposes for which it was created. Until 1685 delegates from these united colonies held meetings from time to time and discussed common affairs. But as the need for defense against the Indians

Changes in English, French, and Spanish Possessions in America, 1664—1775.

English

French

Spanish

on their borders declined, the Confederation weakened. By the end of the seventeenth century it had completely broken down. Still it pointed the way to intercolonial action, as a precedent.

Other colonies also discovered the advantages of mutual aid. Near the middle of the seventeenth century Virginia made treaties of amity and commerce with New York and the New England colonies. In 1684 a conference was held by agents from Virginia, Massachusetts, and New York for the purpose of discussing questions of mutual interest. From time to time when Indians made attacks on Southern frontiers, Virginia went to the aid of the Carolinas. Although no permanent unions came out of these relationships, the value of co-operation was discovered and knowledge of it handed down to coming generations.

It was wars and the need of common defense, rather than any theory of union, which drew the colonies together. As time passed the Spaniards tried to strengthen their claims in the Floridas and the French developed their claims in Canada, in the Ohio country beyond the Alleghenies, and in the Mississippi Valley down to New Orleans. In the presence of French expansion on the continent, Great Britain and her American colonies had special grounds for alarm. Every time a general war broke out in Europe it spread to the frontiers of America and each time two or more colonies were drawn into the war—in the North or West or South or somewhere along the border. The New England colonies and New York were involved in King William's War (1689–97). These colonies and South Carolina took an active part in Queen Anne's War (1702–14). During King George's War (1739–48) troops were levied in New England and supplies were collected in New York, New Jersey, and Pennsylvania.

In the final contest with the French and their Indian allies in the French and Indian War of 1756–63, the conflict became general along the frontier; and many American soldiers, including George Washington, then acquired experience in the arts of campaigns and battles. The struggle opened unofficially in 1755 with the march of General Braddock's troops into the western wilderness of Pennsylvania, where they suffered a disastrous defeat. War was formally declared in 1756 and, at the end of seven years, it closed in the acquisition of Canada by Great Britain and the expulsion of the French from their other continental claims.

Hard pressed for men, money, and supplies for this long war, the British government again called on the colonies for help. Most of them were laggard in responding and a few of them did nothing at all. Massachusetts, Connecticut, and New York furnished nearly three fourths of the American troops raised; but out of the experience all the colonies learned something about the bearing of common burdens and responsibilities.

As if in anticipation of the demands to come during the French and Indian War, an ambitious attempt had been made to unite them in a permanent federation. On a suggestion from the British government, an intercolonial conference was held at Albany, New York, in 1754. Among other things its purpose was to bring the colonies under "articles of union and confederation with each other for mutual defense of his majesty's subjects and interests in North America in time of peace as well as war."

Delegates from Maryland, Pennsylvania, New York, and all the New England colonies attended the conference. Without a dissenting vote they quickly resolved that a union of the colonies was "absolutely necessary for their security and defense." A committee, headed by Benjamin Franklin, brought before the delegates a plan to effect this union. The draft was debated, adopted, and sent to the colonies and the British government for approval but, owing to indifference or hostility, it was never put into force.

Whatever the reason for its failure, the Franklin plan demonstrated that some Americans had a deep understanding of intercolonial affairs. It provided for a general council composed of forty-eight members elected by the colonial assemblies. Representation in that body was to be roughly apportioned among the colonies according to wealth and population. Meetings of the council were to be held once a year or oftener if need be. The president was to be appointed by the Crown. He was to choose the military officers with the consent of the council. The selection of civil officers was vested in the council, subject to the president's approval. As to taxation, the new government was to levy such "general duties as appear equal and just" with due regard to the circumstances in the several colonies.

According to Franklin, the Crown disapproved his scheme as "having too much weight in the democratic part of the constitution, and every [colonial] assembly as having allowed too much prerogative." Though it was rejected, the plan of union was extensively discussed at the time and in years soon to follow it served to light the way toward a permanent union.

If no union was effected by this effort or the wars in which they became involved, colonists learned many things from such experiences. They became acquainted with the pull and haul of interests in the different sections of the country and the nature of the compromises that would be necessary to bring about adjustments among the conflicting forces. In raising troops, collecting supplies, and waging wars, they acquired some rudimentary arts of intercolonial co-operation on a large scale and in difficult circumstances. From Braddock's disaster in Pennsylvania, where George Washington was present and displayed bravery under fire, they developed a suspicion that British regular troops were far from invincible, especially in the arts of wilderness warfare adapted to the American terrain. What was more, and no less significant for American autonomy, discerning leaders among the colonists gained insight into the rivalry of governments for power in the Old World as well as for imperial dominion, into their ambitions and hatreds, and into the great game of diplomacy in Europe based on the balance of power. All this, too, was enlightening and useful in developing the arts of self-government in America.

Chapter 7

TWO SYSTEMS AND IDEOLOGIES IN CONFLICT

As THE AMERICAN COLONIES matured in matters religious, economic, social, intellectual, and political, they developed institutions and ideas that clashed at many points with the institutions and ideas prevailing in the British homeland.

English political life was dominated by an oligarchy, a small group of influential lords and church officials collected around the monarch. There was in Great Britain, to be sure, a "popular" legislative body, the House of Commons. However, the oligarchy generally managed to direct it, through personal influence, wealth, corruption, by taking advantage of the restricted suffrage, and by utilizing the "rotten borough" system whereby certain areas with little or no population received considerable representation in the House.

In trying to make the colonies serve their interests, this compact ruling group was aided by the almost universal belief in England that the colonies were as subordinate socially and intellectually as they were politically and economically. In his *Origins of the American Revolution* (1943), based on microscopic and comprehensive researches in British records, John C. Miller says, while taking note of exceptions: "One of the convictions most firmly planted in the minds of the eighteenth-century Englishmen was the superiority of true-born Britons to the American colonists. . . . The status of the colonies was fixed for all time: regardless of their strength and population they must remain inferior to the mother country." This inveterate attitude was expressed by Dr. Samuel Johnson in the words: "We do not put a calf into the plow, we wait until he is an ox." In other words the young colonies might play in their youth but they must wear the yoke after they grow up.

Though the British oligarchy was often divided over various questions and there were occasional popular outbursts of protest against its harsher measures of government, the ruling classes of Great Britain were fairly united on one thing: they wanted to keep the British Empire intact and to make it contribute to the wealth and power of the mother country. The American colonies furnished many offices and jobs for British lords, their younger sons, and their hangers-on; the American colonies had vast areas of unoccupied land, huge parcels of which royal favorites could obtain for a song if they had the King's approval. British merchants and shippers found American trade highly profitable and naturally sought to get and keep as much of it as they could. British manufacturers looked upon the American markets as their own and as necessary outlets for their woolen cloth, hardware, and other finished commodities. The arable lands and forests of America were the objects of great desire to British enterprisers. British capitalists, whether landlords, merchants, manufacturers, or bankers, ever hunting more advantageous places for the investment of their capital, regarded the American colonies as offering almost unlimited opportunities for money-making.

Associated with British interests in political power and economic advantage were a number of principles—an ideology—which seemed natural, right, and proper to persons who held them. The King and the members of the titled aristocracy, who formed his inner circle, deemed it their right and privilege to hold the colonies tightly and permanently under the British government which they so largely controlled. To British merchants and shippers it was perfectly "reasonable" that they should enjoy ever-enlarging opportunities in the American trade, fix the prices to be paid to American planters and farmers for their produce, and restrain the menacing competition of American merchants and shippers. For British manufacturers it was "natural" to think that Americans should stick at the business of producing grain, lumber, and other raw materials and be compelled, as far as possible, to buy British finished products at good prices. That British capitalists should have special advantages in investing in the lands, fur trade, commerce, and other lucrative enterprises in America was, in their minds, both "right and proper."

These ideas all fitted into the pattern of "mercantilism" which generally prevailed in Western Europe throughout the colonial period. In sum and substance, mercantilism meant that the government should adopt and enforce measures to accomplish the following objects: hold colonies in the status of raw-material provinces supplying the mother country with materials for its manufacturers and foodstuffs for its workers; promote export and import trade in such a way as to bring gold, silver, and other forms of wealth into its coffers; give the mother country the profits that arose from manufacturing; and monopolize more or less the commerce of the colonies to the advantage of its merchants. In the theory of mercantilism, the British government in London and its supporters found "good reasons" for believing that their ideas about managing American affairs were "sound" and "patriotic."

For carrying the ideas of mercantilism into effect, certain very definite laws and practices were necessary. The bonds of union between the American colonies and Great Britain must be kept firm and made stronger as the colonies matured in wealth and power. Laws favorable to the interests of British merchants, manufacturers, and investors must be enacted; and the American colonists must be stopped from passing laws and doing other things which interfered with the enforcement of British measures. To carry British legislation into effect, the number of British officers and agents in the colonies must be increased and, if necessary, British soldiers must be stationed there to uphold British governors and agents in the performance of their duties. Given British interests and ideas of values, given the theory of mercantilism as soundly patriotic, British designs for the colonies followed logically.

But in many matters, American interests ran directly counter to British interests. Most Americans were more concerned with developing the lands and resources right at hand than they were in promoting prosperity in Great Britain or upholding the British interests in India and other distant parts of the world. American artisans and manufacturers wanted to develop their own industries and reap the profits accruing from them. American merchants and shippers longed to enlarge their share of international trade. American farmers and planters believed that they could get better prices for their produce if British merchants exercised less control over the export and import trade; if Dutch, French, and other merchants from the continent of Europe could operate more freely in American markets, offering their goods for sale and buying tobacco, grains, and other farm commodities. American capitalists and enterprisers thought they would have larger opportunities for profitable business if all the lands, forests, and minerals at hand were at the disposal of colonial governments. Farmers and planters on the seaboard looked with hungry eyes toward the vacant lands beyond the near frontier and wanted them thrown open to easy settlement or speculation. Moreover, Americans could scarcely help wanting a larger share of the lucrative offices and jobs filled with appointees of the British King and the colonial governors, whose salaries were paid out of American taxes, without colonial representation in Parliament.

To support their counter interests, Americans had a large stock of ideas. One part of the stock consisted of legal ideas, another part of political ideas, and still another of economic ideas. The whole program included the following elements: under the English "constitution" Englishmen everywhere in the realm have certain rights which cannot be taken from them, such as the right to share, through their representatives, in the making of laws and the laying of taxes; the purpose of government is to protect the life, liberty, and property of the people; when tyranny or oppression takes the place of protection, the people have a right to change the government by revolution if necessary; all human beings are equal and have a right to obtain the land necessary to a livelihood. From such legal, political, and economic theories, Americans active in the advancement of their own interests had little difficulty in choosing arguments that fitted their respective cases.

If Americans were to realize their interests and ideas in practice, they believed that two types of measures were necessary. They needed local laws providing more control over the sale of lands, over the issue of currency used in trade, and over their manufacturing and commerce. Defensive measures were also indispensable—measures directed against British regulations and their enforcement in the colonies.

Having a care for such matters, colonial legislatures, from year to year, passed laws designed to serve American interests, despite the fact that acts were often vetoed by the colonial governor, or disallowed and set aside by the British Crown on its own motion or on appeal from objectors. On the defensive side other lines of action were open to Americans who resented British regulations: they could petition the King; they could send a colonial agent to London for the purpose of lobbying on behalf of their demands; they could simply ignore or violate British laws, especially if the royal or proprietary governor was lenient or negligent, as he often was.

In giving effect to mercantilism and British ideology in general, the Parliament in London enacted many laws pertaining to American economic enterprise and political affairs. In general terms such laws fell into three broad classes.

The first class affected shipbuilding and the carriage of freight by water. They were known as Navigation Acts. These acts provided that goods carried both ways between Great Britain and the colonies and between the colonies and European countries must be transported in British-built ships manned mainly by British sailors. Since, in the eyes of the law, Americans were British, the ships the Americans built were "British-built" and the sailors they furnished were also British. In many ways, therefore, the Navigation Acts worked to the advantage of the colonies as well as the mother country. On the whole, the acts stimulated American shipping and promoted American commercial interests.

To the second class of British legislation belonged the Trade Acts. By such laws certain "enumerated" commodities produced in America had to be exported to Great Britain alone. In time the enumerated list included rice, tobacco, iron, lumber, furs, hides, naval stores, and a few other types of goods. Thus many American farmers and planters had to sell their prime produce through British merchants and accept the prices fixed in the British market, rather than dealing with Dutch, French, and other foreign merchants offering better terms.

Under other trade laws, American goods passing to the continent of Europe and European goods imported into the colonies had to go through the hands of merchants in Great Britain who collected their profits on the business. A special trade law, called the Molasses Act, passed by Parliament in 1733, laid taxes on important articles in the trade of the colonists with non-British possessions in America, especially the French West Indies, for the purpose of benefiting British merchants and capitalists engaged in commerce and sugar production in the British West Indies.

But the trade laws as a rule gave Americans many advantages, while restricting their operations in certain directions. To cite an example, for the enumerated articles Americans had a virtual monopoly in the markets of Great Britain as against their foreign competitors.

It was clearly in the interests of British manufacturers, however, to have laws enacted by Parliament for the purpose of restraining colonial industries. These formed a third class of regulatory laws. In 1699 the colonists were forbidden by act of Parliament to export woolen goods anywhere, and even to trade in such goods between towns and between colonies. In 1732 colonists were deprived of the right to export hats, finished or unfinished, to any place in America or abroad. By 1750 British ironmasters were feeling the pinch of their American competitors and in that year Parliament forbade Americans to set up iron mills for working bar or pig iron and for producing finished iron manufactures.

It was not so easy for the British government to enforce laws restricting American manufactures as it was to carry into effect the Navigation and Trade acts. Strict enforcement would have required a British official in every community, for instance, where housewives were spinning and weaving or men were making hats or hardware. As a matter of fact the British government did not attempt to police the colonies in this respect and the American manufacture of the forbidden goods flourished in spite of the laws.

But a turn came in the relatively negligent methods of the British government after the Seven Years' War with France which ended in 1763. In that conflict colonists had taken an active part by furnishing soldiers and supplies. A heavy burden, however, had fallen on Great Britain, for the war raged in distant places at sea and at points as far apart as the coasts of India and the frontiers of North America. Although some results of the conflict were fortunate for Britain—the capture of Canada and other territorial gains—the struggle had been expensive and had greatly increased the British debt. As an outcome also, the British government faced other problems; for instance, the administration of the Northwest Territory adjoining the Mississippi and the Ohio rivers, and the regulation of relations with the Indians in that region.

In addition, a highly controversial question arose: Who are to benefit most from the exploitation of Western territories now cleared of the French and opened to development—American or British investors, farmers, land speculators, and fur traders? The British had undoubtedly made prodigious sacrifices in the effort to oust the French from the continent. The war had likewise been costly in men and money to the colonies. Both the British and the Americans therefore had logical and legitimate claims regarding all these matters, but there was no high and impartial court above them to which they could appeal for satisfactory adjudication.

Whatever the merits of the respective claims to the benefits arising from enterprise and speculation in America, the British government eventually embarked upon a program of strengthening, adding to, and enforcing laws and decrees designed to regulate American economic and political affairs. Responsibility for this departure was assumed by the British ministries that succeeded one another after George III came to the throne in 1760, in the midst of the great war between England and France.

George himself, upon whom much of the blame for the trouble was later thrown, had little to do with initiating the program, but in general he approved it. Besides, by bribery and corruption, he helped to support the ministers who formulated it in the Parliament; and he had high notions about his royal prerogatives at home as well as over his "farms," as he referred to the colonies. In no way did the new program run counter to his conceptions of government.

Briefly stated, the program included three principal elements: Americans must be taxed to pay a part of the expense incurred by Great Britain in defending, protecting, and administering her possessions in America; old trade and navigation laws must be more strictly enforced; and new laws regulating British and American commerce and enterprise in the colonies must be enacted.

Within five years after the close of the war with France the following measures had been adopted by the British government:

1763—Royal Order, reserving to the King the disposal of Western lands beyond a certain line.

1764—Sugar Act, taxing certain imports, partly with a view to bringing money into the British treasury for supporting British government in the colonies.

1764—Currency Act, forbidding the colonies to issue paper money.

1765—Stamp Act, taxing numerous articles and transactions in America to help pay the costs of protecting and holding the colonies.

1765—Quartering Act, requiring Americans to help house and feed British regular troops stationed in the colonies.

1766—Declaratory Act, asserting the supremacy of the British Parliament in making laws for the colonies.

1767—Customs Collecting Act, establishing British commissioners in the colonies to collect customs and other duties.

1767—Revenue Act, laying taxes on lead, paint and other articles imported into the colonies.

1767—Tea Act, regulating importation of tea in British dominions in America in favor of the British East India Company.

All these measures deeply affected the American colonists: their agriculture, industries, commerce, and investment opportunities; their habits, practices, and desires respecting self-government; their freedom of elections, press, and speech. The Royal Order of 1763 forbade the colonists to buy any more land from the Indians in the West beyond a certain line, and vested in the Crown the sole power to hold and dispose of such lands. If enforced, this decree would mean that hardy pioneers, land-hungry and bent on acquiring homes for themselves, could no longer go West, take up land, and "squat" on it as their own. It would also mean that American land speculators could not acquire huge blocks of Western land in the hope of making money as land values rose with the advance of Western settlement.

The same order contained another provocative clause. It placed in the hands of royal officers the power of licensing persons engaged in trade with the Indians and thereby deciding who was to enjoy the profits of the lucrative fur traffic. In fact, the proclamation, though designed among other things to introduce order along the frontier, indicated that British officials were henceforward to dispose of large sections of the Western territory and settle the question as to who was to reap the profits of the various operations there, including the fur business. This, in turn, meant that Americans would no longer have the liberty to do very much as they pleased on the frontier—to hunt, trade with the Indians, gather up furs, and roam around at will, looking for adventures or "taking up" land.

The purpose of the Sugar Act was clearly stated in the preamble. It was to promote the business of the British sugar colonies in the West Indies, raise money toward the expenses of "defending, protecting, and securing" British colonies and plantations in America, more strictly enforce the laws against smuggling, and secure and improve the trade between Great Britain and her colonies in the New World. The act, like its predecessor in 1733, laid duties on sugar brought into the American colonies from non-British possessions. It also imposed duties on certain wines, silks, calicoes, and linens imported into the American colonies. With a view to enforcement, the act provided heavy penalties for all shippers, British and American alike, who tried to smuggle goods contrary to the terms of the law.

Explicitly, the Sugar Act taxed Americans for the purpose of raising money to pay the expenses of British officials and soldiers employed in governing the colonies and upholding British dominion over them. In itself, this was enough to rouse American ire. But the act also struck a severe blow at one branch of American commerce. Americans could no longer buy sugar cheaper from the French sugar colonies in the West Indies. They had been buying large quantities there, turning it into rum, and exchanging the rum for African slaves to be brought back to America for sale. This was a highly successful business and a tax on it in favor of British sugar growers and slave traders, if enforced, would hamper an important branch of American commerce.

The Customs Collecting Act of 1767, coupled with many provisions in other new British laws, showed that the British government was determined to stop smuggling and other violations of tax and trade laws on the part of Americans. British revenue collectors, officers of the navy and army, royal governors, and other agents were ordered to be diligent, to see that taxes were collected and regulations observed. Shipmasters engaged in the carrying trade had to be registered in official books and give bond that they would obey the laws. Patrols of British ships guarded the Atlantic coast, with power to halt, search, and hold merchant ships suspected of smuggling. Thus American liberty to trade at will was to be drastically curtailed.

By the Currency Act of 1764, American merchants, farmers, and debtors were adversely affected in numerous ways. No rich mines of gold and silver were discovered in the seaboard regions; so that Americans had no gold and silver of their own coinage with which to pay for domestic goods and meet their debts at home. For the same reason they had difficulty in finding specie to pay for imported British and foreign goods and to discharge the debts they owed British capitalists for money they had borrowed to buy land, stock, tools, and other capital supplies. In their straits, nearly all the colonies had been issuing colonial paper money at one time or another, and had made it lawful in business transactions. Now the Currency Act put a stop to this practice definitely and positively, evoking an early episode in the American battle over the "money question."

None of the British regulatory measures, however, affected large numbers of Americans seriously enough to arouse great popular opposition.

It was the Stamp Act of 1765 that first set the colonies aflame. In the preamble of this act also appeared the declaration that its purpose was to provide money for the British treasury, "towards defraying the expenses of defending, protecting and securing the British colonies and plantations in America." That in itself was resented by many colonists. But the clauses of the act intended to raise the money, covering several pages of fine print, prescribed taxes which reached the pocketbooks of Americans from Massachusetts to Georgia.

Americans now had to buy stamps of various kinds, ranging in price from a few pence to several pounds each, to be placed on many classes of papers and articles. Deeds and mortgages relating to property, licenses to practice law, licenses to sell liquor, college diplomas, playing cards, dice, almanacs, and calendars all had to bear British stamps of stated values. More than this: publishers and printers of advertisements, newspapers, and other sheets had to buy stamps for their publications.

If the British Parliament had deliberately searched for taxes that would annoy as many Americans as possible, it could scarcely have improved upon the Stamp Act. The law was especially hard on two classes of Americans who spoke, wrote, and made their opinions heard: the lawyers and the publishers—both given to preaching freedom of speech and press. The very men in the streets were so angry that they instigated boycotts and riots against the act.

In itself the Stamp Act of March 1765 would have made trouble for the British government but it was quickly followed in April of the same year by the Quartering Act which gave the colonists to understand that the laws were to be enforced. Since the British ministry was preparing to send more soldiers than usual to the American colonies, with a view to upholding its authority, it faced the problem of furnishing the soldiers with quarters and supplies.

For this problem the Quartering Act provided what was deemed a solution: Americans were to lodge officers and privates in inns, taverns, uninhabited houses, barns, and other buildings; supply them with numerous articles of consumption; and furnish wagons to haul their goods. American constables, magistrates, and other civil officers in villages, towns, townships, cities, districts, and other places were charged with the duty of seeing that the buildings, candles, liquor, salt, and other articles mentioned in the act were promptly placed at the disposal of the British troops.

Consequently Americans not only had to endure the sight of British troops and the thought of military government; they had to help in housing, feeding, and serving British soldiers. Yet time was required to transport the British soldiers to the colonies and many months passed before

American communities were stirred up by the necessity of finding quarters and supplies for them.

It was the Stamp Act which awakened immediate protests and alarms. Lawyers and merchants were quick to voice their resentment against it. The cry, "No taxation without representation," was taken up in cities, towns, and country regions by artisans, mechanics, farmers, and housewives. Popular societies called the Sons of Liberty and the Daughters of Liberty were organized to resist the sale of stamps. Crowds gathered in the streets of Boston, New York, Philadelphia, and Charleston, and rioted against officers who tried to force people to buy stamps. The offices and houses of royal officials were stoned, in some cases sacked and burned. Going far beyond blocking the sale of stamps, Americans organized groups to boycott British goods of all kinds—to cut down the sale of British manufactures as well as stamps. Indeed there was so much disorder in several colonies that even the protesting merchants and lawyers became frightened and tried to restrain the torrent of popular anger.

Colonial leaders took steps to bring united pressure on Parliament for the repeal of the act. In the Virginia House of Burgesses they forced the adoption of resolutions denouncing the principles of the Stamp Act, asserting that the General Assembly alone could lay taxes on the people of the colony, and branding other methods of taxation as "illegal, unconstitutional, and unjust." It was in supporting this resolution that Patrick Henry delivered the speech which made him famous as a firebrand of the Revolution.

In the spirit of the Virginia Resolutions, the House of Representatives in Massachusetts opposed the Stamp Act and issued a circular letter inviting all the colonies to send delegates to a general congress to be held in New York for the purpose of discussing common problems and taking common action. Nine colonies responded favorably, chose their delegates amid popular excitement, and sent them to New York.

In October 1765 the Stamp Act Congress assembled. Despite some difference of opinion, it agreed on a set of resolutions and the terms of a petition calling upon Parliament to repeal the act. Members of the Congress professed their loyal allegiance to the King and their subordination to the Parliament of Great Britain. But they claimed all the inherent rights and liberties of natural-born British subjects. They declared that no taxes could be laid on the people without their consent, that the colonies were not and could not be represented in Parliament, and that no taxes could be constitutionally imposed upon them without the consent of their legislatures. They also sought to show that various acts of Parliament both burdened the colonies and interfered with trade between them and Great Britain. British merchants were tersely warned that restrictions recently placed on trade would render the people of the colonies unable to purchase British manufactures. While resolutions were respectful and moderate in tone, they were specific and firm.

In consternation over the open resistance in the colonies and under pressure from British merchants hard hit by the American boycott, Parliament in 1766 repealed the Stamp Act. In so doing, however, it did not concede the American claim that it had no right to tax the colonists. In fact, by the Declaratory Act, signed on the same day as the repeal measure, Parliament asserted that the colonies have been, are, and ought to be subordinate to the Crown and Parliament; and that the King and Parliament had, have, and of right ought to have full power and authority to make laws and statutes binding the colonies and people of America "in all cases whatsoever." This language left no loopholes through which Americans could escape admitting their subordination to the British government, but, as they rejoiced over the abolition of the Stamp Tax, they spent little time arguing about the mere legal theory of the Declaratory Act.

Evidently foreseeing the dangers in trying to collect taxes in the colonies directly, the British ministers, still determined to raise revenue in America, took another course. The very next year after the repeal of the Stamp Act, Parliament passed the Revenue Act of 1767, which laid duties on glass, red and white lead, painters' colors, paper, and tea.

At the same time Parliament informed the colonists that these duties were to be collected. It coupled with the Revenue Act a law which had "teeth" in every line. The Customs Commissioners Act of 1767 vested in the hands of British commissioners the duty of supervising the enforcement of the revenue laws. The tax commissioners were to be appointed by the King; they were to reside in the colonies; and they were to be paid from the British treasury, not out of grants of money voted by colonial legislatures. In the Revenue Act itself, Parliament also expressed its resolve to collect the duties: it gave the higher courts in the colonies, made up of British judges, power to issue "Writs of Assistance," authorizing customs officers to search houses, warehouses, shops, cellars, and other places for smuggled goods and to seize them summarily if found.

A third commercial measure passed by Parliament in 1767 was the Tea Act. This act, supplemented by another Tea Act in 1773, among other things relieved the British East India Company of the necessity of paying duties on its tea exported to America. In effect it amounted to giving the company a monopoly of the tea business in America; enforced, it would enable the company to sell tea at lower prices than were asked by other British merchants or, for that matter, even by American merchants who had bought tea from foreign merchants and smuggled it into the colonies. Not without reason did objecting colonists regard the Tea Act as a step toward setting up British monopolies for the control of all American foreign and domestic trade.

Events swiftly following the enactment of the British laws of 1767 revealed to the two parties the sharpness of the conflict. It was now obvious that the British government was determined to raise revenue in the colonies by taxation; to use this revenue toward defraying the expenses of governing the colonies; to enforce its authority through higher officers appointed by the Crown and paid out of the British treasury; to free the royal officers from control by the colonial assemblies; and definitely to subordinate the colonists to British commercial interests. It was made equally plain by events that irate Americans who opposed the British policies would stubbornly resist them by official resolves in colonial assemblies and by popular actions outside the legislative halls—even actions involving violence.

The basic animus of the colonists against British policies became manifest within a year. In 1768 the assembly of Massachusetts, inspired by Samuel Adams, approved the sending of a circular letter to the legislatures of the other colonies, calling upon them to consider their common plight, and declaring the principles of retaliation on which Massachusetts was taking her stand. For this defiance the royal governor at Boston dissolved the assembly.

When assemblies in other colonies approved the doctrines of the Circular Letter, they too were dissolved by their governors. In 1769 the Virginia House of Burgesses proclaimed that it alone had the right to lay taxes in Virginia, and petitioned the King for a redress of grievances. The governor of the colony replied by dissolving that assembly.

Meanwhile a contest especially bitter was going on in New York. In that colony the assembly had refused to make provisions for British soldiers under the Quartering Act of 1765. Parliament answered in 1767 by passing a law suspending the New York Assembly until it was ready to comply with the terms of the Quartering Act. When at length, in 1769, it bowed to British demands, it made no attempt to conceal its indignation; and the necessity of housing and supplying British soldiers stirred up wrath among the residents of the colony.

In 1770 British soldiers, stationed at Boston, jostled and stoned by a crowd of men and boys, fired on their assailants, killing five and wounding several more. News of this "Boston Massacre," as it was described, spread into other colonies, awakening both resentment and anxiety. When in 1772 a British armed vessel engaged in hunting smugglers in

Narragansett Bay accidentally ran ashore, it was quickly boarded by men from Providence who seized the crew and set fire to the ship. In 1773 the House of Burgesses in Virginia, meeting in spite of the governor's prohibition, created a standing committee to correspond with leaders in other colonies and bring about combined actions against British policies and measures. Late that year a group of men, disguised as Indians, forced their way upon ships at Boston, which had brought tea for sale to the colonists under the new terms, and dumped their cargoes into the harbor. In 1774 rioters at Annapolis compelled the destruction of a British vessel, the *Peggy Stewart*, and all the tea chests on board. American resistance was taking the form of physical violence when the year 1774 opened.

If members of the Boston Tea Party thought that the British government would yield to their display of anger they were mistaken and soon disillusioned. Early in 1774 Parliament enacted five new laws intended to cure unrest in America. One of the acts closed the port of Boston to all trade by sea. Another revamped the charter of Massachusetts, made the government still more royal in nature, and even subjected town meetings to the control of the governor. A third act empowered royal officials to take to Great Britain or elsewhere in her American colonies all persons in Massachusetts accused of murder in connection with law enforcement. By a fourth act the quartering of British troops in Massachusetts towns was specifically authorized. The fifth act offended Protestants and affected other interests in the colonies: it granted toleration to Catholics in Canada, widened the boundaries of Quebec southward to the Ohio River, and provided for the government of that vast Western territory by a viceroy of the King.

More British soldiers were now sent to Massachusetts and the commander of the British armed forces in the colony, General Gage, was installed as governor. Such actions on the part of the British government in Massachusetts served as a warning to all the colonists that British authority was not to be denied or defied with impunity. As the spring of 1774 merged into summer, leaders of the opposition to British authority, from Massachusetts to Georgia, had to face that fact and, if still stubborn in their militancy, make further decisions on the basis of it.

Chapter 8

INDEPENDENCE COMPLETED BY REVOLUTION

IN THE SPRING of 1774 a cry went up in the colonies for united action and for a general congress to assure such action. The assembly of Virginia, still meeting, if irregularly, in spite of the royal governor's prohibitive orders, expressed sympathy with Massachusetts and favored combined efforts in resistance to British policies and measures. Encouraged by reports from various sources, the assembly of Massachusetts, under the leadership of Samuel Adams, resolved that a continental congress was highly expedient and indeed necessary to deliberate and determine upon wise and proper steps to be taken in recovering the rights of Americans and restoring harmony with Great Britain. As proof of its intransigence it appointed delegates to attend such a congress on the first of the coming September.

In line with the action of Massachusetts, other colonies chose representatives and on September 5 the first Continental Congress met at Philadelphia. Among its members were men soon to be powerful figures in history, such as George Washington and Patrick Henry from Virginia, Samuel Adams and John Adams from Massachusetts. But they differed among themselves as to the best course to pursue. Many favored radical action verging in the direction of independence; others were cautious and conservative; on the whole, moderates held the balance of power. After tempestuous debates, the Congress agreed upon three expedients.

First, it adopted a set of resolutions, in dignified but pointed language, setting forth the rights, liberties, and immunities of the colonists and naming the measures of the British government which, in their view, violated these rights, liberties, and immunities. As to exactly what they claimed and what they were protesting against, members of the Congress left no doubt. By these resolutions they repeated and expanded the claims made by the Stamp Act Congress of 1765.

Second, while promising to support Massachusetts in her struggle against Great Britain, the Continental Congress drew up an address to King George III and another to the people of England and to the inhabitants of British America, in which it respectfully presented American grievances and called for a restoration of American rights. The resolutions and the addresses were words—firm, moderate, positive words; still they were only words.

A third expedient approved by the Continental Congress went beyond words into action. That was a decision to stop the importation of British goods into the colonies until a redress of grievances could be obtained and to vest the enforcement of the boycott in the hands of local "committees of safety and inspection." The boycott was, of course, a violation of British law. It was more than this. It was aggressive. It provided for establishing in every community a boycott committee to prevent the buying of British goods and to discover who was loyal to Great Britain and who was loyal to the American cause, as tested by their acts in buying goods. Words might be debated and hairs split indefinitely but a colonist either upheld the boycott or he was against it and bought British goods in spite of it. He was in short a Patriot or a Loyalist!

Before adjourning in October, the first Continental Congress provided for a second Congress to be held in May of 1775 in case the situation then required such an assembly.

In response to the demands of the first Continental Congress, the British government made one concession: it was willing to relieve any colony of taxation on condition that it would bear its share of imperial defense and provide money for supporting the officers of the Crown within its borders. But with this concession, such as it was, Parliament coupled a set of resolutions pledging full support to the King in the enforcement of British laws in the colonies. These resolutions it supplemented by restraining acts which practically destroyed the commerce of the colonies.

Meanwhile British officers—civil and military—in the colonies tightened, instead of relaxing, their efforts to compel obedience to British authority. It was in the fulfillment of this duty that General Gage, in Boston, dispatched a small force of soldiers toward Lexington and Concord in April 1775 for the purpose, among other things, of seizing some military supplies supposed to be stored in that neighborhood.

Warned by William Dawes and Paul Revere that British soldiers were on the march, a small number of American militiamen gathered on the green at Lexington early in the morning of April 19. With about thirty or forty onlookers the militiamen were standing there when the British forces arrived under the command of Major John Pitcairn. Seeing that armed resistance would be futile, the captain of the militiamen, John Parker, ordered his men to disperse. While they were slowly breaking ranks a shot was fired.

By whom? British who were present at the time laid the blame for the first shot on Americans; and Americans put it on the British. Since that day the question of blame has been repeatedly debated without reaching any generally accepted conclusion. Whoever cares to weigh the evidence of contemporary witnesses who saw the fray with their own eyes may find the testimony admirably summarized in the pages of Allen French's *The Day of Concord and Lexington.*

Although the person who fired the first shot that nineteenth day of April 1775 must apparently remain forever unknown, it is certain that his shot was followed by firing all day, as militiamen poured in from the surrounding country and harassed British troops on their retreat to Boston. It is also certain that this shot, "heard around the world," heralded a war.

☆

If there had been doubts about the need for a second conference of delegates from all the colonies, they were settled by the clash at Lexington and Concord in April 1775. In the next month the second Continental Congress assembled at Philadelphia. Though blood had been shed, most of the delegates were still inclined to be conciliatory toward the British government when sessions of the Congress opened; for they seemed to hope that the American rights previously declared might yet be acknowledged by Great Britain.

But the Congress prepared for the worst—a general war. It provided for organizing the New England militiamen near Boston into a regular army and appointed one of its members, George Washington, as commander of the American forces in Massachusetts. It also resolved to raise money and supplies for an armed conflict if it came; to seek support by opening diplomatic relations with several European countries; and to carry on the struggle until the liberties claimed by Americans could be realized by British concessions or American independence.

These resolves were met in Great Britain by a proclamation from George III denouncing American leaders in the revolt as "rebels" and ordering the British military and civil agents to suppress the insurrection and punish the authors and abettors of "such traitorous designs." The war was now in full course.

In June 1775 American militiamen on the heights near Boston, though finally driven from their position, proved that they could and would fight as long as they had gunpowder. Taking command of the army at Cambridge the next month, Washington prepared to besiege Boston. In this operation he was so successful that Lord Howe, who had now supplanted General Gage, gave up the city in March 1776 and sailed for Halifax. In his flight Howe carried along, besides his troops, several hundred British officials and Boston residents who were steadfast in their loyalty to King George.

Meanwhile, late in 1775, Vermont militiamen, under Ethan Allen and Benedict Arnold, had seized Ticonderoga and Crown Point, getting possession of strongholds which might block a British drive from Canada. Still later in that year American forces invaded Canada and captured Montreal. But an assault on Quebec failed and they were forced to withdraw, thus losing their hope of bringing Canada to the support of the struggle against Great Britain.

☆

As the war proceeded, prospects for a reconciliation with Great Britain faded and the desire for independence, which only a few Americans had hitherto entertained, flamed into a fixed resolve. On January 10, 1776, while Washington was still besieging the British in Boston, Thomas Paine gave voice to this resolution in a powerful tract called *Common Sense*, published in Philadelphia. Spurning the humble language of loyalty formerly used in petitions to George III, Paine assailed the King in acrimonious words, scorned the once praised British constitution, and demanded immediate and unconditional independence for America. "Now," he exclaimed, "is the seed-time of Continental union, faith, and honor. . . . O! ye that love mankind! Ye that dare oppose not only tyranny, but the tyrant, stand forth."

As edition after edition of *Common Sense*, totaling more than 100,000 copies, came from the press, the call to revolution swept throughout the colonies. The word "independence" had now been spoken and was echoing from New Hampshire to Georgia. The debate with Great Britain over rights claimed as just—rights treasured as the liberties of Englishmen—had become a war of ideas which could not be stopped. Reconciliation, Paine had proclaimed, is "a fallacious dream."

Doubting, wondering, and wavering men in the Continental Congress now began to accept the climax. From all the royal and proprietary colonies, British governors and officials were fleeing as from the wrath to come, accompanied by small bands of American officials and crowds of Americans who still clung to George III. In May the Congress advised every colony to form a government of its own, as if British dominion had actually come to an end. In fact Virginia and other colonies were already taking this fateful step and their example was quickly followed. In short, the colonies were assuming the powers of independent states. South Carolina, having adopted a provisional constitution in March 1776, supplanted it by a definite constitution in 1778.

Strictly speaking, the movement for the break with Great Britain was spreading upward from the colonies to the Continental Congress, rather than downward to the colonies from the Congress. On April 13, 1776, the North Carolina revolutionary assembly gave its delegates in the Congress full power to unite with the other members in boldly declaring independence. Elsewhere the idea was also approved. On May 15 the Virginia delegates at Philadelphia received instructions from a convention of that province to propose independence in the Congress and support it.

Thoroughly aroused by the surge of revolutionary temper from below and incited by daring spirits among its members, the Continental Congress girded itself for final action. On June 7, Richard Henry Lee, speaking for the Virginia delegation, moved that "these united colonies are, and ought to be, free and independent states." But cautious men prevented the immediate adoption of the resolution and the Congress did no more than authorize the appointment of a committee to draw up a declaration of independence. Yielding at length to popular demands, the Congress, by an almost unanimous vote, on July 2 approved a resolution in favor of independence.

Meanwhile the committee appointed in June, composed of five members, including Thomas Jefferson, John Adams, and Benjamin Franklin, was busy framing the document which was to express the ideas and the spirit of independence. A draft of the document was first prepared by Jefferson. It was then reviewed by his colleagues. Adams and Franklin suggested several changes. For example, Jefferson had written: "We hold these truths to be sacred and undeniable." Later it was modified, perhaps by Franklin, to read: "We hold these truths to be self-evident." Finally the draft was completed and laid before the Congress. After making other changes in it, the Congress formally adopted the document on July 4. During a period extending over several months, it was signed by members of the Congress.

The Declaration of Independence set forth in great detail the "causes" that impelled the American people to the revolutionary act of separation from Great Britain. This part of the Declaration was, of course, an American statement of the case against the British government and was directed particularly against King George III as if Parliament bore little or no responsibility for the troubles that had arisen. It put the charges in summary and pointed language which Americans could readily understand, for they had personal knowledge of many a grievance listed in the indictment against the British sovereign.

Unlike the resolutions of the Stamp Act Congress in 1765, which also proclaimed grievances but in a humble tone, the Declaration of Independence was animated by a fixed determination to cast off British dominion and furthermore by a radical theory of government. The theory was not new by any means. It had been known and discussed in the colonies for a long time among students of government and even among people at large. The framer of the Declaration, Thomas Jefferson, was well aware of this fact. Had he invented an entirely novel idea, it would have made less of an appeal to the people. With the aid of Franklin and Adams, he did, however, put all the elements of the theory together effectively and present the whole in a flowing eloquence that electrified American minds and hearts.

In the theory of the American Revolution, as Jefferson formulated it, were three principal features: (1) All men are created equal and endowed by their Creator with certain unalienable rights, among which are life, liberty, and the pursuit of happiness. (2) It is to secure these rights that governments are instituted, and they derive their just powers from the consent of the governed. (3) When any form of government becomes destructive of these ends, it is the right of the people to alter or abolish it, and to institute new government, laying its foundations on such principles and organizing its powers in such form as to them shall seem most likely to effect their safety and happiness.

It was these doctrines, the declaration asserted, which the British government had violated and the American people were to accept as the basis of their independence and the new governments they were to institute. To all other governments then existing in the world the doctrines offered a revolutionary challenge that was to ring through the centuries. Indeed there were even many Americans who, though they were disposed toward independence, were afraid that "the people" might set up governments destructive of the privileges hitherto enjoyed by particular classes in the colonies.

To incarnate the principles of the Declaration in the life of the nation, it was necessary for the Revolutionists first to overcome the armed forces of Great Britain on land and sea; and for many months the prospects for an ultimate American victory looked gloomy. In August of 1776, less than seven weeks after the fateful July 4, the American troops under General Washington were badly mauled on Long Island by superior British regulars. Instead of capturing New York City as they had expected when they marched southward from New England, they were driven northward to White Plains, then across the Hudson River, and then southward through New Jersey.

Not until near the end of that year did a light appear in the blackness. On Christmas night, while the mercenary Hessian troops under British command were celebrating the season at Trenton, Washington made a surprise attack on them and captured about a thousand prisoners. A few days later, early in January 1777, he struck another hard blow at the British in a battle at Princeton a few miles above Trenton.

But these were merely episodes encouraging to Americans, not great victories. Later in the year Washington was defeated at Brandywine. He lost Philadelphia to the British and narrowly escaped disaster at Germantown. Forced to retire westward with his shattered troops to Valley Forge for the winter of 1777–78, he seemed to be almost at the end of his resources.

Then came news from the north which once more raised the enthusiasm of the Revolutionists to a high pitch—news of a great victory for their side. Under orders from the British war office, General John Burgoyne, at the head of a strong force, had invaded northern New York, expecting to be joined by a band of Loyalists and Indians from the west and to be aided by British troops from Lord Howe's army in lower New York. If successful this invasion would have split the country into two parts and imperiled or ruined the American cause. But it failed miserably for the British. Burgoyne was attacked on all sides, his supplies were cut off, the troops sent by Howe from New York City did not arrive to support him, and on October 17, 1777, he surrendered at Saratoga to General Horatio Gates, the American commander who had replaced General Philip Schuyler just as the American victory was in sight.

Burgoyne's surrender at Saratoga, at the close of one of "the decisive battles" of history, marked a turning point toward American independence. It demonstrated that American troops, though poorly trained and supplied, had a genius for warfare and that they could in certain circumstances cope with British regulars. The victory at Saratoga was also crucial in that news of it tipped the balance in the minds of the French ministers then advising Louis XVI and brought France into the war against Great Britain.

For tedious months Benjamin Franklin, the American minister to France, despite his extraordinary popularity in that country, had sought in vain to bring the French government into the war. Smarting under the numerous defeats and losses suffered in fights with Britain, that government had found pleasure in the prospect of a successful revolt against her in America and had secretly given help to the colonies in the form of money and supplies. It had, however, shrunk from entering into an alliance with the United States and declaring war on Britain. Such a venture might end in another disaster for France. Only after the victory at Saratoga were the French ministers induced to gamble again with fate in an open war on the ancient foe.

In February 1778 the French government made treaties of amity and commerce with the United States. It officially recognized American independence, agreed to an alliance for mutual aid and defense, declared war on Great Britain, and immediately began to take part in the military and naval operations against her. Early the next year Spain joined France in the war, hoping to recover among other things Florida, which the British had annexed in 1763 at the close of the French and Indian War. Later Holland lent support to the American cause by preying upon British commerce.

The alliance with France brought to Americans the kind of assistance they sorely needed: strong naval forces, generous loans of gold, silver, and supplies, and a large body of French officers and soldiers well trained in the arts of warfare. It also encouraged Americans in every way; but it did not immediately turn the tide of war. Nor did it mean that they could escape making more strenuous efforts and assuming burdens heavier than any they had as yet carried.

As a matter of fact Americans suffered many reverses during the three years which followed the signing of the treaty of alliance with France. Anxious about a possible blockade by a French fleet, the British evacuated Philadelphia in June 1778, but they repulsed an American attack soon afterward at the Battle of Monmouth. Late in that year the British captured Savannah and, in many campaigns, planned to conquer the whole South. They overran most of Georgia, South Carolina, and North Carolina, in spite of repeated assaults by local bands of American soldiers.

In May 1780 the British took Charleston. Under the command of Lord Cornwallis they pierced the uplands of South Carolina and defeated the Americans at the Battle of Camden. Flushed by success, Cornwallis led his troops into the interior of North Carolina though they had been checked by American forces at King's Mountain. After shattering American lines at Guilford Courthouse in March 1781, Cornwallis headed for Virginia.

On arriving in Virginia, Cornwallis tried to capture the American troops led by the Marquis de Lafayette, "the boy," as he called the young Frenchman who had come over to help in the struggle for independence. Failing in this maneuver, Cornwallis retired to Yorktown on the Virginia coast, where he hoped to get reinforcements by sea.

While American armies were meeting misfortunes in the Eastern campaigns, a stroke was accomplished in the West that was to count in the final settlement. Under a commission from Virginia, George Rogers Clark recruited volunteers and in 1778 seized several towns on the east bank of the Mississippi in the Illinois country. The next year he captured the British garrison at Vincennes on the Wabash River. Thus an American grip was fastened on the Northwest.

None of the exploits by the British in the South, discouraging as they were to patriot leaders, proved to be decisive. The British could beat or scatter the Americans in battle but could not round them up wholesale or prevent their gathering again quickly to renew the struggle. They could

APPROXIMATE FRONTIER LINE OF THE
COLONIES IN 1774

make marauding expeditions into the back regions of South Carolina, North Carolina, and Virginia, but they could not occupy those regions and hold them in subjection against bands of American troops skilled in guerrilla warfare. They hit hard and yet they did not conquer. This lesson Cornwallis learned at great cost in men and supplies. It was, in part, for this reason that he drew back upon the coast at Yorktown and waited for the British navy to support him from the sea.

By that action Cornwallis unwittingly prepared for his doom and the end of the war. General Washington and his French allies, then in the North planning an attack on New York, saw what seemed to be a golden opportunity for a conclusive stroke at Yorktown. So American and French troops were rushed South to pen up Cornwallis from the landward side. A French fleet, under Admiral de Grasse, arrived from the West Indies in time to beat off British naval forces and prevent an escape of the British troops by sea. Under fire from land and sea, Cornwallis ran up the white flag and surrendered on October 19, 1781. As events were to prove, the long war was over; for the British government, stunned by the blow, either could not or would not make another gigantic effort to recover its dominion over the colonies.

☆

Nevertheless many months passed before a treaty of peace could be concluded between the United States and Great Britain. The French were still at war with Britain and their alliance with the United States remained in force. It was not until 1782 that negotiations were opened between the British agents and the American peace commissioners in France—Franklin, John Jay, and John Adams, with whom Henry Laurens was later associated.

Now it was Britain's turn to conciliate Americans in an effort to prevent France from making great gains out of the war. Fortunately for that design, British affairs were in the hands of a new ministry, composed of men who had been sympathetic with the American cause, including Edmund Burke who had so eloquently defended it in the House of Commons. Working quietly with the British agents in Paris, keeping their plans hidden from the French government, the American commissioners won generous terms for the United States and secretly signed the draft of a treaty with Great Britain.

When the French minister, Count de Vergennes, heard about this secret settlement he reminded the American commissioners that the Congress of the United States had instructed them "to be guided by the wishes of the French court," and he charged them with violating the pledges made to France in 1778 when the alliance was formed. Eventually, however, he yielded and, after long negotiations, France also came to terms with Great Britain.

The final treaty between the United States and Great Britain was signed on September 3, 1783, and ratified by the Congress in January 1784. Under its provisions King George recognized the independence of the United States. The Republic was officially accepted as extending from the Atlantic Ocean to the Mississippi River and from the Great Lakes to the Floridas. The navigation of the Mississippi was declared to be open to American citizens and British subjects.

In specific clauses the treaty assured creditors on both sides that there would be no lawful impediments to the collection of just debts. It was also agreed that Congress would recommend to the state legislatures that provision be made for restoring to loyal British subjects all properties and estates that had been confiscated during the Revolution. The right of Americans to fish off the coasts of Newfoundland and in the Gulf of the St. Lawrence in the customary manner was guaranteed by a definite article of the treaty. Even the most zealous patriot in the United States could find little fault with the settlement that brought the war to a conclusion.

The numerous battles and skirmishes waged on land from Massachusetts to Georgia and the exploits of American naval forces at sea, under such officers as John Paul Jones and John Barry, were only a part of the story of the war and the Revolution. During the long contest, men, officers, and supplies had to be provided for the armies, civil government had to be carried on, and many a dispute among Americans over the conduct and aims of the war had to be adjusted or endured.

In itself the war worked havoc in colonial economy and made new economic undertakings necessary to victory. Commerce with Great Britain was practically destroyed and trade with other countries could not fully take its place. Many regions were either occupied or harried by British troops. Loyalists bent on actively aiding the British cause, often with arms, waged a civil war within the war for independence. They in turn were harassed by resentful patriots; many were harshly treated or imprisoned; thousands were driven out of the country, to England or Canada. In important respects, therefore, the revolt against Great Britain involved also a revolution in American affairs—in military power, industry, finance, diplomacy, government, and social arrangements.

In colonial times Americans had relied for their local defense mainly upon militia composed of civilians who gave a limited amount of time to drilling and were officered by men with little more experience than the privates possessed. At the opening of the war militiamen and new volunteers filled the ranks of armies that had to wage battles with trained British regulars.

A large proportion of the recruits were brave men who fought courageously, but they were accustomed to serve for short terms, were undisciplined, not inured to long and grueling campaigns. At the beginning few among them had ever seen a real battle. A majority were farmers who had homes and families and whose minds were filled with their personal cares. After the first burst of enthusiasm died away, especially when they had to go far off from their own communities, hundreds of militiamen insisted on quitting as soon as their terms of service were over, no matter how grave the danger to the American cause and despite the pleas of their officers.

Sorely tried by the conduct of militiamen and volunteers, General Washington again and again begged the Congress to provide for a regular army composed of men enlisted for a long term or the duration of the war. But it was only when failures and defeats threatened utter ruin that the civilians in the Congress, frightened at the mere thought of a standing army as dangerous to civil liberty, yielded to his pleas and offered extra pay to officers and privates pledged to see the war through to the end. At last in the closing years of the conflict Washington had at his command a large body of men so pledged and well disciplined for action in battle.

With regard to officers of all ranks, the colonies were also ill prepared for combat with British regulars. Washington had seen actual, but not extensive, fighting in the French and Indian War. Even he was in fact little equipped by firsthand knowledge for planning and executing great campaigns or coping with the disciplined armies of Britain, enlarged by mercenaries hired from German princes.

None of the the high officers on whom he had to rely for help was thoroughly schooled in the arts of war. Henry Knox had been a bookseller in Boston; Nathanael Greene a farmer and blacksmith in Rhode Island; Benedict Arnold, the brave soldier who turned traitor, a merchant in New Haven; Francis Marion a shy South Carolina planter; and John Sullivan a lawyer in New Hampshire. Anthony Wayne was farming in Pennsylvania when he answered the call to arms, raised a regiment, and offered himself to his country. Daniel Morgan, who distinguished himself at Cowpens in South Carolina, had been only a teamster in General Braddock's army during the French and Indian War.

Competent for battle as many American officers proved to be after they had been tried by fire, Washington was fortunate in having the aid of several military men from Europe, who came to help the American cause, for the love of adventure, or in the hope of honors or other rewards: young Lafayette from France; Pulaski and Kosciuszko from Poland; and from Germany, Baron von Steuben, a former officer in the Prussian army, trained in the iron regimen of Frederick the Great and credited with long military service.

It was Steuben who joined Washington during the dark days at Valley Forge, prepared a drill manual for American soldiers, drilled a model company, and laid the basis for discipline throughout the American forces. Steuben's larger manual, later written for general use in giving soldiers the essentials of military instructions, became "the military Bible of the Continental Army." Besides teaching soldiers, Steuben took part in campaigns; he commanded a division under Washington at the siege and capture of Yorktown.

At all stages of the war American troops in the field needed large quantities of arms, ammunition, clothing, food, and other supplies, in addition to the goods furnished by the French and to some extent by the Dutch. Thus the demand for domestic manufactures and farm produce rose rapidly and the home market was widened to include all the states. At once iron, steel, hat, textile, and other industries, which had begun to flourish in colonial times, were expanded; new plants and forges were built; and special privileges were granted to stimulate war production. Women spun and wove more diligently; and spinning clubs were formed in town and country, turning out increasing amounts of woolen, linen, and cotton cloth to meet military and civilian requirements. Workers in iron, wood, and other materials, often from the farms, were drawn into industrial enterprises, especially in New England and the middle states. As a result of the quickened and enlarged activities, now that British restrictions were cast off and British imports materially reduced in volume, American economy advanced rapidly on the way toward emancipation from dependence on the Old World for several prime articles of manufacture.

In the same process, financial independence—of a kind—was achieved. Facing the necessity of providing funds to pay war bills, the Continental Congress and the state governments were forced to wrestle with difficult financial problems. Gold and silver coins of British, French, and Spanish mintage continued in circulation but the supply was wholly inadequate for public and private needs. So the Congress resorted to the issue of paper money—bills of credit—by the millions and, before the end of the war, it had outstanding about $210,000,000 in Continental money—all badly depreciated in value. To this large sum the states added paper notes of their own in an amount almost equal to the total Continental output.

Paper money was supplemented by interest-bearing securities, Continental and state, which were sold to patriotic bond buyers in exchange for specie or paper notes at a fixed rate. More millions were borrowed from France and Holland, yielding the specie desperately needed. Other revenues were derived from the sale of property confiscated from Loyalists who gave aid and comfort to the British. The Congress also called upon the states for quotas of money to meet the common bills, often without getting much in return. In attempts to comply with the demands of the Congress and cover their own requirements, the states laid heavy taxes on their citizens. In this fashion the Congress and the states created a "financial system" of their own or, rather, a financial disorder, for both paper money and bonds dropped rapidly in value—in many cases to a few cents or less on the dollar.

In various phases of war production and financing, as well as in revolutionary pamphleteering, in spying, in making bullets and other munitions, and in direct aid to fighters at the front, patriotic women were active in all the states. While their husbands, fathers, and sons were away under arms, farm women carried double burdens in field and domestic workshops, furnishing food and clothing for the armies. In towns they formed clubs to speed up production. When drives were made to raise money for the war, they organized committees to help, subscribed themselves, and contributed their gold and silver objects to the common treasury.

"Even in their dresses," complained a writer connected with the British army in South Carolina, "the females seem to bid us defiance; the gay toys which are imported here they despise; they wear their own homespun manufactures, and take care to have in their breast knots, and even on their shoes something that resembles their flag of the thirteen stripes. An officer told Lord Cornwallis not long ago, that he believed if he had destroyed all the men in North America, we should have enough to do to conquer the women. I am heartily tired of this country, and wish myself at home."

As colonists, Americans had been subject, in their relations with other countries, to the diplomacy and foreign policies of the government in London. In seeking a place among the independent nations of the earth, the Continental Congress was compelled, on its own responsibility, to make provision for diplomatic representation abroad and evolve the elements of an American foreign policy. As early as 1776 it sent an agent to Paris, Silas Deane, of Connecticut, to open negotiations, if possible, with the government of France. Later Benjamin Franklin and Arthur Lee were instructed to join Deane at the French capital. Other representatives went to Holland, Spain, Vienna, Berlin, and St. Petersburg in quest of recognition and support.

Only in France and Holland did American diplomacy achieve noteworthy results for some time. Spain was cold to American pleas for aid. Russia maintained an attitude of chilly indifference. Frederick the Great of Prussia expressed sympathies but would take no steps likely to involve himself in trouble with Britain. Yet in the end American ministers abroad—whether they procured aid or got no aid—gained a firsthand knowledge of European governments and their foreign policies, of their ambitions, designs, intrigues, and interests in various parts of the world, especially in the Western Hemisphere. Thrown upon their own resources, American diplomats proved ingenious in negotiations and acquired skill in managing foreign relations as they took over this important branch of government, formerly monopolized in America by the British Crown.

Through all the turmoil of war and the activities connected with it, the work of civil government, local and general, was carried on in the United States. While British governors were being driven from power or fleeing for their lives, eleven of the thirteen states set about drawing up plans for full self-government and at the end of the conflict had constitutions of their own. The other two, Connecticut and Rhode Island, made some changes in their old royal charters, under which they had enjoyed a generous liberty, and governed themselves as before. In each state was installed a legislature resting upon popular elections, and in some cases the property qualifications on the right to vote were made lower than they had been in colonial times. In each state provision was made for a governor, elected by the legislature in a majority of cases; in Massachusetts and New York, by popular vote.

Under these written constitutions, in which, except in New York and Massachusetts, the legislature was supreme, elections were held, campaigns conducted, and issues debated by the voters and by citizens who could not vote. Drawing upon colonial experiences, legislatures enacted laws, laid taxes, made provisions for administering state affairs, elected delegates to the Continental Congress, and co-operated, often faithfully, often negligently, with the Congress in the conduct of the war. Now free from British interference, the state legislatures, even during the most trying hours of the Revolution, began to revise and reform radically the laws inherited from England and from the colonial age, and to make American laws conform more closely to the spirit manifest in the Declaration of Independence.

Meanwhile, at the center of things, members of the second Continental Congress—the provisional body hastily assembled in May 1775—gave attention to the strengthening of the union. In June 1776 the Congress appointed a committee to draw up a plan of confederation for the states. The plan, called the Articles of Confederation, was duly reported to the Congress, debated from time to time amid the exigencies of the war business, finally approved late in 1777, and sent to the state legislatures for review and action. By 1779 all the states, except Maryland, had ratified the Articles and Maryland approved them at last, on March 1, 1781. The next day the Congress assembled under the terms of the Articles. Now the states were formally pledged to "a firm league of friendship" and "a perpetual union" created for "their common defense, the security of their liberties," and their "mutual and general welfare." A fateful step had been taken toward a republic, one and indivisible.

☆

As the revolt against Great Britain proceeded to its triumph, a civil revolution began in American society. In the prewar stage of the controversy over British policies Loyalists had warned conservatives in the Patriot party that the destruction of British dominion would lead to popular insurgency and attacks on the privileges of property and class. Their prophecies were more than fulfilled during the course of the Revolution.

Absorbing as the war was, heavy as were the burdens it imposed, most of the American people from 1775 to 1781 were occupied with civilian pursuits and immediately concerned with their economic and social affairs. At the beginning of the war the total population was about 2,500,000 men, women, and children. In 1776 the American army, then at its highest point in numbers, including militiamen and Continentals, had about 90,000 officers and privates—not more than one man in eight of the males able to bear arms. In the latter part of the war, it included only about one man in sixteen of the fighting age.

It would be a conservative estimate, then, to say that at least three fourths of the men, as well as all the women and young people, devoted themselves mainly to civilian affairs, though often engaged in war production. No longer under the dominion of British officials, they insisted on pursuing their interests, discussing public questions as they pleased, exalting their rights, and undermining special privileges. Spurred by the impacts of the war, they began to attack the social order developed during the colonial period.

Thus a landslide toward democracy—a state of affairs dreaded by American conservatives and British Loyalists—was started. During the Revolution a large portion of the upper class collapsed. After the British governors and their horde of officials fled from colonial capitals, thousands of merchants, clergy, landlords, and lawyers who adhered to Britain were forced to leave the country or retire from public life. As a rule Loyalists who remained outside British military lines were silenced. Often they were subjected to physical violence.

Many large estates owned by British subjects, sometimes embracing several hundred thousand acres, were confiscated and then auctioned off in blocks to Americans. Immense areas of unoccupied lands, once at the disposal of the British Crown or its agents, passed under the control of state legislatures and the Continental Congress, to be granted or sold under American laws. The right of American landlords to pass their estates intact to their eldest sons under the rule of "primogeniture" was assailed and either destroyed or materially modified in favor of the division of estates among all heirs, including daughters. Everywhere in the states the English Church was disestablished and religious liberty was generally widened, though not made complete.

Associated with these changes was a rapidly widening interest among the people in social and political issues. The number of newspapers increased despite the handicaps of the war. Thousands of Americans who had hitherto cared little about election campaigns were aroused by the stirring events of the Revolution and began to take part in public discussions and agitations, to vote, if they had the right, and to demand the right to vote, if it was denied to them under the new state laws. In the most crucial years of the war tumult and perils, differences of opinion over politics, government, and reform divided Americans into parties and factions and precipitated conflicts among the patriots themselves, often verging in the direction of physical violence. For an immense number of the American people, the Revolution in all its phases was, therefore, a great social and intellectual awakening.

Chapter 9

CONSTITUTIONAL GOVERNMENT FOR THE UNITED STATES

AFTER THEY HAD WON independence from Great Britain, Americans faced the problem of governing themselves and holding together the union formed during the Revolutionary War. Could they do it? From the three proprietary colonies—Pennsylvania, Delaware, and Maryland—the proprietary officials had been expelled. From the eight royal provinces—New Hampshire, Massachusetts, New York, New Jersey, Virginia, North Carolina, South Carolina, and Georgia—royal governors and their train of subordinates had been driven out. No longer could disputes within and between colonies be carried to London for settlement. No longer did loyalty to the British King or the need for common action in the war against him constitute a unifying principle for Americans. No longer did the British navy and army serve as shields against the warlike Powers of Europe, especially France and Spain, both eager to extend their dominions in the New World.

In colonial times the British government had exercised control over all the colonies in essential matters of public policy and administration. It had conducted foreign affairs and provided common defense against other nations. Foreign commerce, intercolonial commerce, and the monetary system had all been subject to British regulation. The British Crown had served as the chief executive organ for the colonies, and British courts as tribunals of appeal in cases involving the rights of person and property. Now all this central machinery of power had been swept away and each state was set free to do about as it pleased; that is to say, as the majority of the voters represented in the legislature pleased.

During the Revolution, British officials had scoffed at the idea that Americans could successfully carry on the work of government in its higher ranges where great statesmanship was required; and Tories had sneered at them as pettifogging lawyers, riotous mechanics, disorderly farmers, and lawbreaking merchants. Even patriots on the right wing of the Revolution had expressed dislike and contempt for the people and republics. Neither the Declaration of Independence nor the Articles of Confederation nor any of the first state constitutions had mentioned the word "republic." At the time it was like a red flag to conservatives everywhere.

Moreover, educated patriots knew that revolutions in history, democratic and republican, had often resulted in despotism. Again and again in the Greek states of antiquity, democracy had been supplanted by a dictatorship or tyranny. The Roman republic had disappeared in the rule of an absolute emperor. Only about a century before, the Puritan revolution in England had culminated in the military dictatorship of Oliver Cromwell, followed shortly by a restoration of the monarchy.

Reflective Americans who were confronted with the task of governing the country had read about such historic events. Loyalists who had opposed the American Revolution from start to finish expected it to end in a disaster for the patriots and the re-establishment of a monarchy in some form. Indeed a few of them cast about for a suitable prince to be made king of the United States. Many patriots, some in high places, military and civil, abhorring the very idea of popular rule, looked forward with satisfaction to the triumph of a military dictator, supreme throughout the Union.

Even before peace came, Colonel Lewis Nicola wrote to General Washington expressing scorn for republics and calling for a military government, at least in a part of the country. Washington sent him a blistering reply. But other army officers wrote to Washington more or less in the same vein. In fact, he received so many letters hinting at violent action against the government which had been set up that his brooding spirit burst forth with cries of apprehension over the future of his country.

Rumors of a reaction in the shape of a monarchy or military dictatorship were bruited here and there among the people after peace came. In Connecticut Noah Webster heard from some source that military men and merchants in New England were working at plans to overturn popular rule and establish a government of special privileges by force. In Massachusetts Mercy Warren learned from some source that many young men, "particularly students at law and youth of fortune and pleasure," were clamoring for a monarchy and a standing army to support it. She thought there was "a formidable body ready to bow to the sceptre of a king, provided they may be the lordlings who in splendid idleness may riot on the hard earnings of the peasant and mechanic." Governor George Clinton, of New York, confessed publicly in 1788 that in the closing years of the War for Independence a design had been formed in his state to establish a kind of military government.

Rumors and open threats of drastic action against "popular tumults" increased after a band of debt-burdened farmers in Massachusetts, led by Captain Daniel Shays, a soldier of the Revolution, tried to redress their grievances by an uprising in 1786. According to the constitution of that state, drafted by John Adams and put into effect in 1780, the right to vote and hold office had been limited to property owners and taxpayers; and the richer towns were given special weight in the state senate. Under this government, creditors began to sue debtors in the law courts and take property away from farmers who could not pay what they owed.

In protest Shays organized a large body of men in the western part of the state and attempted to shut up the courts by a display of armed force. It was only with difficulty and some bloodshed that the state government put down "Shays' Rebellion." Even then popular sympathies with the uprising remained so strong that the state officials did not dare to execute Shays or any of his followers. Whatever the merits of this popular revolt, it increased the fears of property owners and conservatives in general, inciting them to work harder than ever for a powerful national government.

Amid efforts to substitute for the Confederation a highly centralized government, akin in some respects to the regimen Great Britain had formerly maintained over the colonies, complaints against state governments grew in number and virulence. In all the states except Massachusetts and New York, which both had strong governments, the control of public affairs was in the hands of the legislature elected by the qualified voters, among whom farmers predominated. In short, the states were controlled by popular majorities with little or no restraint from executive or judicial officers, such as British royal governors and the Crown had imposed on colonial legislatures.

In these circumstances states issued their own money in coin or paper or both and, under pressure from farmers, seven states emitted large quantities of paper money. This was done partly for the purpose of raising the prices of farm produce, making it easier for farmers to pay their debts. Before the Revolution Great Britain had stopped the practice; now Americans were at liberty to revive it.

More liberties were asserted by popular legislatures. Urged by special interests, states put tariff duties on imports from foreign countries, modified them, or repealed them, at will. Determined to protect their local interests, some states laid duties on goods coming in from other states; New York, for instance, taxed firewood from Connecticut and vegetables from New Jersey. During the Revolution states had borrowed money for war purposes and several of them were slow in paying off those debts. In short, for a time, the states acted as independent republics ruled by popular majorities represented in the legislatures;

and, warmly attached to their own liberties, they went to extremes in their indifference to the fortunes of the Union.

While the states and their legislatures were coming under an increasing fire of criticism from merchants, creditors, and holders of state bonds, a storm of disapproval was gathering against the Articles of Confederation and the Congress of the United States. A part of this censure was directed to the form of that government. The Confederacy, according to the critics, was really a farce; it had no executive to enforce the laws made by the Congress; and the states and the people disregarded the laws with impunity. It also lacked a judiciary empowered to try persons accused of violating the laws of the Union, to hear cases arising under them, or to settle disputes among the states.

The Congress was disparaged as faulty in form and futile in action. In the Congress, states, not the people, were represented; its members were elected by the state legislatures; and in all important matters the states, large and small, were equal, for each had only one vote to cast. Its members were negligent in attendance and public business dragged on from year to year unfinished.

On two special counts critics disparaged the Congress in respect of its powers: the Congress lacked power to make laws necessary to the safety and welfare of the Union; and it had no authority to prevent the states from interfering with matters of common, or general, concern.

The Congress could vote money for the purposes of the Union, but it could lay no taxes directly on anybody; it had to depend upon the willingness of the state legislatures to raise money and pay it into the Confederate treasury. The Congress could provide for an army but it was compelled to rely upon each of the states to supply its quota of men voluntarily. Although the Congress could make treaties with other countries respecting foreign commerce, the states decided for themselves whether or not they would obey such treaties. The Congress could not regulate commerce among the states or establish a single and uniform system of currency for the country. Furthermore, as time passed, the states refused, despite urgent appeals from Congress, to grant it additional financial powers essential to its very existence.

On the score of power the Congress was also assailed because it could not compel the states to quit doing many things which interfered with property and comity. It could not stop their issues of paper money or their interference with interstate and foreign commerce. It had no check on their legislation designed to make it easier for debtors to pay their debts in "cheap money." It could not send troops to help put down insurrections or to enforce the laws of the Union if they encountered popular resistance.

In these circumstances agitations were started in several quarters for changes in the American system of government that had come into being as an emergency government during the Revolution and had been continued under the Articles of Confederation. Former army officers, now organized in the Order of the Cincinnati, and former soldiers of the rank and file found the paper scrip with which they had been paid off at the close of the war so reduced in value as to be almost worthless. Holders of state and Continental securities were disgruntled, for the interest on their bonds was not paid promptly, if at all, and their paper sank in the markets, sometimes to a price as low as ten cents on the dollar. Manufacturers complained that the imports of foreign goods seriously cut down their business. Merchants and shippers grumbled over the lack of protection against foreign merchants and shippers in America and distant ports. Owners of undeveloped lands in the West, including soldiers of the Revolution holding claims to tracts there as part payment for their services and speculators engaged in accumulating great areas with a view to profitable sales to settlers, deplored the lack of a national army capable of suppressing the Indians who hampered the spread of settlements. Creditors fretted over paper-money schemes and other threats to their mortgages on property.

Generally associated with one or more of these economic interests, but often rising above purely personal interests, were critics with national vision who joined the movement for drastic changes in the Articles of Confederation. Familiar with the intrigues and ambitions of European Powers, they feared that the United States might be divided by foreign plotting, might be reconquered perhaps by Great Britain, or fall a victim to France or Spain, both with territorial ambitions in the neighborhood. They were also alarmed by schemes for overturning the republican institutions and establishing a monarchy or military dictatorship. Scarcely less disturbing to them was the possibility of an upheaval from below. Worried by the outlook, these national leaders sought to find a peaceful way of setting up a stronger and yet representative government for the Union.

Among the leaders in the nationalizing movement George Washington was foremost in character and influence. As early as 1783, in a circular letter to the governors of the states, Washington, who had done so much to save the Revolution, warned them of perils ahead and recommended the adoption of a more powerful government, able to "regulate and govern the general concerns of the confederate republic." Meanwhile Alexander Hamilton, who had fought in the Revolution, launched a campaign against the Articles of Confederation and demanded the calling of a new congress or convention to draft a constitution based on different and firmer principles. Other men, well known and less well known, including Pelatiah Webster, put forth plans for amending the Articles or substituting an entirely new form of government.

But all along the line advocates of material changes met vigorous opposition. Although none of the leaders in this resistance had the prestige of Washington, many of them had been eminent in the Revolutionary cause. In the struggle against the powerful grip of the British Crown and Parliament, thousands of Americans had acquired a horror of "strong government." Some among them feared that any strong government might end in a monarchy or that it would mean, in any case, big armies, big navies, heavy taxes, mountainous debts, and interference with personal liberty, in the style of the British government. Especially among farmers, who formed a majority of the people, the idea was rigidly held that the state legislature was the best bulwark for the protection of their interests and rights.

Widespread was the conviction that full autonomy in towns, counties, and states was the truest and best basis for the life, liberty, and pursuit of happiness proclaimed in the Declaration of Independence. To Americans who had such views nothing seemed more reasonable than belief that "centralization" was to be dreaded and that the rights of states were to be cherished and preserved.

To change or not to change the form of government—to swing away from more authority or toward it—became by 1786 the burning issue before the American people. At firesides, in taverns, by correspondence, and in the press it was debated with a searching and enlightened intelligence, worthy of the generation that had won independence.

Out of heated discussions came decisive actions. A small group in Virginia induced the state legislature to call a general convention at Annapolis to discuss taxation and commerce. The convention met in 1786 but delegates from only five states appeared on the floor and the prospects were discouraging to its members. One of the delegates, however, Alexander Hamilton, from New York, refused to give up the struggle to realize the aims of the nationalizing movement.

Seizing time by the forelock, Hamilton persuaded the Annapolis convention to adopt a resolution urging the Congress of the United States to take leadership and summon a convention at Philadelphia, for the purpose of proposing amendments to the Articles of Confederation which, when adopted by the states, would make them "adequate to the exigencies of the Union." To this project the Congress agreed. In response, all the states except Rhode Island elected delegates. In May 1787 the new convention assembled in Philadelphia and settled down to the task of devising a stronger government for the United States.

On the roll of the convention, consisting of fifty-five members in all, were many of the most prominent names in America: for example, George Washington, Benjamin Franklin, Alexander Hamilton, James Madison, Robert Morris, Gouverneur Morris, John Dickinson, James Wilson, Roger Sherman, Oliver Ellsworth, Charles Pinckney, and Edmund Randolph. Eight of them had been among the signers of the Declaration of Independence. Nearly all had been active in the Revolution, as military officers, financiers, members of the Continental Congress, and public officials. Among them were men of wealth and influence in their communities—merchants, lawyers, and planters.

On the whole the convention was a conservative body. Thomas Jefferson, then minister to France, a liberal, was not present. Neither was John Hancock, whose name led all the signatures to the Declaration of Independence. That outstanding firebrand of the Revolution, Patrick Henry, though elected a delegate, refused to attend, saying that he "smelt a rat." Even so, great talents, wisdom, and experience in statecraft were represented at Philadelphia in 1787.

The sessions of the convention lasted from May to September 17, 1787, and were marked by many differences of opinion and long debates. Indeed it has been customary for historians to lay stress on the differences of opinion and treat the Constitution which emerged as a mere "bundle of compromises." But this view is far from the whole truth of the matter. Strictly speaking, the agreements of the convention were more numerous and important for the nation than the dissensions and the compromises.

In the course of their proceedings, a large majority easily agreed on the following fundamentals:

The Articles of Confederation must be discarded, not merely amended, and a new constitution substituted.

The new government must have three departments—legislative, executive, and judicial.

The large states must have more power in the new government than the small states, thus giving to it a popular basis.

The new Congress must have the power to legislate on all matters of national concern and all matters with which the states cannot deal competently, including the power to tax, to regulate interstate and foreign commerce, and to spend money for common defense and general welfare.

The debts of the Confederation must be binding on the new government.

Many restraints must be laid on the state governments.

The serious disputes in the convention turned mainly on details and ways and means of realizing the accepted purposes. They involved such questions as these: What shall be the composition of the new Congress?

Shall the executive consist of one person or more? How shall the executive be elected? How shall the large states be given their appropriate share of power in the new government and the claims of the small states to equality be recognized? How shall the enlarged power of the new Congress be expressed in terms of specified powers? How is it possible to create a strong national legislature and a strong executive and yet prevent either from becoming all-powerful in the government of the Union? How shall direct taxes be apportioned among the states in such a way as not to burden unduly the poorer states? What qualifications shall be fixed for voters in federal elections and for places of trust in the new government? What provisions shall be made for amending the new Constitution as times change? How shall the Constitution be finally adopted and put into force?

Out of the debates that swirled around these and subsidiary questions for four months was finally evolved, on September 17, the finished document which thirty-nine delegates, a safe majority, were willing to sign. By that time several of the members had gone home, alienated by the spirit and plans of their colleagues. A few malcontents, who remained to the end, for one reason or another refused to sign the finished instrument. One of the dissenters, Luther Martin, of Maryland, was so perturbed by all he had seen and heard at Philadelphia that he wrote a long letter of denunciation to the legislature of his state and published it widely in an effort to defeat the ratification of the Constitution. Even among the signers there were doubts as to particular provisions in the document, but these were subordinated to the interest of unity on fundamentals. Washington expressed the general sentiment of his colleagues when he declared that the Constitution was about as good as could be expected and the people ought to adopt it, leaving to the future the making of corrections by amendments.

Running through the text of the Constitution from the Preamble to the last line were evidences of the fundamental propositions on which the majority of the convention agreed early in its proceedings. Interwoven with them were answers to the questions of means and details by which the essential purposes of a stronger Union were to be accomplished. Here and there were signs of the compromises and adjustments of interests that the framers found necessary to the settlement of disputes large and small. Only when so viewed does the Constitution take on the fullness of its meaning for the time and the ages.

First of all, the Preamble made it clear that the framers were creating no mere league of states. The Articles of Confederation had declared

Engraving by De Bry. The Bettmann Archive

HOW THE NEW WORLD APPEARED TO A
VERY EARLY ENGLISH PIONEER

The engravings on this page were made from sketches drawn by a member of a sixteenth-century English expedition to America, under the auspices of Sir Walter Raleigh.

(ABOVE) The Virginia coastline. The artist who gave us this view pointed out that the islands in the foreground made it difficult to reach the mainland by boat. Furthermore, he accounted for the absence of organized reception committees on the beaches by reporting that on the approach of the expedition the natives ran off screaming.

(BELOW) An Indian method for making canoes was to hollow out logs with fire, as shown here.

Engraving by De Bry. The Bettmann Archive

SETTLING AMERICA

The first wave of settlers in the wilderness erected crude shelters in a hurry to serve their immediate needs. They were soon joined by others, including many adventuresome women. Later, with more time and greater resources at their disposal, the colonists constructed and furnished many fine homes.

(ABOVE) The first wave of settlement. *Left:* Modern replicas of the first crude huts built by the settlers in New England. *Right:* Wives for the settlers arrive at Jamestown, Virginia.
(BELOW) The settlements mature. *Left:* A street of colonial homes in New England. *Right:* The parlor of a colonial home, the Thomas Hart house, about 1640.

COLONIAL AGRICULTURE

In colonial days, farms varied greatly in size and character.

(ABOVE) In the North—A busy one-family farm with the man attending livestock while the women make candles.

(BELOW) In the South—A glimpse of life on a large plantation. George Washington returning to his Mount Vernon estate after a fox hunt.

COLONIAL COMMERCE AND INDUSTRY

Not only did colonial Americans ship raw materials to England in exchange for some manufactured goods but they managed to make many articles for themselves.

(ABOVE) A colonial port scene.

(BELOW) An early water-driven New England mill.

INTELLECTUAL PROGRESS

The establishment of schools, the printing of newspapers, and the operation of the postal service helped the American colonists to mature and spread their ideas, thus preparing them for the difficult task of founding a new nation.

(ABOVE) A New England dame school, from an old engraving.

(BELOW) *Left:* Arrival of a colonial mail carrier. *Right:* A printing press of the variety used to turn out newspapers prior to the Revolutionary War.

Painting by Howard Pyle.
United Press International

COLONIAL POLITICAL TRENDS

There were two powerful opposing political trends in colonial America. While the King was trying to extend his authority downward through royal governors, Americans sought to push their influence upward through agents of their own choosing.

(ABOVE) A spokesman for the King—Carteret arrives in New Jersey as royal governor of the colony.

(BELOW) American settlers work out a plan for self-government—colonists arriving in the New World aboard the *Mayflower* sign a compact providing for a large measure of self-government.

Painting by E. Moran. The Bettmann Archive

AMERICAN RESISTANCE TO BRITISH COLONIAL POLICIES GROWS

Shortly before the outbreak of the Revolutionary War, many Americans stoutly resisted the new policies being applied by the British Crown to the colonies. Depicted here are American reactions to British rules regarding the importation and sale of tea.

(ABOVE) Feminine wiles at work—A society of patriotic ladies in Edenton, North Carolina, pledging to drink no more tea, 1775.

(BELOW) The men take drastic action—Here we see the famous Boston Tea Party in progress, with Americans dressed as Indians dumping tea from British ships into Boston harbor late in 1773.

THE REVOLUTIONARY WAR

The Revolutionary War was long—eight years—and involved many hardships for Americans, but it was not fought in vain.

(ABOVE) Hardships at Valley Forge—Washington holds his army together through a bitterly cold winter encampment, where shortages of food, clothing and shelter made life very difficult.

(BELOW) Triumph at Yorktown—The British under Cornwallis surrender to the Americans.

explicitly that "each state retains its sovereignty, freedom and independence"—the high power which state legislatures had been exercising. Respecting the sovereignty, freedom, and independence of the states, as such, the Constitution contained not a word, and what it did to the pretensions of the states to full sovereignty stood out boldly in the lines imposing restraints on their powers. The announcement that the Constitution and federal laws were to be supreme over all state actions conflicting with them was unmistakable in its brevity and import.

The Preamble declared that the Constitution was a constitution ordained and established by the people of the United States—not mere articles of agreement between the thirteen states. The Articles of Confederation had called the Union "a firm league of friendship" between the states. The new order contemplated by the Constitution was more than a league of states. The government for which it provided, in the exercise of its powers, was authorized to deal directly with individuals, not states. It was authorized to go over the heads of state officials and legislatures and compel obedience to federal laws by the use of its own agencies of coercion. In fine, the Constitution worked a political revolution—a transformation—in the form of government that had been set up in the violence of the break with Britain. Its critics understood this at the time and history to come validated the fact.

☆

In the structure of the new government this revolution was reflected. The old Congress had been little more than a conference of ambassadors from the states. In one house of the new Congress, it is true, each state, large and small, was to have two senators and the states were thus nominally equal. But each senator was given a term of six years, was to be paid out of the Treasury of the United States, and could not be retired at will or compelled to vote against his conscience by his state legislature. The Senate was given the power to pass upon treaties and nominations to certain high offices proposed by the President.

Sharing the legislative power with the Senate was the House of Representatives, based on population, not on states. Members of this chamber were apportioned among the states according to their respective numbers of free persons, excluding Indians not taxed and including three fifths of "all other persons," that is, slaves. The members of the House were to be elected directly in each state by the persons entitled to vote for members of the most numerous branch of the state legislature. That "the voice of the people" might be heard frequently, provision was made for biennial elections. To prevent state legislatures from interfering too grossly with congressional elections, Congress was given the power to alter and make laws regulating such elections.

In all ordinary legislative matters, the House of Representatives was made equal to the Senate. In one vital matter it was given the supreme weapon of political power—control over the national purse; for the Constitution provided that "all bills for raising revenue shall originate in the House of Representatives." Although in time this provision was allowed to become a dead letter, the intention behind it was indubitable; if it so decided, "the people's house" might exercise supreme power over the purse in the government of the United States.

In another essential respect the weight of the people as against the states counted in the structure of the federal government—in the Executive Department. After careful discussion the convention decided that the Executive should consist of one person, not three or more representing sections of the Union. The President was to be elected, not by Congress as at first decided, nor by popular vote as was proposed, but by electors chosen as the legislatures of the states might decide. In fixing the number of electors assigned to each state, the Constitution recognized both population and the states and so gave the people, as such, a share in the presidency; that is, it prescribed that the number of electors allowed to each state must equal the number of senators and representatives to which it may be entitled. Until a census could be taken in 1790 there were to be sixty-five representatives.

Under the Articles there had been in fact thirteen heads to the confederacy—the thirteen delegations in the Congress, which merely had a presiding officer. Under the Constitution there was to be one head, the President of the United States, endowed with great powers in peace and war. He was to symbolize the unity, not the diversity, of the country. And for strength of support, he was to depend upon numbers of people, not the pleasure of state legislatures.

The unity of the country was also symbolized by the Constitution in the creation of a Supreme Court, the members of which were to be chosen by the President with the consent of the Senate. Congress might at will establish inferior courts, district and circuit, but the Supreme Court was anchored in the Constitution. Its justices might be divided as to cases before it, but its decisions made by a majority of them were to be binding at law throughout the land. Thus in matters of federal concern the will of one high court was to be substituted for the clashing wills of thirteen or more state courts.

The judicial power conferred upon federal courts covered every issue of general interest throughout the Union. It shall extend, ran Section 2 of Article III, "to all cases in law and equity arising under this Constitution, the laws of the United States, and treaties made, or which shall be made, under their authority." That was not all. This power was to embrace all cases of admiralty and maritime jurisdiction arising on the high seas and public waters of the Union. It was to include controversies between two or more states; between a state and citizens of another state; between citizens of different states; between a state and citizens thereof and foreign states, citizens, and subjects. Thus special kinds of conflicts between private persons in the several states and between states as such were to be finally resolved by the exercise of federal judicial power, with the Supreme Court as the tribunal of ultimate appeal.

Yet, powerful as was to be the structure of the new government—Congress, Executive, and Judiciary—it was so formed that, in operation, checks could be placed on the accumulation of despotic power in any hands, even in the hands of the people who had the right to vote in elections. How to set up a government strong enough to serve the purposes of the Union and still not too strong for the maintenance of the liberties of the people? That was a prime issue in the convention. It had been in all previous history, and was to be in centuries to come, the central problem in the science and art of government.

This question the framers of the Constitution sought to settle by establishing what is known as the "system of checks and balances." First of all they founded each great branch of the government on a separate basis of political power. They provided that members of the House of Representatives should be elected for a term of two years by persons entitled to vote under certain laws of the respective states; that the senators should be elected for terms of six years by the legislatures of the states; and that the President should be elected for four years by electors chosen as the state legislatures might decide—by the legislatures themselves or by the voters or in any other appropriate manner. Members of the federal judiciary were to be selected by the President and the Senate, both one degree removed from direct popular vote.

Against the possibility of tyranny, therefore, two safeguards were set up in the Constitution. The ultimate source of power, it was recognized, was the people—the enfranchised voters in the states. But under the methods provided for the choice of representatives, senators, President, and federal judges, no political party or faction could get possession of the whole government at a single election. In the long run, through a period of years, the persistent will of the popular majority might prevail. Yet at no moment could the "snap judgment" of a popular majority prevail in all departments of the federal government.

Moreover, within the very structure of the government, power was so distributed that no branch could seize all of it, unless the others deliberately abdicated. The House and Senate were to check each other in legislation. Congress and the President were to put brakes on each other. As against both, members of the federal judiciary were given the independence of tenure for life; and yet the House could impeach them and, by the judgment of the Senate, they could be removed from office. The President was to enjoy a high degree of independent initiative; but he could do nothing unless Congress enacted laws and voted money for carrying his proposals into execution. Besides, he too could be ousted from office by the process of impeachment.

Upon the government so constructed, the Constitution conferred immense powers in terms specific and general. For convenience they may be divided into two classes: powers over domestic affairs and powers over foreign relations. But in fact these powers were so closely interwoven at many points that lines could not be drawn between them. For example, Congress was given the right to tax and appropriate money for defense and the general welfare of the United States.

Among the great powers particularly relevant to domestic affairs the following were vested in Congress in specific terms: to lay and collect taxes, duties, and excises; pay the debts of the United States; borrow money; regulate commerce among the states; establish uniform rules for the naturalization of aliens; enact laws on bankruptcies; coin money and regulate the value thereof; establish post offices and post roads; promote science and the useful arts by giving exclusive rights to authors and inventors—copyrights and patents; establish courts inferior to the Supreme Court; raise and support armed forces; provide for calling out the militia to execute the laws and suppress insurrections; establish penalties for the punishment of persons who counterfeit the coins and securities of the United States.

The powers relative to foreign affairs were not concentrated in the Executive or in Congress but were distributed among the three departments; or, to put it another way, they were vested in the whole government. To Congress was given exclusive power to provide for the common defense; to regulate commerce with foreign nations, including control over the immigration of aliens; to declare war; to raise and support armed forces; to define and punish offenses against the law of nations; and by implication, to establish and appropriate money for ministers, consuls, and other agents of the United States in foreign countries. To the President was granted the power to make treaties with other countries, but only by and with the advice and consent of at least two thirds of the senators. With the consent of the Senate also he was to appoint the consuls, ministers, and other agents to represent the United States abroad.

Since the Constitution was designed to endure for ages in which great changes were bound to come in American affairs, the framers knew that

Congress would have to deal with them or be helpless in serving the purposes for which the stronger Union was established. So, besides vesting in Congress powers later called "specific," the Constitution gave it two general powers to make the instrument flexible for adaptation to changes in the needs, ideas, and interests of the American people.

It authorized Congress to raise and appropriate money for "the general welfare of the United States." It also authorized Congress "to make all laws necessary and proper for carrying into effect" its specific powers, "and all other powers vested by this Constitution in the government of the United States or any department or officer thereof." Many a conflict was to rage over these lines but in time they were accepted as giving sanction to types of legislation conceived in the general interest of the nation as distinguished from interests purely local in nature.

☆

While creating a strong government, balanced within itself and endowed with great powers, the framers of the Constitution placed definite limits on the federal government with a view to preserving liberty. They provided, for instance, that Congress shall pass no bill of attainder, that is, no law imposing penalties on any person without a judicial trial. They likewise forbade *ex post facto* laws—measures stigmatizing as crimes actions which had been committed but were not crimes at the time of commission. The trial of all crimes against the United States, except in cases of impeachment, they declared, must be by jury and in the state where committed. "No money shall be drawn from the Treasury," ran another clause, "but in consequence of appropriations made by law; and a regular statement and account of receipts and expenditures of all public moneys shall be published from time to time."

Even a strong and limited government for the Union, the framers decided, was not sufficient to fulfill their national purposes. Hence they laid specific restraints upon the states, forbidding them to meddle with many matters of life, liberty, and property. Some of these restraints pertained to domestic affairs; others, to foreign affairs.

The states were stripped of powers to coin money, emit bills of credit, make anything but gold and silver coin legal tender in the payment of debts, pass bills of attainder and *ex post facto* laws, grant titles of nobility, and enact laws impairing the obligation of contracts. Every state was commanded to give full faith and credit to the public acts, records, and judicial proceedings of all other states; in other words, states were to place no barriers in the way of enforcing legal rights throughout the land. As a guarantee of free migration and commerce throughout the country, the Constitution provided that "the citizens of each state shall be entitled to all the privileges and immunities of citizens of the several states."

No less mandatory were the restraints laid upon the states in respect of foreign affairs. They were forbidden to enter into any treaty, alliance, or confederation. They were ordered to lay no imposts or duties on imports or exports, without the consent of Congress, except such as might be absolutely necessary for the execution of their inspection laws. To use the language of the Constitution: "No state shall, without the consent of Congress, lay any duties of tonnage, keep troops, or ships of war, in time of peace, enter into any agreement or compact with another state, or with a foreign power, or engage in war, unless actually invaded, or in such imminent danger as will not admit of delay."

In return for the many limitations imposed upon the states, the framers of the Constitution offered them pledges of protection. The Constitution provided that "the United States shall guarantee to every state in this union a republican form of government, and shall protect each of them against invasion." As if remembering Shays' Rebellion of 1786 in Massachusetts, they offered to the states the aid of the United States against "domestic violence."

Having in mind an enduring Union, the framers of the Constitution realized that conferring general powers upon Congress might not make it competent to cope with all the problems of coming times, with formidable changes that might occur in the ideas and interests of the American people. Radical alterations might be necessary in the form and powers of the proposed government.

In recognition of this fact the framers made provision for amending the Constitution; and here, too, they overrode the sovereignty of the states. No alteration could be made in the provisions of the Articles of Confederation without the consent of every state. For this principle was substituted another rule. By Article V the Constitution provided that Congress might, by a two-thirds vote in each house, propose amendments to the Constitution or, on application from the legislatures of two thirds of the states, must call a convention for the purpose of proposing amendments.

Amendments proposed by Congress or by such a convention were to go into effect when ratified by legislatures or conventions in three fourths of the states. Only one exception was made to this plan for binding states against their wills: "No state, without its consent, shall be deprived of its equal suffrage in the Senate."

The Constitution so drawn was strong medicine for advocates of states' rights. Its framers knew this very well. Throughout their proceedings in the convention they were impressed or oppressed by fear that it would not be ratified. How to put it into effect? That was for them a specter. Many state legislatures had refused to permit any increase in the powers of the old Congress. Perhaps that Congress, still functioning under the Articles of Confederation, would reject the new plan of government. Popular opposition to any changes in the existing form of government might be insurmountable. Perhaps state legislatures would refuse to ratify the Constitution. The knot had to be cut and it was cut by the makers of the Constitution with two provisions for ratification.

First, they appealed over the heads of Congress and the state legislatures. They sent their plan to the existing Congress, with two recommendations, namely, that it be referred to the states by the Congress and that the state legislatures call special conventions, elected by the voters, to pass upon the plan. Second, they provided that the Constitution should go into effect when ratified by nine states as between the nine—leaving the other states, if they preferred, out in the cold without a national roof over their heads.

When on September 17, 1787, the secrecy of the convention was broken and the proposed plan was published, a tempest of public debate over its merits began to blow. Critics fell upon it with might and main. It was not a plan for a "federal" union, some said, but a dark plot to establish a centralized despotism and reduce the states to provinces. The President, others insisted, would become a monarch, perhaps worse than George III. It was a device, radicals claimed, by which the rich and powerful would govern the country and oppress the plain people with armies, taxes, and debts. It had no bill of rights, friends of liberty protested. In fact scarcely a line of the Constitution escaped an attack, mild or passionate. On the other hand, able defenders came to its support in pamphlets, articles, and letters. The most comprehensive and cogent defense was made by Alexander Hamilton, John Jay, and James Madison. Between October 1787 and May 1788 they wrote eighty-five long articles, most of which appeared in the press of New York, under the pen name of "Publius." Many of the articles were reprinted in the newspapers of other states. They were all brought out in the spring of 1788 in two volumes entitled *The Federalist*. From that day to this *The Federalist* has been widely regarded as the most profound single treatise on the Constitution ever written and as among the few masterly works on political science produced in all the centuries of history.

While the public debate over the plan was in full course, conventions duly elected in the states assembled to pass upon it. Within three months three states ratified it—Delaware and New Jersey unanimously, and Pennsylvania after a hot contest. Early in 1788 Georgia and Connecticut added their approval. By a close vote Massachusetts accepted it in February. Maryland and South Carolina soon followed. The New Hampshire convention, at first opposed or hesitant, decided favorably before the end of June. Nine states, the number necessary to put the Constitution into effect, had now made the fateful decision.

But two large states wavered. In New York a majority of the convention was against ratification. In Virginia tenacious opponents, including Patrick Henry, kept the result long in doubt, but in the end the supporters of the new plan triumphed there. Then, under the leadership of Alexander Hamilton, the opposition in New York was overcome and a resolution of ratification was adopted. Thus by the autumn of 1788 eleven of the thirteen states had accepted the new Union. The advocates of the revolutionary change in the loose form of government provided by the Articles of Confederation were at last victorious.

Only two states remained aloof. The convention in North Carolina withheld its approval—until November 1789. Rhode Island would have nothing to do with the new Constitution until the spring of 1790, when it added its ratification.

Exulting in their success, victors in the contest celebrated the occasion by organizing spectacular parades in the principal towns. With justification they looked upon the outcome as the triumph of reason over force. Without drawing the sword in a civil war, without shedding a drop of blood, a new plan of government had been proposed, framed, discussed, and adopted. The victors in seven states, it is true, had been forced to appease opponents distressed about dangers to civil liberties by agreeing that a bill of rights, in the form of amendments, should be joined to the Constitution when the new government got under way. But as none of the proposed amendments affected the form of that government, this pledge, fulfilled in 1791, merely confirmed the faith of Americans in the power of the people to govern themselves on a continental scale by peaceful constitutional processes.

Chapter 10

ESTABLISHING THE REPUBLICAN WAY OF LIFE

WITH GRATEFUL UNANIMITY presidential electors, chosen after the adoption of the Constitution, cast their ballots for George Washington as the Chief Executive of the United States. Inaugurated on April 30, 1789, amid the plaudits of the people in New York City, the first capital of the new government, he delivered an address emphasizing the solemn nature of the republican experiment that was being launched. "The pre-eminence of free government," he said, should be "exemplified by all the attributes which can win the affections of its citizens and command the respect of the world. . . . The preservation of the sacred fire of liberty and the destiny of the republican model of government are justly considered, perhaps, as *deeply*, as *finally*, staked on the experiment entrusted to the hands of the American people."

In this declaration Washington no doubt expressed the sentiments of all Americans save those intransigent Tories who hoped for the failure of the Republic and a return to the fold of the British monarchy. A new government, republican in form, had been founded. Many Americans living under it, even some who had been ardent in support of the Revolution, feared that it might not endure. One great problem of the opening years, then, was that of making universal—in thought, sentiments, and outward signs—the spirit necessary to sustain it.

The Revolutionary generation, now embarking on the republican way of life, had all grown up under a monarchy. Accustomed to that regime, many of the patriots, some of them high in the political and military circles of the Revolution, believed, even while the fighting was going on, that a monarchical form of government was the only kind that could maintain law and order. According to rumors, private negotiations were carried on with or about possible candidates for the throne in America, including the second son of King George III. Certainly a few officers in the Revolutionary army thought that a military dictatorship of one man should be established over the people. John Adams was of the opinion that the President should be given a title as resounding as that of "His Highness" or "His Majesty" in order to excite great respect or awe among the people for the chief magistrate. Attachment to the aristocratic ideology prevalent among nations across the sea was likewise strong among a large number of Americans who sought to shape the American way of life under its republican forms. If no true aristocracy of blood and lineage could be set up, they thought an "aristocracy of wealth and talents" might be substituted for it.

But the monarchists did not have their way. Nor did an aristocracy based on mere wealth and talents attain supreme power. While members of the upper classes of the United States were proposing to take over the government and direct it according to their ideas and interests, no organized royalist movement, even as a temporary grasp at power, interrupted the transition from monarchy to republic. In the shadows was no dethroned king or queen or ambitious pretender who could form the center of a monarchist reaction. The constitutional way of governing had been widely accepted and, in rallying the people to the Constitution, the planting and mercantile interests, so dominant in the Philadelphia Convention of 1787, had to make concessions to popular, and even leveling, doctrines in efforts to make their policies prevail.

The first President was a military hero—the commander in chief of the Revolutionary army. But he was not to become a Caesar or a Napoleon and put a crown on his own head. He had refused, with wrath at the suggestion, to be a party to any conspiracy for setting up a monarch or a military dictator. Of his own choice he had returned to the old Congress the symbol of his military authority—his commission as commander —the military authority granted him by that body of civilians. Now the unanimous choice of the nation's electors, he was to wear no title superior to that of plain "Mr. President." And he was to go down in the republican tradition, not so much as General Washington as simply George Washington.

There was no impulsion to Caesarism in him. His sense of dignity prevented hero worship from degenerating into that form of popular betrayal. Long accustomed to fine horses and equipages, Washington, as "Mr. President," rode out frequently in the first capital of the nation in his grand coach drawn by six horses driven by a slave, accompanied by outriders. But he did not think of himself as a demigod chosen to rule the United States. Nor was he moved to be a lesser divinity and wield power as a demagogue through a resort to hypnotic oratory. He had no genius for oratory.

Despite his great wealth and his social position he was essentially modest in his estimation of his political sagacity. No amount of public adulation changed his estimation of himself—not even during the jour-

ney from his home in Virginia to New York City. During that journey
he passed through one triumphal arch after another amid cheering
throngs to the capital, where he was welcomed by leading citizens with
lavish ceremonies and by huge crowds that had come from distant places
to shout acclaim and throw flowers at his feet. But nothing fired him
with dangerous vanity.

However intractable the remnants of the monarchical tradition may
have been, George Washington had no desire, and was not tempera-
mentally fitted, to reinforce it. He was sincere in his profession that he
lacked many qualifications for carrying the burden of presiding over the
new government as its highest and most responsible official. Before he
started to New York to assume that duty, he had written to General
Henry Knox that his "feelings were not unlike those of a culprit going to
his execution." In his diary he had recorded that his mind was "oppressed with more anxious and painful sensations than he had words to
express."

It was with no mere gesture of false pride that he referred, in his first
inaugural address, to his "inferior endowments from nature," his lack
of experience in "the duties of civil administration," and his other "deficiencies." These were not the ideas of a man thirsting for power or
eager to play the role of a demagogue. They were rather the confessions
of a man prepared to take counsel with the people, his advisers, and
friends, to make compromises with extremists, and rule in the constitutional manner appropriate to the republican way of life.

Moreover, he soon began to study books which might be helpful, such
as Vattel's *Law of Nations* and volumes of the *Debates* in the House
of Commons, making use of the Society Library in New York City. He
had based his scientific plantation management on knowledge acquired
in part by reading books on agriculture in his own large collection. Now
he also looked for such guidance in his public work as books might afford.

Had Washington been inclined to regal or arbitrary habits of rule—
and his political associate, James Madison, testified that he never was
so inclined—he would have found strong opposition among the people
of New York. To be sure, there were still many Tories in the city, re-
minders of the fact that it had been occupied by the British troops from
1776 to the end of the Revolutionary War. But monarchist loyalties were
declining among them. King's College, closed during the British oc-
cupancy, had been renamed Columbia College and its learned professors were republicans now, if cautious in their political expressions. Distinguished lawyers, physicians, and surgeons, who had been eminent in
the old regime, were adjusting themselves to the new regime.

Furthermore, the city had many influential residents who, while definitely republican in principles, had opposed the adoption of the Constitution. Surrounding Alexander Hamilton, prime exponent of centralization, were unswerving defenders of decentralization. Ratification of the Constitution had been literally wrung from the representatives of the New York voters at the state convention in Poughkeepsie in 1788, less than a year before Washington's inauguration. Members of the state legislature were so avid for power that they could not agree on how presidential electors were to be chosen and so New York had not even voted for Washington in the first election. The governor of the state, George Clinton, enjoying his sixth term in office, had fought ratification and had yielded in his last-ditch battle only after nine states had approved the Constitution. He was a forceful figure in New York society.

So was John Lamb, who had been so fervid in his opposition to the Constitution that he barricaded his residence against a Federalist "mob." He had been a leader of the Sons of Liberty, who had rioted against the Stamp Act in 1765, and a soldier in the Revolution. John Lamb was not inclined to approve centralizing "tyranny" in a new form.

Nor were the "plain people" of New York City likely to uphold an ambitious leader bent on "seizing power." Many of the artisans and tradesmen had supported the adoption of the Constitution in the hope that an improvement in business would follow. But memories of rioting by the Sons of Liberty lingered among them and they certainly did not belong to Alexander Hamilton's set. In meetings of Tammany Hall or in public taverns they continued to argue over public questions; and some of them, going beyond republicanism, began to use openly that more incendiary word "democracy."

Even the plays on the New York stage, which Washington and other members of the government occasionally witnessed with the people of pit and gallery, gave no encouragement to kingly or "high-toned" pretensions. For example, Royall Tyler's play, The Contrast, starting on its successful career in 1787, was republican in its argument. Although it dealt humorously with the vanities of small farmers and urbanites alike, it ridiculed British affectations and exalted republican dignity. If it was not agrarian in tone, neither did it lend countenance to royalist designs.

While a "republican court" soon developed among the fashionable circles at the first national capital and was emphatically high-toned in its sympathies, it could not or did not block the tendency toward republican simplicities. Some of its members, according to Jefferson's reports, had doubts whether the constitutional experiment would succeed and even secretly sighed for or expected a return to "kingly rule." Senator William Maclay, one of the earliest outspoken democrats in the country, caustically criticized, in a puritan vein, its balls and dinners, calling them a waste of time and injurious to minds, morals, and the public interest.

But, however skeptically some members of the "republican court" regarded the republican experiment or confidently expected the adoption of a still stronger form of government in case another crisis came, they all rallied to the side of President Washington's administration. They gave to it the support of the "wealth and talents" without which, Hamilton argued, the Constitution could not be successfully launched. Jefferson believed that they were actually royalist in sympathies. But in 1790, when Hamilton told him that the Union was in danger of breaking up, even Jefferson approved a financial measure advantageous to bondholders and speculators on the ground that "the preservation of the Union and concord among the states was more important" than defeating it.

The adoption of New York as the first seat of the new government was in many ways fortunate for what Washington called "the destiny of the republican model of government" on a national scale. The city lay between New England and the South. It cordially received the new government and by generous encouragement helped to make its inauguration an unquestionable success. But, to the regret of merchants, proprietors of taverns, boardinghouse keepers, and hostesses, among other beneficiaries, Congress decided against New York as the permanent capital of the nation.

That decision was the result of a "deal" between Hamilton and Jefferson at a time when Congress was badly split, in 1790, over the issue of assumption of state debts by the federal government. Threats of disunion were thus overcome. Two Southern votes and some Pennsylvania votes were brought over to the support of assumption on condition that Philadelphia was to be the capital for ten years and that the permanent seat of the government was to be located on the banks of the Potomac, as a final concession to the South. Late in 1790 the government of the United States was transferred to Philadelphia. Some New Yorkers found consolation for the loss in the huge profits they had garnered from their speculations in state evidences of indebtedness—speculations made possible by the "deal" between Hamilton and Jefferson.

Philadelphia, the second national capital and the largest city in the Union, also made its peculiar contribution to shaping the spirit and practices of the "republican model." Pennsylvania had never been a royal province. The monarchical tradition was weaker there than in New York. Neither the Penns nor their proprietary agents had imparted to their local administration the glamor that adorned the "court" of a royal governor. Moreover, the population of Philadelphia was more varied in racial stocks than that of New York, and its interests and activities were more diversified. It included some rich landlords and many merchant princes eager to reproduce the "republican court" of New York and prepared to entertain federal officials, members of Congress, and foreign envoys on a scale equally if not more extravagant. At the same time Philadelphia had more small tradesmen and artisans, more schoolmasters, music teachers, lawyers, physicians, surgeons, scientists, and philosophers of a rationalistic and secular bent. Leadership in New York, where the English Church had formerly been established, was still strongly Anglican in religious faith. Philadelphia, on the contrary, had long been the home of religious dissidence, the chief center of scientific inquiry and rationalism.

In Philadelphia there was greater political, social, and intellectual ferment than in the first capital. The state constitution of New York, despite its republican leanings, was, next to that of Massachusetts, the most aristocratic of all the documents drawn up in the early days of independence. The constitution of Pennsylvania, of 1776, on the other hand, was accounted about the most radical of the time—with a legislature composed of a single chamber and a governor subservient to that body—and the new constitution of 1790, though more conservative, was still liberal in spirit. Philadelphia had numerous clubs and societies of tradesmen and artisans addicted to free discussions—political, religious, scientific, and social. The opposition to the adoption of the federal Constitution in Pennsylvania, though not so strong as in New York State, had been bitter; and the memory of it still rankled, particularly in the western regions, which were soon to test President Washington's administrative skill by an open revolt against a federal tax on whisky—the "Whisky Rebellion." If, as the President said, the new government needed, for endurance, the affection of the people, there was ample opportunity to cultivate that attachment in Pennsylvania.

While bestowing its "affection," Philadelphia had many advanced ideas to offer members of the administration and Congress—to Puritans from New England, Anglicans from New York, and planters from the South also usually Anglican in faith. It was the center of the freest thinking in the Union on all matters, human and divine. For a city of those days, it was well laid out and ably governed. Even its wealthy inhabitants displayed a sensitivity to urban poverty and suffering, and maintained institutions of benevolence definitely progressive for the times. In Philadelphia religious toleration was peculiarly broad. Quakers, who made up a large part of the population, were for it on principle and the other denominations, whether on principle or not, accepted it. In scientific inquiries and applications, educational experiments, and civic enterprise, Philadelphia compared favorably with any city in Western civilization.

There the "utilitarian mentor," Benjamin Franklin, had kept the people astir with new adventures in ideas and, though he had died in April 1790, his spirit still enlivened the mood of that city. There the American Philosophical Society which he had promoted was creating intellectual currents that were to spread to all the shores of thought in America. Thomas Jefferson was an officer in this society during the days when he was living in Philadelphia as Vice-President of the United States. Through the port of Philadelphia came travelers, newcomers intending to make America their home, and foreign emissaries, bringing with them, among other intellectual interests, the knowledge and radical philosophy of the French.

Jefferson had become familiar with new French thinking while, from 1785 to 1789, he was minister of the United States at Paris, where he was adjudged a first-rate thinker in his own right. In Philadelphia he encountered congenial minds that fortified his determination to give the government of the United States a firmer bent in the direction of leveling republicanism. His followers in Congress, who had begun to form the nucleus of a political party before the federal government was moved to Philadelphia, were more at ease in the city of Benjamin Franklin than in the metropolis of Alexander Hamilton. In short, Philadelphia aided in smoothing the way for the Jeffersonian "revolution" in politics that attended the next transfer of the capital—to the District of Columbia in 1800.

Under the private agreement and the ensuing act of Congress that fixed the permanent capital of the federal government on the banks of the Potomac, the second President, John Adams, in the summer of 1800, ordered the removal of the administration to the District of Columbia where Congress was to assemble on the first Monday in December. The task of removal was not very burdensome. All told, the federal officers and clerks numbered only one hundred and twenty-six persons. Official papers were boxed and shipped by boat. The officers and clerks made the trip by various routes. President Adams went to see the place in June and later he and his wife Abigail were installed in the "President's House." In a report on the official residence, then unfinished and full of litter, she said that she was using the great "audience room" in the "President's Palace" as "a drying room . . . to hang the clothes in."

In 1801 the District of Columbia was a profusion of forests, hills, and streams interspersed with a few farms, the little village of George Town, some newly laid out streets for the city of Washington, and a few public and private buildings just completed or under construction. Land speculators and real estate promoters swarmed over the place buying and selling lots with no respect for community plans and interests. Good houses dotted the landscape, but the roads between them, in the "city of magnificent distances," were axle deep in summer dust or winter mud. "An awful contrast to the public buildings," exclaimed Oliver Wolcott, Secretary of the Treasury, were the many "small, miserable huts." The inhabitants of the huts, he declared, "are poor, and as far as I can judge, they live like fishes, by eating one another." There were no fine churches, no schools, no colleges, no seasoned residents to extend hospitality at balls and dinners to members of the incoming government. Laborers' shanties and brick kilns stood out starkly in the scene—more vividly than the habitations of the laboring poor in New York or Philadelphia. A slave market, with its pens and auction block, gave obtrusive notice that the capital of the Republic had been located in a region where the "peculiar institution" flourished. The outlook for republican grandeur did not seem brilliant.

But behind the confusion lay the dream of a splendid city worthy of the Republic. Major Pierre Charles L'Enfant, a French engineer and soldier of the American Revolution, whose services President Washington had enlisted, had drawn a grandiose plan for the permanent capital, with broad avenues, spacious plazas, and long vistas, in anticipation of a time when the wealth of the nation would permit an orderly and full development of his design. Having regard for the republican principles of Thomas Jefferson whom he consulted in making his sketches, L'Enfant was careful to avoid a mere duplication of any European pattern, whatever might have been his personal preference, and to make room for the originality of simplicity. It is true that, for the time being, L'Enfant's plan was largely defeated by real estate speculators and that he retired from further activity, discouraged and ruined. Late in the nineteenth century, however, his dream was to be revived and honor paid to his memory.

Notwithstanding the disputes and divided councils that attended the laying out of the new city, the architecture of the two outstanding public buildings in process of completion was in keeping with Jefferson's republican aspirations. For the Congress House, or Capitol, William Thornton's sketches, with provision for a great central rotunda, were accepted by President Washington and, subject to modifications, were used as the basis of construction. The President's House, designed by James Hoban, was modest in lines and proportions. Both buildings represented a departure from Georgian and other purely colonial architecture and a tendency toward the severity of classical models set by the Greek and Roman republics of antiquity.

As if symbolizing this simplicity, the first President to be inaugurated in the new capital of the nation was Thomas Jefferson himself. His party had wrested the federal administration from the "aristocrats" and "monocrats" in the party founded by Hamilton and Washington. Despite his "simplicity," ridiculed as "affected" by his political foes, he was one of the most sophisticated persons of his time in the New World or the Old World. By virtue of his wide knowledge, his interest in natural

THE UNITED STATES AND ITS NEIGHBORS IN 1802

science, art, and learning, his geniality, humor, and readiness to listen as well as pronounce, he was exceptionally equipped to assume the leadership of the political community in Washington. Though familiar with cities of Western Europe as with New York and Philadelphia, he loved the country, and Washington was then little more than a village.

Though treated as a philosopher among the intellectuals who gathered in the home of Condorcet and his high-minded wife in Paris, he had been snubbed by the socially pretentious landlords and merchants of New York and Philadelphia, and felt happier in the White House at Washington.

According to the custom followed at his Virginia country place, Monticello, Jefferson made the President's House in the permanent capital of the Republic a center of social and intellectual leadership, while he presided as Executive over the young nation. At the dinner table, where conversation among Americans from all sections of the country and foreign diplomats was made easy and informal, he was cordial, skillful, and deeply interested in evoking diversities of opinions and tastes. In this way at the crude capital of the young Republic, he attached all sorts and conditions of people, high and low, to the republican experiment. And fortunately, in this wide-open though experienced hospitality, he was aided by his daughter, Martha Jefferson Randolph, whose education, after the death of his wife, he had carefully and thoughtfully supervised.

It was significant for the future that Thomas Jefferson, with his strong faith in the people, took over in 1801 the administration of the republican system of government which had been framed in deep distrust of the people; that as President he strengthened it before the rising tide of Jacksonian democracy began to beat upon it. The very fact that the seat of the government was then in a mere village, frontier in its physical appearance and isolated as a political community, no doubt was a factor in enlarging Jefferson's influence in Congress and public councils generally.

Distrust of cities had been a cardinal feature of agrarian republicanism. Even John Adams had feared the aggressions of plutocratic merchants and speculators as much as he had feared an uprising of the poor. At all events the presence of Jefferson at the head of the Republic in the village of Washington, though his election had evoked the fury of haughty Federalists, increased "the affections of its citizens" for "the republican model of government," as George Washington had called it, and gave vigor to the republican way of life in the United States.

Influential as was the work of Washington, Adams, and Jefferson in fortifying republican government, their work was only one phase of the transition from monarchy to the republican way of life. To the new order was brought the support of intellectual and artistic talents among the citizens, made manifest in forms of written and oral expression, such as books and dramas, and in visible symbols, such as paintings and engravings. Through the press, the theater, and popular education—formal and informal—the results of these activities became known and appreciated among multitudes of people upon whose thought, aspirations, labors, and character the republican experiment ultimately depended for its success.

By the intellectual and artistic activities of private citizens the doctrine was formulated that the Revolution and the Republic were worthy of the highest esteem in themselves, and admirable in the history of humanity. By the same processes were widened and deepened knowledge and thought respecting the new nation whose fortunes were involved in the republican way of life, with all that it signified in terms of civilization. With increasing interest in society, economy, and the people went inquiries, ever more microscopic, into the physical geography and the natural resources of the continental domain as expansion and settlement proceeded—the material setting in which the republican experiment was being carried on.

During the transition from monarchy to the republican type of life, writers gave expression to the revolution in literally thousands of books on the United States—on its government, people, institutions, and resources. By classes, somewhat arbitrary, these books came under the heads of government, law, economy, geography, travel, public policies, and conditions of the people from the poorest slave at the bottom to the richest merchant or planter at the top. Some of them, however, were so comprehensive that they took in all or nearly all the themes then engaging American interests. Collectively, the books contained knowledge and thought bearing upon almost everything human and material that was germane to the republican experiment, its policies and its possibilities, its ideals and its resources. The scope of this literature is merely indicated, rather than adequately illustrated, by the following selected titles and comments:

1787—Thomas Jefferson, *Notes on Virginia.* A model survey of the government, laws, economy, climate, resources, and people of Virginia—the forerunner of many such treatises on individual states.

1787—John Adams, *Defence of the Constitutions of the United States* (Vols. I–III). A historical study of the science of politics in which the principles of the first state constitutions were defended with great learning.

1788—Jay, Hamilton, and Madison, *The Federalist,* essays written in support of the Constitution, published in book form. Frequently republished. French edition in 1792. A treatise on the sociology, economics, and strategy of republican government which formed the primary textbook for the education of the American people in republican ways of government.

1789—William Gordon, *History of the Rise, Progress and Establishment of the Independence of the United States* (Vols. I–III). Published previously in London. Displeased the English by its American sympathies and was regarded in America as scarcely patriotic enough. Gordon copied wholesale from other writings.

1789—David Ramsay, *History of the American Revolution* (Vols. I, II). More favorable to the American cause than Gordon's work.

1791-92—Thomas Paine, *Rights of Man*. Textbook of republican principles. Sold by the tens of thousands in the two hemispheres.

1805—Mercy Warren, *History of the Rise, Progress and Termination of the American Revolution* (Vols. I–III). Far more original than Gordon or Ramsay. Based extensively on personal knowledge; Northern in emphasis. Discussed the conditions from which the Revolution sprang, leading characters and events of the Revolution. Democratic in sympathies and a warning against monarchical tendencies and the greed for riches that might undermine the Republic and restore tyranny.

1805-07—John Marshall, *Life of George Washington* (Vols. I–V). Based on extensive researches. An eloquent defense and vindication of Washington; Federalist in tone; and did more than any other work to set the tradition of Washington as "the father of his country." Severely criticized by Jefferson and his followers, but remained powerful in influence.

1814—Lewis and Clark, *History of the Expedition . . . to the Pacific Ocean* (Vols. I, II). Summary description of a famous journey and the country through which the explorers passed.

1814—Tench Coxe, *A Statement of the Arts and Manufactures of the United States of America for the year 1810*. Based on a federal census taken in 1810.

1814—John Taylor, *An Inquiry into the Principles and Policy of the Government of the United States*. A philosophical treatise on politics, following the Anti-Federalist or agrarian party line in opposition to the "aristocracy of riches."

1817—William Wirt, *Sketches of the Life and Character of Patrick Henry*. Eulogy on the fiery leader of the Revolution.

1819—David Ramsay, *Universal History Americanized* (Vols. I–IX). Three additional volumes unfinished on the death of the author. A grand design to put the United States in the setting of great history.

How many Americans burned midnight oil studying the histories of Gordon, Ramsay, and Mercy Warren was not entered in the records of the time but there can be no doubt that thousands upon thousands saw, as originals or reproductions, the paintings which celebrated in visible form the Revolution and its leaders. The task of such delineation was deliberately assumed by John Trumbull, who had a vision of the "vast consequences" to flow from the establishment of independence. A former colonel in the Revolution, Trumbull had the spirit of the new age and he gave vivid expression to it on his canvases representing the "Battle of Bunker's Hill," the "Signing of the Declaration of Independence," the "Capture of the Hessians at Trenton," the "Surrender of Cornwallis at Yorktown," and in his portraits of leaders, such as Washington and Hamilton.

Two contemporaries of Trumbull, Gilbert Stuart, of Rhode Island, and Charles Wilson Peale, of Maryland, also painted portraits of the outstanding personalities of the Revolutionary generation. Stuart's portrait of Washington, soon to become the most widely accepted for technical competence, depicted the hero as a polished aristocrat of Virginia. Truer to life, Peale portrayed him in his rugged character as outdoor planter, soldier, and stalwart manager of men. The chief paintings of Trumbull, Stuart, and Peale, reproduced by lithographic processes, soon ornamented public buildings and private homes, great and humble, making lifelike, to all who could see, characters and events connected with the making of the independent Republic.

Moved by a kindred spirit, poets joined in the same celebration. Joel Barlow, of Connecticut, for example, dreamed of a great creative future for America. "The American Republic," he told a friend, "is a fine theater for the display of merit of every kind. If ever virtue is to be rewarded, it is in America." In this mood, Barlow wrote and published in 1787 *The Vision of Columbus*, an epic poem of more than five thousand lines on the real significance of the discovery of America. Recognizing, with his critics, some of the youthful exaggerations of this venture, Barlow later worked over and reworked the theme and republished it in 1807 in two sumptuous volumes as *The Columbiad*. Barlow's object, he declared in his preface, was to demonstrate that Columbus "had opened the way to the most extensive career of civilization and public happiness," to inculcate the spirit of liberty, to discountenance violence and war, and "to show that on the basis of republican principles all good morals, as well as good government and hopes of permanent peace, must be founded."

The convulsive changes which marked the transition to the republican way of life were dramatized by playwrights. Following the success of Tyler's comedy, *The Contrast*, in New York, the play was presented in Baltimore, Philadelphia, Charleston, and Boston; and it was published in 1790, with a subscription list at the head of which stood George Washington, the President of the Republic. From year to year in far-scattered places it was reproduced by players both professional and amateur.

Tyler's success encouraged William Dunlap to enter seriously upon a career as a dramatist, dedicating his talents to the service of the Republic, as he believed American artists of every type should do. Knowing that monarchies had been made glamorous by the aid of painters, poets, historians, architects, dramatists, musicians, and novelists, Dunlap felt that the Republic was far more worthy of devotion and should be made attractive to the people by all such forms of art. His father had been a Loyalist during the Revolution and had sent William to Europe to be trained as a painter. But in London William became enamored of the theater; his sympathies with the struggle of the people for liberty were awakened; and on his return home he composed plays and wrote works on the drama and the arts of design.

Dunlap's long career as an important and productive playwright of the Republic opened in 1789 with a drama entitled *The Father; or American Shandy-ism,* in which he presented his view of the "contrast" in the following lines:

> Now I see in this new world
> A resting spot for man, if he can stand
> Firm in his place, while Europe howls around him. . . .
> Then might, perhaps, one land on earth be found,
> Free from the extremes of poverty and riches;
> Where ne'er a scepter'd tyrant should be known,
> Or tyrant lordling, curses of creation.

Other forms of literature expressed the ideas, interests, and ideals of the people in the republican era. The novels and tracts of Charles Brockden Brown contained flashes of discussion which illuminated the wrongs of yeomen and the "rights" of women, as well as nearly every other current theme of democratic interest. James Fenimore Cooper, whose first novel came out in 1820, chose to tell stories of the struggle for liberty in the Revolution, and to portray all kinds of Americans from Indians and pioneers to planters and sailors. Poets, such as Philip Freneau, "the poet of the Revolution," tried their lyrical talents on the aspirations of the Republic. Noah Webster wrote to George Washington in 1786: "I am encouraged by the prospect of rendering my country some service, to proceed with my design of refining the language & improving our general system of education." So he went ahead compiling dictionaries on the basis of American usages for scholarly and popular purposes and making plans for giving the children of the people an education that would inspire a devotion to the Republic and prepare them for citizenship in it.

☆

Newspapers for the distribution of knowledge and ideas, true or false, multiplied in the republican era. Forty-three colonial newspapers, it was estimated, lived through the Revolution; in 1810 Isaiah Thomas recorded, in his *History of Printing,* the existence of 366 newspapers scattered all the way from New Hampshire to the Louisiana Territory, with no less than fourteen in Ohio and one on the frontier of Michigan. In this period the daily press entered the journalistic arena, exciting readers every day instead of every week. Philadelphia printers supplied the first daily—in 1784; and by 1809, the end of Jefferson's second administration, there were twenty-seven dailies in the flourishing cities from Boston to New Orleans.

As the party division into Federalists and Republicans deepened, practically all the newspapers, weekly and daily, became ferociously partisan and outdid in the passion of their language anything the colonial age had experienced. But they distributed news, or at all events selections and versions of news, reported on the great public questions and policies of the day, and supplied topics for discussion at dinner tables, in taverns, at corner stores, and by firesides throughout the land.

All the pressures of thought in the new society struggling to establish the republican way of life—insurgent interests and traditional tastes—found outlets in new magazines which burst forth luxuriantly. In their pages, taken collectively, readers were supplied with polite letters, fragments of creative fiction, patriotic boasting, practical philosophies of daily living, scientific information, codes of etiquette, poetic effusions mawkish or brave, essays on humble ambitions and national aspirations, old and new bigotries with their simplicities of dogma, and solid articles on actions and policies directed to the advantages of classes or the progressive attainment of general welfare. Magazine editors seemed to labor hard at meeting every demand, real or imagined, from the supposed needs of gentlewomen eager for "culture" to the requirements, actual or alleged, of popular success in upholding the Republic.

Among the more substantial periodicals was the *Columbian Magazine*, founded by Mathew Carey at Philadelphia in 1786, a miscellany of original and selected articles on government, currency, industries, agriculture, and science. Its pages carried articles by some of the most distinguished writers of the early Republic, for example, Benjamin Rush, physician; David Ramsay, historian; Charles Brockden Brown, novelist; and Joel Barlow, pamphleteer and poet. It started bravely and seemed destined to have a long career, but after four years of struggle it gave up the ghost.

Other magazines tried to fill the void left by its death, only to meet a similar fate. Yet at no time in the early republican era was the country without an ambitious monthly of the general type. At last, in 1815, when the *North American Review* was launched at Boston, a magazine editor received the support necessary to long endurance. Of the flock of magazines founded between 1776 and 1815 that *Review* alone survived the buffets of fortune into the twentieth century.

On no subject were the leaders of the Revolutionary generation more thoroughly united than on the advancement of popular education and science as indispensable to permanence in the republican way of life. The old Congress under the Articles of Confederation had demonstrated its faith by dedicating to public education regular blocks of land in the Northwest Territory. Then President Washington, in his first annual address to Congress, sounded a national note: "Nor am I less persuaded that you will agree with me in opinion that there is nothing which can better deserve your patronage than the promotion of science and literature. Knowledge is in every country the surest basis of public happiness. In one in which the measures of government receive their impressions so immediately from the sense of the community as in ours it is proportionably essential. To the security of a free constitution it contributes in various ways." To Congress at the moment he left the choice of ways for accomplishing this end but later he recommended the establishment of a national university. This recommendation Thomas Jefferson renewed as President.

Although Congress did not adopt the proposal, one state after another made the beginnings of state colleges and universities; and Jefferson, after he retired from the presidency, set an example of fidelity to conviction by taking the lead in founding the University of Virginia at Charlottesville. This university was not projected as merely a college with a classical curriculum. It was designed as a true modern institution of higher learning, dedicated to freedom of thought, inquiry, and teaching, especially in natural science and the humanities.

Lack of interest among the rank and file of politicians—even hostility—did not deter advocates of public education from planning for the future. Some of their programs, notably that of Robert Coram, a brave seaman in the war of the Revolution and an intellectual leader in Delaware, called for the training of all children in the practical arts as means of assuring personal independence and overcoming the poverty which belied civilization. Other plans, especially that of Noah Webster, while pleading for general education, insisted upon the training of women in the philosophy of republicanism, on the ground that women exercise a major influence through their training of the young and must be taught how to bring up the generations in republican ways of living and thinking.

James Sullivan in Massachusetts produced still another plan for a system of republican education. Sullivan was active in public affairs before, during, and after the Revolution—a justice of the Supreme Court in his state, a member of Congress in 1783, a publicist, one of the "richest, ablest, and most powerful" of the Jeffersonians. In his writings on government, politics, and society in America, Sullivan declared that a system of national education was absolutely necessary if the morals of the people were to be shaped according to the genius of republican government and if the people were to realize the ideals of liberty, happiness, and general welfare that had been proclaimed as the objectives of the republican experiment.

In the voluminous literature on education and the advancement of science, stress was placed on the practical aspects of living. Research in the natural sciences was to be promoted and useful inventions encouraged. Yet the moral sciences of community and national living were also to be emphasized to prepare the nation for its opportunities and destiny. The people, Jefferson insisted, must not only be trained in the practical arts; they must be instructed in those branches of learning, especially history, which would enable them to discharge their duties as citizens while maintaining a vigilant watch against the tendencies of government to encroach on human liberty, including the liberty of free inquiry, thought, and speech.

It was, no doubt, this concern with practical and earthly affairs in educational programs that helped to arouse opposition among the clergy, then the chief leaders in such popular education as prevailed, and to arrest the progress of universal and non-sectarian education until the nineteenth century was well advanced. Yet before the Revolutionary generation passed from the scene, its pioneers in thought had worked out and formulated essential principles for the advancement of science and the education of the people—all with a view to making the nation strong and wise in the use of its resources, solicitous for social improvements, and competent in the arts of republican government.

Chapter 11

THE REVOLUTIONARY GENERATION IN CHARGE OF NATIONAL AFFAIRS

FOR THIRTY-SIX YEARS after the Constitution went into force—from 1789 to 1825—the new government was headed by Presidents who belonged to the generation of revolutionists: by five men, George Washington, John Adams, Thomas Jefferson, James Madison, and James Monroe.

What a roll of services and honors, what varieties of experiences in war and peace, in domestic and foreign affairs, these five men represented!

Washington had been a member of the Virginia Assembly in colonial times, a soldier in the French and Indian War, a member of the Continental Congress, commander of the Revolutionary armies, a member of the convention that drafted the Constitution, the presiding officer of that body, and was literally "first in war and first in peace."

John Adams had spent laborious years in the Continental Congress during the War for Independence, had led in framing the Massachusetts Constitution of 1780, had represented his country in continental capitals and in London, had written a powerful work, the *Defence of the Constitutions of the United States*, and had been Vice-President under Washington.

Like Adams, Thomas Jefferson belonged to the civilian wing of the Revolutionary generation. He had been a member of the Virginia legislature and the Continental Congress. He had drawn up the Declaration of Independence. He had been governor of Virginia, minister of the United States to France, Secretary of State under Washington, and Vice-President during the administration of President Adams.

Before he became the fourth President, James Madison's lines had also fallen in the field of civilian leadership. He had been an active member of the old Congress. He had been a delegate to the convention of 1787 and, in that assembly, had brought to bear in the framing of the Constitution a profound knowledge of history and statecraft, besides an exceptional talent for negotiation. After the adoption of the Constitution he had been a member of the House of Representatives. For eight years he had served as Secretary of State under President Jefferson.

As in the case of Washington, so in the case of James Monroe the experiences of war and peace were combined. In the war of the Revolution, Monroe had learned the perils of the battlefield. He had represented the United States abroad. Under the presidency of Madison he had been Secretary of State and then Secretary of War. Although neither his talents nor his achievements measured up to those of his predecessors, he had qualities which gave him a place of distinction among the leaders of the Revolutionary generation.

Through all these years American citizens generally agreed that the executive leadership of the nation should be vested in outstanding figures of the Revolution. But they by no means agreed on the policies to be adopted and the measures to be enforced by the government of the United States. Americans had been divided into conservative and radical factions during the Revolution as in the preceding colonial order. This division was still evident during the framing and adoption of the Constitution. For a brief time, however, after the Constitution had been ratified, its opponents, accepting their defeat with good grace, permitted a lull in partisanship. Not until the first Congress under the new Constitution revealed its intentions in a program of legislation and the President began to appoint officials and indicate his domestic and foreign policies did serious dissensions reappear among the people.

To both houses of the first Congress many men were elected who had helped to draft the Constitution or who had worked for its adoption in their several states. In choosing the members of his Cabinet and high officials in his administration, Washington was careful to appoint men known as stanch advocates of the new plan. His Secretary of the Treasury, Alexander Hamilton, his Attorney General, Edmund Randolph, and General Henry Knox, his Secretary of War, belonged to that group.

Perhaps with a view to conciliating an expected opposition, Washington gave to Thomas Jefferson the important post of Secretary of State. Jefferson had been in France as minister of the United States during the contest over the drafting and ratification of the Constitution. It was known to his intimates that he had at first thought a few amendments to the Articles of Confederation would suffice and had criticized the Constitution in several respects, especially the lack of a bill of rights. But Jefferson had rallied to the Constitution after 1789.

When the first Congress assembled in New York City and Washington was inaugurated as President, in the spring of 1789, the new government of the Republic was in the hands of its friends, experienced leaders, men long outstanding in public life. The cold text of the written Constitution had become flesh and blood. The time for action had arrived. But what actions in domestic affairs and in foreign affairs? That was the question which aroused expectancy among members of Congress and the people of the states.

Soon answers began to come, first in respect of domestic matters. In response to a popular demand for a bill of rights, Congress early proposed a series of amendments to the Constitution; and ten of them, ratified by state legislatures, went into effect in 1791. Still these involved no alteration whatever in the form of government.

Immediately pertinent to the support of the government were the measures, affecting the property and incomes of the people, that began to flow from Washington's administration and Congress. Revenues from taxation were necessary to the very existence of the government. All knew that. But what kind of taxes? On whom and what were they to fall? Taxation had been a sore point with the people since the Stamp Act of 1765. Well aware of it, Congress resorted to indirect taxation at the outset. The first revenue law, in 1789, laid duties on foreign goods imported into the United States. Both Washington and Hamilton thought that such duties should favor American manufacturers, especially of goods required for national defense. So did many members of Congress from the manufacturing states. In subsequent revenue acts "protection" was given to manufacturers of iron and several other commodities. To provide further revenues Congress laid an excise tax on whisky, a liquor distilled in thousands of farmhouses in various parts of the country.

Other measures affecting special interests were passed by Congress, one after the other, during the administrations of Washington and Adams. High on the list were provisions for paying off the big debt owed by the United States to its creditors—in the main to Americans, but in part to bankers in Holland and to the government of France.

This debt had been incurred by the Continental Congress largely for the purpose of carrying on the War for Independence. Interest on it had long remained in arrears. The prices of the bonds and other securities representing the debt had fallen, at times as low as to ten or fifteen cents on the dollar. Discouraged by the prospect of a total loss or needing money, hundreds of Americans had sold their bonds for almost nothing, to speculators who gambled on the chance that the cheap paper would someday be paid off in full by the government.

Should it be paid in full or at a sum below face value? If paid in full, should discrimination be made between the rate paid to persons who had originally bought the bonds from the Continental government and the rate paid to speculators who had bought the bonds from the original subscribers at low prices?

These points became storm centers of public discussion. The Secretary of the Treasury, Hamilton, proposed that the Continental securities be paid, ultimately, dollar for dollar and that no distinction be made between the persons who had bought their bonds directly from the government at the regular price and speculators who had bought theirs from original holders, second or third hand, for mere pittances. After exhaustive debates marked by thoughtfulness as well as passion, Congress adopted Hamilton's proposal. The Continental debt was thus "funded" and all bondholders were given new bonds for their old paper, dollar for dollar.

The states also had big debts incurred in the War for Independence. Some of the states were making payments on interest and principal; other states were delaying. In any case the bonds of the states had fallen in value, many of them to a low price, and speculators had been buying the state bonds too, at various price levels, in the hope of a rise in values.

That the state debts ought to be paid, people generally recognized. But by whom? Hamilton proposed that the federal Treasury assume the burden of paying them all and at face value. He argued that such a course was just, since the debts had been incurred in a common cause, and that it would strengthen the new government by making all bondholders look to its Treasury, instead of state treasuries, for payment of interest and principal. But on that point Hamilton encountered a still hotter opposition than had been raised against funding the Continental debt at face value. Even so, he managed by a close squeeze to win the approval of Congress for this plan, and the state debts were assumed by the federal government. New federal bonds were then exchanged for old state bonds, dollar for dollar, no distinction being made between original subscribers and the speculators.

Another thing, Hamilton believed, was necessary to strengthen the Union. That was a national currency stable from one end of the country to the other. But the question of money was likewise vexatious. No great mines of gold and silver had been found along the Atlantic seaboard. During the Revolution the states and the Congress had poured out paper money by the bale and the country was full of notes "not worth a Continental," as the saying went. Now the Constitution had forbidden the states to emit bills of credit and had given Congress the power to coin money and regulate the value thereof—not to issue paper money. The only "sound money" in circulation consisted of metallic coins, mostly British, Spanish, and French; and they were being clipped, filed, and shorn by the money-changers.

Soon after Washington's inauguration, Congress made provision for minting new United States coins, but the precious metals available were small in quantity. For the purpose of expanding the amount of money in circulation, Hamilton devised and induced Congress to adopt a plan for a United States Bank. As set up in 1791, the bank was a joint-stock concern, with the United States Government among the holders of shares. The major portion of the stock, however, was subscribed by private investors, partly in specie money and partly in certain new bonds floated under Hamilton's funding and assumption schemes.

Little specie was actually paid in by private investors. So the "capital" of the bank rested principally on the paper bonds of the government. The bank, thus formed, was empowered to receive deposits, issue paper notes of its own, establish branches in various parts of the country, handle government accounts, and lend money at interest. The central office was established in Philadelphia. In time it had a network of branches scattered from Portsmouth, New Hampshire, to Savannah, Georgia. Through the agency of the United States Bank, paper notes of uniform value were put into circulation everywhere in the states; and merchants could now buy, sell, and make exchanges, assured that the bank currency would be both safe and stable.

With a view to promoting other branches of business enterprise, Congress voted bounties to encourage the growth of American fisheries and granted special favors to American shipping interests. Great Britain and other Old World countries were helping their own shippers and discriminating against foreign shippers in their harbors, according to accepted mercantilist theories. Under a strong government the United States was following suit.

To all such American measures Washington lent the support of his great name. The Constitution, he felt, warranted his doing this. He had been president of the convention which drafted it, had heard the debates, and was familiar with the purposes of the men who framed it. He knew more about those purposes than any of his critics, such as Thomas Jefferson, who had not been members of the convention and were less acquainted with the broad conceptions of government written into the Constitution. Giving expression to them, Washington recommended to Congress the enactment of laws promoting not only commerce and industry, but also agriculture, science, and education, with emphasis on the establishment of a national university for the training of young men for public life under the sway of American principles.

The growing body of federal officers engaged in enforcing the new laws under Washington's executive direction was supplemented by a new federal judiciary. By the Judiciary Act of 1789, Congress established the Supreme Court prescribed by the Constitution and a federal district court in each state, with a set of officials and agents for each court. Washington appointed as Chief Justice John Jay, who had battled for the ratification of the Constitution; and all the other judgeships he filled with men having a similar attitude toward the new order.

As soon as the new courts went into operation, citizens everywhere could look to federal judges for the protection and enforcement of their rights under the Constitution. If they felt that their rights were violated by state legislatures or state courts, they could appeal to federal judges independent of both. For example if a merchant of New York City wished to collect a debt from a citizen in North Carolina, he was no longer at the mercy of a local judge and jury; he could take his case into a United States district court. For interstate commerce and general business transactions, therefore, the federal judicial system was no less important than the United States Bank.

With the rise of party conflicts, the significance of the federal judiciary for the Union increased. Federal judges held office for life and could not be ousted except by impeachment. Presidents and members of Congress could come and go. Federal judges could remain on the bench throughout their lifetimes. Nobody understood this better than John Adams. Just before he left the White House in 1801, Adams made John Marshall, of Virginia, Chief Justice of the United States, and also appointed judges to the new circuit courts which Congress had just created. For about thirty-five years, until after Jefferson, Adams, and Monroe were all dead, Marshall kept at his post. A fervent advocate of a strong national Union from the days when he had fought for independence on the battlefield, Marshall welcomed the opportunity to make his views of the Constitution prevail in law. In case after case he declared acts of state legislatures null and void, as contrary to the Constitution. With the same firmness he upheld the power of Congress to enact laws broadly conceived in the general interest of the United States.

The national program of domestic measures, instituted under Washington and continued under Adams, was thoroughgoing. It was designed to, and did, strike deeply into the life, industry, habits, and sentiments of the American people. It set precedents for ages to come. It might have met most needs if Europe had remained at peace and American foreign relations had been undisturbed. But agitations in the United States over the French Revolution and war in Europe beat against the domestic policies of Washington's first administration. They broke in with such force that he and his successors were compelled to develop, also, a program of actions coming under the head of foreign policy.

A few weeks after Washington was inaugurated in 1789, the once powerful French monarchy began to crumble, revealing its decrepitude as popular demands for liberty and self-government increased in vehemence. At first it made concessions which seemed to promise a peaceful transition to a new political order. The authority of the French aristocracy and clergy was shattered; and the King, Louis XVI, was compelled to grant his subjects a constitution, including a national legislature, elected by the voters, and a bill of rights known as "The Rights of Man."

Soon reform merged into revolutionary violence. The constitution was overturned; a republic was proclaimed. The King was put to death in January 1793. In the autumn of the same year, the Queen, Marie Antoinette, was borne to the scaffold. One group of radicals after another seized power. A "reign of terror," accompanied by executions and a civil war, spread from Paris to the provinces. Before many years had passed the struggle closed in the military dictatorship of the warrior and demagogue, Napoleon Bonaparte, as First Consul, then as Consul for life, and finally as Emperor of the French in 1804.

The turmoil in France would have raised questions for the government of the United States to decide in dealing with the rulers who succeeded one another in that country, even if the revolution had not extended beyond French borders. But it spread far and wide beyond the Rhine; and, terrified by events in Paris, the despotic monarchs of Prussia and Austria started a war on revolutionary France, with the diplomatic support of the British government. In 1793 France declared war on Great Britain.

Then country after country in Europe became involved in the fight. Victorious French armies overran Italy, Belgium, Holland, Scandinavia, the western regions of Germany, and Spain, disseminating doctrines of "liberty" as they marched. For twenty-two years, with a brief intermission (1801–03), the wars of the great European Powers raged in nearly every part of the Continent, on the high seas, in Africa, even creating uproars as far away as India. Since the war between France and Britain on the oceans was a war on commerce, both belligerents preyed upon the ships and trade of American citizens, searching for munitions carriers and blockade runners.

As soon as the war broke out between France and Great Britain in 1793, President Washington faced a question that could not be avoided. In the treaty of 1778, under which France came to the aid of the American cause with money and arms, the United States promised to help France in defending her remaining American possessions if, at some time in the future, she again became involved in a war with the British. Recalling this pledge, the government of France in 1793 asked Washington for aid in its new war.

The dilemma was embarrassing for Washington. The promise had been made. There was no doubt about that, and American sympathies in general were on the side of the French. But getting into another war meant laying heavy taxes, raising armies, building war vessels, and increasing the already large national debt. Furthermore it might, Washington thought, completely disrupt the government just established under the Constitution. After consulting his advisers, including Hamilton and Jefferson, he refused to comply with French demands and proclaimed the neutrality of the United States in the European conflict.

More than this, President Washington decided to get on a better footing with the British government. Several sources of ill-feeling still lingered from the War of Independence. Americans had not paid all the debts they had incurred in dealings with British merchants in colonial times. Loyalists in America whose property had been confiscated still waited for the compensation that had been promised them. The British had not removed their troops from forts in the western part of the United States. And other matters interfered with the development of amicable relations between the two nations.

Faced with this situation, Washington ordered John Jay to London, commissioned to make a treaty with Great Britain that would remove some of the worst irritations. Jay managed to wring very few concessions out of the British government. But Washington approved the treaty Jay had negotiated and persuaded the Senate to ratify it in 1795. The United States, he resolved, was to stay out of the war; to pursue the policy of neutrality toward all the belligerents.

The moment Washington and Hamilton began to frame and put into force domestic and foreign policies, they confronted critics and formidable opponents in Congress and outside. In due time, as it turned out, practically all of Hamilton's program encountered protests from members of Congress, pamphleteers, and editors of newspapers. At firesides and in taverns knots of citizens debating his program expressed strong opinions for or against it. Even within Washington's Cabinet the conflict raged. Hamilton and Jefferson engaged in such fierce controversies over the proper course to pursue that Washington could not mollify them, hard though he tried. Within a few years the country was flaming with the polemics of a great dispute.

In a little while two well-knit political parties gave concentration to the scattered fire of the opposing forces. Supporters of Washington's administration, led by Hamilton, called themselves Federalists. Opponents, who at length rallied around Jefferson, were generally known as Anti-Federalists in the beginning—as mere oppositionists. Later they assumed the title of Republicans, eventually changed to the more radical one of Democrats. In the House of Representatives, in the Senate, in the cities, and in the country districts far and wide, Federalists formed committees or caucuses for the purpose of uniting their forces. The Republicans did likewise. Thus party organizations cutting across state lines spread from New Hampshire to Georgia.

Each of the parties was mixed in membership. But Hamilton appealed particularly to the business interests—to holders of government securities, financiers, manufacturers, shipowners, and speculators in Western lands; and around him gathered advocates of strong and stable government. Since he was sympathetic with Great Britain and hostile to France after the revolution flared up in Paris and the European war opened, former Tories who had remained in America and were now American citizens flocked to his standard. In effect the Federalist party could lay claim to representing "the wealth and talents" of the conservative classes in the United States. "Your people," Hamilton was reported to have said, "is a great beast." In any event, he and Washington resented popular agitations at home, as they abhorred such agitation in France, and they thought that the "democratic societies" springing up in towns and country districts ought to be suppressed before they got out of bounds.

For the agricultural interests, especially for the small farmers who owned and tilled their lands themselves, Jefferson became the prime spokesman—leader of the Republican party. Freehold farmers, he declared, were the best and truest support for republican government. He charged Hamilton and his close friends with being monarchists and British sympathizers. He applauded the rights of man proclaimed by the French reformers and rejoiced in their efforts to erect a republic in France. To his partisans Jefferson, author of the Declaration of Independence, was the American Revolution incarnate—the foe of monarchy and the whole British social system in peace and war. After the French Revolution ended in the Napoleonic dictatorship, Jefferson's ardor for France cooled, but his dislike of British policies and actions long remained intense. He stood like a rock for "the people," against "rich and well-born" aristocrats and "monocrats."

By the time the election of 1796 approached, the Republicans were ready for a campaign to get possession of the government. Distressed by attacks on his policies and pained by assaults on his character despite his long public service, Washington refused to run for a third term as President. Rejecting every plea that he stand again for election, he wrote a farewell message to all his countrymen warning them against party passions at home and against becoming involved in the frequent quarrels, combinations, and collisions of European friendships and enmities.

Unable to persuade Washington to lead them again, the Federalists turned to John Adams, the Vice-President, whose conservatism they approved. Yet Adams was no abject disciple of Hamilton, and the Federalists found it hard to forgive his independence in politics. Though the

Revolutionary generation respected his talents, his fidelity to the patriot cause, and his important services, he was not a magnetic figure for a popular campaign.

Yet the Republicans were not strong enough to defeat Adams, although they gave him and his party a fright. When the electoral votes were counted, it was found that Adams had seventy-one and Jefferson had sixty-eight. The narrow victory added nothing to Adams' popularity and his conduct as President reduced it. He did his best to win public favor, but his four years in office were full of troubles and his best was not enough to make him a national hero.

The financial and commercial policies started by Hamilton were continued by President Adams. With regard to Great Britain, he maintained the sympathetic neutrality initiated by Washington. In the case of France, however, affairs were more complicated. The French government in power when Adams became President had denounced President Washington for refusing to aid France in the war against Great Britain and for making terms with the British government in the Jay Treaty. To put it mildly, the relations of France and the United States were strained.

In his desire to ease the strain with France, President Adams sent envoys to Paris empowered to reach a settlement with the French government. Their reception was frigid. Indeed French agents demanded an apology from the United States, a loan of money, and a bribe to be paid to members of their government.

Exceedingly indignant when he heard about the chilly reception of the American mission and the demand for a bribe, Adams, naming the French agents only as X, Y, Z, reported the affair to Congress and the public. The public response was a cry that ran throughout the United States: "Millions for defense, but not one cent for tribute!" Washington was summoned from his plantation to take charge of the armed forces again. Fighting started at sea. With alacrity Federalists gave their support to Adams while Republicans moderated their criticisms of him. For a moment his leadership seemed to be gaining popularity. Then suddenly in 1799, Bonaparte, who had become dictator in France, proposed a peace with the United States on fair terms and Adams accepted it. Now the excitement over the undeclared war died away and with its disappearance attacks on the Adams administration were renewed.

Bent on suppressing their opponents and keeping power if they could, Federalist leaders rushed through Congress, in 1798, two laws directed to those ends.

The first, the Alien Act, gave the President power for two years to expel from the country any alien whom he might deem "dangerous to the peace and safety of the United States." Although Adams did not deport a single person under the act, the mere passage of the law aroused the ire of many Americans as a violation of liberty. Moreover it frightened unnaturalized Irish and French persons in America, who did not like the foreign policy that favored Great Britain.

The second measure, the Sedition Act, placed heavy penalties on every person, alien or citizen, found guilty of trying to stir up "sedition" or who wrote or published anything "false, scandalous, or malicious" against either house of Congress, the President, or the government. This act, opponents contended, transgressed the first amendment to the Constitution forbidding Congress to make any law abridging freedom of speech or of the press. But the Federalists, in power, brushed aside all objections; and under the Sedition Act several Republican writers and publishers were indicted, fined, or imprisoned for criticizing the President and his administration.

These two acts, instead of fastening the grip of the Federalists on the government, laid them open to attacks in the name of American liberty. Republicans interpreted the conduct of the Federalists as revealing their true colors—their liking for arbitrary government. Back in Washington's second administration that kind of "high-toned" government had been displayed when disorders, described as the "Whisky Rebellion," had occurred during efforts to collect an excise tax on whisky in 1794.

On that occasion Washington and Hamilton had called out 13,000 militiamen to overcome a few rioters. In his excitement over the riots, Washington had ascribed them to subversive agitations and had privately expressed his belief that the young "Democratic Societies" should be exterminated.

Shocked by the attitude of the government in that affair, Jefferson had helped to turn Washington and his Federalist advisers away from that aggression against civil liberties. Now, four years later, the passage of the Sedition Act confirmed Jefferson's suspicion that Federalists were resolved to destroy critics by fine and imprisonment, after the fashion of Old World despots.

Adopting underground political tactics, Jefferson wrote an indictment of the Alien and Sedition Acts which was sent quietly to a friend in the state of Kentucky, recently admitted to the Union. On the basis of this document the Kentucky legislature formulated and passed, in 1798, a set of resolutions branding the acts as contrary to the Constitution, as null and void. It declared that, when the federal government exceeded its powers, the states had a right to interpose; and it called upon other states to join in demanding a repeal of the laws in question. Receiving little aid and comfort from other states, the Kentucky legislature then passed, in 1799, a second set of resolutions proclaiming the right of states to nullify "unconstitutional" acts of Congress.

Rejecting the doctrine of nullification as likely to endanger the Union,

James Madison, now affiliated with the Republican party, induced the legislature of Virginia to pass milder resolutions while joining in the protest against the objectionable acts. In fact Jefferson himself later avowed that he had no intention at the time of encouraging action that might lead to a dissolution of the bonds established by the Constitution. Both he and Madison regarded their tactics as only calculated to fan discontent with the Alien and Sedition Acts and weaken the hold of the sponsors, the Federalists, on the nation.

Just how much effect the arguments over the Alien and Sedition Acts had on the voters cannot be determined precisely. Certainly they contributed little or nothing to the popularity of the Federalist party. Nor did they assure an easy triumph for the Republican party in the ensuing election of 1800. In fact, though the political campaign was bitterly waged, the shift of a few votes in New York, where Aaron Burr was especially strong, would have given John Adams a second term as President. Sixty-five votes were cast for Adams, seventy-three for Jefferson, and seventy-three for Burr.

The tie between Jefferson and Burr threw the election into the House of Representatives as provided by the Constitution in such cases. Only with the aid of Federalists in that House was the deadlock resolved in favor of Jefferson. Although Jefferson called his victory a "revolution," the Federalists were still powerful in Congress and he had to walk warily in exercising his powers as Chief Executive.

☆

On March 4, 1801, when John Adams had left the White House in a huff over his defeat, Thomas Jefferson took the oath of office as President. In his inaugural address he spoke softly if positively. Federalists had called him an atheist, a Jacobin, the foe of order and property; but from start to finish he refrained from retaliation in abusive epithets and was conciliatory. We are all Republicans, he said at his inauguration; we are all Federalists; the majority has expressed its will at the polls according to the forms of the Constitution and must be obeyed; for resort to the sword, the parent of despotism, is the only alternative to such obedience. But the minority, he proceeded, has its rights and they must be respected. If any citizen would change our form of government, Jefferson pleaded, let him be heard and let truth combat his error. The rights and liberties guaranteed by the Constitution, he insisted, are to be preserved; the Union is to be strong and the states protected in their rightful powers.

Not even Washington had expressed a greater attachment to the nation and its unity under the Constitution than was displayed on that occasion by the author of the Kentucky Resolutions. Despite his talk about his "revolution," Jefferson made no demand for an overthrow of the financial and foreign policies initiated by Washington and Hamilton.

Jefferson had made several pledges, however, in the name of his party, and they were redeemed. The Sedition Act was allowed to expire; men imprisoned under it were released; and the fines collected were repaid. The tax on whisky, which had stirred farmers to revolt, was repealed. Reductions were made in outlays for the Army, the Navy, and federal officers. Judge Samuel Chase, who had denounced Republicans from the bench, was impeached by the House of Representatives and only the Federalists in the higher court, the Senate, saved him from conviction. The formalities and ceremonials observed by Washington and Adams were modified. Like the British king who delivered his speech from the throne to Parliament, they had read their messages to Congress in person. Jefferson quit the practice and sent his message to the two houses in written form.

While he was operating merely as a critic of the Federalists, Jefferson had adhered to the view that the government of the Union was limited to the exercise of specific powers to be literally, or narrowly, construed. Nevertheless, during his eight years as President he did and approved many things not specifically mentioned in the Constitution, thus taking in fact a broad view of the document.

The Constitution, for instance, did not, in exact words, empower the United States to acquire more territory. Yet Jefferson bought from Napoleon in 1803 the vast Louisiana Territory for $15,000,000, and Congress, on his insistence, sanctioned the purchase. By this single stroke, more than doubling the domain of the United States, Jefferson helped to assure the strength and perpetuity of the Union. Perhaps he accomplished as much in that direction as Washington and Hamilton had achieved by the financial and banking measures that he had once opposed.

The Constitution had said nothing about the power of the federal government to build national highways or canals or improve harbors or found a national university. Nevertheless in Jefferson's first administration Congress appropriated part of the money received from the sale of public lands to the construction of highways into the West. In this way it provided for the building of the Cumberland Road, or national highway, extending from the edge of Maryland through Pennsylvania, Ohio, Indiana, and Illinois, into Missouri. With Jefferson's approval, his Secretary of the Treasury, Albert Gallatin, a statesman of broad outlook, made grand plans for a national network of river, harbor, and canal improvements. Following Washington's example, Jefferson recommended to Congress the creation of a national university. He likewise approved the idea of using surplus revenues of the government to promote the interests of commerce, industry, agriculture, and education, even if a constitutional amendment should be needed to accomplish such national purposes.

In foreign affairs Jefferson continued the general policy framed by Washington; and in his efforts to keep the United States out of the European war he interpreted the Constitution liberally. British naval officers were searching and seizing American merchant ships on the high seas at their pleasure and often carrying off sailors alleged to be British subjects. The French navy was likewise preying on American commerce. From year to year British and French actions grew more and more aggressive until at length nearly all American ships bound to and from Europe were liable to be seized by the one belligerent or the other. In vain did Jefferson assert and insist that American rights on the seas must be observed.

Driven into a dilemma by his resolve to avoid getting into war, Jefferson proposed and Congress approved, in 1807, an embargo forbidding all ships to leave American ports except with the President's permission. By this measure, by cutting off all their American supplies, he thought the British or the French or both might be forced to respect American commercial rights. The Constitution empowered Congress to "regulate" foreign commerce; now Congress had prohibited it altogether on the high seas. Yet this measure failed to bring the British and the French to terms, while it infuriated American merchants and shippers. In response to outcries against it, Congress substituted in 1809 a Non-Intercourse Act directed against Great Britain and France alone. It too was more than a mere "regulation" of commerce but Jefferson supported it in his anxiety to uphold American rights and at the same time keep the United States out of the war.

Notwithstanding the dissatisfaction over his handling of foreign relations, Jefferson could have had a third term if he had so desired. In his second campaign, of 1804, he had carried every state in the Union, except Delaware, Maryland, and Connecticut, against his Federalist opponent, Charles C. Pinckney. If his popularity had somewhat diminished by 1808, it was still very great. Instead of playing upon it, however, Jefferson voluntarily promoted the election of his Secretary of State, James Madison, in whom he had implicit confidence. He declared that two terms were enough; that repeated re-elections of a President might lead to election for life. Thus he set a tradition inimical to a third term for anybody.

☆

Madison was victorious in the campaign and then he had to face the preservation of peace which Jefferson had entrusted to him. But the rise in Congress of a war party, called "War Hawks," led by John C. Calhoun, of South Carolina, and Henry Clay, of Kentucky, both young men of the post-Revolutionary generation, took the issue out of his hands. Some members of the war party were for war on Great Britain; others for war on France; and almost a majority for war on both countries.

Nominally the quarrel with Britain was over her preying on American commerce, her seizures of American sailors, and her support of restless Indians on the northwest frontiers of the United States. In large part war actually grew out of a resolve of Southern politicians to conquer Florida and of Western politicians to subdue and annex Canada. At all events, in June 1812 Congress declared war on Great Britain, and Madison set forth the war aims mainly in commercial terms, saying nothing about either Florida or Canada.

For more than two years the war was waged on land and sea. American sailors and soldiers proved their valor by many exploits—under Oliver Perry on Lake Erie, under Thomas Macdonough on Lake Champlain, under Andrew Jackson at New Orleans, for example. Even so, the invasion of Canada was a failure; whereas the British invaded the United States and applied the torch to public buildings in Washington.

To make matters worse for Madison, the war was decidedly unpopular in the Northeast where, presumably, a war proclaimed in behalf of free commerce would have been welcomed. In the House of Representatives, Daniel Webster, of Massachusetts, denounced the draft of men as unconstitutional. Federalists decried the conflict as merely "Mr. Madison's war." The governor of Connecticut refused to obey the President's call for troops and the Connecticut assembly declared the state to be "free, sovereign and independent." A convention of delegates from various parts of New England, assembled in Hartford in October 1814, adopted resolutions akin in spirit, if not in letter, to those put forth by Kentucky and Virginia in 1798.

In the meantime negotiations for peace with Great Britain were proceeding at Ghent. On Christmas Eve, 1814, a few days before Jackson's victory at New Orleans, the draft of the treaty of peace was signed in Ghent. It contained not a word about British seizure of American sailors, about British preying on American trade, about British searching of American ships, or British support of Indians on the frontier. But when the news of the peace arrived early in 1815, Americans, passing "from gloom to glory," shouted with joy, rang bells, and held holiday parades.

None of the war aims was realized, neither those publicly announced by President Madison nor those unofficially cherished by the "War Hawks." Moreover Madison and his fellow Republicans were in "a sea of troubles" over domestic problems in the aftermath of war. The war had cost a huge sum of money and business was badly deranged. Hamil-

THE UNITED STATES IN 1812

ton's big national debt had been condemned by Republicans; now they confronted a bigger debt. Even the currency was in disorder, the dollar fluctuating violently in value. Manufacturers who had built up industries to furnish the armies with munitions and other supplies clamored for protection against the inrush of cheap British goods. Soon veterans by the thousands were demanding pensions for their services. From day to day the perplexities of the Republicans increased.

In their dilemma the Republicans resorted to the very measures of Alexander Hamilton, which they had so long assailed. His United States Bank had perished when its charter expired in 1811; they established a second United States Bank on the principles of the old one. They funded the scattered government debts into a consolidated debt, larger than the debt they had once condemned. Hamilton had fostered a tariff designed to protect American manufacturers. In 1816 the Republicans passed a tariff measure outstripping in its high protectionism the tariff projects of Washington and Hamilton. Even Jefferson, the champion of agricultural interests, endorsed protectionism, thus joining hands with Calhoun and Clay. In 1819 the first great business panic in the history of modern industrialism burst upon the country, and the Republicans did not know what to do about that.

President Madison closed his second term in 1817 with relief at the thought of turning the office of Chief Executive over to someone else. He proposed James Monroe as his successor and his choice was approved by his party. In the election of 1816 the Republicans had a landslide, the Federalists carrying only three states. Some Federalists had lost ground on account of their opposition to the war. Other Federalists refrained from activity in the campaign in view of the fact that the Republican party had put their program and their principles into effect. For a time the two-party system appeared to be at an end—in the "era of good feeling." Yet a new party was really coming into existence. Monroe was re-elected in 1820 but that was the last act in the short-lived, one-party play.

Three great measures of Monroe's administrations added to the strength of the Union and the feeling of attachment to it. In adopting them Monroe went counter to his former views. He had opposed the ratification of the Constitution in 1788 and had sided with Jefferson in his strict interpretation of that document. But on these three measures Monroe took a broad view of the Constitution—as Jefferson had done on many occasions during his tenure as President. Although he did not renew Jefferson's proposal for a national university, he abandoned his strict constructionism when he had to deal with issues involving the fortunes of the nation.

Among the first problems before President Monroe was that of the Floridas, East and West, which Great Britain had given back to Spain in 1783. Owing to the uncertainties of the Florida boundaries, the United States had some claims to West Florida. Moreover, the swamps of the Floridas were the hiding places of Indian marauders who emerged from time to time to harass American settlements. Ordered by Monroe, after one of these attacks, to pursue a band of Indian raiders to their retreat, General Andrew Jackson marched after them into East Florida, where he did more than fight them; he took possession of the region. Now the Spanish King, who claimed the ownership of this coveted territory, faced what is called in diplomacy a *fait accompli*—an accomplished act— namely, occupation by Americans.

Caught in a jam, the King agreed in 1819 to cede his Florida land to the United States in exchange for not more than $5,000,000, to be paid to American citizens who had damage claims against his government. As Jefferson had done on the constitutional issue, President Monroe simply overlooked the question as to whether the government of the United States had any express power under the Constitution to buy more territory. In this instance "strict construction" was not allowed to interfere with the transaction.

The second outstanding measure of Monroe's administration also involved an interpretation of the Constitution. Under its power to make "all needful rules and regulations" respecting territory belonging to the United States, could Congress lawfully exclude slavery from such territory? That subject was not mentioned in the document, but it was squarely raised in 1818–20 during a dispute over the admission of Missouri to the Union as a slave state. By that time Northern states had abolished slavery within their borders, or had provided for gradual abolition, and anti-slavery sentiment was growing insistent in the country.

Opposition to the admission of another slave state was outspoken in Congress and a deadlock occurred on the issue. After many angry words had been uttered, the standstill was broken by a compromise: Missouri was to be admitted with slavery, and the balance of political power maintained by the admission of Maine as a free state. In addition, as a part of the compromise, slavery was to be prohibited in the rest of the Louisiana Territory north of the line 36° 30′.

On the one side it was claimed that Congress had no authority to prohibit slavery in this territory. On the other, attention was called to the fact that the Northwest Ordinance, adopted in 1787 and ratified by Congress in 1789, had excluded slavery from the Northwest Territory;

so it was argued that Congress could lawfully do this under the Constitution.

While the constitutional point was being argued, President Monroe laid it before members of his Cabinet. They agreed that Congress could prohibit slavery in the territories; and, with their approval, he signed the bill on March 6, 1820, dedicating the major part of the Louisiana Territory to freedom.

Following Washington's example, President Monroe, in 1823, formulated a momentous declaration of foreign policy for the United States—the third notable measure of his administrations. Recently Spain's colonies in the New World had nearly all declared their independence, and President Monroe, like other Americans, was troubled in mind lest European monarchs help the Spanish King in his efforts to recover control over them. From such schemes Great Britain, however, held aloof. British merchants, winning a profitable trade in Latin America, were reluctant to see Spain's commercial monopoly restored. Fully appreciating their situation, the British government proposed to the minister of the United States in London that the two countries join in upholding the independence of the Latin American republics.

On receipt of the news President Monroe turned to Jefferson, Madison, and John Quincy Adams, the Secretary of State, for advice. They all agreed on the desirability of backing up the freedom of the Latin American republics. Jefferson welcomed the assistance of Great Britain in such a project—one so clearly advantageous for the security of the United States in the Western Hemisphere. With the aid of Adams, Monroe framed a message on the question and sent it to Congress in December 1823.

In this message, which was to bear his name in coming times as the Monroe Doctrine, the President made four clear-cut assertions. First, the United States did not propose to interfere with any colonies still owned by European Powers in the New World. Second, any effort on the part of monarchs in Europe "to extend their system to any portion of this hemisphere" would be regarded as "dangerous to our peace and safety." Third, the attempt of a European government to oppress or control colonies that had declared their independence would be viewed as showing "an unfriendly disposition toward the United States."

With reference to a claim to a part of the Pacific coast which the Czar of Russia had lately put forward, Monroe made the fourth assertion: "The American continents . . . are henceforth not to be considered as subjects for future colonization by any European powers." While proclaiming freedom for the Western Hemisphere, however, he informed European governments that in turn the United States would not interfere in what were really only European affairs.

Coupled with Washington's Farewell Address to the nation, the Monroe Doctrine was long a main "cornerstone" of American foreign policy. Thus the last, as well as the first, of the Presidents belonging to the Revolutionary generation fortified the independence of the United States and the security of the Republic.

Chapter 12

EXPANSION TO THE PACIFIC

IT TOOK American people one hundred and seventy-five years to build up and achieve independence for thirteen colonies with about three million inhabitants. In less than one third that span of years seven new states were established in the region immediately westward and occupied by a population larger than that of the whole United States when the census of 1790 was taken. In less than half that number of years five additional states were formed in the Louisiana Territory still further west, Texas was brought into the Union, a vast area to the southwest wrested from Mexico, and California admitted to statehood.

Events in this westward expansion followed one another in no regular order. For example, when the Louisiana Territory was acquired in 1803, Indiana and Illinois, to the east of the Mississippi, had only a few inhabitants. Louisiana and Missouri, in the Louisiana Territory, reached statehood before Michigan. Texas was admitted to the Union three years before Wisconsin; and Wisconsin had been a state only two years when California, on the Pacific coast, became a full-fledged member of the federation. But for the sake of convenience, the expansion to the West may be treated in four stages: settlement of the region between the old seaboard states and the Mississippi; the development of the Louisiana Territory; the push into Oregon; and occupation of the far Southwest.

When independence was won several Eastern states had claims to territory in the region stretching westward to the Mississippi—claims based on royal charters and colonial grants. But by 1786 they had all surrendered to the Union their rights in the territory north of the Ohio. In a short time the territories south of the Ohio were separated from the seaboard claimants—Virginia, North Carolina, South Carolina, and Georgia. Thus the Western lands were cut loose from the overlordship of individual states, put into a national pool, and thrown open for settle-

TERRITORIAL GROWTH OF THE UNITED STATES, 1783–1867

ment to emigrants from all parts of the seaboard region and also from the Old World.

More than this, it was decided that settlers on the Western lands were not to be held permanently under the dominance of the United States Government. They were to be allowed, subject to certain rules, to form governments in their respective territories, draw up constitutions of their own, and at length, as states, join the Union as partners in every respect equal to the thirteen original states. Thus a promise of self-government preceded the great westward migration.

Both in character of settlement and in form of government, therefore, the occupation and management of the region westward to the Mississippi diverged fundamentally from that process in colonial times on the seaboard. The authority in general charge of the operations was at first the old Congress under the Articles of Confederation and then the new government established under the Constitution of 1787. It was an American and a republican government, not a British monarchy located in distant London. No companies chartered by the British Crown, such as the Virginia Company, no great proprietors holding patents from the Crown, such as Lord Baltimore or William Penn, got permanent possession of immense areas in this Western region. Huge blocks of land, it is true, were granted to companies of American citizens; but no company had the right to govern as well as own the district assigned to it, or to hold the district indefinitely as a semifeudal principality. A few American companies which acquired large holdings did assist in outfitting and transporting emigrants to the West; but in the main the work of occupation was effected by individuals, families, and small groups of pioneers, on their own initiative.

The spirit of the new enterprise in land settlement appeared in the Northwest Ordinance, adopted in 1787 by the old Congress under the Articles of Confederation and continued in force by the first Congress under the Constitution. This ordinance applied to the territory north of the Ohio River. Other congressional acts provided for official surveys of the Northwest Territory. By such surveys the region was laid out into townships each six miles square, and each township was subdivided into sections, each containing 640 acres, readily divisible into half sections, quarter sections, and even a smaller acreage. The surveys furnished definite maps and facilitated the location and purchase of lands. At first the price of land was fixed at two dollars an acre, but this was cut in 1820 to one dollar and a quarter.

The Northwest Ordinance itself made provision for temporary territorial government under governors chosen first by the Congress and later by the President of the United States. As soon as there were 5000 free male adults in a particular territory they could establish a local legislature under the supervision of the federal governor. A territorial government so formed consisted of the federal governor, federal judges, a legislative council, and a house of representatives. When a territory acquired 60,000 free residents its people were entitled to a constitution of their own making and to be admitted to the Union "on an equal footing with the original states, in all respects whatever."

The Northwest Ordinance contained more than a plan of government. It stipulated that religious freedom should prevail throughout the region, that the inhabitants should enjoy the right of trial by jury, and that other forms of liberty should be observed. It declared that "schools and the means of education shall forever be encouraged." And this declaration was more than a verbal pledge. Land laws, already passed in connection with the surveys, set aside a section of land in every township to be devoted to the support of schools. A crowning provision of the ordinance, so vital to the growth of liberty, was the article which read: "There shall be neither slavery nor involuntary servitude in the said [Northwest] territory, otherwise than in the punishment of crimes, whereof the party shall have been duly convicted."

Under the generous provisions of the ordinance, pioneers poured into the Northwest Territory. One stream sprang from the South, especially from Virginia, North Carolina, and Kentucky, and flowed into the southern counties of Ohio, Indiana, and Illinois. Other streams sprang from Pennsylvania, New York, and New England. With the westward-moving Americans were mingled newcomers from the Old World—British, Germans, Swiss, and immigrants of other nationalities. Nearly all the families quickly settled down to tilling lands which they had bought either outright or on installments. They built log cabins and cottages, cleared the forests, and prepared fields for crops.

Clues to the swiftness of this movement and the scale of the settlement can be gleaned from the following table showing the dates on which states were admitted to the Union, and the population in the year 1820:

Admission to Union	Population 1820
1803—Ohio	581,400
1816—Indiana	147,100
1818—Illinois	55,200
1837—Michigan	8,800
1848—Wisconsin	

The occupation of the Western territory south of the Ohio River differed in several respects from that of the Northwest. Long before the close of the eighteenth century the Kentucky region of western Virginia was dotted with settlements. By 1792 it had more inhabitants than either Delaware or Rhode Island. Separating itself from Virginia in that year, Kentucky entered the Union as an equal state, with the full consent of Virginia. The Tennessee region, to which North Carolina had claims lasting from the colonial era, was ceded to the Union by the parent state; and for a little while was governed as a territory of the United States. But in 1795, when a census showed that Tennessee had more than 60,000 inhabitants, a local constitution was drafted and the following year, in 1796, Tennessee became a state in the Union.

In regions surrendered by South Carolina and Georgia the remainder of the Southern land was organized under the acts of Congress as a territory of the United States. In 1817 this territory was divided. The western part was admitted to the Union as the state of Mississippi. The eastern part, after two years of territorial status, was given statehood as Alabama.

By 1819 all the divisions of the territory between the original seaboard states and the Mississippi River, except the districts of Michigan and Wisconsin in the north central part, had become equal partners in the Union, as states with their own constitutions. To the list was added, in 1845, the state of Florida in territory acquired from Spain.

In the meantime expansion beyond the Mississippi was under way. Shortly after Jefferson was inaugurated President in 1801 news reached him that Spain had ceded to France the huge Louisiana Territory extending from the Mississippi River to the Far West. American pioneers over the Appalachians now feared that Napoleon, the head of the French government, would close New Orleans to their shipment of grain and other farm produce by water to the Eastern seaboard and to the Old World. So they urged Jefferson to prevent that misfortune, and he sent a special agent to France with a commission to buy New Orleans and West Florida if possible.

Before the agent arrived Napoleon had concluded that he might lose his American possessions in a war with Great Britain, and had informed the American minister at Paris that he would sell the whole territory to the United States for $15,000,000, from which certain American claims against France could be deducted. Surprised at the size of the territory offered so cheaply, Jefferson at first hesitated. But at length the purchase was completed in 1803, despite laments from Federalists on the Atlantic coast. Thus at one stroke and without warfare the territory of the United States was more than doubled, though the boundaries of the Louisiana Purchase were vague.

To collect information on the new territory, Jefferson sponsored an expedition headed by Meriwether Lewis and William Clark to explore it, find an overland route to the Pacific, and report on its resources. Under their leadership a party of hardy adventurers was formed near St. Louis. Special boats were built and a traveling outfit was assembled. On May 14, 1804, they set out on the Missouri River for the Northwest. A year later they reached the great falls of the Missouri in Montana. From that point they made their hazardous way across the mountains, with the guidance in part of an Indian woman named Sacajawea. Over the mountains they arrived at the headwaters of the Columbia River, where they built new boats, embarked on the river, and floated swiftly to the Pacific Ocean, reaching their goal in November 1805.

Having blazed the way, the explorers were able to make the return trip more quickly, and in less than a year they were safely back at St. Louis, having completed a long and dangerous journey of about eight thousand miles in two years and four months. From the records kept by Lewis and Clark a report was soon compiled and published. As a result Americans who felt cramped in the East had at their command considerable knowledge of the newest West and could make plans for going where there was more elbow room.

In the same year that Lewis and Clark started from St. Louis on their journey, Zebulon Pike, leading another party, explored the headwaters of the Mississippi. When Pike had finished that task he was sent on an expedition into the region west and south of St. Louis. He kept on his way until he came to the mountain now known as Pike's Peak in the Rockies. Shortly afterward he turned south and journeyed in that direction until he reached the Rio Grande. Finding himself then in territory occupied by Spaniards, Pike retraced his steps. But in 1810 he published reports on the regions he had covered and persons inclined to adventure in the Southwest thus had access to more information of many kinds about that frontier.

At the time of the Louisiana Purchase the white population of the territory was estimated at figures running from 50,000 to 80,000. The great majority of the inhabitants were French—mainly descendants of the French pioneers who had long before settled at important trading centers, particularly at St. Louis and New Orleans, under the King of France. Among them were many Spanish residents, who had moved up from Spanish territories or from Spain itself, after Louisiana had been turned over to the Spanish King in 1763, at the close of the Seven Years' War. Here and there were also Americans who had crossed the Mississippi even while the west bank was under a foreign flag.

To all the inhabitants of the Louisiana Territory, however, were guaranteed by the treaty of cession "all the rights, advantages, and immunities of citizens of the United States." By act of Congress the territory was

EXPLORATIONS OF LEWIS AND CLARK AND ZEBULON PIKE IN THE FAR WEST divided into two districts later known as the territory of Louisiana and the territory of Missouri.

The more thickly populated region to the south was granted statehood as Louisiana in 1812. As Americans poured across the river into the Missouri district to the north, they began to seek admission to the Union. But a national agitation over slavery delayed admission. In 1819 there were twenty-two states in the Union—half of them slave states and half committed to freedom. If Missouri came in with slavery the balance of power in the Senate of the United States would be upset.

In the North, anti-slavery sentiment was growing. Slavery had been abolished or was rapidly on the way to extinction in all the original states north of Delaware. Ohio, Indiana, and Illinois were free states as required by the Northwest Ordinance. In the House of Representatives, based on population, counting three fifths of the slaves, the strength of the free states was rapidly increasing.

On the other hand, with the spread of cotton planting, pro-slavery sentiment was becoming stronger in the South. Old Southern statesmen, such as Washington, Jefferson, and George Mason, had looked upon slavery as an evil and hoped that in time it could be uprooted. But a new generation of Southerners was beginning to regard slavery as good for both whites and blacks, and to speak of it as a permanent institution to be extended wherever climate and soil were suitable. In these circumstances the admission of Missouri as a slave state was hotly opposed in Congress by Northern men and championed with no less heat by Southern men.

In the end, a major compromise was reached. Under a congressional act of 1820 Missouri was admitted with slavery; but it was balanced by the admission of Maine, a free state, formerly a part of Massachusetts, now given a separate status by mutual consent. Accompanying this settlement was another compromise destined to be the subject of political agitation in years to come. Slavery was prohibited "forever" in all the territory ceded by France to the United States, under the name of Louisiana, lying north of 36° 30′ north latitude, except Missouri. As to slavery in the rest of that territory, nothing was said in the law; silence merely gave consent to its existence in that region.

Another balancing act was performed in 1836. The territory of Arkansas, definitely laid out at the time of the Missouri Compromise, had been filling up with pioneers, many of them planters with their slaves, and others working farmers. By 1836 the Arkansas settlers numbered more than 47,000 and, in the customary way of Americans from the early days of colonization on the seaboard, they demanded self-government. Acceding to their demand, Congress admitted Arkansas to the Union as a slave state, with the provision that the sixteenth section of land in every township be set aside for the support of schools. Far to the northeast, the people of Michigan, with equal zeal, were putting forth their claims to greater autonomy; and the following year, 1837, they entered the Union as a free state. The voting power of slave-owning planters in the Louisiana Territory was thus offset by the voting power of free farmers in the Northwest Territory.

Long before Arkansas and Michigan were "balanced" in the Union, farmers from New England, New York, Ohio, and other Eastern states were moving in long wagon trains into the region known as Iowa. There they staked out for themselves freehold farms in every direction. Three prosperous trading centers sprang up on the Mississippi: Dubuque, Davenport, and Burlington. Academies and colleges were established. In 1846 Iowa won self-government as the fourth state to be erected in the Louisiana Territory, balancing Florida (1845). The fifth state to be carved out of Jefferson's great land purchase was Minnesota, admitted in 1858, without slavery.

Meanwhile, beyond the extreme westerly limits of the Louisiana Purchase—in the Oregon country—fur traders, missionaries, and farmers from the East were building a new free colony, in the American style. In 1843 Oregon settlers, feeling the need of mutual aid, held a meeting at Champoeg and, after listening to a Fourth of July oration, drew up a compact for governing themselves "until such time as the United States of America extend their jurisdiction over us."

As a matter of fact the United States Government had been in trouble over Oregon and was still in trouble. The northern boundary of the country was vague. Under the obscure terms of the Louisiana Purchase and rights of exploration, the United States claimed all the territory up to the line of 54° 40' north latitude—to the borders of the Russian territory of Alaska. But that claim was stoutly contested by the government of Great Britain, and in 1818 the two governments made a kind of truce providing for temporary joint occupation. This agreement was renewed in 1827 for an indefinite period. Yet it was unsatisfactory to British as well as American fur traders; and settlers insisted that an end be put to joint occupation by drawing a definite boundary line between the British and the American parts.

For years neither side would surrender to this demand. In the presidential campaign of 1844 the Democrats declared for "Fifty-four Forty or Fight"; that is, announced that they would, if necessary, wage war rather than give up the old claim. No fighting ensued, however. The victorious candidate of the Democrats, James K. Polk, had not been long in the office of President when he made, in 1846, a treaty with Great

Britain fixing the Oregon boundary at the forty-ninth parallel, not the fifty-fourth. In 1859 the southern part of the Oregon country, the most thickly settled, was admitted to the Union as a state. Many other sections in that territory were also filling up with settlers, and meanwhile the United States had entered upon the fourth phase of its westward expansion—into the far Southwest.

☆

Under the terms of the purchase from France the boundaries of the Louisiana Territory in the Southwest were also indefinite. At first the United States, on good grounds as later evidence proved, claimed that the boundary ran from near the mouth of the Rio Grande on the Gulf of Mexico in a northerly direction along the course of that river to about the forty-second parallel of north latitude, and thence west to the Pacific Ocean. Spain rejected this claim as encroaching upon her territory, and after long negotiations the boundary was fixed, in 1819, in such a way as to cut off a part of the Louisiana Territory in the Southwest.

The line as then defined started on the gulf at the western border of the state of Louisiana, ran northward along that border, and thence northwesterly and westerly in such a fashion as to leave the Texas country and adjoining regions in the hands of Spain. It was in connection with this settlement of 1819 that the Spanish King ceded to the United States all his claims to the territory east of the Mississippi, known as East and West Florida.

For years before the signing of the treaty of 1819 that established the new boundary for the Louisiana Territory, Spain had been involved in struggles with revolutionists in Mexico; and two years later, in 1821, the last Spanish viceroy to Mexico was forced to recognize the independence of that country. Consequently it was the republic of Mexico, now in the disorders of revolution, with which the United States had to deal in the Southwest.

From the border of Louisiana to the Pacific, especially in the region later known as New Mexico and California, Spanish settlements and missions had been established. But the Southwest as a whole was sparsely settled. In 1821 it was estimated that, excluding the Indians, there were about 4000 Mexicans or Spanish in the Texas country, not more than 3000 or 4000 in Upper California, and perhaps 15,000 or 20,000 in the vast intervening area. The size of the Indian population was unknown, but, unlike that of Mexico proper, it was small and thinly dispersed. In other words, the great Southwest was mostly unoccupied and there were no signs that colonists from Mexico, owner of the territory, would soon, if ever, people that region.

To encourage the settlement of this territory by Americans and other alien immigrants, the government of Mexico granted large blocks of land to contractors who would bring in colonists. In 1820, for example, it arranged with Moses Austin, of Connecticut, to found an American settlement near Bexar, in Texas, and the undertaking was carried out by his son, Stephen F. Austin. By 1830 at least 20,000 American farmers, planters, and traders had established themselves in Texas and more were on the way. Then, frightened by the deluge, Mexico abandoned the policy of granting land to aliens, declared invalid many grants already in effect, abolished slavery, and otherwise sought to check immigration.

Besides being futile, these actions irritated the Americans already in Texas and ensuing conflicts culminated in an American revolt in 1836. The Mexican army sent to quell the rebels was defeated by American forces under General Sam Houston; and Santa Ana, the Mexican general, was taken prisoner. Texas was now in effect an independent country.

Having achieved their independence, Texans organized a government of their own and sought admission to the United States as a slave state. Owing to the strength of the anti-slavery opinion in the North and in the House of Representatives, admission was long postponed. Andrew Jackson was sympathetic with the Texan appeal but he did not push the matter. Nor did his successor, Martin Van Buren, who was at heart opposed to slavery.

But when John Tyler became President on the death of William H. Harrison in 1841 the outlook for the Texans improved. Yet even Tyler, a pro-slavery man from Virginia, moved slowly in the affair. At last in 1844, near the end of his term, a treaty of annexation was concluded with Texas, only to be rejected in the Senate where the two-thirds vote for ratification could not be mustered.

In their political campaign of that year the Democrats joined with the Oregon slogan, "Fifty-four Forty or Fight," another slogan, "The Reannexation of Texas." Under these battle cries they were successful in the election. Tyler and his supporters now took a new course. Before the new President, James K. Polk, was inaugurated, they gave up the idea of a treaty and in February 1845 Congress adopted, by a simple majority vote, a resolution admitting Texas to the Union.

Texas was in the Union but what was its southwestern boundary? Texans claimed that it was the Rio Grande. Mexicans insisted that it was the Nueces River. President Polk ordered American troops under General Zachary Taylor to cross the Nueces and hold the disputed territory. Soon they were attacked by Mexican forces and President Polk responded by declaring that war had begun "by act of Mexico." With the support of Congress he carried it forward. While General Taylor drove southward into Mexico an expedition, sent by sea and overland under General

Winfield Scott, captured Mexico City; and Americans on the Pacific coast, with aid from American naval commanders, raised the Stars and Stripes in California.

In February 1848, Mexico gave up the unequal fight. New Mexico, Arizona, California, and other districts were ceded to the victor. To this huge domain the United States, by treaty with Mexico five years later, added a small strip known as the Gadsden Purchase in the Gila Valley along the southern border of Arizona. The enormous region between Texas and California, bounded on the north by the Oregon country, was soon divided into two organized territories, Utah and New Mexico, clearing the way for occupation.

Long before war broke out between the United States and Mexico in 1846, a migration of Americans to California had started. For many years shipmasters and merchants from the Atlantic seaboard had been sailing around Cape Horn, visiting California, and trading pots, pans, shoes, and other manufactures with Spanish owners of great estates and with trappers for hides, furs, and other raw materials. News of the mild climate, the fertile soil, and the resources of the region attracted other fortune hunters. By 1830 a trail was opened to Los Angeles from Independence, Missouri, by way of Santa Fé. In 1844 John C. Frémont, intrepid Western explorer, went over the mountains into Sacramento Valley. By 1846 at least one fifth of the people in the little town of San Francisco were citizens of the United States; and Americans were taking part in the quarrels between the Mexican governor of the province and his distant superiors in Mexico City. Trouble was already brewing and had there been no war with Mexico the American colonization of California would have become ominous to its Mexican owners.

In fact the government of the United States already had an eye on the rich prize of California. As early as 1845 the Secretary of State in Washington secretly informed an American agent in Monterey that he could count on help in case difficulties occurred. The Secretary told him that the United States would not foment a revolution there, but it would protect Californians if they revolted against Mexico. The next year some Americans in upper California flung out a flag on which was painted a bear, and began to shout for independence. The Bear Flag movement was quickly submerged when the war with Mexico opened; but Frémont, with the aid of Commodore John Sloat, Commodore Robert Stockton, and General Stephen Kearny, clinched American possession of the whole region. On July 7, 1846, Commodore Sloat raised the American flag over Monterey and proclaimed the annexation of California to the United States.

The war with Mexico had just closed in 1848 when gold was discovered at Sutter's Mill in the Sacramento Valley, and the gold rush to California began—along the overland trails, around Cape Horn, and by way of the Isthmus of Panama. Within two years, it was estimated, about 100,000 immigrants from all parts of the United States and the world had crowded into the gold regions and neighboring towns. With prospective miners were associated merchants, farmers, doctors, teachers, mechanics, lawyers, and laborers, all seeking good luck in the latest Eldorado.

For the future of California the character of the immigrants was decisive. Planters with droves of slaves were not to occupy the territory and add another slave state to the Union. Without waiting for action by Congress, Californians held a convention in 1849, drafted a constitution, put a prohibition on slavery, and demanded statehood. That was a shock to the pro-slavery politicians in the South and the East, but as a part of a general compromise reached by Congress in 1850 California was admitted to the Union as a free state.

The territorial settlement at the close of the Mexican War and the rapid progress of California in population and wealth affected the career of one of the most divergent groups in the whole story of American pioneering. This was the Mormon colony in Utah. The Mormon sect had started on its course under the leadership of Joseph Smith, of New York, in 1830, and had been pushed from place to place by hostile neighbors before it settled finally in Utah. Its members had tried living in Missouri. From Missouri they moved to Illinois. Having now adopted the practice of polygamy, or "plural marriage," and given it an elaborate religious sanction, the Mormons seemed to multiply their enemies on every hand. When Brigham Young became their second leader, they decided to go to some remote region where they might live and work in their own fashion with no interference from outsiders. After inquiring about the distant West, Young selected a spot so far away and so arid, he supposed, as to invite few if any intruders; and in 1847 he led his flock to the Salt Lake Valley.

By hard labor and efficient management, the Mormons in Utah made that desert blossom like a rose, as Young had said they would, and built up a prosperous society. Their freedom in the wilds of the West was, nevertheless, soon curtailed. In organizing the territory of Utah the government of the United States brought them under its control; and the gold rush to California over the trail running through Salt Lake City introduced "foreigners" and the lure of gold into their midst. Moreover, many Gentiles insisted on settling down in Utah. Thus the Mormons' longed-for escape from the difficulties of relations with other people proved to be no escape at all. They were destined to be merged in the great Union as the tide of immigration rolled westward toward the Pacific.

Chapter 13

THE INDUSTRIAL REVOLUTION

THE WESTERN SETTLEMENT—from the Appalachians to the Mississippi, beyond the Mississippi, and to the Far West—had great repercussions in the politics and economy of the original thirteen states based on the British colonies. The West broke the Eastern monopoly over the choice of candidates for the presidency of the United States and assumed the right to have its share in making party platforms. The West also affected the economy of the East in both its commercial and planting aspects. It opened more domestic markets for seaboard merchants, enlarged their export business, augmented the demand for capital to invest in lands and industries, and created new demands for manufactured goods. Its spreading plantations in the Southwest brought severe competition to the planters in Virginia, the Carolinas, and Georgia as producers of cotton and other staples.

On the other hand an economic revolution in the East had immense repercussions in the West. This was the Industrial Revolution brought about by the widespread use of thousands upon thousands of new inventions, major and minor, between Washington's inauguration in 1789 and the outbreak of fighting between the North and the South in 1861. Through it, the methods of manufacture, transportation, mining, communication and farming handed down from colonial times were drastically transformed. So were the historic patterns of American life, and the nation's outlook.

One of the most important features of the Industrial Revolution was the freeing of Americans from their age-old bondage to the small amount of power that could be developed by the straining muscles of humans and domesticated animals, supplemented by the use of uncertain winds in windmills and fluctuating streams to turn water wheels. With the successful manufacture and sale of steam engines in large numbers, the amount and reliability of the power available in the United States could at last rise to hitherto undreamed of heights.

If this power were to be fully utilized, however, it would be necessary to effect a second release—from the restrictions on output historically imposed by the very limited supply of skilled artisans available for making things. Eli Whitney showed how this could be accomplished in completing a contract made in 1798 with the United States Government for the manufacture of several thousand stands of arms. When he went to work on this project, it was customary for each craftsman in a gun plant to perform a whole series of operations, largely by eye, which yielded parts so varied in size as to make their assembly a laborious process of cutting and fitting, calling for still more judgment and dexterity. Whitney substantially reduced the range of tasks assigned to any one individual, thus diminishing the amount of skill required, then perfected equipment that increased the accuracy of what was being done until parts were uniform enough in dimensions to go together without effort. They were, in short, "interchangeable" between guns. As the movement for dividing manufacturing into smaller, simpler, more repetitive bits, and producing genuinely "interchangeable parts" spread from industry to industry, the rank and file of relatively untrained Americans could find places in the nation's factories.

With historic limitations on the availability of power and skill overcome, and the perfection of machines far surpassing in endurance, speed, and dexterity human fingers, a record-breaking upsurge in production became feasible. In 1807 only fifteen cotton mills existed in the United States and they were operating only 8000 spindles. Four years later the number of mills had increased to eighty-seven and the number of spindles to 80,000. Within four years, more than 500,000 spindles were whirring under the watchful eyes of 76,000 tenders, becoming known as "industrial workers."

When the eighth census was taken in 1860, the leading commodities used for food, clothing, and shelter had been caught up in the Industrial Revolution with astounding results in output. For the year ended June 1, 1860, the total value of machine and hand manufactures, including fisheries and mining, and excluding very small shops, was placed at $1,900,000,000, nearly twice the output of 1850 and more than four times the total national wealth in 1787.

In order of respective values of output the following commodities were highest on the list: flour and meal, cotton goods, lumber, boots and shoes, leather, clothing, woolen goods, machinery, steam engines, etc., books, newspapers, sugar, spiritous liquors, cabinet furniture, bar and other rolled iron, malt liquors, agricultural implements, paper, soap, and candles. The very list of articles and amounts of each exhibited the advance Americans had made on the road to the manufacturing independence foreshadowed in colonial times.

America was ceasing to be a mere raw-material country for manufacturing nations in the Old World. Census takers of 1860 reported that 1,385,000 persons were employed in American manufacturing establishments and enterprises; they estimated that, counting the dependents of these persons, about one sixth of the whole population was directly supported by manufactures. Adding to this number all the persons engaged in the production of raw materials for manufacturing and in the distribution of manufactured goods—capitalists, transportation workers, merchants, and clerks, for instance—the census reporters declared: "It is safe to assume, then, that one third of the whole population is supported, directly or indirectly, by manufacturing industry. . . . The nation seemed speedily approaching a period of complete independence in respect to the products of skilled labor."

A mechanical revolution in the carriage of goods and passengers by water and land aided the flow of commodities to and from plants. While from colonial days Americans had had little difficulty building rafts and barges to float downstream, returning against the current had been so hard that many boatmen, especially on the Mississippi, went downstream in their craft, disposed of the same, and returned home by land. The steamboat, with power enough to paddle in both directions, changed this awkward pattern of commerce by opening many rivers to effective traffic in both directions. Robert Fulton showed the way when his steamboat, the *Clermont*, made a successful trip from New York City up the Hudson to Albany, and return. In 1819 an American sailing ship, equipped with auxiliary steam power, crossed the Atlantic, giving the country's seamen for the first time release from bondage to the vagaries of the wind in navigating the high seas. By that time steamships were plying the coastal waters of the eastern seaboard, the navigable streams of the Mississippi River system, and the Great Lakes. Between 1840 and 1850 the tonnage on lakes, rivers, and coastal waters more than doubled. Already it was possible to travel from New York to California either all the way by steamer via Cape Horn, or mainly by steamer over a shorter route involving a brief trip by land across the narrow Isthmus of Panama. In 1829 the number of steamboats on the Mississippi system was 200; in 1836 it was 240.

The Erie Canal, establishing water connections between New York City and the Great Lakes in 1825, and the Pennsylvania Canal to the West, completed in 1834, had scarcely started the promotion of rapid and long-distance transportation when they were challenged by the railway, which completely emancipated the carriage of passengers and freight from bondage to watercourses. Before the Pennsylvania Canal was finished, steam trains were running between Charleston and Hamburg, South Carolina, and the railway era had dawned.

Soon there were railway connections between the chief cities of the Northern seaboard. By 1860 trains were running regularly between Baltimore, Philadelphia, New York, and Boston; those cities were linked by rail with Cleveland, Cincinnati, Chicago, and St. Louis. Meanwhile the chief cities of the South were joined by railways, and connections were established between them and the Northern network. The time of travel for passengers had been cut from weeks to days and the cost of carrying freight from dollars to cents per ton-mile.

In the wake of the mechanical revolution followed a rapid growth of population in old cities and the appearance of new cities, even in the Western wildernesses. In 1790 only five towns—Boston, New York, Philadelphia, Baltimore, and Charleston—had more than 8000 inhabitants each and their combined population was under 135,000, a little above three per cent of the total population of the United States. Thirty years later there were thirteen communities having 8000 inhabitants or more, with a combined population of almost 500,000. New York alone in 1830 had as many people as all the five towns of 1790 put together; and in 1860 the population of New York, including surrounding districts later drawn under its jurisdiction, had passed the 1,000,000 mark.

In the eight industrial states of the seaboard—from Massachusetts to Maryland, inclusive—there were in 1840 eleven cities with over 20,000 inhabitants; by 1860 the number of cities in that class had increased to twenty-four; and the twenty-four had more than twenty-seven per cent of the total population of the eight states. In 1840 nine towns to the west of the mountains had a combined population of about 150,000— Pittsburgh, Cincinnati, Louisville, Chicago, St. Louis, Milwaukee, Detroit, Cleveland, and Buffalo; within twenty years their aggregate population had risen to about 800,000.

To the factories and shops in the cities moved a steady procession of young people from American farms and small towns. In New England it was led by the daughters of farmers in the neighborhood of the spinning mills, who had been taught that it was their moral and patriotic duty to be as useful as possible in such industries. Indeed to a large extent young women "manned" the first textile mills of that section. Wherever machine industries appeared men and women from the rural regions flocked to them in search of work; and the number of "mill hands" was swelled by child laborers—socially an uprooting phase of the new production methods.

In the growth of manufacturing centers, as in the settlement of the West, immigrants from the Old World became factors of increasing importance. The Industrial Revolution was in reality a new spur to immigration and its effects in this relation were soon manifest in the shipping records. Between 1820 and 1860 more than 5,000,000 alien passengers arrived at the ports of the United States on ships from foreign countries. In 1820 they numbered 8385; in 1850, 310,004; in 1854, 427,833. This inflow of labor forces was stimulated by steamship companies, by employers of labor seeking a plentiful supply to keep wages as low as possible, as well as by other influences within the United States and in the lands of the emigrants.

Reckoning the immigrants of the period by economic classes, the most numerous were as follows:

Laborers	872,000
Farmers	764,000
Mechanics	407,000
Merchants	231,800
Miners	39,900
Textile workers	11,500

In the list of callings and occupations that classified other immigrants who entered the country between 1820 and 1860, the census reported: mariners, shoemakers, tailors, milliners, actors, clergymen, lawyers, clerks, physicians, engineers, artists, teachers, musicians, printers, painters, masons, hatters, millers, butchers, bakers, and servants.

More than twenty countries were recorded as supplying quotas of immigrants during those forty-one years of American expansion. The United Kingdom furnished the largest of all, 2,750,000, of whom 967,000 came from Ireland. Germany stood next with 1,486,000; France third with 208,000; British America fourth, with 117,000. Among the other countries represented were Spain, Prussia, Norway, Sweden, Poland, Italy, China, Mexico and other Latin American nations. To the population of the United States—in 1790 about three-fourths British in origin—were thus added national strains more diverse in origins, languages, and customs.

Although thousands of aliens moved into the West seeking farms to own and till, other thousands stayed in the rising industrial towns on the seaboard and furnished skill, enterprise, and labor for manufacturing, transportation, and commerce. If George Washington could have journeyed again from Virginia northward in 1860, as he had done in 1789 by carriage and on horse, he would scarcely have known the land to whose independence he had dedicated his talents.

Apart from the farmers and great landed proprietors in 1790, the chief economic class among the owners of property had been the merchants who handled exports and imports and interstate commerce. After the Industrial Revolution got under way the role of manufacturers was magnified in American society. Often, if not generally, at first, the manufacturer who assembled machinery and workers for industries came from the old class of mechanics and craftsmen. Frequently he developed his little hand labor shop into a factory, using machines and steam power. Sometimes, like Samuel Slater in Rhode Island, he began anew by building a great mill, frequently with the financial aid of merchants who had capital to invest.

As opportunities for manufacturing multiplied, individual enterprisers, finding their own resources inadequate, banded together in corporations to raise larger capital. These concerns sold stock to the public and borrowed money from banks. Long before 1850 corporations had become numerous and powerful in every branch of industry, transportation, and commerce.

As industries expanded in size and number, manufacturers became more closely associated with inventors engaged in devising new machines and processes and with capitalists seeking opportunities for profitable investment. In the early days of the factory system manufacturers usually managed their own plants, aided by foremen; but with the rise of corporations they often turned this responsibility over to deputies. Out of the varied development of machine economy six groups of enterprisers emerged; manufacturers, specialized inventors, industrial bankers, capitalists pure and simple, corporation lawyers, and industrial managers.

For building and operating machine industries large bodies of skilled and unskilled workers were necessary. From whatever source they came industrial workers faced a situation relatively new to American experience.

In the handicraft economy of earlier times, manufacturing was carried on extensively in connection with agriculture, in the households and in small outside shops; and the workers were not solely dependent upon the sale of sheer labor power for a livelihood. Furthermore, as owners of their tools and their time, they had direct control over their hours of labor and working conditions, onerous as those might be. Even master mechanics who lived in towns, and worked apart from the land, were likewise owners of their tools and shops; and their employees were often apprentices who expected in due time to be their own masters.

Under the new machine economy, on the other hand, few workers personally owned their tools and implements of production; nor, in the nature of things, could any large proportion of them look forward confidently to becoming mill owners. Their wages, hours of labor per day, and even employment on any terms were largely or wholly beyond their control—in the hands of employers, subject to the invisible but imperious conditions of the market for the manufactures produced by capital and labor.

From the point of view of labor and its prospects, therefore, a striking feature of the Industrial Revolution was the immense increase in the proportion of workers dependent wholly upon wages for their subsistence and upon the fluctuations in the market for employment. In former days, on account of the abundance of land open for settlement on easy terms, industrious farm workers including indentured servants had good prospects of acquiring farms of their own. Labor was arduous on the land but families that tilled it could usually count on having some food, clothing, and shelter in the worst of times.

In a different situation were workers connected with machine industries. Thousands of them rose, it is true, into the employing and professional classes, owing to economic opportunities and the fluidity of American society. But the vast majority of them were destined to remain wage workers throughout their lives, and to be subject to the vicissitudes of the panics and depressions which afflicted machine industries. Not only did this destiny present a strange problem to individual men and women in the disruption of the old family economy. It brought to the nation unprecedented problems in class relations and in public policies.

As a result of the Industrial Revolution, a new conflict over the balance of power took form. From the early days of colonization freehold farmers had clashed with seaboard landlords, merchants, and moneylenders. They had struggled to get power, first in the colonial and then in the state legislatures. They had constituted a substantial part of the opposition to the adoption of the Constitution and had rallied in politics to the support of the Republican party under the leadership of Jefferson. Now wage workers in machine industries by the thousands surged into the political arena and began to form organizations for the promotion of their interests.

In large numbers they flocked to the party of Jacksonian democracy, although it was largely a farmers' party. But their interests did not exactly coincide with agrarian interests. They had needs, demands, and methods of their own. Crowded together, as they were, in cities, they could easily create associations of their own to voice their interests and bring pressure to bear on employers, politicians, and on society in general, for the redress of their grievances real or alleged.

The associations organized by or for industrial workers after the rise of machine industries were numerous and varied in nature and purposes. But the most persistent type was the trade union. Between the end of the eighteenth century and the middle of the nineteenth century the trade-union movement went through four rather definite stages, as to forms of organization.

The first stage was the creation of local unions in single crafts or trades, for the purpose of influencing wages and the length of the working day. As early as 1792 the shoemakers of Philadelphia formed a union. Two years later the printers of New York and Philadelphia organized typographical societies. By the end of Jackson's second administration in 1837 workers in the leading trades of Boston, New York, Philadelphia, Baltimore, and several other towns had established local unions. Among them were unions of bookbinders, machinists, ironworkers, hatmakers, jewelers, type founders, glassmakers, millwrights, ship joiners, furriers, leather dressers, shoemakers, printers, boilermakers, loom weavers, and plumbers.

As local unions in single trades multiplied they showed a tendency to draw together in their respective cities, and this marked the second phase of their evolution. New York led off with the establishment of a central or city trades union, a union of trades, in 1833. Within five years there were similar city organizations in Baltimore, Philadelphia, Boston, Newark, Albany, Troy, and Pittsburgh, and also in the Western towns of Cincinnati and Louisville.

During these very years trade unionism entered the third stage in its development: the federation of local craft unions in a national association representing a single trade, an industry, or a craft. For this movement the journeymen cordwainers, or shoe and leather workers, were pathbreakers. In March 1836 they held a convention in New York City, composed of delegates from cordwainers' unions in New York, New Haven, Brooklyn, Newark, Paterson, Philadelphia, Washington, and several other places. Then and there they formed a constitution for the National Co-operative Association of Journeymen Cordwainers and framed a platform pledging mutual assistance. In the same year unionist printers, after many exchanges of letters, sent delegates to a general convention in Washington and entered into a loose national federation. Other trades followed these examples, with ups and downs in fortune, until within twenty years each of the principal crafts had a national organization of some kind.

The fourth step in the organization of labor—the union of all unions in a national federation—was the most difficult of all and was not permanently effected until more than fifty years after the cordwainers had formed their national craft federation in 1836. But the project had been planned in the early stages of trade-union development and efforts had been made to realize it as soon as local unionism had gained its first strength.

An experiment in general organization was attempted in New England in 1831, with the formation of the New England Association of Farmers, Mechanics, and Other Working Men. Although some unionists were represented in its meetings, the association was as much concerned with politics and social reforms as with hours, wages, and working conditions. Within three years it went to pieces.

A stronger effort at national federation on a unionist basis in respect of membership was made in 1834 at a convention of delegates from trades unions held in New York City. After extended debates the National Trades Union was formed under a constitution which declared its purposes to be moral, intellectual, and pecuniary. This national union held conventions in 1835 and 1836 and then collapsed in the panic of 1837. The foundations for such a national union of unions had not yet been securely laid and nearly thirty years were to pass before another undertaking of the kind was even attempted.

☆

Amid the uprush of factories and cities, the multiplication of wage workers, the relative decline of handicraft production, and the growth of trade unions, a thoroughly dislocating force broke into the economy of the nation. That was the periodical panic followed by a widespread industrial collapse. Such crises had often occurred in the past but as long as the overwhelming majority of the people tilled the soil for a livelihood depressions did not create destitution for the masses. Now, however, hundreds of thousands of people were concentrated in great industrial centers and divorced from the soil with its food-giving crops, its raw materials for clothing and shelter, and its enduring opportunities for productive employment. Now a breakdown in industry and business enterprise meant, for such urbanized workers, unemployment, no wages, actual lack of the vital necessities—food, clothing, and shelter.

The first terrific smash in the machine-production age occurred in 1819; another in 1829; the third and most severe in the history of the United States up to that date opened in 1837 and lasted for about five years. A brief recovery was only a prelude to a fourth collapse in 1847. Ten years later, in 1857, another depression settled over the nation and almost crushed the labor movement entirely.

Even in the intervals called prosperous, poverty and distress haunted the working-class districts of the great cities. Famines and misery had marked the course of all history in the Old World and the Orient, but slaves and serfs had usually had some shelter and some bread even in hard times. There had been poverty in colonial times in America and in the early days of the Republic, but it had been widely dispersed and its evils mitigated in considerable measure by charity and poor relief.

Whether the Industrial Revolution increased the relative amount of poverty or not, it made the position of mere wage workers more precarious than that of the serf or the farmer; and it concentrated poverty-stricken persons in urban masses so large that only the blind could fail to see their plight. Such poverty, on a scale so enormous and so obtruding, so contrasted in the cities with flaunting riches, was a new thing; and it aroused consternation among American citizens who had social sympathies and cared about the security of the Republic. Their interest was heightened by the agitations and protests of labor leaders, charity workers, and political reformers.

In a land where the objectives of society and government were declared to be life, liberty, equality, the pursuit of happiness, and the general welfare, what was to be done about such poverty? Were the institutions and ideas derived from the great Revolutionary age of the Republic sufficient to meet the new problems? Fifty years after the Declaration of Independence Americans were impelled to thinking more comprehensively than their forebears had done in the days of the Revolution itself.

Before the industrial upheaval had gone far the American stock of ideas on society and government, on industry and agriculture, on the rights of men and women, was reviewed, reinterpreted, modified, and augmented. Reforms bewildering in number were proposed. They were forced upon the attention of political parties. They were written up in books, pamphlets, and newspaper articles, and made subjects of discussion in circles high and low, from one end of the country to the other. During the advance of the Western frontier, the contests of politicians, the westward sweep into the Louisiana Territory and the Southwest, the upsurge of cities and industries, the building of canals and railways, the celebration of a growing population and mounting wealth—amid all this—plans for recasting the heritage received from the founders of the Republic were forced into the thought of reflective people concerned with the future of the United States. In nature these ideas and plans ranged from specific reforms to an overhauling of the entire social order.

Reformers who spoke from the ranks of labor or in the name of labor presented a long bill of specific demands: equal suffrage for all white men and, sometimes, for women; free and equal public education; the abolition of imprisonment for debt, which especially oppressed the poor; an independent labor press; the dissolution of monopolies; full right of labor to organize, strike, and bargain collectively with employers; a ten-hour day, with hints of an eight-hour day; payment of wages in cash instead of "store goods"; restriction of immigration; sound money for wages, instead of fluctuating bank paper; regulation of factories and mines in the interests of safety and health; and the division of the public domain into small homesteads to be given, not sold, to persons willing to occupy and develop them.

Other reformers, including many men and women distinguished for their idealistic leadership, declared that such schemes were not enough to cure the ills of poverty or release the full productive force of machine economy; and they offered a variety of panaceas. One of the earliest of such reforming groups advocated a peaceful reconstruction of American society, especially that type expounded by the French idealist, Charles Fourier, under a theory of utopian socialism. The utopists of this school were generally called "associationists." They proposed to abandon the capitalist factory system, found colonies of associated workers on the land, and combine farming with manufacturing. In colonies of the kind, they believed, workers could be self-sufficing, share their wealth on equal terms, and acquire economic stability and independence.

One school of American associationists, in their thinking, used extensively the ideals propagated by the British utopian socialist, Robert Owen, who made lecture tours in the United States and, with his son, Robert Dale Owen, founded a socialist colony at New Harmony in Indiana. They were especially impressed by Robert Owen's three revolutionary propositions: the enormously increased productive powers which man in modern times has acquired involve, and in a measure necessitate, great changes in the social and industrial structure of society; the world has reached a point of progress at which co-operative industry should replace competitive labor; society, discarding large cities and solitary homes, should resolve itself into associations—communities uniting agriculture and manufacturing. If in theory Owen's propositions were revolutionary, in practice his program was intended to be pacific, for the independent communities were to be established by the voluntary co-operation of capital and labor.

Convinced that they were on the right line, American associationists made experimental tests of their doctrines. They established several colonies in different parts of the country; but only those motivated by religious fervor and sacrifice managed to survive for more than a few years.

Also revolutionary but at an opposite pole of thought from utopian socialism, and violent rather than peaceful in its implications, was the interpretation of recent industrial events proclaimed by disciples of Karl Marx, whose *Communist Manifesto* was issued in Europe in 1848. Three years later a German apostle of Marx, Joseph Weydemeyer, landed in

America and founded a newspaper to spread the doctrine that the historical role of the working class was to overthrow the whole capitalist system and usher in a "co-operative commonwealth." But Weydemeyer did not make much headway with his propaganda in the American labor movement. When the Civil War started he enlisted as a captain in the Union army and by valiant service rose to the rank of general. Though his call for a revolutionary labor party gained no material support in the American labor movement, Marxism was thrust into the ferment of the new industrial age in the United States.

The influence of the mechanical revolution was not confined to urban centers. Indeed one great machine industry, railway transportation, coupled with the electric telegraph, ran out in every direction until at length it spanned the continent. Railways cut channels from the seaboard to the West, through which manufactures flowed to farmers and planters and farm produce flowed back in exchange. One striking feature of the trunk lines was the close economic union effected between the Northeast and the old Northwest Territory before the sixth decade of the nineteenth century closed.

By that time enterprisers of the North and the South were projecting trunk lines to the Pacific. Had it not been for a dispute over the route—whether it was to go through the Southwest or the Central West—and the political struggle over slavery, beginnings of construction would have been made before 1860.

Rapid transportation between the manufacturing regions of the East and the farming regions of the West did not prevent Westerners, however, from developing industries of their own. Cleveland, Chicago, Cincinnati, Milwaukee, St. Louis, and Louisville early became manufacturing as well as merchandising centers. A survey of American economy published in 1854 reported: "Cincinnati, Ohio, appears to be a great central depot of ready-made clothing, and its manufacture for the Western markets may be said to be one of the great trades of that city. . . . Latterly sewing machines, of varied construction, have been largely employed. . . . At Louisville, Kentucky, and St. Louis, Missouri, the manufacture of clothing is extensively carried on; but Cincinnati may be considered as the great mart of ready-made clothing for the Western states, and, in a measure, for those of the South also. In 1851 there were in the latter city 108 establishments, employing 950 hands in their own workshops, and upwards of 9000 females either at their own homes or under 'bosses.' The proprietors are chiefly German Jews, and most of the operatives are Germans."

A petty village with a few inhabitants when Cook County, Illinois.

was organized in 1831, Chicago soon became a focus for shipping on the Great Lakes and for distributing Eastern manufactures brought by water and rail. Then its enterprisers turned to manufacturing. After the establishment of the McCormick reaper works in 1849, Chicago rose to be the leading center for the manufacture of plows, reapers, threshers, and other machinery needed for the expansion of farm production as vast areas of level Western land were opened up for cultivation, especially enormous corn- and wheat-growing regions.

Although many men in the South saw the immense potentialities of machine industry for economic welfare and sought to balance the agriculture of that region by the introduction of manufacturing, their efforts, for one reason or another, met with only slight success. It is true that by 1840 Virginia, North Carolina, Georgia, Tennessee, and Kentucky had many cotton mills in operation, but these factories were small in size and in their growth fell far behind Northern competitors. In 1850 the annual value of manufactures produced in the free states was more than four times the output of manufactures in the slave states. Omitting Maryland, Kentucky, and Missouri from the list of slave states, it was more than eight times the Southern output. In 1857 the free states had 17,800 miles of railway lines; the slave states only 6800 miles.

By the middle of the century four portentous facts stood out in the economy of the United States. First, the capital value of industrial and urban property overtopped the capital value of all the farms and plantations from the Atlantic to the Pacific. Second, the Northeast and the Northwest, linked together by common interests, greatly surpassed in manufacturing wealth and production all the Southern states, especially the slave belt below Maryland, Kentucky, and Missouri. Third, the iron products and leather goods, including boots and shoes, alone equaled in value of annual output all the cotton grown in Southern fields. Fourth, by similarity of freehold agricultural practices, the people of a vast section between the Southern seaboard and the Mississippi—in western Virginia and North Carolina, and in eastern Kentucky and Tennessee—were affiliated by economic habits and kindred sentiments with Northern farmers, rather than with the planters of the coastal plain who used chattel slaves to till their soil.

Over continuously larger areas of the continental domain the interests and ideologies of the early Republic were undergoing changes and transformations fundamental in character. Inherited productive methods of agriculture and manufacturing were being outmoded. The American population was becoming increasingly urban. The family system of economic and cultural unity was giving way to the factory system which drew even young children into its fold. An organized movement was beginning to assert the claims of labor to a larger share of the profits of capitalistic enterprise; and revolutionary social theories were competing with loyalty to capitalism in the ranks of labor. Localism was yielding ground before the invasion of new laws, customs, institutions, and social problems national in scope. The trend of thought and interest was toward a more consolidated national Union and a fuller realization of the opportunities for the life commodious and abundant on this continent.

Chapter 14

RISE OF NATIONAL DEMOCRACY

ATTENDING the expansion of the American nation to the Pacific Ocean and the transformation wrought in economy by steam and machinery was the decimation of the governing elite, in the name of democracy. Previously the very word "democracy" had been terrifying to ruling classes throughout the world. In America only a few groups of persons belonging to the Revolutionary generation of the eighteenth century had used the word "democracy" as a symbol for their political and social ideals and programs. Such groups had been regarded with horror by those men and women of the times who believed with Chief Justice Oliver Ellsworth that Jeffersonians were the "apostles of anarchy, bloodshed, and atheism"; or with Elbridge Gerry that "the evils we experience flow from the excess of democracy. The people do not want virtue, but are the dupes of pretended patriots."

This fright at the thought of democracy was illustrated in the systems of government set up in the states by the leaders of the Revolution. Those systems in a majority of cases limited the right to vote to men who owned property or paid taxes, and put high property qualifications on the right to serve in legislatures and important offices. In this way they excluded from government a substantial proportion of white males. But since the number of white male property owners and taxpayers was large, the suffrage was widely extended. And in fact, with the abolition of British control, legislatures became very powerful in all the states, representing a positive tendency in the direction of democracy.

On the eve of the revolt against Great Britain the Americans, possibly with some exceptions, were wholehearted monarchists. During the Revolution the word "democracy" was little used. It did not appear in any of the great public documents of the age—neither in the Declaration of Independence, nor in any of the first state constitutions, nor in the Constitution of the United States. In the convention which framed the

Constitution powerful statesmen expressed aversion to democracy and sought to put checks on majority rule by the people. Thomas Jefferson did not publicly call himself a democrat or use the term in any of his public addresses and messages. He was convinced that government by a simple majority—even of farmers—could be as despotic as a one-man tyranny and he especially distrusted "the mobs of the great cities."

Indeed even the word "republic" frightened timid souls. None of the first state constitutions mentioned the word. The Constitution of the United States did not officially declare the new nation to be a republic. Only gradually did that term come into official use. Jefferson was really promoting the idea when he called his party Republican.

During the Revolution, however, multitudes of disfranchised people thought and acted in the domain of public affairs. Throngs who were excluded from the privilege of voting and holding office took part in boycotting British goods. Many men who could not vote fought in the War of Independence. After the new governments were established local, state, and national elections were held periodically and struggles over public questions and for political power quickened the minds of thousands who had no actual share in the government. Elections and campaigns also stimulated political interest among men entitled to vote but hitherto indifferent to their rights and duties as citizens. Political newspapers multiplied. Books, pamphlets, leaflets, and broadsides on politics and government rolled from presses in swelling streams, helping to make citizens more alert to the importance of public questions for themselves and their country.

In this political awakening the advocacy of democracy spread rapidly, especially after the opening of the French Revolution in 1789. Democratic agitations accompanied the outburst of American sympathy for the French Republic when it became involved in war with Great Britain in 1793. During those years of excitement local societies were organized in nearly every state in the Union for the purpose of carrying on political education and propaganda—from Addison County in Vermont to Charleston, South Carolina; from Philadelphia to Lexington in Kentucky. Forty-two such societies are reported by E. P. Link in his *Democratic-Republican Societies*, 1790–1800, published in 1942. Of this number at least fifteen called themselves "Democratic" societies; others chose the more conservative word "Republican" as their title; two adopted the hyphenated title, "Democratic-Republican."

So active were the societies that conservatives, such as Hamilton and Washington, saw the specter of a revolution from below and considered ways and means of suppressing it. In fact the Alien and Sedition Acts, pushed through Congress by the Federalists in 1798, were aimed at such agitations fomented by the popular societies. Nevertheless, respectable leaders in local affairs, apparently in ever larger numbers, were boldly speaking of their political aspirations as "democratic."

The outcome of the French Revolution in the dictatorship of Napoleon Bonaparte cooled the ardors of the democratic and republican societies and most of them as distinct organizations seem to have disappeared by the opening of the nineteenth century. But their places were taken by local party machines which had been growing up in every state and populous community. For the fateful election of 1800 both the Federalists and the Anti-Federalists, or Republicans, were well organized.

Each of the two parties in Congress formed a separate group, or caucus, to promote its political interests. In cities, towns, and counties, from New Hampshire to Georgia, from Pennsylvania to Tennessee, members of the opposition to the Federalists held local conventions and established local committees, each free to choose its name. Most of them adopted the name "Republican"; some preferred the title "Democratic-Republican"; a few candidly called themselves "Democrats."

As the decades of the nineteenth century passed, more and more members of the Republican party appropriated the Democratic label. But national leaders of that party continued to insist they were simply Republicans. State and local committees of the party used the one or the other title, according to their degree of sympathy with popular demands. Since no national party convention was held until 1831, there was no official body empowered to fix the party name.

Madison, Monroe, and even Andrew Jackson clung to the name "Republican." In no state paper or official address did Jackson proclaim himself a Democrat or refer to the United States as a democracy, although in private letters he occasionally used the words with approval. Nor did the early national conventions of the party desert the name given to it by Jefferson. The national convention of 1840 spoke of "cardinal principles in the Democratic faith"; but not until 1844 was its national convention ready to discard officially all references to the "Republican" brethren and declare the party to be "the American Democracy"—"the Democratic party of this Union."

While democratic ideas were spreading, the chances of applying them in everyday practice were improving. All the states admitted to the original Union between 1789 and 1840—Vermont, Kentucky, Tennessee, Ohio, Indiana, Illinois, Louisiana, Mississippi, Alabama, Florida, Missouri, Maine, Michigan, and Arkansas—differed in several features of their social structure from the old seaboard states with their colonial backgrounds. In none of the former was there an upper class of wealth and political power comparable to that represented by the great landlords or the rich merchants of the original thirteen states. In short, there was more equality in wealth and social condition in the new agricultural states than in the old.

Under the circumstances, it is not surprising to find that the constitutions of the new states were more democratic in many respects than the constitutions of some older states. The new states all adopted white manhood suffrage or at most slight qualifications on the right to vote. They also opened places in legislatures and public administrations to adult males in general. As the number of senators and representatives from new states increased in Congress, as Western states acquired more voting power in presidential elections, even seaboard politicians who had no natural liking for democracy were forced to accept some of it as a hard fact or retire from public life.

At the same time the old East was undergoing a transformation which favored the growth of democracy there. The number of freehold farmers was increasing in the regions behind the seaboard, from Maine to Georgia. Popular agitations were making more farmers politically conscious, and changing them from negligent into active voters. New industrial cities were springing up. The population of the older cities was rising rapidly. Immigrants were flooding in from the Old World and acquiring American citizenship. Industrial workers were forming trade unions and labor parties.

These events helped to erode the prevailing class structures of the Eastern states and promote the growth of political democracy—a vote for every white man at least and the opening of all public places to white men of every rank in society. Far and wide, people of democratic inclinations were recalling that the Declaration of Independence had declared all men born equal and pointing the logic that all men ought to have the right to vote and hold office.

So the democratic changes did not all occur in the Western states. As a matter of fact low suffrage qualifications were adopted in several Eastern states before many Western states had come into existence. This was in line with the principles of 1776, reinforced by agrarian and labor agitations in the East since the establishment of the Republic. It had little or nothing to do with the so-called "frontier."

Step by step, seaboard states altered their constitutions, in various parts, in such a way as to abolish or qualify the rule that only owners of property could vote and to confer the suffrage on nearly all adult white males. The property requirement for voting was removed among the original thirteen states in the following order of time:

1778—South Carolina
1784—New Hampshire
1789—Georgia
1792—Delaware
1810—Maryland
1818—Connecticut

1821—Massachusetts, New York
1842—Rhode Island
1844—New Jersey
1850—Virginia
1856—North Carolina

In several cases, when the property-ownership qualification on the right to vote was abandoned, the payment of a small tax, on the Pennsylvania model of 1776, was substituted or continued; but in time that tax was also generally abolished. By the middle of the nineteenth century practically all white male citizens in the original states could vote. Thus two movements between 1776 and 1850—one in the East and the other in the West—converged to make white manhood suffrage prevail generally in the country.

In the same span of years property qualifications on the right to hold office were removed, along with various religious qualifications. Under many of the first state constitutions public officials and members of the legislatures had to be the owners of property in fixed amounts. For example, according to the Massachusetts constitution of 1780, the governor had to own freehold property worth at least £1000; under the South Carolina constitution of 1778 the governor's property qualification was at least £10,000 freehold. Many of the first state constitutions also contained provisions which limited the suffrage or office-holding or both to Christians or to Protestants alone. But with the spread of democracy the restriction of offices to men of wealth and members of specific religious denominations was destroyed.

Coupled with the extension of the suffrage and the removal of property and religious qualifications on office-holding were two other practices also called democratic. The first was the custom of giving short terms to public officers, known as "rotation in office"; the second was the rule that the victors in an election should take over the political jobs held by their predecessors—"to the victors belong the spoils of office."

Democrats early resented the tendency to keep men of old and rich families in office from generation to generation. They maintained, moreover, that long service in places of power was likely to make men arbitrary and aristocratic in the management of public business. A change of officers every few years, they insisted, was necessary in a democracy and conducive to the right conduct of administration. Short terms, frequent elections, and rotation in office, therefore, became popular watchwords.

To them was added one less theoretical: "Turn the rascals out and give the jobs to our 'boys.'" By 1840 "the spoils system" had become general throughout the Union, even in the federal government at Washington. After every election crowds of public officials, including clerks, accountants, and doorkeepers, were removed to make room for men belonging to the victorious party or faction.

Another feature of the democratic tendency was the adoption of the rule that presidential electors must be chosen by popular vote. The original Constitution provided that each state shall appoint in such manner as the legislature thereof may direct the number of electors to which it may be entitled—that is, the number equal to its whole number of senators and representatives. This method of election had been adopted by the convention of 1787 instead of other plans presented, such as election by Congress or by direct popular vote. It was intended to remove the selection of the President from the heats of political campaigns. Presidential electors so chosen, it was thought, would be free to review all the candidates, pass careful judgments on the merits of the men available for the office, and cast their votes according to their best opinions.

In the beginning presidential electors were chosen by the state legislatures themselves in several states, but five states established popular election at the very outset. By 1824, when twenty-four states participated in the election, eighteen had provided that the presidential electors must be chosen by the voters; in only six states were they selected by the legislatures. In the next election, 1828, electors were popularly chosen in all states except Delaware and South Carolina. Meanwhile presidential electors had lost their freedom of choice; they had become "dummies," bound to vote for the candidate for the presidency duly nominated by their political party. Thus popular election had been substituted for the deliberative electoral process contemplated by the framers of the Constitution.

In another respect the election of the President was made still more popular—by the rise of the national party convention as a machine for selecting candidates prior to the election. After the retirement of Washington, whose election had been unanimous, Federalist members of Congress organized a caucus or unofficial committee to select their candidate. The Republicans soon followed their example. Until 1828, one or more candidates were regularly nominated by congressional caucuses. But in that year "King Caucus met his death." Jackson's supporters had outlawed the practice as aristocratic and contrary to the Constitution besides. For a short time there was no national party assembly for nominating purposes.

In 1831, however, a new machine was created—the national nominating convention. In that year the Anti-Masons and the National Republicans, or Whigs, held conventions to choose their candidates for the coming election. The following year the Jacksonian Republicans also summoned a convention, at which Martin Van Buren was nominated to run for Vice-President with Jackson their presidential nominee. By 1840 the national party convention had become an established political institution in the United States.

Delegates to the national convention of each party were chosen by party committees or conventions, state or local or both, in each state. They were, Jacksonians alleged, "fresh from the people." Yet in reality every national convention was dominated by officeholders and professional politicians, including senators and representatives from the Congress of the United States. Nevertheless it was not as secret and autocratic as the congressional nominating caucus which had met and carried on its negotiations behind closed doors. Moreover it was a national assembly which drew together partisans from all sections of the country. It was both more democratic and more national than the caucus.

Besides serving as an assembly for the selection of candidates, the national convention, soon after its appearance, adopted the practice of framing and publishing a platform, or declaration of the party principles, that helped to define and fix the issues of the campaign for public discussion. Hitherto in presidential elections there had been no party statement giving the public any official information respecting the policies for which the candidate stood and which he might carry into effect if given his chance by voters at the polls.

After the election of 1840 the voters had for use in every campaign the national platforms of the rival parties; and the speeches of the campaign could be focused on the doctrines and planks of the platforms. As a wag once said, the platform was often "a thing to get on by and not a thing to ride on." But, vague and elusive as it frequently was, it was usually more definite than the rumors, private letters, and newspaper stories which had formed the chief basis for popular information and judgment in the campaigns held prior to the appearance of the national nominating convention. Henceforward the people had before them in campaigns, besides the personalities of the candidates, statements of party purposes which they could criticize, approve, or reject. Whatever its shortcomings, the practice of issuing platforms was an advance in the democratic process and political education.

During this democratic development women asserted claims to rights and privileges denied them in law and custom. From early colonial times women had been active in public as well as private affairs. They had not only carried on domestic industries that fostered national independence; they had edited and published newspapers, written and printed pamphlets, tracts, poems, and plays in support of the Revolution; they had organized boycotts against British goods and participated in essential work throughout the war against Britain. They had expressed their opinions respecting the course of events at the conclusion of that war; and forceful women had objected to the way in which men proposed to monopolize voting and lawmaking in the nation whose interests women were promoting and defending. Now in the Jacksonian age women were banding together to demand equal rights with men as fellow citizens of the United States. They were applying the principles proclaimed in the Declaration of Independence to their own legal and social status.

Following their excursions into reforming fields, leaders among women came to feel the need of an organized and directed movement for overcoming discriminations against women in law and practice. With the sympathy and aid of several prominent men that movement was formally launched by the holding of a convention at Seneca Falls, New York, in 1848. Lucretia Mott, of Philadelphia, and Elizabeth Cady Stanton, of Seneca Falls, were the prime instigators of this undertaking. After a long debate the convention drafted and adopted a Declaration of Sentiments, or principles, on which to base appeals for united and nationwide action.

Almost in the language of the Declaration of Independence, the women's declaration opened: "When, in the course of human events, it becomes necessary for one portion of the family of man to assume among the people of the earth a position different from that which they have hitherto occupied, but one to which the laws of nature and of nature's God entitle them, a decent respect to the opinions of mankind requires that they should declare the causes that impel them to such a course. We hold these truths to be self-evident: that all men and women are created equal . . ."

Then, after the style of that earlier declaration which had asserted the natural equality and rights of man, there followed a long list of "repeated injuries and usurpations on the part of man toward woman": among other things, man has denied to her the right to vote, compelled her to submit to laws in the making of which she has no voice, taken from her rights in property and the wages she earns, denied to her the facilities for obtaining a thorough education, and monopolized "nearly all the profitable employments."

Having set forth the grounds of women's revolt in the clear terms of the Declaration of Independence and cited the grievances to be remedied, the Seneca Falls convention demanded that women "have immediate admission to all the rights and privileges which belong to them as citizens of the United States." To the Declaration of Sentiments the convention added a set of resolutions dealing with these rights and privileges, and affirming specifically that "it is the duty of the women of this country to secure to themselves their sacred right to the elective franchise."

In demanding equal civil and political rights and in carrying on discussions of public questions women now had a broad program for inspiration and guidance. It was greeted with abuse and derision in many quarters; but, despite rebuffs and setbacks, women pressed forward with their agitation for "the rights and privileges" which they claimed as citizens of the United States.

Equal suffragists were rapidly gaining adherents when the excitement of the slavery crisis broke over the land. Then leaders in the woman movement concentrated largely on the cause of freedom for slaves and the preservation of the Union. But after those causes had triumphed in 1865 they renewed their agitation and started with invincible resolve on the course that led, first, to gains in communities and states and, finally, to national triumph in the Nineteenth Amendment of 1920 which provided that the right to vote shall not be denied or abridged on account of sex.

☆

With the forward surge of democracy the idea took firmer root that free public schools supported by taxation should be established for the education of the children of the people, not otherwise educated. In this school movement many purposes and forms of advocacy were commingled. Large numbers of radicals regarded education as a cure for many social ills and as a means of preparing the people to win more privileges by reducing the power of the educated minority to dictate the terms on which the masses were to work and live. Only an educated people, reformers avowed, can govern themselves, supply competent officials all over the huge continent, and assure the safety of the Republic. On the other hand conservatives thought that public education would be useful in preventing the spread of "wild ideas" among the people and make them less responsive to appeals for their support from "agitators" and "demagogues."

Immigration was likewise brought into the pleas for free and universal education. Swarming thousands of men, women, and children were arriving in America from foreign lands. Many of them were unacquainted with the English language and with the arts of self-government. Among them was a large proportion of Catholics; and Protestants feared that the Catholics would gain too much power in politics and public affairs generally if they were not "Americanized." In this situation it was argued by educational reformers that free schools were needed to start the children of immigrants on the way to citizenship in the Republic and offset the feudal heritage brought from Europe.

Under the impulse of varied motives the movement for free public schools made headway against opposition and indifference. But by no single master stroke throughout the land was universal education established. On the contrary, progress in popular education took the form of local gains slowly accumulated in towns, cities, and states.

Horace Mann was active in formulating the comprehensive program of education finally adopted in Massachusetts; it encompassed, with elementary public schools, training schools for teachers, and free libraries in towns. Henry Barnard was the prime leader of a similar development in Connecticut. Besides working in their own communities, Mann and Barnard labored in other parts of the country for the establishment of free schools. Able men and women by the thousands in many communities and states, including governors, legislators, town councilors, and other officials, gave time and strength to this cause, by speaking and writing, by framing plans and drafting laws.

Grudgingly, stone by stone, amid the grumblings of taxpayers, the foundations of the system of free public education were laid in all the Northern states and in several Southern states by 1860. According to official estimates for that year every white inhabitant of the country received, in public or private schools, on the average, more than five times as many days of schooling as such inhabitants received in 1800.

In this attack on ignorance the following phases were salient:

Grants of public funds to aid charity, church, and private schools, all free from public control.

Laws permitting cities, counties, towns, and other districts to lay taxes for schools if the voters so decided.

Laws making special provisions for the education of the indigent poor.

Laws *requiring* communities to make provision of some kind for education, occasionally with grants from the state treasury, supplemented by small tuition fees.

The abolition of all tuition fees, thus making instruction free.

Equalization of education by abolition of pauper schools and of grants to schools maintained by churches.

Creation of normal schools for the training of teachers.

Organization of regular boards of education, state and local, for the establishment and management of schools.

Mandatory and statewide laws requiring the establishment of elementary, free, and compulsory education in every district.

Limited measures providing for the creation of public high schools to furnish advanced education.

Establishment of state colleges and universities, crowning the system of lower schools.

Yet the phases did not follow one another exactly in order of time. For example, the University of Virginia, designed by Thomas Jefferson, was organized in 1819, but not until 1846 did the Virginia legislature enact a comprehensive law providing for school districts, regular taxation for the support of elementary schools, and county school commissioners. By 1860 only Massachusetts, Connecticut, New Jersey, New York, Pennsylvania, Michigan, Rhode Island, Illinois, and Minnesota had normal schools for the training of teachers.

With the spread of democratic ideas and practices, and of education for the masses, the general public could, and did, play a more active part in the handling of political affairs. The emergence of this increasingly democratic way of life, national in scope and often unifying in its effects, was greatly facilitated by improvements in communication. The development of post roads was almost unbelievable in its rapidity. In 1774 there was only one great post line—the shore road from Portsmouth, New Hampshire, to Savannah, Georgia; except for the road from New York City to Albany there were practically no regular post connections with the interior. Sixty years later, in 1834, there was a large network of post roads from the Atlantic Ocean to the Mississippi River, from the Great Lakes to the Gulf of Mexico, with three lines running beyond the Mississippi to forts on the far frontier. The great Cumberland Road, or national highway, started in 1811 under a congressional act of 1806, had penetrated the heart of Ohio and regular stagecoaches were running over it to and from the seaboard. The Erie Canal linked the regions of the Great Lakes with New York City and intervening points. The Pennsylvania Canal joined Philadelphia to the headwaters of the Ohio and the whole Mississippi basin. Steamboats plying along the Atlantic shore quickened communications between seaboard cities; they were running from seaboard towns to New Orleans and to all settled centers on the Mississippi and its navigable tributaries.

Before Andrew Jackson left the White House in 1837 the building of railways had begun and a few years later the first message by electric telegraph was flashed between Washington and Baltimore. By the close of the sixth decade all the main regions between the Atlantic and the Mississippi were bound together by telegraph wires, over which news as well as private messages could be transmitted in a few minutes. In 1860 telegraph lines as well as railways connected Boston and New York with Chicago; New York, Philadelphia, and Baltimore with Chicago and St. Louis; Charleston and Savannah with Chattanooga; Richmond with Chattanooga and Memphis; Chicago with New Orleans; and all the

RAILROADS OF THE UNITED STATES IN 1860

urban centers of the East with numerous branches of the Western network.

In terms of rapid telegraphic communication the populous centers east of the Mississippi were in instant touch with one another; and news, which once required days or weeks for transmission, became swiftly nationalized. In terms of travel and the transport of goods, a similar nationalization occurred. In 1800 the journey from New York City to St. Louis consumed about six weeks; to New Orleans about four weeks by sailing ship. Ten years later the time of the journeys had been cut in half—to three weeks and two weeks respectively. In 1857 weeks had been reduced to days: it now took only three days to travel from

New York City to St. Louis by rail, and five days to go from New York City to New Orleans by steamboat.

With the aid of these and other means the exchange of general ideas, ideals, and sentiments was augmented and hastened. Politicians from all parts of the country could get together in a short time in group meetings and national conventions. Local trade unions could unite in state and general associations and their leaders keep in close touch with one another. Women could travel more widely and quickly in promoting their movement. Newspapers, once intensively provincial, even local, in their coverage of events, speeches, and literary activities, could enlarge their range of coverage to the very borders of the nation, expediting and extending the circulation of ideas. Public schools prepared new readers for books, magazines, and newspapers. Rotary presses driven by steam engines enabled publishers to print more copies of a paper in an hour than could be printed on a hand press in a week.

So the multiplication and circulation of the printed word reached immense proportions. The country was flooded with books, pamphlets, leaflets, and broadsides. In 1839 a report of the Post Office placed the number of newspapers and periodicals in the United States at 1555. Eleven years later a special census fixed the number of dailies, weeklies, and other periodicals at 2800 and the number of copies printed annually at 422,600,000.

The following table for the year 1839 shows the number and the distribution of newspapers and other periodicals over selected settled regions of the continent:

Massachusetts	124
New York	274
Pennsylvania	253
Ohio	164
Indiana	69
Illinois	33
Missouri	25
Michigan	31
Virginia	52
South Carolina	20
Georgia	33
Louisiana	26

It is evident from this table that in 1839 New York had twice as many newspapers and periodicals as Virginia, South Carolina, Georgia, and Louisiana combined; a single new state in the West, Ohio, had more than all of the four Southern states combined. Indiana had more than Virginia; and the frontier state of Illinois, in which Abraham Lincoln was growing up, had more than South Carolina, the home of John C. Calhoun. Even so, there were now more newspapers in Virginia in 1839 than there had been in all the states when their independence was declared in 1776.

Under the impact of all these developments, the web of unity, while becoming more complex, was growing tighter. Regions, sections, and states remained, but sentiments and loyalties were becoming more uniform. Democratic customs and a public opinion accepting them were spreading without regard to physical boundaries.

☆

As an outcome of the stirring and converging forces at work in the United States the little Union formed by the original thirteen states on the seaboard—the Union now continental in extent—was becoming national in its ideas and feelings, even in the South as pro-slavery secessionists learned from the number and vigor of their opponents in their very midst. It is true that nowhere in the Constitution of the United States did the word "nation" or the word "national" appear. In their secret convention at Philadelphia in 1787 the framers of the Constitution at first resolved that they were seeking to establish a government "national" in all departments; but they struck out the word "national" from their resolutions, thinking, no doubt, that it would disturb advocates of states' rights. Nevertheless Madison, Jay, and Hamilton used the fateful and prophetic words in *The Federalist*. Washington, Jefferson, and Jackson repeatedly referred to the United States as a "nation" and to its great interests as "national." Although as late as 1850 it was still customary in popular usage and in prayers for divine blessing to speak of "these" United States, events were outrunning the language. In the travail of the democratic insurgency these states were fusing into an American nation.

Chapter 15

A BROADENING AND DEEPENING SENSE OF CIVILIZATION

BLENDED with the insurgency of democratic thought and action as expressions of individual rights was concern with American society as a whole and on the continental scale. This concern involved a search for the bonds of social, economic, intellectual, and spiritual loyalty cutting across the variations of states, regions, and classes. It raised such fundamental questions for exploration and treatment as these:

What is the social mission of this nation in its continental home?

What duties and virtues are necessary to the fulfilment of its historic mission?

What opportunities for action lie open to the people?

What knowledge is necessary for the accomplishment of their highest purposes?

What principles, inherited or newly devised, should be applied for progress toward the goal called American?

This interest in what was called with growing frequency "civilization" —the progress of society toward a better way of life—rose far above mere partisan politics.

The word was new in all the history of thought and represented a new idea or ideal. It first appeared in French and English writings, it seems, about the middle of the eighteenth century and was first used in America, apparently, by writers of the Revolutionary age; by Thomas Jefferson, Thomas Paine, Mercy Warren, John Adams, and Joel Barlow, for example. Amid the upheavals of the democratic age it came into wider usage among orators, writers, and publicists, who employed it to distinguish the ways of rational, ethical, and progressively more refined human relations from the ways of barbarism. "The exact measure of the progress of civilization," said the historian, George Bancroft, in an address before the New York Historical Society in 1854, "is the degree in which the intelligence of the common mind has prevailed over wealth and brute force; in other words, the measure of the progress of civilization is the progress of the people."

Thought about popular progress had entered into the daily work of men and women who by labors of mind and hand had brought American society into being and given it a stable government, wealth, and strength. In the democratic era special circumstances favored the rise of thinkers dedicated to the business of speaking and writing, and more or less freed from the tasks associated directly with domestic, agricultural, or industrial enterprises. With the reading public enlarged by popular and secular education, publishers of newspapers, books, and magazines reached out for its patronage. The opportunities to earn a living by studying and writing expanded correspondingly. In other words, there was now a widening market for essays, articles, and books written in a popular style and dealing with every theme of human interest—economic, scientific, political, historical, social, religious, and philosophical.

Avenues opened to abilities in writing for a democratic public by the invention of machines for cheaper printing were paralleled by avenues opened to public speakers by the rise of the platform. In this democratic age auditoriums of many kinds for general assemblies were constructed in the leading cities and many smaller platforms were made available for smaller meetings. A Lyceum Lecture Bureau was organized to furnish speakers on various subjects to clubs and societies on a circuit reaching from the seaboard to the frontier. In Lyceum lecture rooms thousands of Americans heard letters, art, science, and the issues of the time discussed by "the best minds" of the nation. Mass meetings came into vogue, organized by men and women who wished to put before the people at large their proposals for innovations and to ask for popular support.

Though liberty of speech, as well as of press, was guaranteed by federal and state constitutions, free speech from public platforms had not been a general practice before the advent of democracy; and when first attempted it encountered sore trials and tribulations. Unruly elements hissed, booed, and often stoned orators engaged in analyzing traditional theories and practices, pleading for new rights, and demanding reforms, mild or radical, in customary ways of thinking and acting. Yet against opposition and disorder the platform grew in influence as audiences were disciplined by eloquence or were moved to reason by the power of argument. Public speaking became a practice of increasing importance in agitation and the formation of public opinion. In time hundreds of women from the middle class, self-educated by intensive or wide reading and activated by experiences in public life, were addressing audiences with pleas for social improvement.

As platform facilities multiplied and public speaking became an accepted way of distributing knowledge or disseminating ideas, innumerable organizations for education and propaganda sprang up like mushrooms, in communities large and small. Scarcely a proposal, from the amelioration of prison conditions to temperance reform, from the revision of marital relations and family life to easier divorce and woman suffrage, from modifications in the wage system to the abolition of slavery, was without a society devoted to promoting it by concerted efforts.

When Alexis de Tocqueville traveled in the United States during Jackson's administration, studying American habits and customs, he was astounded by the number of civic societies; and in his *Democracy in America* he wrote: "In no country in the world has the principle of association been more successfully used, or applied to a greater multitude of objects, than in America. . . . In the United States, associations are established to promote the public safety, commerce, industry, morality, and religion. There is no end which the human will despairs of attaining through the combined power of individuals combined in a society."

As the idea of civilization in the United States broadened and deepened in the consciousness of the people it became more generally recognized that the destiny and opportunity of the American people lay first of all in their own development. Political independence had signalized that fact. As industries flourished an increasing economic independence corroborated it. Multiplying presses for the publication of books and other writings invited consideration of it. Thought confirmed it, sometimes in boastful arrogance and at other times in calm, rational admission of intellectual and moral obligations.

In an essay published in 1837, Ralph Waldo Emerson acclaimed the growth of national consciousness: "Our day of independence, our long apprenticeship to the learning of other lands, draws to a close. The millions, that around us are rushing into life, cannot always be fed on the sere remains of foreign harvests. Events, actions arise, that must be sung, that will sing themselves. . . . There are creative manners, there are creative actions and creative words. . . . That is, indicative of no custom or authority but springing spontaneous from the mind's own sense of the good and fair."

Was political democracy, into which millions were rushing in America, among the things which Emerson called "good and fair" and a sure promise of advance in civilization? Followers of Andrew Jackson and politicians who were beneficiaries of popular suffrage thought that it was. Walt Whitman agreed that it was with the ardor of a poet, while finding in democracy more than votes to be counted on election days and the spoils of office to be captured. He accepted joyfully as brothers and sisters all sorts, conditions, and classes of people from the sidewalks of New York to California's shores. He rejoiced in their "companionship as thick as trees," and gave his pledge to it: "For you these, from me, O Democracy, to serve you. . . . For you! for you, I am trilling these songs."

Here on this continent Whitman envisaged the making of "the most splendid race the sun has yet shone upon; . . . with the love of comrades"—America linked to humanity by mystic bonds and yet emancipated from many ties to Europe. "Nothing," he declared, "merely copied from and following out the feudal world will do. . . . The entire stock in trade of rhyme-talking heroes and heroines" must be discarded and the songs of a free people sung. Here, in Whitman's vistas, democracy was to build a civilization of greater freedom, equality, and fellowship than the world had ever known.

But the Federalists surviving from Hamilton's era, still clinging to Hamilton's social outlook, and new Federalists bearing the name of Whig were openly skeptical. Josiah Quincy, of Massachusetts, who had been an "insurgent" among the Federalists in the election of 1820, concluded, after he had witnessed the Jacksonian upheaval, that this democracy would fall into anarchy, try revolution, and end in despotism, unless the children of the people could be educated to respect the law, defy demagogues, and play a better role as citizens. And as to that he was by no means optimistic.

Among the Whigs of the South similar views of democracy were stoutly defended. Alexander Stephens, of Georgia, publicly said that the equalitarian ideas espoused by Jefferson and other early leaders of the Republic were simply wrong—"fundamentally wrong" as applied to slavery. Indeed the wealth and talents of the Southern planters were largely enlisted in the opposition to Jacksonian democracy. Whether applied to white men or to slaves, the free and equal doctrines of the Declaration of Independence were regarded by most of their spokesmen as dangerous—to property and prestige.

Writing in a philosophic vein, Emerson took a middle course with respect to the issue of democracy. Many reforms championed by democracy he approved. "The philosopher, the poet, or the religious man," he said, "will, of course, wish to cast his vote with the democrat." The spirit of equality, the spread of popular education, the refinement and elevation of society in all its parts, the opening of opportunities to all the people—these he praised as desirable features of democracy. Such progress was in many ways inevitable in the United States, he thought, and worthy of universal support.

But Emerson refused to admit that the Democratic party was synonymous with democracy. He insisted that it was "the party of the Poor marshalled against the Rich" and was directed by "a few self-seeking deserters from the Rich or Whig party," who misled the people by seeming to be their spokesmen while loving to dine and wine with the wealthy and privileged. In saying this, however, he disclaimed any intention of endorsing Whig denunciations of democracy. "From neither party, when in power," he lamented, "has the world any benefit to expect in science, art, or humanity, at all commensurate with the resources of the nation." In other words political democracy, in Emerson's opinion, was one necessary phase of civilization in the United States and yet not without its gloomy prospects.

For the advancement of civilization, speakers and writers argued, innumerable reforms must be undertaken in order to bring practice more closely into harmony with the humane ideals professed by and for the American people. High among the needed reforms, perhaps the most generally advocated, they listed the revision of laws inherited from colonial times and reproduced to some extent in the new states admitted to the Union. The inherited laws had been heavily freighted with feudal customs, with cruel and barbaric punishments, and with English class doctrines respecting property, crimes, and punishments. When, for example, the leader of the agrarian uprising against the Hudson Valley landlords in 1766 was caught and tried, he was condemned to be hanged, disemboweled, and otherwise mutilated; and nothing but the mercy of the King of England saved him from this horrible fate. At the opening of the nineteenth century the laws of England still prescribed the death penalty for about two hundred and fifty offences, ranging from petty stealing to such high crimes as murder and treason.

Under the statutory and common law of England, from which the colonists had derived many legal principles applicable to property and domestic relations, innumerable rules upheld personal and class discriminations. The English law governing the inheritance of landed property tended to concentrate it in the hands of a few families through transmission to the eldest sons, leaving younger sons and the daughters to fare as best they could. In the absence of prenuptial contracts and other private arrangements the personal property of a married woman, even her wages, according to common law, became the possession of her husband and her landed property passed under his management. According to this old law children were almost the property of their parents, particularly the father. Savage treatment could be and was at times meted out to them.

By no means all of those harsh English legal principles had been adopted in the colonies. Colonial legislatures had abolished or amended many of them. A further renovation took place during the Revolutionary period and, amid the upswing of democracy, reformers began even to advocate a revolt against the whole English legal heritage, including the common law. After all, it was asked, what is the intellectual and moral foundation of the law in America?

Speaking to this point, a judge in Connecticut in 1819 declared that it was the purpose of "our ancestors" to found a pure government in church and commonwealth, "bottomed on the word of God," and that they "brought with them no more affection for the common law than the canon law, the court of star chamber, and high commission, from which they fled with horror and detestation."

This was an extreme view, not universally entertained. But twenty years before it was expressed, the legislature of New Jersey had by law forbidden lawyers to cite in the courts of that state any treatise, decision, or opinion made or written in Great Britain since July 1776. With some modifications this principle had been incorporated in the laws of Kentucky and Pennsylvania. Such extremes were in many ways unworkable. Nevertheless the concept of founding American law, criminal and civil, on the humanizing ideals of the Republic exerted a powerful influence on popular thinking about law and on legislation in the United States.

Reforms in law, proposed and in part realized in practice, followed specific lines of the new thinking. The law of landed property, it was contended, should assure equality of inheritance rights to all children, daughters as well as sons. Equality of legal privileges for women, respecting their personal liberty, their property and wages, their children, and control of their own affairs, was deemed in accord with the principles of the Republic and a progressive civilization. Children, it was argued, are not property to be used or abused at pleasure by their parents but should be protected by the government in the interests of their development and community welfare. Imprisonment for debt, so burdensome to the poor, was stigmatized as a relic of barbarism. The horrible punishments meted out under old laws were condemned as brutal; and a call was made for further reduction in the number of capital crimes—to a very few, such as treason and murder. In this general overhauling of the law the idea of punishment as a mere retribution for evil action—an eye for an eye—was steadily modified by the introduction of practices shaped by the thesis that the true purpose of punishment is to protect society and reform the criminal if possible.

The reforming zeal of the age struck at the slave codes in the name of civilization and at the institution of slavery itself. The codes Lydia Maria Child analyzed acutely with a historical retrospect, in her *Appeal in Favor of That Class of Americans Called Africans*, published in 1833 while Andrew Jackson, a slave owner, resided in the White House. And her carefully formulated attack on slavery became a veritable textbook for those political leaders in the North who adopted the anti-slavery cause.

In other works by succeeding writers slavery was assailed in the name of civilization—as violating all the rights of persons upon which liberty and democracy rested for justification, as the very antithesis of civilization. Defenders of slavery, it is true, also appealed to the idea of civilization and maintained that Negroes as a race were devoid of the capacities and character necessary to help carry civilization forward. But within a few years after William Lloyd Garrison founded his anti-slavery paper, the *Liberator*, in 1831, the intellectual and moral crusade against slavery had gained such momentum that it ripped into the discussion of almost every national question.

So wide-ranging was the reforming thought of the time that it reached all phases of human misery which challenged pretensions to civilization in the United States. "I come to present the strong claims of suffering humanity," wrote Dorothea Lynde Dix in a memorial to the legislature of Massachusetts in 1843, ". . . I proceed, Gentlemen, briefly to call your attention to the state of Insane persons confined within this Commonwealth, in *cages, closets, cellars, stalls, pens: Chained, naked, beaten with rods* and lashed into obedience!" At last the mentally ill, long treated cruelly even in the most enlightened communities, were to be brought within the circle of humanity.

In three years Dorothea Dix, with tireless spirit, traveled more than ten thousand miles, studying prisons, poorhouses, county jails, and houses of refuge. For long years afterward she journeyed, spoke, and wrote in behalf of the unfortunates who had done no wrong and yet suffered so grievously at the hands of people called civilized. Though President Franklin Pierce vetoed a bill granting federal aid for the care of the mentally ill which she had finally persuaded a reluctant Congress to pass, Miss Dix toiled on and on in aid of her wards. Before her death in 1887 she had wrought an irrevocable change in American thought and practice relative to these helpless and burdensome members of society, and paved the way for much prevention of mental illness through the study and promotion of mental hygiene.

☆

Of the many contradictions to civilization in the United States which troubled humanitarians and enlisted reforming efforts, none was more obtrusive and persistent than the misery of poverty—the poverty of strong and active men and women who sought work and bread without finding them.

Scattered poverty Americans had always known, and sensitive persons from colonial times had tried to deal with it by private charity and public relief. Social derelicts, often sodden by drink, had evoked the solicitude of temperance workers. But as the Industrial Revolution swept forward in the great cities of the North, another kind of poverty assumed congested and more morbid forms. During the economic crashes which periodically reverberated throughout the country, from the great thundercrack of 1819 to the milder storm of 1857, the poverty of the strong and unemployed was aggravated beyond the silent endurance of the victims or of the comfortable citizens who cared about the making of civilization in the United States.

Nor was the "perfect civilization" of the South, as planter apologists called it, immune from the scourge. If Horace Greeley, in the terrible winter of 1837–38, found unbearable the "filth, squalor, rags, dissipation, want, and misery" of the sixth ward in New York City, William Gregg, of Charleston, South Carolina, was scarcely less distressed by the perennial squalor and misery of the "poor whites" of the Southern uplands.

The problem of poverty in its manifold forms, this contradiction to civilization, was viewed from various angles. Theologians might regard it as a mysterious ordinance of God—an opportunity for the faithful to display the virtue of charity and make the best of two worlds. But numerous intellectual leaders of the democratic age refused to accept it with complacency. They inquired into the nature of private property, the industrial system, and social as well as individual responsibilities. For some inquirers education seemed to be the remedy, especially vocational training. Others looked to collective bargaining between employers and employees for an escape from poverty due to low wages even in times of business prosperity. Many offered as a solution free lands in the West. Defenders of industrialism relied on an expansion of capitalist enterprise to extirpate poverty in a triumphant and universal prosperity; utopists on voluntary co-operation, productive and consumer; and radicals on a thoroughgoing reconstruction of society with reference to the potentials of the new technology.

In his *Recollections of a Busy Life*, Horace Greeley, the great New York editor, gave his explanation of the existence of poverty in the midst of plenty:

"I. I believe that there need be, and should be, no paupers who are not infantile, idiotic, or disabled; and that civilized society pays more for the support of able-bodied pauperism than the necessary cost of its extirpation.

"II. I believe that they babble idly and libel Providence who talk of surplus Labor, or the inadequacy of Capital to supply employment to all who need it. . . . Where Labor stands idle, save in the presence of some great public calamity, there is demonstrated deficiency, not of Capital, but of brains.

"III. I believe that the efficiency of human effort is enormously, ruinously diminished by what I term Social Anarchy. . . . It is quite within the truth to estimate the annual product of our National Industry at less than half what it might be if better applied and directed.

"IV. Inefficiency in production is paralleled by waste in consumption. . . .

"V. Youth should be a season of Instruction in Industry and the Useful Arts, as well as in Letters and the Sciences mastered by their aid. . . .

"VI. Isolation [of workers] is at war with efficiency and with progress. . . ."

Writing from Europe as a correspondent of Horace Greeley's *Tribune*, Charles A. Dana expressed the conviction that radical changes in the social order were necessary to progress in civilization. "The antique civilization . . . reached its climax and then perished," Dana recalled. "It is for us to take a lesson from its fate. It perished because it was based on slavery. . . . The basis of the social structure is industry. If there is wrong in the relations of industry—that is, of property and labor—the time will arrive when they must be reformed, or the whole structure will go to pieces. . . . Under the existing system of labor, modern society has reached the utmost development which that system will allow. New methods of industry must be established, as much superior to the wages system as that is superior to slavery, or else the doom will be pronounced and executed."

Having offered his clue to the crisis in civilization, Dana then addressed himself to the question whether that doom could be avoided and arrived at an optimistic conclusion: "It should not be forgotten that the civilization of modern times is fortified against an overthrow as that of the antique world was not; the railroads, the steamships, the manufactories, the wealth more abundant and more generally divided, which exists now, are so many substantial guarantees that society is to go forward to higher forms without the sad necessity of beginning the circle anew with barbarism and ignorance for its elements. . . . The principle of co-operation is surely, I believe, supplanting that of competition."

On methods of eliminating poverty and waste, of assuring employment and plenty, writers and speakers of the time ran the gamut of reforming speculations. At one extreme Greeley and Dana held that the answer to the riddle lay in the establishment of co-operative communities owning land, machines, and tools in common and practicing communal industry and agriculture. At the other extreme George Fitzhugh, of Virginia, in his volume *Cannibals All! or, Slaves without Masters*, advocated the creation of a fixed class system in which each owner of property would be compelled to act as a guardian of a number of paupers proportioned to his wealth. As their guardian, the owner could command their labor, while assuring them a livelihood. But, argued Fitzhugh, they "would work no harder than they do now . . . would be relieved of most of the cares of life. . . . What would they lose in liberty and equality? Just nothing!"

Most reformers, though aware of the immense potentialities in technology, thrust aside as visionary the formation of co-operative colonies proposed by associationists, especially after so many experiments of that kind ended in failure. Fitzhugh's plan for establishing the class servitude of a new feudalism they dismissed as simply fantastic. Nor did they esteem more highly the Marxian scheme for a spring into freedom by means of a sudden proletarian revolution.

Threats of a mass revolt against special privilege had flared up in American history from time to time since Bacon's Rebellion in colonial Virginia; and slogans of revolutionary defiance ran through the speeches and writings of many labor champions in the age of the Jacksonian uprising against "the money power." But the great majority of American reformers and most labor leaders preferred pragmatic programs, embracing many lines of attack on poverty—through the organization of labor and political action in support of specific measures directed to the redress of specific grievances. The freedom of speech and press enjoyed under the American constitutional system permitted them to express their discontents openly and obtain a hearing for their indictment of poverty and their proposals to overcome it. The privilege of the vote, won in state after state for white males, enabled agricultural and industrial workers to engage frankly and above ground in political action for a redress of grievances—a uniquely American liberty and form of power in that time.

☆

Sensitive to the agitations of democracy and the demands for reform in every direction, many clergymen of various denominations inquired into the relation of the Christian religion to the unrest around them. From time immemorial Christian leaders had taught the worth of every human being and the spiritual equality of all persons in the sight of God. They had advocated charity and care for the needy and suffering. What was the bearing of such doctrines on the new tendencies

ESTABLISHING CONSTITUTIONAL GOVERNMENT

The preparation and adoption of the Constitution paved the way for Washington's inauguration as the first President in 1789.

(ABOVE) A dramatic moment in our history—the signing of the Constitution in Philadelphia.
(BELOW) Washington en route to his inauguration.

THE YOUNG REPUBLIC FACES CRITICAL DIPLOMATIC PROBLEMS

Only four years after Washington's first inauguration, a great war broke out between France and England, deeply affecting the life and thought of the American people. In the end, the United States entered the armed contest through what is called the War of 1812.

(ABOVE) A British impressment party at work. One of the prime sources of friction between the United States and England before the war began was the British practice of searching American vessels on the high seas and removing members of their crews claimed by the boarding parties to be Englishmen.

(BELOW) The Battle of Lake Erie—an American victory which helped the United States to hold its position on the Great Lakes and improved its bargaining power at the peace conference terminating the War of 1812.

Painting by R. F. Heinrich.
Courtesy National Life Insurance Company

MAJOR INTERNAL IMPROVEMENTS ARE UNDERTAKEN

At the same time that the United States was struggling with foreign problems, it was undertaking a few major internal improvements. Thus federal highway construction gathered momentum in 1811, when contracts were let for the Cumberland Road. Six years later, the State of New York began work on the Erie Canal.

(ABOVE) Better roads made possible the improvement of stagecoach service.
(BELOW) A leisurely journey on the Erie Canal.

Painting by E. L. Henry.
The Bettmann Archive

THE WESTWARD MARCH OF EXPLORATION AND SETTLEMENT

Diplomatic achievements, major internal improvements, exploration, and other developments stimulated the westward sweep of settlement.

(ABOVE) The Lewis and Clark expedition, sent out to explore the Northwest, receives directions from a woman guide, Sacajawea, in 1805.

(BELOW) An English traveler's impression, about 1840, of the process of clearing land for farming by girdling and burning trees.

The Stokes Collection.
Courtesy The New York Public Library

STEAM POWER REVOLUTIONIZES TRANSPORTATION

The application of steam power to transportation was an important means of tying together the rapidly expanding nation.

(ABOVE) Fulton's *Clermont* steaming up the Hudson in 1807 demonstrated how easy it was to travel against the current with the help of mechanical power, thus opening a new era of travel on American rivers.

(BELOW) A race between an early locomotive and a horse-drawn car, conducted to arouse public interest in the future of transportation by rail.

The Bettmann Archive

DEMOCRACY SPREADS

Better means of transportation, widening of the suffrage, and the establishment of
more schools, all contributed to the growth of democracy.

(ABOVE) Political campaigning on the frontier. Behind the speaker sits his opponent, taking
notes for a reply.

(BELOW) Urban campaigning—A Whig parade during the Harrison-Van Buren presidential contest of 1840.

AMERICAN LIFE HAS MANY FACETS

The activities of Americans became increasingly diversified as the nation neared the middle of the nineteenth century.

(ABOVE) An incident in the adventurous life of a whaling expedition. This time the "fish" won.

(BELOW) Firemen racing to a blaze, about 1845, pulling the "latest" fire-fighting equipment.

THE PHOTOGRAPHIC RECORD BEGINS

In the 1840s Americans were employing the clumsy daguerreotype process to turn out their first photographs.

(ABOVE) The earliest President of the United States to be photographed — John Quincy Adams, sixth President, as he appeared in 1847, a year before his death.

(BELOW) The harbor of San Francisco — in the winter of 1852–53, showing many vessels left to rot as their crews deserted to try their luck in the California gold fields.

of democracy and reform, both of which rested their justification on moral grounds?

To Protestant clergymen especially this question was immediately challenging. They were the most numerous of the clergy and they gave it the most attention. Catholics, of course, were not indifferent to it; but, despite the rich store of ethical writings in Catholic literature, including the emphasis on the "just price" and the "just wage," no Pope had as yet issued an encyclical on labor and reform. Moreover the Catholic priests who had accompanied the new immigrants to the United States had come principally from agricultural countries in which feudal traditions and practices were still strong and the problems of the Industrial Revolution had not yet become so acute as in the United States. At all events, for various reasons opinion among the Catholic clergy did not endorse reforms as drastic as those proposed in American democracy. On the whole, as Charles A. Dana said at the time, Catholics did not seem to sympathize with "a radical improvement in the social relations of mankind."

To Protestants and Catholics alike, it was one thing to write into constitutions, state and federal, provisions for religious freedom and seek to remove all signs of the intolerance which had been so cruelly manifested through the centuries. It was another thing to make the ethical teachings of religion real in the life and industry of every community and the nation. Yet to this effort at the realization of Christian ethics in human relations—in social theory and practice—numerous religious leaders devoted abilities and energies. Some stopped short at mild measures of legislation and gentle admonitions to the rich. Others went as far as Horace Greeley and Charles A. Dana in demanding a thorough renovation of American society and made acceptance of this program a duty for Christians.

The age, exclaimed William E. Channing, distinguished Boston preacher, "requires an enlightened ministry. . . . A new spirit of improvement is abroad." In a sermon delivered at Philadelphia in 1841, Channing amplified his meaning: "The multitude is rising from the dust. Once we heard of the few, now we hear of the many; once of the prerogatives of a part, now of the rights of all. . . . Even the most abject portions of society are visited by some dreams of a better condition for which they were designed. The grand doctrine, that every human being should have the means of self-culture, of progress in knowledge and virtue, of health, comfort, and happiness, of exercising the powers and affections of a man, this is slowly taking place as the highest social truth. . . . That the great end of government is to spread a shield over the rights of all—these propositions are growing into axioms, and the spirit of them is coming forth in all departments of life."

While the struggle for the public schools went forward, slowly but steadily, against protests of taxpayers and religious sectarians, an educational philosophy befitting the spirit of the democratic age was formulated by leaders in the battle for free schools. They generally agreed upon several propositions. The vote had been given to nearly all white men, and women were demanding it in the name of the equality and human rights proclaimed in the Declaration of Independence. Multiplying factories using technology were demanding greater knowledge and skill on the part of workers in industry. Poverty was a blight on American civilization. People were commonly lacking in knowledge of the simplest rules for health and healthful living. Illiteracy barred the way to that knowledge as well as to the treasures of the world's best thought.

Therefore, said the philosophers of educational progress, public education must prepare pupils for citizenship in the Republic. It must train them in the elements of the arts and sciences used in industry and agriculture, and necessary for earning a livelihood. It must inculcate the habits and manners of civility as values in themselves conducive to happiness and as indispensable to the practice of self-government in the community and the nation. Education, in sum, is to advance civilization in all its phases.

"Its general purpose," said Horace Mann, indefatigable leader in the public-school movement, speaking of education, "is to preserve the good and to repudiate the evil which now exists, and to give scope to the sublime law of progression." Training for citizenship Mann placed high among the specific aims of education: "Since the achievement of American independence, the universal and ever-repeated argument in favor of free schools has been that the general intelligence which they are capable of diffusing, and which can be imparted by no other human instrumentality, is indispensable to the continuance of a republican government."

While Mann thought that children should be taught respect for property, law, and order, he did not regard everything in this relation settled for all time. "Our advanced state of civilization," he admonished his readers, "has evolved many complicated questions respecting social duties. . . . We want no more of those patriots who exhaust their patriotism in lauding the past; but we want patriots who will do for the future what the past has done for us." By this he meant, bring wisdom, knowledge, and virtue to bear upon the improvements of the conditions of the people. "To diffuse a knowledge of improvements" he made a primary function of education.

To the grand end of a happy and virtuous life for the individual and the progress of civilization in American society Horace Mann subordinated all other aims of education. He advocated strict training in the arts and sciences of industry, in civil habits, and in care of the physical body, but no American, he insisted, can claim the elevated rank of a statesman, "unless he speaks, plans, labors, at all times and in all places, for the culture and edification of the whole people."

☆

The debates over the merits of democracy and innumerable reforms in laws and customs were accompanied by efforts to work out a system of political economy corresponding to the peculiar conditions of the United States. A primary issue was raised by these efforts: Are the conditions of the United States really peculiar or does the British system of economic theory apply precisely to this country as well as all others? A large number of American writers and teachers who dealt with economic theory seemed to think that the "laws" of the British economy were universal and thus reigned in the United States as well as in Great Britain.

In the British theory, especially as it had been worked out by David Ricardo and Thomas Malthus, two principles were firmly fixed: (1) each country, in the division of labor among nations, should produce the things which its natural circumstances enable it to produce the cheapest and all nations should adopt a policy of free trade; (2) large-scale poverty is due to overpopulation, the improvidence of the poor, and the decline in the amount of fertile land available for cultivation.

As applied to the United States by economists, these principles required this country to concentrate on agriculture and continue to be, as in colonial times, mainly a raw-material province for nations far advanced in mechanical industries. They also decreed that large-scale poverty is inevitable and that little or nothing can be done to reduce its area or its miseries.

In various respects British economic theory fitted very well into some beliefs already current in the United States. Many Americans still clung to the doctrine, once asserted by Thomas Jefferson, that popular government must depend for its success on a population composed chiefly of freehold farming families. Farmers alone, ran the dogma, possess the independence and virtue necessary to liberty and self-government. Jefferson had in fact given up the doctrine later, and had endorsed the introduction of manufacturing in order that the United States could become economically independent of Europe, especially in the production of arms and other things imperative for the national defense, necessary to assure political independence.

But representatives of planters and farmers held fast on practical grounds to Jefferson's emphasis on agriculture as the surest basis for a republic. They argued that producers of agricultural commodities would be more prosperous if they could sell their produce abroad, and import manufactures freely from Great Britain where labor was cheap and machine industries were further developed than in the United States at that time. As to poverty, they were often disposed to make that evil the inevitable outcome of manufacturing by the machine process.

Though the British theory of America as a raw-material producing country had been challenged on this side of the water from colonial times, first by manufacturers and then by political leaders such as Washington and Hamilton, it was not until near the middle of the nineteenth century that writers developed a countervailing theory better fitted to the peculiar conditions and potentialities of the United States. The outstanding personality associated with his trend of thought was Henry C. Carey, the son of Mathew C. Carey, a Catholic refugee from Ireland who had taken part in the intellectual battles of the early Republic.

In numerous writings, including his *Harmony of Interests* published in 1851, Henry Carey broke completely away from several fundamentals of British theory. The abundance of land and natural resources in the United States, he maintained, made possible the most prosperous society mankind had ever created. The way to advance civilization here, in his opinion, was to diversify the economy of every region by building factories and workshops in the very midst of the farms. This would reduce the cost of hauling goods long distances, open up various employments to workers of all kinds in their own communities, spread science, art, education, and literature everywhere, and enrich the life of every community throughout the land. If such a policy were adopted, Carey contended, American talents would be encouraged and rewarded and poverty would be materially reduced if not entirely eliminated. In his plans for implementing his industrial program he incorporated a proposal for a government-managed currency, as distinct from Hamilton's system of bank currency managed by capitalists.

Although American economic theorists generally repudiated Carey's doctrines as unsound, several of his proposals were followed in practice by American governments, state and federal. And they were destined to have a great influence on the economic thinking of coming years.

Writings which might be classified as "political science," as distinguished from the more comprehensive political economy, were mainly legalistic in form and spirit. That is, they were primarily concerned with the mere forms and powers of government, particularly the nature of the federal Union and the interpretation of the functions of the federal government. But writings on political science sometimes bore the stamp of the great constitutional controversy then rife among politicians and the people. Is the Union perpetual and are the powers of the federal government to be construed broadly in the interest of general welfare or narrowly in the interest of states' rights?

The answer of Joseph Story, justice of the Supreme Court, in his *Commentaries on the Constitution*, three volumes published in 1833, was unmistakable. The Union, he claimed, cannot be lawfully dissolved by state action; Congress may provide for the common defense and for the general welfare. On the other hand, Nathaniel Beverley Tucker, professor of law at William and Mary College in Virginia, enemy of Jacksonian democracy and friend of aristocratic government, argued with great learning in favor of the right of secession and a strict interpretation of the Constitution. This theme he elaborated in *A Discourse on the Importance of the Study of Political Science as a Branch of Academic Education in the United States* (1840) and other writings, including novels of which *The Partisan Leader* was the most argumentative.

Two treatises dealing with political questions, however, went beyond legalistic theorizing to the substance of politics, as *The Federalist* had done. According to that ever-memorable work, which continued in circulation, political science encompassed geography, economic interests, common customs, laws, and practices, and great functions of government, domestic and foreign. To these subjects Story and Tucker gave little heed.

But John C. Calhoun, in his *Disquisition on Government*, published after his death in 1850, after examining the theory of majority rule under equal suffrage, drew an unglossed picture of the clash of economic interests in the operation of government and sought ways and means of defeating the logic of democracy in the interest of economic privilege. Eager to protect the planting interests founded on slavery against the growing population of the North, Calhoun's treatise bore the stamp of political controversy. Nevertheless it dealt with enduring fundamentals in politics.

So, too, did another volume, on the other side of the slavery debate, Hinton Rowan Helper's *The Impending Crisis*, a prophetic attack on slavery published in 1857. Although by no means academic in tone, it took into account, even more than *The Federalist* had done, all important branches of economy, the arts, sciences, letters, education, manners, customs, and habits of the people, as presenting vivid contrasts between the South and the North. Though greeted as fiercely partisan, Helper's volume went deeper than law and theory, to the sources of the social conflicts amid which government was carried on, and took the whole range of civilization within its compass.

Into the ferment of opinions and judgments pertinent to the direction of American aims and activities, historians injected their interpretations of American life. The publication of new works on the history of the whole United States, not merely histories of colonies and separate states, signified an enlarging consciousness of the time process in which the American Union was developing into a consolidated society. George Bancroft, of Massachusetts, trained in scholarship at Harvard and in European universities, especially in Germany, author of a many-volume work, the *History of the United States*, frankly ranged himself and God on the side of the people. He made the march of the people heroic, from oppression to independence; identified civilization with the progress of the people in all civilian modes of refinement; and, to the horror of New England conservatives, declared himself a Democrat and accepted offices under Democratic presidents. The spirit of his conviction gleamed through the pages of his writings. The first three volumes of his *History* were issued between 1834 and 1840, right in the middle of the Jacksonian upheaval. Originally he had intended to bring it to "the present time," but his last volumes, not published until 1882, ended with the formation of the Constitution.

While Bancroft was developing his interpretation of American history, Richard Hildreth, also of Massachusetts and a graduate of Harvard, published between 1849 and 1852 a six-volume history of the United States covering the period from 1497, the year in which King Henry VII established his claim on this continent, to 1820, the year of the Missouri Compromise. Hildreth was a Whig and had no deep affection for democracy itself or the Democratic party as he observed its practical operations in defense of slavery and machine politics. And his pages, cold and dry in style, contrasting starkly with the purple flourishes of Bancroft, disclosed not the jubilant march of democracy but the struggles and clashes of economic interests that had entered into the making of the American nation.

Neither Bancroft nor Hildreth, however, departed far from political, military, and diplomatic history—not even Brancroft with all his professed interest in democracy. As one of their contemporaries, George Perkins Marsh, said: "History has been written for the ruler, not for the people." On this ground Marsh made an eloquent plea at Union College in 1847 for a new kind of history—a history of the people, adapted to civilization in the United States and to "a commonwealth where government is recognized as being both for and from the people." This was in the temper of Nathaniel Chipman, of Connecticut, a philosopher of the American Revolution and a soldier in it who, in his *Principles of Government*, published first in 1793, had declared that the civil and political institutions of the United States "differ in principles and construction very essentially from all that have preceded them." A history faithful to the realities of American life, Marsh pleaded, should deal with the condition of the people at different periods; in a word, should be social history broadly conceived. It should cover, besides traditional subjects, the work of city governments, the course and character of commerce, the methods and purposes of education, arts, sciences, industries, ceremonies, festivities, family life, "the sanitary and economic condition of the people, the position of the learned professions, the correspondence of families and confidential friends, the character and tendency of public amusements, the ephemeral popular literature of different periods, and the private biographies of the humble as well as the great." History of this kind, Marsh thought, would furnish guidance to citizens and to statesmen in the conduct of private and public affairs. Still, he did not attempt to write that social history. The task he left to others and no one in his time undertook it.

☆

To the broadening of the American outlook natural scientists brought the force of free inquiries and supplied factual knowledge for industrialists and workers in the practical arts and for reformers concerned with programs for the welfare and happiness of the people. Natural science was the monopoly of no section or class. In that respect it was completely democratic. It could escape domination by any special interest in American society and elude the ill-tempers of political conflicts. As a person, a scientist could be partisan. As a scientist, if a genuine scientist, he was above and beyond partisanship in his researches and reports on his findings.

Reformers could of course use the results of scientific inquiries for their own purposes. Indeed they knew that if there was to be progress in national well-being, increasing study of the physical world was one of the imperatives. Yet the scientific spirit in itself was concerned with a search for exact knowledge and not with a quest for reform. Scientists might long to conquer such ills as chronic diseases and epidemics, for instance, but only by gaining precise knowledge could they realize their longing, and they had to start on that basis.

So fruitful and varied was progress in knowledge of the natural sciences in the democratic era that it opened up visions of human welfare never before imagined. In every domain inquiries were pursued and discoveries were reported. Writers of history took little note of the scientists and their achievements. Books on history seldom if ever mentioned so much as their names. Nevertheless, scientists made history—great history as revelation and aspiration.

Among their numbers were John James Audubon in ornithology; Benjamin Silliman, Sr., at Yale College, in chemistry, geology, and mineralogy, and as founder of the *American Journal of Science and Arts* in

1818; Matthew Maury, in the physical geography of the sea; Joseph Henry in physics, meteorology, electricity, and electrical transmission by wire; Constantine Rafinesque in botany and general natural science; Asa Gray in botany; Richard Harlan in zoology and vertebrate paleontology; Josiah Willard Gibbs, one of the world's greatest scientists, in mathematics, physics, and chemistry; Parker Cleaveland in mineralogy and geography; Benjamin Silliman, Jr., in chemistry, with notable achievements in the chemistry of petroleum.

Besides working as individuals, scientists formed organizations to pool their knowledge and promote research in particular fields. Special societies were supplemented in this work of promotion by the establishment in 1847 of a general society—the American Association for the Advancement of Science. National support was also given to scientific inquiries by the founding of the Smithsonian Institution in Washington in 1846 on the basis of a gift by James Smithson, a British chemist who bequeathed a large fortune to the United States for the encouragement of science.

Scientists made advances no less striking and useful in medicine and surgery than those achieved in the physical sciences strictly defined. In general terms the medical advances included more careful and accurate descriptions of human diseases, especially those epidemic in nature; demonstrations in daring surgical operations not hitherto attempted; more precise knowledge of the composition of chemicals in relation to their curative and other properties as applied to disease and suffering; the founding of new medical schools, for example, at Yale in 1810, at Transylvania in Kentucky in 1817, and at Chicago in 1837; scientific writings on surgery, materia medica, dentistry, obstetrics, insanity, diseases of the eye, and medical jurisprudence; and the beginning of popular education in human physiology and anatomy.

In many branches of medical and surgical research hundreds of scientific inquiries were pressed and marvelous results came out of the labor. With the early use of anesthetics, to deaden pain and permit otherwise impossible operations in surgery, were associated Crawford Long, Charles T. Jackson, John Warren, Horace Wells, and W. T. Morton. William Beaumont, of Michigan, did original research in gastric digestion; his book describing his experiments, published in 1833, has been called "the greatest contribution ever made to the knowledge of gastric digestion." Daniel Drake, of Kentucky, was a pioneer in raising the standards of medical education, and wrote a path-breaking work on the *Diseases of the Interior Valley of North America* (1850–54). William Gerhard, of Philadelphia, specialized in the identification and diagnosis of diseases, and differentiated between typhus and typhoid fever, both age-old destroyers of humanity. In South Carolina, James

M. Sims made bold experiments in the surgery of gynecology and founded a school of disciples in that field. At Boston, Oliver Wendell Holmes, Sr., employed his fine mind in studying the infectious nature of puerperal fever and discovered ways and means of reducing the death rate of mothers in childbirth.

Appalled by the amount of ignorance among women respecting their own bodies—an ignorance so serious for personal and maternal health—Paulina Kellogg Wright Davis studied anatomy and physiology with a view to helping them overcome their ignorance. Medical men were lecturing to selected audiences on those subjects. She lectured in a more popular way to groups of women, using a manikin in her demonstrations, much to the disgust and alarm of prudists but no doubt with much value to women. She further shocked even male doctors by demanding that medical schools be opened to the training of women in the profession of medicine. Women had been doctors and surgeons since the dawn of human history, but licenses were now being required for the practice of the healing arts. Hence formal training, preliminary to the obtaining of a license, had to be won if women were to continue in their historic relation to these arts and carry them on with the aid of the most modern learning and skills. By demanding medical training for women Mrs. Davis and other forceful women helped to cleave the stolidity of minds reluctant to recognize the role and function of women in the arts of healing and living.

All in all the epoch of "Jacksonian democracy," the "era of the common man," the "fabulous forties" and the fermenting fifties, was a time of dramatic mental activity and creative thinking in respect of everything human.

Chapter 16

PARTY STRIFE INTENSIFIES

THE rise of democracy in a nation continent-wide, undergoing a transformation by steam and machinery and charged with the turbulence of old and new kinds of thinking about society in the United States, was accompanied by the struggles of political parties, under old and new names, for the possession of the government of the country. The "era of good feeling," associated with the one-party system of the "Virginia dynasty," began to fade in the second term of Monroe—the last member of the Revolutionary generation to occupy the White House. A new era of fierce party battling burst forth. New personalities, of the younger generation, strode upstage as leaders of political cohorts, and employed novel methods of reaching popular audiences and arousing devotion to factional and party interests.

As the party strife grew in intensity, as travel and communication became easier and swifter, candidates for public office started the practice of making direct personal appeals to the people. In the early days of the Republic, Washington, John Adams, and Jefferson made no open bid for popular support. They conducted their campaigns quietly by writing letters or negotiating with friends. But after the democratic march got into full swing, especially after the campaign of 1840, candidates "went to the people." They made public speeches from platforms; they "took to the stump"; they toured whole regions delivering addresses; and sometimes rival candidates for the Senate of the United States joined in debating publicly the issues that divided them and their parties.

This was the era of monster political parades, torchlight processions, popular campaign songs, and huge barbecues, or picnics, attended by thousands of men, women, and youths who swarmed to "camp grounds" in wagons, buggies, and carts to see and hear the candidates. To aged Federalists all this uproar seemed to be the full and natural outcome of sheer demagogy gone insane; but to members of the younger generation it was an appropriate way of organizing parties, conducting campaigns, and letting the people share actively in the determination of public affairs.

In the campaign for a successor to Monroe four candidates were offered to the voters: two from the new West, one from the Northeast, and one from the deep South. The candidates from the West were General Andrew Jackson, of Tennessee, a popular military hero, victor in the Battle of New Orleans; and Henry Clay, of Kentucky, one of the "War Hawks" who had helped to bring on the second armed struggle against Great Britain in 1812 in which Jackson won the accolade for heroism. W. H. Crawford, an upland planter of Georgia with a frontier outlook, who had held high offices in the federal administration, was the presidential aspirant from the South. John Quincy Adams, of Massachusetts, son of the second President, was the candidate from the Northeast.

The strong figures in the campaign were Jackson and Adams, about as unlike as two men could be, but neither won a majority of the votes. So the election of the President was thrown again into the House of Representatives, as it had been in the case of Aaron Burr and Thomas Jefferson in 1800. After a long contest in the House, in which Clay was especially active, John Quincy Adams was chosen as the Chief Executive. When Adams appointed Clay as his Secretary of State, the angry followers of Jackson, who had polled the largest popular vote, shouted that a "corrupt bargain" had brought about the victory of Adams.

Though John Quincy Adams was the son of John Adams, he had moved further in his thinking, amid the social changes of his time. Yet his personality, like that of his father, did not appeal to the people at large and he was no more popular than his father had been during his term of office. A Federalist by birth, John Quincy Adams had pained elder Federalists by joining the Republican party, largely from sympathy with Jefferson's foreign policy—a heresy in their ranks. He had served Madison faithfully as minister to Russia. He had supported Monroe with equal fidelity as his Secretary of State. He had been pleased over the adoption of Hamilton's major financial policies by the Republicans in 1816. But he was not a mere disciple in any school of politics.

His view of the Constitution was a broad view, broad enough to take account of the revolution being wrought by science and invention in industry and agriculture. He felt a deep admiration for Washington as a public character and statesman; and he wished to work in the tradition of great nation-making. Indeed his conception of that task took in the whole range of civilization in America and the long future before it.

With a frankness and a fullness rare in politics, Adams laid his national policies before the country in his inaugural address and in messages to Congress. He insisted that Congress had ample powers under the Constitution to enact laws for the general welfare of the country. Above all he believed that the heritage of land, forests, and minerals should be held by the government in trust for the nation and used for the common good—to employ labor, build highways and canals, support education, and advance science.

To administer this heritage honestly and efficiently, Adams maintained, the nation needed a permanent body of trained and competent public servants, enjoying tenure of office during good behavior. In short, he looked upon the national government as an agency for economic, intellectual, and moral improvement. In his political philosophy government was not a mere police force to keep order while politicians scrambled for the "spoils of office," while businessmen intrigued for special favors, while speculators snatched at and gambled in public lands, while everybody sought to feather his own nest.

But in holding that the great object of government was to improve the condition of the people by well-considered and positive measures, John Quincy Adams was out of harmony with current political and economic avarice. Thousands of politicians were merely hungry for offices and jobs. Land grabbers, including many members of Congress, wanted to seize the public lands, as he said, "with the thirst of a tiger for blood."

And Adams was not the man to educate the country into accepting his policies. He had no genius for drawing multitudes to the support of his ideals. He was alternately cold, suspicious of his foes and critics, and hot in temper. At the end of four years in the White House he was, if anything, less popular than in the beginning. The one important measure that came from Congress during his administration was an act of 1828 raising the protective tariff on manufactures, and his approval of it offended agrarians.

Against everything that Adams stood for, the tide of a new "people's party" was setting in. In membership and doctrines this new party stemmed from the left wing of the revolutionary movement that had won independence for America.

Though merged for a while with conservatives in Jefferson's party, several of the leaders in the faction out of which it sprang had even criticized his policies as too "high-toned." After a Republican Congress had re-enacted Hamilton's chief measures into law in 1816, dissidents in the Republican camp declared that the Republican party managers had swallowed Federalism whole and by so doing had betrayed the people. An increasing number of the objectors began to call themselves "Democrats" publicly or "Democratic-Republicans."

With the crowding into Washington of farmers, planters, and lawyers elected to Congress from the new states of the West and South, the dissidents grew in strength; and attacks on the Republicanism which had absorbed Federalism became irrepressible. Then the new people's party arose. It found its leader in "Andy Jackson"—in a "son of the soil," a "man of the people," also a war hero. Born on a small farm somewhere near the border between North Carolina and South Carolina, he had gone into Tennessee in his youth and there had made his way to a fortune by old Southern methods—as a planter, merchant, and slave-owner.

Daring by nature and intrepid in action when quarrels were involved, Jackson had won distinction in the Tennessee militia and as a general in the Army of the United States. His education was meager but by the exercise of his wits he had risen to prominence in local politics and served in the national Congress. His attachment to the Union was emphatic and steadfast; his followers could be sure of that. But his attitude toward such issues as the tariff, the United States Bank, the management of public lands, and public improvements was obscure. He had never publicly proclaimed himself a "democrat," or a "Democrat." Yet through the shimmer of hero worship he was represented as a champion of the people.

A strong group of admirers swept Jackson into office in 1828 and again in 1832. Encouraged by these successes, the new political force went on to win all the rest of the presidential elections through that of 1856—with two exceptions, in 1840 and 1848. Often called today the party of Jacksonian democracy, it officially adopted the name "Democratic party" at its national convention in 1844, and ever since then has operated under that label.

After two terms in office, Jackson passed his mantle to another member of his party, Martin Van Buren, of New York, elected in 1836. Though Van Buren had held high offices in his state and in the federal government, he had also sprung from the people—the "plain people." He had learned the art of popular politics as a taproom boy in a tavern at Kinderhook, New York, before he began to steer his own course in the world; and it was said of him that as a politician he rowed toward every objective with muffled oars.

The interludes in the Democratic sway over the federal government were brief enjoyments of power by another new party calling itself the Whig party. The title, borrowed from the Whig party in England, celebrated for its resistance to high royal prerogatives, fitted very well the American opposition to the autocratic operations of Jackson. Before Jackson's first term expired men adhering to Federalist principles and discontented Republicans, spurred by Henry Clay, of Kentucky, and Daniel

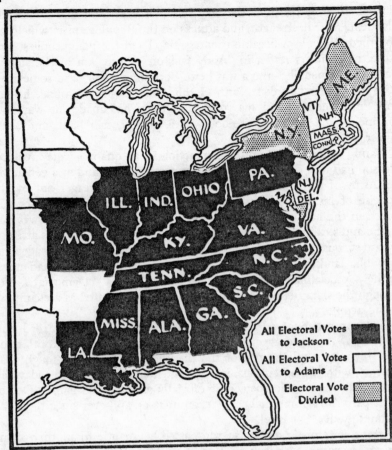

SWEEP OF THE NATIONAL DEMOCRACY. THE ELECTORAL VOTE IN 1828

Webster, of Massachusetts, had formed a combination against his re-election.

They did not call themselves Whigs immediately. In the beginning they were generally known as National Republicans, as if to deny any taint of states' rights and yet capture Republican voters. They gave no hint of the exact policies they would pursue if installed in power, any more than Jackson had done in his first campaign; but it was understood that both Northern and Southern members of this new party were, as a rule, disciples of Hamilton and incensed at the people's party for which Jackson spoke. Although Clay and Webster veiled none of the political views they personally held, the Whig party was largely a negative party—against Jacksonism rather than for anything definite as a substitute.

The Whigs came into the campaign of 1840 with a military hero of their own as their candidate—William Henry Harrison, of Ohio, who, like Jackson, had fought in the War of 1812 and had been victorious over Indians at Tippecanoe in Indiana. They boasted that Harrison had a wing to his house made of logs. They sang campaign songs in praise of log cabins, coonskins, and hard cider, to demonstrate that Harrison was as close to the people as Jackson. They accused Van Buren of putting cologne on his whiskers and taking his meals in the White House from massive gold and silver plate. In their propaganda the Whigs promised the voters "two dollars a day and roast beef," instead of Van Buren's "policy, fifty cents a day and French soup." On such flimsy pledges the Whigs carried the election and William Henry Harrison served as President for one brief month. Then death ended his career and the Vice-President, John Tyler, of Virginia, succeeded him.

In the next election, of 1844, the Whigs were defeated and the Democrats made their way back to power under the leadership of James K. Polk, a kind of heir to Jackson in that he also lived in Tennessee and was a son of the soil. Whigs tried their luck again in 1848 and found it with another military hero, General Zachary Taylor of Mexican War fame, a Louisiana planter whose political ideas were as nebulous as those of Harrison. That success was their last presidential triumph. Though often strong in Congress after 1840, the Whigs, as an organized party, finally disappeared from presidential campaigns like the Federalists before them. In 1860 they adopted the name "Constitutional Unionists" but the name did not save them from defeat in that last grasp at power.

Amid the clashes, personalities, and rhetorical flourishes of the political campaigns waged by Democrats and Whigs, five primary issues remained fairly constant as sources of their differences. All these issues had arisen in the early days of the Republic, but changing circumstances led to varying degrees of emphasis:

Low tariffs in the interests of planters and farmers vs. high tariffs for the protection of American "infant industries."

State banks and state paper money vs. a national bank and national currency.

Federal aid to internal improvements—highways, canals, and railways vs. state aid, or none at all, to such enterprises.

Free land vs. sale for revenue purposes.

Freedom vs. slavery in the territories.

The division between Democrats and Whigs over these issues was by no means clear-cut. On some of them both parties were split. On none of them was the Northeast, the Northwest, or the South actually "solid." Neither of the great political parties was purely sectional. Whigs and Democrats throve in every state. The South furnished great Whig leaders, such as Alexander H. Stephens and Henry Clay, who ranked in learning and eloquence with Northern men, such as Daniel Webster and Edward Everett. The same was true of the Democrats. Yet in time these parties showed a marked tendency to line up on one side or the other of these paramount questions of the age.

Not long after Southern Republicans had agreed to the tariff of 1816, they began to change their minds and oppose the very idea of protection for American industries. Within a few years they formulated a well-rounded argument against it and began to denounce it as a form of robbery under government auspices. Special duties on imported manufactures, they claimed, are contrary to the interests of all agricultural states, North and South; such protection raises the prices of goods which planters and farmers must buy; it is, in effect, a tax on them for the benefit of manufacturers; planters and farmers can prosper best by selling their produce abroad and buying their manufactures from the industrial nations of the Old World with their cheaper labor. On such grounds Southern politicians sought to make an alliance with politicians in the farming regions of the North, especially the Northwest.

It took nearly forty years, however, for advocates of low tariffs, "for revenue only," to win a substantial victory, and it was transient when it came. While Jeffersonian Republicans were still nominally in power, Congress raised the duties on imports twice—in 1824 and in 1828. The second act, decried as "the tariff of abominations," though modified later in details, produced a revolt in South Carolina. In 1832 the state legislature called a convention, and that assembly, duly elected, condemned the protective tariff as contrary to the Constitution of the United States and hence null and void. The delegates further resolved that, if the federal government tried to coerce the people of the state into obeying the law, they would withdraw from the Union and establish an independent state. This was the doctrine of nullification in an extreme form.

Infuriated by the threat of South Carolina, President Jackson issued a proclamation denouncing its action from start to finish. He branded nullification as a violation of the letter and spirit of the Constitution. He exalted the Union as supreme and perpetual and spurned the thesis that it was a mere league of sovereign states from which they could withdraw at will. He informed South Carolina that he would enforce federal laws with all the agencies of power at his disposal and that, if any blood was shed in opposition to the national laws, he would hang the first guilty persons he could catch in the act. To back up his words, he prepared to mobilize the necessary military forces.

Yet Jackson also strove for peace. He advised Congress to alter the tariff that had made the trouble and lay protective duties only on manufactures required for national defense. Then he asked Congress to pass a "force bill," a measure giving him more power in executing federal laws.

Under the leadership of Henry Clay a compromise was reached in 1833. Congress provided that the tariff should be gradually reduced until by 1842 it would be about on a level with the rates set in 1816. It also enacted the force bill into law. Thus both sides could make a show of claiming the laurels. South Carolina repealed her nullification ordinance and a truce reigned for a time.

It was only a truce. Fired by their victory in 1840, the Whigs broke the compromise of 1833 and raised the protective duties on imported manufactures. They made it clear that Clay's "American system" of protection for manufacturing industries was to be a fixed part of their domestic policy. The battle line was thus firmly drawn and Democrats accepted the challenge. In their platform of 1856 they endorsed the idea of progressive free trade throughout the world. Their triumph at the polls they followed up by enacting the law of 1857 which, though far from a free-trade act, made substantial cuts in many protective duties.

The second primary issue of politics—banking and currency—also had sectional aspects. Planters in the new Southwest, often heavily in debt for the purchase of land, slaves, and implements, had a partiality for inflation—an abundance of paper money—to raise the prices of their produce. Farmers in the new Northwest, likewise often in debt for their lands and equipment, were inclined to concur. It was mainly, though not entirely, in the seaboard regions of the East that the United States Bank, re-established in 1816 by the Republicans, and the currency it issued were considered "good for the country."

Appealing especially to farmers and mechanics, President Jackson, the pride of the West, opened a war on the United States Bank soon after he entered the White House. He declared that it was contrary to the Constitution, gave special privileges to the rich, and was against the interests of the plain people. Congress answered in 1832 by passing a bill to renew the bank on the expiration of its charter in 1836. Jackson vetoed the bill. By executive order he removed federal deposits from the vaults of the bank. And as the number of his supporters increased in the Senate and House of Representatives he had the pleasure of seeing the bank utterly destroyed before he retired to his beloved Hermitage in Tennessee in 1837.

Then with no national bank to interfere, state banks, chartered under state laws, burgeoned everywhere more luxuriantly than ever. In the Mississippi Valley such banks, sometimes owned entirely by state governments, sprang up like weeds and issued torrents of paper money based on little or no gold and silver coins. The notes of the worst of these institutions, derided as "wildcat banks," usually fell rapidly in value and often became worthless as the issuing banks blew up in bankruptcy.

Once more in its history, as in Revolutionary times, the United States had fluctuating paper currencies—dollars worth one hundred cents in coin in conservative states and anywhere from ninety-nine cents to almost nothing in the wildcat-banking states. Once more commerce among the states was impeded by paper notes of varying values. But in spite of determined and unremitting efforts, the Whigs were unable to carry through Congress any kind of a bill for establishing another United States Bank.

Over internal improvements—the third leading question of the time— the ranks of both parties were badly broken. Yet, in general, Democratic presidents were inclined to the view that Congress had no constitutional power to build great national roads and should not engage in the business anyway. In taking this position they reversed precedents set under President Jefferson, their political godfather; but consistency had never been a law with politicians. So for a brief period zeal for internal improvements by federal action cooled off.

Not until the success of railways was fully demonstrated did it flare up again. Then Southern Democrats and Northern Whigs agreed that a continental railway should unite the Atlantic coast with the Pacific coast and that federal aid should be provided for the construction of the line. They disagreed, however, over the route to be chosen. Should it be through the Southern or the Northern part of the country? That question was still in dispute when the fateful campaign of 1860 opened.

As railroads were extended from the East into the Mississippi Valley and gave easier access to the Western territories, the fourth political issue became more acute—the disposition of the unoccupied land in the national domain. For a long time after the adoption of the Constitution, Congress had followed the policy of selling this land, either in small plots to settlers or in large blocks to speculators. The price fixed for the land—at first two dollars an acre and later a dollar and a quarter—

though low was largely designed to bring revenue into the federal Treasury.

Low as it was, the figure made it hard for poor farmers and city workers in the East to "take up" lands in the West and establish homesteads there. Having to pay for public land at all was deemed contrary to the spirit of democracy and a hindrance to the abolition of poverty in industrial centers. Hence a clamor went up for a sharp reduction in the price of government land, and finally for a law giving it away to settlers in lots of one hundred and sixty acres.

For leaders in both parties this proposal made trouble. Whig manufacturers in the North were inclined to believe that free land in the West would entice workers away from their mills, or at least force the payment of higher wages to employees as an inducement for them to stay in the factories. Whig planters in the South could reason that free land would mean a more rapid growth of the Northwest, more free states, and the supremacy of free states over slave states in Congress and the Union. On the other hand, under the inspiration of Horace Greeley, a Whig, but also a friend of farmers and urban workers, many Whigs flocked to the free-land cause.

The division among Democrats over federal land policies deepened as the agitation over the slavery question grew more intense and reached a climax in 1859. Free land for the poor was eloquently and steadfastly championed in Congress by a Democrat from the farming regions of Tennessee, Andrew Johnson, an outspoken friend of farmers and workingmen; and around his standard many Democratic senators and representatives collected. But the Democrats were certainly not solidly behind his plans.

At length a combination of Democrats and Whigs was formed; a bill granting free homesteads to settlers was pushed through Congress and sent to President Buchanan for his signature in 1860. Buchanan was on a ticklish spot. The bill was unquestionably popular, but a host of proslavery Democrats were against it. After making his political calculations, Buchanan vetoed the bill, thus leaving the free-land issue to be settled at some indefinite time in the future.

Entangled with the free homestead problem was the question of slavery or freedom in the territories. Twice before the advent of Jacksonian democracy answers had been made in the form of compromises. By acts of Congress slavery had been excluded from the Northwest Territory and permitted in the territories below the Ohio River. Again, by act of Congress, at the time of the Missouri Compromise in 1820, the major portion of the Louisiana Territory had been dedicated to freedom and the smaller portion tacitly left open for slavery. After a great region had been wrested from Mexico by war the issue was revived and brought on a spirited contest in Congress and outside.

Once more an adjustment resulted—the Compromise of 1850—in which both sides sought peace, the Whigs under the leadership of Henry Clay and Daniel Webster, now old men on the verge of the grave. The slave trade, not slavery itself, was abolished in the District of Columbia. That was a concession to freedom if a slight one. It was more than offset, however, by a new and drastic law making it easier for masters to secure the return of slaves who had run away to the North. Under its terms a master merely had to claim a Negro as his slave before the proper federal agent; the Negro so claimed had no right to have a jury trial, to call witnesses, or be heard in his own behalf in open court. If the agent ruled that the claimant was the master, the slave was handed over to him. As to the new territories, the Compromise of 1850 provided that they could come into the Union in the future with or without slavery as their constitutions might provide at the time of their admission.

One-sided as the Compromise of 1850 was in fact, the voters seemed to approve it, for they gave an emphatic majority to the Democratic candidate, Franklin Pierce, in the presidential election of 1852. Had Democrats been content, the issue of slavery in the new territories might have been allowed to languish. But under the leadership of a restless and ambitious Democrat from Illinois, Stephen A. Douglas, the old Missouri Compromise on slavery was abrogated in 1854 by an act of Congress for the organization of the Kansas and Nebraska territories.

These districts were in that part of the Louisiana Purchase where slavery had been abolished by the agreement of 1820. Nevertheless, the new law of 1854 provided that the people of the two territories, or territories formed out of them, might come into the Union with or without slavery as their constitutions prescribed at the time—in short might have slavery if they wanted it. To ring the death knell of the Missouri Compromise on slavery the law expressly repealed it. Settlers, or "squatters," who went into these territories were thus to decide for themselves by popular vote whether they would have slavery or not. In this way the vast interior of the continent, dedicated to freedom in 1820, was thrown open to slavery under the doctrine of what was called "squatter sovereignty." A question long regarded as closed became again the subject of a nation-wide clash.

According to outward signs the repeal of the Missouri Compromise and the opening of all territories to slavery seemed to mean that the Democrats would command the power of the United States Government indefinitely. The tempest of protest that flashed out against the repeal was apparently without avail, for two years later, in 1856, the

Democratic candidate for President, James Buchanan, was triumphantly elected. A Virginia editor had once exclaimed that the South nominated candidates and the Northern Democracy elected them. Judging by the election returns, it was still true. A great barrier to the spread of slavery in Western territories had been removed—the Missouri Compromise prohibiting it—and the people at the polls had apparently approved that concession to slave-owners.

Two days after the inauguration of Buchanan on March 4, 1857, the Supreme Court of the United States seemed to clinch the Democratic grip on the government forever. In the Dred Scott case it declared, in effect, that the Missouri Compromise had been null and void from the beginning and that Congress had no power under the Constitution to exclude slavery from the territories.

A majority of the justices in the court were loyal Democrats and in their decision they followed the party line. They had done this with some hesitation but the upshot was clear. Now slavery could be banned from the territories only by an amendment to the Constitution; and, given the number of slave states, the three-fourths majority of the states necessary to ratify it could not be secured. Besides being successful at the polls, pro-slavery Democrats seemed to be permanently entrenched under the Constitution by Supreme Court sanction.

As a matter of fact all the five primary issues, over which Whigs and Democrats struggled for possession of the United States Government, were debated in the form of constitutional interpretations. Whatever the Whigs demanded, some Democratic orator was almost certain to declare unconstitutional. At length, in the Democratic view, a protective tariff was unconstitutional. So was a national bank and a sound bank currency. So were internal improvements and subsidies for shipping, as well as the exclusion of slavery from the territories. John C. Calhoun was so extreme as to maintain that Congress could not constitutionally accept a gift of money to establish the Smithsonian Institution in Washington for the advancement and diffusion of knowledge.

On the other hand, to Whig orators, everything they wanted the government to do was thoroughly constitutional. Daniel Webster took the position that, in letter and spirit, the Constitution empowered Congress to promote commerce, industry, and "sound practices" in banking. Henry Clay supported him with an eloquence scarcely less impressive. As arguments, they cited precedents set by George Washington and Alexander Hamilton, who, as members of the convention of 1787, presumably knew the primary purposes of the Constitution.

In the course of the constitutional debates over the details of the five specific issues two well-rounded theories as to the very nature of the Constitution were formulated. These theories were given definite shape during a great debate in the Senate in 1830 between Robert Y. Hayne, of South Carolina, and Daniel Webster, of Massachusetts. The Union established by the Constitution, Hayne asserted, is merely a compact between sovereign states; it is simply a league of independent states; and states may at their pleasure lawfully withdraw from the Union. On the other side, Webster protested that the Constitution is ordained and established by the people of the United States; the Union is perpetual; its laws are binding on the states; and states cannot lawfully leave the Union.

Enmeshed with these theories respecting the nature of the Constitution were two theories bearing on the powers of the federal government under the Constitution. By 1850 Democratic leaders in general had committed themselves to the proposition that the powers were confined within narrow bounds: to what they themselves called the explicit, specific, and enumerated purposes set forth in the Constitution. To this fixation Whig leaders opposed the doctrine that the powers conferred on the federal government were, in the very language of the Constitution, broad enough to cover all matters of "general welfare"; that Congress, as the Constitution declared, could make laws on many matters not mentioned at all in the Constitution because Congress was authorized to make all laws necessary and proper for carrying all its powers into effect.

When the dispute over the nature of the Constitution and the powers of the federal government was culminating in a deadlock of interpretations, all the men who had taken part in the framing of the Constitution were dead. James Madison lived long enough to protest against the South Carolina doctrine of nullification, but even his long life had been closed in 1836. Moreover, the debates in the secret sessions of the convention of 1787, as Madison had recorded them, were still sealed in his private papers, utterly unknown to the public. While airing their theories in 1830, neither Hayne nor Webster knew the purposes and intentions of the framers of the Constitution as written down in Madison's notes taken in the Philadelphia convention of 1787. Even after Madison's notes were published in 1840 Calhoun and his disciples went on arguing as before in defense of their narrow interpretation of the Constitution. Nor did the public pay much attention to the revelations contained in Madison's papers. Democrats in power at the national capital continued to claim the sanction of the Constitution for their political program, no matter what their opponents said to the contrary.

☆

At the height of their power, in 1857, the Democrats had a majority in the Senate and House of Representatives. The presidency was in their hands. And a majority of the Supreme Court had come from their ranks. On such good grounds they could exult.

Yet over the bright horizon a tornado was brewing. Dissensions were rising even among the Democrats. Critics were assailing their program and the institution of human slavery associated with it. Public protest was mounting, and an opposition party was preparing to drive slavery out of the territories, despite the repeal of the Missouri Compromise and the decision of the Supreme Court.

In many ways, apart from its merits or demerits, slavery was involved in Democratic measures, actions, and successes. Slaves furnished the labor for the plantations of the agricultural South; and planters were powerful in the councils of the Democratic party. If as planters they took issue with Whigs over protective tariffs, banking, or the currency, Whigs could reply by attacking them as slaveowners. If slavery was to be preserved and the planting interests promoted by federal laws, it was necessary for Southern planters to have more slave states to maintain a balance of power in the Senate against the growing number of free states in the North. Giving free homesteads to free farmers forecast the destruction of that balance. For various reasons, therefore, slavery entered naturally or was deliberately drawn into the debates over all the major political issues of the age.

Meanwhile slavery, the source of economic and political power for planters, was being attacked increasingly and more emotionally as a moral evil, as a violation of the human rights proclaimed in the Declaration of Independence. In 1776 slavery had been lawful in the North, as well as in the South. But it was neither popular nor profitable there. One after another Northern states either abolished slavery or made provisions for gradual emancipation. Massachusetts outlawed it in 1780. New York eradicated in 1827 the last vestiges of slavery within its borders. In Southern states strong sentiments against it were expressed. Great Virginian slaveowners themselves, such as Washington, Jefferson, and George Mason, had condemned it as injurious to both slaves and masters, and had voiced the hope that in coming years it might be abolished. Washington's will provided for freeing his slaves after the death of his wife. Slavery was not mentioned in the Constitution; but Congress, given power to stop the importation of slaves in or after 1808, had exercised that authority at the earliest opportunity. Relatively few leaders of the Revolutionary generation ever undertook to defend slavery through thick and thin.

It was an easy thing, however, to dislike slavery and to hope that in some manner it might pass away. It was possible to give up one's own human chattels and feel more comfortable in conscience. It was really revolutionary to demand the instant and wholesale extirpation of slavery, root and branch. That was what William Lloyd Garrison did when, in 1831, he started publishing at Boston his anti-slavery paper, the *Liberator*. Garrison scorned "gradual emancipation," and called for immediate and unconditional abolition. In vitriolic language he denounced slavery and slaveowners alike, declaring that he would be harsh as truth and would be heard. Stoned and otherwise assaulted by mobs in the streets of Boston, he kept up his agitation with unwavering fervor, powerfully aided by Theodore Weld, a Christian evangelist, pamphleteer, and organizer.

In many parts of the North, from the seaboard to the Mississippi Valley, abolitionists formed groups to work with Garrison or to carry on the crusade against slavery in their own ways. Sarah and Angelina Grimké, of South Carolina, did more than give up their slaves, as many other Southerners did; they also dedicated themselves to the cause of general abolition by going North to join in the agitation against slavery. Their example of conviction and action was an inspiration in the abolition movement.

Negroes who had escaped from bondage told of their tragic experiences and gave firsthand knowledge of slavery to audiences far and wide in the North, helping to inflame antagonism to that system—especially Frederick Douglass, Sojourner Truth, and Harriet Tubman, "the Moses of her people," who led some three hundred Negroes out of the South by hazardous exploits, one after the other. Dramatizing the worst features of slavery in a novel, *Uncle Tom's Cabin*, Harriet Beecher Stowe startled at least a million readers with her selected pictures of its sorrows and cruelties, making slavery odious to an immense number of persons in the North who had thought little about that labor system below the Mason and Dixon border.

In 1859, John Brown, with a few backers, invaded Virginia and at the risk of his life tried to start a general slave insurrection. Like uprisings previously made by slaves, it did not succeed, but it threw fuel into the fire. Higher and higher rose the flame of resentment as political struggles for power over the possession of the federal government engaged the voters in successive campaigns.

Northern critics of slavery found an outlet in the creation of the Liberty party, in time to enter the elections of 1840. When in 1844 the party hopefully attacked slavery both in the territories and in the states, however, it received only some 62,000 votes. After this meagre turnout antislavery forces formed the milder Free Soil party, opposed to extending slavery into free territory, but accepting its presence elsewhere. On this basis, the party won over 290,000 votes in 1848, then declined in power. In the elections of 1852, its votes fell off by nearly a half. The mere exclusion of slavery from free territory did not then seem to be a program with which a candidate could hope to stir up enough popular interest to sweep the country.

Nevertheless the repeal of the Missouri Compromise by Congress in 1854 and the opening of all the territories to slavery changed the temper of many voters with respect to the issue. By this action Congress dispelled the hope that slavery would die out gradually or could be confined to the states where it existed. It indicated the possibility that slavery might become dominant in vast regions of the West and in fact spread throughout the nation.

Unwilling to accept such prospects, many citizens in the North demanded a new party squarely committed to shutting slavery out of the territories; that is, to preventing its expansion. At a public meeting in Wisconsin, called shortly after Congress repealed the Missouri Compromise, a committee composed of Whigs, Democrats, and Free Soilers was appointed to start the organization of this party.

In selecting a name for it, the managers were shrewd. The Federalist party had long been dead. The Whig party was dying. Some other and more attractive title was necessary to capture public interest. Recalling their party memories, the leaders in the new movement at last chose the name "Republican party"—the old but still appealing title that had been adopted by Jefferson for the popular party that overwhelmed the "monocrats" and "aristocrats" of Hamilton's following in 1800. Under the long shadow cast by Jefferson's fame, the new Republicans nominated as their candidate for President in 1856 John C. Frémont, famous as an explorer of California, and adopted as their campaign motto, "Free labor, free speech, free men, free Kansas, and Frémont!" They were defeated in the election but the size of their vote, 1,340,000, encouraged them to expect victory in the next presidential contest.

Watching the tides of public opinion flowing and ebbing through these turbulent years was a Whig of Illinois who had long been active in the politics of that state—Abraham Lincoln. Born in a log cabin in Kentucky in 1809, brought up in log cabins in Indiana and Illinois, Lincoln was certainly "a man of the people." He was poor enough and humble enough to suit any "democrat" in all the land. But, given only the barest rudiments of learning in his boyhood, Lincoln, like

Franklin and Washington of the Revolution, educated himself, and well, by reading, besides a few law books, many classics in the English tongue, including the Bible, Shakespeare, and Aesop's Fables.

After a tough struggle against poverty Lincoln won some local renown as a lawyer and as a Whig member of the Illinois legislature. For a brief period, 1847–49, he served as a member of the House of Representatives in Washington. Still, as he approached the age of fifty, Lincoln was little known except as a local politician in Illinois.

With regard to the slavery issue, Lincoln was no abolitionist. Yet he believed slavery was an evil and was opposed to its extension in the territories. To abolitionists he was thus "a trimmer"; while to pro-slavery Whigs and Democrats he was "unsafe," if not "dangerous."

Lincoln's faith in the people was as stanch as that of any Democrat. Indeed Lincoln confessed that he had learned the first principles of popular government from Jefferson. Even so, he was cautious. He did not leave the Whig party until 1854. Four years later he was nominated by the Republicans as a candidate for the United States Senate.

He was defeated at the senatorial election but during the campaign he became a national figure. In a series of debates with Stephen A. Douglas, the opposing Democratic candidate, Lincoln manifested qualities of greatness—an exceptional knowledge of American history and government, genius as an orator, barbed analytical skill, and a clear conviction on a paramount issue of the times—the exclusion of slavery from the territories.

From the debates with Douglas, Lincoln emerged as a thoughtful leader commanding the confidence and admiration of throngs of citizens. To the discussions men and women had flocked on horseback, in farm wagons, in carriages, and on foot. Amid a fanfare of banner waving, band playing, and parading, however, they had demonstrated that they had serious purposes. They followed the arguments of the debaters and weighed the clashing opinions, soberly, with due recognition of their significance. At the same time newspapers had carried far and wide full reports of the debates; and citizens all the way from Maine to California could make up their minds on the merits of the arguments and the plans for meeting the impending crisis. So cutting and lasting was the impression which Lincoln made on the country by his speeches against Douglas and others delivered subsequently that the new Republican party nominated him for the presidency in 1860. In Southern eyes he was radical on the slavery question, but he was not too radical for the public in the North.

In choosing Lincoln the Republicans elbowed aside William H. Seward, of New York, who had long been prominent in public affairs.

Seward was in some respects more radical than Lincoln and in other respects more conservative. He had gone beyond Lincoln by condemning the system of slavery itself. He had also spoken the ominous words: "the irrepressible conflict." Yet Seward had been associated with the "money power" centralized in the East and hence was no favorite in the Democratic strongholds of the West.

Remembering that they had been beaten at the last election when they had adopted the exclusion of slavery from the territories as the main plank in their platform, the Republicans in 1860 drafted a platform that made a wider appeal to voters. They renewed their pledge to shut slavery out of the territories but they inserted two new planks. One of these endorsed the device of a protective tariff to encourage the development of "the industrial interests of the whole country." That was gratifying to Whigs in the North. Another new plank advocated a homestead law giving a farm of moderate size to anybody who was inclined to go out and till it. That pleased thousands of Democrats, especially in the Middle West, who had supported the homestead bill which the Democratic President, James Buchanan, had vetoed. In other words, Republicans in 1860 "had three strings to their bow"—opposition to slavery in the territories, protection for American industries, and free homesteads for people discontented with their lot in the East.

Over these issues the Democratic party split asunder. One wing, dominated by Southern leaders, nominated for President John C. Breckinridge, of Kentucky, and declared that slavery must be permitted in the territories and protected there by the government of the United States. A second wing held a separate convention and nominated Stephen A. Douglas on a platform of "squatter sovereignty," that is, letting the voters of the territories decide whether they wanted slavery or not. A number of Whigs, clinging to the Clay-Webster program of compromise, took a fresh title, Constitutional Unionists, and selected as candidates for President and Vice-President John Bell, of Tennessee, and Edward Everett, of Massachusetts. In their platform, as if no slavery question tormented the land, they called upon the voters to support the Constitution, the Union, and the enforcement of the laws.

Consequently four parties were in the field for the campaign of 1860. In these circumstances Lincoln carried all the free states except New Jersey. But the number of popular ballots cast for him was smaller by about a million than the number received by his three opponents. In fact, the candidates of the two relatively conservative parties, Bell and Douglas, together received more votes than were polled by the Republicans. Still Lincoln's popular vote was so distributed among the states that he won a majority of all the electoral votes and under the Constitution was lawfully elected to the presidency. Aware that he represented only a minority of the people, though duly chosen for the office of Chief Executive, he looked forward with anxiety to the day of his inauguration.

Chapter 17

THE NORTH AND SOUTH AT WAR

NEWS of Lincoln's election in November 1860 was taken as a signal for secession in South Carolina. The state legislature called upon the voters to elect delegates to a convention endowed with full powers of action on that issue. In December the convention assembled and by unanimous resolution it withdrew South Carolina from the Union. Early the next year other Southern states followed this example: Florida, Georgia, Alabama, Mississippi, Louisiana, and Texas.

In February delegates from six of the states met at Montgomery, Alabama, formed a new union called the Confederate States of America, drew up a provisional constitution, and chose as provisional President Jefferson Davis, a Mississippi planter who had formerly served the national Union with distinction in war and peace. A few weeks later a permanent constitution was framed for the Confederacy. It was ratified by the seceded states; members of the Confederate Senate and House were chosen; and Davis was elected as regular President of the Confederacy.

In taking this action secessionists based their expectations on one or both of two theories. The first was that the North would permit the Confederate States to secede in peace and establish friendly relations with their government. The second was that, if permission was denied and war came, the South could maintain its independence by arms.

Though the Southern states were outnumbered by the Northern states in population, wealth, and all the great industries necessary to provide the sinews of war, there were at the time several reasons for Southern confidence in victory. It was assumed that Great Britain would need cotton to keep her mill wheels turning and would intervene in support of the Confederacy; and that Napoleon III, Emperor of the French, would sympathize with the planting aristocracy and co-operate with Britain in aiding the Confederate government. It was widely believed in the South that Northern farmers and mechanics would not fight; or, if they did, that they would be outmatched by Southern valor. Another source of Confederate optimism was the faith that all the other slave states, except Delaware, would join in secession; and that blocking the mouth of the Mississippi River to the commerce of the Northwest would make states in that region eager to come to terms with the Confederacy. In the opening months of 1861 few if any Confederates could foresee how vain such expectations would turn out to be.

When Lincoln was inaugurated on March 4, 1861, he faced a hard dilemma: the Union seemed to be dissolving; the Confederacy must be allowed to go in peace; a compromise must be reached; or the Union must be maintained by arms. Between his election and his inauguration, Lincoln had refrained from the use of inflammatory language in speaking of the South. By letters and in other ways he let Southern leaders know that he had no intention or power to interfere with slavery in their states. Before his inauguration Congress passed a resolution for amending the Constitution in such a manner as to guarantee that the federal government could never attack slavery in the states where it existed. To this position Lincoln gave his personal approval.

On behalf of the South a proposal was made that the old Missouri Compromise line be drawn through the Western territories—with slavery on one side and freedom on the other. But Lincoln had been elected on a platform promising that slavery would be abolished in the territories. On that point he was adamant and he rejected the proposal.

Lincoln's inaugural address was an appeal for solving the problem within the limits of the Constitution. He declared that the Union was older than the states and that no state could lawfully secede. Under the Constitution slavery was legal in the states where it was established. This fact he recognized and again assured the South that he had neither the right nor the intention to disturb slavery there. The law providing for the return of fugitive slaves to their masters was on the statute books and Lincoln promised to enforce it. To this attitude respecting the Fugitive Slave Act the stoutest slaveowner in the Confederacy could scarcely object.

Lincoln also said clearly, however, that to him was entrusted the power to hold, occupy, and possess the property and places belonging to the government and to collect the duties and imposts; and he added that he was under a solemn oath to "preserve, protect, and defend" the government of the United States. Still he closed on a note of hope—that "the better angels of our nature" would in the end keep the bonds of Union unbroken.

As yet neither side had committed an act of violence. Only words had been spoken, papers written, and pacific measures employed. For more than a month uncertainty as to the outcome of secession prevailed, while representatives of the Union and of the Confederacy feverishly sought, more or less unofficially, to reach a compromise or a settlement of some kind. But a straight-out test of power was in the offing.

On a little island in the harbor before the city of Charleston stood Fort Sumter—a spot of land which belonged by law to the government of the United States and was garrisoned by a small federal force commanded by Major Robert Anderson. Without fresh supplies this garrison could not long hold out. The Confederate government demanded a surrender of the fort. When Major Anderson refused to give up, its officials stopped the flow of provisions to him.

For Lincoln the plight of Fort Sumter created a delicate situation but after many delays he decided to send supplies to Major Anderson by sea. General P. G. T. Beauregard, commander of the Confederate forces at Charleston, relayed this news to the Confederate Secretary of War, Walker, who told Beauregard that if Anderson refused to set a time for evacuating the fort and refused to agree not to fire on the Confederates, the General was to "reduce the Fort."

Beauregard dispatched agents to consult with Anderson and while the Major agreed to surrender on April 15, if no supplies or contrary orders from his government reached him in the meantime, he would not promise to hold his fire should the Confederates attack Union forces. With Union vessels off the coast, the agents considered this reply unsatisfactory and at 3:20 A.M. April 12 notified Anderson his fort would be fired upon an hour later. At half-past four that morning the promised bombardment began. After a spirited defense, Major Anderson surrendered the next day and formally evacuated the fort on April 14.

Among many uncertainties one thing was now certain: the first act of violence had been committed by Confederates—the flag of the United States flying above federal troops had been fired upon. The effect was electric. Millions of people in the North who had been lukewarm or hesitant now declared their unequivocal readiness to defend the Union. On April 15, Lincoln issued a call for 75,000 soldiers—not to wage a general war on the Confederacy but first of all "probably" to repossess the forts, places, and property which had been taken away from the Union—a purpose to be accomplished with the least possible disturbance to peaceful citizens in any part of the country. In the same proclamation he summoned both houses of Congress in special session for July 4, "then and there to consider and determine such measures as, in their wisdom, the public safety and interest may seem to demand."

In the South the firing on Fort Sumter and Lincoln's call for troops were also followed by swift and drastic measures. On April 17, Virginia seceded from the Union. Soon Arkansas, Tennessee, and North Carolina likewise went over to the Confederate side. Then prompt military intervention on the part of Lincoln stifled attempts to withdraw Maryland, Kentucky, and Missouri from the Union.

But the South was far from "solid" in the desire to leave the Union. As a matter of fact in Georgia, Alabama, Mississippi, and Louisiana a strong opposition to secession had appeared in a large minority vote against it. In Virginia western counties were so opposed to it that they withdrew from the Old Dominion and later entered the Union as the state of West Virginia. In the western part of North Carolina, Unionist loyalty widely prevailed. In the eastern parts of Kentucky and Tennessee, Unionists were undoubtedly in a majority and thousands of them joined the Federal army. Although opinion in Maryland and Kentucky was sharply divided, little force was needed to keep those states in the Union. Secessionists in Missouri were numerous enough to create a civil war in that state but at length they were driven out or suppressed, after several pitched battles. Less than a year after the firing on Fort Sumter the hope of Confederates that the border states would come to their aid in the struggle for independence had been dispelled.

When war began in full force the Confederacy had only eleven states on its side against twenty-three states in the North. Nine million people in the South, more than one third of them slaves, were aligned against 22,000,000 people in the North, nearly all free. States predominantly agricultural were arrayed in mortal combat with states rich in manufacturing as well as agricultural resources, reinforced by gold and silver from Western mines. Considered merely in terms of men and metal, Southern strength was inferior; but the South soon demonstrated ingenuity and enterprise in mobilizing materials and high competence in the art of warfare.

As the war got under way the Federal government at Washington and the Confederate government installed at Richmond, Virginia, confronted immense tasks for which neither was well prepared. Armies had to be raised and organized, munitions and other supplies furnished in staggering amounts, and commanding officers chosen to direct military and naval operations. The treasuries of both governments were almost empty and funds had to be provided to pay bills which aggregated before the close of the war far more than all the money the United States Government had spent since the establishment of the Republic. Relations with European governments had to be conducted with a view to securing support and warding off unfriendly acts. Problems of domestic economy and civilian affairs, numerous and perplexing, had to be considered and handled in a manner to preserve internal harmony and promote unison in arms. Finally it was necessary, among all these trials,

THE ALIGNMENT OF THE STATES IN 1861,
WITH DATES OF SECESSIONS FROM THE UNION

for both governments to plan campaigns and direct fighting over immense areas of land and water. To these tasks, on their respective sides, Lincoln and Davis, aided by their advisers and legislatures, devoted their minds and energies from the spring of 1861 to the spring of 1865—for four terrible years of civil war.

During the early months of the armed conflict both governments relied for soldiers upon volunteers who at first rushed to enlist. Soon, however, enthusiasm waned. By special acts passed in April and September 1862, the Confederate Congress authorized President Davis to draft soldiers from among able-bodied males between eighteen and forty-five years of age, with many exemptions including owners or overseers of large plantations. In the last days of the war the Confederacy even made provisions for enrolling slaves; and plans for emancipating slaves in a general conscription were under its serious consideration. In August 1861, Lincoln ordered a draft of militiamen, which turned out to be disappointing as to numbers. In March of the next year the Congress of the United States enacted a law making all able-bodied males, with some exceptions, liable to military duty; and the practice of drafting men continued till the fighting ceased.

On both sides conscription encountered bitter animosity, and desertions from the armies were so numerous as to be serious in effects. When drawings began in New York City on July 13, 1863, a general riot broke out and was not subdued until many people had been killed and a large amount of property burned or otherwise destroyed. The troubles of Davis were equally great if not greater. His recruiting officers met resistance in many places. Governors in some Confederate states, especially Georgia and North Carolina, refused to aid in the strict enforcement of the draft laws. A cry, "rich man's war and poor man's fight," reverberated through the South and men deserted the Confederate ranks in shoals. Nevertheless great and powerful armies were raised by both parties to the conflict and fought valiantly in battles that never seemed to end.

Respecting munitions and other war supplies, the North had a clear superiority of productive power in the beginning and increased its facilities as the war went forward. Able to keep the seas open for Northern shipping, the Union could supplement its domestic output with heavy importations from Great Britain and the Continent. Though the South started with more limited resources, it displayed remarkable energy in building new mills and turning out quantities of war materials. Its achievements were all the more extraordinary by reason of the fact that the Federal blockade of its harbors almost cut off imports of iron, steel, munitions, and other goods. But as the blockade grew tighter, Confederate armies and the civilian population in the South sank into dire distress from the want of adequate supplies.

With regard to financial resources the two governments locked in war were decidedly unequal. At the outset the Union had a Treasury Department and a monetary system; the South had neither and was compelled to create both. The North could command enormous outputs of gold and silver; the South had little hard money and early exported a large portion of what it had to buy military supplies. For raising money both governments resorted to the ancient devices of public finance: taxes, bond sales, and issues of paper notes.

On the Federal side repeated increases were made in customs duties on imports and in excises on tobacco, liquor, other commodities, and occupations; and to these were added taxes on inheritances and incomes. By the sale of bonds and notes the Union Treasury collected a total of $2,600,000,000 during the war. It adopted the third expedient, paper currency, in 1862; and before the conflict closed it issued $450,000,000 in "greenbacks," supplemented by $50,000,000 worth of fractional currency, with notes as low as three cents in face value.

Similar measures were put into force in the Confederacy, coupled with calls upon its states for quotas of money to be raised by direct taxes on property. Confederate bonds were exchanged for specie, produce, and state and Confederate notes. Altogether, about $1,000,000,000 worth of paper currency was emitted, in addition to notes floated by the states, banks, and business concerns.

While Federal bonds dropped in value during the darker days of the war and greenbacks once fell as low as thirty-nine cents on the dollar, Federal financing was, comparatively speaking, sound and stable. In the Confederacy, on the other hand, the course of bonds and notes was on the whole steadily downward as new issues poured out and consumers' goods became scarcer. In the summer of 1862 tea sold in the South at five dollars a pound and boots at twenty-five dollars a pair. In 1862 one dollar in gold was worth twenty-two dollars in Confederate currency; shoes were selling at a hundred and fifty dollars a pair and flour at three hundred dollars a barrel. Early in 1865 beef was six dollars a pound, flour a thousand dollars a barrel, and firewood five dollars a stick. After the surrender at Appomattox in the spring of 1865 Confederate bonds and paper currency dropped dead in the hands of the possessors. According to a current saying of the people, a Confederate dollar was "not worth a Continental," in memory of the paper money issued by the Continental Congress during the Revolution, which hit bottom long before the War for Independence was over.

Especially with reference to foreign relations, the problems of the two governments differed. The government at Washington was already recognized by foreign countries as the lawful government of the United States. Its prime cares were to keep this status unimpaired, to prevent the recognition of the Confederacy as independent, to ward off intervention in the war by Great Britain and France, and to hold the channels of commerce open. On its part the Confederacy struggled to achieve recognition as an independent government, to win financial assistance, to break the blockade on its commerce, and if possible to gain direct intervention on its behalf by Great Britain and France. In this situation Northern measures were essentially protective—against radical changes in foreign relations. Those of the South were essentially exploratory—directed to securing a position as an independent nation among the nations of the earth.

During the first year of the war the Confederacy was recognized as a belligerent by Great Britain and France, though not as an independent state; and it sent two agents abroad, James Mason and John Slidell, to represent it at London and Paris respectively. When the two men were taken from a British steamer by Captain Wilkes, in command of a Union vessel, Great Britain protested against this act of search and seizure. To avoid worse perils, perhaps a foreign war on top of the civil war, Lincoln ordered the Confederate agents released and they went on to Europe to appeal for a recognition of Southern independence and for aid to the Confederacy.

Confederate bonds to the face value of about $15,000,000 were sold in Britain and France. British shipyards, defying an old rule of international law, built war vessels for the Confederacy and the British government allowed them to escape to sea, where they preyed on the commerce of the United States. The sympathies of the British aristocracy and government, of the ruling classes in France, and of Napoleon III, Emperor of the French, were overwhelmingly on the side of the South. In both countries aristocrats hoped that "the upstart Yankee Republic" would be destroyed in the war and many British and French newspapers rejoiced in the prospect. But working people in English cities held mass meetings in protest against giving assistance to slaveowners; and Queen Victoria counseled her Cabinet to be cautious.

Napoleon III attempted to form a European coalition for intervention in the war. In 1861 he suggested to the Czar of Russia that certain great Powers take joint action respecting America, but he met a firm if polite refusal. Meanwhile the British government was toying with the idea. Yet when Napoleon proposed intervention to the British in 1862 he was told that the time was not ripe. One member of the British Cabinet openly declared that the Confederacy was in effect a success; but the Prime Minister, who was watching closely the course of the war in America, was unwilling to take the plunge in aid of the South.

Unable to restrain his meddlesome spirit, Napoleon sent a message to Lincoln offering his services as a mediator between the North and the South. Lincoln responded courteously, declining the offer. In language less urbane Congress replied by passing a resolution telling the French Emperor, in effect, that he should keep his nose out of American affairs.

If it had not been for the decisive Northern victories at Gettysburg and Vicksburg in the summer of 1863, British and French intervention might have come. Those triumphs in arms, however, seemed to assure the future of "the upstart Yankee Republic" and serve as a warning to impertinent foreign Powers. At all events Great Britain and France never recognized the independence of the Confederacy. Nor did they officially intervene in the war.

☆

Not only were the North and South having trouble winning and holding sympathy abroad, but they faced difficulties even in trying to keep their own citizens in line at home.

To check Northern citizens who wanted to help the Confederacy and critics who might weaken Federal war efforts, Lincoln resorted to two forms of stringent action. He suspended the writ of habeas corpus and empowered military authorities to arrest, hold, and try persons accused of giving assistance to the South or of interfering with the movements of Federal troops. In the name of military necessity he authorized the arrest and imprisonment of many newspaper publishers, orators, and agitators who printed or uttered severe criticisms of the Federal government and its war activities. The exact number of arrests under those orders is not known, but it was large.

Even in the South, supposed to be solid, rigorous means were adopted in efforts to stamp out criticisms and crush overt actions interfering with its war program. Early in 1862 the Confederate Congress authorized President Davis to suspend for a term of months the writ of habeas corpus and proclaim martial law in regions where open resistance occurred. Under this act, from time to time, martial law was declared in Richmond, the very capital of the Confederacy, in several Virginia counties, in parts of South Carolina, including Charleston, the hotbed of the secession movement, and in other places in the South.

When this law expired it was not immediately renewed, partly on account of the outcries against it. But in 1864 another temporary act of the kind was passed by the Confederate Congress, in response to a message from President Davis asserting that "disloyalty and hostility to our cause" existed in certain localities and that deserters were being protected by the civil courts.

Actions under such Confederate statutes were numerous and often stern, but apparently fewer and less drastic than similar actions by the Union government in the North. If President Davis had found ample support in the Confederate Congress he might have used martial law mercilessly in trying to prevent the dissolution of the Confederacy during the closing months of the war, but such support was never granted to him.

Supplementing the negative steps taken to suppress critics were the positive efforts made to whip up enthusiasm by turning the public's strong feelings about slavery to good account.

The most celebrated of all Lincoln's war measures was the Proclamation of Emancipation on January 1, 1863. His resolve to effect this historic stroke of state had matured slowly. At the outbreak of the war idealistic men and women in the North urged him to do it and continued their insistence from month to month, rolling monster petitions into the national capital to reinforce their pressure. But for various reasons Lincoln long hesitated. Weighty among them, no doubt, was his fear of losing the support of the slave states which remained in the Union, and his knowledge that the North was seriously divided over abolitionism in every form. He was aware also that a declaration of emancipation would be futile unless confirmed by victory at arms.

It was not until the summer of 1862 that Lincoln decided to act. In July of that year he read to his Cabinet the draft of a proclamation of emancipation which he had written and might issue when occasion seemed to make it feasible. Encouraged by the Federal victory at the battle of Antietam in September, he announced his resolve to the world. He gave notice that unless the states in arms against the Union returned to their allegiance he would, on January 1, 1863, deliver a blow directly at slavery. When the New Year arrived he fulfilled the promise.

In the Proclamation of Emancipation, issued under his war powers, Lincoln declared thenceforward and forever free all the slaves in all the districts of the United States then in arms against the Union. From one point of view this was an empty threat. It freed no slaves in fact. In the loyal districts of the Union slaves remained slaves and, in the districts still controlled by Confederate arms, slaves also remained slaves. But the Proclamation electrified the imagination of all who loved liberty and was indeed a move toward the abolition of slavery throughout the United States.

For Jefferson Davis, as well as Abraham Lincoln, emancipation became a practical issue before the close of the conflict. In desperate straits for soldiers to fight its battles, the Confederate Congress, near the end of the war, passed an act for the employment of slaves in military services. That law had the approval of General Robert E. Lee, as well as of

President Davis, and he aided in recruiting Negroes as soldiers. While the language of the statute and of the orders issued under it was vague, it was interpreted to mean that a slave acquired freedom by joining the Confederate army.

Even plans for complete emancipation were discussed at the Confederate capital. In 1864, Duncan Kenner, a member of the Confederate Congress, proposed to President Davis that an agent be sent abroad with power to offer to the British and French governments the emancipation of slaves in exchange for their official recognition of the Confederacy. Davis acceded to the plan. He appointed Kenner as minister plenipotentiary to carry out the project; and Kenner was abroad working at the scheme early in 1865—too late. Had the war continued, real emancipation might have been a Southern act of war.

☆

It was amidst this complex setting, abroad and at home, that the clash of arms took place, releasing pent-up feelings on both sides. At sea, action was swift. Under powers conferred upon him as commander in chief by the Constitution, Lincoln, in the spring of 1861, declared a blockade of Southern ports and ordered the Union navy to halt all vessels, Confederate or foreign, endeavoring to enter or leave them. In effect this blockade almost destroyed Southern commerce. While some blockade runners escaped the net, the number was too small to prevent a growing paralysis of the Confederate export and import business. The trade in cotton, the prime reliance of the South, was for practical purposes completely ruined.

On land, the problems were much more complex. After Fort Sumter had fallen and war had become a fact, what war plans, what systems of strategy were to be devised and followed? That was a major problem for both President Lincoln and President Davis. Having withdrawn from the Union and fired the first gun, the Confederacy confronted the task of making real by arms the independence it had asserted. If the Union was to be saved, Lincoln and his advisers had to prepare for an invasion of the South and make decisions respecting the routes to be chosen and the strategy of each movement.

At the start the Confederacy had about 400,000 men and large stores at its command and was better prepared for war than the Union in respect of those details. Some of its military officers advocated immediate offensive action against the North, especially an assault on Washington and the seizure of the capital. Such tactics, it was argued, would quickly bring the government of the United States to its knees.

Other Confederates were more wary. The idea of a possible compromise and a peaceful separation lingered among them even after blood had been shed. A blend of caution and hopes finally fixed for them the nature of their strategy. The invasion of the North was not given up; attempts at it were made, too late and with too little strength. So the South was irrevocably committed to fighting a defensive war, on the theory that the Northern armies might thus be beaten or worn down and forced to accept the independence of the Confederacy.

For the military strategists of the Union geography was of course an element to be reckoned with in planning warfare. The Appalachian Mountains separated the South into two great areas—the East, with Virginia as the bulwark; and the West, divided by the Mississippi River. Victory in either area would be more than a local success. If achieved in the West, it would split the Confederacy to the Gulf of Mexico. If it occurred in Virginia and was crowned by the capture of Richmond, it would weaken the prestige of the Confederacy at home and abroad.

Spurred to immediate decision by armchair strategists, shouting "On to Richmond!" in July 1861 an attack was made by a Union army under General McDowell on Confederate forces under General Beauregard near Centreville, Virginia, close to a little stream called Bull Run. The battle ended in a disaster for the Northern troops, and from this awful lesson President Lincoln learned that the conquest of Virginia would not be a simple affair.

It was in the Western region that military events of decisive significance for a Union victory first occurred. During the summer and autumn of 1861 small engagements in Missouri clinched the grip of the Union on that state. Early the next year Federal forces under Ulysses S. Grant started a drive into Tennessee, by way of the Tennessee River from its outlet in the Ohio. By gunboats on the river and by infantry on the landward side, Grant attacked the Confederates at Fort Henry in upper Tennessee and forced them to surrender, on February 6.

Dispatching some of his men by gunboats around to Fort Donelson on the Cumberland River, Grant marched eastward with the rest of his soldiers. On February 16 that fortress fell before the assaults of his troops. At many subsequent battles in western Tennessee the Confederates were defeated or seriously crippled and pushed aside; by the opening of 1863 Federal forces had penetrated upper Mississippi and Alabama.

Leaving other officers to cope with the Confederate forces still intact in Tennessee, Grant began to move on Vicksburg, the great stronghold on the Mississippi River. With the aid of gunboats and transports on the river, he besieged the city and starved General John B. Pemberton, the Confederate leader, into surrender on July 4. A few days later Port Hudson on the banks of the Mississippi, over the border in Louisiana, was taken by General Banks, one of Grant's aides.

As a naval detachment under Captain David Farragut had opened up the lower Mississippi River and seized New Orleans in the spring of the previous year, the "Father of Waters," as Lincoln said, now flowed "unvexed to the sea." On July 16, 1863, a steamer from St. Louis arrived with a cargo of goods at the docks in New Orleans. More serious battles were yet to be fought in Tennessee and Georgia, but the Confederacy was cut in twain by the summer of 1863 and never reunited.

Federal forces in the Eastern theater of war had accomplished nothing decisive when news of the capture of Vicksburg reached Lincoln in July 1863. Battle after battle, often long, desperate, and costly in lives, had been fought in the East: at Antietam, Fredericksburg, and Chancellorsville, for example. Lincoln had tried general after general in a vain search for a man who could win battles there—McClellan, Hooker, and Burnside, among them.

Meanwhile the army of Virginia under General Robert E. Lee, though repelled at Antietam in September 1862, remained powerful and confident. Indeed Lee felt so sure of his strength that he invaded Pennsylvania, by way of the Shenandoah Valley, in 1863. At Gettysburg, in the early days of July, his advance was stopped, but after receiving heavy losses, his forces managed to retire successfully into Virginia. When the year 1864 opened, Lee's army, apparently invincible in defense, barred the roads along which Union armies would have to march if they tried to plunge into the eastern stronghold of the Confederacy.

Two master feats for the Union cause were put through, however, in 1864. In May, General Grant, in command of all the Federal armies, took personal charge of the Virginia campaign and started a relentless drive on Richmond, sparing neither men nor resources in his determination to capture it. That same month Grant's trusted companion in arms, General William T. Sherman, began his march from Chattanooga to Atlanta.

While Grant slashed his way southward, undeterred by heavy losses, crossed the James River, and laid siege to Petersburg, near Richmond, Sherman advanced on Atlanta. In September Sherman took the city. After a delay of a few weeks he led his army off on a march across Georgia, foraging, burning, destroying as he went. On December 20, Savannah crumpled up. From that scene of victory Sherman's army turned northward and pursued its course across Georgia and South Carolina, leaving ruins in its wake, into North Carolina and onward toward Virginia.

The last phase of the war was drawing to a finish. On April 2, 1865, Grant took Petersburg. The next day the Union flag floated over the Confederate capital at Richmond, abandoned by President Davis in a hurried flight. At the head of a shaken if as yet unbeaten army, Lee moved rapidly westward in the direction of Lynchburg, with Grant racing at his heels and General Philip Sheridan on his flank.

For a time Lee seemed to think that he might escape into North Carolina, join forces there with General Joseph E. Johnston, and continue the war. But on April 9, finding that hope forlorn, he gave up, and at Appomattox conceded victory to General Grant. About two weeks later General Johnston laid down his arms. Far away in the West, General Kirby Smith, commanding Confederate troops beyond the Mississippi River, surrendered; and the last fragment of the Confederate army was dissolved during the first days of June. The war, launched with the bombardment of Fort Sumter in 1861, had at last run its course.

Soon it was possible to reckon some of the cost. A careful estimate placed the number of enlistments in the Federal army at 2,898,304 and in the Confederate army at about 1,300,000. The total number of deaths from all causes in the Federal forces was placed at 359,528 and in the Confederate army at approximately 258,000. This was exclusive of the hundreds of thousands of men wounded or made invalids for the remainder of their lives. Estimates of the cost in terms of the money spent on war by the two parties depended on the time fixed—whether up to April 1, 1865, or some later date to cover pensions paid to veterans on both sides. As of April 1, 1865, calculators reported the cost to the Union at about $3,250,000,000 and to the Confederacy at approximately $1,500,000,000; or $4,750,000,000 in all. After pensions, interest on the Federal debt, and the value of property destroyed were added, a conservative computation established the total cost of preserving the Union and abolishing slavery at above $10,000,000,000. For less than half this amount freedom could have been bought for all the 3,953,857 slaves recorded in the census of 1860—the compensated emancipation which Congress and President Lincoln had proposed in 1862.

Consuming as were the events of the war and the measures of public policy immediately connected with it, the thought and activity of the people on both sides of the struggle were by no means wholly monopolized by it. The life and work of millions in both sections continued to be concerned with trends that far antedated the war itself.

The South was disturbed by complaints that civilians gave too much attention and energy to their own interests and too little to the prosecution of the war. Governors of southern states, members of state legislatures, and members of the Confederate Congress concerned themselves continually with the protection of local and civil rights against the encroachments of military power under the leadership of President Davis. All departments of the Confederate government, amid the distractions of war, considered plans and took actions with reference to economic interests, and with a view to the reordering of affairs after independence was secured. But with the collapse of the Confederate system, legal and financial, and the occupation of the South by Federal armies, such plans and actions in respect of Southern economy and social policy came to naught or at least to little if anything.

On the other hand, in the North, rarely invaded and so relatively free from the devastation of battles, the civilian way of life was less upset. There debates over political issues that had shaken the country before the war went on; and significant laws bearing on these issues were enacted by Congress. In response to the increasing demands created by government buying for war purposes, industry and agriculture flourished and the Industrial Revolution drove forward. Out of war profits prodigious masses of capital were accumulated in private hands for new investments in business. Additional millions of acres were brought under the plow by freehold farmers in the West. During the war years the supremacy of manufacturing and commercial interests over the planting interests, in wealth and the number of workers employed, became indisputable.

With senators and representatives accustomed to speak for the planting interests absent from the national capital, the Federal Congress was of course freer to enact laws long demanded by industrialists, financiers, farmers, and reformers. In providing revenues for war purposes it increased again and again the duties levied on imports and raised the discriminative protection accorded to American manufacturers to the highest point yet attained in American history. For example, the tariff on pig iron, which stood at six dollars a ton in 1861, was pushed to nine dollars a ton in 1864, and the tariff of twelve cents a pound on general woolen manufactures was doubled by the act of 1864. Neither the old Federalists nor the Whigs had ever dreamed of favors to industry so generous. Nor were the farmers overlooked in the tariff bills. The duty of three cents per pound for imported raw wool of the lower grade, imposed by the law of 1861, was lifted to six cents a pound in 1864. At the close of the war the free trade which Democrats had once advocated in their national platform seemed as dead as a doornail.

The second great issue over which politicians and statesmen had argued since the days of Hamilton and Jefferson—a national banking system—was likewise settled for a time in connection with efforts to raise money for military expenditures. Hamilton's United States Bank had lapsed in 1811. The second United States Bank established in 1816 had been abolished by Jacksonian Democrats. From 1836 to the outbreak of the war state banks had dominated banking and inundated the country with their paper notes, some sound, some unsound, others fluctuating wildly in value. To cope with financial disorders and help the sale of bonds, Congress in 1863 established a new banking system. It centered the system in the Treasury Department of the Federal government, rather than in a banking corporation such as had been set up in 1791 and 1816, only to be repudiated.

The new law authorized the formation of local banking associations or companies. It empowered them to engage in the general banking business and to issue paper money based on the Federal bonds they bought and deposited with the Treasurer of the United States. The next year, in 1864, Congress made provision for forcing all state banks entirely out of the currency business by laying a prohibitive annual tax of ten per cent on state bank notes, beginning July 1, 1866. Even after they returned to power in Washington, the Democrats, hitherto sworn foes of national banking, did not dare to overthrow it and restore state bank currency. Hamilton had truly triumphed over Jefferson.

During this distribution of national largess by legislative acts, the agrarians got a portion, in the form of free homesteads on the public domain. In their platform of 1860 the Republicans promised free land as well as protection for manufactures. This pledge Congress redeemed two years later by passing the Homestead Act, which President Lincoln gladly signed.

Under the act any person, man or woman, head of a family or twenty-one years old, either a citizen or an alien who had declared his intention of becoming a citizen, could enter a claim to 160 acres on the public domain; and by occupying it for five years, besides making certain improvements on it, the entrant was to have full possession of the property. One vital exception was made, however: excluded from this right to free land were all persons who had borne arms against the United States or given aid and comfort to the enemy. The free land was to go to loyal Unionists including soldiers in the Union army and immigrants from foreign countries.

Other momentous measures passed by Congress during the war years included laws chartering companies to build railway lines to the Pacific coast. By acts of 1862 and 1864 provision was made for a line in the central region, serving Federal interests. The Union Pacific Company was to start from a point in Nebraska, later fixed at Omaha, and build westward. The Central Pacific Company was to begin at San Francisco or a place on the navigable waters of the Sacramento River and build eastward. At some spot, to be determined by speed of construction, the two lines were to meet, thus completing the overland route. In 1864 the Northern Pacific Company was authorized to construct a railway from Lake Superior to Puget Sound by a northern route.

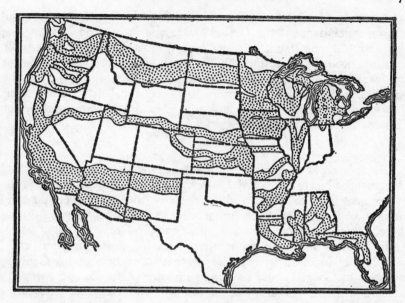

AREAS IN WHICH HALF THE LAND WAS GRANTED BY THE GOVERNMENT
TO RAILWAY COMPANIES, 1850–1871

To speed up the work of the Union and Central Pacific Companies, Congress granted them an enormous acreage of land in the form of free rights of way and alternate sections on each side of their lines. In addition it lent them a large sum of money for every mile of track laid— a sum varying according to the difficulties of construction.

At last the continent was to be spanned by railways. Manufacturers, merchants, and capitalists were delighted at the prospect: their markets and investment opportunities were to be widened. Land-hungry men and women were delighted also: the railways would make it easier for them to go West with their movable property and occupy the now free land; railways would provide transportation for agricultural produce to Eastern markets and would increase the value of farm homesteads. And, what was more, the North would be made stronger in wealth and in ties of communication.

While debating and passing bills relative to the conduct of the war, taxes, tariffs, banking, homesteads, and railways, Congress dealt with the question of slavery. In April 1862 it abolished slavery in the District of Columbia. About two months later it prohibited slavery in all the existing territories of the United States and any that might be acquired at any time in the future. In June 1864 it repealed the Fugitive Slave Act passed in 1793 and amended in the Compromise of 1850. In

January 1864 a resolution for an amendment to the Constitution abolishing slavery throughout the United States was introduced in Congress; and about a year later, after prolonged discussion, it received the requisite two-thirds vote in both houses. It was sent to the states for consideration, ratified, and put into effect in December 1865. Thus the verbal emancipation which Lincoln had proclaimed in 1863 under his war power was extended to include all slaves and implemented by the Thirteenth Amendment.

☆

Although amid the drastic actions taken by President Lincoln and Congress the North presented a firm war front to the Confederacy, the government in Washington and the people of the North were far from united over the merits of the conflict and the measures adopted during the war years. No more than the South was the North actually "solid." From his first inauguration in 1861 until his death in April 1865, Lincoln was involved in controversies with members of his Cabinet, members of Congress, and leaders in his own party. Congress was dissatisfied with his management of the war and created a committee to investigate and supervise it. Senators and representatives bent on destroying slavery at the earliest possible moment protested against his cautious and hesitating methods.

As soon as any former Confederate state was occupied by Union troops advancing into the South, members of Congress began to take issue with Lincoln over the treatment to be meted out to that state—its relation to the Union and the kind of government it was to have. Abolitionists fumed impatiently at his delays in dealing with slavery. Nor were they all content with the elusive emancipation in his Proclamation. "Radical Republicans" in Congress and even members of Lincoln's Cabinet intrigued against him, belittled his character, and attacked many of his measures.

Behind the armed front of the Union, Northern civilians were also engaged in political struggles with one another during the war years. In the congressional elections of 1862 the Democrats gained so many seats in Congress that it looked as if Lincoln and his party might be thrown out of power at the next election. In fact the Republicans were so perturbed in 1864 that they generally dropped their name and called themselves the Union party. And for the purpose of conciliating Democrats, they nominated, as their candidate for Vice-President, Andrew Johnson, a stanch Democrat from Tennessee who had courageously demonstrated his fidelity to the Union from the beginning of the war.

During the presidential campaign of 1864 Lincoln foresaw probable defeat and for a time the outlook for his re-election was indeed dark. In their platform of that year Northern Democrats denounced the war as a failure and called for a conference to restore the old Union under the Constitution. But this defiance alienated voters in their party. The very candidate whom they nominated, General George B. McClellan, insisted in his speech, accepting the nomination, that the war was not a failure, thereby confounding the confusion. At the polls the Democrats carried only three states: New Jersey, Delaware, and Kentucky.

With gratitude to the people for their confidence in him, expressed by re-electing him, Lincoln pushed the war to a conclusion. He was preparing for a peace of reconciliation when, on April 15, 1865, he died at the hands of an assassin—John Wilkes Booth—a martyr to the cause he had served so singleheartedly.

The executive burden passed to the Vice-President, Andrew Johnson. With the office went much of the ferocious criticism that had been directed against Lincoln on account of his conciliatory attitude toward the defeated Confederates and his liberal proposals for restoring the Confederate states to the Union. With Johnson's assumption of his high office the heat of criticism rose and was intensified in many quarters on other scores. Early in 1868 animosity reached such a pitch that the House of Representatives impeached President Johnson before the Senate and he escaped conviction with removal from the presidency only by the margin of a single vote in the Senate.

Chapter 18

POSTWAR RECONSTRUCTION AND
ECONOMIC EXPANSION

WITH THE SHIELD of the Union assured and the issue of chattel slavery finally settled, the people of the United States turned in the spring of 1865 to peacetime tasks. The tasks were, as usual, in the main political, economic, and moral. The setting for actions was now the unbroken continental domain. But grave problems lay before the people: the rights of the Southern states in the Union, the economic advancement of the South, civil liberties for Negroes, the payment of the huge national debt, the formulation of public policies for general economic expansion, the disposition of natural resources, and the development of territories into states.

In respect of these problems the government of the United States played a leading role in the framing of policies and the determination of actions. Imperative among its first obligations was Southern rehabilitation—economic and legal—amid the lingering passions of the war and in circumstances painful to both sides. Southern farms, plantations, and cities had been the scenes of battles. Over large areas buildings and fences had been destroyed, cattle driven off, and implements of production smashed. Miles of Southern railways had been torn up; rolling stock had been wrecked; railway stations and offices had been burned. Families that had led in business and agricultural development were impoverished. The financial system lay in ruins. Confederate bonds were worthless and all thought of reviving them was blasted by the Fourteenth Amendment to the Constitution of the United States adopted in 1868. Confederate paper money was valueless and specie had almost disappeared from circulation. From the ashes of war a new start had to be made in the South.

To complicate the situation, a revolution had been wrought in Southern society by the abolition of slavery. Millions of Negroes, hitherto held in bondage, generally illiterate, little experienced in management if often skilled in the arts of industry, without property, were now "free." Most of them in the Confederate states had been loyal and helpful to their masters and mistresses during the war and had not deliberately sought their freedom.

There were exceptions, to be sure, thousands of exceptions. At least 100,000 Negroes had served in the Union armies as soldiers and laborers. As the Union armies advanced in the South, other thousands of Negroes gave them aid and support in the hope of forwarding their own liberation. In the South as well as the North, hundreds of Negroes, intelligent and educated, furnished some leadership for their bewildered people.

But from the economic point of view, emancipation in general deprived Negroes of their assured livelihood on plantations and set them adrift in the world, homeless, toolless, and penniless, like the evicted peasants of England in the seventeenth century, ill equipped to enter the fierce competition for existence about them, still wearing the color badge of servitude. At the same time slaveowners, besides losing property valued at about $4,000,000,000, lost their supremacy over the labor supply for their farms and plantations. Old laws pertaining to labor relations had expired on the statute books. Old practices of slave days were forbidden. What new laws and practices were to be devised? How much power of self-determination remained in the South?

Now the old ruling class was subject to the military power of the Union and deprived of representation in the Congress of the United States. In this plight that class could do little except wait for the end of the armed occupation and political action by the President and Congress of the United States. Meanwhile small white farmers of the South were jostling it in the contest for power. Upland farmers had long struggled with the seaboard planters in attempts to secure representation in the state legislatures proportioned to their superior numbers; and in the aftermath of the war among the states they were seeking, with more confidence of success, the power hitherto denied them. But neither former slaveowners nor freehold farmers could make any basic decisions in matters of government until their states were restored to the Union in one form or another.

The position to be accorded to the Southern states had become a major question for the government at Washington as soon as its armies had permanently occupied a large area of the South; and it continued to be a primary problem for the President and Congress for many years after the war. Plans proposed in Washington for the treatment of the South, almost endless in number, fell into a few broad patterns. Utopians who had wanted to make the whole war a war for liberty yearned to hold the Southern states down, utterly destroy the great land-lord class by the confiscation of its estates, divide the land among Negroes and poor white farmers who had been loyal to the Union, give the suffrage and full civil rights to the hitherto dispossessed, and force upon the defeated Confederacy the principles of liberty that Thomas Jefferson had celebrated as the perfect good.

Astute Republican politicians, knowing that their party represented a minority in the nation, had a care for measures that would keep them-selves in power. Some of them encouraged and made use of the utopians; but all along they fixed their minds on the instant need of things and made plans adapted to their interests.

All the plans, whatever their source, rested on theories about the nature of the Union, the Confederate revolt, and the power of the President and Congress of the United States.

If Lincoln's theory was right—namely, that the states could not law-fully withdraw from the Union—then none of them was ever out of the Union, even during the height of Southern military strength. If this theory was sound, as the Confederate states came under Federal authority with the progress of Federal arms the loyal citizens in each were entitled to restore loyal state governments. But against Lincoln's theory it was argued that the Confederate states, by armed rebellion, had actually left the Union, were bound to come back as "conquered provinces," and in instituting governments must submit to the decrees of the conquerors.

Who was to make decisions about the restoration of the Southern states? The President or Congress? And what plans were to be followed in the process of restoration? As events developed the process was divided into two stages: "presidential" reconstruction, as it was called, and "congressional" reconstruction. Lincoln's proposals were, relatively speaking, moderate and generous; those of Congress were severe and punitive.

Under his war power Lincoln claimed the right to prescribe the terms on which military government was to be withdrawn from the states of the Confederacy as, one after another, they came under Federal authority again. When the Union forces drove southward in the Mississippi Valley, in 1862–63, he appointed military governors—in Tennessee, Arkansas, and Louisiana—and instructed them to take charge while loyal governments were being formed in those states.

Late in 1863, Lincoln issued a proclamation of amnesty memorable for its conciliatory tone. The decree offered, in the first place, to restore the suffrage to all voters who would take the prescribed oath of loyalty to the United States, with exceptions excluding practically all leaders in the Confederacy. It then provided that, as soon as ten per cent of the voters in any state had taken the oath of loyalty, they could form their own government and, having done so, would be entitled to the recognition of their state by the President of the United States. This plan, which Lincoln amplified in some respects in 1864, was, in its general outlines, followed by his successor Andrew Johnson.

Under the presidential plan of reconstruction, which did not force Negro suffrage on Southern states, new state governments were established as the Confederacy crumbled. By 1866 all of the Southern states had conformed to the terms of the plan and were ready to take their places in the Union again. But in the course of their operations the new Southern legislatures undertook to deal with the "Negro problem," and many of them enacted laws imposing severe restrictions on the rights of freedmen. These laws, known as new "black codes," excited great opposition in the North and were attacked there as attempts to restore slavery under another name.

In these circumstances reconstruction passed into its second, or congressional, stage. The war had ended and the war power of the President had been curtailed. Whatever the President might do about governments in the states that had seceded, the Senate and the House of Representatives claimed the right, by constitutional provisions, each for itself, to admit or exclude men from the South who, duly elected, were ready to take their seats.

With this weapon in their hands, radical Republicans in Congress took charge of reconstruction. In June 1866, Congress adopted a resolution to alter the federal Constitution by adding a fourteenth amendment. This proposal was intended to confer citizenship on all Negroes, establish the right of all persons to life, liberty, and property, and reduce the representation in Congress of any state which deprived adult male citizens of the right to vote in major elections. On April 9, 1866, Congress passed the first Civil Rights Act, a measure designed to assure to Negroes the full civil equality before the law enjoyed by other American citizens. In July of the same year Congress extended the life of the Freedmen's Bureau, established the previous year for the purpose of giving material relief to the emancipated slaves, and enlarged the power of the Bureau to cover protection of civil rights.

While the Fourteenth Amendment was pending before state legislatures for ratification, Congress overrode the presidential plan for reconstruction and enacted a series of bills based on different principles. These laws, the first passed on March 2, 1867, constituted a plan that was almost, if not entirely, arbitrary in nature. All the former Confederate states, except Tennessee, were grouped into five military districts and each was put under the control of a Northern army officer invested with full power to keep order and supervise the process of reconstruction.

In each state a large class of former Confederate leaders was temporarily deprived of the suffrage; and the vote was given to other white men and to Negro men on equal terms. The voters so enfranchised in each state were to hold an election for the purpose of choosing delegates to a state convention authorized to frame a new constitution, including a provision for Negro manhood suffrage. On completion this constitution was to be submitted to the voters for approval or rejection. As soon as a new constitution was established by this process, the state legislature held under it was to ratify the Fourteenth Amendment. After all these steps had been taken and the Fourteenth Amendment had been proclaimed a part of the Constitution of the United States, the state thus reorganized was to be restored to the Union and its people entitled to representation in the national Congress.

The congressional plan of reconstruction was indeed a bitter pill for the former Confederates. It outlawed their recent efforts at recovering a place in the Union on other terms. But, supported by Northern arms, it was carried out. One after another Southern states yielded to its dictates. In 1868, Arkansas, Louisiana, Alabama, Georgia, Florida, South Carolina, and North Carolina complied with the terms of the plan and were restored to the Union. Texas, Mississippi, and Virginia completed the return journey in 1870. Except for Federal troops stationed in a few localities, and subject to the new conditions imposed upon all states by the Thirteenth and the Fourteenth amendments, the South had been "reconstructed."

As if not yet sure that its designs would finally prevail, Congress in 1869 submitted to the states for ratification the Fifteenth Amendment, which provided that the right of citizens of the United States to vote shall not be denied or abridged by the United States or any state on account of race, color, or previous condition of servitude. Just as the last of the states were returning to the Union in 1870 the Fifteenth Amendment was proclaimed in force.

For a brief period the governments of Southern states were in the hands of Negro men and the white men who had not been disfranchised for supporting the Confederacy. That is, in the main, voters who owned small farms or had no property at all held the reins of government. With delight, of course, they accepted the power entrusted to them and began to make laws and distribute offices with a view to their own interests. Many of their laws, for example those providing for free public education, measured up to enlightened conceptions of the age. Others fell far beneath that standard. Corruption and waste of public funds were common in the legislatures, sometimes in the grossest forms. Disgust spread among the disfranchised whites, to crown their resentment at being deprived of their former power.

Whatever the merits or demerits of the new Southern governments, disfranchised white men and white voters otherwise indignant at the new regime quickly set about overthrowing it by methods open and covert. They employed arguments and threats to keep Negroes away from the polls. Secret societies, such as the Ku Klux Klan, terrorized Negroes and their white sympathizers. In state after state "white supremacy" was re-established: in Tennessee in 1869; in Virginia and North Carolina in 1870; in Georgia the next year; in Arkansas, Alabama, and Texas in 1874; in Mississippi in 1875; and in Louisiana, Florida, and South Carolina in 1877—the year in which the withdrawal of the last Federal soldiers of occupation took place.

While Southern people were groping among social and economic ruins for economic security and reorganizing state governments, Northern economy was expanding with unprecedented speed. In the decade after the war nearly 7,000,000 persons were added to the population of the country, counting new immigrants; but the increase in the North and the West was far greater than in the South. By 1870 the population in the United States had risen to 38,500,000; by 1880, to 50,100,000; by 1900, to 76,100,000. The nation now had a large supply of willing hands to subdue the rest of the continental domain and raise the production of wealth to heights undreamed of in the fancies of the Republic's founders.

With millions of dollars at their command for investment, captains of industry leaped forward to build more factories and railways, open up and develop additional resources, and enlarge the output of machine industries in every direction. At their disposal inventors and searchers, besides improving old machines, placed new machines, materials, and processes, on which new industries of gigantic proportions were constructed. Among the discoveries and mechanical inventions of the period the following were so important as to herald the coming of a second industrial revolution:

1859—Great "strike" of petroleum in western Pennsylvania.
1868—C. L. Sholes's typewriter ready for production.
1875—G. F. Swift's refrigerator freight car in use.
1876—Alexander G. Bell sends first telephone message.
1877—Thomas Edison has a phonograph playing.
1879—George Selden's patent for a "gasoline carriage."
1882—Edison's electric power plant starts operation in New York City.
1896—Langley's airplane makes experimental flight.
1901—The Wright brothers finish an airplane glider.

Two of the machines put into use in this period meant an industrial transformation all along the line. The first was the "gas engine," the internal-combustion engine, which emancipated manufacturing and farming from the limitations of the cumbersome steam engine, and furnished an immense market for petroleum products. The second was the electric dynamo and the transmission of power by wire for use in running machines as well as lighting houses, factories, and city streets.

The extension of facilities for the transport of passengers, farm produce, and manufactures kept pace with rising industries. Between 1860 and 1890 the railway mileage increased from 30,000 miles to 166,000 miles. At the opening of the century it stood at 240,000 miles. In 1869 the last spike was driven on the central line to the Pacific and rail communications were opened from the Atlantic to the Pacific, with way stations. Within twenty years three other transcontinental lines were completed, to the north and the south of the central line. Meanwhile new railways were built in the East and the South, short lines were combined into systems, and countless little towns and villages in far-scattered rural regions were linked to the great cities and with one another. On navigable rivers, on the Great Lakes, and in coastal waters, steamships supplemented railway transportation, increasing in some waters and declining in others according to the nature of rail competition.

To the westward rush of pioneers, which had continued even during the Civil War, a powerful new impetus was now given. Northern soldiers and citizens released from the strain of war crowded to the frontier by the thousands. They were joined by thousands of aliens—German, British, Irish, and Scandinavian—fresh from the Old World. Railways facilitated the rush.

Between the tier of states on the west bank of the Mississippi River and Oregon and California on the Pacific coast, only two states had been admitted to the Union during the war period—Kansas in 1861 and Nevada in 1864. All the rest of that vast region was still sparsely settled and under territorial government when the army of Virginia laid down its arms in 1865. But the Homestead Act of 1862, the grants of land to railway companies, and laws providing for the quick sale of timber and mineral lands prepared the way for rapid settlement and for the upswing of mining, lumber, and other industries.

Never before in the history of mankind had agricultural and industrial enterprise, so well equipped with capital and machines, enjoyed such a bounteous opportunity for exploitation. Before the close of the nineteenth century practically all the arable land in the Western regions of rainfall and nearly all the grazing lands in dry or semiarid regions had passed into the hands of farmers, railway companies, stock raisers, purchasers of Spanish grants sometimes embracing hundreds of thousands of acres, land speculators, and engrossers native and foreign. The public domain, especially in Alaska, was still large. But by 1893 it could be officially announced that the frontier hardly existed any longer; that the best of the farming lands had all been given away or sold.

In the lavish parceling out of the national domain, some acreage went directly to men and women who entered lands under the Homestead Act. Relatively speaking, however, it was small in size. By 1923 approximately 213,860,000 acres had been given away to settlers real and pretended since 1868. The word "pretended" is important, for homestead entries were honeycombed with frauds; individual entrants had often acted as dummies for land and mining companies. In the course of the years at least 620,000,000 acres had been sold directly to companies and individuals, granted for the purpose of making internal improvements and building railways, or turned over to states in aid of education and other public functions.

Millions of acres of valuable timber, mineral, and grazing lands were literally stolen under the eyes of dishonest or negligent officials in the federal land office; and other millions were wrested from the government by chicanery of one kind or another. In the history of political corruption, seldom, if ever, had there been transactions on a scale so prodigious or conducted with more brazen effrontery. Thousands of great fortunes in the East as well as in the West were built out of resources wrung from the government for a pittance or for a bribe to its officials, if not actually stolen.

Nevertheless, in the process of dividing the national domain millions of new farms were staked out in the West; grazing lands fabulous in extent were brought into use and overuse by cattlemen and ranchers; and other resources were exploited by mining and manufacturing concerns. Between 1865 and 1900 billions of new wealth were added annually to the national output.

As farmers, miners, prospectors, cattlemen, and lumbermen, with or without families, poured into the Western territories, demands for statehood went up from every region. In 1867 the territory of Nebraska, reduced in size, was formally made a state. By 1875, Colorado claimed a population of about 100,000, largely composed of miners, farmers, cattle raisers, and prospectors. The following year it was granted statehood by Congress.

By this time the territories along the northern border of the United States were filling up and boasting of their progress. Within ten years their political leaders were knocking at the doors of Congress. In 1889 the pleas of North Dakota, South Dakota, Washington, and Montana were favorably heard and they were admitted to the Union. The next year Idaho and Wyoming took their places among the states. Having prohibited polygamy and forced the Mormons to adopt a constitution incorporating that prohibition, Congress finally conferred statehood on Utah in 1896.

This left only three regions, besides Alaska, under a territorial form of government, and they were soon given statehood. Oklahoma came into the Union in 1907 and Arizona and New Mexico in 1912.

At last the continental domain was fully organized, in forty-eight states, all presumed to be "free and equal" under the Constitution of the United States. Each now had a constitution of its own making and a government resting upon popular, if not universal, suffrage.

The swift industrial development and westward expansion were made possible, in a large measure, by the stream of immigrants that flooded into the United States, subject to no retarding legal restrictions of any moment until the Chinese Exclusion Act was passed in 1882. Although the number coming into the country rose or fell from year to year, the general tendency was upward. In 1864 it was 193,000; in 1874, 313,000; in 1884, 518,000; in 1891, 560,000; in 1907, 1,285,000.

During these years striking shifts appeared in the national origins of immigrants. For a short time after 1865 the flow was still mainly from Great Britain, Ireland, Germany, and Scandinavia. Then the number of immigrants from northern Europe diminished relatively, and immigration from Italy, Russia, and Austria-Hungary increased. At the opening of the twentieth century these three countries furnished more than three fourths of all the immigrants. Polish, Hungarian, Czech, Slovak, Croat, Russian, and Jewish immigrants then far exceeded in number all the British, Irish, and Germans making their way into the United States. To give exact figures, between 1871 and 1880 the total number of immigrants from western Europe was 2,000,000, and that from eastern and southern Europe was 181,000. Between 1901 and 1910 the numbers from the two European regions were 2,000,000 and 6,100,000 respectively.

Changes in the national origins of immigrants were closely related to the disappearance of free land in the West which tended to divert immigrants to industries in the cities. In the urban centers immigrants of each nationality formed large colonies, or quarters, of their own, with separate languages, newspapers, and customs. Similar conditions prevailed to some extent among immigrants who settled on farms in the West; but the rise of "foreign cities" within American cities was an extraordinary characteristic of the period that followed the Civil War.

From decade to decade, as the following table shows, the number of foreign-born inhabitants in the United States rose rapidly:

1860, total, 31,400,000; foreign-born, 4,100,000
1880, total, 50,100,000; foreign-born, 6,600,000
1900, total, 76,100,000; foreign-born, 10,300,000

At the end of the century, according to these figures, about fourteen per cent of the total population was foreign-born. But the cities showed different proportions. In the cities of more than 25,000 inhabitants in

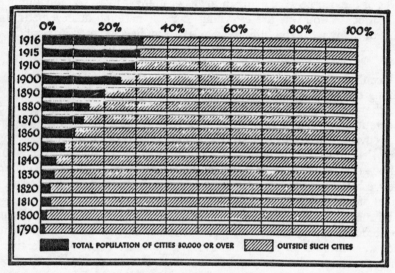

PER CENT OF POPULATION IN CITIES HAVING OVER 30,000 INHABITANTS
AND OUTSIDE SUCH CITIES FOR SPECIFIED YEARS: 1790–1916

1900, approximately twenty-six per cent, were foreign-born. For cities of over 100,000 inhabitants the proportion of foreign-born was about thirty-five per cent, and in a few of the largest cities it was fifty per cent or more. At that time the rapid inflow of immigrants indicated that the percentage of foreign-born in the cities at the next census would be still larger.

As Americans from farming regions and immigrants from abroad turned increasingly to industries and commerce for employment, the growth of urbanism destroyed the almost undisputed supremacy of the rural regions that had characterized the American past. In 1789 only about three per cent of the inhabitants were city dwellers and there were only five cities of more than 8000 inhabitants. By 1890 about one third of the people lived in towns of 4000 inhabitants or more.

Even more remarkable was the growth of great cities. In 1890 New York and Brooklyn combined had 2,300,000 inhabitants; Philadelphia and Chicago had crossed the 1,000,000 line; and Boston, Baltimore, and Washington each laid claim to 500,000. In Massachusetts, Rhode Island, and Connecticut the urban concentration of population was highest. Four fifths of the Massachusetts population lived in urban towns of 4000 or more; and in Rhode Island, nine tenths.

On every hand boasters exulted in the thought that the United States would soon outstrip, in respect of urbanism, England, where about four fifths of the people were living in towns of more than 10,000 inhabitants, as if urbanization was the crowning glory of national achievement. In fact for many years the fulfillment of the prophecy seemed a possibility.

Deeply engaged, as Southerners were, in the struggle for existence among the wreckage of the war and for emancipation from the rule of Northern officials supported by arms, many of them forged ahead energetically with activities which entered into the productive expansion that covered the continent. At first planters faced the burden of getting their fields into production again. Though deprived of their chattel labor supply, they still held their lands; all the radical proposals for breaking up their estates and dividing them among freedmen and landless whites failed of realization.

Dismayed by the prospects of defeat under the new labor system, numerous planting families fled to the cities, South and North, where they went into the professions or business pursuits. Those who remained on their estates usually resorted to one or all of three devices for carrying on production: allowing the former slaves to live in their old cabins and work as before, but for wages or payment in goods; "letting" small blocks of land to freedmen or whites in return for a cash rental or a share of the crops; and selling plots outright while continuing to operate the remainder on a wage or rental basis.

The dilemma of the planters afforded opportunities to many poor whites and freedmen for acquiring land. Since colonial times small farmers had been pressed back into the uplands by the apparently relentless advance of large plantation economy from the seaboard. Now, as many great plantations dissolved, small farmers were often able to buy better land and raise their standard of living. Generally the white farmer and his family supplied all or most of the labor on his freehold; if his acreage was large he hired a few workers at wages. The more thrifty or fortunate Negroes, likewise sharing in this opportunity, were frequently able to buy land and establish homesteads.

Two figures indicate the tendency. In 1860 the average land holding in the Southern states was 335.4 acres; in 1880 it was 153.4; and in 1900 it was 138.2. Yet the tendency to dissolution was checked by the end of the century, leaving many large estates intact. Furthermore, especially in times of depression, urban bankers, lawyers, merchants, investors, and corporations acquired extensive holdings of Southern land and frequently demonstrated the efficiency of large-scale farming as against small-farming, for which skill or capital was lacking.

It was in relation to the system of land economy that emancipated Negro men and women had to find footholds for themselves. If planters had been able to furnish adequate capital and pay wages regularly, many more Negroes would have become permanent wage workers on the land. But the planters after the war were usually handicapped by lack of money. Often they obtained credit for supplies from merchants and furnished the Negroes who worked for them with food, clothing, and shelter as they had done in the slave system; but at the end of the year, in the settlement, the Negroes were likely to have no balance coming to them as wages. They were apt to be in debt to the planter, even when the books were honestly kept by their employers.

Under the wage system Negroes grew discouraged and restless. Thousands left the land for neighboring or distant towns and sought employment as domestic or casual laborers. The more determined among those who remained in the country struggled hard to procure land to be worked on other than wage terms—to achieve an economic underwriting. Many became renters of small farms, paying their rent in a share of the crops—the "sharecroppers." Others by dint of exacting labor and thrift became owners of land, either outright or on mortgage. In 1874, nine years after emancipation, Negroes owned 338,769 acres of land in Georgia alone, either outright or subject to mortgage. By the end of the century, it was estimated, about one fourth of the Negro workers on the land had become freeholders of the one type or the other.

On the whole, particularly as to the production of cotton, none of these schemes for land use proved to be highly efficient. It was not until 1880 that the Southern cotton crop, measured in bales, rose again to the figure of 1860. It is true that twenty years later, in 1900, the output of cotton was about three fourths larger than it had been in 1860, but that was in part due to the extension of the cotton belt in Texas where white labor and management predominated.

If Southern economy had been compelled to depend as largely on cotton production as in the ante-bellum days, its prospects would have been dismal. But diversification in agriculture offered other sources of wealth. To the old staples—cotton, tobacco, rice, and sugar—new products were added: apples, peaches, oranges, lemons, pineapples, peanuts, watermelons, and vegetables in a large variety. As the mileage of railways increased and rapid transportation by refrigerator cars developed, Southern agriculture found large home markets for these commodities in neighboring cities and in the distant North. Thus the subordination of the South as a raw-material province utterly dependent on the world cotton market at Liverpool was mitigated by diversification and by the creation of special ties with the national market.

The stresses and strains of the struggle for existence on the land were also relieved by the growth of manufacturing in the South—an economic enterprise which contributed materially to the expansion of the national productive activities so typical of the period between 1865 and 1900. Leadership in Southern manufacturing enterprise, as Arthur M. Schlesinger has pointed out in *The Rise of the City*, was taken by industrialists who came, in overwhelming proportions, from Southern families outside the former slave-owning groups. During the early stages of its development both capital and management also sprang principally from Southern sources. Thus history seemed to vindicate Southern writers who had claimed before 1860 that the slave system hampered the direction of Southern energies to the industrial use of rich natural resources right at hand.

Scarcely had the brazen clangor of the fratricidal war subsided when Southern promoters exclaimed: "Bring the mills to the cotton!" By 1880 Southern cotton mills were turning out a volume of goods equal to almost one fourth the output of New England's mills. Between 1860 and 1900 the number of Southern spindles increased from 298,000 to 4,300,000. The rise of tobacco manufactures was hardly less spectacular, especially in Virginia, North Carolina, and Kentucky.

In the expansion of capitalist enterprise great coal beds were opened and worked in the Appalachian regions from Maryland to northern Alabama. All the way from Virginia through Alabama to Arkansas and Texas immense deposits of iron ore were unearthed and forced to yield supplies for iron mills; in a few years Birmingham, Alabama, took pride in being "the Pittsburgh of the South." In Kentucky, Tennessee, Louisiana, Arkansas, and Texas petroleum was discovered and the products of the oil industry were added to Southern wealth. Cotton, tobacco, coal, iron, and oil industries were supplemented by the lumber and cottonseed industries. At the opening of the new century the output of Southern lumber mills more than equaled that of the mills in the huge forests of the Great Lakes region.

In the train of the Southern industrial revolution followed the manifold consequences of such an economic upheaval. Around mines, factories, mills, and other scenes of operation congregated armies of industrial workers. Since immigrants from foreign countries generally preferred to settle in the North and West, Southern enterprise had to draw mainly on local sources for its labor supply. Into its industries were lured men, women, and children from rural communities—thousands of "poor whites" from the pine barrens, the uplands, and the mountains, where they had lived on the very margin of subsistence. Now they were to have some cash and be drawn into the social movements of the nation.

As in the North long before, new factory towns shot up in Southern rural scenes, and old towns grew rapidly in population. Richmond, Atlanta, Birmingham, Dallas, Houston, and San Antonio became thriving centers of manufacturing and commerce. To cope with the demands for transportation additional railway lines were built, old lines improved, and consolidations made among short lines. Between 1865 and 1880 the mileage was more than doubled. By 1900 it had been more than doubled again.

Before Hinton Rowan Helper, author of the prophetic *Impending Crisis*, died in 1909 the planters and merchants who had led the South in the days of slavery had been challenged and undermined by white farmers, by great industrialists, by high-powered merchants, and by industrial workers—with their persistent and special interests. Although in national elections the South as a rule seemed "solid," it was in fact divided into strong factions over the problems that went with the swift transformation of its economy—as it was drawn tighter and tighter into the expanding economy of other sections, North and West.

Chapter 19

THE CONCENTRATION OF ECONOMIC POWER

A S THE NATION put one new invention after another to extensive use, following the Civil War, individuals and communities tended to become more and more minutely specialized and diversified in the kinds of things they made and in the services they rendered. Thus, in increasing measure, each person and each area had to look to others for an expanding range of raw materials, finished goods, and types of customers. The web of economic interdependence inherited from earlier stages of the Industrial Revolution was becoming vaster, more complex, and more difficult to manage.

Meanwhile many corporations were striving to capture control over larger and larger segments of the web of interdependence by absorbing competitors in the same line of endeavor, by diversifying into new fields, or by both methods. Workers were organizing on a national scale in an effort to match big business in bargaining power with greater prospects of success; and the Federal Government was trying to cope with the problems raised by both big business and big labor, likewise on a mammoth scale. A trend toward the concentration of economic power in fewer and fewer hands was setting in. If, as Brooks Adams declared in *The Law of Civilization and Decay,* published in 1895, the movement of energies in society is inexorably toward centralization, the course of economic and political affairs in the United States during this period certainly provided illustrations.

☆

As the Far West became more fully settled, it experienced the mass effects of all these developments. The very nature of the Western regions encouraged specialization, for many of them lent themselves best to some single activity or limited variety of activities. Thus in a few areas of heavy rainfall along the Pacific Coast there were fine stands of timber that attracted the attention of lumbermen; where rich veins of ore were discovered, mining camps appeared; and the open ranges were put to work raising cattle. All groups had mutual bonds. Silver from western mines became the basis of currency used to buy lumber for building homes and corrals for cattle ranches, while beef from the ranges fed miners and lumberjacks alike.

Along with the growth of specialization and interdependence in the Far West went a trend toward the concentration of economic power in fewer hands. Compared with the limited sums required to start a stagecoach line, amounts relatively monumental were needed to construct a railway line of a hundred or so miles in length, to haul timber, ore, and cattle. Only concerns of considerable size could properly take the risk or could even raise the funds required to make such a venture practical.

After the principal long and short lines were completed, consolidations among them into systems and trunk lines, advantageous to the rapid and efficient movement of freight and passengers, were effected. They were engineered by actual mergers and physical connections, or by agreements for pooling and routing trains. This process was marred by frauds, gambling ventures, and exorbitant charges at the expense of the public. But these were temporary incidents in the centralization of railway management and operation.

While by its very nature railway expansion facilitated concentrations in capital, other forces pushed manufacturing industries in the same co-ordinative direction. The amount of money needed for the building of great plants put an end to the widespread dispersion of individual ownership characteristic of handicraft days. As a result of the tendency to overbuild, competition among manufacturers became keen, sometimes sanguinary. The manufacturer who saw his profits wiped out by competition often found the remedy in forming trusts and pools with his competitors. Or, finding his profits injured by the high prices he had to pay for his raw materials, the keen-sighted manufacturer could increase his gains by buying raw-material sources and concentrating them under his own direction. Technological considerations also favored bigness. Within limits, according to the processes used, the larger the plant and the operations, the lower the cost of production per unit of output, and the firmer the defense against cutthroat rivalry.

☆

The immense profits made by leaders in industrial enterprises connected with continental expansion speeded up concentration. As profits had to be reinvested if returns were to be obtained from them, the accumulators of profits had to pour them back into their own

THE RAILWAY NETWORK AT THE CLOSE OF THE NINETEENTH CENTURY

industries, thus enlarging them, or into the stocks and bonds of other industries, thus widening the variety of their interests.

Soon after its formation, for example, the first Standard Oil Company in Ohio began to pay annual dividends amounting to about twenty million dollars. A part of their earnings directors of the company invested in their oil business, adding to its magnitude, and another part they placed in other industries such as railways and iron mining. In the course of time, as concentration proceeded, the same industrialist might be serving as a director in ten or fifteen highly diversified manufacturing concerns.

A similar expansion and concentration occurred in nearly all the great staple manufacturing industries as the Industrial Revolution advanced after 1865. In 1873 a group of capitalists headed by Andrew Carnegie, who had accumulated the necessary means in iron, coal, railways, oil, and bridgemaking, started a monster steel mill on the banks of the Monongahela near Pittsburgh. A few years later this group acquired the Homestead Works in the same neighborhood. In the next decade the Carnegie interests were united with several other works in the huge Carnegie Steel Company.

Now firmly established, the Carnegie concern branched out by buying beds of iron ore in the Lake Superior region. To cut freight charges it opened a railway line from Pittsburgh to Lake Erie and, putting a fleet of ore carriers on the Great Lakes, it established direct and cheaper connections between mines and mills. Then, to the dismay of competitors, it proposed, partly as a threat to the J. P. Morgan interests, to diversify its operations by manufacturing many other iron products, such as wire, hitherto beyond its scope of activities.

At this point in the development of the Carnegie interests, iron and steel men and their bankers began to fear that the competition of the new facilities would end in overproduction and the ruin of many companies. Manufacturers of raw iron were invading the field of finished products already occupied by independent producers. They were closing in on the coal, ore mining, and transport business. It looked as if a battle of the giants might end in disaster for the weaker men.

Put on guard by these tendencies and seeing a chance to make more money, the J. P. Morgan banking combine in New York City took the lead in forming the first billion-dollar corporation in the history of the country. Under its direction in 1901 a consolidation of many concerns was effected in the United States Steel Corporation, and $1,400,000,000 in stocks and bonds was issued to the parties in the transaction. To the Morgan underwriting syndicate, stock having the cash value of $62,500,000 was given in the form of a commission for its services.

Later the Federal Bureau of Corporations estimated that the tangible value of the property of the corporation in 1901, the year of its establishment, was $682,000,000, against which $1,400,000,000 in stocks and bonds had been issued. How correct was this estimate became a matter of dispute, but at all events the common stock of the concern soon fell with a crash, and many outsiders who had risked their money in the venture lost heavily.

While Andrew Carnegie was operating in iron and coal resources which, as he afterward said, he got for little outlay of money, John D. Rockefeller was working in the new petroleum industry, first at Cleveland, Ohio. Having hoarded his earnings as a clerk and small merchant, he began to invest in the construction of oil refineries. Soon he found competition keen and, for self-protection as well as for the sake of gain, he set about forming a combination to "stabilize" if not control the local oil business.

After experimenting with small undertakings of this kind, Rockefeller united, in 1870, a group of capitalists in the Standard Oil Company of Ohio and embarked on oil refining on a mammoth scale. With a view to increasing its power, the Rockefeller group took over the South Improvement Company two years later and used it as a means of securing from railway companies rebates or special rates on its shipments of oil, and other favors profitable to the oil company. By extending its operations to the production of oil in the fields, and the transport of oil by pipe lines to the Atlantic coast, the Standard Oil Company of Ohio and its subsidiaries got control over about nine tenths of the refining business within ten years after its formation.

In 1882 the Rockefeller group centralized its many concerns in the form of a trust; that is, the stocks of its concerns were placed in the hands of a few trustees, including John D. Rockefeller, in exchange for "trust certificates of ownership." A few years later the Standard Oil Company of New Jersey, one of its concerns already doing business in New Jersey, was enlarged and in effect assumed responsibility for the management of the trust.

This step was taken under a New Jersey law empowering a company duly incorporated to buy, hold, and vote stock in any other corporation or corporations in New Jersey or any other state—in other words, permitting it to form a "holding company" for the purpose of centralizing control in one industry or many industries. Under this device the Standard Oil Company of New Jersey was able, within a year, to dominate from two thirds to three fourths of the national business in oil and oil products; and to pay its stockholders annually, for several years, from thirty to forty-eight per cent in dividends.

With perhaps even more speed concentration was brought about in the new electrical industry. To secure capital and aid in developing his patents for electric motors, dynamos, lamps, and other products, Thomas Edison, with the help of J. P. Morgan and other financiers, established the Edison Electric Light Company in 1878. After several competing concerns had appeared in the industry, a combination of the Edison and other interests was brought about by the formation of the General Electric Company in 1892. About the same time another consolidation of electrical interests was made by George Westinghouse and his friends, with the incorporation in the year 1886 of the Westinghouse Electric Company. Soon the two companies reached working agreements as to the joint use of patents and divided between them the major portion of the manufacturing business in the chief lines, despite the rise, especially in subsidiary lines, of many independent manufacturers.

Efforts equally determined, if often less successful, were made during this age of industrial expansion to get control over the production of other staple articles of manufacture and mining—sugar, copper, linseed oil, cottonseed oil, whisky, plate glass, and coal, for instance. In 1884 a combination appeared in cottonseed oil; in 1885 in linseed oil; in 1887 in sugar, lead, whisky, cordage, plate glass, and wire nails; in 1899 smelters and coal producers drew together; in 1900 the sugar "trust" was established.

Some of these companies were short-lived and their careers were marked by dubious if not corrupt practices. Others suffered from bad luck and were merged in larger organizations. But by the end of the century the major portion of manufacturing in each of several great lines was concentrated in the hands of corporations—in some lines, a few corporations.

Although not many of these gigantic concerns had complete monopolies in their fields of business, they had a power so great that they could often exercise a decisive influence over the cost of raw materials, the prices of finished products, and the fortunes of independent competitors. Besides wielding the control over their particular areas of the national economy such as oil or steel, corporation promoters built up a wider dominion over economy in general, over politics, and over public opinion by creating interlocking directorates among corporations and other devices.

Concentration in industrial enterprise was facilitated by concentration in the banking business. A vast amount of money was needed for the construction of plants and for current operations. Special agencies were necessary to sell stocks and bonds to investors in large blocks. Here strong banks proved to be valuable adjuncts, and bankers found opportunities to harvest mounting profits. They made loans to corporations, aided in forming combinations among them, and took part in the sale of their securities.

For carrying on the more extensive operations several banks often joined to form an "underwriting syndicate." In the division of financial business certain banks became associated with particular enterprises; for example, J. P. Morgan and Company with the New York Central Railroad Company and the United States Steel Corporation. In many cases, even early in the process of centralization, bankers took the initiative or actively participated in the creation of trusts, corporations, and combinations.

Since bankers usually acquired vital interests in the companies they financed, it became a common practice to put bank presidents and directors on the boards of trustees in charge of railway and manufacturing companies. By way of reciprocity, heads of industrial corporations were also installed among the directors of banks. Through various banking activities a substantial part of the control over industry passed from the original magnates of manufacturing to magnates of finance. So industrial capitalism was transformed into what was called "finance capitalism."

Inasmuch as the greatest banks, the headquarters of numerous corporations, and the chief stock exchange for dealing in corporation securities were in New York City, that metropolis became the principal center of consolidation in the United States. There bankers and corporation presidents mingled freely with one another. Often they engaged in spectacular battles over power and wealth. Often they united in the exercise of control over finance and industry, adding personal union to legal and economic union.

In his book, *The Truth about the Trusts* (1904), a contemporary expert in financial affairs, John Moody, described the situation in the following language: "Around these two groups [the Morgan-Rockefeller interests], or what must ultimately become one greater group, all other smaller groups of capitalists congregate. They are all allied and intertwined by their various mutual interests. For instance, the Pennsylvania Railroad interests are on the one hand allied with the Vanderbilts and on the other hand with the Rockefellers. The Vanderbilts are closely allied with the Morgan group, and both the Pennsylvania and the Vanderbilt interests have recently become the dominating factors in the Reading system, a former Morgan road and the most important part of the anthracite coal combine which had always been dominated by the Morgan people. . . . Viewed as a whole, we find the dominating influences in the trusts to be made up of an intricate network of large and small capitalists, many allied to another by ties of more or less importance, but all being appendages to or parts of the greater groups which are themselves dependent on and allied with the two mammoth, or Rockefeller and Morgan groups. These two mammoth groups jointly . . . constitute the heart of the business and commercial life of the nation."

☆

Paralleling in time the concentration of ownership in manufacturing, transportation, and finance were efforts to tie industrial workers together in bigger unions, more capable of challenging the power of centralized managements. Unlike capitalists who throve on profits from war industries during the civil conflict, industrial workers found it difficult, if not impossible in that wartime, to force an upturn in wages equal to the rise in the cost of living. Yet they sought to make advances in that direction by increasing the number of trade unions; and they came out of the war with many gains in organization.

At its close the number of local unions existing in 1860 had about trebled and to the national craft unions already formed had been added at least ten new national unions of that type. But the membership of all the unions, local and national, was small; under 250,000, it is reckoned. Even so, in 1865 nearly every large industrial city had, besides its local craft unions, a city trades assembly representing the crafts. Certain labor leaders considered the time ripe to renew the attempt, made back in 1834, to effect a permanent consolidation of unions on a national scale.

Leadership in this undertaking was assumed by W. H. Sylvis, a veteran idealist in the labor movement. In 1864, largely at his instigation, a convention called the Industrial Assembly of North America was held at Louisville, Kentucky, and a plan was framed for establishing a continent-wide association of labor organizations. At a following convention, in Baltimore in 1866, the plan was carried out by the formation of the National Labor Union.

Based mainly on the representation of local unions and city trades assemblies, not directly on national craft unions, the new organization was one degree removed from strictly craft interests. It strove, it is true, to secure the recognition of unions by employers, to raise wages, to reduce hours, and to establish the practice of adjusting labor relations by agreements between employers and employees. Yet the National Labor Union also tried to promote various political and social reforms, including the establishment of workshops owned and managed cooperatively by the workers.

Some of its demands, such as an eight-hour day for certain federal employees, were granted, but its main projects for social reform fell by the wayside. Gradually "pure and simple" trade unionists, interested primarily in wages and hours of work, began to desert the organization. After a troubled existence of six years the National Labor Union perished for lack of support.

Meanwhile another project for uniting industrial workers in a single national organization was taking shape on broader organizational lines. The germ of this movement was the Noble Order of the Knights of Labor, a local union formed among garment workers at Philadelphia by Uriah Stephens in 1869. By much agitation several unions of the kind were established in that city and in other industrial cities of the East.

Believing that the hour had struck for a concentration of forces, leaders in these unions called, in 1875, a national convention to which they invited representatives of other associations as well as their own. Out of this assembly the Knights of Labor expanded into a national organization capable of exerting for more than ten years a powerful influence in the industrial world and in labor debate and opinion.

In form and policy the Knights of Labor made departures from the attempts to federate the craft unions composed of skilled workers. It is true that the Knights sought the co-operation of local and national craft unions as fellow members of its order; but its aspiration was broader than theirs in that it tried to unite all laborers, skilled and unskilled, men and women, white and colored, with the castes of trades and crafts, in one big union. While it campaigned for higher standards of labor conditions and rewards within industrial plants and carried on many strikes, local and general, in efforts to gain these ends it did more. Like the National Labor Union, it sponsored co-operative workshops among industrial workers. Still more: it cherished a dream of transforming the capitalist system into a socialist commonwealth. As a step in that direction it advocated the public ownership of utilities such as railways and waterworks.

By its effective battles for higher wages and extensive social reforms, the Order of Knights of Labor for some time drew into its ranks thousands of actual industrial workers and thousands of sympathizers belonging to the middle class not gainfully employed in industry. At the height of its vigor, about 1880, when Terence V. Powderly was at its head as "Master Workman," it claimed an enrollment of approximately 700,000 men and women; and employers then felt themselves in the presence of an ominous challenge to capitalism. But rather suddenly a rapid decline of the Order and its power set in, due in part to the failure of mass strikes, to the strong desire of workers for immediate advances in wages and a reduction of hours, and to the disdain of craft unionists for the methods and ideals of the Knights.

Strong as it proved to be for about ten years, the Knights of Labor movement did not submerge the local craft unions, the city trades assemblies, or the national organization of crafts, from many of which it received aid. On the contrary, such unions were growing in numbers and power while the Knights were still apparently dominant. From year to year new federal unions of crafts were formed: for example cigar makers in 1864; railroad conductors in 1868; locomotive firemen in 1873; iron and steel workers in 1876; and cotton spinners in 1878.

By 1884 the national craft unions, claiming 300,000 members in good standing, showed signs of permanence despite their vicissitudes. Several of the national craft unions were led by capable men and had money in their treasuries. This was especially true of the cigar makers, with whom were associated Adolph Strasser and Samuel Gompers, both hardheaded and skillful in the work of organization and administration. In their national organization the central officers had full authority over local unions, and a part of the dues were set aside to build up benefit funds for members in distress for various reasons or unemployed. Here in firmly knit national craft unions were solid materials for the next and more successful step in concentration—a federation of all unions in one national association, with strong treasuries for tiding the members over the hazards of strikes, competently managed by directors loyal to the interests of the members.

Labor leaders of the "practical" type, quick to appreciate the opportunity before them, now urged the creation of a national organization more limited in structure and purpose than the Order of the Knights of Labor with its miscellaneous membership and its broad program of social reconstruction. At Pittsburgh in 1881 the new labor leaders took action by forming the Federation of Organized Trades and Labor Unions at a convention representing national unions, local unions, and Knights of Labor assemblies in the United States and Canada. Yet even the newest federation did not prosper at once.

Unbeaten, however, its sponsors summoned another conference of delegates, at Columbus, Ohio, in 1886; and after searching debates they merged their organizations in an association called the American Federation of Labor. This federation they grounded squarely on strong national unions of crafts already in existence, state federations of unions, and city assemblies. Representation of mere local craft unions they allowed only in cases where such unions were not federated into national craft organizations.

Under the leadership of Samuel Gompers, who served as president until his death in 1924, except for one year, the American Federation of Labor pursued a utilitarian policy—trade unionism "pure and simple." Gompers had been associated with socialism but now he avoided radical theories, defeating efforts of socialists to capture the federation. The organization clung steadfastly to a simple program: standard hours and wages; fair conditions of labor; collective bargaining with employers; and the accumulation of benefit funds for meeting emergencies. It accepted the capitalistic system of production and ownership and sought to improve the position of labor, especially skilled labor, within that framework. Refraining from declarations of unmitigated class warfare, the federation co-operated where it could with associations of employers and citizens interested in securing to labor bargaining privileges in the industrial world; with the National Civic Federation, for instance.

The success of the American Federation of Labor soon gave wide currency to three rather obvious interpretations of history: first, the Industrial Revolution had brought into being a numerous and permanent body of working men and women, despite the fluidity of class lines; second, the individual worker, with little or no savings between himself and want, was not "equal" in a wage negotiation—under "freedom of contract"—to a million-dollar corporation ruled by industrial magnates; and, third, only by unions of workers could a "fair balance" in wage negotiations be attained.

It was hard for Americans, who were still thinking in terms of handicrafts and freehold farming, to accept facts so "foreign" to old American experience. But in time many citizens acknowledged the changed situation and began to be active in bringing about fundamental modifications in the laws respecting the right of labor to organize, deal collectively with employers, procure better working conditions, and have recognition as one of the great interests of the nation. In the program, tactics, and gains of American organized labor and its middle-class sympathizers the thesis of the unmitigated class war, evolved on the continent of feudal Europe, was completely disavowed.

Though stoutly opposed to the formation of a separate labor party with a blanket program of radical reforms, the American Federation of Labor did, nonetheless, put forward at its annual conventions specific demands for new laws to be won by political action. It called for legislation to provide safety in industries and mines, compensation for workers injured in the course of their duties, the abolition of child labor, equal pay for men and women engaged in equal work, the regulation of the use of injunctions in labor disputes, and indeed a long list of definite proposals. At elections leaders of the federation resorted to the political tactics of "rewarding our friends and punishing our enemies." In presidential elections they often tried to throw the labor vote to the Democrats in return for concessions of one kind or another.

Starting with a membership of about 150,000 in 1886, the American Federation of Labor soon doubled it and by 1904 reported that 1,670,000 workers were on its union rolls. Outside its jurisdiction, but usually co-operative, were other powerful national unions. Among the independent unions the four railway brotherhoods—engineers, firemen, conductors, and maintenance men—had first rank.

Fifty years after the close of the Civil War approximately 3,000,000 industrial workers had been organized on a national scale, centralized through federation, and bound together on a program that presaged not only permanence but growth in numbers and power, economic and political. Although they demanded no overthrow of capitalism, likewise in the process of centralization, they were determined to dictate some of the terms on which capitalism was to function. Whether or not by their actions they increased the proportion of the total annual output that went to labor as a whole, they had certainly wrung favorable laws from legislatures and raised wages for the highly organized craft unionists. Though they spurned independent labor party action, they were active in politics and made labor increasingly conscious of its political strength, actual and potential.

Through its judicial branch, the Federal Government was repeatedly drawn into the great contest for power being waged between big business and various rival interests, including big labor. The net result was that the Supreme Court of the United States ultimately managed to concentrate in its own hands an enormous amount of control over the economic life of the nation.

Under the Constitution of the United States as it stood in 1860, the ownership of property and the conduct of industrial enterprises were wholly within the authority of the several states, except insofar as interstate and foreign commerce were involved. Each state by law defined property for itself and determined what should be the limits imposed on the use of property. The power to charter corporations and control their management also belonged to the states. Therefore capitalists, corporations, and other industrial concerns that had grounds, real or imaginary, for complaining against state laws and the actions of state officials had to resort, as a rule, to state legislatures and state courts for relief. Only in a narrow range of cases could the federal courts accept appeals, intervene on their behalf, and afford them protection. But in 1868 the Fourteenth Amendment became a part of the federal Constitution. Henceforward the ultimate protection of life, liberty, property, privileges, and immunities was to be a function of the federal judiciary, with the United States Supreme Court as the final tribunal of appeal.

Although many advocates of the Fourteenth Amendment insisted that it "nationalized civil liberty"—put everything affecting liberty and property under national authority—the Supreme Court of the United States refused to accept that view for several years after the adoption of this amendment. It held that the amendment was mainly, though not exclusively, designed to sustain the civil rights of the newly emancipated slaves, and not to reduce the historic power of the states over personal and property rights.

At that stage in its interpretation of the amendment, the Court ruled that each state could regulate, for example, the rates of railways within its borders; and when railway companies complained that they were deprived of their property by such regulations the Court told them that they must look to the state legislatures for help, not to the federal courts. Judicial decisions of this type thus continued the dispersion of legal power over property, corporations, and industry among the states, that had prevailed in the days of agricultural supremacy in 1787 when about ninety per cent of the people were engaged in farming.

Under such judicial rulings business corporations operating throughout the country were subject to the varied and often conflicting regulations of as many legislatures as there were states in the Union. Efficient centralization in corporate management became difficult if not impossible. Endless lawsuits over regulations and taxation in states and endless conflicts with state politicians harassed and impeded the formation and operations of corporations, trusts, and combines, as concentration proceeded in industry and transportation. Not without reason did lawyers for dissatisfied capitalists insist that such "anarchy," such a dispersion of legal authority to regulate and control the use of property, if appropriate for earlier times, was unfitted to the prosecution of industrial enterprise on a national scale. Well paid for their advice, lawyers for corporations kept appealing to the Supreme Court of the United States for protection against state legislation adversely affecting the property interests of their clients.

Eventually they were successful in getting a reinterpretation of the Fourteenth Amendment. Under that amendment corporations were "persons" at law and no "person" could be deprived of life, liberty, or property without due process of law. As justices of the Supreme Court died or resigned and new justices were appointed, judicial opinions respecting the rights of corporate persons changed.

In 1889 the Supreme Court decided that, while state authorities could regulate the rates of railway companies, they could not fix rates so low as to deprive the companies of their property without due process. "If the company," said the Court, "is deprived of the power of charging reasonable rates for the use of its property, and such deprivation takes place in the absence of investigation by judicial machinery, it is deprived of the lawful use of its property, and thus, in substance and effect, of the property itself without due process of law and in violation of the Constitution of the United States." Under ruling of this type state regulations of property had to be of such a nature as to allow for a "reasonable" profit to the owners; and the question of reasonableness was a matter to be finally determined by the Supreme Court of the United States in cases duly brought before it.

By this and many other cases decided before the end of the nineteenth century the once almost sovereign powers of the states over property and business within their borders were reduced to mere shadows of their former greatness. Now all laws and actions by state authorities that seriously affected the property rights of corporations and industrial concerns throughout the country were subject to review and possible annulment by a single authority—the Supreme Court at Washington. This was a centralization of legal power practically ultimate in nature; for beyond that tribunal lay no formal appeal, save to the latent power of the people to amend the Constitution by an extraordinary majority in Congress and of the states.

Under the Fourteenth Amendment, so interpreted, innumerable laws and decrees by state, municipal, and county legislatures and officials were declared void. Everywhere state authorities were notified in effect that they could no longer pursue "populistic" or "communistic" policies in dealing with business enterprises; that they must observe the fundamental rights of property as taught in capitalistic economics. According to the letter of the Constitution, the power to make civil and criminal laws yet remained with the states, but that power was in fact strictly limited by the new jurisprudence created by the Supreme Court.

Another practice sanctioned by the Supreme Court gave additional impetus to economic centralization. According to the Constitution, actions at law between citizens of different states could be taken, on certain conditions, into the federal courts. Corporations, besides being persons, were "citizens" within the meaning of the word so used. They were often engaged in interstate commerce which was also subject to federal authority.

As the labor movement grew in strength, and strikes became more frequent, often tying up the trunk lines of railway companies, lawyers adopted the practice of appealing to federal judges for aid against strikers. One form of relief for which they asked was a writ of injunction, forbidding strikers to picket the property of their former employers and otherwise interfere with the operation of their employers' business.

Recourse to the injunction by employers became increasingly frequent during and after the great railway strikes which broke out in the depression of 1873–78. A climax in this development was reached in 1894 on the occasion of a strike ordered by the American Railway Union in Chicago in sympathetic support of strikers against the Pullman Company. In the midst of that labor contest the federal district court in the city issued a blanket injunction forbidding all persons engaged in the strike to interfere with the movement of trains. The president of the American Railway Union, Eugene V. Debs, manager of the strike, was accused of violating the injunction, arrested, and imprisoned for contempt by the federal court from which the injunction issued. On appeal the Supreme Court of the United States upheld the lower tribunal at Chicago and declared that summary imprisonment, without jury trial, for contempt of court in such cases did not violate the federal Constitution.

Having the full sanction of the highest court in the land for the free use of injunctions in labor disputes, lawyers for industrial concerns availed themselves of this legal weapon in every direction to crush strikes and block the efforts of trade unions to force their terms on employers. Thus a new instrument of control was added to the decisions of the Supreme Court, subjecting all state authorities to its dominion in respect of their actions seriously affecting the rights of property. Now the practice of issuing injunctions freely in labor disputes gave to centralizing industry a powerful weapon against coercive measures of the centralizing labor movement.

Therefore, in contests between capital and state governments and between capital and labor, while economic concentration advanced, the balance of legal power was weighted on the side of capital. Insofar as government was involved in its operations, industrial enterprise could now turn with confidence to the federal judiciary for negative relief and for positive assistance in gaining all the profits that, as one lawyer put it, "the traffic will bear." It was after observing such history in the making that Henry Adams was led to wonder in 1895 whether the country was "on the edge of a new and last great centralization, or of a first great movement of disintegration."

Chapter 20

POLITICS IN THE NEW ECONOMIC SETTING

THE LAST HALF of the nineteenth century was crowded with events that shook from center to circumference the economic system handed down from the age of Andrew Jackson. The chief events were a civil war and the abolition of slavery—the very basis of the Southern plantation system; an upheaval in the race and class relations of the South; occupation of the great West; the disappearance of free land for farming families and the transference of natural resources to private persons or corporations; expansion and concentration in industry and transportation; increase in immigration and in the number and size of cities; the creation of a plutocracy, or money aristocracy, flaunting its wealth in the brazen display of new riches; a powerful labor movement; and judicial backing for business enterprise.

This age was also characterized by panics and depressions, nationwide in scope, unprecedented in extent, unemployment, poverty, violence, and the destruction of property. Of the span between 1870 and 1910 about two thirds of the years were years of depressions, long or short in duration: for example, 1873–78; 1884–87; 1893–98. Certainly during half the time farmers, industrialists, and industrial workers were outside the range of what was boastfully called "prosperity."

Every depression season was punctuated by strikes, local and general. The great railway strike of 1877 was accompanied by so many disorders and so much bloodshed as to make Daniel Shays' rebellion in 1786 appear like a mere argument at a garden party. Before it was over the Pennsylvania railway station in Pittsburgh had been seized by rioters and burned. Shortly afterward a railway strike in the Southwest, led by Martin Irons for the Knights of Labor, tied up more than 5000 miles of lines in Missouri, Arkansas, Kansas, the Indian Territory, and Nebraska. It was attended by the seizure of railway property and the sabotage of engines. So disturbing was the railway strike of 1894, in connection with the labor dispute at the Pullman Works in Chicago, that

President Cleveland used the troops of the United States to suppress it.

While major strikes were being ascribed to "the evil spirit" or "ignorance" of American working people, "misled by foreign agitators," the numerous politico-economic scandals which exploded in rapid succession during this eventful era could not all be so simply "explained." In New York City, William Marcy Tweed and a gang of Tammany politicians were exposed to public scorn in 1871 as robbers and bribers who had looted the city treasury and corrupted judges in the highest courts of the state. The next year the New York *Sun* "scooped" the news of a still greater scandal—the Crédit Mobilier peculations in the recent construction of the Union Pacific Railroad. Before this sensation was over the people learned that members of Congress had accepted "favors" which were in effect bribes, and that no less a person than the Vice-President of the United States, if not guilty of gross misconduct in connection with the "deal," was at least by no means impeccable.

While the Crédit Mobilier affair was on the public stage, another inquiry showed that the "Whisky Ring" had been cheating the government of taxes. The trail of that scandal led to the very doors of the White House—to President Grant's private secretary. Another ring, the Star Route gang, including federal officials and members of Congress, was caught defrauding the government in connection with the carriage of mails. It was indeed a rare year that did not produce a fresh exposure in high places.

Among the revelations of the period was the disclosure of monstrous poverty in urban quarters. As foreign immigrants by the millions and native workers from the least prosperous rural districts rolled into the centers of industry and commerce, areas of congestion, the "slums," swelled into huge proportions. Every city had its large districts of poverty, overcrowding, misery, and crime.

Americans had read in their histories about the proletariat of ancient Rome. Now they could actually see a proletariat in every urban region of their own Republic. "It is the city," exclaimed the Congregationalist home missionary, Josiah Strong, in *Our Country*, published in 1891, "where . . . the Sway of Mammon is the widest, and his worship the most constant and eager. Here luxuries are gathered . . . here is the most extravagant expenditure. Here also is the *congestion* of wealth the severest. Dives and Lazarus are brought face to face; here, in sharp contrast, are the *ennui* of surfeit and the desperation of starvation. . . . As a rule, the greater the city, the greater are the riches of the rich and the poverty of the poor. . . . Is it strange that such conditions arouse a blind and bitter hatred of our social system?"

No longer did an abundance of free land offer an escape from this poverty. No longer could politicians delude the poor by proclaiming that "free land" was the solution for the problem of poverty. Nor were all farmers actually on the land becoming stalwart freeholders. When the census takers of 1880 had collected the figures of farm ownership, they reported that twenty-five per cent of all farmers were already tenants. Twenty years later the proportion had increased to thirty-five per cent and was on an upward climb.

To many American observers of these social earthquakes, including such prominent figures as James Russell Lowell, Walt Whitman, and E. L. Godkin, the situation was appalling. Yet throughout most of the period neither of the two major political parties, which contended for power and in one season or another governed the nation, took much account of the volcanic upheavals in American life and labor or made any substantial alterations in the form, methods, or concepts of their obligations. Nominating conventions, "fresh from the people," were held as in the good old days of Andrew Jackson. Amid open convention uproars or back-room negotiations among politicians, candidates were chosen for approval by the voters. On the morning after a triumph at the polls the spoils of office were distributed among the victors, in the style consecrated by long custom. "What are we here for?" a convention delegate once exclaimed when a reformer asked his party colleagues to endorse a civil-service proposal for removing a few hundred jobs from the grip of politicians. At party conventions political experts drafted platforms in the customary manner, praising themselves, damning their opponents, and making vague promises savoring of the millennium.

As in the past, professional politicians controlled conventions and committees, were nominated to high offices, directed party affairs, and, if elected, administered the machinery of government, local and national, with an eye to party advantage. After the overthrow of the planters in the Southern revolution, the monopoly of the professional politicians, mostly lawyers, became more complete. Businessmen, farmers, and industrial workers left to this "elite" the ostensible function of ruling the nation.

In the struggle of the two major parties for power the Republicans gained strength for some time. They had been a minority in 1860 but they emerged from the civil conflict augmented in numbers and influence. During the period of reconstruction in the South they were able to count on the support of the new Negro voters grateful for emancipation and for the civil rights accorded to their race by the party of Abraham Lincoln. To that party bankers and investors in United States bonds looked for the payment of interest and principal and for security against the inflation menace of paper currency. Railway promoters, mining prospectors, cattle kings, timber hunters, and land speculators, already enriched by government bounties, preferred to see the national government in Republican hands. To the Republicans the beneficiaries of the higher tariffs turned with eager expectancy for continued protection. Industrial workers were told that only under such protection could they enjoy higher wages than the "pauper labor of Europe" received. Farmers who were getting free homesteads in the West and Union veterans of the war entitled to land and pensions had reasons for allegiance to Republican leadership. As possessors of the Executive Department in Washington, Republicans dispensed the spoils of office among the faithful.

With these material considerations were united moral advantages in aid of the Republicans. It was under their auspices that the Union had been saved, that the perpetuity of the Republic had been assured. Theirs was the party of Lincoln, which had struck the shackles from four million bondmen—the greatest act of liberation in the tragic history of chattel slavery. The "twin relics of barbarism—slavery and polygamy," orators could say, had been abolished throughout the land by courageous and enlightened Republicans. To whom except Republicans, it was asked, can the liberty of the people and the fortunes of the Republic be safely entrusted?

On the other hand the Democrats long lay under a cloud. They were deprived of the able and powerful leadership once afforded by Southern planters and their lawyers and they were now vilified by Republicans as the abettors of slavery and disunion. They had been split into two factions in 1860. They had officially proclaimed the war a failure in the platform of 1864. What glittering program could they now offer to the voters? Their old pledges of lower tariffs with hints of free trade ahead and their doctrine of states' rights had less popular appeal during the distractions that followed the collapse of the Confederacy.

Besides, their ranks were wavering. They had lost to the Republicans many farmers in the West who had once rallied around their flag, and they were further weakened by the subjection of their fellow Democrats in the South. Thus badly crippled, they seemed to have poor prospects of ever recovering the proud dominion over national affairs previously exercised. Even South Carolina, where secession had started, went Republican in 1868! The main prospect of the Democrats for a reconquest of power, even temporarily, appeared to lie in the mistakes or corruption of the Republicans or in taking advantage of business panics and depressions to urge stricken and distressed farmers and industrial workers to turn away from Republican leadership.

Of the nine presidential elections between 1868 and 1900 inclusive, the Republicans carried all but two and in every instance with a military hero, large or small, as a candidate. General Ulysses S. Grant had exhibited little interest in politics and had voted only once in his life—the Democratic ticket in 1856; but he was perhaps the outstanding figure in national life after the death of Lincoln in 1865. Capitalizing on Grant's popular strength, the Republicans chose him as their candidate for President in 1868, elected him, and then renewed his term in 1872. During the depression which cast gloom over Grant's last years, they picked for the presidency Rutherford B. Hayes, of Ohio, a former general in the Union army, to pit against the Democratic nominee, Samuel J. Tilden, an able lawyer and politician from New York. The contest was close and the returns were disputed, but a special commission, in which the Republicans had a majority, awarded the palm to Hayes. Although Hayes had qualities, character, and intelligence, the Republicans turned from him in 1880, nominated another general, James A. Garfield, also of Ohio, and won that election. When Garfield was cut down in his first year by an assassin's bullet, the presidency passed to the Vice-President, Chester A. Arthur, a colorless man, unable to provoke national enthusiasm.

Republican fortunes were ebbing. War passions were cooling. The services of the party in saving the Union and freeing the slaves were being forgotten in the fleeting years, amid the sensational scandals of the Republican administrations at Washington. Yet Republican leaders were still so confident about their position that they thought they could elect a civilian at last. Instead of gathering around a military hero in 1884, they nominated James G. Blaine, of Maine, who had served in Congress, not on battlefields, during the war. But Blaine had been singed if not scorched by the Crédit Mobilier scandal.

Taking his selection as an "affront," disgruntled Republicans, called "Mugwumps," deserted their party in large numbers and cast in their lot with the Democrats, who had pinned their faith in victory on Grover Cleveland, governor of New York, as their candidate. Cleveland was no war hero either. Indeed, he had hired a substitute to fight for him in the war. But though intellectually complacent and incapable of emulating a fiery Andrew Jackson in his popular appeals, Cleveland had been an efficient public administrator at Albany and had the reputation of being an honest man and a trustworthy official. Despite unparalleled vituperation in the campaign, Cleveland slipped through—by a narrow margin. The switch of a few hundred votes in New York City, or perhaps an accurate count of the votes cast there, would have sent his competitor, Blaine, to the White House in his stead.

Having read their lesson in that outcome, the Republicans then returned to the practice of going to the voters with a military hero. In

1888 they chose as their candidate Benjamin Harrison, of Indiana, who, like Grant, Hayes, and Garfield, had been an officer in the Union army during the war. A cold personality and a rather drab figure in every way, Harrison nevertheless managed to whip up enough support on his military record and other grounds to carry the day against President Cleveland, renominated for a second term by the Democrats.

If there was anything heroic in the stature of Harrison after he became the Chief Executive, the people failed to appreciate it. After four years' experience with him, they retired him to private life in 1892 and restored to the presidency Grover Cleveland, the civilian, nominated again by the Democrats. Once more, and for the last time, in 1896, the Republicans staked their chance of winning an election on a former soldier of the Union army, Major William McKinley, of Ohio. Under his leadership, promoted by a shrewd political financier, Marcus A. Hanna, they recovered their control over the national administration. When the new century opened they thought themselves firmly buttressed in power—though signs of a revolt against historic methods in party politics loomed on the horizon.

While the presidential elections in those years revealed a numerical weakness in the Democratic party, they were not the sole tests of its vitality. In the congressional elections, where the great funds and pressures of the national campaign were less available, the story was different. Except for two bienniums, the Democrats had possession of the House of Representatives during all the years from 1875–95; for four of those years they had a majority in the Senate as well as in the House. During Cleveland's first administration, 1885–89, they controlled the House, while the Republicans held the Senate. For two years in Cleveland's second administration the Democrats marshaled a majority in both Houses of Congress. At no time did they despair of capturing the presidency.

Their anticipation of final triumph was energized by the fact that after the restoration of white dominion the South was really "solid." Before the civil conflict it had been politically divided and indeed it was badly split in the election of 1860. Hundreds of the richest and most powerful planters had feared, if not despised, the democracy of Thomas Jefferson, for they saw in its gospel of human equality a peril to their labor system. But after the emancipation of slaves and the rise of the Republican mastery, all the South below the border states became firmly Democratic. Furthermore, its strength in the House of Representatives was actually increased by emancipation. Before that event a slave had been treated as only three fifths of a person in the apportionment of representatives under the Constitution; after it, all Negroes were counted in fixing the number of representatives accorded to the Southern states. The Negroes now counted in representation; the whites chose the representatives and had more in Congress.

☆

At every presidential election between 1868 and 1892 each of the two major parties put forth an official platform—a declaration of its views respecting the national needs and a statement of its program for reform or conservatism if victorious at the polls. In these successive documents were mirrored the intelligence and thought of the governing elite and its popular supporters.

In the main the platforms dealt with issues that had been upper-most since 1789: tariffs, banking, currency, taxation, internal improvements, and the disposal of the public domain. The hatred of monopolies, the great animus of Jacksonian Democrats, now and then still blazed out in platform attacks on railway corporations, "trusts," and "combines." But on the whole both parties passed over with slight recognition the basic changes that were taking place in American economy under their very eyes. For several years, it is true, Republicans laid stress on promises to uphold the civil rights of Negroes in the South but as time passed that issue relaxed its hold on public interest and on them.

From season to season, while pointing fingers of scorn at Democrats, Republicans stood on their record, claiming it as sufficient proof that they merited an indefinite tenure of power. In assailing that record Democrats emphasized Republican corruption and mismanagement and made much of the popular slogan: "Turn the rascals out!" Of course the charges were occasionally reversed. When the Democrats were in power briefly, they too gloated on their "achievements," and the Republicans took their turn at urging the voters to eject the rascals. Thus praise of their own virtues and abuse of their opponents furnished a major part of the stock in trade drawn upon for campaigns by the leaders of both parties.

"We charge the Democratic party," proclaimed the Republicans in their platform of 1876, "with being the same in character and spirit as when it sympathized with treason . . . With reasserting and applauding in the national Capitol the sentiments of unrepentant rebellion; with sending Union soldiers to the rear, and promoting Confederate soldiers to the front; with deliberately proposing to repudiate the plighted faith of the government; with being equally false and imbecile upon the over-shadowing financial questions. . . . With proving itself, through the period of its ascendancy in the lower House of Congress, utterly incompetent to administer the government; and we warn the country against trusting a party thus alike unworthy, recreant, and incapable." Treason, imbecility, incompetence, unworthiness, and incapacity! These were Republican words supposed to describe the qualities of the Democratic party.

The Democrats retaliated in kind. In their platform of 1884 they paid their respects to their opponents in similar terms: "The Republican party, so far as principle is concerned, is a reminiscence. In practice it is an organization for enriching those who control its machinery. . . . The Republican party, during its legal, its stolen, and its bought tenures of power, has steadily decayed in moral character and political capacity. . . . Honeycombed with corruption, outbreaking exposures no longer shock its moral sense. Its honest members, its independent journals, no longer maintain a successful contest for authority in its canvasses or a veto upon bad nominations. . . . We denounce the Republican party for having failed to relieve the people from crushing war taxes, which have paralyzed business, crippled industry, and deprived labor of employment and its just reward." Thievery, moral decay, corruption, incapacity! These were Democratic words supposed to describe the qualities of the Republican party.

Performances—as distinguished from professions and denunciations—can be weighed by studying the statute books containing the measures which the two parties deemed appropriate and necessary in the age of economic transformation. Five times between 1868 and 1900 the tariff rates on imports were altered, generally in the form of more protection for manufacturers. In 1872 and 1883 minor modifications were made. In 1890 the Republicans, by the McKinley Act, ventured upon a substantial increase in protectionism. In 1894, Democrats, for the moment in control of the presidency and both houses of Congress, juggled the rates again and passed a bill also so protectionist in nature that President Cleveland, unwilling to approve it, allowed it to become a law without his signature.

On the currency question Republicans and Democrats blew hot and cold. In 1875, Congress passed the Resumption Act providing for the redemption of the paper currency, or "greenbacks," in gold, beginning in 1879. But to please the paper-money factions in both parties, Congress in 1878 and in 1890 passed silver-purchase laws authorizing the Treasury to buy annually certain quantities of silver for coinage. Mindful of outbursts against the spoils system in both parties, it enacted in 1883 a civil-service law under which appointments to a few federal offices were removed from the system and made subject to an examination of candidates for efficiency, held by the civil-service commission. At the discretion of the President other offices could be placed, according to this law, under the new "merit system." Judged by such performances, the two major parties were becoming as much alike in their interests and sentiments as two bottles of the same size and shape, differing only in their labels.

During the entire period from 1868 to 1900 only three notable measures passed by Congress were designed to cope with complicated problems raised by industrial concentration and the spoliation of natural resources. The first of these, the Interstate Commerce Act of 1887, forbade interstate railway companies to engage in such practices as pooling freight and giving rebates to shippers "on the inside." It also provided for the Interstate Commerce Commission, empowered to regulate and supervise railways in limited respects. The act had imposing features but no teeth. For many years it was little more than a dead letter.

The second major law bearing on recent developments in American economy was directed against concentration in industry. It was the Sherman Antitrust Act of 1890 which prohibited trusts and combinations "in restraint of trade" and imposed penalties for violations. This act was neither imposing nor effective. For a long time presidents allowed it to sleep in the statute books.

The third law, far from imposing but foreshadowing crucial actions relative to natural resources, was a mere amendment attached to another bill in 1891—a few lines authorizing the President to set aside and hold as national forests certain areas of the public domain. The process of despoiling the national heritage was not stopped by this act but a change in policy was implied.

To the list of the three measures might have been added the provision for a federal income tax incorporated in the tariff bill enacted by Democrats in 1894. This was supposed to make the rich bear their share of taxation. But most of it was declared unconstitutional by the Supreme Court of the United States the very next year.

Such, according to the official platforms and the major pieces of legislation, was the insight of the political elite of the two major parties into the meaning of the catastrophic events in American economy between 1868 and the end of the century. Such were the ideas and actions which they deemed sufficient to meet the challenge of basic changes and to assure what they were fond of calling the prosperity, liberty, and perpetuity of the Republic. Such was their vision of the future, their appreciation of the "shape of things to come," the Americanism they thought adequate for transmission to rising generations, to be maintained forever.

While Republicans and Democrats, highly pleased with themselves
and harsh toward their opponents, thus conducted politics according to
their conceptions of fitness or their power, they were all along bothered
by critics in their own ranks and by minor political parties that appeared
from time to time. If a disturbance was small within their own coteries
or among the people in general, they could ignore it. If it was large,
as indicated by the number of protests made at the ballot box, they
sought to conciliate it by promises of mild reforms and political jobs.
For nearly thirty years they were able to prevent revolts started by discontented people from seriously upsetting party calculations.

Not until 1896 did one of the major parties fall a victim to an uprising from below. Then it was the Democrats whose national machine,
captured by agrarians under William Jennings Bryan, of the young
generation, ceased for a time to function as of old. More years passed.
Then the Republican machine was disrupted by Theodore Roosevelt,
also of the young generation. But the storms which made these wrecks
were slow in gathering. Their beginnings were small and for many years
could be lightly disregarded by men occupied with "large and practical"
affairs.

Judged by their programs and the economic interests to which they
appealed, the critics who protested against the offerings of the major parties and demanded a different order of things belonged mainly to
two groups: labor reformers and agrarians. The first group was concerned
primarily with industrial workers and their claims; the second with
farmers and tenants on the land who had not received all the blessings
of prosperity to which they thought themselves entitled. Yet no deep gulf
separated these two groups and their ideas about public policies. Their
demands often coincided, and members of both groups looked upon the
political struggle as involving farmers and industrial workers alike as in
Jackson's day. Sometimes they were able to unite. At others they
pursued separate courses and no effort at co-operation brought about a
permanent union.

The first break with regular political affiliations after 1865 was made
in the name of industrial labor. In 1872 a convention of delegates from
seventeen states, calling themselves Labor Reformers, met at Columbus,
Ohio, and adopted a platform on issues which the major parties had ignored. As to doctrines, they declared, in the American tradition, that all
political power is inherent in the people and that government is
established for their benefit; that all citizens are entitled to the use and
enjoyment of the fruits of their labor and skills; that no man or set of

men is entitled to special privileges from government except in consideration of public services rendered.

As to practical proposals, the Labor Reformers demanded a national currency issued to the people without the intervention of banking corporations; restriction of the sale of public lands to bona fide home-seekers; exclusion of Chinese laborers; an eight-hour day in all government employment; abolition of contract labor in prisons; government regulation of railway and telegraph corporations to assure equitable rates; civil-service reform; modification of patent laws in the interests of inventors; and the subordination of military power to the civil power. The Reformers' candidate for President, Charles O'Connor, of New York, polled a vote of less than 30,000—more in Texas than in New York, and more in Georgia than in Illinois.

Discouraged by the outcome, Labor Reformers gave up the political battle or merged temporarily with the agrarians. But in 1888 another labor party sprang up—the Union Labor party. It held a convention in Cincinnati and adopted the chief principles put forth by the Labor Reformers, adding an endorsement of woman suffrage and the popular election of United States senators. In the same city at the same time another convention of delegates assembled, the United Labor party, and displayed more radical propensities. These Laborites denounced both Republicans and Democrats as "hopelessly and shamelessly corrupt," and among other things approved an increased taxation of land values and government ownership and control of railway and telegraph lines. But the new Laborites also polled a small vote.

Then in 1892, after local beginnings, the Socialist Labor party launched an independent national campaign, appealing especially to industrial workers for support. Its platform in this campaign was reformist. It advocated government ownership of public utilities, progressive inheritance and income taxes, universal and equal suffrage, free education, municipal home rule, abolition of child labor, employers' liability legislation, and the secret ballot. It also proposed to reconstruct the federal government by abolishing the presidency and the Senate, and setting up an executive board to be elected and subject to recall by the House of Representatives.

At the end of the century, in 1900, a second socialist party, the Social Democratic party, entered the lists with a complete program for nationalizing all the major instruments of production. As an evidence of its militancy, the new party placed at the head of its ticket Eugene V. Debs, who had been imprisoned for his labor activities during the Pullman strike of 1894. In the election Debs received only 94,800 votes.

None of the labor or socialist parties made heavy inroads upon the

RAPID RISE OF TENANCY IN THE UNITED STATES, 1880–1910

Increasing percentage of farmers who were tenants between 1880, when the first census of tenancy was taken, and 1910. From report of President Franklin D. Roosevelt's Committee on Tenancy, 1937.

monopoly of politics possessed by the Republicans and Democrats. But agrarian agitations, persistent since early colonial times, threatened in the closing years of the nineteenth century to fracture that monopoly. In 1876 farmers entered the national campaign with their own organization, the Independent National party, advocating the historic remedy of farmers for their distresses, namely paper money. The "Greenbackers" now proposed to suppress all bank currency and have the federal government issue notes directly to the people on the basis of its own credit and obligations. This demand for national inflation, instead of the state inflation adopted in Jacksonian times, was a striking note in the long effort of American farmers to defend themselves against deflation and get control over the national medium of exchange. Yet agrarians made little progress with a party of their own until 1892 when they invited industrial workers to unite with them and, at a national convention in Omaha that year, formally launched a farmer-labor party named the People's party, shortened by the public to the "Populists."

Before 1892 labor reformers and agrarians had spoken contemptuously of the two major parties, but the Populists at Omaha in 1892 blew against Republicans and Democrats such a blast as had never before come from a political convention. "Corruption," they declared, "dominates the ballot box, the legislature, the Congress, and touches even the ermine of the bench. The people are demoralized. . . . The newspapers are largely subsidized or muzzled; public opinion silenced; business prostrated; our homes covered with mortgages; labor impoverished; and the land concentrating in the hands of capitalists. The urban workmen are denied the right of organization for self-protection; imported pauperized labor beats down their wages; a hireling standing army, unrecognized by our laws, is established to shoot them down, and they are rapidly degenerating into European conditions. The fruits of the toil of millions are boldly stolen to build up colossal fortunes for a few, unprecedented in the history of mankind. . . . We have witnessed for more than a quarter of a century the struggle of the two great political parties for power and plunder, while grievous wrongs have been inflicted upon the suffering people. . . . They propose to drown the outcries of a plundered people with the uproar of a sham battle over the tariff. . . . The interests of rural and civic labor are the same; their enemies are identical." Then followed a long list of demands for radical changes in the law, the currency, the government, and the economy of the United States. On that platform, with General James B. Weaver, a veteran of the Civil War, a former Democrat who had become a Republican in 1860, as their candidate, the Populists polled more than 1,000,000 votes. Signs of an upheaval in party politics were visible.

Despite their appeal to industrial workers in 1892 and notwithstanding the large national vote they received, the Populists polled, relatively speaking, only a handful of votes in the great industrial regions of the country. For example, out of nearly 1,000,000 votes cast in Pennsylvania, only 8700 went to their candidate; out of about 400,000 in Massachusetts, only 3200 bore the Populist mark. Thus the Populist party proved to be mainly agrarian in character and its power lay principally, though not entirely, in Democratic strongholds.

Capitalizing on the panic, depression, strikes, unemployment, and increasing economic distress of the next four years, the Populists and their sympathizers captured the Democratic convention at Chicago in 1896. There the Democratic President in the White House, Grover Cleveland, was unequivocally spurned, conservatives in the party were treated with derision, a radical platform was adopted, and the young politician from Nebraska, William Jennings Bryan, was nominated as the Democratic candidate for President.

From beginning to end the Democratic convention of 1896 vibrated with revolutionary fervor. Bryan lifted the delegates to their feet with a cry that the toiling masses were not to be crowned with thorns and crucified upon a cross of gold! The platform adopted at Chicago denounced the Supreme Court for invalidating the income tax law of the previous year and demanded a reconstruction of the Court so that the burden of taxation could be equally apportioned and wealth forced to bear its due share. The use of injunctions in labor disputes was condemned as highly dangerous to the rights of the people; and the employment of federal troops in the recent strike at Chicago was branded as an unconstitutional and violent interference with the rights of states. "As labor creates the wealth of the country," ran one plank, "we demand the passage of such laws as may be necessary to protect it in all its rights." To farmers in particular, this Democratic platform promised the free coinage of gold and silver at the ratio of sixteen to one. This was a demand for an inflation of the currency in favor of debtors, that vociferous historic class of rebellious Americans, as against the contraction in favor of creditors—a contraction brought about, it was charged, by using as the monetary standard of the United States the gold controlled by private bankers.

Warned that a crisis impended, the Republicans, led by an astute manager, Marcus A. Hanna, an industrial magnate of Cleveland, Ohio, had prepared to meet it at their convention, held previously at St. Louis. Having picked as his candidate William McKinley, of Ohio, Hanna at first hoped to make protection for industries the main issue, thus playing down the fact that McKinley himself had once been an advocate of free silver.

But conservatives at the convention met the issue head on, even at the price of losing the support of the free-silver faction in Republican ranks. They committed the party unreservedly to "sound money" and opposed the free coinage of silver except by international agreement with the leading commercial nations of the world—"which we pledge ourselves to promote."

Speaking on the floor of the convention, Henry Cabot Lodge arrayed his party against "not only that organized failure, the Democratic party, but all the wandering forces of political chaos and social disorder . . . in these bitter times when the forces of disorder are loose and the wreckers with their false lights gather at the shore to lure the ship of state upon the rocks." With McKinley as their candidate, the Republicans raised a great fund and launched their campaign on an extraordinary scale.

The battle between Bryan and McKinley, accompanied by censorious charges and terroristic threats, aroused the country from coast to coast, as it had not been moved since 1860. Bryan defended his cause and his followers against what he called "English toadies and the pampered minions of corporate rapacity." His party, he declared, represented "the masses of the people, the great industrial and producing masses of the people . . . the men who plow and plant, who fatten herds, who toil in shops, who fell forests, and delve in mines . . . who produce the wealth of the republic, who bear the heaviest burdens in time of peace; who are ready always to give their lifeblood for their country's flag."

The Democratic program and movement McKinley countered by declaring that Republicans would squarely face this "sudden, dangerous, and revolutionary assault upon law and order and upon those to whom is confided by the Constitution and the laws the authority to uphold and maintain them." Bryanism, the editor of the New York *Tribune* assured his readers, had sprung from "the assiduous culture of the basest passions of the least worthy members of the community." Bryan himself the editor portrayed as the willing puppet "in the blood-imbued hands of Altgeld, the anarchist, and Debs, the revolutionist, and other desperadoes of that stripe."

On the side of Bryan was aligned nearly all the discontent with the course of national affairs that had been made manifest by Labor Reformers, Greenbackers, Single Taxers, and Socialists in recent years—all the inveterate hostility to concentrated wealth. No doubt millions of Democrats voted for him out of party habit, as unreflecting partisans, but in so doing they gave sanction to his attack and program. At the election Bryan polled about 1,000,000 more votes than Cleveland had received in 1892—a larger vote than the party was to muster when it elected Woodrow Wilson in 1912. Nevertheless, Bryan was defeated by the new or hitherto lethargic voters who flocked to McKinley's banners—2,000,000 more than had voted the Republican ticket four years previously.

Though victorious in the contest for power, Republicans confronted the fact that 6,500,000 Americans had planted themselves on the side of Bryanism against the 7,100,000 committed to "McKinleyism," as Henry Adams called it. If the Republicans' victory was "glorious," as orators were wont to say, it was narrow enough to make them realize that their avenue to power was not to be the same in time to come as it had been since the election of Grant in 1868. It was precarious enough to set them wondering how the ghost of Bryanism could be laid—by frontal assault, concession, or diversion?

Chapter 21

THE BREACH WITH HISTORIC CONTINENTALISM

NEARLY THREE CENTURIES lay between the founding of the English colony of Jamestown in Virginia and the inauguration of McKinley in 1897. Through this long procession of years the energies of the people, of many national origins, called Americans, had been concentrated on expansion and development in this continental theater. Here their labor, interests, and affections centered, as under a sense of great history, often embodied in the somewhat mystical concept of "manifest destiny," they advanced to the shores of the Pacific. By 1897 the continental domain had been rounded out. All the territories, save three, had been admitted to the union as equal states possessing self-government under the federal Constitution.

This is not to say that no Americans—in thought, ambition, and enterprise—had gone beyond the continental borders. Keels of American ships had plowed the waters of all seas bearing masters and merchants in search of foreign markets and opportunities to garner in large profits from foreign trade. American warships had bombarded many ports in distant foreign lands in retaliation for native interference with the operations of American traders. Ambitious naval officers, such as Commodore Matthew C. Perry, who opened to American commerce the barred gates of Japan, had dreamed of and proposed the seizure of islands and territories in far-off lands; and indeed a hold was established in the Samoan Islands by 1889.

In the days of slavery, politicians among the planters had contemplated the seizure of Cuba and advances far into Mexico with a view to adding more territory for planters and their slaves. A few Northern politicians had also imagined further expansion. For example, William Seward, Lincoln's Secretary of State, had proclaimed a different type of "manifest destiny" to include all of North America and war with Russia, on the plains of Manchuria, over dominion in the Far East. In 1867, Seward bought Alaska from Russia and, by methods none too nice, forced Congress to approve his action. General Grant, as President, had tried to annex Santo Domingo in the Caribbean and would have done it if the Senate had not stood foursquare against it. But most of these plans and activities, even when fostered by the United States Government, did little to divert the interests, treasure, and affections of the people from the task of developing their continental home.

Indeed the foreign policy of the United States, prescribed in Washington's Farewell Address, in Jefferson's messages, and in the Monroe Doctrine, rested on the proposition that the fundamental interest of the American people was, and should be, concentrated on their continental opportunities—for many reasons, political, economic, and moral. According to that definite policy this hemisphere, the seat of American power, was to be kept independent and protected against further colonization and conquest by European Powers; the United States was not to intervene in the eternal vicissitudes of European power politics; territories outside the easy reach of effective defense were not to be acquired; and the protection and advance of American civilization in this continental arena was to be the primary and indefeasible objective of the United States Government in all its relations with foreign Powers, near or distant. Not until about 1890 did American politicians begin seriously to plan and publicly to advocate a reversal of this positive policy, propose active intervention in the affairs of Asia and Europe, and urge the transformation of the United States into a "great world Power"—the goal to which European imperialists had been vaingloriously leading their countries.

Like every scheme in politics, the scheme of world power for the United States had its formulators and plans for application. High in the ranks of the men who made the new world image for Americans to live and die by was an American naval officer, Alfred Thayer Mahan, author of large books on sea power. Openly and covertly Mahan labored to steer American politicians out into the new course—of building a big navy, pushing commerce everywhere in the world, and seeking positive power, physical and moral, in the ancient and perpetual controversies of Europe and Asia.

Nominally a naval officer dedicated to the defense of his country, Mahan was actually an amateur historian and a vigorous politician, publicist, and negotiator. He realized in the beginning that his self-appointed task of converting the nation to world-power politics would be difficult; there was, he said, "no aggressive action in our pious souls." Though he confessed that American citizens did not understand what was going on in his line, he told them that they would soon be deeply involved in European and Asiatic politics whether they liked it or not.

A second agitator for the plunge into world-power politics was Josiah Strong, a militant Protestant missionary who lectured and wrote unctuously on the subject. In his book, *Our Country*, published first in 1886 and in an enlarged form in 1891, Strong declared that the United States was in peril of socialism and social upheavals; that the Anglo-Saxon race was chosen by God to civilize the world; and that the major responsibility for running this crusade belonged to the people of the United States.

Associated with the school of aggressive adventurers were two young members of the Republican party then seeking political careers. One was Theodore Roosevelt, of New York, a man of moderate wealth, leisure, and ambition, full of egotism and bluster. To him Mahan's wine of imperialism was little short of a godsend as he cast about for a big role in politics. The other was Henry Cabot Lodge, son of a Boston merchant made wealthy in the China trade, who had battled his way from Massachusetts into the United States Senate in 1893. Bosom friend of Roosevelt and Mahan, Lodge spared no time or strength in preaching the new gospel of world-power politics and in striving to force it upon balky Republicans of the older generation.

In many respects the times were auspicious for the young agitators' designs on America and the world. European Powers, with Great Britain at the head, were then going into imperialism on a vaster scale than ever. They were building bigger navies, raising bigger armies, seizing territories in Asia, Africa, and the islands of the seas, forming secret alliances, carrying on undercover diplomatic maneuvers, and preparing for the climax—the World War which opened in 1914. The sight of this "grand strategy" in Europe filled the American world-power politicians with envy and a burning desire to get into it. Besides, they well knew as expert politicians that a diversion of the people's thought from domestic discontent over plutocracy and poverty, such as embroiled the land in the campaign of 1896, to world politics would surely dampen if not extinguish radicalism at home. It would smother, they trusted, those other agitators: Bryan, Debs, John P. Altgeld, and all such "incendiaries," as they were described in conservative circles. In 1895, when a war with Great Britain seemed impending, Thomas Paschal, a Democratic politician of Texas, wrote privately to President Cleveland's Secretary of State that such a war would knock more pus out of the "anarchistic, socialistic, and populistic boil" than "would suffice to inoculate and corrupt our people for the next two centuries."

Another consideration entered into the world-power design of young Theodore Roosevelt. For about thirty years the American people had been at peace. The bloodshed, sufferings, and destruction of the Civil

War had almost been forgotten—in the North at least. The country, he said, was growing "soft," martial virtue was on a decline, and another war would be "a good thing" to tone up the people. In 1895, while President Cleveland was engaged in a vehement quarrel with Great Britain over her alleged encroachment on the territory of Venezuela, Roosevelt wrote to Lodge: "Personally I rather hope the fight will come soon. The clamor of the peace faction has convinced me that the country needs a war." The efforts of fellow citizens, particularly at Harvard University, to encourage a pacific settlement with Great Britain filled him with disgust. He asked Lodge whether he should not write to the Harvard magazine, the *Crimson*, "a smashing letter . . . giving my views and saying a word for Patriotism and Americanism."

Within a short time the agitators' program for America's thrust into world-power politics was well formulated and contained the following propositions. The United States, long an infant nation, had "grown up," had become "adult," must cast off the provincialism of its youth and, as a grown man, press into the grand game of power politics played by the grown men—the "big men"—of Europe and Asia. To continue in the old ways at home would be childish. All the free land and natural resources in the United States had passed into private hands and been developed; there was no more living room for Americans on this continent. Hence Americans must look far away for room in which to expand.

Americans, said an Indiana recruit to world-power politics, Albert J. Beveridge, produced more agricultural commodities and manufactures than they could consume; they must have new markets and colonies to exploit or American economy would be paralyzed with surplus wealth. Nations, argued Mahan in the language of Darwinism, must struggle with one another for existence and unless the United States was strong in the struggle it would perish. Millions of brown, yellow, and black men, lamented Josiah Strong, sat in the shadows, outside the blessings of Christianity, and by conquering those benighted multitudes, the United States would spread the helpful gospel of Jesus. Therefore, ran the "practical" side of the argument, the United States must build a big navy, seize new naval bases and colonies, force distant markets open, and enter full-panoplied into the competition of the great nations for the possession and domination of the earth.

In summation, the prophecy of the imperialists embraced the features deemed good politics and likely to allay domestic outbreaks against special privileges. The two great expedients of the preceding fifty years had failed to obliterate popular unrest and the will to self-expression. Free homesteads had been bestowed bountifully on settlers in the West; now those very settlers were filling the country with the uproar of a populist revolt against conditions objectionable to them in respect of government. The protective tariff had been tried as a device to assure full employment at good wages for industrial workers, but the McKinley tariff of 1890, the highest yet in American history, had been followed by the devastating panic of 1893-98, with its riots, hunger marches, and threats of revolution.

If politicians were to hold power or to get it if out of office, some new instrument was necessary and they found it in imperialist prophecy. The economic tenets of that prophecy boiled down to two mass appeals: imperial expansion would provide better markets for farmers, outlets for their "surpluses" of produce at prices profitable to them; and it would create jobs for industrial workers, fill their dinner pails.

An occasion to put the plan for world-power politics into effect was afforded by a dispute with Spain about her island of Cuba, rampant when McKinley was inaugurated in 1897. For years Cuba had been torn periodically by revolts against Spanish dominion, and in 1895 a new rebellion had flamed up. Opposed to imperialism on principle, President Cleveland had studiously sought to pursue a policy of neutrality in the war between Spain and the Cubans. Personally pacific in spirit, President McKinley at first seemed inclined to follow that precedent.

But the American people were deeply moved by the stories of cruelties practiced by the Spanish generals in Cuba especially as narrated by William Randolph Hearst and Joseph Pulitzer in their "yellow journals." To the stories of atrocities were joined pleas for American aid to the "brave Cubans fighting for liberty and independence" and demands for help from American capitalists whose plantations and sugar mills in Cuba were being destroyed in the civil war.

In the midst of the excitement early in 1898 an American battleship, the Maine, which had been sent to the harbor of Havana "to safeguard American interests," was blown up by an explosion. Two officers and 258 members of the crew lost their lives in the disaster. Spanish officials were accused of committing the deed, but they denied it and the mystery of its origin was never solved.

For seeming to rely on pacific measures in respect of Cuba and the Maine affair, President McKinley was accused by impatient Americans of being weak-kneed. Theodore Roosevelt declared that he had the backbone of a chocolate éclair. Still McKinley persisted in his negotiations with Spain and was able to wring from the government in Madrid a promise to restore peace in Cuba and grant Cubans a form of self-government amounting to autonomy, if not independence. Then suddenly, on April 11, 1898, without fully revealing to the public the Spanish promise, the President sent a message to Congress calling for a resolution authorizing him to expel Spanish forces from the island of Cuba.

Although an overwhelming majority of the representatives and a safe majority of the senators were hot for war on Spain, the form of the resolution recognizing the independence of Cuba, then under consideration, became the subject of analytical debate. Among the senators especially a dread was voiced that the war would lead to unknown adventures; that the McKinley party would take advantage of it to annex Cuba and accomplish other designs than the expulsion of Spanish authorities from that island.

A leading question, therefore, was raised: What was to be the status of Cuba after Spanish dominion was destroyed? Some Americans believed that the Cubans were not fit for self-government and that the island should be annexed or in some way put under American hegemony. But Congress declared in the war resolution that the people of Cuba were, and of right ought to be, free and independent.

For the most cautious senators, suspecting ulterior purposes, that was not enough. On motion of Senator Henry M. Teller, who had bolted the Republicans in 1896 as a free-silver reformer, another provision, more precise, was added to the resolution: "The United States hereby disclaims any disposition or intention to exercise sovereignty, jurisdiction, or control over said island except for the pacification thereof, and asserts its determination, when that is accomplished, to leave the government and control of the island to its people." This prescription seemed to leave no loophole for imperialists and annexationists of the Mahan school.

With the Teller Amendment added, Congress passed on April 19 the resolution for Cuban independence, empowering the President to use the armed forces of the United States, if necessary, to expel the Spanish government from the island. That was in effect a declaration of war, and under it war began. It was supplemented, however, on April 25, by another resolution declaring war to exist in fact and directing the President to employ the land and naval forces in waging it. War had begun, without any official reference to Spain's island of Puerto Rico or her possession in the Far East—the Philippines. To all appearances it was a war for the liberation of Cuba from Spanish dominion—an altruistic, moral war.

The hour had come for the planners of world-power politics to steer the country out on the course of imperialism. In a few weeks the naval and land forces of the United States disposed of the Spanish navy and troops in and about Cuba. Then American forces occupied Puerto Rico without having to fight a battle. Meanwhile, as American naval authorities had planned it, the American fleet in the Far East, under Admiral George Dewey, destroyed the Spanish war vessels in the harbor of Manila on May 1, and in effect ended Spanish rule in the Philippines. In August when Spain made overtures for peace, Cuba was freed from her dominion and Puerto Rico and the Philippines were at the command of the United States. Although most Americans had not thought of the war as a war for imperial expansion according to the Mahan-Lodge-Roosevelt formula, they now faced the issue of turning the war for the liberation of Cubans into a triumph for imperialism.

They had a foretaste of what was coming, moreover, in the annexation of the Hawaiian Islands on July 7, 1898, by a joint resolution of Congress. The Hawaiian Islands had long been coveted by several European Powers and by Japan. American missionaries had gone there early in the nineteenth century and Americans had taken part in the development of Hawaiian sugar interests. Before the close of the century Americans in the islands had grown restless under the government by native rulers. In 1893 they had revolted against Queen Liliuokalani, compelled her to abdicate, and established a republic. Under the administration of President Benjamin Harrison they had negotiated a treaty with the United States providing for annexation; but not long after he was inaugurated President on March 4, 1893, Grover Cleveland deliberately blocked the project.

The Republicans simply bided their time. In June 1897 the McKinley administration made a second treaty of annexation with the government of Hawaii controlled by Americans, and its ratification by the United States Senate was pending when the war with Spain broke out. Fearing endless delay, if not defeat, sponsors of annexation then substituted for the treaty a joint resolution of Congress, which required only a majority vote in each house for passage. The resolution was carried. On August 12 the islands were formally annexed and in 1900 they were given a territorial form of government.

In the preliminary peace settlement with Spain in August 1898 it was agreed that Cuba should be free, that Puerto Rico should be ceded to the United States, and that Manila should be occupied by American troops until the terms of the formal peace were determined.

For weeks McKinley withheld his decision on the fate of the Philippines. Meanwhile advocates of annexation, on the platform and in the press, worked hard to convince the American people that it was their opportunity and duty to annex the distant islands and spread American civilization among the natives.

At length McKinley made up his mind in favor of annexation and Spain was compelled to yield. In the final treaty drawn up at Paris, independence was granted to Cuba; Puerto Rico and Guam were ceded to the United States; and the Philippines were transferred to the United States in exchange for a payment of $20,000,000.

When the treaty of peace, including provisions for the annexation of the Philippines, was placed before the Senate for ratification, senators of the anti-imperialist school felt that their worst forebodings were to be justified. In war resolutions of April 1898 they had barred all plans for the annexation of Cuba and repudiated in stern and specific language every imperialist ambition in that connection. Now they realized that, by the treaty, the United States was to be thrust into the eternal wars of the Orient and into the endless intrigues of the great Powers of Europe.

As they understood the departure from the traditional foreign policy, America was henceforth to be one of the imperialist nations of the world, following the course of Spain and Great Britain in conquering and ruling subject peoples, forever warring for more territory, commerce, and dominion over other races. Immediately there was formed in the Senate an opposition so determined that the McKinley administration, backed by Theodore Roosevelt, Lodge, Mahan, and their followers, was greatly worried lest ambitions for world power be thwarted.

Soon the politicians of the McKinley school discovered that they might not be able to secure even a bare majority of the senators for the approval of the annexationist treaty, to say nothing of the two-thirds majority required by the Constitution. Exasperated by the prospect of losing their prize, they denounced the proposal to reject or recast the treaty as shameless effrontery, a reckless repudiation of national honor. In their perplexity and quest for backing they even welcomed William J. Bryan, so recently described by Republicans as an addlepated criminal, when he came to Washington and urged his followers in the Senate to vote for ratification on grounds of national honor; for without the support of Democrats and Populists defeat was certain. By strenuous efforts enough senators personally antagonistic to imperialism were at last rounded up by party whips, and the treaty was ratified with a declaration to the effect that the question of the future of the Philippines was to be left indeterminate. The fateful commitment had been made. Two years later Cuba was forced to accept the so-called Platt Amendment establishing an American protectorate over the island.

Before the conflict over the treaty with Spain was settled in 1899, news arrived that a rebellion had started in the Philippines. For years these islands had seethed with resentment against Spanish rule. The leader of the opposition, Emilio Aguinaldo, was in open revolt when the United States declared war on Spain and his aid had been sought by American army officers in defeating Spanish forces in the Philippines. When this object had been achieved he and his supporters hoped or assumed that at last independence was to be established for the Philippines, as it had been promised to Cuba.

Their expectation of freedom was soon dispelled. On February 4, 1899, a slight collision occurred between Aguinaldo's men and American soldiers and several lives were lost. Ignoring his efforts to arrange an amicable settlement, American authorities pressed the war against the "insurrectionists," who regarded themselves as "patriots." This war went on for more than three years. Early in 1901, with the assistance of Filipinos who had been loyal to the Spanish regime, Aguinaldo was captured and forced to take an oath of allegiance to the United States. But guerrilla fighting continued until July 1902, when President Theodore Roosevelt officially declared it to be at an end.

While the Philippine war was in full blast during the summer of 1900, members of a secret society in China, called the "Boxers," started an organized rout of foreigners. They murdered missionaries in the provinces, killed the German minister in the streets of Peking, and besieged the British quarters in Peking to which hundreds of aliens of various nationalities had fled for safety. At once the United States joined Japan, Russia, Great Britain, France, and Germany—the great imperialist Powers—in sending troops to the Chinese capital, where they broke the siege of the British quarters and put down the Chinese "insurrection" against foreigners.

In connection with the settlement at the close of this conflict, John Hay, the American Secretary of State, adhered to a policy for the Far East, now known as the "Open Door." He proposed that the rights already guaranteed to foreign Powers in China by treaty and international law be protected; but he urged that "Chinese territorial and administrative entity" be preserved and that "the principle of equal and impartial trade with all parts of the Chinese Empire" be safeguarded for the world. For the damage to foreign lives and property, done by the Boxers, heavy indemnities were imposed on the Chinese government, and Hay's doctrine was conveniently ignored by the great Powers engaged in seizing and dividing the spoils of China.

☆

Against the background of these war events the presidential campaign of 1900 was carried on. The Republicans renominated McKinley and associated with him Theodore Roosevelt, now acclaimed a hero of the Spanish War in which he had done a little fighting, as candidate for Vice-President. In their platform they took a firm position in support of the gold standard, celebrated the "splendid triumphs" of business and commerce under the McKinley administration, and stood fast against everything that smacked of Bryanism in 1896. Concerning foreign affairs, they declared that the war with Spain had been "unsought and patiently resisted," but had been "triumphantly waged" when it came.

THE AMERICAN EMPIRE AT THE END OF THE NINETEENTH CENTURY

As a result of the war, "to ten millions of the human race there was given a new birth of freedom," and to the American people "a new and noble responsibility." With respect to the Philippine insurrection against this birth of freedom, the Republicans proposed to put it down and "to confer the blessings of liberty and civilization upon all the rescued peoples." In other words, they advanced confidently in defense of their domestic program and their foreign policies.

In response to this challenge on domestic and foreign policies, the Democrats renominated Bryan and, besides reaffirming their faith in their principles of 1896, declared their belief that imperialism was a curse to the nation. They lashed it as a new and dangerous threat to the American Republic. They asserted that the Filipinos could not be made citizens without undermining our civilization or subjects without imperiling our form of government. Since the United States now had these wards, however, the Democrats promised them a stable form of government, independence, and then protection against outside interference. They condemned "the greedy commercialism" which dictated the Philippine policy of the Republican administration and impugned the war against the Filipinos as a war of "criminal aggression." "Militarism" they decried as meaning "conquest abroad and intimidation and oppression at home." They were not willing, they declared, "to surrender our civilization or to convert the Republic into an empire." While assailing imperialism, Bryan insisted on upholding his program for the home front that had been formulated for the campaign of 1896.

In justifying their new course Republican orators bore down hard on two types of argument. The first was that of "our responsibility." Their policy, they insisted, was not imperialism; it was the fulfillment of duty to the peoples that had been brought under American jurisdiction as if by an "accident" of history. The Philippines had come to the United States unexpectedly, amid the fortunes of a war fought to free Cuba, and it was our moral obligation to protect these helpless peoples, to civilize them, to educate them, to raise their standard of life, and to confer on them the blessing of liberty.

The second argument of the Republicans pertained to the insurrection in the Philippines, and they shaped it into a question of American patriotism. "Don't haul down the flag!" Theodore Roosevelt shouted as he toured the country in the campaign. It had been raised in the Philippines, enemies had fired on it, every patriot must defend it, and only "copperheads" and traitors sympathized with Filipinos who wanted to pull it down and substitute their banner of independence.

Against imperialism, from the very inception of the war with Spain, a strong opposition was presented by publicists; and in the campaign Democratic politicians contributed their denunciations. William Graham

Sumner at Yale University, in an article entitled "The Conquest of the United States by Spain," portrayed the United States as adopting the very course that had led to the downfall of Spain. Imperialism and its works, he contended, would result in bigger armies and navies, bigger debts, a contempt for the Constitution, and more wars whenever the politicians decided that the country needed them. Mark Twain ridiculed the program "for giving civilization to the man who sits in darkness," and condemned the whole imperialist business as a pious fraud devised to conceal commercial greed and lust for power. Andrew Carnegie inveighed against imperialism so fervently that John Hay declared the ironmaster to be "off his head." Bryan crowned it all by proposing to stop the bloodshed in the Philippines at once and make immediate arrangements to prepare the Filipinos for independence.

By the popular decision at the polls in November, McKinley remained President of the United States. He received 100,000 more votes than in 1896; while Bryan, with his program for concentration on the domestic front, dropped below his record of 1896 by nearly 130,000. Imperialists interpreted McKinley's re-election as a final approval of their quest for world power. As in other elections, however, it was impossible wholly to separate the influence of foreign policies in the campaign from the influence of domestic policies.

In any event McKinley's victory, substantial though it was, did not obscure the existence of a powerful opposition. The balloting by counties revealed a pronounced shift of party loyalties, especially in the West where agricultural prices had improved materially after 1896. That signified a return of many farmers to the Republican fold but not necessarily an endorsement of imperialism. Still committed to measures which Republicans attacked as radical and dangerous, the Democratic party was far from death's door and there were many signs that the apparent endorsement of imperialism might not be real, especially in the farming regions of the West and South.

Nevertheless the Republicans were preparing for a rapid advance along their line of world-power politics when President McKinley was assassinated in September 1901. Although his successor, Vice-President Theodore Roosevelt, promised to uphold McKinley's policies unbroken, he had ideas and purposes of his own. McKinley had been timid about foreign adventures, in spite of all that had happened in recent years. He had belonged to the old generation brought up in the belief that the foreign policy of Washington, Jefferson, and Monroe was the correct policy for the Republic. The plans of Lodge, Mahan, and Roosevelt for world imperialism had been alien to his outlook upon national destiny.

Theodore Roosevelt, on the other hand, was of the new generation and, besides loving power for its own sake, he insisted that the nation should pursue a course of power politics in dealing with foreign governments. At the same time he was far less conservative in declaring new domestic policies than were the older leaders of his party. With his imperialism, he coupled pledges of reform on the home front almost in the spirit of Bryanism. He assailed trusts, combines, concentrated wealth, and plutocrats as fiercely as Bryan and the Populists had done. He spoke openly of a more equitable distribution of wealth, of the poverty in great cities, and of social perils within the United States, due to inequalities of wealth.

In fact as President, Theodore Roosevelt, by uniting world-power politics and domestic social reform—pomp and prestige in world affairs with the conciliation of discontented farmers and industrial workers at home—formed a combination of policies that made a strong appeal to the American electorate. He "took the wind out of Bryan's sails," as the saying went, by his operations on the home front, by his "square deal," and provided the people simultaneously with almost daily excitement in his handling of foreign relations. His versatility in this type of statesmanship, or "demagogy" as his opponents defined it, was conclusively demonstrated in the presidential election of 1904.

For that test the Democrats shoved Bryan aside at last, nominated Alton B. Parker, a conservative New York judge, and jettisoned most of the Populist program of reform. Nominated by the Republicans to succeed himself, President Roosevelt came back to the White House in a whirlwind. His popular vote was larger by about 400,000 than McKinley's poll in 1900; Parker fell below Bryan's last vote by more than 1,000,000 and below Roosevelt's by more than 2,000,000. About half a million voters went over to the Socialists and the Populists, but in the Republican avalanche of November 1904 their protests against imperialism and capitalism could be ignored by the Republicans.

Under the leadership of President Roosevelt for nearly eight years a "vigorous" foreign policy was pursued. The insurrection in the Philippines was crushed. An organic law, modeled on that enacted for Puerto Rico in 1900, was put into force in the Philippines in 1902, with provisions for giving the Filipinos self-government piece by piece. The policy of the "Open Door," which was presumed to give American capitalists equal trading rights in China with the British and other capitalists, was upheld and highly praised as indicating something permanent. When Russia and Japan approached a deadlock in a frightful war in 1905, President Roosevelt offered his services in bringing the belligerents together, opened their peace conference at Portsmouth, New Hampshire, and filled the newspapers with blazing headlines about that conference for several days. He negotiated the "Gentlemen's Agreement" with Japan, which forbade the immigration of Japanese laborers to compete with American laborers. With the idea of exhibiting the naval strength of the United States, he sent a fleet around the world in 1907–09. By this action, in defiance of opposition in Congress, he sought to demonstrate to Americans and the rest of mankind that the Navy of the United States was ready for what the diplomats of world-power politics called "eventualities."

In the sphere of action nearer home President Roosevelt pressed for the construction of a canal across the Isthmus of Panama which, in addition to promoting water-borne commerce, would make possible the movement of American naval forces between the two oceans. When he came to the presidency a treaty had been negotiated with Great Britain, permitting the United States to go ahead with the canal. That arrangement set aside an old treaty of 1850 providing for joint construction and authorized the United States to proceed alone, on condition that there was to be no discrimination among nations in rates fixed for the use of the canal.

Two routes for the canal were then being discussed: one through Nicaragua and the other through Panama. After a heated argument the second was chosen and Roosevelt set about making terms for its construction with the government of Colombia, of which Panama was a part. A draft of the treaty was framed but the Senate of Colombia rejected it. Annoyed by the delay, a few men in Panama, feeling certain that the government of the United States would support them, provoked a revolt against Colombia in 1903. Within a few days President Roosevelt recognized their independence and made a treaty with the new Panama government that granted the United States the right to build the canal through its territory.

Soon "the dirt began to fly," as Roosevelt expressed it, and in 1913 the waters of the Atlantic and the Pacific were joined; the voyage between New York and San Francisco was shortened by nearly 8000 miles. Roosevelt was criticized for his "highhanded action" in dealing with Colombia and he later confessed that he simply "took" Panama to stop endless talk and get the work done.

Just as the building of the canal began Roosevelt resorted to another action in the Caribbean region, also deplored by his critics as autocratic. Santo Domingo had long been heavily in debt to European investors, and their respective governments were considering the use of naval forces to collect the debts. Interpreting it as an omen of possible occupation of the island, President Roosevelt intervened and made a treaty with Santo Domingo authorizing the United States to supervise its finances and the payment of its debts.

When this treaty was rejected by the United States Senate, Roosevelt went forward with his plans anyway. He had an American put in charge of the customs-house in Santo Domingo and sent warships there as a sign that he had force at his command. Senators accused him of violating the Constitution and acting arrogantly, besides ignoring Congress and the rights of the people in Santo Domingo. No doubt some of the European claims against that little country were more than tinged with fraud, but Roosevelt insisted that he was conducting the foreign affairs of the United States and would not be hampered by opponents.

During the conflict over Santo Domingo, Theodore Roosevelt gave to the world a new interpretation of the Monroe Doctrine thoroughly imperialistic in letter and spirit. Was the United States, under that doctrine, to prevent European Powers from using battleships to collect debts in the Latin American countries? If so, what was to prevent them from seizing territory in defiance of the doctrine? Or was the United States to see that such debts were paid? Or should these matters be submitted to arbitration by an international tribunal?

On the issues Roosevelt took a positive stand. Foreign Powers, he declared, are not to seize any more territory in this hemisphere, as the old Monroe Doctrine affirmed; moreover controversies of the kind are not to be submitted to any international tribunal. Then he also proclaimed a new doctrine all his own: if governments in Latin America cannot keep order and pay their debts the United States, having prevented other Powers from acting, must intervene, stop disorders, and make sure that just debts are paid. This pronouncement by the President of the United States was immediately characterized in Latin America as crass "Yankee imperialism." Nevertheless, on this theory, presidential actions in the Caribbean region were multiplied.

Under Roosevelt's successor, William Howard Taft, who had beaten William Jennings Bryan in the election of 1908, imperialistic activity by the President received another name. Republicans now simply called it "dollar diplomacy." The rose under a new name meant that it was the duty and right of the United States Government to seek out and protect opportunities that would allow American businessmen to operate freely in foreign countries and American bankers to make profitable loans abroad. "The diplomacy of the present administration," President Taft explained in 1912, "has sought to respond to modern ideas of commercial intercourse. This policy has been characterized as substituting dollars for bullets. . . . It is an effort frankly directed to the increase of American trade upon the axiomatic principle that the government of the United States shall extend all proper support to every legitimate and beneficial American enterprise abroad."

In conformity with this axiom foreign policy was conducted during

Taft's administration. He intervened personally, for example, in China, and tried to secure for American bankers a share of a loan that was being floated in Peking under the auspices of European financiers. Under his leadership advantages were taken of a disturbance in Nicaragua to land American marines in that country and establish there an American "protectorate."

When Woodrow Wilson, after defeating President Taft in the election of 1912, assumed the presidency in Washington, he officially renounced imperialism as theory, but as practice it was by no means entirely discarded. Although President Wilson refused to support Taft's plans for American bankers in China, he adopted strong measures in the Caribbean. The protectorate in Nicaragua was continued. In 1914, Wilson landed marines in Santo Domingo. Two years later he ordered a full military occupation of that country, suppressed its government, set up American military authority, and had a new constitution for Santo Domingo drawn up in Washington.

In 1915, during a revolution in Haiti, American marines were dispatched to the scene, order was restored at a heavy cost of lives, and Haiti put under the control of American military authorities. On this occasion the Secretary of State explained the action in sanctimonious language reminiscent of McKinley: "The United States Government has no purpose of aggression and is entirely disinterested in promoting this protectorate." As a part of the program for strengthening American power in the Caribbean, President Wilson negotiated a treaty with Denmark by which, in 1917, the Danish West Indies, not far from Puerto Rico, were transferred to the United States. Not without reason it could be boasted that the Caribbean had become an "American lake." The phrase was not exactly pleasing to Latin Americans but it rather closely fitted the facts in the case.

Meanwhile troubles had been seething in Mexico and the pot was boiling over when Wilson was inaugurated President. In 1911 its President, Porfirio Diaz, who had long ruled his country with an iron rod, was confronted by a threat of revolution. Too old to fight back as he had hitherto done on such occasions, Diaz resigned and fled to Europe. His flight was followed by one uprising after another. President Taft, then near the end of his administration, was urged to intervene, and "restore order." He refused, however, and left the thorny problem to President Wilson.

For a time Wilson pursued a policy described as "watchful waiting." But in fact he did intervene in Mexico. He declined to recognize the government of a new military dictator, Huerta, who rose to power in the confusion. In so doing Wilson took the position, revolutionary in the history of America's foreign policy, that it was his duty and right to withhold recognition from any government which did not measure up to the moral, political, and commercial standards of the United States. This made the American government a kind of censor over all governments established in foreign countries and seeking recognition in Washington.

Acting on events in Mexico, President Wilson ordered the landing of American marines in Vera Cruz and the seizure of that city in 1914. After Huerta gave up his office a settlement was made and the marines were withdrawn. Again, in 1916, after a Mexican bandit had raided a neighboring town in New Mexico, President Wilson sent American troops under General John Pershing on an expedition into Mexico in search of the marauder. Such was the state of American-Mexican relations when the energies of the United States became engaged in the war on Germany in 1917.

By this time imperialism everywhere was in a crisis. Indeed the United States had scarcely embarked on the new course of seeking world power when even leaders of imperialism in the Old World began to profess anxiety over the growing armaments and darkening perils of universal war. For various reasons, some hidden from public view, the Czar of Russia called upon other governments to hold a general conference on peace. The assembly, including delegates from the United States, met at The Hague in 1899, but did little or nothing to reduce the dangers of war. It adopted a rule that any neutral country could rightfully offer its services as a mediator between nations at war; and it established at The Hague a court for hearing international disputes voluntarily submitted to it.

After two more wars had intervened—the Russo-Japanese War and the war between the British and the Boers in South Africa—the Czar called a second "peace conference" at The Hague, in 1907. Like the first, it did nothing to reduce the growing armaments of the world and was, if anything, a more obvious failure. As later revelations respecting the proceedings of the two conferences disclosed, both were dominated by men holding imperialist doctrines, all bent on gaining advantages for their respective countries. Certainly it could be said with truth that the adventure of the United States in world-power politics had not brightened the outlook for world peace.

Chapter 22

WIDENING KNOWLEDGE AND THOUGHT

WHILE the continent was being rounded out and imperialist adventurers were carrying the flag to distant places, the realm of American knowledge and ideas about the physical sciences, human history, and society in general was also undergoing rapid expansion. Until near the end of the nineteenth century the American people depended for this growth of information, beyond the necessities of working routines, on the sporadic inquiries of curious persons who studied particular subjects and wrote about or taught them. Governments, it is true, often looked into such topics as population, wealth, natural resources, and the output of farms and factories, and issued bulky reports; but knowledge of other matters and theories respecting them were mainly provided by private persons who hunted for facts and figures, made observations, thought about their findings, and published articles, pamphlets, and books.

As the nineteenth century drew to a close and the twentieth century advanced toward its meridian, individuals, as hitherto, continued to enlarge knowledge and bring thought to bear on its meaning and uses. Seekers after precise information and its significance for American society still worked alone, at their own expense and on their own initiative, and their findings were often so important for the advancement of American civilization as to be epoch-making. But to the explorations of self-directed individuals were now added the explorations of individuals and groups of workers, financed by mammoth sums of money dedicated to research, who made inquiries in every domain of knowledge, physical and human. They labored under the auspices of governments, federal, state, and local; of civic societies concerned with the humanities and civilization; and of special interests desiring information useful to their designs. In other words, to a considerable and an increasing extent, searching and thinking became more specialized, more organized, and more heavily financed.

☆

For the simple economy of farms, handicrafts, and small towns the old method of acquiring and extending knowledge by individual and haphazard research met fairly well the needs of the people. At all events it was the method generally employed. But after the Civil War new and vast industries rose in all parts of the country from ocean to ocean; markets widened from communities to the national borders and beyond them to the outer world; trade unions, local and national, were organized; conflicts of capital and labor upset social peace; and the business of government, state and federal, became more and more complicated. For a long time government had been confined mainly to keeping order, building roads, collecting taxes, and administering poor relief. Now its officials encountered new and more intricate responsibilities, such as the regulation of railways and utilities, the adjustment of relations between capitalists and industrial workers, and other problems not to be "solved" by rule of thumb.

On the impacts and problems of this crucial transformation in economy and politics individual inquirers, as in previous times, concentrated intellectual energies. The huge collection of American books, articles, and pamphlets dealing with the physical and human universe, accumulated during the eighteenth century and enlarged in the age of Jacksonian democracy, was now expanded by literally millions of publications, general and special, covering the physical resources of the continent, many branches of economy in minute detail, many tendencies in action, thought, and aspiration.

The findings and reports ranged so far and wide that nothing short of the great rooms of the Library of Congress filled with card catalogues could indicate their sweep. Works were available to answer hosts of questions. Was it the matter of a better understanding of social beginnings in prehistoric ages won by a long and intensive study of the American Indians? Lewis Henry Morgan, in his *Ancient Society*, published in 1877, illuminated the history of all civilization. The labor movement? John R. Commons and his associates gave a portrayal of it in their *History of Labour in the United States* (1918). The woman movement? A three-volume *History of Woman Suffrage* (1881–87) unfolded that story. A more comprehensive history of the nation? John B. McMaster began to make an answer with his *History of the American People*, the first volume of which came out in 1883. Was it the nature of American intellectual interests? Vernon Parrington dealt with that in his *Main Currents of American Thought*, published in 1927–30. Did citizens seek knowledge of anything else? Vast libraries, well organized and operated, could furnish bibliographies of writings on short notice.

But mingled with the work of individuals and enlarging it in every direction were the researches of specialized groups set apart to make studies and financed from public and private funds. Systematic research for knowledge was fostered by the founding and expansion of universities, public and private. State institutions created in earlier times were granted more money by legislatures with which to build laboratories, assemble great libraries, and conduct graduate schools for advanced studies in the sciences, letters, and arts. Old private colleges, such as Harvard and Columbia, were transformed into universities, with research and publication as a primary aim. New universities were established on the basis of gifts by men who had accumulated wealth from America's expanding economy.

The Johns Hopkins University at Baltimore, endowed by a leading capitalist of that city and named for him, opened its doors in 1876— one hundred years after the Declaration of Independence. About ten years later Stanford University was founded in California by Leland Stanford, a pioneer capitalist on the Pacific coast. In 1892 the University of Chicago, endowed with funds from the oil magnate, John D. Rockefeller, also began the promotion of research and instruction in almost everything under the sun.

By the opening of the twentieth century there were few colleges in the country, new or old, which were still content to teach routine subjects from books in the traditional style. The smallest and poorest of such institutions made efforts to extend the boundaries of knowledge and to teach the new learning that was coming from private inquiries and the graduate schools of the universities.

Systematic research for scientific knowledge and discovery was also carried on by many other agencies. Large industrial corporations built their own laboratories and engaged experts in physics, chemistry, and mechanics to invent new machines and devise new commodities for manufacture. During the opening decades of the twentieth century it became a practice for rich men and women to establish foundations for the promotion of research in the sciences and the humanities directed toward the welfare of mankind, the Carnegie Corporation, the Rockefeller Foundation, and the Russell Sage Foundation being conspicuous examples. In endowed institutions able minds concentrated on medical research that might lead to the conquest of pain and disease or on pure science from which might flow practical results in the physical and moral universe.

In 1916 the National Industrial Conference Board was organized by industrialists and supplied with funds for making studies of industrial and economic questions. Independent institutes of special types, such as the Brookings Institution in Washington, D.C., and the Bureau of Economic Research in New York were created to conduct research in the fundamental problems of economy and government. Trade unions, discovering that matters of collective bargaining were complicated, adopted the practice of employing experts in law, economics, and finance to furnish them information for guidance in policy making and action.

Governments, federal and local, more and more realized the need for organized continuous research. Earlier they had relied mainly upon the knowledge of persons who happened to be in office or upon hasty inquiries by legislative committees in emergencies. Now, confronting new and perplexing problems in administration, they established one after another, often as a result of popular or special demands, bureaus or other agencies of research, frequently in connection with the matter of expenditures and the laying of taxes—that is, in budgetary operations. By the second decade of the twentieth century research and planning agencies, associated with governments, had been set up in all parts of the United States. By that time it had also become a practice for Congress and state legislatures to appoint special committees authorized to employ experts and carry on extensive investigations, before undertaking the business of lawmaking relative to such intricate matters as the regulation of railways, conservation of natural resources, and the provision of social security.

As a result of such inquiries and reports the American people had available an increasing amount of knowledge for use in their private pursuits and callings, in the shaping of their own character and purposes, and in reaching decisions respecting policies of government and social improvement. They could either buy, or read at the swiftly multiplying libraries, books on every subject of historical or current interest; for example, business, industry, agriculture, labor organization, wealth, taxation, politics, natural science, religion, psychology, sociology, anthropology, archaeology, technology, the arts, health, home ownership, crime, poverty, the family, the relation of the individual to society, foreign commerce, international affairs, and the changes which were taking place in national affairs.

Though American life was not so complicated in his day, the first President of the United States had been conscious of the role that knowledge must play in a progressive society. In his first annual address to Congress, President Washington had said: "There is nothing which can better deserve your patronage than the promotion of science and literature. Knowledge is in every country the surest basis of public happiness. In one in which the measures of government receive their impressions so immediately from the sense of the community as in ours it is proportionately essential. To the security of a free constitution it contributes in various ways." When the two-hundredth anniversary of his birth was celebrated in 1932 his desire was being realized in part: the people of the

United States had at their disposal a wealth of knowledge of things physical and human—science and literature—to use for the purposes of civilization if they could.

More or less affected by the new knowledge ran currents of thought about its implications, as the continent was rounded out and the inherited society of farms and small towns was transformed into a continental nation of closely integrated parts. In these trends of thought two theories or interpretations competed for supremacy. One placed the individual at the center of interest and made individual enterprise the primary source of invention, progress, wealth, and national greatness. The other emphasized society and general welfare as the controlling concern and insisted that the individual, however enlightened and powerful, owed his existence, his language, most of his knowledge, and his opportunities to the society in which he lived and worked. Both were used by powerful interests in American society.

To the first line of thought the name "individualism" was given. This was a new word that first came into play in the nineteenth century. It was used by de Tocqueville in a book, *Democracy in America*, published in an English translation in 1835. As he employed the word, it meant a kind of individual anarchy—the conduct of any person who arbitrarily cut himself off from his family, friends, and society. Near the middle of the nineteenth century economists took up the new idea, individualism, and built a whole system of thought around it.

About the same time reinforcement of the idea came from natural science. In 1859 the English scientist, Charles Darwin, published the *Origin of Species,* mainly emphasizing biology and the struggle of the individual animal for existence—a kind of biological war of each against all. In his later work, *The Descent of Man,* published in 1871, Darwin definitely connected man with the kingdom of lower animals and again laid stress on the struggle for individual existence.

Darwin himself was cautious in his statements respecting the role of the individual in evolution, but the "Darwinians" in the United States and other countries made dogmas of his speculations, maintaining that they were truths beyond argument. Consequently when Americans, released from the strain of their Civil War, rushed to the conquest of the continent and impetuously went into the business of trying to get rich quickly, they had ready for use a theory, an ideology, that justified the strong in accumulating all the wealth they could in any way not too outrageous and in doing what they liked with their possessions.

Between 1865 and 1900 this theory of individualism was worked out by many American writers of marked intellectual power, who published articles and big books on the subject. Soon after he became a professor of political and social science at Yale University in 1872, William Graham Sumner sought to show that all civilization had come from free individual initiative; that all hope of progress and improvement lay in giving the fullest liberty to individuals; and that government interference with this liberty was injurious to mankind. As a sociologist, Sumner gave the support of his branch of learning to the individualist argument.

A contemporary at Columbia University, John William Burgess, a professor of political science, wrote brief articles and large treatises on government and liberty in which he made political science serve the cause of individualism. In the department of economics at Columbia, one of Burgess' colleagues, John Bates Clark, building on the work of other writers, American and European, constructed a whole system of economics out of individualism. At the University of Chicago another economist, J. Laurence Laughlin, taught a version of the theory about as extreme as imagination could make it, short of sheer anarchy.

Meanwhile Charles A. Dana, who had been a kind of utopian socialist in the days of Jacksonian democracy but was now a conservative editor of the New York *Sun*, daily preached individualism with withering scorn for all doubters; and as editor of the *Nation*, E. L. Godkin gave weekly versions of the same doctrine to his readers. In 1893 Frederick Jackson Turner, a professor of history in the University of Wisconsin, published a paper on "The Frontier in American History," which made individualism an interpretation of American history, by ignoring families and communities—that is, mutual aid—and tracing the secret of American uniqueness to the stoutest of all alleged individualists—the man of the frontier, as if there had been no women or families or communities or books or schools or churches there.

When the twentieth century opened, the doctrine of individualism had become a potent influence in American thought. Thousands of men and women, who knew little or nothing of its origins or were indifferent to its one-sided nature, had accepted it as a law of nature in private affairs and public policy. In fact the history of the preceding twenty-five years—the rapid opening up of the West, the swift rise of industries, and the increase of national wealth—seemed to them proof that the theory was in accord with reality.

To coming generations it was transmitted by instruction in universities, colleges, and lower schools as if it had never been analyzed and controverted by minds as able as those by which it had been formulated. So thoroughly intrenched was it in places high and low that President Hoover won rounds of popular applause when he prefixed an adjective to it and spoke of "rugged" individualism. Judging by the fervor of that applause, rugged individualism was the supreme characteristic of American life, character, and purposes.

The thesis that human beings are actuated merely by a competitive struggle for existence and that society is a product of such individualism was countered by a thesis directing attention to the co-operative nature of human beings and the power of mutual aid in the origin and evolution of society. The sponsors of the associative principle in human life insisted that the creed of individualism, pushed to the extreme of dogmatism, was false to the facts of history, including the history of the United States; or at least so false as to be a gross distortion of reality. They pointed out, with copious illustrations, the heavy debt of all the individuals in the United States to American society for all the tools they worked with, for education, for opportunity, for the protection and benefits bestowed by the government as the representative of society. To ruthless individualism they traced much of the poverty and misery, ugliness and waste, which had marked the years of the uprush in business enterprise. To social action by groups and agencies of government they looked for the measures necessary to master these evils and bring about a greater equality of condition—a higher standard of life for all the people. The ideal of these "humanitarians" was best expressed by their own term "social meliorism"—gradual but effective improvement by social action.

If William Graham Sumner was the sociologist of individualism, Lester Ward was the sociologist of social meliorism. For leadership of this kind Ward was prepared by varied experiences and studies. After serving during the Civil War in the Union army, from which he was honorably discharged on account of wounds, Ward entered the employment of the United States Government and achieved distinction in scientific inquiry and reporting. While pursuing his work in natural science he took up the study of social evolution and in 1883 published the first volume of his *Dynamic Sociology*.

In this and other works Ward dwelt on the co-operative nature of human societies from the earliest times and on the opportunities, devices, and services provided by society for individual happiness and advancement. He marshaled a mass of countervailing knowledge against the individualist, or laissez faire, doctrine of Sumner and his school, and contended that co-operation among individuals, rather than a merciless and unfeeling competition for wealth and power, is the secret of human progress toward welfare for each and all. From his intensive study of the past Ward moved to the conclusion that government, representing society, should be positive not negative in policy and should adopt measures deliberately directed to social improvement. On the constructive side, therefore, Ward chose a middle way between individualism and socialism. By writing and lecturing in this median line of thought until his death in 1913, he helped to give social meliorism a firmer hold on American minds.

Building upon the work of the sociologists and independent inquiries, Anna Garlin Spencer, in *Woman's Share in Social Culture* (1913), dealt systematically with the role of women in social evolution from primitive times to the modern age. In this book she described the important part played by women in the original invention of the domestic, or civilian, arts; in the long development of the productive activities by which the family and society are sustained; and in the formation of the social sentiments necessary for the harmony and welfare of society.

Taking up the conditions of her own times, Dr. Spencer examined the varieties of activities carried on by women in all branches of national life, from industry to education. She demonstrated that women had been energetic in every kind of social improvement and argued cogently that, since in the modern age government was assuming positive duties in raising the standards of welfare, it was a logical and necessary step to grant equal suffrage to women—an equal share in the government. In this contribution to knowledge and thought Anna Garlin Spencer furnished a broader social philosophy for the woman movement then rapidly gaining in force and influence. She also vitalized the whole case for social meliorism by teaching and lecturing on the subject from the pulpit and in leading universities and public halls.

In the domain of economic thought the doctrine of individualism was likewise questioned, especially after about 1880, by several university economists, including Richard T. Ely, Simon Patten, and Edmund J. James. These critics attacked the doctrine on many grounds. They declared that it did not correspond to innumerable facts of human experience. They said it was simply an armchair theory and advised students of economics to go out into the real world, make observations, examine the ways in which industry and labor actually operated, and adjust theories to the facts of economy.

Individualism, by setting everyone against his neighbors, these critical economists declared, was contrary, moreover, to good morals, especially Christian morals. Poverty, they maintained, was due in part to legislation; not solely to individual idleness, improvidence, and incompetence. Great riches heaped up by individuals they ascribed in part to favors conferred by society, and in part to special privileges bestowed by government. According to their views it was therefore the duty of government to change unjust laws, bring about a more equitable distribution of wealth, and take an active part in improving the lot of the people.

Among the economists who refused to take individualism as the ultimate word was Thorstein Veblen, for a time a teacher at the University of Chicago. He did not concern himself, however, with meliorist reforms.

What he did especially was to compare the actual conduct of American capitalists with the theories about their conduct promulgated in the works of the orthodox economists and taken by capitalists at face value. After studying court records and legislative reports on the methods of trusts, combinations, and financiers, so often ignored by theorists, Veblen presented a conclusion startling to defenders of apologetic economics.

In summary, he pointed out that modern business was carried on largely by corporations, not by individuals; that great fortunes had accrued to individuals by the formation of trusts and combines which closed many competitive plants and raised prices; that other great fortunes had been accumulated by selling pieces of paper, called stocks and bonds, to investors at prices far above their true value; that instead of increasing the production of wealth, in innumerable cases big business operations actually reduced the production of wealth.

In a way this was what populists had been saying for years but Veblen expounded the criticism, in his treatise, *The Theory of Business Enterprise,* in 1904, in an ingenious form of learning that made it more palatable to economists in universities and to other persons interested in public behavior and general welfare. This book made no case for social meliorism but it helped to blunt the edge of individualism conceived as guaranteeing the utmost production of wealth and a distribution of wealth according to "merits."

The theory of individualism as applied to political science by John W. Burgess and his school was also countered by other political scientists. According to the individualist thesis recently built up in American books on political science, government represented "the people" and its primary duty was to keep order, defend life and property, and refrain from interfering with economic enterprise. By numerous writers this thesis was attacked as in part contrary to historical facts and in part contrary to the professed ideals of the Republic. They asserted that the government of the United States from the beginning had in fact represented powerful economic classes—manufacturers, financiers, bankers, and planters— actually opposed to the interests of the people at large, and that it had constantly interfered with agriculture and small economic enterprises in order to benefit the holders of special privileges. Even justices of the Supreme Court in Washington, publicists charged, did not merely enforce the Constitution, as some theorists declared, but read into it opinions favorable to "big business."

The meliorist revolt conducted against individualism by political scientists was concisely described by J. Allen Smith at the University of Washington, in *The Spirit of American Government,* published in 1907. In a few words Smith characterized the Constitution as a "scheme of government . . . planned and set up to perpetuate the ascendancy of the property-holding class leavened with democratic ideas." The major political parties he represented as dominated by corporations and men of great wealth. The sources of many evils, such as corruption, he found "not in the slums . . . but in the selfishness and greed of those who are the recognized leaders in commercial and industrial affairs."

Individualism as "no government interference with business," Smith described as merely "the selfish view" of a "relatively small class which, though it controls the industrial system, feels the rein of political control slipping out of its hands." By way of remedies for the situation so described, he proposed the breaking up of big trusts, government ownership of many public utilities, progressive taxes on incomes and inheritances, and other measures included in the program of social meliorism.

By the ferment of critical thought respecting the nature of society historians were the least affected. Busy as a rule with writing stories of political and military events narrowly construed, they paid little attention to social and economic events or to the general ideas entertained by the people. John Bach McMaster's *History of the People of the United States,* the first volume of which came out in 1883, was a notable exception, but it was more of a catalogue or chronicle than a social history as its name implied. History, it was often said, provides the lamp of experience for guidance in the present, but the histories written merely as professional exercises or for the edification of the public dealt with only a small part of the human experience and even with that in a very limited fashion. It was even declared that scholarship must narrate events or meticulously analyze documents and avoid interpretation.

Not until 1895, when Brooks Adams' *The Law of Civilization and Decay* appeared, was much recognition given to the fact that written history in every form had a bearing on what was taking place in the United States and on what would probably come to pass in the future of the nation.

Although Brooks Adams' volume dealt with history in Europe, it set forth a theory covering history in general. His theory was that all human societies pass from a stage of wide dispersion on the land to a stage of high concentration; that they fall under the sway of capitalistic usurers; and that they then enter a period of decay and dissolution.

The theory, whether true or false, was applicable to the United States as well as to ancient Rome and modern Europe. While apparently remote from American politics in 1895, it crashed into the free and easy optimism of many editors, including Charles A. Dana of the New York *Sun,* and of many politicians, especially young Theodore Roosevelt, then at the beginning of his public career, who commented on it in a long review.

At any rate Adams' book was an evidence that some Americans of intellectual attainments were not convinced by the rosy exposition of individualism or of social meliorism either. They did not believe that all was well in the United States and were expecting serious troubles in the years ahead. Indeed, Henry Adams, a brother of Brooks, who had read the manuscript of *The Law of Civilization and Decay* two years before it was published, said in an open letter to the American Historical Association that the big social explosion would come in about fifty years—that is, about 1944.

☆

The changing conditions of American life and the new knowledge and thought were also mirrored in imaginative letters. Authors of novels dealing with the eternal triangle—one man and two women or one woman and two men—even when "historical" in pretensions, were more or less influenced by their times. Imaginative letters after 1865 carried descriptions and interpretations of the swift changes—continental and regional —which had occurred as the national domain was rounded out, industries were expanded, and concentration set in.

Nearly everything human and material seemed to be noted in the myriad pages of "fiction," turned out from year to year: reconstruction in the South; westward pioneering and settlement; regional customs and practices; conflicts between capital and labor; strikes, riots, and disorders in industry; struggles of immigrants for footholds and social places; the grievances that flared up in populistic and socialistic revolts; every shade of opinion from Puritan distress over the poverty and grime of factory towns to communistic resentments at the whole course of capitalism; variations and clashes of opinion from decade to decade; all phases of the strife for social improvement in every direction; efforts to apply Christian teachings to the perils within the Republic.

Support for the broad statement that imaginative letters were sensitive to all phases of American history is supplied by at least two comprehensive works on American literature: the third volume of Vernon L. Parrington's *Main Currents in American Thought*, published in unfinished form in 1930 shortly after the death of the author, and Alfred Kazin's *On Native Grounds*, published in 1942. Literary critics took account of the fact in current reviews. They generally agreed, of course, that the quality of a novel depended upon the genius, skill, and discipline of the author rather than on the mere quantity or nature of the facts in his pages. But they also held that accuracy of portrayal, whether of regions or characters, and accuracy in representing ideas, whether conservative or radical, were necessary to the creation of "great" literature.

The volume, continuity, and variety of the imaginative literature which depicted the many phases of American life in all parts of the country is illustrated by the following list of twenty-two works selected from two or three hundred novels of recognized quality written between 1870 and 1940:

1871—Elizabeth Stuart Phelps, *The Silent Partner*. A Puritan protest against factory conditions in New England and a plea for better treatment of labor.

1873—Mark Twain and Charles Dudley Warner, *The Gilded Age*. Political corruption and greedy citizens in the age of President Grant.

1880—Henry Adams, *Democracy*. A defense of democracy against the indifference, contempt, and pessimism of the rich.

1881—Helen Hunt Jackson, *A Century of Dishonor*. Cruel treatment of the Indians by the United States Government.

1884—John Hay, *The Bread-Winners*. An attack on labor leaders in the spirit of individualistic capitalism.

1888—Edward Bellamy, *Looking Backward*. Utopian picture of abundance and a good life under a socialistic regime in the year 2000.

1890–98—Hamlin Garland, *Main-Travelled Roads*. Hard-bitten and impoverished farming families of the Middle West struggling for a livelihood.

1894—W. D. Howells, *A Traveler from Altruria*. Conflict between classes and masses in the light of a democratic and socialistic ideal.

1900—Theodore Dreiser, *Sister Carrie*. Cruel fate of the poor and humble in the land of great riches and prosperity.

1901—Frank Norris, *The Octopus*. An epic of great wheat production in California.

1905—David Graham Phillips, *The Deluge*. For democracy against corruption and oppression by the privileged few—financial manipulators.

1905—Edith Wharton, *The House of Mirth*. The new plutocracy against a background of seasoned riches.

1906—Upton Sinclair, *The Jungle*. Poverty, filth, and suffering in a great industrial center.

1910—Jack London, *Revolution*. Industrial strife at a high pitch and in a revolutionary temper.

1911—Edith Wharton, *Ethan Frome*. Cold fate of the poor in a New England farming community.

1920—Sinclair Lewis, *Main Street*. Drab, small-town culture in the West—and almost anywhere else in the United States.

1925—Ellen Glasgow, *Barren Ground*. Struggles against poverty and defeat in a rural community of the South.

1933—Jessie Fauset, *Comedy American Style*. Follies of Negroes and whites.

1934—Stark Young, *So Red the Rose*. The South of romance.

1935—Sinclair Lewis, *It Can't Happen Here*. Fascist tendencies in conflict with American ideals of liberty.

1936—James Farrell, *A World I Never Made*. Irish working-class family in a harsh struggle for existence in the urban world of industry and business.

1938—John Dos Passos, *U.S.A.* Graphic pictures of suffering and struggling among victims of misfortune during the great depression, contrasted with the pomp and pretensions of politicians and the rich.

☆

While knowledge in every field, much of it microscopic in detail, was being accumulated, and thought about American society was finding expression in various media, facilities for distributing facts and ideas among the people were multiplying or enlarging. A major facility was the system of education. The principle of free and compulsory education in primary subjects for all children, widely accepted by 1860, was applied in every part of the country, with variations according to the wealth of states and communities and their social composition. By 1910 it was a poor district indeed which had made no provision whatever for primary education.

As the extension and improvement of primary schools proceeded, the American people were being induced to accept the idea that higher education should be opened more freely to the youth of the land and were voting fabulous sums of money for realizing it. Evidence of the advance in higher education is afforded by the following table showing the growth in the number of high schools between 1880 and 1910:

In 1880 800
1890 2,526
1900 6,005
1910 10,213

After the high school had achieved a secure position came a demand to bring college education nearer to the people. In part this demand was met by university extension work and in part by the creation of "junior colleges" in communities able to pay for them through taxation. In 1917 there were 39 such colleges in the United States; by 1932 the number had risen to 181.

With the growth of educational facilities illiteracy declined, despite the mounting immigration of persons who could not read. In 1880 17% of the people ten years of age or more were reported as illiterate; thirty years later, in 1910, the percentage of such illiterates had fallen to 7.7; and, among the white population, to 4.9. At the same time the proportion of boys and girls pursuing higher learning rose. In 1930 one half of all the children of secondary school age were attending a secondary school of some kind, and one person in every seven of college age was enrolled in a college. Nevertheless in 1940 3,000,000 Americans twenty years of age or more had never completed as much as one year of formal schooling.

Popular interest in education was partly measurable in terms of the money spent for it. In 1925 the total annual outlay for all public and private schools, colleges, and various institutions of higher learning amounted to more than $2,000,000,000.

The distribution of knowledge and ideas was widened and accelerated by the increase in the number and kinds of newspapers, magazines, and books, ranging from the solid volumes of individuals and learned societies to a growing flood of simple comics and "salacious literature" appealing to the widest common denominators of interest: sex and crime. Improvements in the technology of printing made possible the publication of books, even the classics, at figures ranging from five cents to fifty and sixty odd cents a copy and such books at low cost were turned out and sold by the millions. A rapid growth in rural free delivery under the United States Post Office, coupled with highway improvement and the automobile, brought the metropolitan daily to the doors of farmers who had hitherto relied mainly upon rural weeklies for news of the country and the world.

Given such opportunities for public education and self-education, only the most unfortunate or the most indifferent and shiftless in the American population remained outside the circle of widening knowledge and thought. If as an outcome of this development there was to be a degradation of American democracy in the coming years, as Brooks Adams prophesied, a share of responsibility would have to be laid at the door of those who sought financial profits in the literature of degradation as well as those who chose to buy it in the market place.

As progress in facilities for distributing knowledge and ideas gathered momentum, the radio appeared, producing an upheaval in education, the results of which were immeasurable. As early as 1916 the electrical transmission of sounds by wireless methods had reached such a stage that Lee de Forest could begin experiments with the broadcasting of music. A few years later, in 1921, the KDKA broadcasting station was opened in Pittsburgh. By 1925 so many stations were in operation that they interfered with one another and the federal government had to intervene and apportion among them "time and space on the air." In 1941 there were 915 licensed broadcasting stations in the United States and the number of receiving sets was at least 56,000,000.

The country had become a vast radio auditorium. In that auditorium the people, literate and illiterate alike, who had ears could hear, amid the confusion of advertising, music, and other "entertainment," speeches by men and women who thought they had something to say, on subjects ranging from canning fruits and vegetables to ways and means of running the whole world.

As to the effects of all this broadcasting, there were acute discrepancies of opinion. Optimists called it progress. Doubting Thomases suspected that it would lead to a demoralization in both knowledge and thought, with consequences disastrous to the Republic. But at all events, for good or ill, the radio was distributing information and misinformation, ideas useful or pernicious, to millions of people who fell under its sway.

Into this "educational" tumult the motion picture likewise thrust its power with incalculable effects. What has been claimed to be the "first motion-picture feature" was shown publicly at Richmond, Indiana, in 1894, by the inventor of the machine, C. F. Jenkins. His contrivance was built on the basis of experiments by other inventors extending back in time more than fifty years and was soon improved beyond recognition. In 1905 the first motion-picture theater was opened at Pittsburgh. In 1927 sound-reproduction devices made possible the "talking picture."

By 1942 every town of any size from Maine to California had its film theater—and the combined capacity of the "palaces" was 10,000,000 lookers and hearers. In that year the estimated weekly attendance was approximately 85,000,000. Quickly adopted by colleges, universities, and lower schools, the motion and talking picture was used to supplement and enliven by visual means the customary methods of education.

All the forms of uproar that the radio diffused could be utilized by motion pictures, and more too. Now the people, high and low, everywhere, could not only listen to the speeches, lectures, and addresses of talkative men and women on every kind of subject, hear music in all its ranges from symphonies to the syncopations of Tin Pan Alley, and catch the roar and clatter of mass assemblies; they could see animated pictures of persons directing "messages" to them and asking them to support every sort of program, panacea, or scheme of full salvation.

In short, the American people now had at their command agencies almost illimitable in range and speed for the distribution of knowledge and the circulation of ideas true, false, or simply nonsensical. What the consequences of this revolution in communication would be was a theme of emotional debate and sober examination throughout the nation. Would intelligence be stimulated or arrested or destroyed? Certainly mere facilities afforded no guarantee that the information distributed so swiftly and widely was founded on accurate knowledge or that the general ideas put before the people were valid in themselves or good for practical applications. Reports formulated by psychologists who explored the new types of human behavior seemed to indicate that neither mere knowledge nor general ideas nor instruments for their diffusion could add anything to that elusive quality of the human spirit known as intelligence. Opinions respecting the probable outcome, near and distant, of the new agencies and the uses to which they were put varied as widely as the ideas themselves which were shot forth through the air or on paper or on the silver screen to the public at large.

Chapter 23

AN ERA OF POLITICAL REVOLT AGAINST PLUTOCRACY

IF THE glittering prophecy of benefits offered by proponents of imperialism had been fulfilled to the pecuniary advantage of everybody, if capitalists, farmers, and industrial workers had been satisfied with what they received, complaints of populists, trust busters, socialists, muckrakers, and systematic critics of American economy might have fallen on deaf ears. It was not realized. Like all wars, the war with Spain and in the Philippines furnished an immediate boom; but that boom was far from full and permanent prosperity. Dazzling strokes in war and diplomacy gave diversion to many people, especially Republican editors and propagandists. But the public was either fickle or the diversion was incomplete. Protests against the imperialist excursion, during the war with Spain and in the Philippines, grew in volume and intensity as the years passed, especially as the mirage of universal prosperity vanished and public interest converged again on fundamental domestic issues.

In the nature of things there were limits to imperialist ambitions. Territorial expansion could not go on indefinitely without incurring awful war hazards for which the American people were in no mood. By 1900 the world had nearly all been parceled out among the imperialist Powers of Europe and Asia and only petty fragments of territory remained for Americans to acquire if they could. Gone were the huge unexploited spaces around the globe, such as had existed in 1800 and could be easily wrested from defenseless natives. There were no more spoils to be seized by Americans without fights with Great Britain, France, Germany, Japan, or Russia.

In view of the opposition at home to expansion in the Philippines, even the most forthright imperialist scarcely dared to propose more war of that kind, at least candidly, as a policy likely to awaken great popular enthusiasm. John Hay made plans for seizing some territory in China but they were official secrets, and he drew back when Japan suggested that they did not comport with the noble professions of the "Open

Door." Besides, the official thesis of the Republicans held that they had intended no imperialism in 1898 and that the Philippines had come to the United States inadvertently during the discharge of a duty imposed upon the country, by an accident or an act of God. Though the Republicans were successful in the elections of 1900, 1904, and 1908, they encountered a formidable antipathy even to that version of their purposes. A similar animosity was displayed by the Democrats against imperialism in the Caribbean region—until their own leader, President Woodrow Wilson, embarked upon it in Haiti and Santo Domingo.

Moreover, from the "empire" acquired in 1899 no streams of riches flowed into the United States, such as Great Britain had drawn from India. No endlessly expanding markets for the "surpluses" of American factories and farms were found. Instead of garnering wealth from their empire, American taxpayers had to face increasing levies by the government of the United States for military and naval outlays and for subduing the guerrilla warfare in the Philippines.

A cold balance sheet of the imperialist undertaking showed a large net loss to the nation as a whole. Filipinos and Puerto Ricans, most of them in wretched poverty, could not buy American goods in billion-dollar lots. Furthermore the agricultural products imported from the "empire" soon entered into competition with the surpluses of American farms. As for increasing the relative export of American goods, that proved to be another delusion—a political romance confuted by experience. There was no relative increase in fact. The export of goods in 1900 amounted to about 10 % of the exportable goods produced in the United States. In 1914 the percentage was 9.7; in 1929, 9.8.

Soon after the first flush of war excitement passed it was discovered even by philosophers of the Mahan school that the current naval expenditures, though many times larger than ever, would not provide adequate defense for the Philippines if powerful aggressors chose to operate against them from land bases in the neighborhood. Before he died in 1919, Theodore Roosevelt himself realized this and exclaimed that the Philippines were the Achilles' heel of the American Republic. Only swivel-chair strategists in the Navy Department continued to imagine that American dreadnaughts with superior fire power could easily destroy the Japanese navy and effect American supremacy in the Far East. By no form of economic or military calculation could the imperialism of 1898 be called a blessing to the American nation; or, indeed, from any point of view, an unqualified success. Moreover it failed to divert Americans from their primary interests at home or to quell completely the political uprising against centralized capitalism that had grown to ominous proportions in 1896.

Starting in 1898, it is true, the newspaper headlines daily shrieked sensational news of the war with Spain and then sensational news of the war for suppression of the native revolt in the Philippines. Magazines carried solemn articles on "our new obligations" in the dependencies and descriptions of the lands occupied by "our" new subjects. Professors wrote bragging books on America as a "world Power," on colonial administration, and on foreign affairs. Protestant ministers preached sermons on "our new opportunities to save souls." The same newspapers, magazines, professors, and preachers, as a rule, paid slight regard to populist complaints at home about either domestic or foreign affairs, except to curse them as the fruits of evil minds. Judging by such literary appearances, the American people were absorbed in "great" world politics and blind and deaf to the agitations of men and women, now called "mollycoddles," "calamity howlers," and "ignoramuses," who insisted on going forward with Bryan's "battle," or with other kinds of reforms on the home front.

Yet in time the throbs of the war drums were silenced, veterans of the Cuban and the Philippine wars were granted pensions, and the furor over "our new wards" faded out. After all the American people could not live on newspaper headlines, books, magazine articles, or sermons about Christianizing people in remote places. Nor, as events indicated, did many Americans take more than a transient interest in the emotional diversions created by and in the name of imperialism. If millions seemed to approve it in the elections of 1900, 1904, and 1908, with varying intensity of conviction, other millions voted with the Democrats, who denounced every feature of it.

As a matter of fact, in June 1898, while the war with Spain was at its height, Congress, though dominated by Republicans, created an Industrial Commission, composed of senators, representatives, and eminent private citizens, and charged it with studying the disturbing problems of capital and labor. In 1900, while the Philippine war was still in progress, the commission made a report that filled many large volumes and carried recommendations for reforms in capitalist methods.

Indeed, at no stage in the development of political insurgency against centralized capitalism had Republicans been wholly untouched by it. In its origin the very Republican party was itself an expression of insurgency against the supremacy of what it called the "slave power" in the government and politics of the United States. Its hero, Abraham Lincoln, had confessed that he owed the first principles of his policy to Thomas Jefferson, who in 1776 had announced the philosophy of revolutionary equalitarianism, and by destroying slavery Lincoln had dared to commit a revolutionary act himself. Not without justification could Theodore

Roosevelt, in an hour of concern with domestic politics, claim that the Republican party "in the days of Abraham Lincoln was founded as the radical progressive party of the Nation."

During the agitations of the subsequent years, that party was harassed by a left wing and supplied recruits to the Greenbackers and Populists. It was a former Republican, Senator Teller, who had tried to strike a blow at incipient imperialism by imposing a self-denying ordinance on the resolution that led to war against Spain. It was a Republican, Senator Hoar, who believed that, had it not been for the intervention of Bryan on McKinley's side, he could have stopped the imperialist adventure in 1900. It was in Republican states and under Republican auspices that the most enlightened labor and social legislation had been inaugurated as the great industrial expansion proceeded.

Insurgency in Republican ranks was accelerated soon after Theodore Roosevelt had settled down in the White House as the successor of McKinley. The high Republican manager, Marcus A. Hanna, sensitive to trends of popular opinion, had agreed to the nomination of Roosevelt as Vice-President in 1900 partly with a view to capturing votes in the West, so deeply infected by agrarianism, and at a time when Republican bosses in New York wanted to get him out of the state on the ground that he was a political "troublemaker." Now this young man of impulses deemed "radical" by his party colleagues had possession of the greatest citadel of political power in the country.

By training, experience, and private reading Theodore Roosevelt was a variant from his predecessors who had come up to power through the pull and haul of politics and had given little thought to the great historical process in which they pulled and hauled. Although, as he said, he learned nothing but orthodox laissez-faire economics at Harvard College, young Roosevelt had studied some history and had early formed some decided views on social conflicts in history and the ways of plutocracy.

In 1897 Roosevelt had published, in the *Forum* magazine, a long review of Brooks Adams' *The Law of Civilization and Decay*—a prophecy of the death of civilization under the heel of capitalistic usury. While he distinctly repudiated Adams' gloomy verdict, Roosevelt confessed that "there is in it a very ugly element of truth. . . . That there is grave reason for some of Mr. Adams' melancholy forebodings, no serious student of the times, no sociologist or reformer, and no practical politician who is interested in more than momentary success, will deny. . . . The rich have undoubtedly grown richer; . . . there has been a large absolute, though not relative, increase in poverty and . . . the very poor tend to huddle in immense masses in the cities. Even though these masses are, relatively to the rest of the population, smaller than they formerly were, they constitute a standing menace, not merely to our prosperity

SLAVERY BECOMES A MAJOR ISSUE

As the 1850s progressed, the dispute over the extension of slavery to the territories in the West brought the North and South to the brink of war.

(ABOVE) In the South—Runaway slaves risked death rather than remain slaves. *The Gulf Stream,* a painting by Winslow Homer.

(BELOW) In the North—one of the important debates between Lincoln and Douglas, dealing with the slavery issue.

THE NORTH AND SOUTH AT WAR

Shortly after Lincoln's inauguration, a Southern attack on Fort Sumter launched a long and bitter war.

(ABOVE) Bloody battles brought forth desperate and valiant acts of courage on both sides. Here we see the Battle of the Crater.

(BELOW) Lincoln delivering his famous address at Gettysburg in 1863—in the midst of the war he called upon the nation to resolve that the dead shall not have died in vain.

The Library of Congress

POSTWAR RECONSTRUCTION IN THE SOUTH

With many of its buildings destroyed, railroad lines wrecked, Confederate money worthless and the labor system disintegrated, the South faced many serious problems as it emerged from the war.

(ABOVE) Devastation in Richmond, Virginia—as photographed by Brady in 1865.

(BELOW) Freed Negroes voting in tne South—a postwar election scene in New Orleans.

Frank Leslie's Illustrated Newspaper, Nov. 30, 1867.
Courtesy The New York Public Library

THE SETTLEMENT OF THE FAR WEST

Settlers moving West sent many tales of adventure back East.

(ABOVE) An impromptu hunt—passengers and crew of a Western train, halted by buffalo, make the most of the delay.

(BELOW) Life in a wagon train could be dull, but you could not count on it—artists' impressions of the monotonous haul across the wastelands and of an Indian attack.

Con Edison of New York

Courtesy General Electric Company

INVENTIONS LEAVE THEIR MARK ON THE AMERICAN SCENE

Between the close of the Civil War and the early twentieth century, numerous outstanding inventions which changed America came into general use.

(ABOVE) *Left:* Electricity is put to work—Edison's first commercial electric generating station in New York City. *Right:* The Edison Company's Schenectady Works, 1891, supplying a growing market for electrical devices.

(BELOW) C. H. Mailes and Mack Sennett in a scene from D. W. Griffith's "The Lonely Villa" produced by Biograph in 1909, an early film with Mary Pickford.

Museum of Modern Art Film Stills Archive

LABOR HAS ITS PROBLEMS

Between the Civil War and the close of the nineteenth century, large numbers of Europeans poured into America, adding to the discontent of many American workingmen and women, who thus faced greater competition for jobs.

(ABOVE) Immigrants arrive—a scene in the Castle Garden immigration depot, 1884.
(BELOW) A contemporary sketch of workmen striking for an eight-hour day.

New York Daily Graphic, Jan. 16, 1878.
Courtesy The New York Public Library

THE REFORM MOVEMENT ENTERS THE POLITICAL ARENA

Between 1850 and 1890 reformers kept politics astir with such projects as the granting of suffrage to women and the ousting of grafters from places of power.

(ABOVE) Elizabeth Cady Stanton addressing a committee of the United States Senate in 1878 on the subject of votes for women.

(BELOW) Two of Nast's cartoons attacking New York's Boss Tweed, taken from a powerful series that played an important part in breaking Tweed's grip on the City.

Harper's Weekly, Oct. 7, 1871.
Courtesy The New York Public Library

Harper's Weekly, Aug. 19, 1871.
Courtesy The New York Public Library

THE BALLOT

IN COUNTING THERE IS STRENGTH

"THAT'S WHAT'S THE MATTER."
"As long as I count the Votes, what are you going to do about it? say?"

WHO STOLE THE PEOPLE'S MONEY? — DO TELL .N.Y.TIMES.

'TWAS H

AMERICA ACQUIRES DISTANT COLONIES

Although the United States plunged into the Spanish-American War to liberate the Cubans, by the treaty of peace that brought the conflict to a close it assumed the burden of governing distant peoples.

(ABOVE) An early scene in the Spanish-American War — United States troops led by Theodore Roosevelt storming a Spanish stronghold in Cuba.

(BELOW) Types of natives in the Philippines — brought under the American flag by the treaty of peace with Spain.

but to our existence." Cautious and qualified as this statement was, it referred to matters which Republican party managers had not noticed, officially at least. They were the matters over which farmer and labor insurgency was highly articulate.

As President, Theodore Roosevelt abated none of his zest for his "big stick" policy in "extraterritorial," that is, extracontinental, affairs. He indulged in feverish exchanges with European diplomats, supported the Open Door in China, and almost daily provided "hot news" for the press by "strokes of state" in foreign policy. In this sphere his constant activities fretted many old Republicans of the Hanna school as well as social actionists who wanted to concentrate on political and economic reforms at home. Those old Republicans felt that they had been hustled into the imperialist adventure by the young "war hawks" of the twentieth century and they were deeply troubled over the possibility that Theodore Roosevelt might involve the nation in a foreign war really perilous to taxpayers, domestic finances and economy, and the management of business in the customary manner.

While Theodore Roosevelt worried conservative Republicans by his lunges into foreign affairs, he won enthusiastic support among liberals and radicals by his domestic policies. When business as usual was threatened by a big coal strike in 1902, President Roosevelt manifested sympathies with the miners. Instead of sending Federal troops to suppress strikers, as the Republican President Hayes had done in the railway strike of 1877, and the Democratic President Cleveland had done in the Pullman strike of 1894, he prepared to use the troops to keep the mines open and productive. He forced the mine owners to accept the arbitration which they had rejected; and he was instrumental in bringing about a settlement advantageous to labor. He also sought to stop the spoliation of natural resources by adopting a policy of conservation—withholding timber and other lands from the grasp of private interests and speculators. Moreover he introduced "righteousness" into politics. While praising "good trusts" and "sound labor leaders," he denounced the "bad" trusts, "malefactors of great wealth," and "anarchistic labor leaders." He also publicly censured many a conservative representative and senator in Congress, while he was careful not to alienate the most powerful men of his party in that body.

Meanwhile reinforcements for progressive insurgency, political and economic, came from many directions in articles, books, and magazines. For example:

Henry George's *Progress and Poverty*, issued first in 1879, grew in influence, spreading the doctrine that many millionaires owed their wealth to the "unearned increment" arising merely from increases in land values. In 1889, Andrew Carnegie began to publish articles on wealth and labor in which he demonstrated that, while in part great fortunes had grown out of inventions and management, also in large part they had sprung from mere land ownership and speculation, from the markets developed by the social growth of the country, and from easy opportunities afforded manufacturers to acquire immense natural resources at nominal prices, or for nothing.

In 1894, H. D. Lloyd issued his *Wealth against Commonwealth*, assailing the Standard Oil Company, challenging the whole system of individualistic acquisition, and calling for a new order of co-operation.

In 1902, Ida Tarbell began the serialization of her critical articles in *McClure's* magazine, "The History of the Standard Oil Company."

In 1902, W. J. Ghent's *Our Benevolent Feudalism* portrayed American society as a hierarchy of classes dominated by men of wealth at the top.

In 1901, W. J. Bryan started publishing the *Commoner*, a weekly journal, which soon attained a large national circulation.

In 1906, David Graham Phillips commenced a series, entitled "The Treason of the Senate," in the *Cosmopolitan* magazine, attacking it as a body of rich men who legislated for the rich and defeated the aspirations of the people.

☆

A large school of reformers from right to left attributed most if not all the evils of the Republic to the control of party machinery and all branches of government by Theodore Roosevelt's "malefactors of great wealth," operating through political bosses, local and national. Their proposal for breaking this control was to "restore the government to the people"; and one of the first points of their attack was the Senate of the United States elected not by the people but by the state legislatures—in fact by party caucuses and bosses behind the scenes.

Back in the age of Andrew Jackson, when the Senate of the United States was under fire from popular strongholds, it had been proposed that senators should thereafter be elected directly by the voters of the states—no longer indirectly. In 1893 the House of Representatives mustered a two-thirds majority for a resolution authorizing this change by an amendment to the Constitution. Satisfied with things as they were, the Senate, however, refused to concur and so repelled this attack on its position. Beaten in Washington, advocates of direct election turned to the states and sought to circumvent the Constitution by ingenious devices for having candidates for the Senate nominated at popular primaries.

To make the popular choice at the polls binding on the state legislature, Oregon in 1901 established a system by which the voters could name the United States senator at a regular election and the candidates for the state legislature could pledge themselves to vote for the "people's choice," no matter to what party he belonged. Soon Oregon witnessed the extraordinary spectacle of a Republican legislature electing a Democrat to represent the state in the national Senate.

By 1910 at least twenty-eight states, mainly in the West and South, had in force one scheme or another compelling state legislatures to elect senators actually chosen, previously, at a primary or popular election. Thus the personnel of the national Senate and its temper were gradually altered between 1893 and 1910. In this period also the legislatures of two thirds of the states passed resolutions calling upon Congress to submit to the people an amendment providing for popular election of senators in a regular and constitutional manner.

At length, "softened up" by the arrival of new senators "fresh from the people," the Senate yielded to the House in 1912 and approved a resolution of amendment. It was sent to the states for action. With alacrity the states replied by ratifying the Seventeenth Amendment and the very next year it went into effect. As if derisively timed, the amendment was proclaimed in force by William Jennings Bryan, then Secretary of State. Only sixteen years previously he had been cursed as an anarchist for proposing to lay his rude hands on this bulwark of conservatism, placed in the Constitution by the fathers of the Republic. So swiftly had insurgency advanced in the intervening years that Bryan himself, archcritic of the plutocracy, had become the chief cabinet officer in the Democratic administration of Woodrow Wilson.

Running along with the movement to expel "plutocrats" from the Senate was an agitation for taking the nomination of all major candidates —local, state, and federal—out of the hands of conventions ruled by professional politicians and entrusting it to the people at the polls. This action was also undertaken by states, one after another.

The instrument chosen for it was known as the direct primary. Laws applying it varied in form from state to state, but their purpose was to force all seekers after nomination for important places in government—local, state, and federal—to offer themselves to the voters of their respective parties in a party election called the primary. By 1910 at least twenty-one states, chiefly in the West and South, had direct primary laws stringent in nature.

These laws by no means eliminated the power of professional politicians over the nomination of candidates, but they disconcerted the "old-line bosses" for a time; they made it possible for many energetic young leaders to appeal immediately to the voters and ride to high places of power in government, in spite of the bosses. For years insurgents had inveighed against the "corrupt machines" of both major parties. Now they had a strong weapon in their hands if they could use it.

Another protest against the machines operated by professional politicians had represented the ballot system in vogue as permitting them to buy votes and watch the voters deliver the "stolen goods" at the polls. This system had been created by politicians themselves. Under it each party printed its own ticket or list of candidates for each election and on paper of a distinctive color. At the polls on election day the agents of each party handed out its ballots—red, white or blue, as the case might be—and kept their eyes on each voter until he dropped his colored ticket into the ballot box.

In many places a practice of "straight-arm voting" had been adopted; that is, party voters were lined up, a party ticket was put into the hand of each, and they were then marched to the polls in formation, keeping ranks until their ballots were deposited. Not only was it easy for party managers thus to lead their henchmen to the polls: they could see who was voting the opposite ticket and, if strong enough, could intimidate men who refused to vote "right." It was an almost perfect system for exposing workingmen and insurgents to surveillance, oppression, and even violence if they refused to follow the party line.

The device adopted for breaking this tyranny over voters was the Australian ballot, containing the names of all the candidates of all the parties, printed at public expense, and distributed only at the polls by public officers. Where it was used the voter indicated his own choice by marking the column of his party himself or the names of persons for whom he wished to cast his ballot. A closed booth was provided so that ballots could be marked secretly and ballots were folded so that no one could discover for whom citizens voted.

This reform was introduced first in Massachusetts, and in Kentucky in a limited fashion, in the year 1888. Within eight years thirty-six other states had adopted it. Additional legislation improved the system, and by the opening of the century such secret balloting had become a general rule in the United States. Thus intimidation at the polls was reduced and the political independence of voters increased. Money provided by the campaign funds of the parties and threats of retaliation, or even physical injury, could no longer be as effective as in the "good old days of open voting."

While the revolt against established political methods was drawing the governing power closer to voting men, the demand of women for the right to vote was renewed and gained strength. A national suffrage organization was formed. A proposed amendment enfranchising women throughout the nation was introduced in Congress in 1869. Three years later women pressed their claims on the Republicans and in doing so reminded them of the services rendered by women in the recent war for the preservation of the Union. Republican leaders still wanted the aid of women, especially help from the magnetic orator, Anna Dickinson —the "American Joan of Arc"—in the campaign of 1872, and the Republican party declared that it welcomed women to spheres of wider usefulness; that their demand for additional rights deserved "respectful consideration."

But women soon learned that they were to have no automatic victory in the national capital and they took the hard road to their goal by winning the suffrage, step by step, in the states, under the nationwide leadership of such indomitable citizens as Elizabeth Cady Stanton, Lillie Devereux Blake, Mathilda Joslyn Gage, and Susan B. Anthony. These women and others traveled up and down the land and appealed for the enfranchisement of women to voting men in the cities, villages, distant rural districts, and on outlying farms. They argued their case before members of state legislatures and constitutional conventions, published journals of agitation, wrote articles and letters to the newspapers, issued books on the subject, and spared no labor in their efforts to persuade the hostile or indifferent that their cause was just and vital to the advancement of democracy.

For some years their gains in the states were discouragingly small. Wyoming, which had established equal suffrage while still a territory, continued the practice after admission to the Union in 1890, despite strenuous objections in Congress. Three years later women won the ballot in Colorado. In 1896 they were victorious in Utah and Idaho. During the furor over imperialism and conferring the blessings of liberty on "our brown brothers" in distant dependencies, no advances were made, though women carried on their agitation with unremitting tenacity. After that militant outburst had lost its glamor women began to win victories rapidly: in Washington, 1910; California, 1911; Oregon, Kansas, and Arizona, 1912; Nevada and Montana, 1914. At length the ice was broken on the middle border: Illinois in 1913 conferred on women the right to vote for presidential electors and so gave them a greater leverage in national elections.

After older leaders had procured the ballot in several states, younger women, mostly college graduates, turned to the weapon of political power to shorten the struggle for full national enfranchisement. They built a backfire against obstinate members of Congress and Eastern politicians who aspired to the presidency. Led by Alice Paul and Lucy Burns, women organized, in the states having equal suffrage, thousands of enfranchised women who pledged themselves to cast their ballots only for candidates openly favorable to the adoption of equal suffrage on a national scale— by an amendment to the federal Constitution.

Although these new tacticians were unable to move Woodrow Wilson from his rigid opposition to such an amendment during the campaign

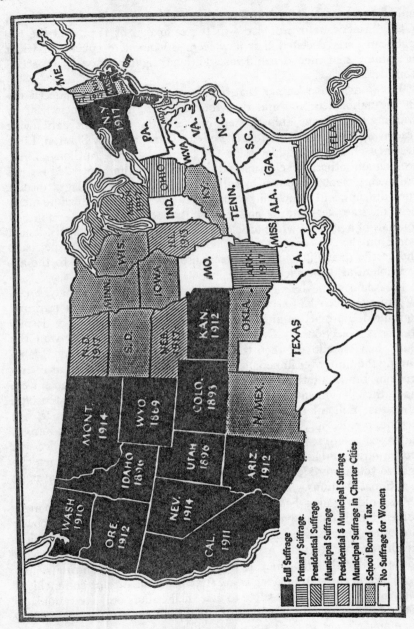

STATUS OF WOMAN SUFFRAGE IN 1918

of 1916, they secured the endorsement of the Republican candidate, Charles E. Hughes, and a helpful support from Theodore Roosevelt. On a referendum the next year, 1917, women won the vote in the great state of New York, and in 1918 they were successful in Oklahoma, South Dakota, and Michigan.

With so much power already in the hands of women voters it was difficult for any politician in Washington to treat their demands with historic ridicule or indifference. Indeed President Wilson was finally moved to call upon Congress in September 1918 to pass the suffrage amendment to the Constitution. With the aid of Republicans, who secured possession of both houses in the elections of the following November, the requisite two-thirds majority was won for the Nineteenth Amendment—in the following June. Quickly ratified by three fourths of the state legislatures, it went into effect in time for the presidential election of 1920. Equal suffrage had been made the law of the land.

As insurgency flourished in the form of verbal criticism and new methods for making it effective by direct elections were brought into use, conservative managers in both the major parties were finding it harder to keep a tight rein on candidates, legislatures, executives, and courts in the former style. In seeking to escape the perils of defeat they had to make concessions to this growing independence. King Canute had to move his throne.

Aware in 1908 that the Republicans would have to meet again the resolute Bryan running on a platform of revolt in the spirit of 1896, President Theodore Roosevelt planned to take at least some of the wind out of the "Great Commoner's" sails. Having decided not to run for a "second election," he fixed upon his Secretary of War, William Howard Taft, as his successor and presented him to the country as a progressive, as a man who would follow "my policies." Roosevelt then threw the weight of executive influence and patronage on the side of Taft and had the pleasure of seeing the Republican convention bow to his will. Conservatives in the convention did it with a wry face, but they yielded as gracefully as they could.

Yet the Republican platform of 1908 gave little recognition to the unrest abroad in the land. The platform was "safe" enough to please even the followers of the late Marcus A. Hanna. After consultations with President Roosevelt, however, the candidate, Taft, made several gestures to the left in his campaign speeches. He declared himself in favor of the popular election of United States senators, which stalwarts in his party had long opposed as an assault upon the Constitution. The taxation of incomes, execrated in 1895 by Joseph Choate as communistic and populistic, Taft endorsed in 1912 mildly, not enthusiastically. Labor, he said, had a legal right to organize, strike, and bargain collectively; and in some cases, he admitted, the courts had oppressed labor by the use of injunctions.

The methods of modern business, Taft thought, were generally sound, but since there had been too much speculation, stock watering, and fraud, reforms were needed in this relation also. The currency system, assailed by Bryan, was, in Taft's opinion, defective in various respects and should be made more flexible. As for socialism, he spoke gently of its "very humane and kindly theories," while dismissing it as wholly impracticable. In other words, from the Republican view of 1896, Taft was tainted with insurgency, but with the aid of the doughty Roosevelt and his followers he defeated Bryan, who stood fast on his populistic principles and made another vehement campaign that terrified conservatives.

Reflecting changes of the intervening years, President Taft translated some progressive policies into action. He supported the adoption of the resolution by Congress which provided for the income-tax amendment to the Constitution. He pressed for a revision of the tariff, a thorny question carefully avoided by Roosevelt. He urged upon Congress, in defiance of express companies, a bill for the establishment of a parcels post and Congress complied with his recommendation.

Many bankers had long opposed a plan for creating a postal savings system in the Post Office Department. Under Taft's leadership the plan was enacted into law by Congress. Since the passage of the Sherman Antitrust Act in 1890 the prosecution of trusts and combinations in restraint of trade had been neglected. President Taft launched an active campaign against them and the Supreme Court responded by ordering the Standard Oil Company and the American Tobacco Company to dissolve. Compared measure by measure with Theodore Roosevelt's regime, President Taft's administration, though less spectacular, could be correctly characterized as on the whole more "progressive."

Nevertheless soon after Taft's term opened a rebellion broke out against him within his own party. Several Republican senators and representatives, including Senator Robert M. La Follette, of Wisconsin, and Senator Albert J. Beveridge, of Indiana, were enraged by the high rates in the tariff bill of 1909, voted against it, and took the stump against it. On his return home from a hunting trip to Africa and a visit to Europe, Theodore Roosevelt expressed irritation over Taft's policies and measures, accused him of taking a reactionary tack on the tariff, conservation, and other issues, and launched an opposition in the Republican camp in 1910.

Hints of a general insurrection were received when the voters in the congressional election of that autumn sent a Democratic majority to the

House of Representatives. In 1910, also, insurgent Republicans and Democrats in the House overthrew the system by which the Speaker, Joseph Cannon, and a few chairmen of committees were permitted to determine whether any bill was to be debated or passed. Populists had condemned this system, in season and out, and now a Republican House had annihilated it. The next year a group of Republicans, up in arms against Taft's policies, met at the home of Senator La Follette in Washington and formed a Progressive Republican League to unite all the forces of insurgency within the party.

As the campaign of 1912 drew near, Democratic managers were all agog with excitement. In Republican dissensions they saw at last a chance to carry the election—the first since 1892 when Cleveland had won his second term and then, by his conservative policies, had split his own party asunder. The only question among the Democrats was whether they were to turn right or left in this golden opportunity. Three times they had failed with Bryan as their leader and radicalism as their inspiration. But they had failed far more miserably in 1904 when they veered over to the gold standard and conservatism.

Even with the Republicans divided, the prospects were clouded. Would Bryan run again—for the fourth time? If so, could he be elected? If he withdrew or could be pushed aside, what man and what policies were most likely to bring the triumph at the polls for which Democratic hearts panted? It took a shrewd calculation to discover the person and the appeal that would carry the Democratic banner to victory in a time when the historic patterns of both parties were being badly shaken along a broad front.

For years an influential journalist in the East, George Harvey, long closely associated with powerful men in the "plutocratic" wing of the Democratic party, had been thinking that Woodrow Wilson, president of Princeton University, had the right character and the right ideas for a successful career as a Democratic politician. As a professor Wilson had taught politics and government, and from his youth he had nursed political ambitions. While professor and president at Princeton he had always taken a conservative position on public questions. He had despised Bryan and everything connected with Bryanism. He had angrily opposed Bryan in 1896, had even refused to sit on a platform with him, had attacked his theories as "foolish and dangerous," and in a private letter had expressed the hope that Bryan might be "knocked into a cocked hat."

For the policies of Theodore Roosevelt, Wilson had a dislike almost as intense. He had denounced government regulation of railways and assailed federal regulation of corporations. As late as 1909 he had upbraided trade unions for interfering with individual liberty. In fact there was scarcely an item in the populist or progressive program which Wilson had not frowned upon in public addresses and in private letters. From the standpoint of Harvey and his Wall Street friends, therefore, Woodrow Wilson seemed to be the ideal candidate to swing the Democratic party back to the conservatism of Grover Cleveland, and capture control over the government of the United States.

After some astute negotiations Harvey induced the Democratic boss of New Jersey, James Smith, to nominate Wilson as the party candidate for governor of the state in 1910. Weakened by the factional fights in their ranks, the New Jersey Republicans were ill prepared for the fray; and Wilson, without going beyond generalities in his campaign speeches, won the election with little difficulty. The first step in Harvey's plan to make Woodrow Wilson President of the United States had been achieved, and now the President-maker turned to the final act of his play. At the masthead of *Harper's Weekly*, which he edited, he flung out a sign reading: "For President, Woodrow Wilson."

But it was known that J. P. Morgan and Company had once come to the financial aid of the Harper publishing firm and, besides, Woodrow Wilson had plans of his own. With keen discernment he decided that Harvey's conservative designs did not comport with the progressive temper of the country and would bring disaster in the election. So he brusquely told Harvey that his open support was no longer desired. Wilson's name was taken from the masthead of *Harper's Weekly* and he assumed direction of his own campaign for nomination and election.

Having severed ties with "reactionaries" in his party, Wilson set about securing the Democratic prize. He toured the country, even to the Far West, and made numerous speeches in the progressive vein. He repudiated conservative doctrines he once had espoused; he approved nearly all the items that had long been listed in the populist program. He sought the friendship of Bryan whom, a few years before, he had wanted to see knocked into a cocked hat, and declared in his presence at a great public dinner: "There has been an interesting fixed point in the history of the Democratic party, and the fixed point has been the character, and the devotion, and the preachings of William Jennings Bryan." To the horror of incredulous Democrats he endorsed direct democracy—the initiative and referendum—although he did not press that issue. With the support of Bryan at last secured, Wilson won the nomination for President at the Democratic convention in Baltimore after a hard tug of war among the politicians.

Aware that progressive interests were laying hold of the country, Theodore Roosevelt threw his hat into the ring for the Republican nomination. But he was rejected in favor of President Taft at the party convention in Chicago. Declaring that the nomination had been "stolen" from him, Roosevelt and his followers then formed an independent party and adopted for it the name "Progressive." At a separate convention he was nominated as the Progressive party candidate for President.

As if in recognition of a national uprising against imperialism and all its works, Theodore Roosevelt veered back to domestic issues. Not long before, he had declared that the country needed a war and that everybody who opposed it was a "mollycoddle"; but he was compelled at the Progressive convention in Chicago to come to terms with Jane Addams, an invincible pacifist and anti-imperialist. There he joined in castigating the "barbaric system of warfare among nations, with its enormous waste of resources even in time of peace and the consequent impoverishment of the life of the toiling masses"; and in advocating an international agreement to limit naval forces, with the proviso that two battleships should be built a year until such agreement was reached. There at Chicago he gave up the gospel of imperialism and united with the Progressives in a declaration proclaiming the responsibilities of the Americans at home: "Unhampered by tradition, uncorrupted by power, undismayed by the magnitude of the task, the new party offers itself as the instrument of the people to sweep away old abuses, to build a new and nobler commonwealth."

The platform of the new party endorsed practically all the insurgent political reforms, such as direct primaries, popular election of senators, the initiative, referendum, and recall, woman suffrage, and recall of judicial decisions annulling social legislation. It approved the regulation of corporations, conservation of natural resources, income and inheritance taxes, and limitations on the use of injunctions in labor disputes. In fact William Jennings Bryan was delighted with the doctrines enunciated by Roosevelt and the Progressives. He declared, ironically, if wistfully, that they were a long time coming around to the propositions for which he had battled for the last twenty years.

In his campaign Wilson expounded many views of economic and political affairs that squared with the assertions made by laborites, populists, and socialists during the previous thirty or forty years. While rejecting their remedies he agreed with their contention that the Industrial Revolution had fundamentally altered the economic scene, that old political theories did not fit the new order, and that the government of the United States had long been run by concentrated business interests in their own behalf.

"Our life has broken away from the past," Wilson exclaimed. "We have changed our economic conditions, absolutely, from top to bottom; and, with our economic society, the organization of our life. The old political formulas do not fit present problems; they read now like documents taken out of a forgotten age. . . . The government of the United States at present is a foster child of the special interests. It is not allowed to have a will of its own. . . . The government of the United States in recent years has not been administered by the common people." Continuing in the spirit of the revolt against the plutocracy, Wilson maintained that "the masters of the government of the United States are the combined capitalists and manufacturers of the United States"—the big bankers, the big manufacturers, the big masters of commerce, the heads of railroad and steamship corporations.

Theodore Roosevelt's speeches vibrated with similar denunciations of the "big interests" and similar promises to restore the government to the people. Caught between the fire of Roosevelt and the fire of Wilson, President Taft, in a sober and dignified manner, defended his administration against their charges and sought to show that in fact it was both progressive and enlightened. Having again nominated Eugene V. Debs as their candidate, the Socialists contended that if big capitalists did rule the country, as the politicians were now agreeing, it was time to break their dominion by nationalizing the means of production from which they derived their money and their power.

The votes in the election of 1912 revealed unmistakably the growing revolt within the two major parties and outside. They also disclosed sharp differences of opinion as to what must be done about the problems brought to the front by American thought respecting the Industrial Revolution, especially the accusation that the country was dominated by plutocratic interests. Wilson was elected but his popular vote was smaller than that given to Bryan in either 1896 or 1908. Indeed it fell short by nearly 2,500,000 of the total vote cast against him. Roosevelt polled about 700,000 more votes than Taft but the combined Progressive and Republican vote was below that polled by Roosevelt in 1904 and even below that received by Taft in 1908.

There was no better evidence of the strength of the political revolt than the number of ballots cast for the Socialist candidate, Eugene V. Debs. Notwithstanding the radical talk of Wilson and Roosevelt against "big business," the vote for Debs was more than double the Socialist vote of 1908. It approached the million mark—that point which hitherto in American history had indicated an impending explosion.

Despite the clashes of opinion over what was to be done about the problems of domestic economy, one thing seemed verified: the glittering promises of prosperity to be won by imperialism and the expansion of foreign trade made little appeal to the voters. Indeed Republicans did not make much of their "dollar diplomacy" in the campaign; and Democrats spurned imperialism as they had in previous years. The glories of empire and aggressive foreign policies had not extinguished progressive insurgency nor eased the clashes of interests on the home front.

Confident that he had a popular mandate to act forcefully, Wilson as

President assumed the leadership of his party; and during his first term in office, with the aid of progressives and dissidents from both parties in Congress, the following program of legislation was enacted:

The tariff was reduced, not to free trade or a revenue basis, but to a lower level than the country had seen for years.

A new banking law set up the Federal Reserve System, in which old Federalist ideas of centralized banking were combined with more flexibility for the currency and more government control over banking administration.

Laws against trusts and combinations were strengthened and efforts were made by administrative action to tear apart interlocking relations of banks, corporations, and business concerns in the interest of free enterprise—if with little effect.

To organized labor three offerings were made: provisions presumed to liberate trade unions from prosecution as combinations in restraint of trade and to limit the use of injunctions in labor disputes; a law fixing eight hours as the standard day for trainmen employed on interstate railways; and the La Follette Seamen's Act assuring better treatment to sailors on board American merchant ships.

Farmers, who had complained about the extortions of Eastern bankers, were conciliated by the establishment of federal land banks empowered to lend them money at a lower rate of interest.

With a view to formulating and enforcing "fair" trade practices for commerce and industry, the Federal Trade Commission was created and endowed with powers to inquire into "unfair" actions in business and make recommendations for legislation to stop them. Though vague in its phrasing, the Federal Trade Commission Act of 1914 departed from the old faith that sharp competition would of itself bring prosperity, and indicated a trend toward a new faith—in government regulation of business enterprises for the public interest.

Chapter 24

SOCIAL REFORMERS MAKE HEADWAY

OLDER than the political insurgency that went by the name of Progressive, related to it, and yet in many respects fundamentally independent of political partisanship, were efforts of humanitarians to realize ideals social in nature that transcended personal desires for self-perfection, wealth, prestige, and power. The humanitarians worked in the spirit of civilization which had found expression in colonial times, the Revolution, the early Republic, the democratic awakening, the Civil War, and the ensuing age of the rising plutocracy. Now they took advantage of the new knowledge and thought evolved at the turn of the nineteenth century. They sought to apply the theories of social meliorism developed by the economists, sociologists, and political scientists who analyzed and pointed out inadequacies in the doctrines of individualism. The humanitarians were more than students, theorists, and writers, though some of them were all those persons; they were primarily activists anxious to get reforms established. They made minute surveys of blighted areas in national life and searched for ways and means of integrating social theory and social practice.

Literally millions of men and women participated in this wider movement of thought, program making, and implementation. It was composed of a large variety of groups, such as the Association for Labor Legislation, the National Consumers' League, the National Housing Association, and the Association for the Improvement of the Condition of the Colored People, which worked for the realization of special programs. But the movement as a whole was inspired by the common purpose of raising the standards of living, promoting physical and mental health, enlarging the concept of social justice and its applications—in short, advancing civilization in the United States. In social origins and continuous support this movement was mainly, though by no means entirely, instigated by the middle class. It gave effect to aesthetic, ethical, and humane impulses in the democratic way—by proposal, discussion, adoption—within the limits of a reforming, socializing capitalism.

Few of the men and women who carried this movement forward received during their lives the newspaper publicity accorded to warriors, politicians, plutocrats, and criminals. Nor in their death were many of them given revealing obituaries or places in the twenty volumes entitled Dictionary of American Biography. Nevertheless their force of character, intellectual powers, steadfastness in research, in educating the public, in drafting legislation and advocating it before committees of government, municipal, state, and federal, so influenced the thought of the nation that ideas once "dangerous" became commonplaces, accepted by persons who had formerly fought to the last ditch the new proposals put up to the country. The humanitarians not only broke down the resistance of private interests and legislatures. They also compelled a reconstruction or re-education of the United States Supreme Court which for more than forty years had been reading into the federal Constitution, as Justice Oliver Wendell Holmes remarked, the laissez-faire doctrines of Mr. Herbert Spencer, English individualist.

Chief among the labors of the humanitarians were attempts, through public and private collective action, to reduce the impacts of poverty, industrial accidents, disease, and other handicaps on the lives of millions of Americans. In this fashion, they hoped to realize in greater measure the American ideals of liberty, equality, the pursuit of happiness, and the promotion of the general welfare which had been professed at the time national independence was achieved.

In the struggle over social improvement advocates and opponents were aligned as groups and organizations. The alignment was not as wholesale or always as sharp as in the strife of political parties, but conservatism and insurgency appeared within it as in political struggles for power.

In the run-of-the-mill opinion social conservatism signified the support of measures and practices which protected concentrated wealth, and the methods of acquiring wealth, against interference on the part of government. "We have among us," wrote the economist, Richard T. Ely, in 1894, "a class of mammon worshippers, whose one test of conservatism, or radicalism, is the attitude one takes with respect to accumulated wealth. Whatever tends to preserve the wealth of the wealthy is called conservatism, and whatever favors anything else, no matter what, they call socialism." A person may love old ways and draw his ideals from a past which he deems saner in its views of wealth, Ely went on; yet if he would, "by social action," endeavor to change certain tendencies and conserve the treasures of the past, "he is still a radical in the eyes of those men whose one and sole test is money."

This was not, however, the whole creed of social conservatism. Many elements entered into it—some of them inherited from the days when America was a country of free land and immense natural resources open to energetic individuals capable of improving their condition by initiative and persistent labor. Other features were newly formulated under the head of individualism—a theory which, as we have said but repeat for emphasis, encompassed four main propositions as follows. It is individuals struggling to make a living and acquire property who set productive activities in motion and create the wealth which makes the country great and prosperous. In this struggle each individual is rewarded according to his personal contribution to the stock of wealth; his wages or profits are the measure of his contribution. Poverty is the "natural" outcome of individual idleness, lack of enterprise, imprudence, improvidence, and in many cases drunkenness. Although Christian charity may relieve poverty here and there, nothing vital can be done to prevent or remove its mass. Efforts to overcome it by government action—that is, by collective action—will merely hurt the capable portion of the population and pauperize the poor.

The theories advanced by the activist humanitarians against the thesis of conservatism were not closely knit into a single argument or philosophy, as a rule. Yet, however formulated, the theories of the activist humanitarians denied the truth of the conservative assertion that gross inequalities of wealth, signifying poverty, are decreed by any iron law of nature; that the riches of the rich are merely the rewards of their thrift and enterprise; that the poverty of the poor is solely due to indolence and improvidence. They accepted the contention of the sociologists such as Lester Ward and Anna Garlin Spencer to the effect that the individual, no matter how enterprising, derives the knowledge, the inventions he makes and uses, and the security he enjoys, from the common life of society and the government that holds it together. The active meliorists insisted that ills in society have various origins—such as accidents in industry, insanitary and congested conditions of labor and living, contagious diseases, and other adverse factors which can be removed or prevented or diminished by special measures. These changes, they argued, can be brought about peacefully, by group and public action, and thus dire poverty can be abolished, misfortunes mitigated, special privileges inimical to the interests of society destroyed, and the quality of the common life improved.

☆

A summary of the concrete proposals for social improvement conceived in the meliorist spirit was presented to the country in two works issued near the turn of the nineteenth century. The first was *Socialism, Its Nature, Strength and Weakness*, published in 1894 by Richard T. Ely, a teacher of economics who combined studying, observation, and theorizing with the formulation of programs for social action. The second was *Poverty,* published in 1904 by Robert Hunter, a student of economics who turned to social work in the slums of New York City and witnessed the making of poverty at first hand. Taken collectively, the proposals for action offered by Ely and Hunter included these:

Taxation of incomes and inheritances, and application of the revenues to social purposes.

Making all factories and tenements sanitary and safe.

Stamping out contagious diseases by public-health measures.

Shortening hours of work, especially in dangerous and laborious industries and for women and young people.

Public care of defectives and dependents, separating them from the body of employable and industrious workers.

Insurance against sickness, unemployment, and accidents in industry.

Compensation to workers injured in industries through no fault of their own—a great source of poverty and family distress.

Old-age pensions.

Establishment of minimum hours and wages in "sweated" industries and enforcement of sanitary standards by public authority.

Regulation of tenements, planning and improvement of cities with provision for parks, playgrounds, and other recreational facilities.

Conservation and wise use of natural resources.

Raising standards of physical well-being by compulsory public-health measures.

Extension and improvement of public education for all the children of all the people.

Long before the nineteenth century came to a close practically all the ideas of social improvement which Americans of later generations were to debate, modify, amplify, and apply had been formulated and thoroughly discussed by reflective persons from one end of the country to the other. Moreover for the first time serious studies had been made of the actual distribution of wealth in the United States. For a hundred years or more that subject had been talked about but few facts had been available as a basis for informed talk. Social reformers made guesses respecting the amount of wealth and poverty that existed. Conservatives admitted that there was some poverty in the United States but they declared that it did not amount to much or was deserved; that in any case America was the most prosperous nation in the world and good enough for anybody. At length statisticians tried to reduce the loose talk about concentrated wealth and poverty to something like a statement of facts.

In 1893 George K. Holmes, of the United States Census Office, formulated the following estimate: "Twenty per cent of the wealth of the

United States is owned by three-one-hundredths of one per cent of the population; seventy-one per cent is owned by nine per cent of the families, and twenty-nine per cent of the wealth is all that falls to ninety-one per cent of the population." Holmes' generalization was immediately attacked as inaccurate. Richard T. Ely, in using it, admitted that, owing to the backward state of the American census, calculations respecting the distribution of wealth in the United States were "extremely uncertain." But he added: "All estimates agree in one respect, and that is in attributing a greater concentration of wealth to the United States than to any other modern country." This did not mean that a larger proportion of the people in the United States than in European countries were in poverty. Such was not a fact, Ely conceded. Yet there was no doubt in his mind that America was cursed by widespread poverty in spite of all that could be truly said about prosperity.

Determined to find out with as high a degree of exactness as possible just how much poverty there was in the United States, Robert Hunter made an extensive study of the subject, using the various kinds of available figures. In 1904 he reported the results of his work in his book bearing the plain title, *Poverty*. This was his summary: "There are probably in fairly prosperous years no less than 10,000,000 persons in poverty; that is to say, underfed, underclothed, and poorly housed. Of these about 4,000,000 persons are public paupers. Over 2,000,000 working men are

PERCENTAGE OF ORGANIZED WORKERS IN MASSACHUSETTS
UNEMPLOYED, 1908–21

unemployed from four to six months in the year. . . . Probably no less than 1,000,000 workers are injured or killed each year while doing their work . . . We know that many workmen are overworked and underpaid. We know in a general way that unnecessary disease is far too prevalent. We know some of the insanitary evils of tenements and factories."

If Hunter had examined conditions in rural regions as carefully as in the cities, he could have noted that a special census of 1900 reported more than thirty-five per cent of American farmers as tenants—an increase over 1880 and 1890. He did state, however, that over fifty per cent of the farmers were either tenants or held their land under mortgages —propertyless, or only partial owners of their homes.

Hunter's estimates were in turn attacked and shown to be in some respects lacking in accuracy if not exaggerated. Owing to the indifference or hostility of certain officials nothing approaching precise and comprehensive figures on poverty was accessible to the people of the "greatest nation on earth." Though precision as to the total picture was impossible in these circumstances, it was certain that there were millions of persons on some form of relief and that millions of self-respecting workers were from time to time unemployed or received wages which were too small or too irregular to keep them from the uncertainty of livelihood and the pinching want known as poverty. At all events, while statisticians disputed, Americans who observed poverty at first hand or suffered from it personally protested against it and demanded amelioration by concerted efforts, private and public; and leaders in the labor movement, who had direct contact with social conditions in industrial cities, promoted what was frequently called the "war on poverty."

Since one of the first needs in the quest for social improvement was to get basic facts as to wages, hours, employment, unemployment, industrial accidents, and similar matters, a demand arose for two types of actions: the creation of labor bureaus to collect such figures; and the addition of questions to those already used in the decennial census taken by the government of the United States. Massachusetts replied to the first demand in 1869 by establishing the first bureau of labor statistics in America. Between 1869 and 1885 similar bureaus were set up in several other states. In the latter year provision was made for a federal Bureau of Labor in the Department of the Interior. Subsequently the bureau was transferred to the Department of Commerce and Labor and in 1913 it became a separate Department of Labor in the federal administration. Among its duties the Department of Labor was to "foster, promote, and develop the welfare of wage earners, to improve their working conditions, and to advance their opportunities for profitable employment."

The year before the separate department was established, Congress created the Children's Bureau "to investigate and report upon all matters pertaining to the welfare of children and child life." In 1920 the Women's Bureau was set up in the Department and charged with "formulating standards and policies for promoting the welfare of wage-earning women, improving their working conditions, increasing their efficiency, and advancing their opportunities for profitable employment."

Meanwhile official government census takers were instructed to ask an increasing number of questions of the people; federal bureaus undertook to collect a wider range of figures relative to all the major branches of the American economy; and state governments likewise increased their annual output of material covering the health, employment, income, home-ownership status, and welfare of the people under their respective jurisdictions. These reports were supplemented by special studies of all the major phases of American life, from overcrowding in city tenements to tenancy and poverty in the most backward country districts. Eventually, Americans who genuinely wanted to know the condition of their country could obtain a surprisingly wide variety of information on the status of people belonging to many different age, racial, and economic groups in all parts of the United States.

In practice, improvements in the lot of the American people were made in many different directions as men and women, individually and in organizations, struggled to overcome the evils that seemed to them most glaring. Naturally, progress toward their objectives was uneven and what they were able to achieve inevitably varied widely from place to place, depending on local circumstances.

Massachusetts, for example, was an outstandingly successful pioneer in the drive to overcome factory conditions that had been harmful to industrial workers. Building upon a law adopted in 1842 which had established a ten-hour day in industry for children under twelve years of age —in itself certainly an eloquent reminder of what the so-called "good old days" had been like—Massachusetts provided for a regular system of factory inspection in 1867. Two years later a state department of labor was established. This was followed in 1874 by a law that limited women to a maximum of ten hours a day at work in industry, and in 1877 by a general law setting up standards for industrial safety.

In time, statutes of a similar type began to flow in large volume from the legislatures of other highly industrialized states. In addition, the maximum working hours for men were limited in many states in certain special occupations and industries. By 1910, for instance, nearly a third of the states had set a maximum limit of eight hours a day on public works projects. In 1907, twenty-three states enacted laws reducing the hours of toil for men in mines, smelters, and under-

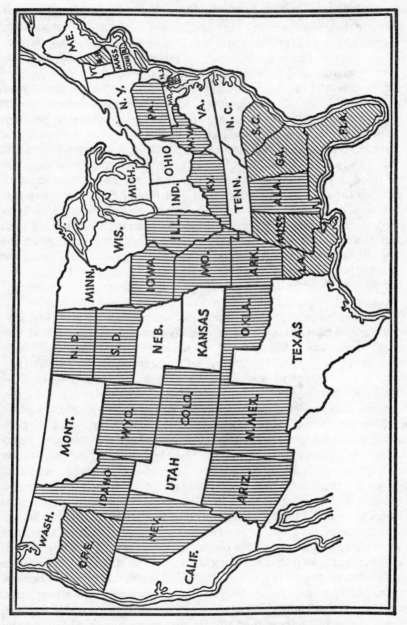

STATE INSPECTION OF MINES AND QUARRIES FOR SAFETY
IN 1936 (White, by labor depts.; Vertically shaded,
by mines depts.; Diagonally shaded, no inspection)

ground work generally, on trains and in other occupations where the strains and dangers of industry were peculiarly severe. Although the courts were early inclined to hold that men would have to look after themselves, the principle was finally established that the hours of labor for men, as well as women, could be regulated by law; the old idea that endless drudgery was the unavoidable lot of all workers had been widely abandoned and the doctrine of shorter hours both to relieve fatigue and enable workers to have the benefits of some leisure, in which to develop their other powers, was fairly well established.

A second type of labor legislation pertained to sanitation and safety in factories and mines. The Massachusetts general law on this subject, enacted in 1877, was followed by amendments in that state which steadily elaborated the details of public control over the building and operating of factories once regarded as a purely private matter for owners and managers. Other states soon framed laws based on the Massachusetts model and within twenty-five years such regulations were in force in nearly all great industrial regions.

Henceforward in progressive communities it was necessary for factories to be built with more regard to safety and ventilation; for dangerous machinery to be guarded by protective devices; for heat to be supplied in cold weather; for boilers to be maintained in good order and regularly inspected; for certain standards of cleanliness to be observed; and for sanitary appliances to be installed. Henceforward it was necessary for mine owners to provide their mines with arrangements for ventilation, safety, and the escape of workers in cases of explosions and other accidents if such escape was at all possible. Henceforward manufacturing in tenements was restricted and in the case of many commodities wholly forbidden for reasons of sanitation and general welfare. From year to year the early laws were supplemented by amendments and new statutes which made tighter and tighter the public control over the material surroundings in which industrial workers labored—a control of vital importance for the safety, health, comfort, and well-being of millions engaged in industry and mining.

Lagging far behind legislation respecting sanitation, safety, and hours was the extension of aid to working people injured in the course of duty. Here the traditions of the common law were used by lawyers and employers to throw the burden of accidents mainly on the workers. Under those traditions the employer was not liable for damages unless he was personally responsible for an accident; he was not liable at all for accidents due to "unpreventable causes" or to the negligence of the injured employee or a fellow employee. And any person injured in an industry could secure damages only by a lawsuit which might be long, expensive, and futile. Thus employers were under no economic compulsion to take every possible care against accidents by providing safety appliances; and the poverty of the poor was increased by the necessity of meeting the costs of most injuries incurred in mills, factories, mines, and transportation industries.

Proposals to shift the burden of accidents to industry itself were made early in the rise of the factory system but they were fiercely and effectively combatted by employers. This reform, it was said, would take money unjustly from employers and give it to workmen guilty of carelessness or malicious negligence. Judges and lawyers usually adopted this view respecting life, liberty, and property.

As machine industries multiplied, accidents increased. "Fourth of July orators," declared H. R. Seager, the social economist, in 1910, "delight to point out the various fields in which we excel, but there is one field of which they say very little, and that is that we kill and injure more working-men in proportion to the number employed on our railroads, in our mines, and factories than any other country in the world." Statistics of accidents, like those of poverty, were far from complete, but there were enough to show that in the number of accidents America certainly led the whole world.

To extirpate this source of pain and poverty men and women from coast to coast held meetings of protest, drafted remedial laws, and besieged the halls of Congress and the state legislatures. Two schemes were proposed, one mild, the other thoroughgoing. The first modified the old common-law rule and compelled the employer to pay compensation for injuries whenever accidents were due to his negligence, that of his employees, or to the necessary risks of the industry. The second was a system of accident insurance. It required employers to insure their employees against accidents just as they insured their buildings against fires, cyclones, and explosions; it provided for easy and inexpensive methods of compensating injured persons, or their families in case of death, without requiring them to engage in tedious and costly lawsuits.

In 1913 the state of New York, by constitutional amendment, authorized legislation of both types and the backbone of the resistance to industrial insurance was broken. Some men and women who had begun the struggle for this social improvement, amid the din of "great party battles" in the eighties and nineties, lived to see the principle of accident insurance well established in every enlightened state in the Union.

Even more devastating than dangerous machinery as a source of poverty and misery was chronic disease or intermittent sickness. Through the long centuries bad health had been looked upon as a necessary evil or an act of God or as a private matter between the individual and his doctor, if he could afford a doctor. But with the advance of medical knowledge mankind discovered that, while many diseases seemed to be hereditary or due to personal faults, others were social in origin—sprang from contagion and from methods of working and living in society. Indeed a large number of them were new "occupational diseases," arising from the use of chemicals and materials in certain processes, such as the making of matches and pottery, or from sheer fatigue.

Slowly it also dawned in the public mind that even those diseases due to heredity or personal faults constituted a costly burden for industry and society. They reduced the efficiency of workers and the number of working days in industry. They increased the heavy public expenditures to maintain hospitals and institutions for the sick, injured, and defective. In short, besides direct costs for care running into millions of dollars each year, diseases reduced the productive power of the people to a degree calculated in terms of money at billions of dollars annually.

Here then was another recognized problem, partly individual and yet involved in factory management beyond the control of individual workers. Operating as single investigators and in groups, men and women concerned with raising the standards and values of life in the United States studied this problem. They made careful surveys and devised remedial plans to be enacted into law and enforced by public agents.

Near the middle of the nineteenth century their activities were accelerated as epidemics of smallpox and cholera aroused national interest in a new subject, "public health," or social health. Amid the terror over epidemics Massachusetts created in 1849 a commission to investigate the sanitary conditions in the state and the report of that body served as the basis for extensive legislation directed against the social sources of disease. In 1853, shortly after cholera had spread death and fright in the city of New Orleans, the State of Louisiana, at the insistence of public-spirited men and women, organized a department of public health and began a public attack on the roots of disease with a view to prevention. As research enlarged medical knowledge during the closing years of the nineteenth century, a public-health movement, led by enlightened citizens and many special societies, slowly forced city councils and state legislatures to act in the interest of public health and gained victory after victory over indifference, ignorance, and often virulent opposition.

Before the twentieth century had advanced far the death rate in the country, for infants, children, and adults had been materially cut; great codes of law incorporating the latest discoveries of preventive medicine had been enacted; and every state and city had a department or office of public health charged with carrying the laws into effect. The war on disease, and on the poverty and misery accompanying disease, had won impressive victories. Not only this. The strategy of new public-health campaigns had been laid out and ideas for achievements hitherto beyond the sweep of imagination had been formulated. Moreover a young generation of doctors and health workers was being trained to carry on through the years of the twentieth century. In summarizing her years' labors in the movement for public health, Dr. S. Josephine Baker, head of the Bureau of Child Hygiene in New York City, symbolized those labors in the title of her autobiography, *Fighting for Life.*

Related to the attacks on conditions partly responsible for disease, but also connected with concern for comfort, beauty, mental hygiene, and social stability, was a collateral drive on the evils of ill-housing, the congestion of people in tenements, the spreading slums, hideous and crime-breeding. As the right of the individual to look after his own diseases had once been deemed sacred, so the right of property owners to herd tenants like cattle into buildings, and yet wrench exorbitant rents from them as human beings, had been regarded as a vested privilege, not to be invaded by government.

Out of the exercise of this privilege came housing conditions "indescribable in print," as a New York tenement-house report of 1903 put the case: "vile privies and vile sinks; foul cellars full of rubbish; . . . dilapidated and dangerous stairs; plumbing pipes containing large holes emitting sewer gas throughout the houses; rooms so dark that one cannot see the people in them; cellars occupied as sleeping places; . . . pigs, goats, horses, and other animals kept in cellars; dangerous old fire traps without fire escapes; . . . buildings without adequate water supply—the list might be added to almost indefinitely."

In such places lived thousands of industrial workers in the United States; into them crowded new immigrants from Europe. What was to be done about them? They furnished millions of dollars annually to owners in rents and increased land values. One of the most opulent and fashionable religious bodies in New York City had large investments in such property. Thus powerful private interests were arrayed against change and denounced change as subversive and revolutionary.

But men and women of the age lightly called "gilded" declared war on American "rack-renting" and slums, and advanced inch by inch against the vested "rights" of landlords. Campaigns were made and laws drafted to cut away first this evil and then that evil. Windowless rooms were forbidden here; the installation of toilets instead of block privies was ordered there; dangerous firetraps were condemned to repair or destruction. While McKinley and Bryan were arguing about the currency and imperialism, the complaint that reformers would be next demanding bathtubs for the people rose in the land. In 1902 the state of New York enacted a comprehensive and detailed housing law applicable to the tenements of its great cities. Resistance, though by no means broken, was wavering, and the idea of decent housing for the people was competing in the market place of opinion for recognition as a necessity of civilization in America.

From exercising public control over houses and buildings in the interest of public safety, health, and welfare, it was a logical step to the concept of planning whole cities in the general interest. American cities, with a few exceptions, had grown up rapidly and in a haphazard fashion. Landowners and real estate speculators had encouraged urban anarchy, with the barest reference if any to the convenience of industry and commerce, to comfort for the residents, to recreation, beauty, and wholesome living. Only here and there, and largely by accident, parks and breathing spaces had been reserved among the square miles of brick and mortar and wooden buildings.

But many men and women were thinking about this outcome of greed and carelessness and ignorance. They realized that every social improvement—in factory legislation, health protection, and tenement-house control—was in some way connected with city life as a whole. In response to a growing interest in municipal affairs, a city planning movement came into being. All reflective persons admitted that some city planning seemed necessary. The question was: how much? Engineers and economists studied the subject and wrote on it. In 1907 the city of Hartford, Connecticut, created a city planning commission empowered to make, though not enforce, general plans for the control of building in the community. The example was soon followed in other municipalities. In 1909 the National City Planning Association was founded and began to hold annual conferences. Another field of social improvement was to be occupied.

In the general uprising against poverty, misery, and the inequality of wealth and opportunity, another proposal for curtailing exploitation and effecting a more equitable distribution of wealth gained headway. Corporations holding franchises for operating public utilities in cities had long insisted that they were entitled to earn "all the traffic will bear," and to determine the kind of services they were to render within the usually loose terms of their charters. Next to the large landholders in cities they had profited most from urban development. They had garnered for their stockholders and managers millions of dollars more than a "reasonable return" on prudent investment would have yielded. But efforts were made in cities and states, as well as at the national capital, to reduce and hold within reasonable limits the rates charged by public utilities for supplying water, transportation, electricity, and other services to the public.

By hundreds of state statutes and municipal ordinances enacted during the early years of the twentieth century, the granting of loose and perpetual franchises to utility corporations was definitely ended in American practice; the rates and services of such corporations were subjected to minute regulations in the public interest; and exploitation by corruption and manipulation was curtailed. Even the directors of utilities themselves were so affected by the movement of thought and action that they began to style their companies "public-service corporations." By that time the principle was being firmly established that such corporations were entitled to charge rates no higher than those yielding a fair return on prudent investment.

A primary foundation of the enormous wealth accumulated in the hands of a few thousand families in the United States had been the natural resources of the states and the national domain, bought at low prices and in many cases acquired by fraud and manipulation. As natural resources were diminished through almost unrestrained exploitation, and the glaring waste committed by the exploiters was exposed by investigations, a movement was launched for the conservation of the national heritage in forests, lands, minerals, water power, and other natural riches. Here too a contest was waged against resolute vested interests determined to get possession of the remaining resources still in public ownership, while handling as they pleased the property they already had. In this crusade progress was slow and halting. Yet progress was made.

While General Grant was still occupying the White House a committee of the Association for the Advancement of Science recommended, in cautious language, a change of national policy in disposing of the national forests. Scientists, engineers, economists, and other citizens concerned with the conservation of resources gave thought to the problem, wrote about it, and delivered speeches on it. Gradually they built up a body of exact knowledge and a strong public opinion in favor of protecting and making a wise use of the nation's physical heritage.

Governments in states, such as New York, that still held public lands, began to safeguard them and even to legislate respecting the use of resources in private hands. In 1891 the Congress of the United States, at last affected by the growing demand from conservationists, empowered the President to withdraw forest lands on the national domain from sale. President Harrison and President Cleveland took action under the law, though in no spectacular spirit, and established enormous forest reserves. In 1882, under the inspiration of Bernhard Fernow, the American Forestry Congress was organized to promote the study of forestry and the conservation of forests.

Four years later Fernow was appointed head of the forestry division in the federal Department of Agriculture and inaugurated a systematic study and administration of the national forests. Gifford Pinchot, an associate of Fernow in the movement, became head of the division. From him Theodore Roosevelt caught an enthusiasm for conservation and, as President, by innumerable addresses, conferences, and actions, he dramatized it as a great national obligation.

Hard-driven by the pressure of public opinion, Congress grudgingly enacted new laws for withdrawing resources from sale and making better use of the lands in public ownership. In 1910 it provided for the separation of the subsurface from the surface of coal-bearing lands and for the retention of coal deposits in public hands, while disposing of the surface for agricultural uses. The same year it authorized the President to reserve lands "for water-power sites, irrigation . . . or other public purposes." In 1911, Congress made a radical departure by beginning the policy of buying great areas of forest land in Eastern states where there was no national domain and placing them under federal authorities. Meanwhile other acts made provision for the more efficient control and administration of forests, minerals, grazing lands, and other resources under the jurisdiction of the federal government. Before President Taft retired in 1913 the foundations for the development of national conservation had been securely laid.

All these measures of social improvement merely affected the distribution of wealth more or less indirectly, despite the fact that they were continuously assailed as undermining the vested rights of property owners. But at length they were supplemented by a direct attack on concentrated wealth through the use of income and inheritance taxes. Neither tax was exactly new to American fiscal policy. The income tax and inheritance tax had been employed by Congress in its desperate search for additional revenues during the Civil War. A light inheritance tax, also for revenue purposes, had been adopted by the Republicans in connection with financing the war on Spain. When, however, the Democrats in 1894 attempted to set up an income tax, for the avowed object of making the rich bear their share of national burdens, the Supreme Court declared nearly every feature of the tax unconstitutional.

Defeat only spurred its advocates to more determined efforts; and so impressive was the agitation that a Republican Congress in 1909 submitted to the states an income-tax amendment to the Constitution. Duly ratified in 1913, the Sixteenth Amendment allowed the Democrats, under the presidency of Woodrow Wilson, to make the taxing of incomes a regular part of federal financing. By this time a large number of states had also begun to lay progressive taxes on incomes and inheritances.

Against protests of conservatives that it was communistic, populistic, or socialistic, the principle of apportioning taxes according to riches— ability to pay—was now generally accepted as just. What was more, the use of other forms of taxation for social as well as revenue purposes was securely established in the law of the land.

To utopians—those eternal dreamers and prodders of mankind, always testing practice by purely ideal concepts of life, labor, and government— the achievements of the humanitarians seemed excessively prolonged; meager in proportion to the magnitude of the problems thrown up by the Industrial Revolution; painfully limited in view of the potentials for the production of all the goods deemed necessary to an ideal standard of living; and complacent respecting a possible abundance for the people in the forms of leisure and meditation and work in the creative arts. Notwithstanding such strictures, however, the achievements of the humanitarians, by contrast with the state of things in 1865, certainly represented substantial progress—*Ethical Gains through Legislation,* as Florence Kelley conceived their movement, in which she was herself a national leader. Moreover these accomplishments, in the face of the venomous opposition from individualists, kept alive the spirit of civilization, augmented its force, and prepared the way for grappling with still greater social problems.

Chapter 25

GATES OF OLD OPPORTUNITIES CLOSING

IN THEIR EFFORTS to improve American standards of living, reformers now had to reckon with an indubitable fact: an epoch in the history of the American people had come to an end. For four hundred years adventurers, conquerors, capitalists, and settlers had been operating within the present continental limits of the United States, always with open spaces before them. There they had enjoyed elbow room and chances to win a living, even riches, by acquiring and exploiting valuable natural resources. As the nineteenth century came to an end, however, most of the attractive areas had already been taken, closing the gates to this great avenue of opportunity. Meanwhile, the growth of manufacturing in the United States was closing the gates of the American market to some of the Old World's industries. Leading Americans were conscious of these major developments, and of their implications.

"A few generations ago," wrote Theodore Roosevelt with reference to the great coal strike of 1902, "an American workman could have saved money, gone West, and taken up a homestead. Now the free lands were gone. In earlier days a man who began with pick and shovel might have come to own a mine. That outlet too was now closed, as regards the immense majority. . . . The majority of the men who earned wages in the coal industry, if they wished to progress at all, were compelled to progress not by ceasing to be wage earners, but by improving the conditions under which all the wage earners in all the industries of the country lived and worked, as well, of course, as improving their own individual efficiency."

In an autobiography, the story of his long struggle as a labor leader to uphold and improve American standards of life and work, Samuel Gompers dealt with changed conditions of national economy near the end of the nineteenth century and gave his reasons for believing that the unlimited flood of immigrants was threatening to "submerge standards of life and work that we had established." "The majority of immigrants," he explained, "no longer came from western Europe where language, customs, and industrial organization were similar to those of the United States but from the countries of eastern Europe where lower standards of life and work prevailed. As these immigrants flooded basic industries, they threatened to destroy our standards. . . . In the early days, boundless and undeveloped resources made possible and expedient a policy of stimulating immigration. It was not until industrialism developed and there were evidences that the newer immigration was not being assimilated that as a nation we began to consider policies of regulation. The labor movement was among the first organizations to urge such policies. . . . Although I realized that the American people in their generosity wished to maintain the United States as an open, free asylum to the oppressed of the whole world, yet we realized also that the United States could not solve all the problems of the world and that the struggle for human freedom and advancement would largely have to be worked out by each country for itself." Gompers was close to his subject. He had come to the United States from England at the age of thirteen.

After the founding of the English colonies in America, especially after the launching of the American Republic and the opening of the West, venturesome men and women by the millions had crowded into the United States in search of more liberty and wider opportunities for earning a livelihood, for trade, for acquiring land, and for working natural resources. For a full century this immigration had been practically unimpeded by legal restrictions. On the contrary, it had been actively encouraged, by federal laws, state laws, shipping concerns, land speculators, industries in search of abundant, cheap, and docile labor, and by sympathizers with refugees from European tyranny. Abroad, it had been stimulated by such major developments as the great famine of 1846 in Ireland, the collapse of revolutionary outbreaks in Europe in 1848, and the persecution of Jews in Russia.

With sturdy, able-bodied, industrious, skilled, intelligent, and talented men and women had come criminals, paupers, paralytics, prostitutes, persons suffering from loathsome and contagious diseases, imbeciles utterly unable to take care of themselves, and cripples—all without let or hindrance. European governments had swept up paupers from their poorhouses and paid their way to America so that their taxpayers could escape the burden of supporting the unfortunates of their own lower orders. Furthermore they had expelled from the countries under their control—often to America—liberals, democrats, labor leaders, reformers, and socialists in efforts to evade social problems and agitations in their own societies.

PERCENTAGE OF FOREIGN-BORN WHITE PEOPLE IN THE TOTAL
POPULATION IN EACH STATE IN 1920

The magnitude of the migration to the United States from the Old World is indicated by the following tables, giving the number of immigrants in four selected decades:

1821–30	106,508
1851–60	2,452,660
1881–90	4,737,046
1901–10	8,136,016

When the trickle of immigration expanded after the establishment of independence, the United States had at its disposal an immense domain of Western lands and resources. Other territories were added at each stage of the westward movement. In all, between 1781 and 1853, the year of the last continental extension, made by the Gadsden Purchase, the public domain of the United States had amounted to approximately 1,400,000,000 acres—an area about five times as large as the combined areas of Germany, France, and Italy.

Of this vast public domain all except a mere fragment had passed into private hands by 1900. Of the 1,400,000,000 acres only 186,000,000 acres remained in public possession in 1924; and that domain consisted mainly of mountains, deserts, arid regions, and forest lands not suitable for cultivation. The dearth of more land for cultivation and exploitation was now a fact as indisputable as the existence of the Rocky Mountains. The shrinkage of free or cheap land was a stubborn reality.

It was also portentous for the economy of the United States and the rest of the world. Every informed and thoughtful citizen of the Republic became aware of its implication in terms of diminished opportunities for attaining wealth quickly. No longer was it easy for industrious, prudent, and determined persons of any nationality to make a living or a fortune by acquiring free or cheap natural resources in the manner long followed by pioneers in agriculture, cattle raising, mining, and industry. Newcomers would now have to compete for a livelihood with the established industrial, business, and professional classes in America— classes that were becoming "overcrowded." Even Alaska, which had been added in 1867, was nearly all staked out within fifty years and offered little escape from the occupied continental domain.

Furthermore, those who had been fortunate enough to have acquired valuable resources while they were still plentiful were now running into trouble through their misuse. By careless exploitation the land and mineral resources in private hands were being denuded and depleted in the most extraordinary carnival of waste yet recorded in all history. Arable land by the millions of acres was stripped of topsoil and eroded into ruins by greedy and ignorant cultivators. Grasslands were plowed up and turned into dust storms or overgrazed into deserts. Forests were slashed without regard to future growth, and magnificent trees by the millions were lost in forest fires. Oil, iron, and other mineral resources were exploited so recklessly and swiftly that by 1940 experts in this field of "economics" were justified in announcing that the "richest nation on earth" would be deprived within an appreciable time of the prime raw materials essential to its welfare and defense. It was with the support of confirming facts and figures that young Henry Cabot Lodge could declare on the floor of the Senate in 1943 that the United States was now in some essential aspects to be included among the "have not" nations of the earth.

☆

Equally meaningful was the closing of the American gates against manufactures from the Old World. When the overwhelming majority of the people of the United States had been engaged in agriculture, practically all their exports to the Old World consisted of foodstuffs and other raw materials. With the opening of the Far West, the very soil of America was literally "mined" and sent to Europe in the form of wheat, corn, and other products, at prices actually below the cost of production, counting in the cost the value of the wasted soil. American exports supplied food for millions of industrial workers in Great Britain and on the continent of Europe and raw materials for innumerable industries there. In those days Americans took in exchange an immense volume of manufactured products annually, thereby contributing to the unprecedented prosperity of the Old World.

As the final decades of the nineteenth century passed, however, the percentage of raw materials and foodstuffs included in the total export of the United States declined, while the percentage of manufactured goods rose. The United States as a manufacturing nation was becoming a stiffer competitor of Great Britain and Europe in all the world markets. For the years 1926–30 crude materials, crude foodstuffs, and manufactured foodstuffs amounted in dollar values to only 40.5% of the total export of the United States; while semimanufactures and finished manufactures amounted to 59.5% of the total. That too was a stubborn fact: the gates of the United States were closing on the once wide-open American market for Old World manufactures, and the gates for the outflow of American agricultural commodities were drawing closer together.

Nor did even the Democrats at any time venture to destroy the protective tariffs under which the relative export of foodstuffs and raw materials was falling and the relative export of manufactures was rising. In

1856 they had announced in their platform that "the time has come for the people of the United States to declare themselves in favor of free seas, and progressive free trade throughout the world." But never thereafter did they officially repeat that declaration or even attempt to make a slashing reduction of the protective rates to a mere revenue basis.

Their President, Cleveland, in 1887 severely criticized the existing rates of duty and called for modifications. But he was careful to declare: "In a readjustment of our tariff, the interests of American labor engaged in manufacture should be carefully considered, as well as the preservation of our manufactures. . . . The question of free trade is absolutely irrelevant."

From time to time Democratic platforms condemned the tariff as the "mother of the trusts" or as the cause of various economic distresses. Yet they contained no planks demanding free trade. When in 1913 the Democrats, led by President Wilson, got possession of both houses of Congress and had the legal power to cut tariff rates to a low point, they enacted a tariff bill that was strongly protective, despite many substantial reductions in rates.

Though they returned to power again in 1933, with Franklin D. Roosevelt as President and a still larger majority, the Democrats refrained from a frontal attack on the tariff duties raised in the meantime by the Republicans to the highest point in American history. In fact President Roosevelt rather brusquely broke up the London Conference of 1933 at which experts had hoped to reduce tariff barriers and reach an agreement on a monetary standard of international trade. He slammed the door on all such undertakings, cut loose from the countries which still clung to the gold standard, and adopted a managed currency for the United States.

Although the Democrats in Congress later authorized President Roosevelt to make "reciprocal" trade treaties with other nations and modify tariff rates, they set limits to the modifications and to the term of his powers under the Reciprocal Trade Act. The act shifted the making of specific rates from Congress to the State Department, over which presided a free-trader, Cordell Hull. But the treaties made under the law, while favoring certain American productive interests as against others, were by no means free-trade treaties.

With endless reiteration the slogan of "lower trade barriers" was repeated, and professors of economics continued to recite the free-trade formulas of their "science," borrowed largely from Mid-Victorian England. Nevertheless the force of stubborn fact was working against projects for wide-open free trade throughout the world. Indeed all the other great nations went over to some form of managed economy, some in the direction of socialism—managed economy in full form.

While agriculture was rapidly expanding as virgin soil was brought under cultivation, while industries were multiplying as resources were exploited by crude methods, protests against the swelling torrent of immigration were ineffective. George Washington, Thomas Jefferson, and John Adams had warned their countrymen against free migration from countries whose people were wholly inexperienced in self-government; but the second generation of Americans mostly ignored their warnings.

It is true that by 1840 immigration had become so extensive that loud objections were raised against it. Protestants were alarmed by the great influx of Catholics. Old-stock Americans were incensed at seeing recently naturalized foreigners flocking to the polls "under bosses" in the cities, and taking possession of municipal governments. In fact opposition to the foreign vote took an aggressive form in the organization of the Native American party in 1848; and later, of the United American, or Know-Nothing, party.

Such protests were largely confined to the East, however, and leaders of the major political parties were skittish about listening to them. Often a presidential election turned on a few thousand votes and candidates quailed at the thought of offending any minority of voters that might have political influence.

At no time before the end of the nineteenth century did either of the major political parties officially call for closing the gates to any immigrants, except oriental coolies. On the contrary, the Republicans in 1864, for the moment styling themselves the Union party, actually endorsed the encouragement of immigration and enacted a law providing for the importation of immigrants bound to labor by contract in such a way as to ensure the payment of their passage.

Although sporadic criticism of untrammeled immigration continued, it was not until organized labor in the United States began a national struggle to maintain and improve standards of work and wages—standards of living—that effective pressure for restrictions on immigration appeared in Congress. Then candidates for the House and the Senate in many districts or states had to calculate whether they had better chances in appealing to the "labor vote" or to the "foreign vote." Other interests were enlisted on the side of restriction, but the labor interest was the best organized and the most persistent. In time its demands were heeded.

Excepting an act of Congress passed in 1875, forbidding the importation of prostitutes and alien convicts, and an act of 1882 excluding idiots, convicts, and persons obviously unable to take care of themselves, the first material restriction imposed on immigration by federal legislation was the Chinese Exclusion Act of 1882. States, to be sure, had attempted to bar paupers. Massachusetts in 1820, New York in 1824, and Maryland in 1833 had enacted laws directed to this end. But such efforts did not cut down immigration, for shipmasters who brought over human derelicts could land them at ports in other states.

The Chinese Exclusion Act of 1882 was the outcome of a long agitation against cheap Chinese labor, in the East as well as on the Pacific coast. In connection with early efforts of the United States to force open the ports of China to American merchants and adventurers, the ports of the United States had been opened to Chinese immigrants by treaty provisions. Americans apparently could not, with a straight face, declare to the Chinese government that they had full freedom to enter China at their pleasure, without granting the Chinese similar rights in the United States. At all events in the treaty of 1868 between the United States and China, the high contracting parties "cordially" recognized "the mutual advantage of the free migration and emigration of their citizens and subjects . . . for purposes of curiosity, of trade or as permanent residents." Taking the cordiality of the American invitation as genuine, and stimulated by appeals of American employers for cheap labor, especially in railway construction, Chinese immigrants soon began to press into the states of the Pacific coast, and many found their way as far east as the factories of Massachusetts.

Very soon conflicts arose between American workers and their Chinese competitors, on many grounds, and as early as 1879 Congress passed a bill virtually providing for the exclusion of Chinese immigrants, in defiance of the treaty with China. President Hayes vetoed the bill. As an act of courtesy a commission was sent to China for the purpose of revising treaty relations. A new treaty was negotiated in 1880 and finally under its terms Congress in 1882 suspended the admission of Chinese laborers for a term of years—later making exclusion permanent.

The enforcement of this law led to constant friction with the Chinese government but efforts to weaken its categorical terms were in vain. The treaty of 1868 had definitely stated that nothing in its provisions should be held to confer the right of naturalization on the Chinese in the United States or on Americans in China. That provision for "reciprocity" could be kept by both parties; and it came about that there was no large "Chinese vote" to worry American politicians.

Responding also to demands from organized labor, Congress passed in 1885 the Contract Labor law—a blow at the importation of any cheap labor by employers seeking to break strikes or cut wages. The act forbade persons, companies, partnerships, and corporations to prepay the passage of aliens or in any way to encourage their immigration under a contract—written, oral, or implied—to perform services or service of any kind in the United States.

Employers soon found a vulnerable spot in the law. They evaded the act by issuing notices that laborers entering the country could find employment at specific places on their arrival. Steamship companies, nearly all of them owned in foreign countries, aided American employers by distributing such notices in Europe and bringing over shiploads of laborers who had full knowledge that they were to work at certain shops, factories, or mines. On renewed petition from organized labor, Congress made the alien Contract Labor law stricter by amendments passed in 1887 and 1888.

It was in connection with efforts to check the practice of drumming up and importing strike-breaking and wage-cutting laborers that Congress, in the act of 1888, introduced a new principle into immigration legislation. As early as 1850 demands had arisen in Eastern cities for the deportation of alien paupers who, soon after their arrival, had to be put into American poorhouses and supported at public expense. Against such demands the government of Württemberg in Germany had protested. It had been sending paupers to the United States to get rid of them and avoid its own responsibility; and it now objected to the idea that the United States could send them back. But at that time American politicians were so intimidated by the foreign vote that they enacted no laws to prevent even such flagrant abuses by foreign interests.

Not until 1888 did Congress provide for the deportation of aliens who had unlawfully entered the United States. In that year it served notice on employers, steamship companies, and foreign governments that the United States had the right and intended to deport aliens at will; that steamship companies or employers guilty of abetting the unlawful entry of aliens would have to pay the expense of carrying them back to their native countries.

Agitation over the exclusion of the Chinese, who unlike Europeans were few in numbers in the United States and so without political power, was accompanied by growing objections to free immigration from all quarters. By 1888, Chinese laborers, contract laborers, insane persons, idiots, and persons likely to become public charges had been denied entrance to the United States. The laws were loosely enforced, but they were at least written in the books. Then, in 1891, Congress grew sterner.

To the list of classes excluded it now added paupers specifically, polygamists, persons suffering from loathsome or dangerous contagious diseases, and, subject to qualifications, persons whose passage had been paid in whole or in part by others. The law also stiffened the enforcement of restrictions imposed by prior acts, especially the prohibition forbidding employers, steamship companies, and their agents to recruit im-

migrants abroad by advertisements, inducements, and promises of any
kind.

In a careful revision of immigration restrictions, in 1903, after the
assassination of President McKinley by Leon Czolgosz, a German Pole,
Congress increased the list of persons excluded. It proscribed, among
others, anarchists, some of whom believed in and advocated the overthrow of all governments by violence and the assassination of public officials. Again, in 1907, Congress added to the roll of persons excluded. By
this time it was bold enough to shut out consumptives, unmistakable imbeciles, and feeble-minded persons in general.

As the gates against free and easy immigration were pushed together
inch by inch, opposition to additional restrictions and to the full enforcement of existing laws became consolidated; and it was strengthened
by the support of the vested interests. Many American citizens insisted
the old doctrine that the United States was an asylum for the oppressed
of all lands was still valid and should never be infringed. They could
point, in confirmation of their view, to the inscription on the Statue of
Liberty, unveiled in 1886, four years after the passage of the Chinese
Exclusion Act:

> *Give me your tired, your poor,*
> *Your huddled masses yearning to breathe free,*
> *The wretched refuse of your teeming shore.*
> *Send those, the homeless, tempest-tost to me,*
> *I lift my lamp beside the golden door!*

They argued that sturdy sons and daughters of toil from other lands
helped to promote the rapid development of the nation's resources,
added to its wealth, enriched its culture, and fortified the love of liberty.

Other opponents of restriction were neither so tenderhearted nor so
disinterested as the advocates of liberty in the abstract. At the turn of
the century when a new immigration bill was up in Washington, the
general agent of the North German Lloyd Steamship Company, then
engaged in carrying immigrants from various European ports, wrote to
his local agents all over the United States: "Immigration bill comes up
in the House Wednesday. Wire your congressman, our expense, protesting against proposed exclusion and requesting bill be defeated, in-
forming him that vote in favor means defeat in next election." Editors of
newspapers in which the steamship company carried advertising were also
informed by wire that they were expected to oppose the bill.

To such vested interests in the opposition were joined others: American railway interests which transported trainloads of immigrants to the West; employers ever struggling to keep wages low; and a horde of "labor bosses" who profited by supplying laborers of their national origins to big industries, often in the process robbing and cheating their own people in the United States.

The situation was complicated for advocates of additional restrictions and for immigrants themselves, by immigration agents operating alone or in connection with steamship companies and American employers of cheap labor. In Europe these agents gave to prospective emigrants a rosy view of the money they could quickly make in the United States, aided them in evading the immigration laws, and offered them all kinds of inducements for the adventure. In the United States they herded immigrants into blocs according to their national origins, found employment for them, and supplied strikebreakers on occasion.

Deluded by the promises and frequently finding their new conditions harsher than those they had suffered at home, many immigrants turned upon the country of adoption in a natural wrath, aggravating the discontent and radical agitations among Americans themselves and evoking more resentment against the influx of foreigners. Extreme radicals joined the hue and cry against restrictions, on a Marxian theory that the worse the plight of workers became, in the United States as well as everywhere else, the sooner would be the revolutionary spring into their kingdom of heaven. On such grounds they harried the American Federation of Labor in its efforts to maintain and raise the standards of life for industrial workers by limiting immigration. Thus, while seeking to keep the gates open, they played into the hands of the very interests which exploited immigrants.

The United States Immigration Commission, appointed to make extensive inquiries into various aspects of immigration, reported in 1911 that economic interests deliberately organized were mainly responsible for the tremendous inflow of Europeans: "The present emigration from Europe to the United States is in the largest measure due to economic causes." Immigrants already here, it conceded, incited immigration by writing enthusiastic letters home to relatives and friends and by sending money to bring them over; but a considerable portion of it was artificially stimulated by "quasi labor agents" and by the "many thousands of steamship ticket agents and subagents operating in the emigrant-furnishing districts of southern and eastern Europe." In other words, the commission found that, apart from the actions of former immigrants settled in the United States, the promotion of immigration had become a money-making game highly profitable to those engaged in it.

Now an old cry, which had been little heeded in the political din of the Jacksonian era, was revived and reinforced: "Immigration is a peril to the Republic, to the institutions of self-government and liberty." Henry Cabot Lodge the elder, senator from Massachusetts, took it up, despite his affiliation with Republican industrialists in search of workers at low wages. Though opposed by many members of his party, especially by Joseph Cannon, Speaker of the House of Representatives, Senator Lodge organized a new drive against immigration. The only question with him was the formula under which it was to be effected. What new and large class of immigrants was to be excluded?

An answer was provided by a proposed literacy test. So far Congress had excluded the Chinese coolies, contract laborers, paupers, idiots, polygamists, anarchists, and other special classes, but no barrier had been erected against persons totally illiterate, such as were now coming from southern and eastern Europe in enormous numbers. A literacy test would push the gates closer together. And on this proposal both Senator Lodge and Samuel Gompers agreed. "So far as I remember," wrote Gompers, "this is the only issue upon which I have ever found myself in accord with Senator Lodge."

Late in 1912, Congress passed a bill designed to shut the gates on illiterates from Europe. Early the next year President Taft vetoed it, and its supporters in Congress could not muster enough votes to carry it over executive disapproval. The succeeding Congress passed another bill similar in principle. President Wilson vetoed it, regarding it as a serious departure from traditional policies. Again Congress failed to muster the two-thirds majority necessary to make it a law in spite of the presidential opposition.

In the following session Congress renewed the battle by passing another bill embodying the literacy test. When President Wilson also vetoed this one Congress defied him by rolling up a huge majority and making it a law without his signature, on February 5, 1917. At this time a great war was raging in Europe, immigration was curtailed anyhow, and there was no opportunity to measure its results in "normal" conditions; but the intentions of the act were clearly and firmly expressed in its provisions.

With certain exceptions, especially affecting persons fleeing from religious persecution, the law of 1917 excluded "all [European] aliens over sixteen years of age, physically capable of reading, who cannot read the English language, or some other language or dialect, including Hebrew and Yiddish." Besides this barrier raised particularly against immigration from southern and eastern Europe, the law of 1917 added to the number of classes of persons already excluded under previous legislation and plugged up many crannies through which evasions had been effected. Moreover, it supplemented the Chinese Exclusion Act by placing an absolute bar against practically all immigration from Asia, except from Japan. Immigration from that country, however, had been cut down since 1907 under the Gentlemen's Agreement between President Theodore Roosevelt and the Japanese government.

Designed to curtail immigration from southern and eastern Europe, two great areas of illiteracy, the law of 1917 by no means guaranteed a reduction in the total number of immigrants admitted annually to the United States. Like other "qualitative" laws, it merely defined the character or quality of persons to be deemed admissible. In legal terms the gates were still wide open to any number of qualified immigrants.

At the close of the first World War all signs pointed to an enormous increase in the annual migration from Europe to America. Then Congress struck at it decisively by putting numerical limits on immigration. By an emergency act in 1921 it fixed the number of aliens of any nationality, to be admitted annually, at three per cent of the number of the foreign-born persons of such nationality actually resident in the United States in 1910 as determined by the census of that year. This cut the total immigration from Europe to 309,556 for the fiscal year 1921–22, to about one fourth the number of immigrants admitted in 1913. As a positive quantitative cut in immigration, the act showed a determination on the part of Congress to put an end to free and easy immigration for all time.

Having made this provision, in the face of an outburst of objections, Congress elaborated it in 1924. In the act of that year it placed a maximum limit on the total annual immigration from Europe—temporarily at 150,000. This number it apportioned among various European countries on the basis of two per cent of the number of foreign-born persons of the respective nationalities, as determined by the census of 1890, with a minimum quota of 100. The return to the census of 1890, which meant a clear discrimination against the countries of southern and eastern Europe, raised a storm of protest from people affected by it. But Congress refused to bow to the tempest. It insisted on making the drastic cut, with its discrimination against southern and eastern Europe. And, responding to labor and other demands from the Pacific coast, Congress in the act of 1924 also placed an absolute bar on the immigration of laborers from Japan; it overthrew the Gentlemen's Agreement of 1907 and assigned to Japan the same position as other oriental countries, in respect of immigration.

Subsequently, as provided in the act of 1924 and later amendments, the total number of quota immigrants for each year was fixed at 154,000 and the quota to be allowed to each foreign country coming under the law was established by a complicated process of calculation. The census of 1920 was taken as the basis. The number of persons in the United States belonging to each nationality in that year was estimated. The ratio of such number to the total number of inhabitants in the United States was then ascertained—as amounting to a certain percentage of the whole. Finally, to each nation entitled to send emigrants under the act was given a number—a quota equal to this percentage of the total number, 154,000, to be annually admitted. That is, for example, if the number of persons of a given national origin in the United States was two per cent of the American population in 1920, the immigrant quota of their country in Europe was two per cent of 154,000, or 3080.

The spirit of the national resolve against free immigration was expressed in the House of Representatives by Knud Wefall, of Minnesota, when, referring to the bill of 1924, he said: "The question [of immigration] is our own to solve in the manner we see fit to solve it. . . . We do not intend to close the door because we were here first but because it is our door. We are now under a reaction of the effects of the first World War. . . . We now want to close the door more tightly while we take stock of ourselves."

The die was cast. The proportion of foreign-born Americans was to decline swiftly. The continent had been rounded out. No more free land beckoned pioneers to the West. Crude exploitation of the continental domain by crude labor and crude capitalism had come to an end. Science might raise visions of wider opportunities for the production of wealth by other methods. But whether such visions were to be realized or not depended upon new factors and new skills of a different sort. There could be no return to the state of things existing in 1900 or 1880 or 1870. And as threats were made in Congress from time to time to reduce immigration to a bare trickle or stop it entirely, prospects of removing the restrictions faded. Only immigrants from Canada, Newfoundland, Mexico, Cuba, Haiti, the Dominican Republic, and the independent countries of Central and South America were exempted from the quota restrictions; even they were subject to numerous restrictions. The gates of the once wide-open "asylum for the oppressed of all lands" had been brought together with a bang that awakened repercussions throughout Europe and Asia. Not even the war gesture to China in 1943, repealing total exclusion and allotting her a quota of 105 immigrants a year, altered this situation.

Chapter 26

WORLD WAR I AND AFTERMATH

IN THE SUMMER of 1914 the interests of the American people were especially directed to pressing domestic problems. The presidency and Congress were under the control of the Democrats, committed to the reforms of the "New Freedom"—and to the emancipation of the country from its "masters . . . the combined capitalists and manufacturers of the United States," as the Chief Executive of the nation phrased the issue. Since 1899 the Democrats had fumed against imperialism and the entanglements in world politics which imperialism of necessity involves. Now the Department of State was headed by William Jennings Bryan, who had so intransigently combined advocacy of world peace, through treaties renouncing war, with opposition to imperialism.

Despite this concern with urgent domestic affairs, the rivalry of imperialist Powers in Europe and Asia was not ignored in the United States. For years the news from Europe and Asia had carried stories respecting the alliance of Germany, Austria, and Italy on the one side; and working agreements between Britain, Japan, France, and Russia on the other side. News reports, books, articles, and essays in increasing volume had made it clear in America that all those Powers were engaged in a frantic race to build up their armaments for war, piling taxes and debts upon peoples already groaning under heavy financial burdens. Observers of world operations along such lines, including President Wilson, suspected that this rivalry among the foreign Powers, if it continued unabated, would end in a holocaust of war, the most destructive that mankind had ever experienced.

Yet it was on a people largely intent on their own purposes that the calamity of European war burst during the first days of August 1914. When the news of the war came, shocking though it was, the general sentiment of Americans was undoubtedly opposed to participation in the conflict. On August 4 President Wilson issued a proclamation declaring the neutrality of the United States and the following day he supplemented it by another in the same vein. Two weeks later he made a special appeal to the American people to observe the letter and spirit of neutrality: "The effect of the war upon the United States will depend upon what American citizens say or do. Every man who really loves America will act and speak in the true spirit of neutrality."

Despite the President's admonition, the American public was soon deeply agitated by the war and the course of its events, especially as propagandists from both parties to the conflict in Europe descended in hordes upon the country to elicit American support. Many Americans of English descent frankly sympathized with the Entente Allies. On the other hand many Americans of German descent publicly professed their attachment to the Fatherland. Irish, remembering their own history, could scarcely conceal their satisfaction over the thought of a British defeat in the war. Jews, recalling the terrible persecutions which had recently befallen their people in Russia, as a rule deemed the Germans more civilized and more worthy of victory. On the whole, however, the sympathy of the large majority was on the side of the Allies. Even so, that did not mean that the Americans wanted or expected to become actual fighters in the war.

But as neutrals Americans had certain historic rights under international law, among which these were important:

1. Neutrals may sell goods to, and trade with, belligerents in a war—both munitions and goods of peace, or non-contraband goods.

2. Belligerents may lawfully suppress this trade by imposing a blockade on each other to stop the passage of ships carrying such goods; but a blockade to be lawful must be effective, that is, carried out by a sufficient number of patrolling war vessels.

3. If a peaceful merchant ship, whether belonging to a neutral or an enemy, is caught by a belligerent, it may be seized and confiscated in certain circumstances, but it must not be sunk or destroyed without provision for the safety of the crew and passengers.

Under international law and the laws and policies of the United States, it was the duty of President Wilson to see that these rights of Americans to engage in commerce as citizens of a neutral Power were enforced against both the belligerents in Europe. Thus he was compelled, as the Chief Executive of the nation, to consider American complaints against violations of neutral rights and to act on violations by the parties to the war.

At the outset of the conflict, the government of Great Britain made two decisions affecting the rights of Americans as neutrals. It proclaimed an iron blockade on the ports of the Central Powers and the ports of neighboring neutrals through which goods might pass to those Powers. The perils from German submarines made it impossible for Great Britain to sustain an effective blockade by keeping rings of ships near the blockaded ports; yet in spite of this fact, she declared her blockade effective. The second British decision reduced the number of non-contraband goods which neutrals had a right to sell to belligerents and other neutrals, if they could get them through the blockade. In time the British government included in the list of forbidden goods nearly every important article of commerce, including grain, other foodstuffs, and cotton, hitherto regarded as non-contraband.

Numerous British actions invaded the rights of Americans as neutrals to trade and travel. Great Britain insisted on stopping and seizing American ships bound for neutral countries bordering on Germany, such as Holland, Denmark, Norway, and Sweden. This she did on the ground that the goods they carried would eventually go to Germany or release goods in those neutral countries for sale to Germany. In November 1914 the British government declared that Germans were sowing mines in the open seas and proclaimed the whole North Sea a war zone closed to neutral shippers, subject to British orders.

Against these decisions by the British government, the State Department at Washington made strong objections. It asserted that they were unlawful, violated American rights, and were not necessary to British self-preservation.

Meanwhile the German government was also defying international law and endangering American lives as well as property on the high seas. In 1915, Germany proclaimed all the waters around Great Britain a war zone and announced that German ships, meaning her submarines now in use, would sink every enemy vessel found within that zone. Under the established international law Americans had the right to travel all the seas on their own merchant ships, on British ships, or on the ships of other countries. If such a merchant ship was caught by an enemy war vessel, the safety and lives of passengers were to be protected by the captor. But a submarine ordinarily could not take on board the passengers and crew of a captured ship about to be sunk. Hence the commanders of the new instruments of war disregarded the historic rules built up by agreements among the nations.

Against the German threat to merchant shipping in the zone marked out, President Wilson lodged a protest in February 1915. In very clear language he informed the German government that it would be held accountable for American lives destroyed in its submarine compaign. Nevertheless, on May 7, a great British ship, the *Lusitania*, with American passengers and some munitions on board, was torpedoed by a German submarine near the coast of Ireland and 114 American men, women, and children went down to death on the sinking vessel.

To this deed President Wilson objected vehemently and declared that the government of the United States would not "omit any word or act necessary to the performance of its sacred duty of maintaining the rights of the United States and its citizens and of safeguarding their free exercise and enjoyment." The German government replied evasively. In two additional notes to it, President Wilson repeated his objections and warnings. At length in September 1915 the German government replied: "Liners will not be sunk by our submarines without warning and without safety of the lives of non-combatants, provided the liners do not try to escape or offer resistance." It looked as if President Wilson had won a great diplomatic victory.

Although war agitations continued to fan excitement in the United States, as the presidential campaign of 1916 drew near, the majority of the people still seemed in a mood to keep out of the European conflict. At least such appeared to be the judgment of political leaders. With the Progressive party now dying, the Republicans, counting on their recovered unity for success at the polls, nominated Charles E. Hughes as their candidate and in their platform declared that they would maintain American rights "at home and abroad." At the same time they announced: "We desire peace, the peace of justice and right, and believe in maintaining a straight and honest neutrality between the belligerents in the great war in Europe." Renominating President Wilson unanimously, the Democrats praised "the splendid diplomatic victories of our great President, who has preserved the vital interests of our government and its citizens and kept us out of war." The campaign was boisterous and the election was close. At first it was reported that Hughes had carried the country but belated returns from California shifted the balance and gave the presidency to Wilson for a second term by an electoral vote of 277 to 254.

Hoping, perhaps, that he might be helpful in bringing the war to an end, President Wilson, soon after his triumph at the polls, addressed "peace" notes to the belligerents in Europe. His appeal for a peace conference was fruitless. Growing firmer in his resolve to intervene in the diplomacy of the war, he declared to the Senate, in January 1917, that the United States ought to take part in the establishment of peace on certain principles: "peace without victory"; the right of nations to have liberty and self-government; independence of Poland; freedom of the seas; reduction of armaments; and the abandonment of entangling alliances. A few days later the German government announced that it would renew its unlimited submarine warfare. Then without reviving the verbal argument with Berlin, President Wilson dismissed the German ambassador in Washington, Count von Bernstorff, and severed relations with his government.

Within two months six American ships were torpedoed and sunk. By April it was plain that this time Germany would not be stayed or turned in pursuing her peculiar methods of warfare. On April 2, 1917, President Wilson called upon Congress to "declare the present course of Germany to be in fact nothing less than war against the government of the United States." Four days later the war resolution was passed by Congress with a few dissenting votes—fifty in the House of Representatives and six in the Senate.

Having adopted the war resolution, Congress began to frame and pass measures for winning the war, which slashed deeply into the ways of American life. It quickly decided that a volunteer army would not be sufficient for the task ahead or indeed founded on correct principles, and that a great armed force must be raised by a draft of able-bodied males. At first it fixed the age limits at twenty-one to thirty-one inclusive and later at eighteen to forty-five inclusive. To support the armed forces, Congress provided for the floating of loans running into the billions. It increased taxes in every direction, devised new taxes, and raised the rates of income taxes to the incredible figure of sixty-three per cent in the highest brackets—a figure that must have made the eyes of radicals and conservatives surviving from 1896 start from their sockets. Heavier taxes were laid on inheritances. A high excess profits tax was imposed on corporations and partnerships.

Upon the President, Congress conferred broad power to control, regulate, and commandeer natural resources, industries, labor, the sale and distribution of food supplies—in fact to regiment men and women, all callings and occupations, and all activities, in the interest of winning the war. At the same time freedom of press and speech was put under severe limitations by Espionage and Sedition Acts, the most severe yet passed in the history of the country. Never before had life and property in the United States been subjected to restrictions so numerous, so onerous, and so deep-thrusting.

A disciplined master of the English language, skilled in the art of clothing noble sentiments in lofty and telling phrases, President Wilson employed his talents in framing war aims and delivering addresses on the subject to Congress, the American people, and the world. In his earlier diplomatic notes to Great Britain and Germany he had dwelt upon American rights of commerce and travel. In his war message of April 2, 1917, he sought to lift the war above such practical considerations. "The World," he said, "must be made safe for democracy. Its peace must be planted upon the tested foundations of political liberty. We have no selfish ends to serve. We desire no conquest, no dominion. We seek no indemnities for ourselves, no material compensation for the sacrifices we shall freely make. We are but one of the champions of the rights of mankind."

Later the President expounded the "war for democracy" as also a "war to end war," to establish permanent peace throughout the world, to make certain territorial changes in the interest of oppressed nationalities, and to force the adoption of new measures for the conduct of international relations. His specific objectives he summarized in fourteen points in a message to Congress on January 8, 1918. Chief among his points of political significance were these: open treaties of peace, openly arrived at, to supplant secret treaties, intrigues, and alliances; freedom of navigation on the seas; the removal of trade barriers among nations, "so far as possible"; reduction of armaments; more liberty for the nationalities in Austria-Hungary; and an association of nations to afford guarantees of rights and peace for all nations, large and small.

Respecting territorial matters, President Wilson favored the restoration of Belgium, which Germany had invaded and overrun during the war; righting the wrong done to France in Alsace-Lorraine; changes in Italian frontiers for transferring Italians to the homeland; restoration of Serbia and Rumania; alterations in the Turkish Empire; the independence of Poland; and fair treatment for Russia, then in the throes of revolution. What about subject peoples of European empires? Colonial claims, President Wilson maintained, should be adjusted in the interest of the subject peoples.

In the prosecution of the war—widened in December 1917 to include Austria-Hungary—detachments of American naval forces were sent to European waters to co-operate in the hunt for German submarines and to convoy merchant ships carrying supplies. In June 1917 the vanguard of the army, the American Expeditionary Force, commanded by General John J. Pershing, reached France. Before the end of the war over 2,000,000 American soldiers were sent to France; while nearly 2,000,000 more were in training at home for service abroad if needed. By October 1917, American soldiers were in European trenches. From that time forward they took part in increasing numbers in the great battles which finally subdued Germany and Austria-Hungary.

When the armistice came on November 11, 1918, more than 75,000 American soldiers and sailors had sacrificed their lives in the struggle. More than 200,000 had been wounded or were missing or were in German prison camps. In the meantime the United States had furnished to the Allies enormous financial credits and great quantities of supplies for civil and military uses.

CHIEF THEATER OF AMERICAN ACTION IN WORLD WAR I

In January 1919 agents of the Allied and Associated Powers met at Paris to draw up the treaties of the war settlement. President Wilson was there in person, accompanied by a peace commission which he had chosen himself. For months the delegates at the Paris conference labored and disputed over the terms to be imposed on the vanquished. Early in May the treaty with Germany was finished and, on June 28, German delegates, with bitterness of protest against its terms, signed it at Versailles. Afterward treaties were completed with Austria, Hungary, Bulgaria, and Turkey. In all these proceedings, Russia, still in the toils of the revolution that began in 1917, took no part.

By the various treaties the map of Europe and a part of Asia was refashioned. Alsace-Lorraine was handed over to France. Other parts of Germany were joined to neighboring countries. Poland won independence. Russia was reduced in size by the creation of small states on her western borders. Czechoslovakia and Yugoslavia were brought into existence. The German colonies in Africa were transferred to Great Britain and France, to be held as mandates under the League of Nations. The province of Shantung, which Germany had seized in China, was given to Japan for temporary administration. The German navy was surrendered and the German military power diminished to a mere shadow of its former strength.

In several respects the terms imposed on defeated Germany did not conform to the war aims which President Wilson had so eloquently proclaimed to the world. But compared with the terms which Germany had imposed on conquered Russia at Brest Litovsk the preceding year, the provisions of the Versailles Treaty were mild. Indeed if it had not been for President Wilson's moderating influence, they would have been harsher, and the government of France would have taken immediate steps to occupy and hold Germany down by military force for an indefinite period. President Wilson himself thought that the Versailles Treaty had many faults but he expressed the hope that its injustices would be corrected in peaceful councils of the Powers under the association of nations for which a section of the treaty provided, largely on his insistence.

According to the provisions of this section, known as the Covenant, a League of Nations was to be established. Within the League were to be included the Allied and Associated Powers, countries that had been neutral in the war, and in time the countries defeated in the war. The League was to be governed by an assembly in which each country had one vote and a council where the great Powers had permanent seats and minor powers were let in by rotation on a temporary basis.

The nations in the League were bound by the Covenant to keep the peace themselves and to join in protecting one another against external aggression. They were to submit their disputes to the council for arbitration and inquiry. If a member violated its pledge to follow peaceful methods, measures to coerce it might be taken by the League. Provisions were to be made for disarmament. Thus if the United States joined the League it would be under obligations to observe the rules of the Covenant and to take part regularly and continuously in the adjustment of controversies arising among the nations of the earth. Only by becoming a member of the League and sharing its responsibilities, President Wilson averred, could a lasting peace be achieved for the United States and all other countries.

In the summer of 1919 the Versailles Treaty, including the Covenant of the League of Nations, was laid before the Senate and people of the United States for discussion and action. Hitherto many plans for permanent world peace had been proposed and debated in the United States. Now large and loose theories were reduced to a very definite scheme for a League of Nations which, its sponsors claimed, would guarantee permanent peace.

By the very nature of politics, the debate over the League became entangled with debates over foreign and domestic affairs in general and particular. The Covenant of the League was tied into the treaty, which prescribed severe terms for the Germans. Americans of German origin made all they could of that fact. Americans of Irish origin disliked the provision giving Australia, Canada, New Zealand, and South Africa, as well as Great Britain and Ireland, each a delegate in the League Assembly, thus strengthening British power in the League. Other critics assailed the transfer of Shantung to Japan instead of to China, its former owner. The war had been unpopular in many sections of the United States among Americans of old and new stocks and, now that freedom of discussion was partially restored, opponents of the war could voice their dissatisfaction with the treaty which came out of the war.

A large number of liberals and radicals, who might have favored the idea of a league of nations in the abstract, were loath to do so on account of revelations respecting some sordid origins of the war that made them question the possible efficacy of the proposed League and its setup. In January 1918, Oswald Garrison Villard published in the New York evening Post a number of secret treaties by which Russia, Great Britain, France, and Italy, either before or during the war, had agreed to divide the spoils at the end of the conflict. These startling documents disclosed deep-seated imperialistic ambitions as among the real war aims of the Entente Allies. Moreover, while peace negotiations were pending, American troops, without a declaration of war by Congress, were waging war on Russia, a former associate of the United States, at Archangel and in Siberia—solely under orders of President Wilson.

Into the confused situation was injected the question: Who is now to govern the United States—League of Nations or no League? Dissatisfaction with the Democratic party, for various reasons, was intensifying. In the congressional campaign of 1918, while the war was still raging, President Wilson appealed to the voters to elect a Democratic Congress for the support of his policies. On November 5, 1918, the people had their first opportunity since the outbreak of the war to pass judgment on the Democratic administration, and their verdict was emphatic against it. The Republicans won a majority in both houses of Congress. This outcome, Theodore Roosevelt declared, was tantamount to a national repudiation of President Wilson's leadership and doctrines. No doubt some Republican enmity for the Democratic party and its President was transferred to the League of Nations, just as some Democratic enmity was enlisted in its behalf.

Reflecting the popular divisions of opinion, the Senate was in turbulence. At one extreme in positions was a large group of senators prepared to ratify the treaty as drafted and to approve the League of Nations as incorporated in the treaty. At the other extreme was a small number of irreconcilables, among whom Senator Borah was prominent, determined to keep the United States out of further European entanglements by defeating American participation in the League. Between the extremes stood Republican and Democratic senators ready to vote for the League if some modifications or reservations were made in its plan. Caught between opposing tempers, President Wilson refused to make any significant compromises as the debate went on for weeks and months. At length on March 19, 1920, both the treaty and the League definitely failed, by eight votes, to receive the two-thirds majority of senatorial votes required by the Constitution for adoption.

In the national election of that autumn a "solemn referendum" was taken on the League of Nations. Nominating James Cox, of Ohio, for President and Franklin D. Roosevelt for Vice-President, the Democrats championed the League before the country. Choosing as their standard-bearer Warren G. Harding, of Ohio, and Calvin Coolidge as candidate for Vice-President, the Republicans assailed the Democratic administration from top to bottom. Harding condemned the proposed League but vaguely approved an indefinite kind of international association in the interest of peace. Some of his supporters endorsed the League outright and asserted that the election of Harding would mean participation in it. Other supporters, with equal assurance, told the voters that a Republican triumph would keep the United States out of the League and all such foreign entanglements.

Whatever the election returns of 1920 actually did imply, as a verdict for or against the League, there was no question about the party outcome: the Democrats were blown from power in a tornado of ballots. Harding carried every Northern state and even Tennessee in the South. His popular vote was 16,150,000 as against 9,140,000 cast for Cox. Nearly 1,000,000 votes, the heaviest Socialist vote ever polled, were cast for the Socialist candidate, Eugene V. Debs, then in prison for having denounced the war as an imperialist and capitalist conflict. So the repudiation of President Wilson's policies which had been foreshadowed in the congressional elections of 1918 seemed to be confirmed.

☆

Not only did Wilson have trouble in the realm of foreign policy, but he had to struggle with major economic dislocations at home. Scarcely had his first term begun in 1913 when business in the United States took a downward slide.

An expert in labor conditions, John B. Andrews, reported: "From the point of view of the wage earner seeking work, the year 1914 was the worst since the year following the financial panic of 1907." According to an authority on industrial tendencies, they too were moving downward, "in most instances reaching such an alarming state as to place the year on a par with the severe depression of 1907–08." If agriculture was in a better state than business, farmers were far from satisfied with the prices of their produce in the dull markets.

And as the Democrats, in their customary style, had promised prosperity through "lowering trade barriers," so the Republicans in their customary style laid the slump to the reduction of the protective tariff by the Democrats. Whatever the reason for it, an implacable discontent with the New Freedom was abroad in the land—a revulsion which materially reduced the Democratic majority in the House of Representatives in the congressional elections of 1914 and destroyed it in the congressional elections of 1916 when Wilson was re-elected President.

About this time the economic slump disappeared temporarily. The war in Europe had scarcely started in the summer of 1914 when Great Britain and France began to buy enormous quantities of farm produce, manufactures, and semifinished raw materials in the United States. From month to month their purchases increased in volume, as they poured their own money into this country and began to borrow huge sums from American banks and investors. By the end of 1916 most branches of manufacturing and agriculture were booming; unemployment had almost disappeared; wages were higher; businessmen and farmers were gathering in large profits.

Although this spurt of prosperity before the United States entered the war was largely due to the purchases made by the Entente Allies, Wilson's partisans attributed it in some measure to the New Freedom. But leading Democrats, including the President himself, knew that it was mainly artificial and that the defeat of the Allies or the ending of the war would bring in its train an economic crash in the United States. In fact, to some members of the administration this was an argument for enlarging the borrowing facilities of the Allies and, finally, for entering the war directly. At all events, after the United States did enter the war, the business and agricultural boom grew to huge dimensions.

Yet even during the war and economic boom the domestic struggle over matters of capital and labor, over conservation of resources, over problems of taxation, and all the other issues relative to American living standards continued among the people and on the floors of Congress. Indeed, in some respects, the war magnified the problems and sharpened the issues.

Opposition to the war, such as it was, and to various measures adopted in carrying on the war, prevailed largely among the farmers and industrial workers who had fostered populistic or socialistic movements during preceding years. The arrest, prosecution, and imprisonment of war dissenters and labor agitators, notably Debs, revealed that the war for liberty and democracy abroad could be accompanied by stern measures of repression at home, under the very administration of President Wilson, world spokesman for those exalted war aims.

The social order was disturbed by strikes, numerous and widespread. Progressive and radical Democrats and Republicans in Congress tried to "make the rich pay for the war," to impose heavy taxes on profits, and to "restore the government to the plain people." During the war they also developed postwar plans for government ownership of the railways and for other features of "social reconstruction" in the United States.

It was generally understood that the domestic struggle would go on after the war and that provisions would have to be made for dealing with the economic crisis bound to follow the peace. But President Wilson proposed remedies couched primarily in international terms. The United States, he said, would have to join the League of Nations and promote world trade in order to find market outlets for the enlarged productive capacity of American industry and agriculture. Americans must do this, he insisted, "or you have ruined the United States." Even the settlement of controversies between capital and labor within America, he contended, cannot be effected unless we have "frank discussion" and "friendly discussion" and "those are the very things that are offered to us among the nations of the world by the Covenant of the League of Nations."

Years before, Republican leaders had promised manufacturers and farmers ever-expanding markets and prosperity, if they would support imperialism. Now President Wilson proposed to resolve pressing domestic difficulties in industry and agriculture by having the United States join the League of Nations and by promoting the reduction of protective tariffs, by opening American ports more freely to commodities from foreign lands.

By their actions, however, a large majority of the American people—Democrats as well as Republicans, Progressives, and Socialists—took issue with President Wilson on this point. They eventually made it evident that, in their opinion, joining the League of Nations or trying to drum up more foreign trade would not settle any of the major domestic disputes respecting national economy, poverty, or labor relations; or, for that matter, advance the brotherhood of mankind very far. Indeed in February 1917, while the entrance of the United States into the "war for democracy" was imminent, Congress passed, over President Wilson's veto, an act restricting immigration, and put it into effect May 1, 1917. Again, under pressure from President Wilson himself, Congress passed, in 1918, the Webb Act, which eased up the Sherman Anti-Trust law and permitted American businessmen to form combinations, loose cartels, in the export trade, for the purpose of combatting foreign concerns more vigorously in the international competition for world markets.

☆

The period of Republican rule from 1921–33, commonly described as the age of "normalcy," was marked by a foreign policy that practically ignored the League of Nations, though "observers" were sent to its headquarters at Geneva from time to time. Imperialist activities conceived as in the interest of trade were pushed everywhere. Former associates in the war were urged to pay the war debts they owed to the United States. The tariffs on imported manufactures were twice raised. Peace was made with Germany, reserving to the United States all the rights against that nation, established by the Treaty of Versailles, which the Senate had rejected.

American investors were encouraged to lend billions of dollars to Germany, thereby helping to restore her economic power and enabling her to make payments on the reparations to the victors in the war, especially on the heavy damages levied by Great Britain and France. Wilson's policy of refusing to recognize revolutionary Russia, on the ground that he did not approve its government, was continued. In this way Russia was treated as a pariah among nations; while the State Department encouraged American capitalists to make money out of Russian trade if they could. The floating of loans to foreign countries and capitalists was promoted; the export trade of the United States was pushed by federal agents; imperialist policy was revived in the Philippines; and efforts were made to keep ajar the so-called Open Door in China for American business enterprise.

Nevertheless under Republican auspices regard was paid to ideals of peace prevalent in the United States. At an arms-reduction conference held in Washington in 1921–22, Great Britain, Japan, and the United States agreed to stop their naval race for a specified time and limit the size of their battleship fleets. In 1928 the United States joined France in promoting the Kellogg-Briand Pact, an arrangement by which all the great nations of the earth bound themselves to outlaw war as an instrument of national policy and to settle their disputes henceforth by peaceful methods. Ardent advocates of internationalism hailed this act as putting an end to war and guaranteeing world order.

The age of normalcy also became in many ways an age of disillusionment in respect of foreign affairs. As the strife among the governments of Europe and Asia for world power, economic privileges, and other advantages went forward within the League of Nations and outside its councils, indifference to its fate widened in the United States. For this spectacle Americans who had opposed the entry of the United States into the League had only derision; and idealists who had sought to carry America into the League got cold comfort from it. The treatment accorded to revolutionary Russia by European governments contributed little to the comity of nations. Imperialist rivalries flourished as before— in Africa, Asia, and the islands of the seas.

At the same time secret agreements, made long before 1914, between Russia, France, and Great Britain, were unearthed by historians working in the archives of Russia, Germany, and Austria thrown open to researchers by revolutions in all those countries. On the basis of clear documentary evidence scholars dissected the myth, propagated by those Powers, that Germany was wholly responsible for inaugurating the war; that on Germany must be placed all the war guilt; that the governments of Great Britain, France, and Russia united by the secret agreements were administered by innocent civilians suddenly and unexpectedly attacked by a bloodthirsty villain.

By reading copies of these diplomatic documents, scholarly works in European history founded on them or the publicity given to the findings, literate Americans in large numbers learned something of the innumerable lies, deceptions, and frauds perpetrated by the governments of Czarist Russia, Great Britain, and France, as well as of the Central Powers, at the expense of their own peoples and other nations. The gleaming mirage that pictured the World War as purely or even mainly a war for democracy and civilization dissolved beyond recognition. Countless Americans who in 1914–18 had yearned for a "brave new world" at the conclusion of the war were disheartened by the proofs of sinister purposes running against their dreams.

☆

Although the Republicans could claim, with some justification in the election returns of 1920, that the country had turned its back on President Wilson's internationalism, they were not able, in domestic affairs, to stamp out the spirit of progressive or radical insurgency, old in American tradition and yet ever new in its application to changing conditions. In fact in 1924 they encountered a progressive revolt. Progressive Re-

publicans and Democrats, disgusted with both the old parties, put into
the field a third ticket, headed by Senator Robert M. La Follette, of
Wisconsin, and Senator Burton K. Wheeler, of Montana. But the
regular Democrats nominated for President John W. Davis, nominally of
West Virginia, in reality a New York lawyer for the firm of J. P. Morgan
and Company in Wall Street. In the election the Republican candidate,
Calvin Coolidge, who had succeeded to the presidency on the death of
Harding in 1923, received more than half the total vote cast. Yet the
4,800,000 votes polled by the Progressives indicated that the country was
far from converted to Republican "normalcy."

Nor in truth did the election of 1928, in which the Republicans received a longer lease on power, indicate an exact return to any previous
state of affairs. The Republican candidate, Herbert C. Hoover, who had
been Secretary of Commerce since 1921, was not a mere replica of a
McKinley, a Taft, or a Harding. In that office he had convinced many
businessmen that he was a financial wizard. He had promoted the export
of manufactures by the lavish use of public funds. He had encouraged
American investors to "prime the pump" abroad for American industries
by lending billions to foreign governments and corporations, thus enabling foreigners to "buy" American goods. Though Hoover praised
"rugged individualism" and was commended as a "great business leader,"
he was widely known also as a philanthropist and a man of avowed social
sympathies. He had headed American relief in Belgium during the World
War and later disbursed American money abroad by the millions in
relieving famine-stricken regions.

Never before in their history had the Republicans nominated for the
presidency a man who had spoken with such anxiety about the depress-
ing aspects of American society against which the spirit of progressive insurgency had been continuously directed. Nor had any Republican candidate advocated so repeatedly the removal of these afflictions by private
co-operation and governmental action.

In 1923, for example, Hoover had urged insurance companies to attack the problem of unemployment by adding that evil to the list of
casualties against which they provided underwriting: "There is one field
of insurance not yet covered. You have covered the great range of accidents and disaster, but one great disaster that comes to our workfolk has
yet been unguarded. . . . It is less than eighteen months ago when we
had five millions of unemployed men in our streets, of men who wished
to work but for whom no work could be found. There is nothing that
leads to such despair and such decay of self-respect as the man who wants
a job and wants to work, the support of whose family is in jeopardy."

Hoover had also opposed child labor and endorsed a constitutional
amendment authorizing Congress to abolish it. He had commended and

aided the work of associations for the improvement of housing conditions, public health, the care of children, and other phases of American society.

Gross inequalities in the distribution of wealth, long the subject of populistic, progressive, and socialistic criticism, Hoover had frankly faced, to the alarm of conservatives; and he proposed to attack them by the use of the inheritance tax. The inheritance tax, he declared in 1919, "does redistribute overswollen fortunes. It does make for equality of opportunity by freeing from the dead hand control of our tools of production. It reduces extravagance in the next generation and sends them to constructive service." To Republicans who had assailed the income tax of 1894 as communistic that must have sounded like treason to the Grand Old Party; and to scholastic economists, a foolish flouting of "natural law."

Nor did the Democrats in 1928 nominate a Cleveland Democrat. They selected a liberal, of progressive social sympathies, Alfred E. Smith, of New York. While legislator and governor in that state, Smith had consistently promoted social legislation in line with progressive aspirations. He had defended freedom of speech amid the hysteria of the World War and with a proclamation of liberty had pardoned a communist imprisoned on account of his opinions. With Smith's social and political doctrines, liberals and progressives were generally in agreement. But he was handicapped by two disqualifications for a popular appeal at the time: he was a Roman Catholic in a country loyal to its Protestant heritage; and he had consistently opposed prohibition since the adoption of the Eighteenth Amendment in 1919, in defiance of the powerful anti-saloon organizations behind it. If the votes cast in 1928 proclaimed another extension of Republican power, they did not in any case mean that the processes of American history were reaching a standstill.

In spite of their three successive victories in presidential elections and many pledges of a return to the "good old days" of free enterprise—no government interference with business—Republicans did not wipe out the measures of reform that had been accumulated since 1900. They did not reverse history and go back to the policies and legislation of the McKinley regime.

On the contrary, reformist measures, once condemned by conservatives of every type, were retained on the statute books, if occasionally with changes; and new laws conceived in the reform spirit were added. Moreover, the struggle to level down the special privileges of the plutocracy and raise the living standards of the masses went on within both great political parties, while the agitations of minor parties on the left wing gave the public no rest.

Hopes of abolishing or reducing to nominal rates the federal taxes on income and inheritances, entertained in some quarters, came to naught after the return of the Republicans to power in 1921. Twenty years previously nearly all the revenues of the federal government were derived from indirect taxes—customs duties and excises on consumption. At that time conservatives had decried income and inheritance taxes as socialistic or communistic. And advocates of such taxes had admitted publicly that they were framed to shift a part of the burden of taxation from the poor to the rich; while intransigents among them had declared that these taxes were steps toward the destruction of the plutocracy and greater equality in the distribution of national income.

On this question President Coolidge took a traditional position: "I do not believe that the government should seek social legislation in the guise of taxation. If we are to adopt socialism it should be presented to the people of this country as socialism and not under the guise of a law to collect revenue."

Yet of the $4,100,000,000, collected by the federal government in revenues in the fiscal year ended June 30, 1927, more than half came from income taxes on individuals and corporations. And President Coolidge's Secretary of Commerce, Herbert Hoover, publicly expressed the belief that "the present inheritance, income, and excess-profits tax tend to a better distribution of wealth." No clearer proofs could have been adduced to show that normalcy, in its effort to retreat, did not in fact go all the way back to the beginning of the twentieth century.

When, early in Coolidge's administration, rumors circulated to the effect that during the administration of his predecessor, President Harding, great oil reserves had been corruptly turned over to private concerns, the Senate ordered an investigation. Scandals were uncovered, and prosecutions were begun against offenders. Day by day revelations of bribery and fraud broke into the front pages of the newspapers, giving the people lurid pictures of the way in which unscrupulous men had got hold of and exploited the natural resources of the nation. Private promoters, the testimony revealed, had contributed money to Republican campaign funds and to politicians, in return for leases to tremendous oil reserves from which to enrich themselves.

Under stinging rebukes from members of Congress, the Coolidge administration started lawsuits in the courts against parties charged with fraud, and after the cases were heard the oil lands surreptitiously obtained were restored to the United States Government. No longer was it possible, as it had been fifty years earlier, for private persons or corporations to enter into secret connivance with government officials and gain titles to huge sections of the public domain without risk of exposure or retribution. The public resolve to keep all that remained of the national heritage of resources had been effectively demonstrated.

Another phase of the domestic struggle over the management of natural resources had to do with the development of water power. It had once been the practice of federal authorities to permit private companies to build hydroelectric plants on the public domain, or navigable streams coming under federal control, on a very liberal basis.

This policy outstanding progressives had attacked early in the century. They insisted that all water power should be publicly owned, that public power plants should be built, and that electricity should be distributed by public lines and sold at the lowest possible rates. Modifications of these propositions in the form of compromises, such as short-term leases of sites to companies, combined with strict regulation of rates and services, were also submitted to the country.

Before the World War had come to an end, the question of "federal power" was brought to the front in Congress. In 1920 a comprehensive federal water power act was passed and signed. The measure provided for the establishment of a water power commission and made a beginning at strict control over private utilities using federal power sites.

Not long afterward a project for building a great power plant in the Boulder Canyon of the Colorado River came up for review. Again a compromise was reached: ownership of the power site was retained in the hands of the government. The Secretary of the Interior was authorized to construct and operate a dam and other works on the site, and to allot the water for irrigation, domestic purposes, and the generation of electrical energy. The electrical power so produced he was permitted to sell, at rates sufficient to cover the cost, to states, municipalities, and private corporations for distribution. In selling this power, however, he was compelled to give priority to states and municipalities. In the end only a small portion of it went to private companies. Consequently Congress, under Republican leadership, moved nearer to the production and sale of power by means of public agencies, without the intervention of private enterprise.

Nevertheless the Republicans did manage to make one successful stand against the extension of public ownership, in this period. They had inherited from the Democrats a great power plant which the government had begun to build at Muscle Shoals, in the Tennessee Valley, for the production of chemicals to be used in munitions during the World War. When peace came, Republicans and Democrats who clung to nineteenth-century traditions of free enterprise in such matters demanded that the plant be sold or leased to a private concern at a low or even nominal figure. With this view Harding, Coolidge, and Hoover agreed in principle if not as to details.

But progressives in Congress, led by Senator George W. Norris, of Nebraska, had other plans—plans for socialization—and fought for them tenaciously. After a seven-year battle they pushed through Congress a resolution providing for government ownership and operation of the Muscle Shoals plant, for the construction of new plants, and for priority to states and municipalities in the sale of power.

President Coolidge killed it with a pocket veto. Again, and still under the leadership of Senator Norris, Congress passed a similar bill in 1931. President Hoover vetoed it, saying that it would help to destroy the "initiative and enterprise" of the American people. Though defeated temporarily in their efforts, congressional advocates of "public power" were able to prevent the adoption of recommendations from Coolidge and Hoover for otherwise disposing of Muscle Shoals, and to keep the plant in the hands of the government.

While conservatives of both parties labored unsuccessfully to turn the power resources of the Tennessee Valley over to private enterprise on easy terms, in the postwar period, few among them proposed repeal of the laws enacted in aid of agriculture during President Wilson's administration. If they had desired to do this, the plight of agriculture would scarcely have permitted the undertaking. After 1921, with the disappearance of the war demand for food products, agriculture started on a course of steep and ruinous decline. The prices of farm produce fell swiftly. Farmers by the tens of thousands went into bankruptcy. Farm mortgages were foreclosed and freehold farmers driven into tenancy or off the land. To make things worse, under the Republican tariff law of 1921 the prices of manufactured commodities which farmers had to buy remained fixed at high levels or in many cases rose still higher. Once more the country resounded with agrarian laments. Even politicians well entrenched in urban centers could hardly fail to note the discontent.

In these circumstances Republicans in control of Congress added to, instead of subtracting from, the Wilson program of agricultural legislation. They kept in force the Farm Loan Act of 1916 extending long-term credits to farmers at low rates of interest and supplemented it by provisions for short-term credits at low rates of interest. The Warehouse Act of 1916, designed to protect farmers against deceptive and fraudulent transactions in the storage of their products, was supplemented by the Packers and Stockyards Act, which gave farmers a similar protection in the shipment and sale of livestock. In 1922 grain growers were safeguarded by legislation against speculators in grains, as cotton growers had been by an act of 1916 against speculators in that commodity. Producers of perishable fruits and vegetables, who had long suffered from cheating and false reports at the hands of middlemen, were afforded more adequate defense by the Perishable Commodities Act of 1930. At the same time federal agencies were established to push the sale of agricultural products abroad in the manner employed to expand the foreign markets for manufactures. Invincibly, government functions were expanding.

But none of these measures did more than touch the fringes of the distress in agriculture. Surpluses of crops continued to pile up. The downward tendency of prices remained unchecked. Ruin spread more widely in farming regions. Farmers were suffering from the kind of calamity that was soon to overtake the middle classes and industrial workers of the cities; and right in the middle of "Republican prosperity" they gave the signal for a new agrarian rebellion. They demanded bigger markets and higher prices for their produce. One of their leaders vented their sentiments in saying: "If we cannot have prosperity too, we will kick the legs out from under the table and all Americans will have to sit on the ground." How to get the markets and higher prices? That was the question.

So deep was the unrest among farmers that Congress was moved to attempt a cure in 1927 by passing a bill to aid in handling the agricultural surpluses. The bill provided for the sale abroad of certain commodities at low prices and for making up the loss by an equalization fee or tax laid on producers in proportion to their sales. This would, its sponsors claimed, dispose of surplus output and raise prices. But whatever the merits of the bill, Coolidge interposed with a veto. The next year Congress passed a similar bill. Again Coolidge applied the veto.

The defeated farm bills represented a positive effort to interfere with the "natural" course of farm production and prices. As such they were generally deemed "unsound" by urban economists. Herbert Hoover was known to be against them. But in the heat of the campaign in 1928 both he and the Democratic candidate, Alfred E. Smith, promised to "do something" about the farm problem.

After his inauguration in 1929, President Hoover proposed and Congress enacted, with modifications, an agricultural marketing bill to control the disposition of various agricultural products. The act was expected to promote the organization of producers on the land into associations and corporations, to discourage overproduction, to foster orderly marketing, and to eliminate "undue" fluctuations and depressions in prices. To administer the law the Farm Board was created and a fund of $500,000,000 put at its command to be used in interfering with the "natural" course of production and prices in agriculture. This experiment, dubious in character, had just been started when the panic of 1929 struck even the cities and knocked "the legs out from under the table" in a wholesale fashion which even farmers had not contemplated in their resentment over their own economic distress.

In respect of labor legislation and social improvement, historic subjects of strife in the United States between and within political parties, the so-called age of reaction and disillusionment was in many respects an age of progress, not of retreat.

The provisions of the Clayton Antitrust Act of 1914 passed by a Democratic Congress, called by Samuel Gompers the "Magna Charta of Labor," had declared that labor was not a commodity and that the activities of organized labor were not to be suppressed under arbitrary injunctions issued by the federal courts. These two provisions, often violated or ignored in fact, were not struck from the statute books by Republicans. They were strengthened instead by a stringent anti-injunction law underwriting the principles of collective bargaining, passed in 1932. The new bill was sponsored by two progressive Republicans, George W. Norris in the Senate and Fiorello H. La Guardia in the House of Representatives, supported by many regular Republicans, championed by Democrats who then had a majority in the lower house, and signed by President Hoover. At no time in the history of the labor movement had its leaders been more powerful in political councils; the Anti-Injunction Act was testimony to the fact.

The La Follette Seamen's Act of 1915 for improving the conditions of sailors on American merchant vessels and assuring them new "human rights" remained on the statute books as another evidence that the influence of organized labor in social legislation was not declining under normalcy. In 1927, Congress gave to longshoremen and harbor workers the benefit of compensation for injuries—a privilege earlier granted to workers on interstate railways. The Railway Labor Mediation Act of 1926 was also in the line of progressive legislation, not a reversal in any respect. If few labor candidates were elected to Congress and setbacks frequently occurred in labor disputes, organized labor was growing in political force and winning sympathy under presidents often dismissed as "reactionary" by radicals.

What was known as the "social movement" was also gaining momentum. A sign of its meliorist advance was the adoption by Congress in 1924, with the approval of President Coolidge, of a resolution amending the Constitution so that federal authorities could regulate or abolish child labor throughout the United States. The amendment was not ratified by enough states to make it law, but some of its aims were later realized in other ways. In the states, almost unobserved by those who kept their eyes only on "national" affairs, laws were being multiplied in the interests of public health, housing, care of dependents, and protection against the hazards of poverty and other misfortunes. By 1930 three fourths of the states had provided pensions for widows and deserted wives with dependent children. By the end of 1931 at least nine states had general old-age pension laws and propaganda for national pension legislation was expanding throughout the country. In short neither war nor reaction had stifled the American resolve to subdue the evils of poverty in the United States.

Chapter 27

ECONOMIC CRASH AND NEW DEAL
UPRISING

IN THE AUTUMN OF 1929, just as the country seemed safe and sound on the "high plateau of permanent prosperity," except for farmers, the business boom attributed to Republican statecraft burst with a resounding crash. The prime stocks of the leading corporations fell nearly forty points on the average in a single day, October 29, when more than 16,000,000 shares were dumped on the market at the New York Stock Exchange. This panic was followed by the explosion of banks, railway companies, and private concerns, by increasing woes among farmers already in straits, by the closing of factories, shops, and offices, and by a steep decline in the opportunities of employment for artists, writers, musicians, architects, engineers, playwrights, and teachers—indeed the whole white-collar class—from New York to California. In the opening months of 1933, it was estimated, 12,000,000 men and women were out of work. Ruin and hunger, if not starvation, haunted not only the shacks of tenants and sharecroppers on the land, not only the back streets inhabited by industrial and professional classes, but also the grand avenues of great cities.

For a moment leaders in business and politics thought that this was "just another panic." President Hoover said: "We have passed through no less than fifteen major depressions in the last century. . . . We have come out of each . . . into a period of prosperity greater than ever before. We shall do so this time." But as the depression dragged through tedious months and into years, belief in "prosperity just around the corner" turned into doubt or despair. As this revulsion of feeling intensified, trust in the "natural" and "normal" processes of "recovery" declined, and leaders in the economic, intellectual, and moral life of the nation vehemently declared their unwillingness to endure the crisis with pious resignation as a visitation of God or of natural forces beyond human control. Long years of research, debate, agitation, and legislative gains in respect of social improvement had prepared multitudes of Americans for a different attitude toward poverty, unemployment, and misery in "God's own country."

Outstanding personalities in business and professional circles such as Owen D. Young and Gerard Swope of the General Electric Company, leaders in the United States Chamber of Commerce, in the American Federation of Labor, in the Federal Council of the Churches of Christ in America, and in associations for civic advancement joined in demanding concerted action against the depression. They called for deliberate planning and collective measures to create economic well-being and prevent the return of such a national misfortune. It was openly asserted in high places that, if capitalists could not so conduct industrial enterprise as to avoid periodical depressions of the kind and maintain a steady level of employment, the government of the United States would have to assume the responsibility.

In previous panics presidents had said or acted as if they believed that neither they nor Congress had any constitutional power to meddle with business activities and relieve the distresses of the millions unemployed. But President Hoover accepted no such defeatist philosophy while this terrible depression harrowed the nation with bankruptcies, mortgage foreclosures, poverty, hunger, and degradation. He immediately called upon Congress to make provision for a large-scale construction of public works to put labor and capital in action again; and he urged the governors of states to press for similar remedial measures within their respective jurisdictions.

As the depression wore on, Hoover acted more energetically and creatively. He recommended, and Congress adopted, two proposals for interfering in the "natural course" of business enterprise—from calamity to calamity. The first was the establishment of the Reconstruction Finance Corporation, which placed federal credit at the disposal of banks, insurance companies, railways, and other concerns in financial difficulties. The second was the formation of the Federal Home Loan Bank Board to aid people in peril of losing their homes under foreclosures of mortgages. He also approved legislation extending federal credit to states and municipalities struggling with unemployment and poverty. The popular criticisms launched against President Hoover were not to the effect that he had done nothing, but that he had not done enough or the right things on a scale commensurate with the magnitude of the national catastrophe.

President Hoover was desperately engaged in wrestling with the depression when the time for taking a national referendum on Republican statesmanship—the presidential election of 1932—arrived, as prescribed by the Constitution of the United States. Though the Democrats had won a majority in the House of Representatives in the congressional election of 1930, they had proposed no constructive measures to overcome the depression. Millions of Americans were still unemployed; poverty had become aggravated to menacing proportions; agriculture and industry were in a bad plight. The whole society of the United States was in a state of anxiety and confusion. But Democratic tactics in the House of Representatives were principally confined to obstructing and harassing President Hoover in such undertakings as he ventured to sponsor in trying to cope with the economic disaster.

As far as appearances indicated, the Democratic party, historically committed to the creed of "the less government the better," was even more disinclined than the Republicans to make a frontal drive against the depression by resorting to governmental action. Under Wilson's leadership they had, it is true, interfered with "free enterprise" in significant respects, but they had officially admitted no change in their individualistic creed. Nor in their platform of 1932 did they give any hint that they intended to reverse fundamentally their long role of opposition to federal interference in the "natural course" of national economy.

Neither in their choice of a presidential candidate nor in their campaign did the Democrats give the slightest indication that they intended to embark on a program of wholesale government interference with the processes of industry, agriculture, and labor organization. The man whom they selected to head their ticket, Franklin D. Roosevelt, governor of New York, represented by his sponsors as "progressive," had not in the course of his political career espoused any public policies which could be deemed radical by any stretch of the imagination. In their campaign literature the Democratic managers pictured Mr. Roosevelt as a man who could "perfectly understand the viewpoint of the dirt farmer and the city laborer, the man in the street and the one in high places, . . . quietly, impartially, firmly uphold the rights of each and achieve a fair deal for all."

Whether from sheer unrest or a belief that the Democrats could and would restore prosperity, the voters at the election broke Republican control over the executive and legislative branches of the federal government. They cast 22,800,000 ballots for Roosevelt as against 15,700,000 for President Hoover, the Republican candidate, running to succeed himself. Furthermore they returned huge Democratic majorities to the Senate and the House of Representatives.

What were the Democrats to do with their victory? Some, of course, expected to settle back and enjoy the spoils of office. Others relied on the revered economic philosophy that prosperity would revive in America if enough foreign outlets could some way be found for the products of American factories and farms. Indeed this historic dogma had been reiterated in their platform and in speeches during the campaign. Although their candidate, Mr. Roosevelt, had lent countenance to it, he had endorsed an agrarian program of government intervention for farm relief and promised to adopt several measures of relief for unemployment and poverty.

If the backers of Franklin D. Roosevelt expected a period of Democratic "normalcy," they were disappointed. Between November 1932 and his inauguration in March 1933 another financial panic had hit the country with the force of a cyclone. In every direction banks crashed and closed their doors. On the day of his installation hundreds were in bankruptcy, and practically all the others were shut up under precautionary measures taken by state governments. On March 4, 1933, therefore, circumstances looked black for the enjoyment of political jobs and power in the old style.

As the Democratic organization in Congress had no plans whatever for dealing with the financial disaster, the burden of leadership became President Roosevelt's and he took it upon his own shoulders. Under his direction a multitude of measures known collectively as the New Deal, devised to meet the depression, were quickly adopted and put into effect. These measures were based on the belief that the main business of getting the country out of the depression would have to be undertaken by the people and the government of the United States at home, and could not be disposed of by trying to get foreign markets in bankrupt Europe or poverty-stricken Asia.

Among Roosevelt's associates in the new Cabinet only one, Cordell Hull, Secretary of State, stuck to the idea of lowering trade barriers as the principal or sufficient mode of escape from the crisis. He admitted that the people at home could do something to help themselves; but putting American economy on a high level of production and prosperity by domestic actions he belittled as an effort to lift oneself by one's bootstraps; so he began to search for new or bigger foreign markets for American goods. While heading the American delegation to the World Economic Conference at London in the spring of 1933, Secretary Hull sought to reach some working agreements with representatives of various foreign governments, also in economic grief, that would enlarge the volume of American exports and imports. He was laboring at this task, though not making much advance, when President Roosevelt practically put an end to the conference by an abrupt message, and turned to the promotion of a domestic program for tackling the depression at home.

Apart from the repeal of the Prohibition Amendment in 1933, the principal domestic measures of the New Deal, adopted during and after 1933, may be summarized in a small compass under six heads: (1) control over banking and currency; (2) federal credit to property owners and corporations in financial difficulties; (3) relief to farmers; (4) regulation and stimulation of business enterprise; (5) systematizing rights of collective bargaining for organized labor; and (6) social security for selected groups of people against the hazards of dependency, unemployment, poverty, and old age. Taken collectively, they represented an effort to establish in the United States a stable economy in place of alternating booms and panics and to protect the people against numerous misfortunes of specific kinds. In the struggle to create the institutions of the New Deal many lines of older social meliorism were brought to a focus.

With the banks shut and the circulation of money palsied on March 4, 1933, the first task undertaken by President Roosevelt was that of opening the banks and managing the currency. Though urged by some of his supporters to nationalize at once all banks of issue and vest in the federal government the sole power of issuing currency, the President chose a less extreme course—one more in accord with the interests of private banking, and yet extending the scope and nature of regulation. All banks were put under closer federal supervision; credit was extended to banks which, it was thought, could be put back into sound condition; and banks beyond redemption were liquidated. The gold standard was abandoned. Gold coins and bullion were called in for deposit with the government, and the right of citizens to demand gold in exchange for paper money was abolished. For a currency based on gold was substituted a currency issued and managed under the authority of the United States. Thus the power of private banks possessing stores of gold to dominate the issue of currency by the United States was ended.

To afford relief to individuals and concerns in peril of bankruptcy or of losing their homes or farms, the policy of granting federal credit and aid was extended and made more effective. The farm loan banks were reorganized and supplemented by other credit institutions. The amount of security farmers were required to give for loans was reduced, and to those who could provide such security money was lent at lower rates of interest, on long terms, with easy methods of repayment in installments. Through new special agencies similar arrangements were made to lend money to people in towns who were in debt, had mortgages on their homes, and were in danger of losing their property. The Reconstruction Finance Corporation, established under President Hoover's administration, was revised; and billions of dollars were lent to banks, railways, insurance companies, industries, and other enterprises whose earnings temporarily fell short of their needs. By these measures the United States Government became the biggest money borrower and lender in the country and assumed heavy responsibilities for the fortunes of property owners in distress.

Rejecting the idea that all the huge surpluses of wheat, corn, cotton, meat, and other prime farm products could be sold abroad, or even "dumped" on foreign countries by any method, sponsors of farm relief adopted another course. By the Agricultural Adjustment Act of 1933 and later amendments, Congress provided for the curtailment of farm production by direct action. Instead of providing for the expansion of the home market, it adopted plans for organizing farmers who raised the leading agricultural staples, for reducing the amount which they produced, and for compensating them for that reduction by subsidies of money proportioned to their respective acreages withdrawn from production. With these measures were coupled other acts designed to restrict farm production, including livestock, to existing markets, stabilize supply in relation to demand, and create what was called by the Secretary of Agriculture, Henry A. Wallace, an "ever-normal granary."

Yet the dream of selling more agricultural produce abroad was not wholly given up. Under a law passed by Congress in 1934, on the insistence of Secretary Hull, the President and Secretary of State were authorized, for a period of three years, later extended, to make reciprocal trade agreements with other countries, free from the necessity of submitting their projects to the Senate for ratification. In these agreements they could lower, within limits, the tariff rates on manufactures and other commodities in return for pledges on the part of foreign governments to reduce their rates on American imports. By this means, it was argued, outlets for a large amount of cotton, corn, meat, and other farm produce could be found in foreign markets.

But American manufacturing interests were also suffering from surpluses which could not be sold; millions of people were out of work. Who was to buy the mountains of manufactured goods piled up in warehouses?

An attack on this problem was made under the National Industrial Recovery Act of 1933. The act authorized the expenditure of billions of dollars for the construction of public works with a view to stimulating building activities and creating purchasing power for the workers. Under it also an immense effort was made to organize business enterprises in the United States for a drive to increase employment, production, and sales in the home market. Enterprises were grouped together according to their nature. Their representatives were given power to adjust supply to demand, to fix prices within limits, and otherwise regulate their operations. For the purpose of preventing excesses in stock-market speculation and in the financing of great supercorporations, the Securities and Exchange Commission was established and given autocratic authority over all such transactions.

In the New Deal program special favors were afforded to organized labor which warmly supported President Roosevelt in elections. The National Industrial Recovery Act made provisions for collective bargaining between employers and employees, but the Supreme Court in 1935 declared unconstitutional nearly all of that act. Then Congress passed the National Labor Relations Act, making collective bargaining generally mandatory on employers and employees. Industrial and other workers were authorized to form or join unions of their own choosing and to elect representatives empowered to bargain for them in matters of hours, wages, and working conditions. To enforce the act the National Labor Relations Board was created. By other legislation Congress tightened the hold of organized labor on the processes of industrial bargaining.

Although a split occurred in the ranks of the American Federation of Labor under William Green and another organization, the Congress of Industrial Organizations, was formed, at first under the leadership of John L. Lewis, head of the United Mine Workers, both national federations flourished. The Congress of Industrial Organizations was highly successful in organizing industrial and white-collar workers, especially outside the old-line crafts. Both branches of national organized labor, with support from the National Labor Relations Board, increased rapidly in membership.

Taking into account millions of workers largely unorganized, Congress added the Wages and Hours Act to the labor program. Under this statute steps were taken to fix standard hours and wages in numerous industries and enterprises—particularly those in which the hours were long and the wages low.

By a series of measures the Roosevelt administration attacked more directly the problems of unemployment, poverty, and misery. Billions of dollars were appropriated for immediate relief to the hungry and homeless, to be spent directly through federal agencies and in co-operation with state and local governments. Later, jobs were provided for millions of the unemployed, including large numbers of the white-collar classes, on numerous projects set up under the Works Progress Administration and other federal agencies.

Various forms of social security were instituted under the Social Security Act of 1935; for example, insurance against unemployment to a limited extent and, for certain classes of workers, insurance against dependence in old age, and grants in aid of persons suffering from poverty, blindness, and other afflictions. Federal grants of money were made to states with a view to encouraging the establishment of a complete scheme of old-age pensions in every state in the Union. Briefly stated, a "floor" of minimum security was placed under millions of people. At the same time new projects for including all persons exempted from such benefits were proposed and brought under debate by sponsors of the New Deal.

Despite criticisms brought against it, frequently outrageous, and its many undoubted shortcomings and extravagances, the New Deal did so much for discouraged and desperate people that it won great popular support. In the circumstances relatively few persons with political aspirations proposed to abolish it completely and entrust the welfare of the people entirely to competitive enterprise.

While indulging in many denunciations of the New Deal in general, the Republicans, in their platform of 1936, endorsed the chief relief principles of the New Deal and pledged themselves to apply those principles more efficiently and at less cost. The Republican candidate, Alfred M. Landon, who had been associated with progressive politics in the West, stood by the planks of the Republican platform during the campaign of that year and in one respect he outbid the New Deal—by offering larger aids to agriculture.

Nevertheless, the Democrats won the election. Renominated by acclamation, President Roosevelt promised to uphold and expand the Democratic program. Reviewing with praise the New Deal activities since 1933 and declaring that he had just begun his fight in the interest of general welfare, he so captivated the public that he received 27,500,000 votes as against 16,700,000 cast for Landon. Whatever their deficiencies, New Deal endeavors to overcome the depression and relieve misery, mainly by domestic measures, seemed to be anchored in the affections of an enormous majority of the voters, so many of whom had personal reasons for being grateful.

Yet in fact the depression was by no means mastered when President Roosevelt took the oath of office for a second term on January 20, 1937—the date as fixed by the Twentieth Amendment, which moved closer to the election the installation of the President, senators, and representatives. At least 6,000,000 Americans were still unemployed. Business was still far below the peak of 1928. And in the year 1937, notwithstanding domestic pump-priming, another crisis struck the stock market, and prices of stocks went down even more rapidly than in the crash of 1929.

Financial analysts for the *American Year Book* of 1937 reported: "A new depression overtook the country in September. Unemployment increased with almost unprecedented swiftness. Relief rolls expanded. . . . The number of commercial failures was increasing. . . . New financing continued during 1937 in a state of comparative stagnation. . . . The decline in [stock] prices during September, October, and November was not only drastic. In fact there are few instances on record where a larger percentage decline has occurred in so short a period of time." Meanwhile the national debt mounted and yet no end of borrowing was in sight. On the contrary New Deal "experts" were now advocating the adoption of borrowing and spending as a permanent fiscal policy for fostering and directing industrial and agricultural production.

☆

During the early stages of the concentration on domestic problems and on measures designed to lift the nation out of the depression, the mood of the country seemed to become more and more concerned with the character of society in the United States, with its grave difficulties, its extraordinary opportunities, its values and potentialities. To this mood the term "isolationism" was sometimes applied. The expression had been coined as a term of reproach for opponents of President Wilson's type of internationalism. Now it was often employed against New Dealers by Americans who believed that general prosperity could only be recovered by lowering trade barriers and entering into some form of collective security with the other nations of the earth. Although President Roosevelt proposed that the United States join the World Court, created under the League of Nations, the Senate rejected the recommendation and he declined to press the issue.

The spirit of disgust with war and Europe was intensified by reports from an investigation of the munitions traffic, pursued by a special committee of the Senate, which unfolded a seamy story of international intrigues, sinuous diplomacy, and profiteering devoid of patriotism, running through the years of the "war for democracy" and the planning for "permanent world peace." Sworn testimony, covering hundreds of pages in the volumes issued by the Senate committee, demonstrated that many men who had applauded Wilson's idealism had in fact made huge sums of money out of the war. Widely publicized, the Senate committee's revelations deepened the disillusionment over the nature and results of that "great crusade." Even President Roosevelt was accused of isolationism and in his reply he lent verisimilitude to the criticism by saying: "We are not isolationists except in so far as we seek to isolate ourselves completely from war."

Out of the uproar over the munitions inquiry and the refusal of Great Britain, France, Italy, and other associates in the World War to pay the debts they owed to the government of the United States came two acts of Congress designed to keep the country out of the next European war, already visible on the horizon. The first was the Johnson Act of 1934, forbidding the flotation of any more loans in the United States for foreign governments that had in effect repudiated the aforesaid debts. The second act was the Neutrality Resolution of 1935. It prohibited the sale of "arms, munitions, and implements of war" to foreign belligerents in time of war and provided that Americans who insisted on traveling aboard the ships of belligerents in wartime must do so at their own risk.

The two acts, in the intentions of the authors, were to prevent a repetition of events which had facilitated the involvement of the United States in the recent European war. When the Neutrality Resolution expired in 1936 it was renewed and made more stringent. Supported by overwhelming majorities in the Democratic Congress, neutrality legislation appeared to represent a reasoned desire on the part of the American people to avoid being entangled in another European war.

By words and actions President Roosevelt indicated that he was in full accord with this desire to keep out of Europe's next war, should another one break. In 1933 he virtually closed the World Economic Conference in London, where the representatives of great Powers had assembled to consider ways and means of overcoming the terrible economic depression through agreements on international trade and currencies. He refused to bring special pressure on the Senate to secure the approval of American participation in the World Court project. He adopted a "good neighbor" policy in Latin America, substituting conferences and cordiality for the straight imperialist coercions of former years.

He induced Congress to free Cuba from the protectorate imposed upon her by the so-called Platt Amendment of 1901. He signed with commendation an act of the Democratic Congress under which the imperialist experiment in the Philippine Islands was to be liquidated by granting them independence, to become effective in 1946.

In his campaign for re-election in 1936, President Roosevelt encouraged the people to fortify their resolve against taking part in another foreign war. He said in his address at Chautauqua, for example: "The Congress of the United States has given me certain authority to provide safeguards of American neutrality in case of war. . . . We can keep out of war if those who watch and decide have a sufficiently detailed understanding of international affairs to make certain that the small decisions of each day do not lead toward war and if, at the same time, they possess the courage to say 'no' to those who selfishly or unwisely would let us go to war."

Chapter 28

AMERICA'S PART IN WORLD WAR II

WHILE Americans were entrapped in the wreckage of the depression, casting about fitfully for methods of full "recovery," and in a mood of revulsion against participation in any more foreign wars, the economy of Europe was falling into chaos and the democracy for which the world was to have been made safe, according to President Wilson's formula, began to collapse in those parts of Europe where it had prevailed. The depressed state of the Old World dampened plans for maintaining or starting booms in the United States by lending American money to foreigners so that they could buy the "surpluses" of American goods. As a matter of fact, all over central and eastern Europe the march of events for years had been away from the solution of any nation's domestic problems by the mere promotion of freer trade. The march had been in the direction of dictatorships, controlled economy, and revived imperialism.

From its establishment in 1917 by revolution, under V. I. Lenin's strategy, the government of Soviet Russia was frankly an unlimited dictatorship, described as communist and headed by men who, without equivocation, avowed their contempt for democracy, constitutional government, and civil liberties. In 1922 parliamentary government was overthrown in Italy by Fascist bands under the leadership of Benito Mussolini who derided democracy and civil liberty as "stinking corpses," but who went beyond the Russian revolutionists by glorifying war and brute force as good in themselves. One after another smaller states—Yugoslavia, Greece, Spain, and Poland—lost their popular government and were taken over by strong-arm governments.

Germany's experiment with a republic and a democracy under a constitution adopted at Weimar in 1919 was brief. In 1933, Adolf Hitler, commanding a private army of banditti, called National Socialists, achieved political supremacy in Germany, destroyed the republic, suppressed civil liberty, and started a savage persecution of Jews, churches,

Social Democrats, Communists, and Liberals. Years before 1933, Hitler had announced his ambitions and intentions in his book *Mein Kampf* (*My Battle*). As there exhibited they embraced a merciless battle at home against all his opponents and a war, east or west or in both directions, against the neighbors of Germany.

To gain time for his operations, however, Hitler spoke publicly of peaceful intentions. Secretly, he began at once to rearm Germany and train soldiers for a career of conquest. Many European and American writers warned mankind that Hitler and Mussolini were planning assaults far and wide, but conservative heads of governments in Great Britain, France, and elsewhere—the neighbors against whom they had warlike designs—refused to heed the warnings. Sympathetic toward the fascist suppression of communists in Italy and hoping later to turn the full force of Nazi Germany against Russia and communism, they tried to maintain peaceful relations with Mussolini and Hitler—even after these dictators, allied in a Rome-Berlin Axis, were joined by Japanese warlords in making open war on neighbors.

As he observed German, Italian, and Japanese military operations fan out in Europe and Asia, President Roosevelt, after his second overwhelming triumph at the polls in 1936, took a series of steps to bolster the anti-Axis powers, steps that, becoming bolder and bolder, created growing risks of involving America in a shooting war. Although the majority of his countrymen were also undoubtedly sympathetic towards the victims of Axis aggression, realization of the horrors of being in a war made them hesitant about going so far so fast.

This gap in thinking between the President and his public first became conspicuous in October, 1937. During that month, he made a ringing speech denouncing, without naming them, Germany, Italy, and Japan, for bringing on "the present reign of terror and international lawlessness." Pointing out that a community may use a quarantine to fight an epidemic, and classifying war as a contagion, he called for concerted efforts to restrain the dangerous Powers. After alarmed citizens demanded that he specify the measures he had in mind, and he sensed that he was out of tune with his audience, he discontinued the plan of appealing for sweeping action. As an alternative, he took one restraining step at a time, describing each as peaceful in intent.

Late in 1939, he took step one. After Germany had invaded Poland, and Great Britain and France had retaliated by declaring war on Germany, President Roosevelt called upon Congress to repeal the embargo provision of the neutrality legislation or modify it in such fashion as to permit Americans to sell munitions to the British and French governments. In his message to Congress, however, he assured Congress that the repeal which he demanded was in the interest of American abstention from the war—in the interest of "American neutrality, American security, and above all, American peace." Apparently accepting the President's explanation, Congress made changes in the Neutrality Act in the direction which he indicated; but tightened it in other respects.

Whether this weakening of the neutrality legislation was in fact in the interests of peace as the President claimed, or a step toward war reminiscent of Wilson's journey from 1914 to 1917, as his critics contended, it had little immediate effect on the war. By the time the presidential campaign of 1940 was in full swing, France had fallen, much of continental Europe was in German hands, and England seemed in peril. What should America do next? The Democrats offered Roosevelt for an unprecedented third term, as the man best suited to answer this question, while the Republicans ran Wendell Willkie for President, a former Democrat, utility lawyer, and public relations agent, long opposed to Roosevelt's domestic policies.

Whatever party managers had in view, peace was an issue uppermost in the minds of the people. On this issue both candidates seemed to be reassuring. "The American people," declared Wendell Willkie, "do not want war. . . . They are determined to keep America at peace. In that determination I stand with them. I am for keeping out of war." So, too, was President Roosevelt, judging by the repeated efforts he made to convince the public that the steps he was taking during the campaign period did not, in fact, endanger the peace.

On September 3, 1940, President Roosevelt informed Congress that he had, by executive act, acquired lease rights to naval and air bases in Newfoundland, in the British West Indies, and in British Guiana; and that in exchange for certain of these bases he had given Great Britain fifty of our "over-age destroyers."

Objectors charged that, besides being an arbitrary action which the president had no lawful right to take, it was a plain act of war as defined by international law—the transfer of war vessels by a presumptive neutral to a government at war with another power. In his reply to this attack, the President sought to dispel popular fears. Not only had the Attorney General, he said, pronounced the operation lawful, but it was "not inconsistent in any sense with our status of peace."

Less than two weeks after the President announced the transfer, an act went into effect establishing the first peace-time draft in the entire history of the Republic. Started on a temporary basis, this system of conscription was, through renewal, kept in force until after America became a combatant more than a year later. Just why was this drastic departure from American traditions made at this particular juncture? Voters having sons of draft age demanded an answer before Election Day. They got it. On October 30, 1940, the day after the first draft numbers were selected, Roosevelt gave a solemn pledge to his country: "And while I am talking to you mothers and fathers, I give you one more assurance. I have said this before, but I shall say it again and again and again. Your boys are not going to be sent into any foreign wars. They are going into training to form a force so strong that, by its very existence, it will keep the threat of war away from our shores. The purpose of our own defense is defense."

Franklin D. Roosevelt was granted a third term by a vote of 27,000,000 in round numbers against the 22,000,000 polled by Willkie. In his annual message of January 6, 1941, to Congress, he announced his intention to have the United States send to the nations at war with Hitler and Mussolini "in ever-increasing numbers, ships, planes, tanks, guns." This action, he realized, might lead to war and yet he said: "Such aid is not an act of war, even if a dictator should unilaterally proclaim it so to be."

Then he had drawn up and introduced into Congress, in January, a measure "to promote the defense of the United States," known as the Lend-Lease bill. After extensive hearings and a long debate, this bill, modified by amendments, became a law on March 11, 1941. The Lend-Lease Act authorized the President to sell, transfer, exchange, lend, lease, or otherwise dispose of ships, aircraft, implements of war, and other commodities to the "government of any country whose defense the President deems vital to the defense of the United States." In effect, it empowered the President to sell or give, to any and all governments actually or nominally at war with the Axis Powers, war implements and supplies in immense quantities.

Under international law as hitherto recognized, this law was an act of war. Opponents of the bill so characterized the gift of military supplies to China in her conflict with Japan and similar aid to Great Britain and her Allies in their war on Germany and Italy. But it was entitled a bill to promote the defense of the United States; and its sponsors in Congress assured the country that it was intended to keep the country out of war.

On July 7, 1941, about two weeks after Hitler's armies invaded Russia, President Roosevelt notified Congress that the armed forces of the United States had occupied Iceland, jointly with British forces for the time being; and that he had ordered the American Navy to defend the sea lanes between the United States and that island.

In August the President and the British Premier, Winston Churchill, met aboard warships off Newfoundland, and agreed upon steps to be taken in providing for the safety of their respective countries against Germany and the governments associated with her. They also drew up at their conference a declaration of principles, soon called the Atlantic Charter, for the conduct of affairs, not only during the war but also after the destruction of Nazi tyranny.

On October 27, 1941, President Roosevelt informed the country that engagements had taken place in the Atlantic. "Hitler," said the President, "has attacked shipping in areas close to the Americas. . . . Many American-owned ships have been sunk on the high seas. One American destroyer was attacked on September 4. Another destroyer was attacked and hit on October 17. Eleven brave and loyal men of our Navy were killed by the Nazis. We have wished to avoid shooting. But shooting has started. . . . America has been attacked."

While the attention of the American people was being directed especially to the war in Europe, trouble was brewing in another foreign quarter. The government of Japan, taken over by ruthless militarists, had for years been seizing territory in China and waging war on that country. Under the slogan of "Asia for the Asiatics," Japanese imperialists nourished projects for conquering and ruling immense areas of the mainland and islands in the Far East.

Japan's aggression, of course, ran counter to American foreign policy in the Orient and to the letter and spirit of treaties signed by the Japanese government and other Powers, including the United States. In upholding that policy President Roosevelt took the position that Japan was violating treaties and international law, destroying the independence of China, and transgressing American rights in the Orient.

In response to such complaints the Japanese government, by this time allied with Germany and Italy as the third party to the Axis, offered some concessions, but in the main adhered to its own imperialistic line. It insisted that the United States was violating Japan's rights as a belligerent by giving financial aid to the government of China and by sending munitions to that government at Chungking, by way of the Burma Road. For months, as indeed for years in the past, the State Department at Washington refused to surrender any part of its Far Eastern policy. Diplomatic exchange between the governments of the United States and Japan continued without softening the asperity of their differences.

Eager to avoid the awful perils of a two-front war, Great Britain tried conciliation with Japan. For a long time the two countries had been formal allies united by treaty. Though, on the insistence of the United States, their alliance had been severed in 1922, they had managed to keep on workable terms. Yielding to protests from the Japanese government, Great Britain in 1940 closed the Burma Road to shipments of munitions and supplies bound for Chungking, still in the hope of warding off a war with Japan.

But the British closure of the Burma Road brought objections from the United States. When he heard rumors of the proposal Secretary of State Cordell Hull declared that the United States had a "legitimate interest in the keeping open of the arteries of commerce in every part of the world," and that shutting the road would "constitute unwarranted interposition of obstacles to world trade." When her agreement with Japan expired at the end of six months, Britain complied with American desires and opened the road again to the transport of munitions to Chungking.

By November 1941 the tension between the government of the United States and the government of Japan approached a climax, as Japanese armed forces moving southward into French Indochina increased in number. China had opposed a quiet settlement of the differences between the United States and Japan, and during the Atlantic Charter negotiations British Prime Minister Churchill had urged Roosevelt to warn Japan against continued aggression. In the end, stern counsels prevailed. On November 26, 1941, the United States sent a note to Japan asking her to withdraw her military, naval, air, and police forces from both China and Indochina. This was equivalent to asking her to do an abrupt about-face in thought and action.

What would happen if Japan preferred to keep to her current course? As early as January 27, 1941, the American ambassador in Tokyo, Joseph Grew, had reported to the State Department that in case of trouble with the United States, the Japanese were planning an attack on Pearl Harbor in the Hawaiian Islands. There, a heavy concentration of American forces constituted an inviting target. Having successfully broken down the secret code used by Japan in sending messages, and having thus gained glimpses of what Japanese militarists were thinking, American officials had some sense of awareness of what might occur. On November 28, 1941, in fact, the American Secretary of State, Cordell Hull, told "high officials" in his own government that relations with Japan were critical and that Japan might launch sudden attacks at various points.

A few days later, these sudden attacks came. Following a pattern she had set in two previous wars of starting hostilities without warning, Japan bombed Pearl Harbor at dawn on Sunday morning, December 7, 1941, catching the American defenders substantially off guard. While the responsibility for this state of affairs has long been debated, the outcome was plain. American forces were severely mauled. At the same time, the Japanese were attacking American and British outposts in the Far East.

THE EXTREME LIMITS OF AXIS DOMINANCE IN WORLD WAR II

On December 8, 1941, the day after the attack on Pearl Harbor, the United States declared war on Japan, and so did Great Britain. Three days later Germany and Italy proclaimed war on the United States and agreed with Japan, their Axis colleague, not to make a separate peace. In a little while nearly all the world was engulfed in war. The conflict of 1914–18 had been comparatively limited—mainly to Europe and the Atlantic. Now Asia, Africa, and the Pacific had also become major scenes of armed combats. Only minor Powers, such as Switzerland, Sweden, Turkey, and Argentina, remained outside the circle of fighting or belligerency.

SHOWN IN BLACK ON LAND AND GRAY ON WATER

Before America formally entered the war, German and associated armies held much of Europe and parts of northern Africa. Then, partially protected against attack from the west by the English Channel, the Germans threw most of their strength into a gigantic drive eastward to overwhelm the Soviet Union. Shortly after America went to war, the embattled Russians appealed to the United States to join with Great Britain in a full-scale invasion of western Europe. By forcing the Germans to divide their energies between two fronts, such a venture would obviously be of great help to the Communists in trying to hold out in the east.

Rather than attempt a premature invasion of Europe in 1942, the year of the Russian request for help, England and the United States took the safer course of first pinning the Germans down in Africa. Late in that year, American and British troops stormed ashore in the French-held northwestern corner of Africa to begin a push to the east against German and Italian resistance, co-ordinated with a British drive westward from Egypt. Squeezed mercilessly between the two jaws of this giant pincers, the Germans and Italians in Africa surrendered during May 1943.

From their African bases, American and British troops next crossed the Mediterranean in 1943, captured Sicily, and moved on to the Italian mainland to start the first major invasion of Europe. Following internal disorders that overthrew Fascism, Italy signed an armistice. This, however, had little effect on military operations, for the German troops holding most of the country stoutly resisted American and British efforts to drive northward.

Plans had been evolved, meanwhile, for two other invasions of Europe, farther west. The first materialized on June 6, 1944, when a large fleet carrying American, British, and associated troops crossed the English Channel, with air support, to lunge at the German-held beaches of Normandy, France. About two months later a second expedition landed, in southern France, and quickly linked up with the earlier group. The invasion forces, so joined, pushed the Germans out of France, through Belgium and Holland, into Germany proper. Simultaneously, the Russians drove relentlessly toward Berlin from the east, aided by American and British air raids that wrought havoc behind the German lines. Meanwhile, progress was being made in Italy. On May 8, 1945, the last of the battered Germans finally surrendered unconditionally.

Of a very different character was the Pacific phase of World War II. Taking advantage of the heavy damage done American forces by the surprise attack on Pearl Harbor in 1941, the Japanese seized several American outposts—the Philippines, Guam, Wake, and two spots in Alaska's Aleutian Islands chain. On the Asiatic mainland, Japan formed an alliance with Siam (Thailand), and overran not only eastern China and French Indochina, but the English colonies of Hong Kong, Burma, and Malaya as well. The Japanese also seized a whole series of British and Dutch islands jutting far out into the South Pacific, to the east (map, p. 437).

The overextended Japanese offensive was finally brought to a grinding halt in 1942 by an accumulation of American, Australian, and other associated forces. At the Battle of Midway, for example, Americans severely damaged and turned back an eastbound Japanese fleet. American supplies were moved into China to bolster its power to resist the Japanese in the west. Finally, late in 1942, American, Australian, and associated forces began their own version of an island-hopping advance. In the course of a whole series of desperate encounters on the beaches and in the jungles, from the Solomons to Iwo Jima, they slowly worked their way closer and closer to the Japanese homeland. By late 1944, Americans re-entered the Philippines. Early the next year the United States used air bases close to Japan to conduct massive air raids that severely disrupted the Japanese economy.

Germany's surrender in May 1945 permitted much greater concentration of American energies on knocking Japan out of the war. Having secretly tested an experimental atomic bomb, America issued a stern warning to Japan in July 1945 to surrender unconditionally or face annihilation. When the Japanese continued to fight, and immense American losses in a conventional invasion of her home islands seemed to be the only alternative to its use, Truman ordered the dropping of the first atomic bomb ever employed in warfare. It fell on August 6, 1945, shattering the Japanese city of Hiroshima. Two days later, Tokyo had another rude shock—news that Russia had declared war on Japan. The next day a second atomic bomb fell, on Nagasaki. The end came quickly; on September 2, 1945, Japan signed surrender papers terminating the last Axis resistance in World War II.

The bitter and far-flung campaigns waged in Africa and Europe to the East and in the Pacific and the Orient to the West, brought striking changes in the lives and modes of thinking of the American people. Through volunteering and heavy use of the draft, the American armed forces were brought to a peak of over twelve million men, most of them yanked out of their familiar surroundings and placed in strange and trying new environments. Also, the Army and the Navy, long opposed to using very much feminine help, actively recruited women in World War II and at one time had over 250,000 of them in uniform. They, too, were taken from their usual settings, drilled, disciplined, and assigned to a variety of duties, one of them being ferrying combat planes from factories to major air bases.

To the material needs of the men and women in the American armed forces were added those of some two or three times as many put in uniform by China, England, the Soviet Union and other anti-Axis powers. The combined needs of this great multitude included everything from canned food to electronic gear and bombing planes. A very large part of the massive and complex over-all task of providing these supplies was successfully assumed by the United States.

In its struggle to attain the stupendous military and naval production goals it set for itself, America made use of its existing arsenals, navy yards, and other war plants, converted a long list of factories from the fabrication of civilian goods to war production, and built supplementary works at an astonishing rate. Whereas in 1939, the year World War II broke out in Europe, manufacturing plants in the United States represented an investment of about $50,000,000,000—the accumulation of decades of effort—within the next three years additional facilities costing $22,000,000,000 were partially or wholly completed.

From the swiftly expanding array of works poured forth a rapidly increasing volume of supplies. According to an official estimate, the total value of American production of goods and services in 1945, the year in which military victory was completed, was over $210,000,000,000 or more than double that of 1929, during most of which a great peacetime boom had been in progress.

Big business was responsible for much of the expansion in physical output. To get quickly and in fabulous amounts guns, ships, tanks, airplanes, and other implements of war, the Federal Government turned for help to concerns gigantic enough to be able to take huge production orders in their stride. By the close of 1943, for example, some seventy per cent of the war business had gone to the hundred largest companies. This trend, of course, created abundant opportunities for charging that the anti-trust laws had been violated. Yet to divert the energies of overworked executives from critical production problems to the refinements of anti-trust litigation and to break intercompany ties that sped the flow of goods, just to please small competitors, had its military hazards that could not be lightly ignored. Finally squarely facing this issue, at the insistence of the War and Navy Departments, the Department of Justice curtailed its program of prosecuting trusts and combinations in restraint of trade, to simplify and expedite the war effort.

Champions of small-scale enterprise and greater competition viewed with their traditional alarm these new developments strengthening the trend toward big business. Vice-President Wallace lashed out wrathfully at the "monopolists." Members of Congress spread denunciations over pages of *The Congressional Record*. Other New Dealers roundly condemned the "economic royalists." Yet strong as they were, such verbal bombardments never succeeded in shattering the leadership in the battle of production taken by giant concerns, with their demonstrated capacity for providing the supplies needed to overwhelm the enemy.

The imposing layout of American plants, many of them operated by big companies on a three-shifts-a-day basis, made exceptionally heavy demands on the labor market. With millions of members of the usual peacetime working force enlisted in the American armed services, industry had a difficult time getting enough help. This is evident in official statistics which show a drop in unemployment from 14.6 per cent of the civilian labor force in 1940 to the low level of only 1.2 per cent in the busy Normandy invasion year of 1944. Not only did the war enable most of the previously unemployed members of the regular working force to get jobs, but it drew into factories and other business establishments millions of housewives, teen-agers, and old people who would not have sought employment in times called normal.

Under New Deal policies, millions of these men and women were in effect compelled to join unions and pay union dues to get and hold desirable jobs. With their membership growing, work plentiful, wages often high, and Communist agitators generally anxious to speed the flow of goods to hard-pressed Russia, unions benefited mightily from the spectacular boom.

While wartime prosperity was thus solving certain problems for big business, individuals, and unions, it was also generating a host of special difficulties all its own. For example, when unions, conscious of their mounting power and determined to make their weight felt, organized strikes, they sometimes interrupted the flow of supplies needed to win battles in far-off regions. With the success of the fighting forces thus placed in jeopardy, Congress finally passed the Smith-Connally Act in 1943 placing restraints on the use of strikes. Nor did the national government hesitate to take drastic action against the unions when it considered the step imperative—it formally seized a whole series of coal mines to terminate one major strike and the railroads to prevent the outbreak of another.

A second vexing problem created by the war was the serious shortage of skilled help that appeared in certain fields. The flow of doctors and nurses into the armed forces and into war plant clinics often left whole communities with woefully inadequate hospital and other medical services, despite the heroic efforts of numerous overworked physicians and nurses who stuck to their accustomed posts. Education suffered greatly as thousands of experienced teachers left to fight or enter war plants. Many business enterprises, too, no longer deemed "essential" to the war effort, were denuded of competent help.

To inconveniences springing from shortages of help were added those due to shortages of goods. By converting many plants to the production of military and naval items, voluntarily or under various forms of governmental compulsion, American industry thereby lost much of its capacity for supplying the civilian market. In frank recognition of this fact, the Federal Government ordered the complete cessation of the construction of nonessential buildings and of the manufacture of certain articles for ordinary civilians—notably passenger cars—forcing the public to get by as best it could with used equipment. A second category of things, which included tires, gasoline, meat, and certain canned goods, was made available to civilians only in restricted quantities, carefully parceled out by the stores to those presenting the necessary federal ration stamps and tokens. Moreover, the quality of even what was available underwent some deterioration. That is, by giving war plants priority in the use of certain essentials, the Federal Government forced other factories to resort to less desirable substitutes in turning out articles for civilians.

As if trouble in getting supplies were not enough, many civilians had a hard time even finding places to live. The expansion of factories in older communities, the adding of extra shifts, and the erection of plants in rural regions, all caused the migration of millions of persons, individually and in families, to new locations poorly prepared to carry the extra burden. Under the circumstances, Americans often had to double up in old houses, crowd into hastily erected emergency dwellings, or sleep in small trailers.

Vast shifts of population threw heavy loads on roads, schools, water supplies, sanitary facilities, and power and telephone systems. When efforts were made to surmount these difficulties with new construction, they were frequently so handicapped by shortages of funds, labor, and material as to prove woefully inadequate.

Perhaps most serious of all was the wholesale disruption of family life created by the war. The absence of fathers, mothers, and older children in the armed services, in war plants, on merchant ships and elsewhere, left millions of youngsters to shift more or less for themselves, in unaccustomed ways, frequently without being adequately prepared to use their freedom wisely. Neglecting school, roaming the streets looking for excitement, tens of thousands of minors got into trouble, detected and undetected. The strong increase in recorded juvenile delinquency, overcrowding, rationing, moving problems, the stresses and strains brought on by wartime separations of loved ones, and other difficulties represented in the aggregate a grave departure from the usual peacetime concepts of good living.

Nor could the public even express itself in the free and easy manner customary in times of peace. As in the Civil War and in World War I, so in World War II the Federal Government placed a series of restrictions on what one could say or write while hostilities were still in progress. The Espionage Act of 1917 was again put to work. Newspapers, magazines, and the radio were placed under official scrutiny to prevent the divulging of information useful to the enemy and to maintain "American morale" at home. Two prominent leaders of pro-Nazi organizations were arrested for their advocacy of the Axis cause. News releases were officially prepared for the definite purpose of bolstering the will to conquer. Even some of those who had done nothing clearly unpatriotic were taken into protective custody. In a step marking a striking departure from American tradition, some one hundred thousand persons of Japanese ancestry, American citizens and aliens alike, were taken from their homes in strategic areas and transferred to federal concentration camps, without previously being charged with any definite harmful act.

Amidst all the turmoil of World War II days, the government of the United States itself underwent a drastic change of character. Struggling to meet a host of acute problems generated by the war, Congress conferred upon the President far more authority over human lives and property than it had seen fit to grant to President Wilson in World War I. Much of it was used. Some of the results have already been described, from rationing to censorship. The other restrictions were legion. Ablebodied men in certain age groups were in effect told to "work or fight." That is, under certain circumstances they were offered draft deferments for service in war plants, but if they quit they automatically became subject to induction into the armed forces. Many others found that big obstacles stood in the way of their leaving essential plants to work elsewhere. Ceilings were clamped on wages, the prices of many articles were fixed, and rents in areas where critical wartime housing shortages existed were closely regulated, all by federal order. Indeed almost everywhere civilians turned, they were confronted by a welter of rules, many of them in a state of flux, that made observance of "the law" both frustrating and difficult, even for those having the best of intentions.

To handle the mountainous details of wartime controls, to keep munitions flowing, and to perform the many other special tasks it had suddenly undertaken, the Federal Government had to hire hundreds of thousands of extra men and women. From a total of slightly over a million in 1940, the number of civilians on the federal payroll swelled to more than three and a half million in 1945, the year Germany and Japan surrendered. To cover their salaries, meet the bills for giant orders for airplanes, quadruple the size of the ocean-going American merchant marine, and otherwise carry the financial burdens of its share in the global contest, the Federal Government spent money at a fantastic rate. In the critical year of World War II that closed on June 30, 1945, the national government spent over ninety-eight billion dollars—more than five times as much as it had spent between the inauguration of the first President and the opening of the Twentieth Century.

As one means of meeting the rising cost of America's participation in World War II, federal taxation was widened in scope and increased in severity. To cite an example, by lowering exemptions millions of Americans who had never before paid a federal income tax now had to file returns, and by boosting rates old-time taxpayers had to carry added burdens. Nevertheless, the cost of the conflict continued greatly to outdistance the growth of taxation, leaving staggering deficits to be covered by borrowing—through one issue after another of war bonds. The trend is plain in the per capita national debt, which rose over 500 per cent from $325 on June 30, 1940, to $1,848 on June 30, 1945, shifting the day of reckoning to future generations.

Running through the thinking of most far-sighted Americans, whether fighting overseas or struggling with problems at home, was a disturbing sense of uncertainty as to what would be the ultimate results of actually overwhelming the Axis. That success in battle was no sure guarantee of a stable peace had been amply demonstrated by European developments after the close of World War I. Would the United States, this time, feed and clothe the losers and get them back on their feet, only to become alarmed over their renewed and hostile vigor? Or would America help execute Axis leaders and dismantle Axis industries to reduce substantially and "permanently" the war potentials of the defeated lands? Would Communists, spearheaded by the Soviet Union, take advantage of the collapse of the Axis to expand their operations and thus endanger the peace? Or would the human race at last achieve a brave new order which, to use President Franklin D. Roosevelt's hopeful words, would provide "freedom from fear" and "freedom from want," not just in scattered places, but "everywhere?"

While the general public was pondering such questions, President Roosevelt, directly or through his agents, was striving to answer some of them by making specific agreements with British, Russian, and Chinese leaders as to what the major victors were to have and what should be done with the vanquished upon the defeat of the Axis. Though the labors of the conferees were currently "described" to the press and to Congress in official releases, and denials were made at the time that there were any secret understandings, the latter did in fact exist. The Russian promise to enter the war against Japan, with whom she was currently formally at peace, for example, and Roosevelt's offer to do certain things in return, were kept hidden from the world at large at the time they were made, for strategic reasons.

Thanks to subsequent revelations, however, the fundamental story of what President Roosevelt did to set the stage for the peace that was to follow the collapse of the Axis is now a matter of public record. In it may be traced a persistent effort to create a workable and permanent international organization. The first step was taken openly, in January 1942, when the United States and other powers at war with the Axis assumed the name of the United Nations and agreed to work toward victory in unison. A further advance was made in October 1943, when the Moscow Conference of foreign ministers, at which the United States was represented, announced itself as being in favor of establishing a post-war international body. About a year later, at Dumbarton Oaks, American and foreign representatives worked over the details for such an organization.

Turning from world problems to the specific troubles of Europe, representatives of the United States, Great Britain, and Russia, at the Moscow Conference of foreign ministers, in 1943, considered what should be done with Germany, Italy, and Austria after the war. The results were publicized—that "war criminals" would be tried, Italy should be given an opportunity to establish a government on democratic principles, and Austria should be made independent. At the Second Quebec Conference, the next year, President Roosevelt and Prime Minister Churchill of Great Britain gave further attention to the German problem, agreeing for a time to the "Morgenthau Plan" for destroying Germany's industrial might and reducing her to the status of a simple farming nation. This severe "solution" was, however, quickly abandoned by Roosevelt and West Germany ultimately became an industrialized, armed bulwark against Communism (p. 453). At Quebec, too, allied occupation zones for Germany were discussed.

Meanwhile, Oriental affairs were receiving close attention. At the First Cairo Conference, held in November 1943, President Roosevelt, Prime Minister Churchill, and Generalissimo and Madame Chiang Kai-shek of China agreed that their respective countries would continue the war on Japan until her unconditional surrender. They also agreed that Japan should be deprived of all the islands in the Pacific she had acquired since the outbreak of World War I, that China should get back the regions Japan had taken from her, such as Manchuria, Formosa, and the Pescadores, and that Korea should ultimately become independent. These objectives were released to the press at once.

Right in the midst of his complex global maneuvering, President Roosevelt had to turn aside to attend to an urgent domestic matter—the regularly scheduled national elections of 1944. He again accepted the Democratic nomination for President and, in deference to his wishes, Senator Harry S. Truman was named as his running mate. To lead the attack on this ticket the Republicans nominated Governor Thomas E. Dewey of New York. Following a vigorous campaign the polls were opened and Roosevelt emerged as the winner, by the slimmest margin of his career as a perennial candidate for the highest office in the land.

Shortly after his inauguration for a fourth term, Roosevelt went to
Yalta, in Russia, for a last major conference with Churchill of Great
Britain and Stalin of the Soviet Union. There it was agreed that a meeting should be held soon in San Francisco to draft a formal charter for the
United Nations. Thus Roosevelt followed in the footsteps of his Democratic predecessor, Wilson, in proposing that a formal international organization be created to deal with the vexing problems left in the wake
of a great war.

Turning to European issues, the three leaders agreed that Russia might
have eastern Poland. To compensate Poland for this loss, she was to be
allowed to expand westward by taking in German soil. It was also understood that what was left of Germany should be divided for occupation
purposes and that her supply of machine tools, labor, and other major
sources of economic strength might be tapped for reparations, an arrangement that was to be highly advantageous for the Russians. In return for such help, Premier Stalin promised that "free elections" would
be held in the areas "liberated" by advancing Russian armies in eastern
Europe, thus arousing hopes that democratic societies could flourish
once again in that portion of the globe.

At Yalta, too, Roosevelt secured from Russia a pledge to join America
in the final assault on Japan, within some sixty to ninety days after Germany surrendered. In appreciation, Roosevelt undertook to do four
favors for Stalin in the Orient. First, Roosevelt recognized the "autonomy" of Outer Mongolia, a huge region the Russians were trying to
separate from China and bring within their own sphere of influence.
Secondly, he agreed to respect the special interests the Russians claimed
to have in the key area of Manchuria. In the third place, Roosevelt con-
sented to Russian seizure from Japan of the Kurile Islands and southern
Sakhalin. Lastly, Roosevelt offered to do his best to get China to go
along with the above plans, whenever Stalin should indicate that the
appropriate time had come for his intercession.

Since the full publication of the Yalta understandings, there has been
heated debate over their merits. On the one hand, it has been argued
that Russia was in a position to obtain most of the things she requested
at Yalta, even without American help, so that whatever Roosevelt sal-
vaged for the West was a gain. On the other hand, it has been said that it
was so clearly to Russia's advantage to enter the war on Japan in its
final stages that no American concessions were really necessary.

Whatever one may think of the specific parts of the Yalta agreement,
it is plain that Roosevelt was trying to achieve through them a better
world, trusting that Stalin would keep his side of the bargain. Moreover,
Roosevelt felt that generosity toward the Russians should evoke a cor-

responding spirit of friendliness toward the West that would ease postwar tensions. To those who might otherwise have been able to say "How do you know you can't get along with the Russians unless you try?" Roosevelt could certainly have replied that he had tried.

Like Wilson before him, however, Roosevelt lived long enough to see his dreams of a better world fade before the hard dawn of reality. Shortly before Roosevelt died, a Soviet agent stormed into "liberated" Romania and gave its king less than three hours in which to establish a Communist government; there was no mention of the "free elections" promised at Yalta. Soon afterward, the Polish Government formed under Russian supervision turned out to be another Communist dictatorship and again there were no signs of free elections. Roosevelt protested to Stalin without success. It was amidst such mounting gloom that Roosevelt died. The date was April 12, 1945.

His passing put Vice-President Harry S. Truman in the White House. As Truman took the oath of office, he faced the task of bringing to a close America's participation in the biggest war in history, and making a series of complex peace settlements for Europe and the Orient. Humble in origin, modest as to his ability to discharge his new obligations, and not yet having had time to raise a troublesome crop of political enemies, Truman had the sympathies and good wishes of millions of Americans as he started his arduous labors.

During his first six months in the White House, tremendous changes took place. The international conference in San Francisco drew up the charter of the United Nations. The Germans surrendered unconditionally. The Japanese were brought to their knees. Occupation of Axis territory got under way, and the nuclear blasting of Japan had opened an era wholly new to human experience.

Chapter 29

THE ATOMIC AGE UNFOLDS

THROUGH HER LARGE-SCALE and successful participation in World War II, America added to her reputation as a great power. Moreover, by emerging from the contest unscathed, the continental United States was left in a better position for meeting the immediate challenges of peace than were the severely damaged heartlands of the other chief belligerents. Militarily, too, America was fortunate. Not only were her fighting forces much bigger than at the end of any previous war but they were far better armed than ever before. The outstanding feature of America's arsenal was, of course, the dreaded atomic bomb, the effectiveness of which had been established beyond dispute in the attack on Japan. Through her initial monopoly of this device, the United States possessed a tremendous strategic advantage over other countries, as the atomic age began to unfold.

In the early postwar years, America sought to protect her superior position by rendering it impossible for the losers to attempt another great wave of conquest soon. First, she co-operated with Great Britain, France, Russia, and China in disarming Germany and Japan and curtailing the war-making potentials of some of their industries. Then through the signing of treaties and acquiescence in Russian demands, America helped to strip the former Axis powers of much of their land. By the time the process had been completed, Italy had lost her African possessions and small tracts in Europe. Finland and Romania had been reduced in size. Japan had been pushed out of the regions she overran in World War II and some earlier holdings—notably Formosa, Korea, Manchuria, and the Kuriles. Germany had been deprived of her World War II conquests and even some land that had been German centuries before the struggle began. America received little direct advantage from this change; her one territorial gain was the taking over of the Carolines, Marshalls, and Marianas from Japan, via a United Nations Trusteeship offering some of the benefits of ordinary ownership.

On the damaged remnants of their domains, the defeated powers had to support not only those present at the moment of surrender, but many thousands of soldiers and civilians forced to return from areas lost in the war. Adding further to their tribulations, the ex-Axis states also had to contribute labor, equipment, and other things to the victors. For example, with American consent, the Russians tore Germans from their homes and compelled them to work, virtually as slaves, on Russian reconstruction projects. Russians also took machinery, tools, railroad rolling stock and other items from Austria, Germany, Hungary, Romania, and Manchuria.

Serving as a constant reminder of their loss of the war, too, was the presence on the soil of the ex-Axis states of the occupying forces of the victors. Russians did the occupying in eastern Europe and the United States took charge in Japan. Austria and Germany, together with their respective capitals of Vienna and Berlin, on the other hand, were cut into separate American, British, French, and Russian occupation zones. The sequel was frequent and bitter wrangling among the would-be managers, ending in the granting of independence to a unified Austria, the division of the bulk of Germany between the Communist and Western blocs (pp. 451, 453), and the maintenance of Berlin as a Communist-surrounded "island" occupied by the four leading victorious powers.

During the period of occupation, various German and Japanese leaders were placed on trial as "war criminals." In the list of charges brought against them were the commission of "crimes against peace" and "crimes against humanity." Acting largely through allied military tribunals including American, British, French, and Russian judges, the victors found many guilty, executing some and imprisoning others. In addition, the records of tens of thousands of Germans and Japanese were reviewed to determine, in the light of their wartime activities, who should be excluded from participation in public affairs.

Yet America was too generous a foe to be content merely with holding down the losers, and trying to prevent them from attempting further conquests. She undertook to create for them new and rewarding patterns of peaceful living. Screened and approved Germans and Japanese were allowed to form governments which, in the areas under American supervision, were constructed along democratic lines. In Japan, for instance, Americans ended deification of the Emperor and gave votes to women.

America also played a prominent part in overhauling the economies of certain former Axis states. This was costly. The United States spent several billion dollars in Austria, Germany, and Japan for food, machinery, and other items needed during the restoration of their war-torn agriculture and industry to effective operating condition. With such help, and local initiative, West Germany ultimately became strong, and Austria and Japan were able to resume their former status as independent nations. Americans who had groaned under the double financial burden of smashing enemy powers, then putting them back in shape, now had a new complaint—the rejuvenated Germans and Japanese were successfully invading markets Americans wanted to hold, at home and abroad.

Besides working with the vanquished, the United States, as a prominent member, helped the victors put the United Nations Organization (UN) in motion. Shortly after its initial meeting in London in 1946, the UN clarified its authority by formally taking over the tasks and assets of the prior League of Nations. Then the UN transferred its headquarters across the Atlantic and ultimately into specially designed buildings in New York City, a striking testimonial to America's growing importance.

In structure, the UN was a compromise between the desire of small nations for equal representation and the resolve of the great powers to maintain a position of leadership. In deference to the wishes of the former there was established a General Assembly, or lower house, where each member country had one vote in recommending action to the upper house, or Security Council. Bowing to the demands of the great powers, the latter was composed of five permanent members—the United States, the Soviet Union, Great Britain, France, and China—plus six others chosen by the General Assembly on a rotating basis, for two-year terms. On major issues, the Council could reach binding decisions only with the unanimous consent of all the permanent members and the concurrence of two of the rotating members.

This machinery has been successfully applied to the solution of numerous problems. For example, the UN evolved a truce between the Jews and Arabs in Palestine at one juncture, and induced Russia to withdraw troops from Iran at another. It backed medical, cultural, scientific, and other agencies that contributed substantially to the welfare of large regions.

Yet while the UN was attempting to bring peoples together to solve problems in common, a fundamental division of viewpoint over Communism was also driving them apart. There gradually developed, on the one hand, a powerful bloc of Communist states, centering about the Soviet Union, and on the other hand a group of governments more or less favorable to private enterprise, held together, if fitfully and haltingly, by a sense of common alarm over relentless Communist pressures. Time after time, matters involving action by these rival groups would be *urtesy United States Steel Corporation*

An International Harvester photo

TAPPING AMERICA'S RICH NATURAL RESOURCES

As the development of the nation gathered momentum, America's rich natural resources were tapped on a gigantic scale, with the help of advanced machinery. How long would they last as the tempo increased? The answer will depend in part on how wisely they are utilized.

(ABOVE) Tapping America's resources. *Left:* An open pit iron ore mine in the famous Mesabi Range of Minnesota. *Right:* A group of big combines rolling across the prairies. Each unit is capable of cutting and threshing 500 acres of wheat a day.

(BELOW) The problem of the bad management of our natural resources is tackled in earnest. *Left:* Soil erosion in progress. *Right:* Controlling erosion by contour plowing.

U. S. Department of Agriculture

Photo from John Deere

THE RISING TIDE OF URBAN POPULATION

With the long-time shift of population from rural to urban regions continuing far into the twentieth century and the population of the continental United States approximately doubling between 1900 and 1950, heavy burdens of caring for more and more people were thrown on the cities and the flood of human beings spread out into the suburbs.

(ABOVE) Urban areas as seen from on high. *Left:* New York City—with a large housing development in the foreground. *Right:* Suburbia—on Long Island, N. Y.

(BELOW) In the thick of it. *Left:* At work—a traffic jam on Manhattan Island, New York City. *Right:* At play—the beach at Coney Island, on the outskirts of New York City.

BUSINESS CYCLES AFFECT THE FORTUNES OF MILLIONS

From boom to bust and back to boom—so swung the business cycle as the twentieth century advanced, affecting the fortunes of millions in the mines and fields of the country and on the city streets.

(ABOVE) Scenes from the depression of the 1930s. *Left:* A breadline. *Right:* Shacks of the unemployed in Los Angeles.

(BELOW) Industry prospers. *Left:* Lend-Lease shipments to Europe in World War II kept American factories busy filling huge orders. *Right:* The impressive Washington, D. C., headquarters of the American Federation of Labor and Congress of Industrial Organizations, a union that has worked hard to improve the living standards of its members.

GREAT WARS RAGE

The United States became an active participant in both of the great wars that raged during the twentieth century.

(ABOVE) World War I. *Left:* The first contingent of American troops landing on the friendly soil of St. Nazaire, France. *Right:* American troops going into action against the Germans.

(BELOW) *Left:* Counter-guerrilla warfare in the Korean War—An infantryman waited under cover to ambush an enemy patrol. *Right:* In Vietnam the helicopter was fully used for the first time in front line rescue of the wounded, supply and defense.

EFFORTS TO HOLD DESTRUCTION IN CHECK

The havoc wrought by two great conflicts in the twentieth century inspired efforts to bring the forces of destruction under better control through world organization and "summit conferences" of heads of state.

(ABOVE) International organization becomes a reality. *Left:* Woodrow Wilson boards ship —as the first President to leave the United States—on his way to the Peace Conference at Versailles, 1919, out of which emerged the League of Nations. *Right:* United Nations Headquarters in New York City.

(BELOW) Summit conferences. *Left:* Democratic style—President Franklin D. Roosevelt seated with Winston Churchill of England and Joseph Stalin of the U.S.S.R. at a conference during World War II. *Right:* Republican style—President Dwight D. Eisenhower and Nikita Khrushchev meet in September 1959.

U. S. Army

Official U. S. Air Force photo

RESEARCH UNLOCKS THE DOORS

Extraordinary advances in scientific and engineering research during the twentieth century enormously increased the capacity of human beings for doing good or evil.

(ABOVE) Research unlocks the doors to appalling devastation. *Left:* A test underwater atomic bomb explosion set off by the United States in the Pacific after World War II. *Right:* An Atlas intercontinental missile, a swift carrier of destruction, being prepared for firing.

(BELOW) Research opens up new vistas of peaceful living—installing the reactor core for the first large-scale commercial atomic-powered generating plant in the United States at Shippingport, Pennsylvania, 1957.

Duquesne Light Company

Giddings & Lewis Machine Tool Company

Ford Motor Company

TOWARD AUTOMATION

During the twentieth century automation has been achieved in numerous fields.

(ABOVE) Progress in manufacturing. *Left:* Ford's assembly line in the year 1913. *Right:* Automation — a machine tool receiving instructions from tape turns out an airplane part automatically.

(BELOW) Fast mechanized thinking for a complex world—a Univac electronic computer employed by the United States Bureau of the Census for such tasks as providing business statistics.

Courtesy Remington Rand, A Division of Sperry Rand Corporation

National Aeronautics and Space Administration

National Aeronautics and Space Administration

THE LAST FRONTIERS BECKON—OUTER SPACE AND HYDROSPACE

Outer space and the ocean depths are the last frontiers for exploration by the scientifically and technically advanced nations. The pictures on this page give us an idea of the world of tomorrow.

(ABOVE) *Left:* Astronauts will see this as they come from behind the moon. The world's first photo of earth (U.S. east coast at upper left, southern Europe on the night side) was taken by camera-carrying Lunar Orbiter I. *Right:* Scale model of the moon surface and Lunar Orbiter I.

(LEFT) Navy diver testing equipment outside an experimental one-man submarine Star-1 in the vicinity of Sealab-1 at a depth of 192 feet.

U.S. Navy

brought before the Security Council only to have one of the permanent members, frequently Russia, promptly terminate discussion by a single vote. Thus the range of human affairs which the UN could effectively handle was greatly restricted.

How had the new "balance of power," within and outside of the UN, between Soviet communism and its opposites been developed? In the first place, the growth of international communism had been facilitated by the shattering of the Axis. Germany's collapse permitted Communist penetration deep into Eastern and Central Europe, while Japan's disintegration cleared the way for a similar spread of Communist influence throughout the Orient. The Communists exerted pressure in both directions. Russians, who had long complained of being "encircled" by capitalist "imperialists" now became in their turn "encirclers," employing "imperialist" methods on a global scale, and with ruthless determination.

One part of this expansion had got under way as victorious Russian armies swept across Eastern Europe in the closing months of World War II. The Baltic countries of Estonia, Latvia, and Lithuania, Russian prior to the close of World War I, were firmly incorporated in the Soviet Union. Russia's borders were also extended westward to encompass almost 70,000 square miles of eastern Poland, under the Yalta agreement, and sections of German East Prussia as well. By treaties of peace signed with Eastern European losers, Russia acquired territory from Finland, Romania, and Czechoslovakia. Far to the east, again in accordance with the Yalta understandings, Russia annexed the Kurile Islands and southern Sakhalin from Japan. By 1956, the Soviet Union had grown to an estimated area of over 7,877,000 square miles and an estimated population of some 200,000,000.

Further strengthening the Soviet position was the chain of Communist-dominated satellite nations which the Russians forged along their borders. Backed by Russian troops and in violation of the pledge to hold free elections made at Yalta, a Communist-dominated government was imposed on Poland. Eventually the Russians converted their occupation zone in eastern Germany into the Communist "German Democratic Republic." In 1948, Communists seized control of Czechoslovakia. In Albania, Bulgaria, Hungary, and Romania as well, Communist governments aligned with Russia appeared. The score in Europe? By the end of the 1950s, seven Soviet satellites with a combined area of about 400,000 square miles and an estimated population of some 95,000,000.

Similar developments occurred in the Orient. Aided by the Yalta agreement, close ties were established by Russia with the huge region of Chinese Outer Mongolia, now designated the "Mongolian People's Republic." With Russian encouragement, Chinese Communists pushed southward, forcing the previous anti-Communist administration to take refuge on the Island of Formosa and producing on the mainland the Red-ruled "People's Republic of China," linked with Russia by treaty. Following Russian occupation of northern Korea, under a previous agreement, that region became the satellite "People's Democratic Republic of Korea." In southeastern Asia, Communists overran a French colony to produce the satellite state of Northern Vietnam. The score in the Orient? Four Communist satellites with an estimated area of about 5,600,000 square miles and an estimated population in the 1950s of well over 600,000,000.

Elsewhere, too, Communists advanced their cause in a variety of ways. They staged riots in Western Europe in protest against American aid to democratic nations, provided equipment and safe and neutral bases for Communist guerrillas in Greece, and threatened to invade Formosa. In Burma, Indonesia, and Thailand, in Africa and Latin America, their agitators labored to smash those who opposed them. The Russians even offered financial aid and technical assistance to wavering lands, in return for support, and indulged in a wholesale propaganda campaign of vilification against those who resisted their advances.

As matters stood in 1960, then, the chief reality confronting the United States in the domain of foreign affairs was that about a third of the world's population was under some form of Communist government and Communist influence was penetrating deeply into much of the remaining territory. Thus a grave threat existed to cherished American institutions and ideals that called for vigorous countermeasures.

Dissatisfied with many fruitless efforts to meet relentless Communist pressures by working through the UN, President Truman finally resolved to detour that body on a large scale. On March 12, 1947, he announced the "Truman Doctrine" that America must offer direct help to certain nations endangered by international communism. As a first step, Congress provided quick aid to Greece and Turkey, then menaced by Communist maneuvers. Later, also at his prompting, Congress extended aid to Western European democracies, to help them revive their war-torn economies, through the "Marshall Plan" or European Cooperation Act. After the Korean invasion began (p. 454), these ventures were supplemented by military assistance programs. Even frankly Communist Yugoslavia received millions of dollars from America for opposing its own native brand of communism to the party line laid down in Moscow, thereby remaining somewhat precariously outside the main Russian camp. Lastly, "Point Four" assistance was extended to "underdeveloped" countries in an effort to keep their poverty-stricken masses from turning to communism in their distress. All told, the foreign aid program, from its inception shortly after World War II through June 30, 1959, cost the United States more than $60,000,000,000—with no end then anywhere in sight.

Funds spent in Europe did much to revive national economies and private enterprise, lifting production well above prewar levels in many sections. Similarly the military assistance program, despite some waste, considerably improved the fighting strength of the anti-Communist powers.

Somewhat less conclusive have been the results achieved under "Point Four" help to underdeveloped nations. A prime difficulty with this program has been the tendency for foreign populations to grow rapidly, throwing steadily mounting burdens of support on America and making the maintenance of even relatively poor standards of living tremendously expensive. To illustrate, the United States Department of Agriculture remarked in 1957 that the population of the Far East had outstripped the gain in production, even bolstered by American money, so that the amount of food available per capita was then less than it had been before World War II. To emphasize the seriousness of the situation, students of population problems have estimated that at the rate of increase prevailing in the 1950s, in another six hundred years the average land area per person on this planet would fall to approximately one square yard. It seems scarcely possible that in those six centuries nothing constructive will be done about this startling prospect.

Going beyond trying to win friends with money and technical advice, the United States entered into a whole series of mutual defense pacts with countries threatened by Communist imperialism. Best known of these is the North Atlantic Treaty, ratified during Truman's administration. Effective in 1949, it bound the United States, Great Britain, Canada, France, Belgium, the Netherlands, Luxembourg, Denmark, Iceland, Norway, Portugal, and Italy to arm, and announced that an attack on any member would be considered an attack on all. In 1952, Greece and Turkey were added to the group, and in 1955, after the replacement of the British, French, and American occupation zones in Western Germany by the new Federal Republic of Germany, the latter's armed force also became a segment of the NATO defenses. In 1958, the NATO powers undertook to bring their operations up to date by acquiring missile bases, later equipped to use American-made nuclear weapons, for mass atomic retaliation in case of a Communist attack.

Other mutual defense agreements covered areas extending far to the East of the NATO powers, along the borders of the Communist bloc. In 1957, for instance, the "Eisenhower Doctrine" was implemented by an act of Congress permitting the President of the United States to give military assistance to Middle Eastern countries requesting help against Communist aggressors. In 1955, the United States became bound by a collective defense treaty having its geographic center still farther to the East, and encompassing British and French outposts, Pakistan, Thailand, and the Philippines (independent since 1946). Under this treaty, the United States declared that Communist aggression in a designated area of Southeastern Asia would endanger its peace and safety, but cautiously added that it would take account of developments only "in accordance with constitutional processes," whatever that might mean in practice. North of the Philippines lies Formosa, in the hands of an anti-Communist Chinese government with which the United States also had a mutual defense pact. Still farther north is Japan, restored by treaty in 1952 to the status of an independent nation and likewise bound by a mutual defense agreement with the United States.

There was, of course, an element of grim irony in this mutual defense program. Western Germany and Italy, once disarmed by the United States and supposedly brought to the close of their martial careers, now stood rearmed, partly with American equipment, to strengthen American efforts to hold Communist expansion in check in Europe. Japan also went through the complete cycle. Shortly after her surrender in 1945, American occupation authorities obliged her to insert in her new constitution a clause renouncing war "forever" and agreeing never again to acquire "land, sea, and air forces." Yet a few years later, urged to do it by the United States, Japan was rearmed, partly with American equipment, as a prime non-Communist outpost in the largely Communist-dominated Orient.

The first time the relative strength of the two rival groups was tested in actual combat on a major scale was in Korea beginning in 1950. The timing is significant. It was in 1949 that the Russians announced they had set off an atomic bomb, thus ending American monopoly of the weapon, and President Truman took American support forces out of South Korea. The very next year, Red China signed a mutual defense pact with Russia. Four months later, North Korean Communists, armed with Soviet-made weapons, tried the venture of invading South Korea. The date was June 25, 1950, American time. Two days later, in the absence of the Soviet representative, the United Nations Security Council called on members of the United Nations to back South Korean efforts to resist the aggressors. That very day, without pausing to ask Congress to declare war, Truman ordered American forces to fight alongside the South Koreans.

Engaging in what Truman called a "police action," American and other United Nations troops ultimately drove the North Koreans across the 38th Parallel, their southern border. At this juncture, Red China declared that it could no longer stand idly by, and sent large masses of Chinese "volunteers" into the fray, helped by Russian advisers and equipment. Should the United States strive to end the contest by a direct bombing of the sources of supply for these "volunteers," located in China proper, so the argument ran, China might allege she was being attacked, producing World War III. Faced with this touchy situation, Truman limited the fighting to Korea proper for the remainder of his term of office. General Eisenhower, the next President, had promised in his election campaign to do something about the Korean stalemate. He kept his pledge; he ended it with a truce a few months after his inauguration, in 1953.

Between the end of World War II and the end of Eisenhower's administration in 1961, warfare was revolutionized. As indicated above, both the United States and Russia had already added the atomic bomb to their arsenals before the Korean war began. During that contest, President Truman tried to place America in the lead again, by speeding work on the still more destructive "hydrogen" bomb. Late in 1952, a bomb containing hydrogen ingredients was set off by the United States, and was estimated to have achieved an explosive power some six hundred times greater than that of the bomb dropped on Hiroshima in World War II, making the new weapon theoretically capable of reducing any major city in the world to ruins. The next year this advantage was lost when the Russians successfully tested a similar device.

Once both the United States and the Soviet Union had been equipped with devastating nuclear weapons, the chief emphasis in the race for military advantage shifted to the design and manufacture of means for getting them quickly and accurately to distant targets. Going far beyond jet bomber speed, the United States finally managed, in 1958, to hurl a heavy intercontinental ballistic missile more than six thousand miles, in about half an hour, to splash down in a designated target area. By the close of Eisenhower's administration, in 1961, both the United States and Russia were equipped with enough missiles, ready to fire, to make large-scale nuclear warfare possible. Some of the American missiles were placed in sites buried deep in the ground while others were carried by roving nuclear-powered submarines.

At this stage, what would have happened in the event of a Russian attack on the United States? Theoretically, such a raid would have been detected by a radar screen, already established on the ground, aboard ship and in the air, in cooperation with Canada. However, since it would have taken less than thirty minutes for a missile to go from Moscow, Russia, to New York City, even a perfectly functioning screen would have allowed Americans very little reaction time. While it might have sufficed to launch automatically a retaliatory array of pre-aimed missiles and to radio strategic bombers, in the air, to proceed to designated targets, it would have been of limited value to the general public. Lacking readily accessible fallout shelters to protect them against nuclear attack, and as yet having no sure means of destroying enemy missiles in flight, prospects for ordinary citizens would have been grim. The public realized that much of American civilization could be wiped out in a matter of hours, after which the continent would have been subjected to fallout for generations to come. Warfare had entered new dimensions.

Faced with this situation, Eisenhower warned the Communists that major military moves by them would be met, not with large conventional forces as in the Korean war, but by massive nuclear retaliation. At the same time, he tried to avoid a nuclear holocaust by "waging peace"; that is, by trying to establish more friendly relations with Russia. In this latter attempt, he invited the Soviet Premier, Khrushchev, to visit the United States in 1959 and Eisenhower planned to return the call. Eisenhower warned Congress in 1958 that Communist use of non-military forms of pressure—economic and ideological—could undermine the free nations despite their military strength. Then in 1960 he toured Latin America and the Orient in an effort to counteract these attempts.

As matters stood at the end of the Eisenhower administration, this "waging of peace" had run into difficulties. Eisenhower's handling of the bagging of a high-flying American U-2 reconnaissance plane by Russian weapons well inside Russia, and Khrushchev's angry reaction to the event, blocked further friendly contacts. Meanwhile, the Communists were on the move in many parts of the world—in Laos, South Vietnam, Africa, Latin America, and Cuba—always on too small a scale to call Eisenhower's nuclear deterrent down upon themselves. As he neared the end of his term, Eisenhower did not wish to counter these moves with conventional forces either, and he left these trouble spots for his successor.

☆

In American domestic politics, as in foreign affairs, the collapse of the Axis powers brought far-reaching changes. The surrender of Germany and Japan ended the need for vast quantities of military and other supplies, thereby making it possible to return the United States to a peacetime footing. As the great transition back to more normal living began, early in President Truman's first administration, there were widespread fears that a major depression might be near at hand. It was plain that several million men and tens of thousands of women would have to be quickly released from the armed forces, in response to persistent public demands that they be returned home. In addition, large numbers of workers would have to be laid off as military production lines ground to a halt in plant after plant. Before these dislocated masses could be properly absorbed by civilian enterprises, many factories would have to be converted from putting together implements of war to turning out things for ordinary consumers, a complex and lengthy job.

Seeking broad authority to guide the nation's economy through this disruptive period, President Truman urged Congress to extend his war-created emergency powers to regulate prices, to ration commodities, and to do various other things. Congress, however, was inclined to scrap much of the wartime system of supervision and let economic forces work themselves out in comparative freedom. While the executive and legislative branches were battling over how much public intervention there should be, most of the wartime regulations were abandoned.

Often blocked in his efforts to carry out his program, Truman wanted voters to elect a more co-operative Congress in 1946. Instead, they substituted a Republican for the former Democratic majority in both houses. After nearly two years of struggle with this even more antagonistic group, Truman called it the worst or almost the worst Congress in history.

Despite this background of political confusion, the conversion from a war to a peace footing was accomplished with very little involuntary unemployment. Many ex-service men were temporarily absorbed by government-subsidized educational programs. Large masses of women left wartime posts for the cares of the home, further easing the situation. Meanwhile a big force of workers converted factories to peaceful production and filled openings in enterprises that had been stripped of help during the war, because they had been rated as "non-essential." Moreover, the termination of war-inspired restrictions on the sale of such items as automobiles, tires, and new residences produced a rush of buying that quickly piled up huge backlogs of orders at converted plants.

With workers previously "frozen" on their jobs and held under federal wage ceilings now able to go where they wished and bargain freely, pent-up wartime tensions were suddenly released. As the heavy overtime pay of World War II days was no longer available, many grew restive. Some 180,000 auto makers struck in November 1945. The following January, steel and electrical workers laid down their tools, and in April soft coal miners did likewise. During 1946, over 4,500,000 workers struck, resulting in some 115,000,000 man days of enforced idleness.

This wave of strikes brought on federal intervention. President Truman ordered the National Government to seize the soft coal mines. When the miners struck against the government, they were hailed into court and fined. In 1947, Congress passed the Taft-Hartley Act over Truman's veto, permitting the employment of non-union members in interstate commerce, authorizing employers to sue unions for breaking contracts and causing strike damage, preventing unions from contributing directly to national political campaigns, and requiring union leaders to swear that they were not Communists. It was amidst such uproars and alarms that reconversion was completed.

With the country restored to a peace footing, the draft that had carried it through World War II was allowed to expire, on March 31, 1947, but the lapse was brief. In the face of mounting tensions abroad, the draft was revived the following year for what proved to be a long period of time. Further strengthening America's military position, Congress in 1947 placed all the armed forces in a National Military Establishment, under a civilian secretary. Launched by its sponsors with high hopes that it would achieve major gains in efficiency, economy, and morale, the program soon ran into stormy seas. Interservice rivalries, arguments over the relative effectiveness of ships and planes, over the comparative merits of mass armies and airborne atomic weapons, and over other matters, interfered seriously with efforts to achieve full integration.

Intimately associated with the work of its successor the Department of Defense were the labors of a slightly older body, the Atomic Energy Commission, created in 1946. To safeguard information of military value, this agency was vested with authority over the entire field of atomic energy in the United States. Under its auspices work was begun which eventually provided America with by far the most deadly weapons of offense and defense in its history, and produced such impressive peaceful applications of atomic energy as the large-scale generation of electricity.

Accompanying the foregoing efforts to strengthen America's military might went a drive to overhaul federal civilian agencies, likewise in the interests of national security. Disturbed by reports of Communist infiltration of key places in his administration, Truman issued an executive order in 1947 requiring all federal agencies to submit lists of their employees to the Federal Bureau of Investigation (FBI) for study. Persons suspected of disloyal or "subversive" activities or associations were then brought before loyalty boards for questioning, and some were fired. To carry out this delicate assignment with fairness to all, amidst a welter of facts, claims, and fancies, would have been difficult even in quieter surroundings. In practice, the environment was anything but calm. While the number of employees challenged and removed under the program constituted a very small percentage of the entire federal payroll, the spectacular investigation of charges, and angry speeches in Congress received large and lurid attention in the press, arousing widespread public interest. Some wanted more rascals thrown out; others claimed American concepts of civil liberties were being crudely violated. Few, if any, seemed satisfied.

Even Truman's efforts to project into the postwar era the New Deal trends of the days of Franklin D. Roosevelt did not go over as smoothly as he had hoped. In his first term, Congress defeated one of his low-cost public housing schemes, balked at raising the minimum wage scale, and reduced rather than increased social security coverage at one point.

Congress also fought with him over civil rights. Truman's appointment of the President's Committee on Civil Rights got the controversy under way. In due course, the Committee made strong and sweeping recommendations which Truman urged Congress to accept. He asked for federal anti-lynching legislation, the creation of a Commission to prevent job discriminations, the establishment of a Civil Rights Division in the Department of Justice, and suffrage for residents of the District of Columbia, home of many Negroes. In these suggestions for the continental United States he was substantially defeated.

On the other hand, departing from the "imperialist" doctrines of the old school of American expansionists, the Federal Government granted important new rights to the outlying possessions in Truman's first administration. On July 4, 1946, the Philippines became a free and independent nation. The following year, Truman signed an act authorizing the Puerto Ricans to elect their own governor, as a step toward becoming a "free commonwealth" associated with the United States.

By the time the Democratic National Convention met in 1948, Truman had experienced numerous reverses, and was soon to have another. When the Convention nominated him for president, many members of his party broke camp. Southern groups opposed to his liberal stand on civil rights aimed at improving the lot of Negroes, joined forces to nominate J. Strom Thurmond for the presidency as a States Rights Democrat. Radical elements rallied to the banner of Henry A. Wallace, running on the Progressive ticket and advocating friendlier relations with the Soviet Union. Impressed by this dissension and the supposed strength of his Republican rival, Thomas E. Dewey, experienced poll takers predicted Truman's outright defeat.

Undaunted by these voices of doom, Truman began a hard-hitting campaign by train, carrying his story to the people. Traveling some thirty thousand miles to attack Republicans frequently and vehemently, at "whistle stops" and in big cities, he outwitted the experts. Though he won, the splintering of the Democratic party left him with less than half the total popular vote, making him the first minority President since 1912.

As president for a second term, Truman continued to press for the same general type of program he had backed in his initial term, a group of ideas now collectively known as the "Fair Deal." He urged Congress to repeal the Taft-Hartley Act which had placed major restrictions on labor unions; to expand social security; to provide more federal aid for housing; to enact his civil rights recommendations; and to establish national health insurance. Though blocked by Congress in some of this, such as his drive for national health insurance and repeal of the Taft-Hartley Act, he did win such victories as enlargement of the social security system.

Then came an abrupt change in the direction of events; in 1950, as previously described (p. 455), President Truman ordered American troops to Korea to hold back the Communists, and promptly declared the existence of a state of national emergency. The old problems of wartime hoarding and wage and price increases now returned to plague the country. By acts passed in 1950 and 1951, Congress gave the President authority to fix wages and prices. These controls were dramatized when steel companies turned down a federal mediation award in March 1952 boosting wages for steel workers, since they could not raise steel prices. The steel workers struck. Truman seized the mills. Their managements charged the President had exceeded his constitutional powers. On June 2, 1952, the United States Supreme Court agreed, and ordered the mills returned to their owners.

In an effort to meet the heavy costs of the Korean war, of foreign aid, of farm relief, and of other expensive programs, the National Government took in more money during Truman's two terms than it had collected under all the previous Presidents combined. Part of the time, this sufficed to balance the budget; part of the time, it did not. When his second term ended and the figures were all in, it was seen that the national debt was only slightly below the all-time peak hit during World War II. Such vast sums, naturally, proved to be tempting and under Truman part of the money was carelessly handled, to say the least.

Charges were made in the press that funds had been squandered in buying supplies, that political influence had won unjustified loans and contracts for favored parties, and tax concessions for the "right" people. Newspaper attacks on the President's plans for dealing with graft, discontent over the stalemate in Korea, and public alarm over rumors of Communist infiltration in Washington, were whittling away at his popularity and that of his party, by the time it held its national convention in 1952.

After losing five presidential elections in dreary succession, the Republicans sought to capitalize on these developments by departing from their recent custom and nominating a soldier, Dwight D. Eisenhower, for the presidency in 1952. As the successful commander of the invasion troops who brought World War II to an end in Western Europe, he had achieved national fame. By previously shunning politics, he had the added advantage of not having raised a troublesome crop of long-standing political enemies to haunt him on Election Day. In the third place, many voters hoped his military skill would enable him to terminate the costly fighting in Korea and deal effectively with other Communist challenges.

Against Eisenhower, the Democrats ran Governor Adlai E. Stevenson of Illinois. In an uphill effort to publicize their much less well known candidate, the Democrats had trouble. When Truman stepped in to rescue them, his own record became an added campaign issue. In the ensuing election, the Democrats lost by a wide margin.

During the gap between this Democratic failure and his own inauguration, Eisenhower fulfilled a campaign pledge by making a tour of inspection of the Korean theatre of war. In the interval between election and inauguration, too, Eisenhower talked with Truman and accepted his generous invitation to have incoming Republican administrators visit federal agencies for a preview of their new duties. Following these highly unusual preliminaries, the Republicans staged a triumphant celebration in Washington, D.C., when on January 20, 1953, for the first time in over two decades, they inaugurated a President.

Eisenhower's first major achievement was to terminate the fighting in Korea, after protracted negotiations, with cease-fire orders taking effect on July 27, 1953. Soon afterward, he brought home large masses of American troops. He warned the Communists, however, against viewing this departure as a sign of weakness by pointing out that Americans had "means" of coping with further trouble. The language was widely interpreted as a veiled threat to use atomic and other advanced weapons, rather than sheer manpower, in case of need.

Turning to domestic problems, Eisenhower advocated a program bearing considerable resemblance to the New Deal ideas of his Democratic predecessors. Thus he won from Congress an extension of social security to cover several million more people, and supported federal aid for farmers. Eisenhower, too, inherited the civil rights issue that had interested Franklin D. Roosevelt and Truman. Soon it burst into open flame; the United States Supreme Court held in 1954 that the segregation of whites and Negroes in public schools was unconstitutional. Shortly afterward, the Court ordered gradual integration. This aroused stiff opposition from many whites, particularly in the South, producing dissension throughout the remainder of Eisenhower's first term.

On the other hand, Eisenhower displayed a friendliness toward big business that differentiated his administration from that of his predecessor. Eisenhower placed outstanding business leaders in his cabinet. He ended Federal ceilings on wages and prices, and let rent controls expire. To encourage business, he also let excess profits taxes go quietly, and he favored the sale of certain federally owned factories to private concerns. In this friendly climate, the gross national product continued the growth begun under Truman.

Though his so-called "middle of the road" methods won for Eisenhower personal popularity, he did not seem to have enough zest for politics to be able to transmit his strength to the rest of his party. Despite his support, the Republicans lost control of Congress to the Democrats in 1954. The elections of 1956 revealed the same difference in general appeal. Eisenhower unanimously received the Republican nomination for President in 1956 and, aided near Election Day by the Suez Canal crisis which placed a premium on military competence, defeated Adlai Stevenson, the Democratic candidate, for the second time. Yet in 1956, the Republicans were still left in a minority in both houses of Congress and lost more ground in 1958.

As a Republican thus facing a Democratic Congress throughout his second term, Eisenhower's lot was not altogether a happy one. Where he adhered to such New Deal staples as promoting social security, bolstering foreign aid and farm relief, and favoring public works construction, especially highways, he achieved considerable success. When, however, he talked of economy and balanced budgets, he got relatively little help. To such a pass had matters come, by June 30, 1959, that the national debt was at an all-time peak.

Turning to matters of civil rights, Congress and the President brought an end to the historically inferior position of the natives of Alaska and Hawaii by admitting both areas to statehood in 1959, thus giving their inhabitants greater voice in government and stronger constitutional guarantees of liberty. On the other hand, the racial issue on the mainland could not be so easily resolved, as tempers flared. In Arkansas, despite a United States Supreme Court order requiring the bringing of Negroes and whites together in the public schools, Governor Faubus used the local National Guard to keep them apart. When a federal court order terminated this maneuver, but still integration was delayed, Eisenhower sent federal troops to the area to protect Negroes ready to go to the same school with whites. With less show of force, integration proceeded in other schools. The inquiries into Negro voting made by a federal commission and the direct action of Negro groups in staging lunch-counter "sit-ins" were also aimed at racial barriers.

Prevented from running again by the Twenty-second Amendment to the Constitution, which limits presidents to two elected terms, Eisenhower was automatically out of the picture as the country prepared for the 1960 elections. Under the circumstances, the Republicans nominated his Vice-President, Richard M. Nixon, as their candidate. Against him the Democrats ran John F. Kennedy, eldest son in a very wealthy and ambitious Irish Catholic family, who had served first as a Representative and then as a Senator from Massachusetts in Congress. As the two rivals seemed closely matched, Eisenhower stepped in near election day to help Nixon. After a campaign in which television played a major, if not a decisive, role for the first time, it was discovered that Kennedy had won, but by the narrowest margin in over seventy years— a mere two-fifths of one per cent of the popular vote.

In the economic field, the United States had been experiencing some remarkable changes. Through a costly foreign aid program, overseas markets for American goods were stimulated right after the close of World War II. Then the Korean contest touched off another spurt in demand. Also of substantial help to industry, was the increase in the population from about 130 million in 1940 to over 170 million in 1960, and the appearance of a host of new products, from television sets to power lawn mowers. Expanding at a fast clip, American industry raised its output by more than fifty per cent between the end of World War II and 1960. This rise was markedly greater than the rate of population growth and insured a substantial improvement in general standards of living.

Paralleling the gains in factory output were changes in farming. Increased mechanization and use of more fertilizer, better seed, and less labor enabled farmers to achieve advances in their productivity per acre and per man-hour. Although cultivating the smallest acreage in forty years, and using fewer workers than in the past, American farmers in

1958 managed to exceed the previous all-time high in the output of major crops by eleven per cent.

Indeed, so efficient had industry and agriculture become that in the decade that ended in 1958 the number of people employed in physical production declined some nine per cent even though the total population grew in the meantime. This made possible a marked expansion in the service occupations, from teaching to appliance repair, until by 1960 several million more people were employed in services than in production.

As an increasingly wealthy, technologically advanced, and diversified nation, with a margin of energy, resources, and funds to spare, America was finally able, during Eisenhower's administration, to undertake the mastery of outer space. Government technicians, in point of time only slightly behind the Russians, managed to put the first American earth satellite, Explorer I, into orbit on January 31, 1958. It was soon followed by an array of other American satellites that proceeded to perform a variety of useful functions, from maintaining surveillance over Russia and Red China to aiding weather forecasting and radio communication. Then in 1959, in one searing cloud of smoke and flame America launched an unmanned probe that swept past the moon to enter an eternal orbit around the sun as the nation's first artificial planet. By thus penetrating the heavens, it ended for all time American isolation from the surrounding universe, with ultimate consequences, secular and religious, about which we can only guess.

Between the close of World War II and the end of Eisenhower's administration, tremendous changes had occurred. Probably the most important of these had been the loss by the United States of its original monopoly of nuclear weapons. Later, calmed by the thought that in Eisenhower they had an experienced and respected general as President, Americans managed to survive with some equanimity the development of the intercontinental ballistic missile with its threat of virtually instant and wholesale destruction. Still later, Americans took in their stride the penetration of the universe by an unmanned American probe. Fortunately for them, they also enjoyed a few years of peace and prosperity, following the close of the Korean war, which made it easier for them to adjust to their strange new situation, and under the relatively calm leadership of Eisenhower they had gained needed strength for meeting the troublesome days that lay ahead.

Chapter 30

THE BURDENS OF POWER

ON January 20, 1961, Dwight D. Eisenhower, at 70 the oldest man ever to serve as President of the United States, passed the responsibilities of his office over to John F. Kennedy who, at 43, was the youngest man ever elected to that high post. Indeed Kennedy was, on that day, the only person born within this century to head any major nation. His election was interpreted the world over as the coming to power of a new generation.

Much as if the United States had no pressing domestic problems, the new President devoted the entire inaugural address to foreign affairs. His stand was bold. Readily, almost eagerly, shouldering the obligations of leadership that had fallen on his country, as the foremost economic and military power of the free world, he would let every nation know "that we shall pay any price, bear any burden, meet any hardship, support any friend, oppose any foe, to assure the survival and success of liberty."

Having thus committed himself to sweeping action, he had to determine what roles should be played by the two types of military forces he commanded in carrying out his policies. While he realized that nuclear weaponry might effectively deter Communists from making a direct attack on the United States, and probably from invading Western Europe, he considered it unsuitable for blocking minor Communist intrusions. Yet, when he took office, such stealthy moves were already under way in Southeast Asia and in obscure areas of Africa and Latin America. If these moves were to be stopped, Kennedy believed, the task would have to be performed by "conventional" forces prepared to fight small engagements without nuclear weapons.

These notions were first tested in Cuba, the closest of the trouble spots, at its nearest point only some ninety miles off the Florida coast. Cuba's government had been taken over by a Communist-dominated group led by Fidel Castro. Native Cuban and American property had been seized and thousands of Cuban refugees had fled to America; moreover, the island was rapidly becoming a center for Communist infiltration into other parts of Latin America.

Having at his disposal, as a legacy from the Eisenhower administration, a small band of Cuban refugees equipped with conventional arms and trained under the auspices of the United States Government, Kennedy decided to use this band as a tool to overturn Castro, expecting that the liberators would be aided by their oppressed countrymen. Under plans approved by Kennedy, this force of some 1500 men stormed ashore on April 17, 1961, at the Bay of Pigs in southern Cuba. Running out of ammunition, lacking proper air support that only the United States could have provided, and without assistance from the islanders, the invaders met disaster. As they died or were captured on the beachhead, Kennedy held aloof, unwilling to send American forces into battle. In the end the survivors were freed from Castro's jails and returned to the United States in exchange for commodities financed by private parties at Kennedy's urgent request. With ransom delivered to a minor power almost in its backyard, one of the most humiliating episodes in America's history closed.

While enduring a barrage of criticism for the fiasco, Kennedy turned to another of his problem areas in an effort to rebuild his own "image" and his country's prestige. Going to Europe for conferences with heads of state, he met Premier Khrushchev of the Soviet Union in Vienna, Austria, in June of 1961. There Khrushchev bluntly told him that Russia intended to make a separate peace treaty with Communist East Germany before the year was out. By terminating World War II, the Premier said, this treaty would end all temporary Allied privileges in East Germany, including the right of access to West Berlin, then occupied by American, British, and French troops. He added that Russia would uphold the new arrangement, even if it meant war.

Resolved not to be "bluffed" by this threat, Kennedy returned to Washington to prepare the United States for a firm stand in West Berlin, now described by him as "the great testing place of Western courage and will." As a visible evidence of his determination, the American contingent in Berlin was augmented and the over-all size of American conventional forces was increased. Meanwhile, the Communists erected the notorious "Berlin Wall," cutting off nearly all communication with the eastern portion of the city. Surrounded by Communist territory and troops, American soldiers, with the heartfelt support of West Berliners, endured a virtual state of siege, but there was no war. There was also no separate peace for East Germany.

As the Berlin stalemate between the two chief powers continued, the Russians were getting ready to mount a spectacular nuclear display.

Abruptly ending the informal Russian-American moratorium on the atmospheric testing of such devices, the Soviet Union staged an explosion in the sky on September 1, 1961. By the time their series of experiments was ended, the Russians had fired off a weapon equivalent in destructive power to fifty million or more tons of TNT, setting by a wide margin the world's record for sheer size in proven nuclear bombs. It later became known that they had also tested advanced methods of defense against American missiles. As a rain of radioactive fallout swept across the globe, a chorus of protests rose from many nations. Nevertheless, to keep abreast of Russian technology, American scientific advisers agreed that the United States should conduct similar tests in the atmosphere, even though this evoked a second round of denunciation.

While attention was being focused on the strange "siege" of Berlin and the awesome displays of might, the Soviet Union was secretly preparing a fresh shock for the world. It was rushing to complete intermediate- and medium-range ballistic missile bases in Communist Cuba. Before long these showed up on photographs taken by American reconnaissance planes. The most powerful of these bases, it was found, could be made ready to fire nuclear warheads far enough to devastate virtually any city in the United States, some in Canada, and many in Latin America.

Roused to action by these revelations, in October, 1962, Kennedy used radio and television to let the public know what had happened and describe his countermeasures. Armed forces were moved into Florida and a ring of American naval vessels and aircraft was formed around Cuba, to prevent the further delivery of Russian offensive military equipment to that island. He also openly told Russia that if any missile were fired from Cuba in an assault on any part of the Western Hemisphere, he would consider it a direct attack on the United States itself, which would evoke full retaliation on Russia.

Shortly afterward, anxious citizens were relieved to learn that missile-carrying ships bound from Russia to Cuba were turning around at sea and heading home. There was no armed resistance to ship-board inspections of cargo.

Out of this tense confrontation emerged a working American-Russian compromise. The Soviet Union agreed to dismantle bases, and to remove missiles and long-range bombing planes from Cuba, and in return, the United States withdrew its patrols from Cuban waters. In addition, some American missile sites in Turkey and Italy, fairly close to Russian borders, were given up. While these developments left a Communist regime in control of Cuba, and permission was refused to make on-the-spot inspections of the abandoned bases, Kennedy's firmness went far to restore public confidence.

By the middle of the following year, the excitement over nuclear threats had begun to die down. In this setting the United States, Great Britain, and the Soviet Union, as the foremost atomic powers, agreed to a treaty banning further testing of nuclear devices in outer space, in the atmosphere or under water. It went into effect on October 10, 1963. About the same time, a "hot line" was installed between Washington and Moscow, permitting high Russian and American officials to communicate instantly in any fresh emergency. The Russians and Americans even exchanged ideas on disarmament, but without noteworthy progress.

Screened by these major developments, a struggle had been building up in another part of the globe, beyond the Pacific in a region where the United States had never before been very deeply involved. In Southeastern Asia, operating out of bases in China and North Vietnam, Communists had been putting pressure on Laos. To offset this move, Kennedy landed a conventional force of American troops in adjoining Thailand in 1962 and sent it north to the Laotian border. Then in October of that year, amid the Cuban missile crisis, Communist China pushed into India. The United States and Russia proffered military aid to India, helping to halt the invasion. Nor was this all: Communist guerrillas, called the Viet Cong, acting for the Nationalist Liberation Front, and supplied from North Vietnam and its capital at Hanoi, had begun a strong push to overrun South Vietnam about the time Kennedy was inaugurated. As a countermove, the number of American military advisers already in South Vietnam was increased; finally, they were authorized to accompany their students into battle and fire if fired upon. Soon the list of American casualties lengthened.

American involvement in Vietnam was more than military. To encourage the people in their stubborn resistance to the terrorism of the Viet Cong, it was decided to give economic aid in many forms; it was also hoped that a democratic government would be evolved in Saigon that would contrast favorably with the totalitarian regime in Hanoi. However, progress in this respect was slow, owing in part to Viet Cong terrorism and in part to internal dissension among the South Vietnamese.

Nearby, in Indonesia and the Malay Peninsula, impoverished masses of mixed faiths and races seemed to offer breeding grounds for revolution. Should South Vietnam fall to the Communists, it was argued, these and other regions, perhaps even the great subcontinent of India, would feel the repercussions. Meanwhile, far away in Africa, Communists took a hand in local politics. In the newly emerging nation of the Congo, civil strife even led to intervention by United Nations forces, largely underwritten by the United States. Near home, American warships cruised close to the Dominican Republic; there, with diplomatic help, conditions favorable to the holding of free elections were assured.

Hand in hand with moves of military and economic assistance went the attempts of the Kennedy administration to give a personal and idealistic touch to its contacts with other lands by creating the Peace Corps. This agency recruited volunteers, mainly from among the young, and sent them to carry American skills, especially in agriculture and education, to selected regions that had asked for American assistance. Living simply and speaking local languages where feasible, the Corps workers were to offer concrete proof of American sympathy and "know-how."

Other visible efforts to strengthen alliances and encourage friends of liberty to stand their ground were made by members of the administration in travels abroad, and in the lavish welcome given in Washington to European statesmen, rulers of Asiatic lands such as Iran and Afghanistan, and leaders of newly formed African nations. Favored guests were offered a sampling of American arts and feted with a special kind of elegance that had not previously marked official White House hospitality. Moreover, government funds helped to send American dance groups and musicians to foreign capitals, where the Soviet Union was displaying its violinists and ballerinas. Thus Americans of many sorts were being encouraged to take part in an ideological and cultural confrontation between West and East.

A variety of international organizations were at the same time called upon by the United States to co-operate in resisting Communist intrigues and in strengthening freedom through social and economic progress. In Latin America, the Organization of American States as a comprehensive regional alliance was encouraged to take more concerted action as Communist rebels sought to undermine existing governments by guerrilla warfare or engineered "coups." American assistance was channeled to Latin American countries for social and economic purposes through the Alliance for Progress. However, the high birth rate and widespread illiteracy, as well as the oligarchic structure in some countries, made advance difficult.

While poverty was producing trouble in Latin America, the rise of nationalism brought dissensions in prosperous Europe. America had hoped to draw the peoples of the continent together for military defense against Russia in the North Atlantic Treaty Organization (NATO). While the United States, under Kennedy, offered to provide atomic weapons for NATO warships, to be manned by multi-national crews, it insisted on controlling their firing. Only Great Britain as yet had an independent nuclear defense system, and other countries, led by France, now protested the Anglo-American monopoly, weakening NATO by their rivalries.

Largest of all the organizations through which the general aims of peace and progress were pursued, was the United Nations. Suffering from growing unwieldiness, as many new countries were admitted to membership, this world assembly began to offer as many problems as support to its chief financial backer, the United States: 900 million Asians and Africans had been released from colonialism since World War II and were still being shaped into independent nations. And, as Kennedy came to admit, "We are only six per cent of the world's population," and hence "cannot impose our will upon the other ninety-four per cent of mankind."

The reluctance or inability of other nations to shoulder more of the burdens of armament and of economic assistance to hard-pressed nations, began to produce severe international monetary dislocations. The flow of funds out of the United States to finance such programs, as well as to pay for imports, to cover the expenses of tourists abroad and, above all, to meet the mounting costs of American investment and enterprise over the globe, was becoming a matter for concern. No longer sufficiently offset by foreign payments for American exports, the government made up for part of the difference by shipping gold abroad from its dwindling supply. Trying to correct this situation, and also to stimulate a transatlantic partnership between the United States and the members of the European Common Market, Kennedy won from Congress in 1962 the Trade Expansion Act, then launched the "Kennedy Round" of tariff negotiations. Concessions were offered to countries willing to lower bars in return, but the response was slow.

Thus in the brief period allotted to Kennedy, the "thousand days" of his power, the American people found themselves increasingly enmeshed in foreign affairs. Americans had not sought world leadership through a spirit of nationalism or thirst for conquest. They had no reason, as might poorer and smaller nations, to want more territory; abundant riches lay at home. Instead, they had been drawn into their new position through a multitude of supposedly small commitments now grown large and interlaced. Historically, the United States had rarely been compelled, as great European powers had been, to accept the "primacy of foreign policy" over domestic issues; now it entered a new era. For years to come, like the troubled peoples of older societies, Americans would be asked to forego much of the satisfaction of making progress at home to build up and maintain alliances abroad, as a matter of continuing principle.

With much of his time and energy absorbed by problems abroad, in the management of which Congress allowed him a relatively free hand, Kennedy soon found himself restricted in the amount of attention he could devote to the domestic scene. To deal with the latter, he gathered around him the youngest group of cabinet officers in many years, among them his own brother, Robert F. Kennedy, the Attorney General.

Carrying on the "brain trust" idea of President Roosevelt, and the staff organization of Eisenhower, he drew other men and women, often young and largely from academic backgrounds, to Washington, forming them into "task forces" to work on special problems. It was by now, more than ever, recognized that a solitary individual in the White House could no longer shoulder his heavy burdens without such staffs, so greatly had the responsibilities of the office grown. In reference to Kennedy's campaign promise to "move America forward" to new frontiers, the aides about him were frequently called collectively the "New Frontiersmen." Frequently their operations cut across and upset traditional departmental arrangements.

As they turned to legislative matters, they recognized at the outset the inherent weakness in their position. Elected by a razor-thin majority, the President could not count on ready support in Congress, where he was still remembered as a recent junior Senator by its seasoned committee chairmen. Moreover, the liberal program of the New Frontier was offered to a Congress dominated by an ever stronger conservative coalition of Southern Democrats and Republicans.

Under the circumstances, success was limited. A number of measures, such as an increase in the minimum wage, were approved, but several key proposals met defeat. Among the latter were a comprehensive plan for health insurance for the aged, a major bill for federal aid to education, and a scheme for setting up a cabinet position in charge of urban affairs. Even the significant civil rights bill was still languishing in Congress at the time of Kennedy's death.

Outside the field of legislative activity, in the area of administration over which he had greater control, his influence had more impact, particularly with respect to civil rights. The first member of the Catholic minority ever to be elected to the presidency, and the son of a Bostonian Irish family, he gave fresh hope to other minorities. The most outspoken of these was the new generation of Negroes whose discontent was already erupting in a wave of sit-ins, stand-ins and other demonstrations in stores, bus depots, on the streets and elsewhere in the South. Most impressive of all was the huge, orderly crowd of over 200,000 Negroes and white sympathizers who took part in the Freedom

March in Washington, in August 1963, to the steps of the Lincoln Memorial.

With the assistance of his brother, the Attorney General, Kennedy provided substantial aid to Negroes. They were helped to register to vote in the South, when blocked in this effort by local authorities. The administration also used its power to get interstate transportation facilities, bus, rail, and air, desegregated in the South. Less dramatic was the continuing progress made in integrating the military forces at home and abroad. Job opportunities were widened in the federal service and Negroes filled relatively important posts such as that of Housing Administrator and Ambassador to Norway. Private industry, especially that portion having contracts with the government, was nudged to find new positions for Negroes. Most striking was the use of federal troops to enforce a court order, late in 1962, successfully getting a Negro registered, despite mob violence, in the previously all-white University of Mississippi.

On the economic front, a business recession was combatted by the government's increasing the amount of federal funds put into the economy; later, economic experts strove to hold inflationary forces in check. Pointing to the growth in productivity per man-hour made possible by modern technology, Kennedy argued that it was sufficient to support both gradual wage increases for workers and rising corporate profits, with little or no advance in prices. Accordingly, "guidelines" were laid down for what the administration in Washington declared to be reasonable wage boosts, and pressure was exerted on management and labor to follow them.

After union wage increases in the steel industry had been held down, through the mediation of the Secretary of Labor, Arthur J. Goldberg, who had once been counsel for the steelworkers, the United States Steel Corporation suddenly announced a sizable hike in the price of its principal steels in April, 1962. Kennedy at once attacked it for disregard of the public interest, had government contracts shifted to competitors, and talked of antitrust action. The increase was soon rescinded, but the business community remained alarmed by the quite upsetting direct intervention of the President. A sharp though short drop in the stock market ensued. Hard as Kennedy tried to recover business support, distrust lingered, even though he later signed an act providing for the settlement of a protracted railway labor dispute by compulsory arbitration, the first such legislation in peacetime in the nation's history.

Perhaps the clearest success of the administration in "moving America forward" came in outer space, where the chief obstacles were scientific rather than political. The array of unmanned satellites, which had begun to orbit the earth in the Eisenhower years, was expanded and improved. Thus on July 10, 1962, Telstar, a communications satellite, was orbited and soon relayed the first live transatlantic exchanges of television programs between America and Europe. Later, the small unmanned probe, Mariner II, left the domain of the earth satellites far behind and after a trip of 109 days to the vicinity of Venus, radioed back to earth, across more than 36 million miles of space, the first close up observations of another planet in history.

Meanwhile, Russia and the United States were racing to put human beings into outer space. A Russian orbited the earth in a capsule on April 12, 1961; on February 20, 1962, an American duplicated the feat. To Kennedy, this was merely the beginning of manned exploration of the universe. He obtained funds from Congress to land an American on the moon "before this decade is over," and soon had mammoth preparations under way.

Late in 1963, Kennedy turned his attention to a very earth-bound matter, the formulation of plans to win a second term in the 1964 elections. It was partly with this contest in mind that he flew to Texas late in November, to try to bring greater harmony into that state's Democratic party organization.

Riding through the streets of Dallas in an open car, on November 22, 1963, waving to the throngs on the sidelines, John F. Kennedy was struck by rifle fire from a mentally deranged assassin. Rushed to a hospital, he was soon pronounced dead, the fourth American president to be so felled while in office. As word of his passing spread like wildfire across the nation and the globe, multitudes were stunned by the news.

Great crowds gathered in Washington, where his body was brought at once, filing past his coffin through the day and night. At his funeral, the world paid tribute to a man who had aroused so many hopes abroad, as the heads or other representatives of more than ninety countries, scattered over six continents, gathered in the nation's capital for the last rites.

Riding only a short distance behind Kennedy through the streets of Dallas when the fatal shots rang out, Vice-President Johnson was almost at once aware of the tragedy. Within hours, boarding the presidential plane, which also carried the body of the late leader, Johnson took the oath of office. Flown to an airport near Washington, D.C., he was whisked by helicopter to the White House lawn. Before the day had ended, he had taken firm command in the nation's capital. This swift transfer of power, while much of the country was still in a state of numbed horror, prevented any group at home or abroad from taking advantage of the crisis, had they been so minded.

Very soon, the new President called upon Congress to complete Kennedy's stalled legislative program, thus paying tribute to the slain chief. This co-operation was forthcoming under the guidance of Johnson, a mature and seasoned veteran of congressional battles, who had been Majority Leader in the Senate until 1960. At a rapid pace, he put through measure after measure that Kennedy had been unable to win; most significant was the broad civil-rights law, giving substantial protection to Negroes, which Johnson, himself a Southerner, considered vital, and promising women greater job equality with men.

The display of managerial skill, as well as party loyalty, won for Johnson an unopposed Democratic nomination for another term in the White House. He could also dictate the choice of his running mate, Senator Hubert H. Humphrey, Jr., of Minnesota. An easy victory was won over the Republican candidate, another man of the Southwest, the archconservative Senator Barry M. Goldwater of Arizona. Voters returned Johnson to the White House by a majority of sixty-one per cent, the largest in many years.

During the campaign and then, after the triumph at the polls, in his State of the Union address on January 4, 1965, Johnson devoted himself as wholeheartedly to domestic affairs as Kennedy had stressed foreign problems. At the time, with America "in the midst of the greatest upward surge of economic well-being in the history of any nation," and with the struggle in South Vietnam still apparently a relatively localized conflict, the country could perhaps afford to tackle the over-multiplying problems of its own citizens, long so sorely neglected. A new group of presidential advisers formulated sweeping programs that exceeded the proposals of Kennedy's frontiersmen, and Johnson went before the people to demand a "great consensus" in support of reform.

The "Great Society," as the concept evolved, must concentrate on air and water purification, traffic management and safety, and the suppression of organized crime and sporadic delinquency, and to make war on poverty, ignorance, and disease. Such a society must not be satisfied too easily, on a plateau of affluence, but must climb toward a "summit where freedom from wants of the body can help fulfill the needs of the spirit." Encouraging the arts as well as the skills of modern technology, "the Great Society asks not how much but how good; not only how to create wealth but how to use it; not only how fast we are going, but where we are headed."

Both Kennedy and Johnson initially made unprecedented demands upon the country. But whereas the former appealed to youth to sacrifice in the defense of liberty on foreign shores, Johnson challenged it to remodel the whole environment of the continent. In this, he went beyond any previous proposals; his audacious program surpassed to all appearances the more remedial measures of the "New Deal" or "New Frontier."

This consensus was not immediately forthcoming. The public was not yet thoroughly aroused, as it was soon to be, by growing problems such as smog above and rioting within urban centers. Many, indeed, ridiculed the utopian nature of Johnson's speeches. Others feared the invasion of the Federal Government into every sphere of life, the laying of the hand of bureaucracy on local governments and private enterprise, on teachers and artists, perhaps spying on the innermost details of individual life. The plans were offered months before the problems were widely recognized.

Still, in 1965, Congress was persuaded to enact what seemed to be the great bulk of Johnson's proposals, in one of the most productive sessions in legislative history, marking a turning point in American national development. It gave approval to a Department of Housing and Urban Development, and a National Foundation for the Arts and Humanities; the next year a Department of Transportation was created. A Commission on Law Enforcement and the Administration of Justice was appointed to study the rapid growth of crime and advise on improvements in police and court procedures. Congress in 1966 agreed to explore possibilities of conservation, going beyond the creation of a few parks to the preservation of historic sites and landmarks; the Department of Health, Education and Welfare was authorized to set up standards for control of water and air pollution.

Most easily understood, perhaps, was Johnson's call for a broad expansion of federal aid to education, for already the average citizen was aware of the spectacular advances in science, the encroachment of automation, and the need to keep abreast of America's rival, Russia. Aid was readied to enable schools to buy textbooks and build up libraries and laboratories; able students were encouraged by grants. The nation was already impressed and astonished by the immense growth in its youthful population; the birth rate of the United States had so soared that, for a time, it approached that of teeming India. Wide open spaces of the continent began to suffer from congestion, and traffic arteries were clogged with cars as cities became more decentralized. The young, affluent as never before and drawing if need be upon credit cards and installment buying as well, became mass consumers and dictators of taste. Hordes of students crowded into schools and "multiversities" that could not be enlarged fast enough to hold them all. A time seemed to be approaching when over half of the American people would be under twenty-five years of age.

Almost equally, Congress and the general public were aware of the need to succor many of the aged, whose lives were being prolonged by better living conditions and medical science. A sweeping program of health insurance known as "Medicare" was initiated; social-security benefits were extended, bringing a sense of independence and stability to a greater number of aged Americans. Before long a "guaranteed minimum income" was discussed for the deprived of any age.

Another part of the Great Society program that had wide appeal was the "war on poverty" and the "war on disease." Congress voted large funds for research into the main "killer diseases," as well as into the problems of drug addiction and alcoholism. The "anti-poverty" act was intended to begin job retraining and establish youth camps; attack on special areas of under-employment and great need, as in Appalachia, was started with more than a billion dollars granted by Congress. Efforts to protect the average American as consumer and driver were also popular; a variety of bills were proposed to set up new standards of quality, labeling, and pricing for drugs and foods, as well as a program to increase the safety of motor vehicles, in the effort to reduce the terrible annual death toll on highways.

Interests of a widening public turned to problems of a less material nature, such as "beautification" of the vast American landscape, preserving more of the "unspoiled wilderness" in national parks, and rescuing miles of highways from junkyards of crumpled automobiles and other mountains of waste piled up by the world's greatest consumer nation, which disfigured the views. The federal program to encourage the arts soon ran into trouble, however. Though the "culture explosion" was indeed greatly increasing the numbers of theatres, art galleries, museums, and concert halls everywhere, almost all of them in need of help, the altogether novel problems of federal intervention in this field proved difficult to handle.

Very significant in the long-range view, was the agreement of Congress to go along with Johnson on the immigration question. It passed with little protest his bill effective December 1, 1965 phasing out the 41-year-old national origins quota system, thus abolishing discrimination against immigrants from Asia, Africa, and southern Europe. Admissions were now based, not on race and nationality, but on the skills of newcomers; instead of masses of day laborers, such as once poured through Ellis Island, there now came many trained in medicine, science, and technology. Indeed, so successful was the quest for foreign talent that the rest of the world began to complain bitterly against the "brain-drain," the attracting to America of many of the most able young graduates of other nations' schools and universities.

With a readiness that was hardly to be anticipated, the nation accepted the fact that a new "mix" of races and creeds was already here. A Senator of Chinese origin from the new interracial state of Hawaii was welcomed in Congress; a white Republican constituency in Massachusetts elected the Negro, Edward Brooke, to the Senate. As for the American Indians, once characterized as a "vanishing" race, they too were increasing in numbers and receiving more help.

Americans of old strains, stemming from those original pioneers, sodbusters, and pathfinders who opened the wilderness, were becoming more tolerant of minority groups. Their sons, stationed abroad as soldiers or sent away to study, were bringing back brides of Japanese, Korean, European, and Vietnamese origins to villages that had never known such exotic residents. Many thousands of teachers, businessmen, and others were sampling the sights of the "Grand Tour" once restricted to noblemen and millionaires, or going on "safari" to Africa, as jet liners increased their passenger capacity and speed.

If the "provinciality" so evident in prewar years was breaking down, there was a curious reaffirmation of the American past, in the shape of the struggle to preserve remnants of national monuments and sites. The Federal Government was eager to assist those who saw the value of relics of the past, even while it helped to destroy that past. Nostalgia was reflected in the popularity of Colonial and Victorian furniture and other objects. There was even reenactment of a number of battles of the Civil War during its centennial celebrations. Federal funds were given to some projects, helping restore or even reconstruct relics, as Americans gave what was perhaps a last look backward, and tried to retrieve the "atmosphere" of "ghost towns" in the West, the Bohemian artists' quarter of New York's Greenwich Village or the "Vieux Carré" of old New Orleans, Williamsburg, Santa Fe, and San Antonio.

So far, Americans were willing to go along with Johnsonian reforms, altering their social and physical surroundings. However, they were not at once prepared for his urban proposals. As his term of office opened, Americans were too busy following the bulldozers to new housing developments, or putting up industrial parks and modern factories with geodesic domes and illuminated fountains, to consider the implications of the urban decay they had turned away from. In later months, though, drought-stricken cities began to look hard for new sources of clean water, or to suffer under sudden blankets of choking fumes. The new residential subdivisions rocked with sonic booms; and in the "hot summers" of 1964 and after riots broke out in the crowded cores of mid-Western population centers and in the new "megalopolis" seaboard areas, both East and West.

Eventually, opposition to federal intervention diminished to some extent, as the cities and highways created problems beyond the ability of localities to solve. More reluctantly, Americans were prodded along the way to the moon, already pointed out by Eisenhower and Kennedy. There was little enthusiasm among earth-bound constituents for the new tax burdens, but it was realized that space proposals, such as the huge Moonport, now involved hundreds of companies and thousands of employees and could not be dropped without economic dislocations. And as the new color television sets multiplied, millions of viewers began to follow, and suffer with, each new effort of the astronauts from the "blast-off" to the "splash-down." The candid reporting of American anxieties and tragedy, as three gallant young astronauts died in a capsule that had not even left the launching pad, caught up audiences not only here but in foreign lands.

Perhaps only a limited part of the public took seriously the threat of Russian dominance of outer space, and realized that orbiting "space platforms" could be a vital part of the national struggle for survival. The more practical everyday benefits of space study, however, appealed to investors, who poured savings into a private enterprise that, co-operating with the Federal Government and also international networks, succeeded in shooting into space "switchboard satellites" to carry phone calls, television, teletype, military and civilian data on the "rent-a-satellite" system begun by "Early Bird" in 1965.

The already present military threat was somewhat veiled. Yet some understood the race for outer space as, in part, a question of power. As scores of Russian objects were orbited, observing every corner of the American landscape, American defense organizers had no choice but to raise their own "eyes in the sky," watching the weather, mapping the globe, transmitting data to armies, navies, and planes, and noting in minute detail indications of military developments far below. So precious was the harvest of information that, early in 1967, President Johnson could say that the data so obtained were worth, from the standpoint of national defense, every penny—indeed ten times more—than the total cost of the American space effort.

Even as the Great Society began to take shape, it became clear that the problems were mounting faster than the programs that had been intended to correct or forestall them. Perhaps the initial success had been almost too rapid and the country seemed to lack the administrative organization, even more than the funds, to go so far so fast. And that still little understood force, set up by the "founding fathers," the Supreme Court of the United States, was yet to be reckoned with.

The spreading of the great cities to meet and merge in sooty seaboard combinations had been foreseen; but the struggles in the hearts of those cities were more intense than expected, for rural families, white as well as Negro, dispossessed by the spread of harvesting and cotton-picking machinery, took refuge there. As "ghettos" grew, white-collar workers fled to the suburbs, followed in turn by the relocation of many corporations employing them.

Local governments strove to cope with these emergencies, swamped with claims on police, fire forces, water supply, and disposal plants. On top of these came the new federal programs, aiding and yet confounding progress. As Senator Edmund S. Muskie of Maine estimated, by 1966 there were no less than 170 different federal aid programs on the books, financed by some 400 separate appropriations and administered by twenty-one federal departments and agencies aided by 150 Washington bureaus and over 400 regional offices. Over 80,000 units of state and local government, many of them too small to carry such burdens, floundered amid overlapping layers of government, inter-community rivalries, weak and antiquated offices, and ill-trained employees. As Johnson, aware of the morass, called for "creative federalism," it was clear that old patterns of American government and politics were in flux. Cities were co-operating with surrounding suburbs, regardless of state and county boundaries; new bodies were set up that embraced several regions and participated in local and private as well as federal programs. A re-thinking of America's old divisions of village, county, state, and federal boundaries was imminent.

Amid this ferment, the Supreme Court passed down a decision in 1964, which would in effect compel the reapportionment of legislatures according to population, on the principle of "one man, one vote." As many saw, with fear or rejoicing, this would profoundly change the character of government and the quality of rural life, by reducing the power of rural constituencies and enhancing the strength of cities, unless stopped by constitutional amendment or other means.

Historically, rural America had retained a relatively great power over urban America, predicated on the old Jeffersonian ideas of the superior virtues of the "tillers of the soil." But by the beginning of the last third of the twentieth century, nearly seventy per cent of the population lived in urban areas, while dwindling numbers of agricultural workers tilled ever-enlarging farms, producing vastly more food, indeed creating problems of surpluses. Still, though fewer farmers were affected, the decision marked, at least symbolically, a turning point, like the new immigration procedures. Rural as well as racial qualities were to be forgotten in the race for skills called for by onrushing technology.

Adroit as he was in persuasion of legislators, Johnson had not had to cope with the Supreme Court so far; soon, however, he was challenged, like Franklin D. Roosevelt, by that body. Portentous decisions came from this highest bench in the land, which seemed to threaten the Executive and Legislative branches of government with a relative shrinking of their powers, at the hands of an increasingly bold juridical branch.

As Johnson proposed to reduce crime, the Supreme Court made revolutionary decisions upholding the rights of the accused who made "confessions" without "safeguards" in police rooms and court trials. This came just at the point where police forces were involved in a struggle against violence such as had never been known before, even in the age of frontier posses and "lynch law." On a huge scale, crime syndicates had been organized; the spread of juvenile delinquency was fostered by the easy access to many kinds of drugs among ever wider circles of society. It became increasingly awkward to deal with all this while preserving the due rights of the accused and high standards of liberty and justice. Law enforcers found their ability to stop and search restricted, and they were limited in the use of the subtle "snooping" and "bugging" devices that were the newest marvels of the electronics industry.

The Supreme Court supported those who sought to divorce Church from State still more completely, going so far as to bar prayer from public schools. It refused to uphold the government's contention that the Communist Party must register as an arm of a foreign power or to prevent Americans of suspected Communist affiliations from traveling abroad, even to Communist lands. Going further, it challenged the rights of state legislatures to set up standards for their own members. In other words, it set itself up as another, a powerful third element in the political picture.

Managing to avoid too close an identification with any one segment of the political scene, Johnson remained the seeker of "consensus." Though a self-made man raised under harsh conditions, he did not champion any special "deprived" group against the managerial levels of business and science; investing his wealth in ranch lands in his native Texas, he yet would not lead the embattled farmers against the megalopolitan cities. Avoiding too astringent words, he sought to reconcile the many sectors struggling for ascendancy or equal rights, while riots, strikes and demonstrations continued to emphasize the mobile nature of our advancing technological society.

Efforts of the government to rescue small business and preserve a certain sphere for individual spontaneous enterprise through anti-trust action now had a novel effect; unable to expand in their original fields, one large corporation after another acquired companies in other lines. A coal mining company entered the underwear business and a cigarette firm made cat food. Thus corporations were attaining, somewhat against their will, diversity and complexity never beheld before. Spreading over Europe and Asia as well by "daughter" affiliations, they were nourished by funds from many sources. They eagerly welcomed the savings of labor unions, as well as investments through mutual funds by all sorts of Americans of average means as well as rich. The ownership and direction of corporate enterprise became enormously diverse. By 1967, twenty million Americans held shares in publicly owned corporations, more than three times as many as had been shareholders only fifteen years earlier.

With the consent of the government, labor itself was combining into mammoth units, the largest of which, the AFL-CIO, was a multimillion member force with great financial strength. Able to plan negotiations on an industrywide basis, to jeopardize national defense as well as paralyze communications, unions were asking not only for wage raises but benefits and insurance against automation. But labor was not without its troubles; new highly skilled groups in the automated industries were reluctant to join with teamsters and coal miners.

The onrush of progress in the most advanced society in the world created immediate dislocations and perplexities in American life. And President Johnson, coming from the Texas prairies with his hopes for a great agreement, was met by a vast regrouping and reforming of elements and complexes for work and play. Teams of scientists for research and doctors for medical practice were formed. Though old rigid "class" lines withered, new "establishments" of "status" rose, as men of talent or fortune reassembled. The new "ecumenical" spirit brought together Americans of many faiths and races to work on social problems, even at times sharing religious buildings. Some old political habits and beliefs were shaken. The liberal movement was splintered. The formerly dependable political solidarity of South and North was weakened. Even "minority" groups began to feel inner discord, once outer acceptance was won; Catholics argued over many legal issues; Negroes disputed over aims, and it seemed unlikely that they would soon again be so monumentally united as they had been on their great Freedom March.

The old America of elm-shaded small towns and sun-baked farms was astir; even some of the deserts, provided with new water sources, became heavily populated. The imagery of Grandma Moses, a favorite painter of the Eisenhower era, yielded to the restless shapes and colors of "Pop" and "Op" art, or electronic sculpture. Old town meetings in New England were becoming obsolete, but so were the boundaries of great cities. The pace of American life could no longer be restrained. Could it indeed be planned? With hope, at least, in his State of the Union message in 1966, the President stated that this nation can "pursue goals abroad while still building a great society here at home." But the goals abroad were many.

☆

The program for social improvements at home was from the outset hampered by commitments abroad made in earlier administrations. Outstanding among these were the promises the United States had made to aid the South Vietnamese in their struggle to maintain independence against the aggressive and terrorist activities of Viet Cong guerrillas supplied from Communist North Vietnam.

A Southeast Asian people of about sixteen millions, half of a country divided like Germany and Korea, South Vietnam thus came to absorb a climbing share of American energies and funds. Had the United States refused to honor its pledges there, it was argued, its allies everywhere might doubt its vaunted will to defend freedom. On the other hand, too strong a display of power might ultimately involve war with China and Russia; it might even bring on what a physicist has called "the unthinkable although possible war" of atomic annihilation. The United States did not wish to provoke such a clash, nor did it seek "unconditional surrender." Under Johnson, it took cautious steps; yet, as months went by, the involvement, the costs, and the casualties mounted.

At first, Johnson merely continued Kennedy's policy of letting American military advisers accompany native troops into sporadic combat, authorized to shoot when fired upon; then, after an American military base was hit by the Viet Cong in February, 1965, a retaliatory air raid was staged on North Vietnam, the source of supply for the invaders. Soon air raids on the North became routine, aimed at a gradually widening range of carefully selected targets. On March 6, 1965, combat troops landed to defend American bases and, before long, they went into the jungles in big drives planned and run by American commanders.

As the scope of operations grew, so did the succor given to the North by China, Russia, and other Communist lands. On September 2, 1965, Red China called for a worldwide revolution on Vietnamese lines, urging guerrillas to arise in Africa, Asia, and Latin America, establishing bases of Communism in rural areas that would someday encircle and strangle "urban centers"; a cordon would be formed around the United States and Europe. Force was lent to this challenge by China's first explosion of nuclear devices. Chinese appeared in North Vietnam to repair damage done by American raids and China supplied arms and ammunition; Russia sent oil, planes, munitions, and antiaircraft batteries, while occasionally Cubans manned these batteries.

As both sides to the conflict "escalated" their efforts, the United States built at Cam Ranh Bay in South Vietnam, a harbor to handle supplies that became at once one of the greatest in that part of the world. New types of helicopters and other weapons were developed to deal with the strange warfare, against a foe encamped often underground, or in swamps and forests. From a mere 23,000 men in February, 1965, American forces rose to about 200,000 by the end of the year. That number had doubled by March, 1967. The strain of increased draft calls reached far into American homes.

Other peoples were drawn into the vortex. Laos became involved; so did Cambodia, when the Communists proceeded to operate from its cover. American planes took off from bases in Thailand. From Australia, New Zealand, South Korea, and the Philippines came combat troops to fight side by side with American forces. With world attention focused on the conflict, truces of various lengths were declared, during which the United States would wait for "peace feelers," while neutral negotiators tried to arrange conferences. As the undeclared "war" was turned on and off, much division and criticism appeared in the West.

It was at least possible for Americans to agree on efforts to aid the distressed people of South Vietnam, especially the innocent victims of military operations and Viet Cong terrorism. Medical and agricultural teams went afield, at great risk, to improve village life. A constitution was written, despite the local differences and religious quarrels between Catholics and Buddhists. By 1967, free popular elections were widely held in liberated areas, though the victors ran serious risks of being shot or kidnaped by the Viet Cong.

Flying to the Orient in 1966, Johnson told the people of Thailand that "we are Pacific neighbors with common interests, with a common destiny . . . We are committed to the proposition that no nation shall dominate another nation in the Pacific." As the spokesman for what was now a "Pacific power," Johnson ate with American troops in South Vietnam, visited six other nations in the area and met at Manila late in 1966 to confer with other regional leaders.

Meanwhile, he tried to convince Americans that he was not neglecting their hemisphere. After violence erupted in the Panama Canal Zone in 1964, efforts were made to negotiate a new Canal treaty with Panama. The next year, Johnson rushed more than 35,000 troops to the Dominican Republic, when a coup, said to involve Communists, threatened to overturn its civilian government. Later, the Organization of American States intervened, and sent troops from several Latin American countries. Then in 1967, Johnson attended a parley of leaders in South America. It called for the creation of a Latin American Common Market patterned after one previously established for Central America.

If Johnson appeared for a time to turn his back on Europe, in his absorption with other areas, American businessmen did not: billions of dollars were poured into the continent by giant corporations making use of the most advanced research and technology. In turn, European businesses were forced to band together to raise capital and set up larger laboratories to meet American competition. Europeans, too, had learned to work together through the multinational European Common Market. Finally, in 1967, the members of this prosperous market joined with the United States and many other nations in reaching a broad provisional agreement for sweeping tariff reductions, affecting the bulk of all foreign trade.

At the same time, a regrowth of the spirit of nationalism in Europe, stimulated by France against desperate resistance from other nations, was undermining American hopes of drawing Western Europe together, under NATO, in a common plan for defense for maximum security. In the end, De Gaulle, the French leader, insisted on the withdrawal of all American and NATO forces from French soil. Honoring his demand, American troops were pulled out of France in 1967 and in the same year NATO headquarters were shifted from France to Belgium.

While the Atlantic alliance was being thus weakened, the Communist "bloc" against which it had been primarily aimed, was also being eroded. European Communist parties were rent with schisms, as national self-interest cut across old party lines from Bucharest and Belgrade to Warsaw and Prague. Even China and Russia, in a serious doctrinal dissent, exchanged bitter words and became rivals for the sympathies of Eastern Europeans.

Taking the world as a whole, the United States was by 1967 linked by defensive ties to forty-two countries scattered around the globe. With such bodies as NATO, SEATO, and CENTO, and members of the Rio and ANZUS pacts, as well as by numerous bilateral agreements, a most intricate system of relationships had been formed. (See Appendix, p. 545.) In support of these pledges, Americans were under arms on four continents.

Meanwhile, attempts were made to reduce tensions with the Communist world. America joined the Soviet Union in a treaty banning the use of nuclear weapons in outer space and urged further agreements to check the spread of such weapons among lesser powers and to avert the "antimissile" race. An air-liner link was projected between Moscow and New York and, in 1967, Congress authorized an exchange of consular officials between the two lands. This approach proved of value during the Arab–Israeli hostilities in June 1967, when America and Russia found themselves in opposing camps, but the "hot line" remained open between the two capitals. Later a personal encounter was arranged between Premier Kosygin and President Johnson at an informal "summit" meeting at Glassboro, in New Jersey, for a calm discussion of their positions.

We need international efforts, said Dean Rusk in 1967, urging more participation upon all peoples, to control populations, even "to cure our air" and "keep it clean." Through more general agreements, a "co-operative assault on the treasure chest of the seas" and operations in outer space could be mounted. Above all, collaboration alone could provide the "reliable safeguards" to prevent the diversion of nuclear fuel and equipment to military use, as more nations enter the "atomic club." Thus the American diplomat expressed recognition of the fact that the foreign policies of nations were increasingly at the mercy of technologies that were also in a state of flux. The trend of the world's affairs was being set not only in the chancelleries but in the laboratories.

As America entered the last third of the twentieth century, and the year 2000 loomed on the horizon, it became clear that the burdens of power would long continue to weigh upon the United States. Though the national production increased, so did the costs and complexities of leadership. To forecast these developments began to seem a prime task of government.

Armies have long planned for "the next war"; now, toward the middle of the twentieth century, governments began to see that peace demands "preparedness" as well. Government, business, scientific, and educational institutions learned to pool endeavors to study the future. Looking as far ahead as projections could be made, they sought to anticipate problems and discover ways of dealing with them before they became crises. In terms of money and effort involved, the United States was outpacing any other country in this field, except possibly Russia.

Some "futurologists" (as they were coming to be known) were employed by government agencies; among these was the National Aeronautics and Space Administration concerned with explorations in outer space. The Air Force conducted studies of its own and contributed some millions to the Rand Corporation, set up primarily to deal with predictions. Ordinary business organizations supported many probings of the future, such as those made by the General Electric Company's special TEMPO unit. Funds were flowing from foundations, private enterprise, and the government to many groups such as the Commission on the Year 2000, the Hudson Institute, and Resources for the Future.

By channeling some two-thirds of the millions spent in 1966 on research and development in the country, the national government assumed leadership in molding the shape of things to come. Thereby it determined where emphasis was to be placed; for example, a priority was given to coping with the expected population burst at home and abroad, through the dissemination, under federal auspices, of information on the latest birth control drugs and devices. Meanwhile, laboratories have been experimenting with making cheap, high-protein foods from marine products and even petroleum. Reports that the population of the United States might, if current trends continued, reach 438 million by the year 2010, accelerated such programs.

Turning to the environment in which future generations of Americans will live, the President's Science Advisory Committee stated in 1966 that by the year 2000, unless fuel consumption habits are altered, the carbon dioxide content of the atmosphere will have risen high enough to produce marked changes in the climate, lending new importance to the struggle against air pollution. In anticipation of another crisis, a water shortage, research continued on processes to remove salt from sea water at lower cost, thus supplying "fresh" water to seaboard cities and perhaps aiding agriculture.

Beyond the land mass of the United States lies hydrospace, the great body of water that covers some seventy per cent of the surface of the globe. Here, America and the Soviet Union are already engaged in highly competitive exploratory ventures. Of particular importance to the United States is its adjacent "continental shelf," a region of relatively shallow water comparable in size to the Louisiana Purchase. By ratifying an international convention in 1964, the United States extended sovereignty over this watery realm and is now encouraging its development. Drilling rigs, operating from platforms on the ocean's surface, are now tapping deposits of oil and gas. Later, it is expected, research will make it possible for forces of "frogmen" to use submerged bunkhouses on the ocean floor as bases for performing tasks, such as raising vegetation and aquatic animals in undersea "ranches," or mining valuable ores.

It is also foreseen that great progress will take place in the exploration of outer space. The National Aeronautics and Space Administration has already sought funds for the study of "advanced manned missions," going far beyond the proposed landing on the moon, to send Americans near Venus and to land on Mars. Later, experienced scientists have suggested, space vehicles may reach the nearer stars, far beyond the solar system.

Thus this story of America, which began with the theme of exploration, may well end on the same note. But whereas Columbus took two months in 1493 to sail from American waters to Spain with his report on the New World, the American probe, Mariner IV, radioed back a photograph of the surface of Mars in nine hours, over a span of more than 130 million miles. Yet if those who dare to dream the boldest dreams are right, and human adventurers some day leave our troubled planet, with its teeming multitudes, nuclear perils, and national rivalries, to seek a new life on some distant star, there will be one requirement technological progress will not have eliminated. Off in a frail craft on a lonely voyage among dangers as yet hardly imagined, man will still need the same quality of courage that upheld Columbus.

Appendix

SELECTED DOCUMENTS FROM
AMERICAN HISTORY

1. THE ROYAL CHARTER FOR THE VIRGINIA
CORPORATION (1606)

I. JAMES, by the Grace of God, King of *England, Scotland, France,* and *Ireland,* Defender of the Faith, &C . . . do . . . for Us, our Heirs, and Successors, GRANT and agree, that the said Sir *Thomas Gates,* Sir *George Somers, Richard Hackluit,* and *Edward-Maria Wingfield,* Adventurers of and for our City of *London,* and all such others, as are, or shall be, joined unto them of that Colony, shall be called the *first Colony;* And they shall and may begin their said first Plantation and Habitation, at any place upon the said Coast of *Virginia* or *America,* where they shall think fit and convenient, between the said four and thirty and one and forty Degrees of the said Latitude; And that they shall have all the Lands, Woods, Soil, Grounds, Havens, Ports, Rivers, Mines, Minerals, Marshes, Waters, Fishings, Commodities, and Hereditaments, whatsoever. . . . And shall and may inhabit and remain there; and shall and may also build and fortify within the same, for their better Safeguard and Defence. . . .

And we do also ordain . . . that each of the said Colonies shall have a Council, which shall govern and order all Matters and Causes, which shall arise, grow, or happen, to or within the same several Colonies, according to such Laws, Ordinances, and Instructions, as shall be, in that behalf, given and signed with Our Hand or Sign Manual, and pass under the Privy Seal of our Realm of *England;* Each of which Councils shall consist of thirteen Persons, to be ordained, made, and removed, from time to time, according as shall be directed and comprised in the same instructions; And shall have a several Seal, for all Matters that shall pass or concern the same several Councils. . . .

And that also there shall be a Council established here in *England,* which shall, in like Manner, consist of thirteen Persons, to be, for that Purpose, appointed by Us . . . , which shall be called our *Council of Virginia;* And

shall, from time to time, have the superior Managing and Direction, only of
and for all Matters, that shall or may concern the Government, as well as of
the said several Colonies. . . .

And moreover, we do Grant . . . that the said several Councils, of and
for the said several Colonies, shall and lawfully may . . . give and take
Order, to dig, mine, and search for all Manner of Mines of Gold, Silver, and
Copper, as well within any part of their said several Colonies, as for the
said main Lands on the Backside of the same Colonies . . . the fifth Part
only of all the same Gold and Silver, and the fifteenth part of all the same
Copper, . . . without any other Manner of Profit or Account, to be given
or yielded to Us. . . .

And that they shall, or lawfully may, establish and cause to be made a
Coin, to pass current there between the People of those several Colonies, for
the more Ease of Traffick and Bargaining between and amongst them and
the Natives there. . . .

And we do likewise . . . give full Power and Authority to the said Sir
Thomas Gates [and others] . . . and to the said several Companies, Plantations, and Colonies, that they . . . shall have, take, and lead . . . towards
the said several Plantations and Colonies . . . such and so many of our Subjects, as shall willingly accompany them . . . ; with sufficient Shipping, and
Furniture of Armour, Weapons, Ordinance, Powder, Victual, and all other
things, necessary for the said Plantations. . . . PROVIDED always, that
none of the said Persons be such, as shall hereafter be specially restrained
by Us. . . .

ALSO we do . . . DECLARE . . . that all and every the Persons, being
our Subjects, which shall dwell and inhabit within every or any of the said
several Colonies and Plantations, and every of their children, which shall
happen to be born within any . . . of the said several Colonies and Plantations, shall HAVE and enjoy all Liberties, Franchises, and Immunities,
within any of our other Dominions, to all Intents and Purposes, as if they
had been abiding and born, within this our Realm of *England*, or any other
of our said Dominions. . . .

2. THE "MAYFLOWER" COMPACT INTRODUCES SELF-GOVERNMENT TO AMERICA (1620)

In the name of God, Amen. We whose names are underwriten, the loyall
subjects of our dread soveraigne Lord, King James, by the grace of God,
of Great Britaine, Franc, & Ireland king, defender of the faith, &c., haveing
undertaken, for the glorie of God, and advancemente of the Christian faith,
and honour of our king & countrie, a voyage to plant the first colonie in the
Northerne parts of Virginia, doe by these presents solemnly & mutualy in
the presence of God, and one of another, covenant & combine our selves
togeather into a civill body politick, for our better ordering & preservation
& furtherance of the ends aforesaid; and by vertue hearof to enacte, con-

stitute, and frame such just & equall lawes, ordinances, acts, constitutions, & offices, from time to time, as shall be thought most meete & convenient for the generall good of the Colonie, unto which we promise all due submission and obedience. In witnes wherof we have hereunder subscribed our names at Cap-Codd the 11. of November, in the year of the raigne of our soveraigne lord, King James, of England, France, & Ireland the eighteenth, and of Scotland the fiftie fourth. Anno: Dom. 1620.

3. DECLARATION OF INDEPENDENCE

In Congress, July 4, 1776,

THE UNANIMOUS DECLARATION OF THE THIRTEEN UNITED STATES OF AMERICA,

When in the Course of human events, it becomes necessary for one people to dissolve the political bands which have connected them with another, and to assume among the Powers of the earth, the separate and equal station to which the Laws of Nature and of Nature's God entitle them, a decent respect to the opinions of mankind requires that they should declare the causes which impel them to the separation.

We hold these truths to be self-evident, that all men are created equal, that they are endowed by their Creator with certain unalienable Rights, that among these are Life, Liberty and the pursuit of Happiness. That to secure these rights, Governments are instituted among Men, deriving their just powers from the consent of the governed, That whenever any Form of Government becomes destructive of these ends, it is the Right of the People to alter or to abolish it, and to institute new Government, laying its foundation on such principles and organizing its powers in such form, as to them shall seem most likely to effect their Safety and Happiness. Prudence, indeed, will dictate that Governments long established should not be changed for light and transient causes; and accordingly all experience hath shown, that mankind are more disposed to suffer, while evils are sufferable, than to right themselves by abolishing the forms to which they are accustomed. But when a long train of abuses and usurpations, pursuing invariably the same Object evinces a design to reduce them under absolute Despotism, it is their right, it is their duty, to throw off such Government, and to provide new Guards for their future security.—Such has been the patient sufferance of these Colonies; and such is now the necessity which constrains them to alter their former Systems of Government. The history of the present King of Great Britain is a history of repeated injuries and usurpations, all having in direct object the establishment of an absolute Tyranny over these States. To prove this, let Facts be submitted to a candid world.

He has refused his Assent to Laws, the most wholesome and necessary for the public good.

He has forbidden his Governors to pass Laws of immediate and pressing importance, unless suspended in their operation till his Assent should be obtained; and when so suspended, he has utterly neglected to attend to them.

He has refused to pass other Laws for the accommodation of large districts of people, unless those people would relinquish the right of Representation in the Legislature, a right inestimable to them and formidable to tyrants only.

He has called together legislative bodies at places unusual, uncomfortable, and distant from the depository of their Public Records, for the sole purpose of fatiguing them into compliance with his measures.

He has dissolved Representative Houses repeatedly, for opposing with manly firmness his invasions on the rights of the people.

He has refused for a long time, after such dissolutions, to cause others to be elected; whereby the Legislative Powers, incapable of Annihilation, have returned to the People at large for their exercise; the State remaining in the mean time exposed to all the dangers of invasion from without, and convulsions within.

He has endeavoured to prevent the population of these States; for that purpose obstructing the Laws for Naturalization of Foreigners; refusing to pass others to encourage their migration hither, and raising the conditions of new Appropriations of Lands.

He has obstructed the Administration of Justice, by refusing his Assent to Laws for establishing Judiciary Powers.

He has made Judges dependent on his Will alone, for the tenure of their offices, and the amount and payment of their salaries.

He had erected a multitude of New Offices, and sent hither swarms of Officers to harass our People, and eat out their substance.

He has kept among us, in times of peace, Standing Armies without the Consent of our legislature.

He has affected to render the Military independent of and superior to the Civil Power.

He has combined with others to subject us to a jurisdiction foreign to our constitution, and unacknowledged by our laws; giving his Assent to their acts of pretended legislation:

For quartering large bodies of armed troops among us:

For protecting them, by a mock Trial, from Punishment for any Murders which they should commit on the Inhabitants of these States:

For cutting off our Trade with all parts of the world:

For imposing taxes on us without our Consent:

For depriving us in many cases, of the benefits of Trial by Jury:

For transporting us beyond Seas to be tried for pretended offences:

For abolishing the free System of English Laws in a neighbouring Province, establishing therein an Arbitrary government, and enlarging its Boundaries so as to render it at once an example and fit instrument for introducing the same absolute rule into these Colonies:

For taking away our Charters, abolishing our most valuable Laws, and altering fundamentally the Forms of our Governments:

For suspending our own Legislature, and declaring themselves invested with Power to legislate for us in all cases whatsoever.

He has abdicated Government here, by declaring us out of his Protection and waging War against us.

He has plundered our seas, ravaged our Coasts, burnt our towns, and destroyed the lives of our people.

He is at this time transporting large armies of foreign mercenaries to compleat the works of death, desolation and tyranny, already begun with circumstances of Cruelty & perfidy scarcely paralleled in the most barbarous ages, and totally unworthy the Head of a civilized nation.

He has constrained our fellow Citizens taken Captive on the high Seas to bear Arms against their Country, to become the executioners of their friends and Brethren, or to fall themselves by their Hands.

He has excited domestic insurrections amongst us, and has endeavoured to bring on the inhabitants of our frontiers, the merciless Indian Savages, whose known rule of warfare, is an undistinguished destruction of all ages, sexes and conditions.

In every stage of these Oppressions We have Petitioned for Redress in the most humble terms: Our repeated Petitions have been answered only by repeated injury. A Prince, whose character is thus marked by every act which may define a Tyrant, is unfit to be the ruler of a free People.

Nor have We been wanting in attention to our British brethren. We have warned them from time to time of attempts by their legislature to extend an unwarrantable jurisdiction over us. We have reminded them of the circumstances of our emigration and settlement here. We have appealed to their native justice and magnanimity, and we have conjured them by the ties of our common kindred to disavow these usurpations, which, would inevitably interrupt our connections and correspondence. They too have been deaf to the voice of justice and of consanguinity. We must, therefore, acquiesce in the necessity, which denounces our Separation, and hold them, as we hold the rest of mankind, Enemies in War, in Peace Friends.

We, therefore, the Representatives of the united States of America, in General Congress, Assembled, appealing to the Supreme Judge of the world for the rectitude of our intentions, do, in the Name, and by Authority of the good People of these Colonies, solemnly publish and declare, That these United Colonies are, and of Right ought to be Free and Independent States; that they are Absolved from all Allegiance to the British Crown, and that all political connection between them and the State of Great Britain, is and ought to be totally dissolved; and that as Free and Independent States, they have full Power to levy War, conclude Peace, contract Alliances, establish Commerce, and to do all other Acts and Things which Independent States may of right do. And for the support of this Declaration, with a firm reliance on the Protection of Divine Providence, we mutually pledge to each other our Lives, our Fortunes and our sacred Honor.

SIGNERS OF THE DECLARATION OF INDEPENDENCE

Arranged by states, not in the order in which they appeared in the original copy of the document.

NEW HAMPSHIRE

Josiah Bartlett
Wm. Whipple
Matthew Thornton

MASSACHUSETTS

John Hancock
Saml. Adams
John Adams
Robt. Treat Paine
Elbridge Gerry

RHODE ISLAND

Step. Hopkins
William Ellery
Fras. Hopkinson
John Hart
Abra. Clark

PENNSYLVANIA

Robt. Morris
Benjamin Rush
Benja. Franklin
John Morton
Geo. Clymer
Jas. Smith
Geo. Taylor
James Wilson
Geo. Ross

DELAWARE

Cæsar Rodney
Geo. Read
Tho. M'Kean

MARYLAND

Samuel Chase
Wm. Paca
Thos. Stone
Charles Carroll of Carrollton

CONNECTICUT

Roger Sherman
Sam'el Huntington
Wm. Williams
Oliver Wolcott

NEW YORK

Wm. Floyd
Phil. Livingston
Frans. Lewis
Lewis Morris

NEW JERSEY

Richd. Stockton
Jno. Witherspoon

VIRGINIA

George Wythe
Richard Henry Lee
Th. Jefferson
Benja. Harrison
Thos. Nelson, jr.
Francis Lightfoot Lee
Carter Braxton

NORTH CAROLINA

Wm. Hooper
Joseph Hewes
John Penn

SOUTH CAROLINA

Edward Rutledge
Thos. Heyward, Junr.
Thomas Lynch, Junr.
Arthur Middleton

GEORGIA

Button Gwinnett
Lyman Hall
Geo. Walton

4. CONSTITUTION OF THE UNITED STATES

PREAMBLE

We, the People of the United States, in Order to form a more perfect Union, establish Justice, insure domestic Tranquility, provide for the common defence, promote the general Welfare, and secure the Blessings of Liberty to ourselves and our Posterity, do ordain and establish this Constitution for the United States of America.

ARTICLE I

Section 1. All legislative Powers herein granted shall be vested in a Congress of the United States, which shall consist of a Senate and House of Representatives.

Section 2. The House of Representatives shall be composed of Members chosen every second Year by the People of the several States, and the Electors in each State shall have the Qualifications requisite for Electors of the most numerous Branch of the State Legislature.

No Person shall be a Representative who shall not have attained to the Age of twenty-five Years, and been seven Years a Citizen of the United States, and who shall not, when elected, be an Inhabitant of that State in which he shall be chosen.

Representatives and direct Taxes shall be apportioned among the several States which may be included within this Union, according to their respective Numbers, which shall be determined by adding to the whole Number of free Persons, including those bound to Service for a Term of Years, and excluding Indians not taxed, three-fifths of all other Persons. The actual Enumeration shall be made within three Years after the first Meeting of the Congress of the United States, and within every subsequent Term of ten Years, in such Manner as they shall by Law direct. The Number of Representatives shall not exceed one for every thirty Thousand, but each State shall have at Least one Representative; and until such enumeration shall be made, the State of New Hampshire shall be entitled to choose three, Massachusetts eight, Rhode-Island and Providence Plantations one, Connecticut five, New-York six, New Jersey four, Pennsylvania eight, Delaware one, Maryland six, Virginia ten, North Carolina five, South Carolina five, and Georgia three.

When vacancies happen in the Representation from any State, the Executive Authority thereof shall issue Writs of Election to fill such Vacancies.

The House of Representatives shall choose their Speaker and other Officers; and shall have the sole Power of Impeachment.

Section 3. The Senate of the United States shall be composed of two Senators from each State, chosen by the Legislature thereof, for six Years; and each Senator shall have one Vote.

Immediately after they shall be assembled in Consequence of the first Election, they shall be divided as equally as may be into three Classes. The

Seats of the Senators of the first Class shall be vacated at the Expiration of the second Year, of the second Class at the Expiration of the fourth Year, and of the third Class at the Expiration of the sixth Year, so that one-third may be chosen every second Year; and if Vacancies happen by Resignation, or otherwise, during the Recess of the Legislature of any State, the Executive thereof may make temporary Appointment until the next Meeting of the Legislature, which shall then fill such Vacancies.

No Person shall be a Senator who shall not have attained to the Age of thirty Years, and been nine Years a Citizen of the United States, and who shall not, when elected, be an Inhabitant of that State for which he shall be chosen.

The Vice-President of the United States shall be President of the Senate, but shall have no Vote, unless they be equally divided.

The Senate shall choose their other Officers, and also a President pro tempore, in the Absence of the Vice-President, or when he shall exercise the Office of President of the United States.

The Senate shall have the sole Power to try all Impeachments. When sitting for that Purpose, they shall be on Oath or Affirmation. When the President of the United States is tried, the Chief Justice shall preside: And no Person shall be convicted without the Concurrence of two-thirds of the Members present.

Judgment in Cases of Impeachment shall not extend further than to removal from Office, and disqualification to hold and enjoy any Office of honor, Trust or Profit under the United States: but the Party convicted shall nevertheless be liable and subject to Indictment, Trial, Judgment and Punishment, according to Law.

Section 4. The Times, Places and Manner of holding Elections for Senators and Representatives, shall be prescribed in each State by the Legislature thereof; but the Congress may at any time by Law make or alter such Regulations, except as to the Places of choosing Senators.

The Congress shall assemble at least once in every Year, and such Meeting shall be on the first Monday in December, unless they shall by Law appoint a different Day.

Section 5. Each House shall be the Judge of the Elections, Returns and Qualifications of its own Members, and a Majority of each shall constitute a Quorum to do Business; but a smaller Number may adjourn from day to day, and may be authorized to compel the Attendance of absent Members, in such Manner, and under such Penalties as each House may provide.

Each House may determine the Rules of its Proceedings, punish its Members for disorderly Behaviour, and, with the Concurrence of two-thirds, expel a Member.

Each House shall keep a Journal of its Proceedings, and from time to time publish the same, excepting such Parts as may in their Judgment require Secrecy; and the Yeas and Nays of the Members of either House on any question shall, at the Desire of one-fifth of those Present, be entered on the Journal.

Neither House, during the Session of Congress, shall, without the Consent of the other, adjourn for more than three days, nor to any other Place than that in which the two Houses shall be sitting.

Section 6. The Senators and Representatives shall receive a Compensation for their Services, to be ascertained by Law, and paid out of the Treasury of the United States. They shall in all Cases, except Treason, Felony and Breach of the Peace, be privileged from Arrest during their Attendance at the Session of their respective Houses, and in going to and returning from the same; and for any Speech or Debate in either House, they shall not be questioned in any other Place.

No Senator or Representative shall, during the Time for which he was elected, be appointed to any civil Office under the Authority of the United States, which shall have been created, or the Emoluments whereof shall have been increased during such time; and no Person holding any Office under the United States, shall be a Member of either House during his Continuance in Office.

Section 7. All Bills for raising Revenue shall originate in the House of Representatives; but the Senate may propose or concur with Amendments as on other Bills.

Every Bill which shall have passed the House of Representatives and the Senate shall, before it becomes a Law, be presented to the President of the United States; If he approve, he shall sign it, but if not, he shall return it, with his Objections, to that House in which it shall have originated, who shall enter the Objections at large on their Journal, and proceed to reconsider it. If after such Reconsideration two-thirds of the House shall agree to pass the Bill, it shall be sent, together with the Objections, to the other House, by which it shall likewise be reconsidered, and if approved by two-thirds of that House, it shall become a Law. But in all such Cases the Votes of both Houses shall be determined by Yeas and Nays, and the Names of the Persons voting for and against the Bill shall be entered on the Journal of each House respectively. If any Bill shall not be returned by the President within ten Days (Sundays excepted) after it shall have been presented to him, the Same shall be a Law, in like Manner as if he had signed it, unless the Congress by their Adjournment prevent its Return, in which Case it shall not be a Law.

Every Order, Resolution, or Vote to which the Concurrence of the Senate and House of Representatives may be necessary (except on a question of Adjournment) shall be presented to the President of the United States; and before the Same shall take Effect, shall be approved by him, or being disapproved by him, shall be repassed by two-thirds of the Senate and House of Representatives, according to the Rules and Limitations prescribed in the Case of a Bill.

Section 8. The Congress shall have Power: to lay and collect Taxes, Duties, Imposts and Excises, to pay the Debts and provide for the common Defence and general Welfare of the United States; but all Duties, Imposts and Excises shall be uniform throughout the United States;

To borrow Money on the credit of the United States;

To regulate Commerce with foreign Nations, and among the several States, and with the Indian Tribes;

To establish an uniform Rule of Naturalization, and uniform Laws on the subject of Bankruptcies throughout the United States;

To coin Money, regulate the Value thereof, and of foreign Coin, and fix the Standard of Weights and Measures;

To provide for the Punishment of counterfeiting the Securities and current Coin of the United States;

To establish Post Offices and post Roads;

To promote the Progress of Science and useful Arts, by securing for limited Times to Authors and Inventors the exclusive Right to their respective Writings and Discoveries;

To constitute Tribunals inferior to the supreme Court;

To define and punish Piracies and Felonies committed on the high Seas, and Offences against the Law of Nations;

To declare War, grant Letters of Marque and Reprisal, and make Rules concerning captures on Land and Water;

To raise and support Armies, but no Appropriation of Money to that Use shall be for a longer Term than two Years;

To provide and maintain a Navy;

To make Rules for the Government and Regulation of the land and naval Forces;

To provide for calling forth the Militia to execute the Laws of the Union, suppress Insurrections and repel Invasions;

To provide for organizing, arming, and disciplining the Militia, and for governing such Part of them as may be employed in the Service of the United States, reserving to the States respectively, the Appointment of the Officers, and the Authority of training the Militia according to the discipline prescribed by Congress;

To exercise exclusive Legislation in all Cases whatsoever, over such District (not exceeding ten Miles square) as may, by Cession of particular States, and the Acceptance of Congress, become the Seat of Government of the United States, and to exercise like Authority over all Places purchased by the Consent of the Legislature of the State in which the Same shall be, for the Erection of Forts, Magazines, Arsenals, dock-Yards, and other needful Buildings;—And

To make all Laws which shall be necessary and proper for carrying into Execution the foregoing Powers, and all other Powers vested by this Constitution in the Government of the United States, or in any Department or Officer thereof.

Section 9. The Migration or Importation of such Persons as any of the States now existing shall think proper to admit, shall not be prohibited by the Congress prior to the Year one thousand eight hundred and eight, but a Tax or duty may be imposed on such Importation, not exceeding ten dollars for each Person.

The Privilege of the Writ of Habeas Corpus shall not be suspended, unless when in Cases of Rebellion or Invasion the public Safety may require it.

No Bill of Attainder or ex post facto Law shall be passed.

No Capitation, or other direct, Tax shall be laid, unless in Proportion to the Census or Enumeration herein before directed to be taken.

No Tax or Duty shall be laid on Articles exported from any State.

No Preference shall be given by any Regulation of Commerce or Revenue to the Ports of one State over those of another: nor shall Vessels bound to, or from, one State, be obliged to enter, clear, or pay Duties in another.

No Money shall be drawn from the Treasury, but in Consequence of Appropriations made by Law; and a regular Statement and Account of the Receipts and Expenditures of all public Money shall be published from time to time.

No Title of Nobility shall be granted by the United States; And no Person holding any Office of Profit or Trust under them, shall, without the Consent of the Congress, accept of any present, Emolument, Office, or Title, of any kind whatever, from any King, Prince, or foreign State.

Section 10. No State shall enter into any Treaty, Alliance, or Confederation; grant Letters of Marque and Reprisal; coin Money; emit Bills of Credit; make any Thing but gold and silver Coin a Tender in Payment of Debts; pass any Bill of Attainder, ex post facto Law, or Law impairing the Obligation of Contracts, or grant any Title of Nobility.

No State shall, without the Consent of the Congress, lay any Imposts or Duties on Imports or Exports, except what may be absolutely necessary for executing it's inspection Laws: and the net Produce of all Duties and Imposts, laid by any State on Imports or Exports, shall be for the Use of the Treasury of the United States; and all such Laws shall be subject to the Revision and Control of the Congress.

No State shall, without the Consent of Congress, lay any Duty of Tonnage, keep Troops, or Ships of War in time of Peace, enter into any Agreement or Compact with another State, or with a foreign Power, or engage in War, unless actually invaded, or in such imminent Danger as will not admit of delay.

ARTICLE II

Section 1. The executive Power shall be vested in a President of the United States of America. He shall hold his Office during the Term of four Years, and, together with the Vice-President, chosen for the same Term, be elected, as follows:

Each State shall appoint, in such Manner as the Legislature thereof may direct, a Number of Electors, equal to the whole Number of Senators and Representatives to which the State may be entitled in the Congress: but no Senator or Representative, or Person holding an Office of Trust or Profit under the United States, shall be appointed an Elector.

The Electors shall meet in their respective States, and vote by Ballot for two Persons, of whom one at least shall not be an Inhabitant of the same

State with themselves. And they shall make a List of all the Persons voted for, and of the Number of Votes for each; which List they shall sign and certify, and transmit sealed to the Seat of the Government of the United States, directed to the President of the Senate. The President of the Senate shall, in the Presence of the Senate and House of Representatives, open all the Certificates, and the Votes shall then be counted. The Person having the greatest Number of Votes shall be the President, if such Number be a Majority of the whole Number of Electors appointed; and if there be more than one who have such Majority, and have an equal Number of Votes, then the House of Representatives shall immediately choose by Ballot one of them for President; and if no Person have a majority, then from the five highest on the List the said House shall in like Manner choose the President. But in choosing the President, the Votes shall be taken by States, the Representation from each State having one Vote. A quorum for this Purpose shall consist of a Member or Members from two-thirds of the States, and a Majority of all the States shall be necessary to a Choice. In every Case, after the Choice of the President, the Person having the greatest Number of Votes of the Electors shall be the Vice-President. But if there should remain two or more who have equal Votes, the Senate shall choose from them by Ballot the Vice-President.

The Congress may determine the Time of choosing the Electors, and the Day on which they shall give their Votes; which Day shall be the same throughout the United States.

No Person except a natural born Citizen, or a Citizen of the United States, at the time of the Adoption of this Constitution, shall be eligible to the Office of President; neither shall any Person be eligible to that Office who shall not have attained to the Age of thirty-five Years, and been fourteen Years a Resident within the United States.

In Case of the Removal of the President from Office, or of his Death, Resignation, or Inability to discharge the Powers and Duties of the said Office, the Same shall devolve on the Vice-President, and the Congress may by Law provide for the Case of Removal, Death, Resignation or Inability, both of the President and Vice-President, declaring what Officer shall then act as President, and such Officer shall act accordingly, until the Disability be removed, or a President shall be elected.

The President shall, at stated Times, receive for his Services, a Compensation, which shall neither be increased nor diminished during the Period for which he shall have been elected, and he shall not receive within that Period any other Emolument from the United States, or any of them.

Before he enter on the Execution of his Office, he shall take the following Oath or Affirmation:—"I do solemnly swear (or affirm) that I will faithfully execute the office of President of the United States, and will, to the best of my Ability, preserve, protect and defend the Constitution of the United States."

Section 2. The President shall be Commander-in-Chief of the Army and Navy of the United States, and of the Militia of the several States, when called into the actual Service of the United States; he may require the Opinion, in writing, of the principal Officer in each of the executive Departments, upon any Subject relating to the Duties of their respective Offices, and he shall have Power to grant Reprieves and Pardons for all Offences against the United States, except in Cases of Impeachment.

He shall have Power, by and with the Advice and Consent of the Senate, to make Treaties, provided two-thirds of the Senators present concur; and he shall nominate, and by and with the Advice and Consent of the Senate, shall appoint Ambassadors, other public Ministers and Consuls, Judges of the Supreme Court, and all other Officers of the United States, whose Appointments are not herein otherwise provided for, and which shall be established by Law: but the Congress may by Law vest the Appointment of such inferior Officers, as they think proper, in the President alone, in the Courts of Law, or in the Heads of Departments.

The President shall have Power to fill up all Vacancies that may happen during the Recess of the Senate, by granting Commissions which shall expire at the End of their next Session.

Section 3. He shall from time to time give to the Congress Information of the State of the Union, and recommend to their Consideration such Measures as he shall judge necessary and expedient; he may, on extraordinary Occasions, convene both Houses, or either of them, and in Case of Disagreement between them, with Respect to the Time of Adjournment, he may adjourn them to such Time as he shall think proper; he shall receive Ambassadors and other public Ministers; he shall take Care that the Laws be faithfully executed, and shall Commission all the Officers of the United States.

Section 4. The President, Vice-President and all civil Officers of the United States, shall be removed from Office on Impeachment for, and Conviction of, Treason, Bribery, or other high Crimes and Misdemeanors.

Article III

Section 1. The judicial Power of the United States shall be vested in one Supreme Court, and in such inferior Courts as the Congress may from time to time ordain and establish. The Judges, both of the Supreme and inferior Courts, shall hold their Offices during good Behaviour, and shall, at stated Times, receive for their Services, a Compensation, which shall not be diminished during their Continuance in Office.

Section 2. The judicial Power shall extend to all Cases, in Law and Equity, arising under this Constitution, the Laws of the United States, and Treaties made, or which shall be made, under their Authority;—to all Cases affecting Ambassadors, other public Ministers and Consuls;—to all Cases of admiralty and maritime Jurisdiction;—to Controversies to which the United States shall be a Party;—to Controversies between two or more States;—between a State and Citizens of another State;—between Citizens of different States;—between Citizens of the same state claiming Lands under Grants of different States, and between a State, or the Citizens thereof, and foreign States, Citizens or Subjects.

In all Cases affecting Ambassadors, other public Ministers and Consuls, and those in which a State shall be Party, the Supreme Court shall have original Jurisdiction. In all the other Cases before mentioned, the Supreme Court shall have appellate Jurisdiction, both as to Law and Fact, with such Exceptions, and under such Regulations as the Congress shall make.

The Trial of all Crimes, except in Cases of Impeachment, shall be by Jury; and such Trial shall be held in the State where the said Crimes shall have been committed; but when not committed within any State, the Trial shall be at such Place or Places as the Congress may by Law have directed.

Section 3. Treason against the United States, shall consist only in levying War against them, or in adhering to their Enemies, giving them Aid and Comfort. No Person shall be convicted of Treason unless on the Testimony of two Witnesses to the same overt Act, or on Confession in open Court.

The Congress shall have Power to declare the Punishment of Treason, but no Attainder of Treason shall work Corruption of Blood, or Forfeiture except during the Life of the Person attainted.

ARTICLE IV

Section 1. Full Faith and Credit shall be given in each State to the public Acts, Records and judicial Proceedings of every other State. And the Congress may by general Laws prescribe the Manner in which such Acts, Records and Proceedings shall be proved, and the Effect thereof.

Section 2. The Citizens of each State shall be entitled to all Privileges and Immunities of Citizens in the several States.

A Person charged in any State with Treason, Felony, or other Crime, who shall flee from Justice, and be found in another State, shall on Demand of the executive Authority of the State from which he fled, be delivered up, to be removed to the State having Jurisdiction of the Crime.

No Person held to Service or Labour in one State, under the Laws thereof, escaping into another, shall, in Consequence of any Law or Regulation therein, be discharged from such Service or Labour, but shall be delivered up on Claim of the Party to whom such Service or Labour may be due.

Section 3. New States may be admitted by the Congress into this Union; but no new State shall be formed or erected within the Jurisdiction of any other State; nor any State be formed by the Junction of two or more States, or Parts of States, without the Consent of the Legislatures of the States concerned as well as of the Congress.

The Congress shall have Power to dispose of and make all needful Rules and Regulations respecting the Territory or other Property belonging to the United States; and nothing in this Constitution shall be so construed as to Prejudice any Claims of the United States, or of any particular State.

Section 4. The United States shall guarantee to every State in this Union a Republican Form of Government, and shall protect each of them against Invasion; and on Application of the Legislature, or of the Executive (when the Legislature cannot be convened) against domestic Violence.

ARTICLE V

The Congress, whenever two-thirds of both Houses shall deem it necessary, shall propose Amendments to this Constitution, or, on the Application of the Legislatures of two-thirds of the several States, shall call a Convention for proposing Amendments, which, in either Case, shall be valid to all Intents and Purposes, as Part of this Constitution, when ratified by the Legislatures of three-fourths of the several States, or by Conventions in three-fourths thereof, as the one or the other Mode of Ratification may be proposed by the Congress; Provided that no Amendment which may be made prior to the Year One thousand eight hundred and eight shall in any Manner affect the first and fourth Clauses in the Ninth Section of the first Article; and that no State, without its Consent, shall be deprived of its equal Suffrage in the Senate.

ARTICLE VI

All Debts contracted and Engagements entered into, before the Adoption of this Constitution, shall be as valid against the United States under this Constitution, as under the Confederation.

This Constitution, and the Laws of the United States which shall be made in Pursuance thereof and all Treaties made, or which shall be made, under the Authority of the United States, shall be the supreme Law of the Land; and the Judges in every State shall be bound thereby, any Thing in the Constitution or Laws of any State to the Contrary notwithstanding.

The Senators and Representatives before mentioned, and the Members of the several State Legislatures, and all executive and judicial Officers, both of the United States and of the several States, shall be bound by Oath or Affirmation, to support this Constitution; but no religious Test shall ever be required as a Qualification to any Office or public Trust under the United States.

ARTICLE VII

The Ratification of the Conventions of nine States, shall be sufficient for the Establishment of this Constitution between the States so ratifying the Same.

Done in Convention by the Unanimous Consent of the States present the Seventeenth Day of September in the Year of our Lord one thousand seven hundred and Eighty-seven, and of the Independence of the United States of America the Twelfth. In witness whereof We have hereunto subscribed our Names, Attest
William Jackson
    Secretary

Go: Washington—
Presidt. and deputy from Virginia

New Hampshire

John Langdon
Nicholas Gilman

Wm. Paterson
Jona: Dayton

Pennsylvania

Massachusetts

Nathaniel Gorham
Rufus King

B. Franklin
Thomas Mifflin
Robt. Morris
Geo. Clymer
Thos. Fitzsimons
Jared Ingersoll
James Wilson
Gouv Morris

Connecticut

Wm. Saml. Johnson
Roger Sherman

New York

Alexander Hamilton

Delaware

Geo: Read
Gunning Bedford Jun
John Dickinson
Richard Bassett
Jaco: Broom
Richd. Dobbs Spaight
Hu Williamson

New Jersey

Wil: Livingston
David Brearley

Maryland

James McHenry
Dan of St. Thos Jenifer
Danl. Carroll

South Carolina

J. Rutledge
Charles Cotesworth Pinckney
Charles Pinckney
Pierce Butler

Virginia

John Blair—
James Madison Jr.

Georgia

North Carolina

Wm. Blount

William Few
Abr Baldwin

AMENDMENTS

Articles in addition to and Amendment of the Constitution of the United States of America.

Article I

Congress shall make no law respecting an establishment of religion, or prohibiting the free exercise thereof; or abridging the freedom of speech, or of the press; or the right of the people peaceably to assemble, and to petition the Government for a redress of grievances.

ARTICLE II

A well-regulated Militia, being necessary to the security of a free State, the right of the people to keep and bear Arms, shall not be infringed.

ARTICLE III

No Soldier shall, in time of peace be quartered in any house, without the consent of the Owner, nor in time of war, but in a manner to be prescribed by law.

ARTICLE IV

The right of the people to be secure in their persons, houses, papers, and effects, against unreasonable searches and seizures, shall not be violated, and no Warrants shall issue, but upon probable cause, supported by Oath or affirmation, and particularly describing the place to be searched, and the persons or things to be seized.

ARTICLE V

No person shall be held to answer for a capital, or other infamous crime, unless on a presentment or indictment of a Grand Jury, except in cases arising in the land or naval forces, or in the Militia, when in actual service in time of War or public danger; nor shall any person be subject for the same offence to be twice put in jeopardy of life or limb; nor shall be compelled in any criminal case to be a witness against himself, nor be deprived of life, liberty, or property, without due process of law; nor shall private property be taken for public use, without just compensation.

ARTICLE VI

In all criminal prosecutions, the accused shall enjoy the right to a speedy and public trial, by an impartial jury of the State and district wherein the crime shall have been committed, which district shall have been previously ascertained by law, and to be informed of the nature and cause of the accusation; to be confronted with the witnesses against him; to have compulsory process for obtaining witnesses in his favor, and to have the Assistance of Counsel for his defence.

ARTICLE VII

In Suits at common law, where the value in controversy shall exceed twenty dollars, the right of trial by jury shall be preserved, and no fact tried by a jury, shall be otherwise re-examined in any Court of the United States, than according to the rules of the common law.

ARTICLE VIII

Excessive bail shall not be required, nor excessive fines imposed, nor cruel and unusual punishments inflicted.

506   APPENDIX

ARTICLE IX

The enumeration in the Constitution, of certain rights, shall not be construed to deny or disparage others retained by the people.

ARTICLE X

The powers not delegated to the United States by the Constitution, nor prohibited by it to the States, are reserved to the States respectively, or to the people. [First ten Amendments adopted in 1791]

ARTICLE XI

The Judicial power of the United States shall not be construed to extend to any suit in law or equity, commenced or prosecuted against one of the United States by Citizens of another State, or by Citizens or Subjects of any Foreign State. [1798]

ARTICLE XII

The Electors shall meet in their respective states, and vote by ballot for President and Vice-President, one of whom, at least, shall not be an inhabitant of the same state with themselves; they shall name in their ballots the person voted for as President, and in distinct ballots the person voted for as Vice-President, and they shall make distinct lists of all persons voted for as President, and of all persons voted for as Vice-President, and of the number of votes for each, which lists they shall sign and certify, and transmit sealed to the seat of the government of the United States, directed to the President of the Senate;—The President of the Senate shall, in the presence of the Senate and House of Representatives, open all the certificates and the votes shall then be counted;—The person having the greatest number of votes for President, shall be the President, if such number be a majority of the whole number of Electors appointed; and if no person have such majority, then from the persons having the highest numbers not exceeding three on the list of those voted for as President, the House of Representatives shall choose immediately, by ballot, the President. But in choosing the President, the votes shall be taken by states, the representation from each state having one vote; a quorum for this purpose shall consist of a member or members from two-thirds of the states, and a majority of all the states shall be necessary to a choice. And if the House of Representatives shall not choose a President whenever the right of choice shall devolve upon them, before the fourth day of March next following, then the Vice-President shall act as President, as in the case of the death or other constitutional disability of the President. —The person having the greatest number of votes as Vice-President, shall be the Vice-President, if such number be a majority of the whole number of Electors appointed, and if no person have a majority, then from the two highest numbers on the list, the Senate shall choose the Vice-President; a quorum for the purpose shall consist of two-thirds of the whole number of Senators, and a majority of the whole number shall be necessary to a choice.

But no person constitutionally ineligible to the office of President shall be eligible to that of Vice-President of the United States. [1804]

Article XIII

Section 1. Neither slavery nor involuntary servitude, except as a punishment for crime whereof the party shall have been duly convicted, shall exist within the United States, or any place subject to their jurisdiction.

Section 2. Congress shall have power to enforce this article by appropriate legislation. [1865]

Article XIV

Section 1. All persons born or naturalized in the United States, and subject to the jurisdiction thereof, are citizens of the United States and of the State wherein they reside. No State shall make or enforce any law which shall abridge the privileges or immunities of citizens of the United States; nor shall any State deprive any person of life, liberty, or property, without due process of law; nor deny to any person within its jurisdiction the equal protection of the laws.

Section 2. Representatives shall be apportioned among the several States according to their respective numbers, counting the whole number of persons in each State, excluding Indians not taxed. But when the right to vote at any election for the choice of electors for President and Vice-President of the United States, Representatives in Congress, the Executive and Judicial officers of a State, or the members of the Legislature thereof, is denied to any of the male members of such State, being twenty-one years of age, and citizens of the United States, or in any way abridged, except for participation in rebellion, or other crime, the basis of representation therein shall be reduced in the proportion which the number of such male citizens shall bear to the whole number of male citizens twenty-one years of age in such State.

Section 3. No person shall be a Senator or Representative in Congress, or elector of President and Vice-President, or hold any office, civil or military, under the United States, or under any State, who, having previously taken an oath, as a member of Congress, or as an officer of the United States, or as a member of any State legislature, or as an executive or judicial officer of any State, to support the Constitution of the United States, shall have engaged in insurrection or rebellion against the same, or given aid and comfort to the enemies thereof. But Congress may by a vote of two-thirds of each House, remove such disability.

Section 4. The validity of the public debt of the United States, authorized by law, including debts incurred for payment of pensions and bounties for services in suppressing insurrection and rebellion, shall not be questioned. But neither the United States nor any State shall assume or pay any debt or obligation incurred in aid of insurrection or rebellion against the United States, or any claim for the loss or emancipation of any slave; but all such debts, obligations and claims shall be held illegal and void.

Section 5. The Congress shall have power to enforce, by appropriate legislation, the provisions of this article. [1868]

ARTICLE XV

Section 1. The right of the citizens of the United States to vote shall not be denied or abridged by the United States or by any State on account of race, color, or previous condition of servitude.

Section 2. The Congress shall have power to enforce the provisions of this article by appropriate legislation. [1870]

ARTICLE XVI

The Congress shall have power to lay and collect taxes on incomes, from whatever sources derived, without apportionment among the several States, and without regard to any census or enumeration. [1913]

ARTICLE XVII

The Senate of the United States shall be composed of two Senators from each State, elected by the people thereof, for six years; and each Senator shall have one vote. The electors in each State shall have the qualifications requisite for electors of the most numerous branch of the State legislature.

When vacancies happen in the representation of any State in the Senate, the executive authority of such State shall issue writs of election to fill such vacancies: *Provided,* That the legislature of any State may empower the executive thereof to make temporary appointment until the people fill the vacancies by election as the legislature may direct.

This amendment shall not be so construed as to affect the election or term of any Senator chosen before it becomes valid as part of the Constitution. [1913]

ARTICLE XVIII

Section 1. After one year from the ratification of this article the manufacture, sale, or transportation of intoxicating liquors within, the importation thereof into, or the exportation thereof from the United States and all territory subject to the jurisdiction thereof for beverage purposes is hereby prohibited.

Section 2. The Congress and the several States shall have concurrent power to enforce this article by appropriate legislation.

Section 3. This article shall be inoperative unless it shall have been ratified as an amendment to the Constitution by the legislatures of the several States, as provided in the Constitution, within seven years from the date of the submission hereof to the States by the Congress. [1919]

ARTICLE XIX

The right of citizens of the United States to vote shall not be denied or abridged by the United States or by any State on account of sex.

Congress shall have power to enforce this article by appropriate legislation. [1920]

ARTICLE XX

Section 1. The terms of the President and Vice-President shall end at noon on the 20th day of January, and the terms of Senators and Representatives at noon on the 3d day of January, of the years in which such terms would have ended if this article had not been ratified; and the terms of their successors shall then begin.

Section 2. The Congress shall assemble at least once in every year, and such meeting shall begin at noon on the 3d day of January, unless they shall by law appoint a different day.

Section 3. If, at the time fixed for the beginning of the term of the President, the President elect shall have died, the Vice-President elect shall become President. If a President shall not have been chosen before the time fixed for the beginning of his term, or if the President elect shall have failed to qualify, then the Vice-President elect shall act as President until a President shall have qualified; and the Congress may by law provide for the case wherein neither a President elect nor a Vice-President elect shall have qualified, declaring who shall then act as President, or the manner in which one who is to act shall be selected, and such person shall act accordingly until a President or Vice-President shall have qualified.

Section 4. The Congress may by law provide for the case of the death of any of the persons from whom the House of Representatives may choose a President whenever the right of choice shall have devolved upon them, and for the case of the death of any of the persons from whom the Senate may choose a Vice-President whenever the right of choice shall have devolved upon them.

Section 5. Sections 1 and 2 shall take effect on the 15th day of October following the ratification of this article.

Section 6. This article shall be inoperative unless it shall have been ratified as an amendment to the Constitution by the legislatures of three-fourths of the several States within seven years from the date of its submission. [1933]

ARTICLE XXI

Section 1. The eighteenth article of amendment to the Constitution of the United States is hereby repealed.

Section 2. The transportation or importation into any State, Territory, or Possession of the United States for delivery or use therein of intoxicating liquors, in violation of the laws thereof, is hereby prohibited.

Section 3. This article shall be inoperative unless it shall have been ratified as an amendment to the Constitution by conventions in the several States, as provided in the Constitution, within seven years from the date of the submission hereof to the States by the Congress. [1933]

Article XXII

Section 1. No person shall be elected to the office of the President more than twice, and no person who has held the office of President, or acted as President, for more than two years of a term to which some other person was elected President shall be elected to the office of the President more than once. But this Article shall not apply to any person holding the office of President when this Article was proposed by the Congress, and shall not prevent any person who may be holding the office of President, or acting as President, during the term within which this Article becomes operative from holding the office of President or acting as President during the remainder of such term.

Section 2. This article shall be inoperative unless it shall have been ratified as an amendment to the Constitution by the legislatures of three-fourths of the several States within seven years from the date of its submission to the States by the Congress. [1951]

Article XXIII

Section 1. The District constituting the seat of Government of the United States shall appoint in such manner as the Congress may direct:

A number of electors of President and Vice-President equal to the whole number of Senators and Representatives in Congress to which the District would be entitled if it were a State, but in no event more than the least populous State; they shall be in addition to those appointed by the States, but they shall be considered, for the purposes of the election of President and Vice-President, to be electors appointed by a State; and they shall meet in the District and perform such duties as provided by the twelfth article of amendment.

Section 2. The Congress shall have power to enforce this article by appropriate legislation. [1961]

Article XXIV

Section 1. The right of citizens of the United States to vote in any primary or other election for President or Vice-President, for electors for President or Vice-President, or for Senator or Representative in Congress, shall not be denied or abridged by the United States or any State by reason of failure to pay any poll tax or other tax.

Section 2. The Congress shall have the power to enforce this article by appropriate legislation. [1964]

Article XXV

Section 1. In case of the removal of the President from office or of his death or resignation, the Vice-President shall become President.

Section 2. Whenever there is a vacancy in the office of the Vice-President, the President shall nominate a Vice-President who shall take office upon confirmation by a majority vote of both houses of Congress.

Section 3. Whenever the President transmits to the President pro tempore of the Senate and the Speaker of the House of Representatives his written declaration that he is unable to discharge the powers and duties of his office, and until he transmits to them a written declaration to the contrary, such powers and duties shall be discharged by the Vice-President as Acting President.

Section 4. Whenever the Vice-President and a majority of either the principal officers of the executive departments or of such other body as Congress may by law provide, transmit to the President pro tempore of the Senate and the Speaker of the House of Representatives their written declaration that the President is unable to discharge the powers and duties of his office, the Vice-President shall immediately assume the powers and duties of the office as Acting President.

Thereafter, when the President transmits to the President pro tempore of the Senate and the Speaker of the House of Representatives his written declaration that no inability exists, he shall resume the powers and duties of his office unless the Vice-President and a majority of either the principal officers of the executive departments or of such other body as Congress may by law provide, transmit within four days to the President pro tempore of the Senate and the Speaker of the House of Representatives their written declaration that the President is unable to discharge the powers and duties of his office. Thereupon Congress shall decide the issue, assembling within forty-eight hours for that purpose if not in session. If the Congress, within twenty-one days after receipt of the latter written declaration, or, if Congress is not in session, within twenty-one days after Congress is required to assemble, determines by two-thirds vote of both houses that the President is unable to discharge the powers and duties of his office, the Vice-President shall continue to discharge the same as Acting President; otherwise, the President shall resume the powers and duties of his office. [1967]

5. PRESIDENT GEORGE WASHINGTON, IN HIS FAREWELL ADDRESS, WARNS THE PEOPLE AGAINST DOMESTIC AND FOREIGN CONFLICTS (September 17, 1796)

Friends and fellow citizens: The period for a new election of a citizen to administer the executive Government of the United States being not far distant, and the time actually arrived when your thoughts must be employed in designating the person who is to be clothed with that important trust, it appears to me proper, especially as it may conduce to a more distinct expression of the public voice, that I should now apprize you of the resolution I have formed to decline being considered among the number of those out of whom a choice is to be made. . . .

Here, perhaps, I ought to stop. But a solicitude for your welfare which cannot end but with my life, and the apprehension of danger natural to that solicitude, urge me on an occasion like the present to offer to your solemn contemplation and to recommend to your frequent review some sentiments which are the result of much reflection, of no inconsiderable observation, and which appear to me all-important to the permanency of your felicity as a people. . . .

The unity of government which constitutes you one people is also now dear to you. . . . This Government, the offspring of our own choice, uninfluenced and unawed, adopted upon full investigation and mature deliberation, completely free in its principles, in the distribution of its powers, uniting security with energy, and containing within itself a provision for its own amendment, has a just claim to your confidence and your support. Respect for its authority, compliance with its laws, acquiescence in its measures, are duties enjoined by the fundamental maxims of true liberty. The basis of our political systems is the right of the people to make and to alter their constitutions of government. But the constitution which at any time exists till changed by an explicit and authentic act of the whole people is sacredly obligatory upon all. The very idea of the power and the right of the people to establish government presupposes the duty of every individual to obey the established government. . . .

It is important, likewise, that the habits of thinking in a free country should inspire caution in those intrusted with its administration to confine themselves within their respective constitutional spheres, avoiding in the exercise of the powers of one department to encroach upon another. The spirit of encroachment tends to consolidate the powers of all the departments in one, and thus to create, whatever the form of government, a real despotism. . . .

It is substantially true that virtue or morality is a necessary spring of popular government. The rule indeed extends with more or less force to every species of free government. Who that is a sincere friend to it can look with indifference upon attempts to shake the foundation of the fabric? Promote, then, as an object of primary importance, institutions for the general diffusion of knowledge. In proportion as the structure of a government gives force to public opinion, it is essential that public opinion should be enlightened. . . .

Observe good faith and justice toward all nations. Cultivate peace and harmony with all. . . .

The great rule of conduct for us in regard to foreign nations is, in extending our commercial relations, to have with them as little *political* connection as possible. So far as we have already formed engagements let them be fulfilled with perfect good faith. Here let us stop.

Europe has a set of primary interests which to us have none or a very remote relation. Hence she must be engaged in frequent controversies, the causes of which are essentially foreign to our concerns. Hence, therefore, it must be unwise in us to implicate ourselves by artificial ties in the ordinary vicissitudes of her politics or the ordinary combinations and collisions of her friendships or enmities.

Our detached and distant situation invites and enables us to pursue a different course. If we remain one people, under an efficient government, the period is not far off when we may defy material injury from external annoyance; when we may take such an attitude as will cause the neutrality we may at any time resolve upon to be scrupulously respected; when belligerent nations, under the impossibility of making acquisitions upon us, will not lightly hazard the giving us provocation; when we may choose peace or war, as our interest, guided by justice, shall counsel.

Why forego the advantages of so peculiar a situation? Why quit our own to stand upon foreign ground? Why, by interweaving our destiny with that of any part of Europe, entangle our peace and prosperity in the toils of European ambition, rivalship, interest, humor, or caprice?

6. PRESIDENT THOMAS JEFFERSON PLEADS FOR REPUBLICAN UNITY IN HIS FIRST INAUGURAL ADDRESS (1801)

Called upon to undertake the duties of the first executive office of our country, I avail myself of the presence of that portion of my fellow citizens which is here assembled to express my grateful thanks for the favor with which they have been pleased to look toward me, to declare a sincere consciousness that the task is above my talents, and that I approach it with those anxious and awful presentiments which the greatness of the charge and the weakness of my powers so justly inspire. A rising nation, spread over a wide and fruitful land, traversing all the seas with the rich productions of their industry, engaged in commerce with nations who feel power and forget right, advancing rapidly to destinies beyond the reach of mortal eye—when I contemplate these transcendent objects, and see the honor, the happiness, and the hopes of this beloved country committed to the issue and the auspices of this day, I shrink from the contemplation, and humble myself before the magnitude of the undertaking. . . .

During the contest of opinion through which we have passed the animation of discussions and of exertions has sometimes worn an aspect which might impose on strangers unused to think freely and to speak and to write what they think; but this being now decided by the voice of the nation, announced according to the rules of the Constitution, all will, of course, arrange themselves under the will of the law, and unite in common efforts for the common good. All, too, will bear in mind the sacred principle, that though the will of the majority is in all cases to prevail, that will to be rightful must be reasonable; that the minority possess their equal rights, which equal law must protect, and to violate would be oppression. Let us, then, fellow citizens, unite with one heart and one mind. Let us restore to social intercourse that harmony and affection without which liberty and even life itself are but dreary things. And let us reflect that, having banished from our land that religious intolerance under which mankind so long bled and suffered, we have yet gained little if we countenance a political intolerance as despotic, as wicked, and capable of as bitter and bloody persecutions. During the throes and convulsions of the ancient world, during the agonizing spasms of infuriated man, seeking through blood and slaughter his long-lost liberty, it was not wonderful that the agitation of the billows should reach even this distant and peaceful shore; that this should be more felt and feared by some and less by others, and should divide opinions as to measures of safety. But every difference of opinion is not a difference of principle. We have called by different names brethren of the same principle. We are all Republicans, we are all Federalists. If there be any among us who would wish to dissolve this Union or to change its republican form, let them stand undisturbed as monuments of the safety with which error of opinion may be tolerated where reason is left free to combat it. I know, indeed, that some honest men fear that a republican government cannot be strong, that this Government is not strong enough; but would the honest patriot, in the full tide of successful experiment, abandon a government which has so far kept us free and firm on the theoretic and visionary fear that this Government, the world's best hope, may by possibility want energy to preserve itself? I trust not. I believe this, on the contrary, the strongest Government on earth. I believe it the only one where every man, at the call of the law, would fly to the standard of the law, and would meet invasions of the public order as his own personal concern. Sometimes it is said that man cannot be trusted with the government of himself. Can he, then, be trusted with the government of others? Or have we found angels in the forms of kings to govern him? Let history answer this question.

Let us, then, with courage and confidence pursue our own Federal and Republican principles, our attachment to union and representative government. Kindly separated by nature and a wide ocean from the exterminating havoc of one quarter of the globe; too high-minded to endure the degradations of the others; possessing a chosen country, with room enough for our descendants to the thousandth and thousandth generation; entertaining a due sense of our equal right to the use of our own faculties, to the acquisitions of our own industry, to honor and confidence from our fellow citizens, resulting not from birth, but from our actions and their sense of them; enlightened by a benign religion, professed, indeed, and practised in various forms, yet all of them inculcating honesty, truth, temperance, gratitude, and the love of man; acknowledging and adoring an overruling Providence, which by all its dispensations proves that it delights in the happiness of man here and his greater happiness hereafter—with all these blessings, what more is necessary to make us a happy and a prosperous people? Still one thing more, fellow citizens—a wise and frugal Government, which shall restrain men from injuring one another, shall leave them otherwise free to regulate their own pursuits of industry and improvement, and shall not take from the mouth of labor the bread it has earned. This is the sum of good government, and this is necessary to close the circle of our felicities. . . .

7. PRESIDENT JAMES MONROE PRESENTS TO CONGRESS HIS DOCTRINE FOR THE WESTERN HEMISPHERE (1823)

. . . In the discussions to which this interest [claim of Russia on the northwest coast] has given rise, and in the arrangements by which they may terminate, the occasion has been judged proper for asserting, as a principle in which the rights and interests of the United States are involved, that the American continents, by the free and independent condition which they have assumed and maintain, are henceforth not to be considered as subjects for future colonization by any European powers. . . .

It was stated at the commencement of the last session, that a great effort was then making in Spain and Portugal, to improve the condition of the people of those countries, and that it appeared to be conducted with extraordinary moderation. It need scarcely be remarked, that the result has been, so far, very different from what was then anticipated. Of events in that quarter of the globe, with which we have so much intercourse, and from which we derive our origin, we have always been anxious and interested spectators. The citizens of the United States cherish sentiments the most friendly, in favor of the liberty and happiness of their fellow men on that side of the Atlantic. In the wars of the European powers, in matters relating to themselves, we have never taken any part, nor does it comport with our policy so to do. It is only when our rights are invaded, or seriously menaced, that we resent injuries, or make preparation for our defence. With the movements in this hemisphere, we are, of necessity, more immediately connected, and by causes which must be obvious to all enlightened and impartial observers. The political system of the allied powers is essentially different, in this respect, from that of America. This difference proceeds from that which exists in their respective governments. And to the defence of our own, which has been achieved by the loss of so much blood and treasure, and matured by the wisdom of their most enlightened citizens, and under which we have enjoyed unexampled felicity, this whole nation is devoted. We owe it, therefore, to candor, and to the amicable relations existing between the United States and those powers, to declare, that we should consider any attempt on their part to extend their system to any portion of this hemisphere, as dangerous to our peace and safety. With the existing colonies or dependencies of any European power, we have not interfered, and shall not interfere. But with the governments who have declared their independence, and maintained it, and whose independence we have, on great consideration, and on just principles, acknowledged, we could not view any interposition for the purpose of oppressing them, or controlling, in any other manner, their destiny, by any European power, in any other light than as the manifestation of an unfriendly disposition towards the United States. In the war between those new governments and Spain, we declared our neutrality at the time of their recognition, and to this we have adhered, and shall continue to adhere, provided no change shall occur, which, in the judgment of the competent authorities of this government, shall make a corresponding change, on the part of the United States, indispensable to their security.

The late events in Spain and Portugal, shew that Europe is still unsettled. Of this important fact, no stronger proof can be adduced than that the allied powers should have thought it proper, on any principle satisfactory to themselves, to have interposed, by force, in the internal concerns of Spain. To what extent such interposition may be carried, on the same principle, is a question, in which all independent powers, whose governments differ from theirs, are interested; even those most remote, and surely none more so than the United States. Our policy, in regard to Europe, which was adopted at an early stage of the wars which have so long agitated that quarter of the globe, nevertheless remains the same, which is, not to interfere in the internal concerns of any of its powers; to consider the government *de facto* as the legitimate government for us; to cultivate friendly relations with it, and to preserve those relations by a frank, firm, and manly policy; meeting, in all instances, the just claims of every power; submitting to injuries from none. But, in regard to those continents, circumstances are eminently and conspicuously different. It is impossible that the allied powers should extend their political system to any portion of either continent, without endangering our peace and happiness; nor can any one believe that our southern brethren, if left to themselves, would adopt it of their own accord. It is equally impossible, therefore, that we should behold such interposition, in any form, with indifference. If we look to the comparative strength and resources of Spain and those new governments, and their distance from each other, it must be obvious that she can never subdue them. It is still the true policy of the United States to leave the parties to themselves, in the hope that other powers will pursue the same course.

8. PRESIDENT ANDREW JACKSON ATTACKS BANKING MONOPOLY IN A MESSAGE TO THE SENATE (1832)

To the Senate:

. . . A bank of the United States is in many respects convenient for the Government and useful to the people. Entertaining this opinion, and deeply impressed with the belief that some of the powers and privileges possessed by the existing bank are unauthorized by the Constitution, subversive of the rights of the States, and dangerous to the liberties of the people, I felt it my duty at an early period of my Administration to call the attention of Congress to the practicability of organizing an institution combining all its advantages and obviating these objections. I sincerely regret that in the act before me I can perceive none of those modifications of the bank charter which are necessary, in my opinion, to make it compatible with justice, with sound policy, or with the Constitution of our country.

The present corporate body, denominated the president, directors, and company of the Bank of the United States, will have existed at the time this act is intended to take effect twenty years. It enjoys an exclusive privilege of banking under the authority of the General Government, and a monopoly of its favor and support, and, as a necessary consequence, almost a monopoly of the foreign and domestic exchange. The powers, privileges, and favors bestowed upon it in the original charter, by increasing the value of the stock far above its par value, operated as a gratuity of many millions to the stockholders.

An apology may be found for the failure to guard against this result in the consideration that the effect of the original act of incorporation could not be certainly foreseen at the time of its passage. The act before me proposes another gratuity to the holders of the same stock, and in many cases to the same men, of at least seven millions more. This donation finds no apology in any uncertainty as to the effect of the act. On all hands it is conceded that its passage will increase at least 20 or 30 per cent more the market price of the stock, subject to the payment of the annuity of $200,000 per year secured by the act, thus adding in a moment one-fourth to its par value. It is not our own citizens only who are to receive the bounty of our Government. More than eight millions of the stock of this bank are held by foreigners. By this act the American Republic proposes virtually to make them a present of some millions of dollars. For these gratuities to foreigners, and to some of our own opulent citizens the act secures no equivalent whatever. They are the certain gains of the present stockholders under the operation of this act, after making full allowance for the payment of the bonus.

Every monopoly and all exclusive privileges are granted at the expense of the public, which ought to receive a fair equivalent. The many millions which this act proposes to bestow on the stockholders of the existing bank must come directly or indirectly out of the earnings of the American people. It is due to them, therefore, if their Government sell monopolies and exclusive privileges, that they should at least exact for them as much as they are worth in open market. The value of the monopoly in this case may be correctly ascertained. The twenty-eight millions of stock would probably be at an advance of 50 per cent, and command in market at least $42,000,000, subject to the payment of the present bonus. The present value of the monopoly, therefore, is $17,000,000, and this the act proposes to sell for three millions, payable in fifteen annual installments of $200,000 each.

9. DOROTHEA DIX SPEAKS TO THE MASSACHUSETTS LEGISLATURE IN BEHALF OF THE HELPLESS (1843)

Gentlemen: I come to present the strong claims of suffering humanity. I come to place before the Legislature of Massachusetts the condition of the miserable, the desolate, the outcast. I come as the advocate of helpless, forgotten, insane, and idiotic men and women; of beings sunk to a condition from which the most unconcerned would start with real horror; of beings wretched in our prisons, and more wretched in our almshouses.

I must confine myself to a few examples, but am ready to furnish other and more complete details, if required.

I proceed, gentlemen, briefly to call your attention to the *present* state of insane persons confined within this Commonwealth, in *cages, closets, cellars, stalls, pens! Chained, naked, beaten with rods,* and *lashed* into obedience.

I offer the following extracts from my notebook and journal.

Springfield: In the jail, one lunatic woman, furiously mad, a state pauper, improperly situated, both in regard to the prisoners, the keepers, and herself. It is a case of extreme self-forgetfulness and oblivion to all the decencies of life, to describe which would be to repeat only the grossest scenes. In the almshouse of the same town is a woman apparently only needing judicious care and some well-chosen employment to make it unnecessary to confine her in solitude in a dreary unfurnished room. Her appeals for employment and companionship are most touching, but the mistress replied "she had no time to attend to her."

Lincoln: A woman in a cage. *Medford:* One idiotic subject chained, and one in a close stall for seventeen years. *Pepperell:* One often doubly chained, hand and foot; another violent, several peaceable now. *Brookfield:* One man caged, comfortable. *Granville:* One often closely confined, now losing the use of his limbs from want of exercise. *Charlemont:* One man caged. *Savoy:* One man caged. *Lenox:* Two in the jail, against whose unfit condition there the jailer protests.

Dedham: The insane disadvantageously placed in the jail. In the almshouse, two females in stalls, situated in the main building, lie in wooden bunks filled with straw; always shut up. One of these subjects is supposed curable. The overseers of the poor have declined giving her a trial at the hospital, as I was informed, on account of expense.

Besides the above, I have seen many who, part of the year, are chained or caged. The use of cages is all but universal. Hardly a town but can refer to some not distant period of using them; chains are less common; negligences frequent; wilful abuse less frequent than sufferings proceeding from ignorance, or want of consideration. I encountered during the last three months many poor creatures wandering reckless and unprotected through the country. . . . But I cannot particularize. In traversing the state, I have found hundreds of insane persons in every variety of circumstance and condition, many whose situation could not and need not be improved; a less number, but that very large, whose lives are the saddest pictures of human suffering and degradation. . . .

Men of Massachusetts, I beg, I implore, I demand pity and protection for these of my suffering, outraged sex. Become the benefactors of your race, the just guardians of the solemn rights you hold in trust. Raise up the fallen, succor the desolate, restore the outcast, defend the helpless, and for your eternal and great reward receive the benediction, "Well done, good and faithful servants, become rulers over many things!"

Injustice is also done to the *convicts*: it is certainly very wrong that they should be doomed day after day and night after night to listen to the ravings of madmen and madwomen. This is a kind of punishment that is not recognized by our statutes, and is what the criminal ought not to be called upon to undergo. The confinement of the criminal and of the insane in the same building is subversive of that good order and discipline which should be observed in every well-regulated prison. I do most sincerely hope that more permanent provision will be made for the pauper insane by the state, either to restore Worcester Insane Asylum to what it was originally designed to be or else to make some just appropriation for the benefit of this very unfortunate class of our fellow beings.

Gentlemen, I commit to you this sacred cause. Your action upon this subject will affect the present and future condition of hundreds and of thousands. In this legislation, as in all things, may you exercise that "wisdom which is the breath of the power of God."

10. THE WOMEN'S DECLARATION OF SENTIMENTS AT SENECA FALLS (1848)

When, in the course of human events, it becomes necessary for one portion of the family of man to assume among the people of the earth a position different from that which they have hitherto occupied, but one to which the laws of nature and of nature's God entitle them, a decent respect to the opinions of mankind requires that they should declare the causes that impel them to such a course.

We hold these truths to be self-evident: that all men and women are created equal; that they are endowed by their creator with certain inalienable rights; that among these are life, liberty and the pursuit of happiness; that to secure these rights governments are instituted, deriving their just powers from the consent of the governed. Whenever any form of government becomes destructive of these ends, it is the right of those who suffer from it to refuse allegiance to it, and to insist upon the institution of a new government laying its foundation on such principles, and organizing its powers in such form, as to them shall seem most likely to affect their safety and happiness. Prudence indeed will dictate that governments long established should not be changed for light and transient causes; and accordingly all experience hath shown that mankind are more disposed to suffer, while evils are sufferable, than to right themselves by abolishing the forms to which they were accustomed. But when a long train of abuses and usurpations pursuing invariably the same object evinces a design to reduce them under absolute despotism, it is their duty to throw off such government and to provide new guards for their future security. Such has been the patient sufferance of the women under this government, and such is now the necessity which constrains them to demand the equal station to which they are entitled.

The history of mankind is the history of repeated injuries and usurpations on the part of man toward woman, having in direct object the establishment of an absolute tyranny over her. To prove this, let facts be submitted to a candid world:

He has never permitted her to exercise her inalienable right to the elective franchise.

He has compelled her to submit to laws, in the formation of which she had no voice.

He has withheld from her rights which are given to the most ignorant and degraded men—both natives and foreigners.

Having deprived her of this first right of a citizen, the elective franchise, thereby leaving her without representation in the halls of legislation, he has oppressed her on all sides.

He has made her, if married, in the eyes of the law, civilly dead.

He has taken from her all right in property, even to the wages she earns.

He has made her, morally, an irresponsible being, as she can commit many crimes with impunity, provided they be done in the presence of her husband. In the convenant of marriage, she is compelled to promise obedience to her husband, he becoming to all intents and purposes, her master —the law giving him power to deprive her of her liberty and to administer chastisement.

He has so framed the laws of divorce, as to what shall be the proper causes, and in case of separation, to whom the guardianship of the children shall be given, as to be wholly regardless of the happiness of the woman— the law, in all cases, going upon a false supposition of the supremacy of man, and giving all power into his hands.

After depriving her of all rights as a married woman, if single, and the owner of property, he has taxed her to support a government which recognizes her only when her property can be made profitable to it.

He has monopolized nearly all the profitable employments, and from those she is permitted to follow, she receives but a scanty remuneration. He closes against her all the avenues to wealth and distinction which he considers most honorable to himself. As a teacher of theology, medicine, or law, she is not known.

He has denied her the facilities for obtaining a thorough education, all colleges being closed against her.

He allows her in Church, as well as State, but a subordinate position, claiming Apostolic authority for her exclusion from the ministry and, with some exceptions, from any public participation in the affairs of the Church.

He has created a false public sentiment by giving to the world a different code of morals for men and women, by which moral delinquencies which exclude women from society, are not only tolerated, but deemed of little account in man.

He has usurped the prerogative of Jehovah himself, claiming it as his right to assign for her a sphere of action, when that belongs to her conscience and to her God.

He has endeavored, in every way that he could, to destroy her confidence in her own powers, to lessen her self-respect, and to make her willing to lead a dependent and abject life.

Now, in view of this entire disfranchisement of one-half the people of this country, their social and religious degradation—in view of the unjust laws above mentioned and because women do feel themselves aggrieved, oppressed, and fraudulently deprived of their most sacred rights, we insist that they have immediate admission to all the rights and privileges which belong to them as citizens of the United States.

In entering upon the great work before us, we anticipate no small amount of misconception, misrepresentation, and ridicule; but we shall use every instrumentality within our power to effect our object. We shall employ agents, circulate tracts, petition the State and National legislatures, and endeavor to enlist the pulpit and the press in our behalf. We hope this Convention will be followed by a series of Conventions embracing every part of the country.

11. JOHN C. CALHOUN, MARCH 4, 1850, WARNS THE NORTH AGAINST AGITATION OF THE SLAVERY ISSUE

I have, Senators, believed from the first that the agitation of the subject of slavery would, if not prevented by some timely and effective measure, end in disunion. Entertaining this opinion, I have, on all proper occasions, endeavored to call the attention of both the two great parties which divide the country to adopt some measure to prevent so great a disaster, but without success. The agitation has been permitted to proceed . . . the Union is in danger. . . . How can the Union be preserved? . . .

What is it that has endangered the Union? To this question there can be but one answer,—that the immediate cause is the almost universal discontent which pervades all the States composing the Southern section of the Union. . . . It commenced with the agitation of the slavery question. . . . The next question, going one step further back, is—What has caused this widely diffused and almost universal discontent? . . . It will be found in the belief of the people of the Southern States, as prevalent as the discontent itself, that they cannot remain, as things now are, consistently with honor and safety, in the Union. . . .

To place this subject distinctly before you, I have, Senators, prepared a brief statistical statement, showing the relative weight of the two sections in the Government under the first census of 1790 and the last census of 1840. . . . To sum up the whole, the United States, since they declared their independence, have acquired 2,373,046 square miles of territory, from which the North will have excluded the South, if she should succeed in monopolizing the newly acquired territories, about three-fourths of the whole, leaving to the South but about one-fourth. . . .

But if there was no question of vital importance to the South, in reference to which there was a diversity of views between the two sections, this state of things might be endured, without the hazard of destruction to the South. But . . . there is a question of vital importance to the Southern section, in reference to which the views and feelings of the two sections are as opposite and hostile as they can possibly be. I refer to the relation between the two races in the Southern section, which constitutes a vital portion of her social organization . . . the Southern section regards the relation as one which cannot be destroyed without subjecting the two races to the greatest calamity, and the section to poverty, desolation, and wretchedness; and accordingly they feel bound, by every consideration of interest and safety, to defend it.

12. EMANCIPATION PROCLAMATION (January 1, 1863)

Whereas, on [September 22, 1862], a proclamation was issued by the President of the United States, containing, among other things, the following, to wit:

"That on [January 1, 1863], all persons held as slaves within any state or designated part of a state, the people whereof shall then be in rebellion against the United States, shall be then, thenceforward, and forever, free; and the Executive Government of the United States, including the military and naval authority thereof, will recognize and maintain the freedom of such persons, and will do no act or acts to repress such persons, or any of them, in any efforts they may make for their actual freedom.

"That the Executive will, on the first day of January aforesaid, by proclamation, designate the states and parts of states, if any, in which the people thereof, respectively, shall then be in rebellion against the United States; and the fact that any state, or the people thereof, shall on that day be in good faith represented in the Congress of the United States, by members chosen thereto at elections wherein a majority of the qualified voters of such states shall have participated, shall, in the absence of strong countervailing testimony, be deemed conclusive evidence that such state, and the people thereof, are not then in rebellion against the United States."

Now, therefore, I, ABRAHAM LINCOLN, President of the United States, by virtue of the power in me vested as commander-in-chief of the army and navy of the United States, in time of actual armed rebellion against the authority and Government of the United States, and as a fit and necessary war measure for suppressing said rebellion, do, on this first day of January, . . . [1863] . . . , and in accordance with my purpose so to do, publicly proclaimed for the full period of one hundred days from the day first above mentioned, order and designate as the states and parts of states wherein the people thereof, respectively, are this day in rebellion against the United States, the following, to wit:

Arkansas, Texas, Louisiana, (except the parishes of St. Bernard, Plaquemines, Jefferson, St. John, St. Charles, St. James, Ascension, Assumption, Terre Bonne, Lafourche, St. Mary, St. Martin, and Orleans, including the city of New Orleans,) Mississippi, Alabama, Florida, Georgia, South Carolina, North Carolina, and Virginia, (except the forty-eight counties desig-nated as West Virginia, and also the counties of Berkeley, Accomac, Northampton, Elizabeth City, York, Princess Ann, and Norfolk, including the cities of Norfolk and Portsmouth,) and which excepted parts are for the present left precisely as if this proclamation were not issued.

And by virtue of the power and for the purpose aforesaid, I do order and declare that all persons held as slaves within said designated states and parts of states are, and henceforward shall be, free; and that the Executive Gov-ernment of the United States, including the military and naval authorities thereof, will recognize and maintain the freedom of said persons.

And I hereby enjoin upon the people so declared to be free to abstain from all violence, unless in necessary self-defence; and I recommend to them that, in all cases when allowed, they labor faithfully for reasonable wages.

And I further declare and make known that such persons, of suitable condition, will be received into the armed service of the United States to garrison forts, positions, stations, and other places, and to man vessels of all sorts in said service.

And upon this act, sincerely believed to be an act of justice, warranted by the Constitution upon military necessity, I invoke the considerate judgment of mankind and the gracious favor of Almighty God. . . .

13. LINCOLN'S ADDRESS AT GETTYSBURG (1863)

Fourscore and seven years ago our fathers brought forth on this continent a new nation, conceived in liberty, and dedicated to the proposition that all men are created equal.

Now we are engaged in a great civil war, testing whether that nation, or any nation so conceived and so dedicated, can long endure. We are met on a great battle-field of that war. We have come to dedicate a portion of that field as a final resting-place for those who here gave their lives that that nation might live. It is altogether fitting and proper that we should do this.

But, in a larger sense, we cannot dedicate—we cannot consecrate—we can-not hallow—this ground. The brave men, living and dead, who struggled here, have consecrated it far above our poor power to add or detract. The world will little note, nor long remember, what we say here, but it can never forget what they did here. It is for us, the living, rather, to be dedi-cated here to the unfinished work which they who fought here have thus far so nobly advanced. It is rather for us to be here dedicated to the great task remaining before us;—that from these honored dead, we take increased devotion to that cause for which they gave the last full measure of devotion; —that we here highly resolve that these dead shall not have died in vain, that this nation, under God, shall have a new birth of freedom, and that government of the people, by the people, for the people, shall not perish from the earth.

14. PRESIDENT ULYSSES S. GRANT INSTRUCTS CONGRESS ON WAYS OUT OF THE GREAT DEPRESSION (1874)

Since the convening of Congress one year ago the nation has undergone a prostration in business and industries such as has not been witnessed with us for many years. Speculation as to the causes for this prostration might be indulged in without profit, because as many theories would be advanced as there would be independent writers—those who expressed their own views without borrowing—upon the subject. Without indulging in theories as to the cause of this prostration, therefore, I will call your attention only to the fact, and to some plain questions as to which it would seem there should be no disagreement.

During this prostration two essential elements of prosperity have been most abundant—labor and capital. Both have been largely unemployed. Where security has been undoubted, capital has been attainable at very moderate rates. Where labor has been wanted, it has been found in abundance, at cheap rates compared with what—of necessaries and comforts of life—could be purchased with the wages demanded. Two great elements of prosperity, therefore, have not been denied us. A third might be added: Our soil and climate are unequaled, within the limits of any contiguous territory under one nationality, for its variety of products to feed and clothe a people and in the amount of surplus to spare to feed less favored peoples. Therefore, with these facts in view, it seems to me that wise statesmanship, at this session of Congress, would dictate legislation ignoring the past; directing in proper channels these great elements of prosperity to any people. Debt, debt abroad, is the only element that can, with always a sound currency, enter into our affairs to cause any continued depression in the industries and prosperity of our people. . . .

Our commerce should be encouraged; American shipbuilding and carrying capacity increased; foreign markets sought for products of the soil and manufactories, to the end that we may be able to pay these debts [owed abroad]. Where a new market can be created for the sale of our products, either of the soil, the mine, or the manufactory, a new means is discovered of utilizing our idle capital and labor to the advantage of the whole people. But, in my judgment, the first step toward accomplishing this object is to secure a currency of fixed, stable value; a currency good wherever civilization reigns. . . . Gold and silver are now the recognized medium of exchange the civilized world over, and to this we should return with the least practicable delay.

15. PRESIDENT GROVER CLEVELAND MAKES TARIFF REDUCTION THE MAIN ISSUE IN A MESSAGE TO CONGRESS (1887)

Our present tariff laws, the vicious, inequitable, and illogical source of unnecessary taxation, ought to be at once revised and amended. These laws, as their primary and plain effect, raise the price to consumers of all articles imported and subject to duty by precisely the sum paid for such duties. Thus the amount of the duty measures the tax paid by those who purchase for use these imported articles. . . .

It is not proposed to entirely relieve the country of this taxation. It must be extensively continued as the source of the Government's income; and in a readjustment of our tariff the interests of American labor engaged in manufacture should be carefully considered, as well as the preservation of our manufacturers. It may be called protection or by any other name, but relief from the hardships and dangers of our present tariff laws should be devised with especial precaution against imperiling the existence of our manufacturing interests. . . .

The reduction of taxation demanded should be so measured as not to necessitate or justify either the loss of employment by the working man or the lessening of his wages; and the profits still remaining to the manufacturer after a necessary readjustment should furnish no excuse for the sacrifice of the interests of his employees, either in their opportunity to work or in the diminution of their compensation.

16. RADICAL PLANKS IN THE DEMOCRATIC PLATFORM OF 1896

Recognizing that the money question is paramount to all others at this time, we invite attention to the fact that the federal Constitution names silver and gold together as the money metals of the United States, and that the first coinage law passed by Congress under the Constitution made the silver dollar the money unit, and admitted gold to free coinage at a ratio based upon the silver dollar unit.

We declare that the act of 1873 demonetizing silver without the knowledge or approval of the American people has resulted in the appreciation of gold and a corresponding fall in the prices of commodities produced by the people; . . . the enrichment of the money-lending class at home and abroad; the prostration of industry and impoverishment of the people. . . .

We demand the free and unlimited coinage of both silver and gold at the present legal ratio of sixteen to one without waiting for the aid or consent of any other nation. . . .

We demand that all paper which is made a legal tender for public and private debts . . . shall be issued by the government of the United States and shall be redeemable in coin. . . .

Until the money question is settled we are opposed to any agitation for further changes in our tariff laws, except such as are necessary to meet the deficit in revenue caused by the adverse decision of the Supreme Court on the income tax. . . . We declare that it is the duty of Congress to use all the constitutional power which remains after that decision, or which may come from its reversal by the court as it may hereafter be constituted, so that the burden of taxation may be equally and impartially laid, to the end that wealth may bear its due proportion of the expenses of the government.

We hold that the most efficient way of protecting American labor is to prevent the importation of foreign pauper labor to compete with it in the home market, and that the value of the home market to our American farmers and artisans is greatly reduced by a vicious monetary system which depresses the prices of their products below the cost of production, and thus deprives them of the means of purchasing the products of our home manufactories; and, as labor creates the wealth of the country, we demand the passage of such laws as may be necessary to protect it in all its rights. . . .

We denounce arbitrary interference by federal authorities in local affairs as a violation of the Constitution of the United States and a crime against free institutions, and we especially object to government by injunction as a new and highly dangerous form of oppression by which federal judges, in contempt of the laws of the States and rights of citizens, become at once legislators, judges, and executioners. . . .

17. PRESIDENT THEODORE ROOSEVELT OPENS THE TWENTIETH CENTURY IN MESSAGES TO CONGRESS

The tremendous and highly complex industrial development which went on with ever accelerated rapidity during the latter half of the nineteenth century brings us face to face, at the beginning of the twentieth, with very serious social problems. The old laws, and the old customs which had almost the binding force of law, were once quite sufficient to regulate the accumulation and distribution of wealth. Since the industrial changes which have so enormously increased the productive power of mankind, they are no longer sufficient.

The growth of cities has gone on beyond comparison faster than the growth of the country, and the upbuilding of the great industrial centers has meant a startling increase, not merely in the aggregate of wealth, but in the number of very large individual, and especially of very large corporate, fortunes. The creation of these great corporate fortunes has not been due to the tariff nor to any other governmental action, but to natural causes in the business world, operating in other countries as they operate in our own. . . .

In the interest of the whole people, the Nation should, without interfering with the power of the States in the matter itself, also assume power of supervision and regulation over all corporations doing an interstate business. . . .

The most vital problem with which this country, and for that matter the whole civilized world, has to deal, is the problem which has for one side the betterment of social conditions, moral and physical, in large cities, and for another side the effort to deal with that tangle of far-reaching questions which we group together when we speak of "labor." . . .

When all is said and done, the rule of brotherhood remains as the indispensable prerequisite to success in the kind of national life for which we strive. . . . (1901)

When our tax laws are revised the question of an income tax and an inheritance tax should receive the careful attention of our legislators. . . .

Our aim is to recognize what Lincoln pointed out: The fact that there are some respects in which men are obviously not equal; but also to insist that there should be . . . an equality of rights before the law, and at least an approximate equality in the conditions under which each man obtains the chance to show the stuff that is in him when compared to his fellows. . . . (1907)

We wish to see the farmer own his own land; we do not wish to see the farms so large that they become the property of absentee landlords who farm them by tenants; nor yet so small that the farmer becomes like a European peasant. . . .

There should no longer be any paltering with the question of taking care of the wage-workers who, under our present industrial system, become killed, crippled, or worn out as a part of the regular incidents of a given business. (1908)

18. THE PROGRESSIVE PLATFORM EXALTS NATIONAL WELFARE (1912)

The conscience of the people in a time of grave national problems has called into being a new party, born of the nation's awakened sense of justice. . . .

We hold, with Thomas Jefferson and Abraham Lincoln, that the people are the masters of their Constitution, to fulfill its purposes and to safeguard it from those who, by perversion of its intent, would convert it into an instrument of injustice. In accordance with the needs of each generation the people must use their sovereign powers to establish and maintain equal opportunity and industrial justice, to secure which this government was founded and without which no republic can endure.

This country belongs to the people who inhabit it. Its resources, its business, its institutions, and its laws should be utilized, maintained, or altered in whatever manner will best promote the general interest. It is time to set the public welfare in the first place . . . to build a new and nobler commonwealth. . . .

The Progressive party, believing that no people can justly claim to be a true democracy which denies political right on account of sex, pledges itself to the task of securing equal suffrage to men and women alike. . . .

19. THE SOCIALIST PLATFORM DENOUNCES THE CAPITALIST SYSTEM (1912)

The representatives of the Socialist party in national convention at Indianapolis, declare that the capitalist system has outgrown its historical function, and has become utterly incapable of meeting the problems now confronting society. We denounce this outgrown system as incompetent and corrupt and the source of unspeakable misery and suffering to the whole working class.

Under this system the industrial equipment of the Nation has passed into the absolute control of a plutocracy which exacts an annual tribute of millions of dollars from the producers. . . .

Multitudes of unemployed walk the streets of our cities. . . .

The farmers in every State are plundered. . . .

Capitalist concentration is mercilessly crushing the class of small business men. . . .

It is this capitalist system that is responsible for the increasing burden of armaments, the poverty, slums, child labor, most of the insanity, crime and prostitution, and much of the disease that afflicts mankind. . . .

20. PRESIDENT WOODROW WILSON'S FOURTEEN POINTS ON INTERNATIONAL RELATIONS (1918)

I.—Open covenants of peace, openly arrived at, after which there shall be no private international understandings of any kind but diplomacy shall proceed always frankly and in the public view.

II.—Absolute freedom of navigation upon the seas, outside territorial waters, alike in peace and in war, except as the seas may be closed in whole or in part by international action for the enforcement of international covenants.

III.—The removal, so far as possible, of all economic barriers and the establishment of an equality of trade conditions among all the nations consenting to the peace and associating themselves for its maintenance.

IV.—Adequate guarantees given and taken that national armaments will be reduced to the lowest point consistent with domestic safety.

V.—Free, open-minded, and absolutely impartial adjustment of all colonial claims, based upon a strict observance of the principle that in determining all such questions of sovereignty the interests of the population concerned must have equal weight with the equitable claims of the Government whose title is to be determined.

VI.—The evacuation of all Russian territory and such a settlement of all questions affecting Russia as will secure the best and freest cooperation of the other nations of the world in obtaining for her an unhampered and unembarrassed opportunity for the independent determination of her own political development and national policy, and assure her of a sincere welcome into the society of free nations under institutions of her own choosing; and, more than a welcome, assistance also of every kind that she may need and may herself desire. The treatment accorded Russia by her sister nations in the months to come will be the acid test of their goodwill, of their comprehension of her needs as distinguished from their own interests.

VII.—Belgium, the whole world will agree, must be evacuated and restored, without any attempt to limit the sovereignty which she enjoys in common with all other free nations. No other single act will serve as this will serve to restore confidence among the nations in the laws which they have themselves set and determined for the government of their relations with one another. Without this healing act the whole structure and validity of international law is forever impaired.

VIII.—All French territory should be freed and the invaded portions restored, and the wrong done to France by Prussia in 1871 in the matter of Alsace-Lorraine, which has unsettled the peace of the world for nearly fifty years, should be righted, in order that peace may once more be made secure in the interest of all.

IX.—A readjustment of the frontiers of Italy should be effected along clearly recognizable lines of nationality.

X.—The peoples of Austria-Hungary, whose place among the nations we wish to see safeguarded and assured, should be accorded the freest opportunity of autonomous development.

XI.—Rumania, Serbia, and Montenegro should be evacuated; occupied territories restored; Serbia accorded free and secure access to the sea; and the relations of the several Balkan States to one another determined by friendly counsel along historically established lines of allegiance and nationality; and international guarantees of the political and economic independence and territorial integrity of the several Balkan States should be entered into.

XII.—The Turkish portions of the present Ottoman Empire should be assured a secure sovereignty, but the other nationalities which are now under Turkish rule should be assured an undoubted security of life and an absolutely unmolested opportunity of autonomous development, and the Dardanelles should be permanently opened as a free passage to the ships and commerce of all nations under international guarantees.

XIII.—An independent Polish State should be erected which should include the territories inhabited by indisputably Polish populations, which should be assured a free and secure access to the sea, and whose political and economic independence and territorial integrity should be guaranteed by international covenant.

XIV.—A general association of nations must be formed under specific covenants for the purpose of affording mutual guarantees of political independence and territorial integrity to great and small States alike.

21. JUSTICE OLIVER WENDELL HOLMES UPHOLDS "FREE TRADE IN IDEAS"

Persecution for the expression of opinions seems to me perfectly logical. If you have no doubt of your premises or your power and want a certain result with all your heart you naturally express your wishes in law and sweep away all opposition. To allow opposition by speech seems to indicate that you think the speech impotent, as when a man says that he has squared the circle, or that you do not care wholeheartedly for the result, or that you doubt either your power or your premises. But when men have realized that time has upset many fighting faiths, they may come to believe even more than they believe the very foundations of their own conduct that the ultimate good desired is better reached by free trade in ideas—that the best test of truth is the power of the thought to get itself accepted in the competition of the market, and that truth is the only ground upon which their wishes safely can be carried out. That at any rate is the theory of our Constitution. It is an experiment, as all life is an experiment. Every year if not every day we have to wager our salvation upon some prophecy based upon imperfect knowledge. While that experiment is part of our system I think that we should be eternally vigilant against attempts to check the expression of opinions that we loathe and believe to be fraught with death, unless they so imminently threaten immediate interference with the lawful and pressing purposes of the law that an immediate check is required to save the country. [Dissenting Opinion, Abrams v. United States, 1919.]

22. PRESIDENT HERBERT HOOVER ON SOCIAL AND ECONOMIC PHILOSOPHY (1922)

Five or six great social philosophies are at struggle in the world for ascendancy. There is the Individualism of America. There is the Individualism of the more democratic states of Europe with its careful reservations of castes and classes. There are Communism, Socialism, Syndicalism, Capitalism, and finally there is Autocracy—whether by birth, by possessions, militarism, or divine right of kings. . . .

It is not the individualism of other countries for which I would speak, but the individualism of America. . . . In our individualism we have long since abandoned the *laissez faire* of the eighteenth century—the notion that it is "every man for himself and the devil take the hindmost." We abandoned that when we adopted the ideal of equality of opportunity—the fair chance of Abraham Lincoln. We have confirmed its abandonment in terms of legislation, of social and economic justice,—in part because we have learned that it is the hindmost who throws the bricks at our social edifice, in part because we have learned that the foremost are not always the best nor the hindmost the worst—and in part because we have learned that social injustice is the destruction of justice itself. We have learned that the impulse to production can only be maintained at a high pitch if there is a fair division of the product. We have also learned that fair division can only be obtained by certain restrictions on the strong and the dominant. . . .

The social force in which I am interested is far higher and far more precious a thing than all these [assumptions of some group dominating somebody else]. It springs from something infinitely more enduring; it springs from the one source of human progress—that each individual shall be given the chance and stimulation for development of the best with which he has been endowed in heart and mind; it is the sole source of progress; it is American individualism.

The rightfulness of our individualism can rest either on philosophic, political, economic, or spiritual grounds. It can rest on the ground of being the only safe avenue to further human progress. . . .

To curb the forces in business which would destroy equality of opportunity and yet to maintain the initiative and creative faculties of our people are the twin objects we must attain. . . . This is the deadline between our system and socialism.

23. PRESIDENT HERBERT HOOVER'S ECONOMIC PHILOSOPHY APPLIED TO HIS VETO OF THE MUSCLE SHOALS BILL (1931)

I am firmly opposed to the government entering into any business the major purpose of which is competition with our citizens. There are national emergencies which require that the government should temporarily enter the field of business, but they must be emergency actions and in matters where the cost of the project is secondary to much higher considerations. . . . But for the Federal Government deliberately to go out to build up and expand such an occasion to the major purpose of a power and manufacturing business is to break down the initiative and enterprise of the American people; it is destruction of equality of opportunity amongst our people; it is the negation of the ideals upon which our civilization has been based.

This bill raises one of the important issues confronting our people. That is squarely the issue of Federal Government ownership and operation of power and manufacturing business not as a minor by-product but as a major purpose. Involved in this question is the agitation against the conduct of the power industry. The power problem is not to be solved by the Federal Government going into the power business, nor is it to be solved by the project in this bill. The remedy for abuses in the conduct of that industry lies in regulation. . . . I have recommended to the Congress on various occasions that action should be taken to establish Federal regulation of interstate power in co-operation with state authorities. This bill would launch the Federal Government upon a policy of ownership and operation of power

utilities upon a basis of competition instead of by the proper government
function of regulation for the protection of all the people. I hesitate to contemplate the future of our institutions, of our government, and of our country if the preoccupation of its officials is to be no longer the promotion of
justice and equal opportunity but is to be devoted to barter in the markets.
That is not liberalism, it is degeneration.

24. PRESIDENT FRANKLIN D. ROOSEVELT FACES THE CALAMITY OF 1933

This is a day of national consecration. I am certain that on this day my
fellow Americans expect that on my induction into the Presidency I will
address them with a candor and a decision which the present situation of
our nation impels. . . .
So first of all let me assert my firm belief that the only thing we have to
fear is fear itself—nameless, unreasoning, unjustified terror which paralyzes
needed efforts to convert retreat into advance. . . .
Values have shrunken to fantastic levels; taxes have risen; our ability to
pay has fallen; government of all kinds is faced by serious curtailment of
income; the means of exchange are frozen in the currents of trade; the
withered leaves of industrial enterprise lie on every side; farmers find no
markets for their produce; the savings of many years in thousands of families are gone.
More important, a host of unemployed citizens face the grim problem of
existence, and an equally great number toil with little return. Only a foolish
optimist can deny the dark realities of the moment. . . .
I am prepared under my constitutional duty to recommend the measures
that a stricken nation in the midst of a stricken world may require. . . .
But in the event that the Congress shall fail to take one of these two
courses [adopting my measures or others devised by Congress], and in the
event that the national emergency is still critical, I shall not evade the clear
course of duty that will then confront me.
I shall ask the Congress for the one remaining instrument to meet the
crisis—broad executive power to wage a war against the emergency as great
as the power that would be given to me if we were in fact invaded by a
foreign foe. . . . [First Inaugural Address.]

25. PRESIDENT FRANKLIN D. ROOSEVELT CALLS ATTENTION TO A THIRD OF THE NATION IN HIS SECOND INAUGURAL ADDRESS (1937)

Let us ask again: Have we reached the goal of our vision of that fourth
day of March, 1933? Have we found our happy valley?
I see a great nation, upon a great continent, blessed with a great wealth

of natural resources. Its hundred and thirty million people are at peace among themselves; they are making their country a good neighbor among the nations. I see a United States which can demonstrate that, under democratic methods of government, national wealth can be translated into a spreading volume of human comforts hitherto unknown, and the lowest standard of living can be raised far above the level of mere subsistence.

But here is the challenge to our democracy: In this nation I see tens of millions of its citizens—a substantial part of its whole population—who at this very moment are denied the greater part of what the very lowest standards of today call the necessities of life.

I see millions of families trying to live on incomes so meager that the pall of family disaster hangs over them day by day.

I see millions whose daily lives in city and on farm continue under conditions labeled indecent by a so-called polite society half a century ago.

I see millions denied education, recreation, and the opportunity to better their lot and the lot of their children.

I see millions lacking the means to buy the products of farm and factory and by their poverty denying work and productiveness to many other millions.

I see one-third of a nation ill-housed, ill-clad, ill-nourished.

It is not in despair that I paint you that picture. I paint it for you in hope —because the Nation, seeing and understanding the injustice in it, proposes to paint it out. . . .

In taking again the oath of office as President of the United States, I assume the solemn obligation of leading the American people forward along the road over which they have chosen to advance.

26. THE ATLANTIC CHARTER

. . . The President of the United States of America and the Prime Minister, Mr. Churchill, representing His Majesty's Government in the United Kingdom, being met together, deem it right to make known certain common principles in the national policies of their respective countries on which they base their hopes for a better future for the world.

FIRST, their countries seek no aggrandizement, territorial or other;

SECOND, they desire to see no territorial changes that do not accord with the freely expressed wishes of the peoples concerned;

THIRD, they respect the right of all peoples to choose the form of government under which they will live; and they wish to see sovereign rights and self-government restored to those who have been forcibly deprived of them;

FOURTH, they will endeavor, with due respect for their existing obligations, to further the enjoyment by all States, great or small, victor or vanquished, of access, on equal terms, to the trade and to the raw materials of the world which are needed for their economic prosperity;

FIFTH, they desire to bring about the fullest collaboration between all nations in the economic field with the object of securing, for all, improved labor standards, economic advancement, and social security;

SIXTH, after the final destruction of the Nazi tyranny, they hope to see established a peace which will afford to all nations the means of dwelling in safety within their own boundaries, and which will afford assurance that all the men in all the lands may live out their lives in freedom from fear and want;

SEVENTH, such a peace should enable all men to traverse the high seas and oceans without hindrance;

EIGHTH, they believe that all of the nations of the world, for realistic as well as spiritual reasons, must come to the abandonment of the use of force. Since no future peace can be maintained if land, sea or air armaments continue to be employed by nations which threaten, or may threaten, aggression outside of their frontiers, they believe, pending the establishment of a wider and permanent system of general security, that the disarmament of such nations is essential. They will likewise aid and encourage all other practicable measures which will lighten for peace-loving peoples the crushing burden of armaments.

FRANKLIN D. ROOSEVELT
WINSTON S. CHURCHILL

Dated August 14, 1941.

27. THE MAIN THREE-POWER DECLARATION AT TEHERAN

We, the President of the United States of America, the Prime Minister of Great Britain, and the Premier of the Soviet Union, have met in these four days past in this the capital of our ally, Teheran, and have shaped and confirmed our common policy.

We express our determination that our nations shall work together in the war and in the peace that will follow.

As to the war, our military staffs have joined in our round-table discussions and we have concerted our plans for the destruction of the German forces. We have reached complete agreement as to the scope and timing of operations which will be undertaken from the east, west and south. The common understanding which we have here reached guarantees that victory will be ours.

And as to the peace, we are sure that our concord will make it an enduring peace. We recognize fully the supreme responsibility resting upon us and all the nations to make a peace which will command good will from the overwhelming masses of the peoples of the world and banish the scourge and terror of war for many generations.

With our diplomatic advisers we have surveyed the problems of the future. We shall seek the co-operation and active participation of all nations, large and small, whose peoples in heart and in mind are dedicated, as are our own peoples, to the elimination of tyranny and slavery, oppression and intolerance. We will welcome them as they may choose to come into the world family of democratic nations.

No power on earth can prevent our destroying the German armies by land, their U-boats by sea, and their war plants from the air. Our attacks will be relentless and increasing.

Emerging from these friendly conferences we look with confidence to the day when all the peoples of the world may live free lives untouched by tyranny and according to their varying desires and their own consciences.

We came here with hope and determination. We leave here friends in fact, in spirit, and in purpose.

Signed at Teheran, Dec. 1, 1943.

ROOSEVELT, STALIN, CHURCHILL.

28. PLANKS ON DOMESTIC AND FOREIGN AFFAIRS FROM THE PROGRAM OF THE POSTWAR PLANNING COMMITTEE OF THE AMERICAN FEDERATION OF LABOR (April, 1944)

We want a regime of economic freedom, but our enterprise system must demonstrate that it can function so as to husband and utilize, not to waste and dissipate our natural resources. We want free enterprise, but our productive system must be committed to the progressive raising of the national income and the maintenance of full employment. Such a system is necessarily opposed to all tendencies toward monopolistic restriction. We want free enterprise, but we also want an economy which will provide ample support for the health, educational, recreational, and similar public services so essential to the welfare of the working people in our industrial society. Finally, we want a program of economic enterprise which will not be repressive, but will support the free exercise of civil and political liberties. . . .

The right to work and the right to quit work are among the basic rights of free men. . . .

Free and independent organizations of the people are an indispensable means of checking concentration of economic and governmental power. . . .

All will suffer disaster, if the powerful organizations of finance, business, farmers, and labor seek merely to advance their own interests without regard for the consequences on the community as a whole. . . .

There has been, there is, and there can be no lasting conflict between a movement created by the working people and democratic purposes and processes. . . .

[As to foreign relations] It is imperative that the United States do its full part to help develop a general system of mutual security. . . . [but not a world government].

29. THE PRESIDENT OF THE UNITED STATES CHAMBER OF COMMERCE, ERIC JOHNSTON, EXPRESSES HIS VIEWS ON THE HOME FRONT[1]

I believe—I may say we believe—that the individual man and woman is the pivotal element in a desirable society. The individual safety, freedom, and happiness come first and last. The state in any of its forms, for us, has no standing or authority per se as an end in itself, but only as the tool and servant of the individual. A rich and powerful state would be meaningless to Americans, if it rested on weak and poor individuals.

We deny that America faces a choice between a congealed old order and some experimental new order. On the contrary, we feel that those who narrow down the choice between such repugnant extremes are dangerously confusing the issue.

We believe in the middle way: the way of realistic adjustment between old-style laissez-faire capitalism and socialized economy.

I have an abiding faith in the common sense of the American people. I believe that our instincts are right, not because we are better or more intelligent than other peoples, but because we have been conditioned by a hundred and fifty years of freedom. Relying on themselves, rather than on state or fate, has become second nature to people who faced and conquered a continent with their bare hands and their indomitable will.

A great duel is under way in the world today.

I refer to the fateful duel between two conceptions of human existence, two ways of life, that may be summed up in the over-simplified formula: individualism versus statism.

The contest cannot be identified in terms of party labels or regions, because it cuts across political and geographical boundaries.

I believe capitalism has no need of apologetics. Capitalism is neither "good" nor "bad." It is a process, and all that we need to judge is how it works. I see three main capitalisms in the world.

There is the capitalism of the bureaucrats. I am against it in its extreme forms in the totalitarian countries. I am against it in its seedling growths in our own country.

Second, there is the capitalism of private monopoly and special privilege. I am against it wherever it seeks to control and to dominate.

Finally, there is what I venture to call a people's capitalism. I come from it. I want to see it survive for every boy and girl in America after me.

We Americans have been able to make the magnificent contribution of our industrial genius toward winning the war precisely because we were rich, industrious, immensely productive, and economically free.

The upsurge of energy, inventiveness, productivity evoked by an external

[1] A compilation of public expressions by Eric Johnston, prepared with the permission and approval of the U. S. Chamber of Commerce.

enemy can and must be maintained for war against internal enemies such as poverty, low living standards, chronic unemployment. These are challenges as real as the Axis and can be met in the same spirit.

Americans must not become slaves of any ideology—not even the ideology of free capitalism. The techniques of capitalism are tools to be used, not fetishes to be worshipped.

I believe there should be special tax concessions for new enterprises for a limited number of years—the period of dangerous infant mortality in business—and special tax treatment for capital invested in plant expansion and other job-making efforts.

An amicable management-labor picture is not a secondary matter to be dealt with in spare time. It is a central challenge. Nothing less than the life or death of our free economy is at stake.

In recent travels I have been less impressed with the "oneness" of the world than with its dizzy multiplicity. Space has been telescoped by the airplane, but the differences between nations and peoples are as formidable as ever.

The devastation that has swept the world in our time is not alone physical. We may survive physically, but we shall be moral casualties if in the process of winning the war we lose any portion of our hatred for its brutalities and its sufferings. In the preoccupation with slogans, propaganda, postwar planning, let us never lose the tragic sense that war is hell and that no price is too big to stave it off.

30. SOME OF THE AGREEMENTS REACHED BY ROOSEVELT, CHURCHILL, AND STALIN AT YALTA
(1945)

The Premier of the Union of Soviet Socialist Republics, the Prime Minister of the United Kingdom and the President of the United States of America have consulted with each other in the common interests of the peoples of their countries and those of liberated Europe. . . .

The establishment of order in Europe and the rebuilding of national economic life must be achieved by processes which will enable the liberated peoples to . . . create democratic institutions of their own choice. This is a principle of the Atlantic Charter—the right of all peoples to choose the form of government under which they will live— . . .

. . . the three Governments will jointly assist the people in any European liberated state or former Axis satellite state in Europe where, in their judgment conditions require . . . to form interim governmental authorities broadly representative of all democratic elements in the population and pledged to the earliest possible establishment through free elections of Governments responsive to the will of the people; and . . . to facilitate where necessary the holding of such elections. . . .

The United Kingdom, the United States of America and the Union of

Soviet Socialist Republics shall possess supreme authority with respect to Germany. In the exercise of such authority they will take such steps, including the complete disarmament, demilitarization and dismemberment of Germany as they deem requisite for future peace and security.

. . . Germany must pay in kind for the losses caused by her to Allied nations in the course of the war. . . .

Reparations in kind is to be exacted from Germany in three following forms:

(a) Removals within two years from the surrender of Germany or the cessation of organized resistance from the national wealth of Germany . . . equipment, machine tools, ships, rolling stock, German investments abroad, shares of industrial, transport and other enterprises in Germany, etc. . . . these removals to be carried out chiefly for purpose of destroying the war potential of Germany.

(b) Annual deliveries of goods from current production for a period to be fixed.

(c) Use of German labor. . . .

. . . The Provisional Government which is now functioning in Poland should . . . be reorganized on a broader democratic basis. . . .

This Polish Provisional Government of National Unity shall be pledged to the holding of free and unfettered elections as soon as possible on the basis of universal suffrage and secret ballot. In these elections all democratic and anti-Nazi parties shall have the right to take part and to put forward candidates. . . .

The three heads of Government consider that the eastern frontier of Poland should follow the Curzon Line with digressions from it in some regions of five to eight kilometers in favor of Poland. They recognize that Poland must receive substantial accessions of territory in the north and west. They feel . . . that the final delimitation of the western frontier of Poland should thereafter await the peace conference. . . .

The leaders of the three great powers—the Soviet Union, the United States of America and Great Britain—have agreed that in two or three months after Germany has surrendered and the war in Europe has terminated, the Soviet Union shall enter into the war against Japan on the side of the Allies on condition that:

1. The status quo in Outer Mongolia (the Mongolian People's Republic) shall be preserved;

2. The former rights of Russia violated by the treacherous attack of Japan in 1904 shall be restored, viz:

(a) The southern part of Sakhalin as well as the islands adjacent to it shall be returned to the Soviet Union;

(b) The commercial port of Dairen shall be internationalized, the pre-eminent interests of the Soviet Union in this port being safeguarded, and the lease of Port Arthur as a naval base of the U.S.S.R. restored;

(c) The Chinese-Eastern Railroad and the South Manchurian Railroad, which provide an outlet to Dairen, shall be jointly operated by the establishment of a joint Soviet-Chinese company, it being understood that the pre-eminent interests of the Soviet Union shall be safeguarded and that China shall retain full sovereignty in Manchuria;

3. The Kurile Islands shall be handed over to the Soviet Union.

It is understood that the agreement concerning Outer Mongolia and the ports and railroads referred to above will require concurrence of Generalissimo Chiang Kai-shek. The President will take measures in order to obtain this concurrence on advice from Marshal Stalin. . . .

31. TRUMAN ANNOUNCES THE DOCTRINE THAT THE UNITED STATES MUST DETOUR THE UNITED NATIONS, WHEN NECESSARY TO HOLD COMMUNIST EXPANSION IN CHECK (1947)

. . . The very existence of the Greek state is today threatened by the terrorist activities of several thousand armed men, led by Communists, who defy the Government's authority at a number of points, particularly along the northern boundaries. . . . The Greek Army is small and poorly equipped. It needs supplies and equipment if it is to restore the authority to the Government throughout Greek territory. . . .

We have considered how the United Nations might assist in this crisis. But the situation is an urgent one requiring immediate action, and the United Nations and its related organizations are not in a position to extend help of the kind that is required. . . .

It is necessary only to glance at a map to realize that the survival and integrity of the Greek nation are of grave importance in a much wider situation. If Greece should fall under the control of an armed minority, the effect upon its neighbor, Turkey, would be immediate and serious. Confusion and disorder might well spread throughout the entire Middle East.

Moreover, the disappearance of Greece as an independent state would have a profound effect upon those countries in Europe whose peoples are struggling against great difficulties to maintain their freedoms and their independence while they repair the damages of war. . . .

Should we fail to aid Greece and Turkey in this fateful hour, the effect will be far reaching to the West as well as to the East.

We must take immediate and resolute action.

I therefore ask the Congress to provide authority for assistance to Greece and Turkey in the amount of $400,000,000 for the period ending June 30, 1948. . . .

Finally, I ask that the Congress provide authority which will permit the speediest and most effective use, in terms of needed commodities, supplies, and equipment, of such funds as may be authorized. . . .

If we falter in our leadership, we may endanger the peace of the world—and we shall surely endanger the welfare of our own Nation. . . .

32. PRESIDENT KENNEDY WARNS THE NATION BY RADIO AND TELEVISION OF THE PERILS CREATED BY THE EFFORT TO PLACE LONG-RANGE RUSSIAN MISSILES IN CUBA (1962)

This Government, as promised, has maintained the closest surveillance of the Soviet military buildup on the island of Cuba. Within the past week unmistakable evidence has established the fact that a series of offensive missile sites is now in preparation on that imprisoned island. The purpose of these bases can be none other than to provide a nuclear strike capability against the Western Hemisphere. . . .

The characteristics of these new missile sites indicate two distinct types of installations. Several of them include medium-range ballistic missiles capable of carrying a nuclear warhead for a distance of more than 1,000 miles. Each of these missiles, in short, is capable of striking Washington, D.C., the Panama Canal, Cape Canaveral, Mexico City, or any other city in the southeastern part of the United States, in Central America, or in the Caribbean area.

Additional sites not yet completed appear to be designed for intermediate-range ballistic missiles capable of traveling more than twice as far— and thus capable of striking most of the major cities in the Western Hemisphere, ranging as far north as Hudson Bay, Canada, and as far south as Lima, Peru. In addition, jet bombers, capable of carrying nuclear weapons, are now being uncrated and assembled in Cuba, while the necessary air bases are being prepared.

This urgent transformation of Cuba into an important strategic base— by the presence of these large, long-range, and clearly offensive weapons of sudden mass destruction—constitutes an explicit threat to the peace and security of all the Americas. . . .

The 1930's taught us a clear lesson. Aggressive conduct, if allowed to grow unchecked and unchallenged, ultimately leads to war.

. . . We will not prematurely or unnecessarily risk the costs of worldwide nuclear war in which even the fruits of victory would be ashes in our mouth—but neither will we shirk from that risk at any time it must be faced.

Acting, therefore, in the defense of our own security and of the entire Western Hemisphere, and under the authority entrusted to me by the Constitution as endorsed by the resolution of the Congress, I have directed that the following initial steps be taken immediately:

First: To halt this offensive buildup, a strict quarantine on all offensive military equipment under shipment to Cuba is being initiated. All ships of any kind bound for Cuba from whatever nation or port will, if found to contain cargoes of offensive weapons, be turned back. This quarantine will be extended, if needed, to other types of cargo and carriers. . . .

Second: . . . I have directed the Armed Forces to prepare for any even-tualities; and I trust that, in the interest of both the Cuban people and the Soviet technicians at the sites, the hazards to all concerned of continuing this threat will be recognized.

Third: It shall be the policy of this nation to regard any nuclear missile launched from Cuba against any nation in the Western Hemisphere as an attack by the Soviet Union on the United States, requiring a full retaliatory response upon the Soviet Union. . . .

Seventh and finally: I call upon Chairman Khrushchev to halt and elimi-nate this clandestine, reckless, and provocative threat to world peace . . . by . . . withdrawing these weapons from Cuba—by refraining from any action which will widen or deepen the present crisis—and then by partici-pation in a search for peaceful and permanent solutions.

33. THE SUPREME COURT OF THE UNITED STATES ORDERS REAPPORTIONMENT OF STATE LEGISLATURES BY POPULATION (1964)

We hold that, as a basic constitutional standard, the Equal Protection Clause [of the United States Constitution] requires that the seats in both houses of a bicameral state legislature must be apportioned on a population basis. Simply stated, an individual's right to vote for state legislators is unconstitutionally impaired when its weight is in a substantial fashion diluted when compared with votes of citizens living in other parts of the state. . . .

The right of a citizen to equal representation . . . in the election of members of one house of a bicameral state legislature would amount to little if states could effectively submerge the equal population principle in the apportionment of seats in the other house. . . .

At the time this litigation was commenced, there had been no reapportion-ment of seats in the Alabama Legislature for over sixty years. Legislative inaction, coupled with the unavailability of any political or judicial remedy, had resulted, with the passage of years, in . . . a minority strangle hold on the State Legislature. . . .

Under the existing provisions, applying 1960 census figures . . . Bullock County, with a population of only 13,462, and Henry County, with a popu-lation of only 15,286, each were allocated two seats in the Alabama House, whereas Mobile County, with a population of 314,301, was given only three seats . . . With respect to senatorial apportionment, since the pertinent Alabama constitutional provisions have been consistently construed as prohibiting the giving of more than one Senate seat to any one county, Jefferson County, with over 600,000 people, was given only one Senator, as was Lowndes County, with a 1960 population of only 15,417. . . .

. . . Since, under neither the existing apportionment provisions nor either of the proposed plans was either of the houses of the Alabama Legislature apportioned on a population basis, the District Court correctly held that all three of these schemes were constitutionally invalid. . . .

34. EXCERPTS FROM PRESIDENT LYNDON B. JOHNSON'S STATE OF THE UNION ADDRESS TO CONGRESS, JANUARY 4, 1965, DESCRIBING THE GREAT SOCIETY

World affairs will continue to call upon our energy and our courage.

But today we can turn increased attention to the character of American life.

We are in the midst of the greatest upward surge of economic well-being in the history of any nation. . . .

We worked for two centuries to climb this peak of prosperity. But we are only at the beginning of the road to the Great Society. Ahead now is a summit where freedom from the wants of the body can help fulfill the needs of the spirit. . . .

The Great Society asks not how much, but how good; not only how to create wealth but how to use it; not only how fast we are going, but where we are headed. . . .

This kind of society will not flower spontaneously from swelling riches and surging power . . . It will require of every American, for many generations, both faith in the destination and the fortitude to make the journey. . . .

I propose that we begin a program in education to insure every American child the fullest development of his mind and skills.

I propose that we begin a massive attack on crippling and killing diseases.

I propose that we launch a national effort to make the American city a better and more stimulating place to live.

I propose that we increase the beauty of America and end the poisoning of our rivers and the air that we breathe. . . .

I propose that we make new efforts to control and prevent crime and delinquency.

I propose that we eliminate every remaining obstacle to the right and the opportunity to vote. . . .

Our economy owes much to the efficiency of our farmers. We must continue to assure them the opportunity to earn a fair reward. . . .

In a country that spans a continent modern transportation is vital to continued growth . . . I will ask for funds to study high-speed rail transportation between urban centers. We will begin with test projects between Washington and Boston. On high-speed trains passengers could travel this distance in less than four hours. . . .

Most Americans enjoy a good life. But far too many are still trapped in poverty and idleness and fear.

Let a just nation throw open to them the city of promise.

To the elderly, by providing hospital care under social security and by raising benefit payments to those struggling to maintain the dignity of their later years.

To the poor and unfortunate, through doubling the war against poverty this year.

To Negro Americans, through enforcement of the civil rights law and elimination of barriers to the right to vote.

To those in other lands that are seeking the promise of America, through an immigration law based on the work a man can do and not where he was born. . . .

To promote and honor creative achievements, I propose a National Foundation on the Arts. . . .

I will recommend programs . . . to bring closer the day when the oceans will supply our growing need for fresh water.

CHANGES IN THE TERRITORY UNDER
AMERICAN CONTROL

PART I. AREAS FULLY ACQUIRED BY THE UNITED STATES

Region	Year Acquired[1]	Area in Sq. Mi.	Purchase Price	Acquired from
Original United States	1783	888,811		Gt. Britain
Louisiana Purchase	1803	827,192	$15,000,000[3]	France
West Florida	1810–1813	13,443		Spain
Present Day Florida	1821	58,560	5,000,000[3]	Spain
Texas	1845	390,144		Texas
Oregon	1846	285,580		Gt. Britain
Mexican Cession	1848	529,017	18,250,000[3]	Mexico
Gadsden Purchase	1854	29,640	10,000,000	Mexico
Alaska	1867	586,400	7,200,000	Russia
Hawaiian Islands	1898	6,423		Hawaii
Puerto Rico and Guam	1899	3,641		Spain
Philippine Islands	1899[2]	115,600	20,000,000	Spain
American Samoa	1900–1904	76		Samoa
Virgin Islands of the U.S.	1917	133	25,000,000	Denmark

In addition various minor islands, such as Wake, have been acquired, chiefly through discovery.

[1] The year given is that in which the United States took firm physical possession.
[2] Granted independence in 1946.
[3] Not counting bond interest, if any.

PART II. FOREIGN AREAS LEASED BY THE UNITED STATES

Region	Year Lease Began	Leased from
Panama Canal Zone	1904	Panama
Corn Islands	1916	Nicaragua
Atlantic Ocean bases	1940	Great Britain

The United States also has the use of certain bases in other countries, such as the Philippines.

PART III. AREAS OPERATED BY THE UNITED STATES UNDER A TRUSTEESHIP FROM THE UNITED NATIONS, CREATED IN 1947

The Marshall, Caroline, and Mariana Islands in the Pacific Ocean.

DEFENSE PACTS BETWEEN UNITED STATES AND 42 OTHER COUNTRIES (1967)

ANZUS* PACT	BILATERAL TREATIES	CENTO*	NATO*	SEATO*	RIO PACT**
Australia	Japan***	Britain	Belgium	Australia	Argentina
New Zealand	Nationalist China	Iran	Britain	Britain	Bolivia
	Philippines	Pakistan	Canada	France****	Brazil
	South Korea	Turkey	Denmark	New Zealand	Chile
			France	Pakistan	Colombia
			Greece	Philippines	Costa Rica
			Iceland	Thailand	Domin. Repub.
			Italy		Ecuador
			Luxembourg		El Salvador
			Netherlands		Guatemala
			Norway		Haiti
			Portugal		Honduras
			Turkey		Mexico
			West Germany		Nicaragua
					Panama
					Paraguay
					Peru
					Uruguay
					Venezuela

*   ANZUS: Australia, New Zealand, United States
       CENTO: Central Treaty Organization
**   Rio Pact: Pledges the U.S. to defend any member that asks for help.
***   U.S. pact with Japan may be terminated by either party after 1969.
**** France now sends only an observer to meetings.

NATO: North Atlantic Treaty Organization
SEATO: Southeast Asia Treaty Organization

A CHRONOLOGY

1000	Norsemen discover America (?)
1492	Columbus discovers America
1497	John Cabot touches Labrador
1513	Balboa discovers the Pacific
	Ponce de León discovers Florida
1521	Cortes conquers Mexico
1522	Magellan expedition around world completed
1524	Verrazano discovers the Hudson
1527	Cabeça de Vaca explores the South
1535	Cartier discovers the St. Lawrence
1540	Coronado explores the Southwest
1541	De Soto discovers the Mississippi
1565	St. Augustine—first permanent settlement
1579	Drake touches California coast
1584	Raleigh's expedition lands on Roanoke
1602	Gosnold lands near Cape Cod
1604	The French settle Acadia
	Champlain explores Maine coast
1607	Virginia founded at Jamestown
1608	Quebec founded by Champlain
1609	Champlain discovers Lake Champlain
	Hudson sails beyond Albany
1619	Representative assembly (Jamestown)
	Negro slavery introduced (Virginia)
1620	Pilgrims land at Plymouth
1626	Peter Minuit founds New Amsterdam
1629	Massachusetts Bay Colony at Salem
1630	Puritans migrate; found Boston
1632	Maryland charter granted
1634	Maryland settled at St. Mary's
1635	Connecticut settled by Puritans
1636	Rhode Island settled, Providence
	Harvard College (named in 1639)
1638	New Haven colony founded
	Swedish settlement in Delaware
1639	First constitution (Connecticut's)
1643	New England Confederation formed
1662	Connecticut charter granted
1663	Charter of Carolina granted
	Rhode Island and Providence charters
1664	New Jersey chartered and founded
	British take New Amsterdam (later called New York)

1673	Marquette and Joliet discover the northern Mississippi
1681	Pennsylvania chartered to Penn
1682	La Salle claims Louisiana
	William Penn founds Philadelphia
1689	King William's War (to 1697)
1691	New charter for Massachusetts
1693	College of William and Mary founded
1699	First French colony, at Biloxi
1701	Yale College founded; later at New Haven
1702	Queen Anne's War (to 1713)
1729	Division of Carolina
1733	Georgia settled at Savannah
1735	Freedom of the press (Zenger trial)
1744	King George's War (to 1748)
1754	French and Indian War (to 1763)
	Albany Plan of Union
	King's (Columbia) College founded
1755	Braddock's defeat in Pennsylvania
1759	Surrender of Quebec
1761	Writs of assistance, Massachusetts
1763	France cedes Louisiana to Spain
	Spain cedes Florida to England
1765	Stamp Act
	Stamp Act Congress protests
1770	The Boston Massacre
1773	The Boston Tea Party
1774	Continental Congress, Philadelphia
1775	Battles of Lexington and Concord
	Second Continental Congress
	Battle of Bunker Hill
1776	Declaration of Independence signed
	British occupy New York
1777	Howe occupies Philadelphia
	Burgoyne surrenders at Saratoga
	Articles of Confederation adopted by Congress
	Washington at Valley Forge
1778	British evacuate Philadelphia
1781	Cornwallis surrenders at Yorktown
	Articles of Confederation take effect
1783	Treaty of Peace with England
	England cedes Florida to Spain
1786	Shays' Rebellion in Massachusetts
	Annapolis (pre-federal) Convention
1787	Philadelphia convention; Constitution
	Northwest Ordinance adopted
1788	The Constitution adopted

1789 First Congress meets, New York
Supreme Court established
1790 Philadelphia as capital (10 years)
First census taken
1791 United States Bank chartered (to 1811)
First ten amendments to Constitution (Bill of Rights) ratified
1793 France and England at war
U.S. neutrality proclamation
Whitney invents the cotton gin
1794 Whisky Rebellion in Pennsylvania
1798 Undeclared naval war with France (to 1800)
Alien and Sedition laws passed
1800 Spain cedes Louisiana to France
Washington becomes the capital
1801 War with Tripoli (to 1805)
1803 The Louisiana Purchase
1804 Lewis and Clark Expedition (to 1806)
Twelfth amendment ratified
1807 Fulton's passenger steamer *Clermont* successful
The Embargo Act passed
1808 Slave importations prohibited
1812 War of 1812 (to 1815)
1814 Hartford (tri-state) Convention
1815 Battle of New Orleans
1816 Second United States Bank (to 1836)
1819 Negotiators agree on annexation of east Florida
1820 Missouri Compromise
1823 Monroe Doctrine declared
1825 Erie Canal opened
1829 Delaware and Hudson Canal Company tests railway locomotive
1831 Garrison's *Liberator* (to 1865)
1832 Nullification Ordinance (S.C.)
1837 Financial panic
1838 First ships cross Atlantic using steam only
1844 Telegraph line opened, Washington to Baltimore
1845 Texas annexed
1846 War with Mexico (to 1848)
Howe invents the sewing machine
Anesthetics used in Boston
Oregon boundary dispute settled
1848 First women's rights convention
Mexico cedes the Southwest
1849 California gold rush begins
1850 Compromise of 1850 over slavery
1854 Gadsden Purchase (Mexican border) completed
Perry opens trade with Japan

Kansas-Nebraska Act passed
Present Republican party formed
1857 Dred Scott decision
1859 John Brown at Harper's Ferry
1860 South Carolina secedes
1861 Confederate States of America formed
Civil War (to 1865)
1862 Battle of the *Monitor* and *Merrimac*
Transcontinental telegraph service opens
Homestead (free land) Act
1863 Emancipation Proclamation
Battle of Gettysburg
National banking system established
1864 Campaign of the Wilderness
Sherman takes Atlanta and Savannah
1865 Grant takes Richmond
Surrender of Lee
Assassination of Lincoln
Thirteenth amendment
1866 Field lays an enduring Atlantic cable
1867 Reconstruction Act passed
Purchase of Alaska
1868 Fourteenth amendment ratified
1869 First railroad to the Pacific opened
1870 Fifteenth amendment ratified
1873 Financial panic (to 1878)
1876 Hayes-Tilden election dispute
Bell's speaking telephone first shown
1877 Edison invents a practical phonograph
Union troops removed from the South
1879 Edison's incandescent electric light
1881 President Garfield shot
1882 Chinese immigration suspended
1883 Civil Service Commission created
1886 Mergenthaler linotype goes to work for a newspaper
American Federation of Labor formed
1887 Interstate Commerce Commission
1890 Sherman Anti-Trust Act
1892 Homestead steel and other strikes
Duryea's first American automobile driven
1893 Financial panic and depression
Edison's motion-picture machine
1894 Pullman strike
First public showing of a feature movie
1898 Spanish-American War
Annexation of Hawaii

550 APPENDIX

1899 Spain cedes Puerto Rico, Guam, and the Philippines
      Open-Door Policy in China
1901 President McKinley assassinated
1903 Wrights' first airplane flights
1904 Panama Canal strip leased
1906 De Forest invents vacuum radio tube
1907 Financial panic and depression
      Japanese immigration restricted by the Gentlemen's Agreement
1911 U. S. Supreme Court dissolves Standard Oil Co. of N.J.
1913 Sixteenth amendment ratified
      Seventeenth amendment ratified
      Federal Reserve system created
1914 Marines occupy Vera Cruz; mediation
      Panama Canal officially opened
1916 Intervention in Santo Domingo
1917 War declared on Germany; first World War
1918 Armistice signed, November 11
1919 Eighteenth amendment ratified
      Peace conference; Versailles Treaty
1920 Nineteenth amendment
      Transcontinental air mail service begins
      Commercial radio broadcasting starts
1921 Immigration Act establishes quotas
      Washington Conference (naval arms limitation)
1923 President Harding dies; Coolidge takes the Presidency
1927 U.S. represented at Geneva Disarmament Conference
      Television successfully demonstrated
1929 Stock market crash; long depression
1930 U.S. represented at London Naval Conference
1932 Reconstruction Finance Corporation created
1933 Prohibition amendment repealed
      New Deal begins
      Federal relief for unemployed started
      Payment to farmers for crop reduction begins
      U.S. abandons the gold standard for money
      National Industrial Recovery Act adopted
1934 Securities and Exchange Commission created
1935 National Labor Relations Act adopted
      Trans-Pacific airline service begun
      Social Security system begins
      Committee for Industrial Organization (CIO) formed
1937 United States Housing Authority tackles the slums
1938 Fair Labor Standards Act adopted
1939 World War II begins in Europe; U.S. proclaims neutrality
1941 Lend-Lease Act adopted
      The Atlantic Charter drafted

Japan attacks Pearl Harbor; U.S. enters World War II
1942 American forces invade North Africa
1943 Invasion of Italy
Casablanca, Quebec, Moscow, Cairo, and Teheran conferences
1944 Invasion of France through Normandy
1945 Yalta Conference
Franklin D. Roosevelt dies; Truman becomes President
Germany and Japan surrender; U.S. drops atom bomb on Japan
United Nations Charter goes into effect; U.S. a member of U.N.
1946 The Philippines made independent
1947 Truman Doctrine and Marshall Plan announced
Taft-Hartley labor law adopted
1949 U.S. joins North Atlantic Treaty Organization
1950 U.S. participation in Korean conflict (to 1953)
1952 First U.S. hydrogen bomb test succeeds
1954 Supreme Court outlaws segregation in the public schools
1955 American Federation of Labor and the CIO merge
1958 Atlas intercontinental missile fired full range
First U.S. earth satellite put in orbit
National agency for space travel created
1959 Alaska and Hawaii become states
American artificial planet goes into orbit around the sun
1960 U.S. starts military watch abroad via satellite
1961 U.S.-encouraged Cuban invaders defeated at Bay of Pigs
U.S. holds firmly to Berlin despite Russian threats
1962 John H. Glenn, Jr. is first American to orbit the earth
U.S. naval blockade halts Soviet missile flow to Cuba
1963 U.S., Britain, Russia agree to restrict nuclear testing
President Kennedy assassinated; Johnson becomes President
1964 U.S. court orders reapportionment of state legislatures
Civil Rights Act of 1964 goes into effect
U.S. starts the bombing of North Vietnam
1965 Federal law reduces discrimination in employment
U.S. space probe photographs Mars at close range
1966 Federal officers register Negro voters in the South
Medicare program of medical aid for elderly starts
1967 Space treaty with Britain and Soviet Union ratified

PRESIDENTS AND VICE-PRESIDENTS

President	Born in	Party
1. George Washington	Virginia, 1732	No party
2. John Adams	Massachusetts, 1735	Federalist
3. Thomas Jefferson	Virginia, 1743	Republican
4. James Madison	Virginia, 1751	Republican
5. James Monroe	Virginia, 1758	Republican
6. John Quincy Adams	Massachusetts, 1767	Republican
7. Andrew Jackson	South Carolina, 1767	Republican
8. Martin Van Buren	New York, 1782	Republican
9. William Henry Harrison	Virginia, 1773	Whig
10. John Tyler	Virginia, 1790	Whig
11. James K. Polk	North Carolina, 1795	Democratic
12. Zachary Taylor	Virginia, 1784	Whig
13. Millard Fillmore	New York, 1800	Whig
14. Franklin Pierce	New Hampshire, 1804	Democratic
15. James Buchanan	Pennsylvania, 1791	Democratic
16. Abraham Lincoln	Kentucky, 1809	Republican
17. Andrew Johnson	North Carolina, 1808	Republican
18. Ulysses S. Grant	Ohio, 1822	Republican
19. Rutherford B. Hayes	Ohio, 1822	Republican
20. James A. Garfield	Ohio, 1831	Republican
21. Chester A. Arthur	Vermont, 1830	Republican
22. Grover Cleveland	New Jersey, 1837	Democratic
23. Benjamin Harrison	Ohio, 1833	Republican
24. Grover Cleveland	New Jersey, 1837	Democratic
25. William McKinley	Ohio, 1843	Republican
26. Theodore Roosevelt	New York, 1858	Republican
27. William H. Taft	Ohio, 1857	Republican
28. Woodrow Wilson	Virginia, 1856	Democratic
29. Warren G. Harding	Ohio, 1865	Republican
30. Calvin Coolidge	Vermont, 1872	Republican
31. Herbert C. Hoover	Iowa, 1874	Republican
32. Franklin D. Roosevelt	New York, 1882	Democratic
33. Harry S. Truman	Missouri, 1884	Democratic
34. Dwight D. Eisenhower	Texas, 1890	Republican
35. John F. Kennedy	Massachusetts, 1917	Democratic
36. Lyndon B. Johnson	Texas, 1908	Democratic

OF THE UNITED STATES (see footnotes, next page)

	Elected from	Service	Died	Vice-President
1.	Virginia	1789–1797	1799	John Adams
2.	Massachusetts	1797–1801	1826	Thomas Jefferson
3.	Virginia	1801–1809	1826	Aaron Burr, 1st term George Clinton, 2nd term
4.	Virginia	1809–1817	1836	George Clinton, 1st term Elbridge Gerry, 2nd term
5.	Virginia	1817–1825	1831	Daniel D. Tompkins
6.	Massachusetts	1825–1829	1848	John C. Calhoun
7.	Tennessee	1829–1837	1845	John C. Calhoun, 1st term Martin Van Buren, 2nd term
8.	New York	1837–1841	1862	Richard M. Johnson
9.	Ohio	1841 (1mo.)	1841	John Tyler
10.	Virginia	1841–1845	1862	
11.	Tennessee	1845–1849	1849	George M. Dallas
12.	Louisiana	1849–1850	1850	Millard Fillmore
13.	New York	1850–1853	1874	
14.	New Hampshire	1853–1857	1869	William R. King
15.	Pennsylvania	1857–1861	1868	John C. Breckinridge
16.	Illinois	1861–1865	1865	Hannibal Hamlin, 1st term Andrew Johnson, 2nd term
17.	Tennessee	1865–1869	1875	
18.	Illinois	1869–1877	1885	Schuyler Colfax, 1st term Henry Wilson, 2nd term
19.	Ohio	1877–1881	1893	William A. Wheeler
20.	Ohio	1881 (6mos.)	1881	Chester A. Arthur
21.	New York	1881–1885	1886	
22.	New York	1885–1889	1908	Thomas A. Hendricks
23.	Indiana	1889–1893	1901	Levi P. Morton
24.	New York	1893–1897	1908	Adlai E. Stevenson
25.	Ohio	1897–1901	1901	Garret A. Hobart, 1st term Theodore Roosevelt, 2nd term
26.	New York	1901–1909	1919	Charles W. Fairbanks, 2nd term
27.	Ohio	1909–1913	1930	James S. Sherman
28.	New Jersey	1913–1921	1924	Thomas R. Marshall
29.	Ohio	1921–1923	1923	Calvin Coolidge
30.	Massachusetts	1923–1929	1933	Charles G. Dawes, 2nd term
31.	California	1929–1933	1964	Charles Curtis
32.	New York	1933–1945	1945	John N. Garner, 1st, 2nd term H. A. Wallace, 3rd term Harry S. Truman, 4th term
33.	Missouri	1945–1953		Alben W. Barkley, 2nd term
34.	New York	1953–1961		Richard M. Nixon
35.	Massachusetts	1961–1963	1963	Lyndon B. Johnson
36.	Texas	1963–		Hubert H. Humphrey, Jr., 2nd term

FOOTNOTES FOR THE TABLE OF PRESIDENTS

The numerals in front of the Presidents are those of the successive *administrations*. The total of these administrations is one greater than the number of men who have served as President, since Cleveland headed both the 22nd and the 24th administrations.

Two distinct parties have been called Republican. The first of these was designated "Republican" by its leader, Thomas Jefferson, to distinguish it from the allegedly "monarchical" Federalists. It appears in the table down through the administration of Van Buren. Popular practice was, however, another matter. Members of the first Republican party were often called Democrats, and the party officially made use of the name "Democratic" in its platform for 1844. Ever since that date, the party has been both officially and popularly known only as the Democratic party.

The second Republican party, appearing in the table opposite Lincoln and coming down to our own day, is an entirely different organization, suddenly formed in 1854 during a period of agitation over slavery. Both officially and popularly it has always had but one name—Republican.

FINDING HISTORICAL INFORMATION
IN LIBRARIES

To help readers find information on American history quickly, the following time-saving hints are offered.

Book Numbering. Books are usually shelved in numerical order, according to the "Dewey Decimal System." Under this plan, general United States history bears the number 973. Books from 973.1 through 973.9 deal with specific *periods*, from early exploration and discovery (973.1) to our own times (973.9). Numbers 974 through 979 cover general history of specific *regions*, such as the Pacific Coast (979). For further details on the numbering of these and other phases of American history consult Dewey, M., *Decimal Classification and Relative Index.*

Alphabetical Arrangements of Topics. Readers using standard encyclopedias for historical information can avoid overlooking pertinent material by turning to the final index or study guide volumes for outlines giving cross references to the main text. Short articles appear in several specialized "Dictionaries" of American history. Examples of the latter are: Adams, J. T. and Coleman, R. V., eds., *Dictionary of American History*, 5 vols. (1940) and *Supplement One* (1961); and Martin, M. and Gelber, L., *The New Dictionary of American History* (1966).

Dates. When correlating dates with events, and arranging them in proper sequence, these books can save hours of toil: Carruth, G., and others, *The Encyclopedia of American Facts and Dates*, 4th ed. (1966); Morris, R. B., ed., *Encyclopedia of American History*, rev. ed. (1965); Langer, W. L., ed., *An Encyclopedia of World History* (1952), a volume putting American dates in a world setting; and *The World Almanac*, latest edition, for recent dates.

General Histories. Absence of detail in one history book can often be compensated for by consulting another. Representative one- and two-volume general histories are: Beard, C. A. and Beard, M. R., *The Rise of American Civilization;* Morison, S. E., *The Oxford History of the American People* (1965); Morison, S. E. and Commager, H. S., *The Growth of the American Republic*, 2 vols. (1962); and Nevins, A. and Commager, H. S., *A Short History of the United States*, 5th ed. (1966). Much more extensive are: Johnson, A., ed., *The Chronicles of America*, in 56 small volumes, and Hart, A. B., ed., *The American Nation, a History*, in 28 medium-sized volumes.

Lives. For biographical information, consult the authoritative *Dictionary of American Biography*, 22 vols. (up to 1958), covering the deceased, and *Who's Who in America*, revised every two years, for the living.

Maps. When detailed maps are needed, these books may help: Adams, J. T. and Coleman, R. V., eds., *Atlas of American History* (1943), Paullin, C. O., *Atlas of the Historical Geography of the United States* (1932);

Brown, R. H., ed., *Historical Geography of the United States* (1948); Lord, C. L. and E. H., eds., *Historical Atlas of the United States* (1953); Wesley, E. B., and others, eds., *Our United States, Its History in Maps*, 2nd ed. (1961); and Cole, D. B., ed., *Atlas of American History* (1963).

Outlines. A time-saving concise outline of American history can be found in the final "Reading and Study Guide" volume of *The World Book Encyclopedia*, under the heading "History," subhead "United States." Krout, J. A., *United States to 1865* (1962) and *United States Since 1865* (1965) are inexpensive paperback outlines that are obtainable in college and other bookstores.

Pictorial Accounts. Those in quest of historical photographs, engravings, and other illustrative material will find excellent reference collections in Adams, J. T., ed., *Album of American History*, 6 vols. (1961); Butterfield, R., *The American Past* (1966); Davidson, M. B., *Life in America*, 2 vols. (1951); and Gabriel, R. H., ed., *The Pageant of America; A Pictorial History of the United States*, 15 vols. (1926–29).

Source Materials, such as the texts of documents and contemporary accounts of historical events, may be found in the following volumes: Commager, H. S., ed., *Documents of American History*, 7th ed. (1963); Commager, H. S. and Nevins, A., eds., *The Heritage of America* (1949); and Hart, A. B., ed., *American History Told by Contemporaries*, 5 vols. (1950).

Specialized Fields. There are many specialized histories. In foreign affairs these books are useful: Bailey, T. A., *Diplomatic History of the American People*, 6th ed. (1958); and Bemis, S. F., *A Diplomatic History of the United States*, 5th ed. (1965). For economics, there is David, H. and others, *The Economic History of the United States*, 5 vols. (1945–51), as well as several other valuable accounts. For literature, these books are well known: Curti, M. E., *The Growth of American Thought*, 3rd ed. (1964); Parrington, V. L., *Main Currents in American Thought*, 3 vols. (1930); and Spiller, R. E. and others, *Literary History of the United States*, 3rd ed. (1963). A good example of a history of technology is Oliver, J. W., *History of American Technology* (1956). Oliver W. Larkin's *Art and Life in America*, rev. ed. (1960) is invaluable in understanding American architecture and art.

Studying Other Topics. For library problems not dealt with above, consult extensive bibliographies printed in general texts on American history; the compilation under the heading "History," subhead "United States" in the Bibliography and Index volume of recent editions of *Collier's Encyclopedia*; and R. R. Bowker Co., *Subject Guide to Books in Print* (annual). Much more detailed is Handlin, O. and others, eds., *Harvard Guide to American History* (1954), (in paperback, 1966). *American Heritage*, a hardcover bimonthly periodical of American history is especially well illustrated with, when possible, contemporary material, and is indexed annually.

Index

INDEX